Basic Research Methods In Social Science

Basic Research Methods In Social Science

Third Edition

JULIAN L. SIMON / PAUL BURSTEIN

University of Maryland   Vanderbilt University

Random House New York

Third Edition
98765432
Copyright © 1969, 1978, 1985 by Random House, Inc.

Library of Congress Cataloging in Publication Data

Simon, Julian Lincoln, 1932–
  Basic research methods in social science.

  Bibliography: p.
  Includes index.
  1. Social sciences—Research.   2. Social sciences—
Methodology.   I. Burstein, Paul   II. Title.
H62.S475   1985   300'.72   84-24934
ISBN 0-394-33243-1

Manufactured in the United States of America

Cover and text design: Jo Stein

Preface

The most important change in this edition is the addition of Paul Burstein as an author. Praise of one coauthor by another would be out of place here. But it does seem within the bounds of decency for the original author to tell the world that he is delighted in all ways with his new colleague.

This edition includes four wholly new chapters: an explanation of the sequential roles of the various types of statistical devices in data analysis (Chapter 26); a nontechnical exposition of path analysis with emphasis on its use as a tool in helping one think clearly about the analysis of data (Chapter 27); a survey of several analytic techniques that have now become sufficiently common that some acquaintance with them is necessary if one is to be literate in research (Chapter 28); and a chapter on the philosophy and practice of prediction as an extension of scientific research (Chapter 29). Several other chapters have been revised extensively, notably Chapter 13 on conducting surveys, the sections in Chapter 14 on the use of available social and economic data, which has increased so greatly in the social sciences in recent years, and Chapters 15 and 16 on measurement and scaling. We have also reorganized the book's structure in some ways that will be obvious to those who have used the previous editions. This edition also has undergone extensive line-by-line editing to make it even easier to read than previous editions, whose readers and reviewers were kind enough to say the book was a pleasure to read. And we have added a good many new examples to ensure that students will find it fresh and up-to-date.

Though we have beefed up the sections on the conduct of surveys, we still devote less space to this topic than do other books on research methods. The survey is just one of many tools in standard use in the social sciences, and we believe that it is vital for the person who wishes to understand research to recognize that other methods should be chosen when they are indicated, and to have sufficient acquaintance with them so they will not seem foreign. Of course it is natural for any field to stress the method most in use in that field. But we feel we have a duty to counterbalance that natural tendency with a wide-ranging review of all the main methods in order to avoid disciplinary blindness. The response to previous editions has shown that there is a heartening proportion of teachers of research methods who agree with us in this matter.

Though this is a practical how-to-do-it book, it also aims to teach the basic concepts in the philosophy of science. In our view this is not a contradiction, since the philosophy of science at its best is a very practical subject composed of ideas that clarify the nature and meaning of research and help the researcher better understand how to proceed when faced with difficult choices and decisions.

This book may be deceptively easy to read. We have always hated obscurantism and have been emotionally committed to simplicity, in Simon's case perhaps because of the coincidence of his name with the nursery rhyme "Simple Simon met a pieman. . . ." But simplicity has its drawbacks. For instance, some students concluded that the first edition was so simple to read that it was insufficiently "challenging." Simplicity has a basic psychological difficulty, as expressed by T.S. Eliot about poetry: "A successful poem must be sufficiently simple so it can be understood, but sufficiently difficult so that it cannot be understood immediately." Yet, we are unwilling to make our writing hard to understand so as to be more appealing. Also, simplicity of expression may fool you into thinking that the ideas discussed here are simple ones. They are not. As someone has said: Seek simplicity— but distrust it.

On the other hand, the book may seem overly long, containing too many examples. But as someone else once said: Short writing makes long reading. So we hope you will not be put off by the book's length.

The writing style is more casual than is conventional, and it does not always meet editors' standards as to what is "correct." Therefore we are pleased to take full responsibility for the language.

Despite the fact that this is a text, it contains some new scientific ideas. Those ideas we most hope you will notice as being original contributions are, first, causality as a concept requiring appropriate operational definition (Chapter 35), and second, the Monte Carlo approach to basic statistics (Chapters 30–33). Since the first publication of the Monte Carlo methods in this book, there has developed a body of experimental evidence that this radically different way of learning and doing statistics is easier to understand and more effective than the conventional analytic method (Simon, Shevokas, and Atkinson, 1976). And the most recent enthusiasm in mathematical statistics, "bootstrapping," is a formalization of the same device.

A personal note from Julian Simon: The considerable success of the first edition heartened me in many ways. First—and this may in turn hearten other prospective authors—the skeletal first draft of the manuscript was rejected by fifteen publishers before Hanan Selvin pointed out its potential to Random House. Second, I worried that because the book is not narrowly specialized to a single discipline, each teacher would say that it might be good for others but not for him or her. It turns out, however, that there are a good many instructors who believe in a broad education in research methods; this heartens me because I, too, believe that. Third, I worried that the lack of mathematical notation and "sophisticated" and "rigorous" complexity would deter instructors from adopting the book; but apparently there are plenty of instructors who are more interested in teaching than in impressing students, and that cheers me, too.

In closing, I am grateful for your attention to my thoughts and writing. I benefited from the suggestions and corrections I received from readers of the first two editions. And Paul Burstein and I shall be glad to receive more on this third edition.

Julian L. Simon

Acknowledgments
To First Edition

For a hundred and more years ingenious social scientists have faced obstacles to getting the empirical knowledge they sought, devised ways to circumvent the obstacles, and then told others what they learned. I am grateful to them.

Hanan Selvin subjected the penultimate draft of this manuscript to the searching scrutiny that most manuscripts need but few are lucky enough to get. The quantity and quality of his critical comments were an author's dream, and I have in many places appropriated his thought and word without special note. There would be fewer errors and obscurities in the book if I had followed his advice even more diligently.

James W. Carey gave me many exciting and enjoyable hours discussing some of the fundamental concepts. I also benefited from talks with Howard Maclay. Other friends may also recognize their casual observations in these pages. Allen Holmes read the chapters on statistics very carefully and corrected some errors. Dennis J. Aigner was also good enough to look at those chapters. For useful references and suggestions I am grateful to Stanley Friedman, Lewis Goldberg, James H. Lorie, and Louis Schneider.

My greatest debt is to my wife, Rita. Without her encouragement this book would never have been done.

I have tried to cover the wide intellectual area of all the social sciences, and I hope the reader will bear with me when I depart from the substantive fields that I know best. I will appreciate hearing from anyone who can set me straight on any matter or who can give an instructive or interesting example to illuminate a point.

Jerusalem, 1968   J.L.S.

Acknowledgments To Second Edition

Hanan Selvin listened to tapes of many chapters for the second edition, especially the new ones, and gave me a flood of useful and delightful comments, only some of which did I have the strength to exploit. Gideon Keren made helpful comments on Chapter 11. And the following long list of people were kind enough to send me evaluations or remarks about the first edition: Marcus Felson, William Ahlhauser, Wayne W. Snyder, Jason Millman, Robert A. Baker, Oleh Wolowyna, Lawrence G. Smith, Lucy W. Sells, Leigh Marlowe, Siamak Movahedi, Michael A. Baer, Joann S. DeLora, Marc D. Magre, Leroy Gruner, John H. Kramer, Jules W. Delambre, Alan C. Acock, Robert W. Shotoln, David M. Krieger, Michael D. Grimes, L. V. Hayes, Robert C. Smigelski, David G. Pfeiffer, Jamie M. Calderon, D. E. W. Holden, David M. Monsees, Jr., L. Fannin, Luther H. Keller, Linda Brookover, Borque, David Nasatir, Kenneth R. Rothrock, Louis A. Brown, LeRoy Martinson, Gosts Wolff. I am grateful to one and all.

More and more, my family and our life together sustains me. Wife Rita and children David, Judith, and Daniel give my days the joy and meaning that enable me to write.

Urbana, Illinois, 1978   J.L.S.

Contents

PART 3:   The Obstacles to Social-Science Knowledge and Ways to Overcome Them

Prologue

Cast your mind back 450 years. The Governor of Rodera—a small Asian principality—decided to find out why the country's tax revenues were not greater. Here is a classic problem for research, and much of mathematics and social-science techniques was originally invented to improve tax collection.

The Governor first consulted an adviser who had studied in Europe and had learned something of Aristotelian logic. The adviser reasoned that (a) good citizens willingly pay as much tax as they are able to, (b) the folk of Rodera were very good citizens, and therefore (c) the tax collections *could not* be higher.

The Governor immediately dismissed this syllogistic thinking as pure nonsense because he disbelieved the premises. Even without special training he was smart enough to understand the weakness of bad logic.

Next, the Governor called in the regional tax collectors and put the problem to them, because they were experts in the tax-collection field. After consultation the consensus among the tax collectors was that the people of the country simply *could not afford* to pay any more taxes. To support this statement the tax men stated that they had already used every possible technique to extract higher taxes—raising valuations of property, checking on hidden assets, and the like—and even their best efforts could not raise more money.

The Governor understood the tax men's analysis of the situation as a self-seeking attempt to make themselves seem competent and hard-working, and he therefore disregarded this "expert opinion."

The Governor then concluded reluctantly that he would have to find out the answers for himself. He instructed an aide to bring him a handful of typical citizens. The aide brought in some people who were close at hand. They included a few beggars who had been loitering nearby, plus the aide's brother and two young guards. It was obvious to the Governor that these people were not representative of the population, and therefore it was useless to question them. To put it in modern terms, the Governor recognized that he had a badly biased sample.

The aide was therefore instructed to bring in some "typical" peasants and townspeople, which he did. The Governor then asked them, "Why don't you pay more taxes?" The first few answers showed the folly of the question, for what he heard were excuses, complaints, entreaties—everything except what seemed to be sensible answers.

The Governor then confined his questions to factual matters. He asked about each person's property—crops, family size, and the amount paid in taxes. Assuming that the answers were true and that he could have them checked, the Governor thought he was getting somewhere.

The information obtained from such a small handful of people clearly was not enough, however, because the group did not include any rich men, any people from the far provinces, any foreign residents, or any representatives of other important classes of people. Nor could the Governor tell from this sample how many people in each class there were. Therefore, the Governor ordered a nation-wide house-to-house census.

Nowadays the data for a complete nation-wide United States census can be collected in months. But transportation and communications were poorer then, and few literate people could be found to collect information. The census therefore required twelve years.

By the fifth year the Governor grew impatient and decided to experiment with the effect of new pressures to increase tax collections. He ordered that anyone who did not pay half again as much tax as in the previous year would have his cattle confiscated. It turned out that the total taxes paid did not increase. The crops were bad that year, and the Governor could not determine whether the taxes would have been as high or higher than otherwise if the crop had been normal. The trouble was that his experiment was uncontrolled, because he had not kept the old tax system in effect in some areas for comparison—that is, his experimental design was incomplete. And worst of all, many people slaughtered their cattle to avoid confiscation, which ruined the country's meat supply for several years.

By the time the census data were all in hand at the end of the twelfth year, the country's situation had changed, and the data collected in early years no longer meant much. (Nowadays we know how to take samples to reduce costs and avoid long time lags during which the picture may change.) Furthermore, after twelve years the tax-census data filled a whole warehouse, and another ten years would have been required to interpret them. The Governor gave up the task in disgust and retired to his harem.

The point of this story is that knowledge is often not easy to come by because there are many obstacles in one's path. And common sense alone is not enough. But by now social science has accumulated a body of tested experience on how best to overcome the obstacles and acquire empirical knowledge efficiently and safely. This book presents some of this accumulated experience.

Basic Research Methods In Social Science

Introduction

1. Purpose of the Book

This book is primarily for students who have never before studied or done empirical social-scientific research. We hope that the book contains good advice that will help you get your first research project off the ground successfully and increase your efficiency in later work. As for those of you who will not do empirical research, the book may teach you to distinguish good research from poor research and help you to understand why empirical researchers do things as they do them.

People who have had some training or experience in empirical research may also gain from the elementary level of the discussion. Basic concepts often are bypassed as one rushes to learn the methods of particular fields. Coming back to fundamentals can widen the perspective of an advanced student and fill holes in his or her knowledge. If an advanced student is to gain something from this book, however, he or she must have the wisdom to realize that the apparent simplicity of the basic concepts is often deceiving. For example, all researchers know that *ceteris paribus*—holding

"all other things equal"—is important. But the more research you do, the more you realize how complex the *ceteris paribus* idea is, how difficult it is to choose the right *ceteris paribus* conditions, and how often research is useless because other things were not made sufficiently equal.

The book is primarily intended for future *producers* of research. But many people who study research methods will never produce research; rather, they will be research *consumers* in their jobs and as citizens. For this important group of people, the aim of the book is to teach how to evaluate research done by others—to know which research is good and which is not; where the weak spots are in a piece of research and how important they are; and whether a research finding, whether presented in the professional literature, in an informal report, or in the popular press, is or is not likely to be valid. For example, Volvo recently advertised that "90 percent of the Volvos sold in the last eleven years in the U.S. are still on the road." A good course in research methods is likely to

1

alter your impression of what that claim might mean.

We hope that you yourself carry out some empirical research—no matter how small in scope—as you read this book. It is not enough to study empirical research the way one studies astronomy, economics, psychology, and other academic subjects. Although reading about research principles is certainly useful, research is not entirely an academic subject. Rather, it is largely an art, a how-to-do-it subject like musical composition, writing advertisements, or swimming.[1] You never really know how to do research until you do it, any more than you can know how to swim after only pool-side instruction. You must jump into the water, thrash around, and gradually improve with practice.

For the same reason, skill in empirical research requires experience—that is, doing research of your own and criticizing the research of others. Eventually you would learn much that is in this book by trial and error. Instruction can only hasten the process and make it less painful by showing what has and has not worked for others. But that is as far as the teaching can go. (Reading what others say about research *can* be enormously profitable, however, *if* you will benefit by the experience of others.)

Now, to state a theme that will recur throughout the book: There is never a single, standard, correct method for carrying out a piece of research. You should not wait to start your research until you find out *the* proper approach, because there are always many ways to tackle a problem—some will be better than others, but probably several will be good ways. There is no single perfect design. Every approach has its strengths and weaknesses, which the researcher will have to weigh and balance before beginning his or her research. Practical

problems often affect the choice of approach as well. One method may seem better than another for dealing with a particular problem, but it may also cost so much more in money and effort as not to be worth it. Research always involves trade-offs between the desirable and the practical. A research method for a given problem is not like the solution to a problem in algebra; it is more like a recipe for beef stroganoff: There is no one best recipe.[2]

For technical problems, too, there is often no single cut-and-dried solution; there may be several satisfactory techniques. For example, if you want to do a questionnaire survey, should you interview by mail, by telephone, or in person? Chapter 13 discusses the pros and cons of each method, but eventually sound judgment is required for this technical decision; no handy rule book can make such decisions for you. Should you pay your subjects in an experiment or survey? Again there is no pat answer; instead, this book tries to give you some principles that will help you to make sound technical decisions about your research methods.

In this book the word "method" refers to *empirical* techniques and devices of various sorts. To the philosophers the term refers to "scientific method"—the whole process of getting knowledge, including the theoretical and the empirical steps. But even then it is surely true that there is no single "scientific method." "There is no one scientific method . . . there

---

1. A great mathematician applies the same analogy to his sort of work, too: "Solving [mathematical] problems is a practical skill like, let us say, swimming. We acquire any practical skill by imitation and practice" (Polya, 1957: 4).

2. Scientific reports typically tell *how* the research was done, but not *why* it was done that way or how the scientist decided what to do. They thus leave out what would be most interesting to someone trying to learn how to design research. Three short descriptions of this sort can be found in Wallis and Roberts (1966: Chap. 3). Some valuable descriptions of how scientists actually work include K. Colby's account of Semmelweiss and childbed fever (pp. 44–50); Watson on his role in discovering the structure of DNA; Whyte on his study of youths in an ethnic neighborhood (2nd edition, Appendix A); Braidwood on archaeological research; Riesman on his study of professors; Ulam on mathematics and the development of the atomic bomb; and Hammond's compilation of first-person accounts of research by several major social scientists. Mills (1959: 199ff.) interweaves a description of one of his labors with marvelous general advice on craftsmanship and how to get ideas and do social analysis.

will be as many different scientific methods as there are fundamentally different kinds of problems" (Northrop, 1965: ix, 19). "The scientific method, as far as it is a method, is nothing more than doing one's damnedest with one's mind, no holds barred" (Bridgman, 1945: 450).

2. What Kinds of Research Are Called "Empirical"?

This book deals with *empirical*[3] research and not with scientific speculation. Much of scientific work consists of thinking up ideas about the nature of the world, generalizing from observed facts to scientific "laws," and developing logical systems that are called "theories" or "models." But simply as a division of labor the speculative part of science is not covered here. The subject of this book is "getting the facts." Of course, empirical work goes beyond "mere" observation and description, and it is inextricably intertwined with explaining nature and making predictions about it. But the process of thinking up explanations or hypotheses about nature and its laws is beyond our scope here.[4]

Nor is this book concerned with the logical process of building scientific theories. That is, it does not deal with the process of finding the *logical* relationships between various scientific statements or with the process of developing generalizations or scientific laws. Rather, its subject is the less glamorous craft of producing and examining factual and material evidence

and sense data to develop the descriptions, measurements, comparisons, and tests of hypothesized relationships that are themselves part of the speculative side of scientific work.

Lest there be misunderstanding, we emphasize that a good idea is the keystone of an empirical study. Mere data collection and measurement are worthless unless the subject is important. Theory is often the fount of important ideas for empirical research, and sound theory is of inestimable value in any field. The relationship between theory and empirical research is explored in Chapter 5.

Finally, "empirical research" excludes knowledge obtained by *consulting authorities,* in books or in person. It includes only knowledge obtained from data resulting from first-hand observations, either by you or by someone else. Reexamination of data collected by others, such as U.S. Census data, *is* empirical research, of course.

Most of the examples in this book are drawn from "pure" research, which can be defined as research motivated primarily by the desire to *understand* something without regard to immediate economic or social payoff. But we also draw examples from "applied" social research, which is oriented toward answering practical questions with an eye to short-term payoff. Often the methods used in pure and applied research are similar, even though the goals are different; for example, a political pollster interested in predicting election results and a political scientist who wants to understand why voters decided to vote for a particular candidate may both carry out national surveys (Abramson, 1983). Applied research methods are sometimes more sophisticated than methods used in pure research (Rossi, 1980) because the need for practical answers and the concern for immediate costs and benefits forces the researcher to be as efficient as possible.

Our examples come from the *social* sciences, not only because the book is intended for students of the social sciences, but also because empirical scientific methods have been used with greater variety and subtlety in the social

---

3. "The adjective *empirical,* in its combinations with various nouns, appears to denote observations and propositions primarily based on sense experience and/or derived from such experience by methods of inductive logic, including mathematics and statistics" (*The Dictionary of the Social Sciences,* p. 237). The crucial distinction here is between empirical research and *theorizing,* though the two activities are very much interdependent.

4. The elusive phenomenon of scientific *discovery* is discussed at length by many writers. See, for example, J. Young (1977), Bachrach (1972: Chap. 1), Mills (1959, Appendix, especially pp. 200–201, 211–217), Stigler (1965), Diesing (1971).

sciences than in the natural sciences (Chapter 36 defends this claim). We shall turn frequently to a few classic studies, despite their age, for several reasons: The studies are interesting; students will often have read about them in other courses; many of them have been written about and reanalyzed by other experts; and they show us a wide variety of methods and a broad representation from the social sciences as practiced by some of the best social scientists. We also refer frequently to our own work, despite its limitations, because we know exactly what went into the work—the difficulties, decisions, errors, corrections of errors, and order in which things took place. One cannot have such intimate knowledge of anyone else's work. Yet it is these details and decisions, seldom written about, that are hardest for the novice to understand and master and that he or she usually learns only by serving as an apprentice (that is, "graduate assistant") or by trial and error.

The book emphasizes the design and plan of research rather than the analysis of research data. Except for studies that reanalyze data collected by others, the most important and interesting decisions arise at the design stage, or at least they *should* arise then. If you make a mistake when analyzing data, you can probably correct it fairly easily. But if you make a mistake when designing the collection of data, you may have to redo much of the study to correct it, at the cost of heartbreak and expense.

Here are three brief examples of the importance of good design: First, two library scientists sought to determine the proportions of various-sized books in research libraries. So they measured the heights of each of the hundreds of thousands of books in a major library. With a little planning and a knowledge of sampling design, they would have realized that they needed to measure only a fraction of the books in order to get a very accurate estimate of the proportions of different sizes. Measuring just a sample of the books rather than all of them would have saved a tremendous amount of work.

Second, a family-planning group tested one birth-control propaganda campaign in Village A against another in Village B to see which campaign would be more effective. But they forgot that subsequent differences in birth rates and contraception-acceptance rates might reflect differences between the two villages that existed before the campaigns began. Sound planning would have led them to take these preexisting differences into account.

Third, political scientists trying to understand why people change their minds about political candidates during a campaign know they cannot wait until after the election to ask them about it because people forget or distort much of what they thought during the campaign. Instead, political scientists often use a *panel design,* quizzing the same people about their voting intentions several times during the same campaign. The repeated observations make it possible to get accurate information about change while it is happening.

Mistakes at the design stage can be mended only at great extra cost or not at all. By comparison, mistakes at the analysis stage can be remedied at slight or no cost as long as the mistakes have not gotten into print or been acted upon.

Think through the research design carefully in advance. Failing to consider all the necessary details at the design stage because of procrastination or mental laziness is one reason that many researchers get very little done. Of course, not everything can be foreseen, especially in exploratory studies, but one should use as much foresight as possible. It is useful to talk to your friends about the design, and to prepare an outline of it; both processes reveal fuzziness in your design thinking.

The design of a piece of research must depend on the particular purpose that the research is intended to serve; this is a message we shall repeat again and again. For example, the Internal Revenue Service publishes statistics on the amount of advertising done by groups of firms that sell various products, and these statistics include *all* firms' advertising, because the government requires data on the entire economy. But the statistics gathered and published by industry trade associations cover *only the leading firms*, because the industry-collected statistics are designed to meet only the information needs of the industry. For another example, a psychologist studying the relative memorability of beginning, middle, and ending portions of messages will use a different test of memory (perhaps a list of nonsense syllables) than will a psychologist who is studying how many pieces of information a radio operator can remember accurately. *You must ask yourself repeatedly: Exactly what do I want to find out and why? If you can answer these questions clearly and precisely, you have gone a long way toward creating a satisfactory research design.*

Part One introduces you to the process of social science research, beginning with a description of the language of science (in Chapter 2), which is inseparable from science itself. Chapter 3 discusses basic concepts one needs to know before beginning to do research. Chapter 4 is an introduction to the research process itself; it classifies the types of questions that empirical research is asked to answer; using the classification helps one decide what types of research methods are appropriate for any given study. Chapter 5 explores the relationship between theory and empirical research. And Chapter 6 discusses the choice of appropriate empirical proxies (indicators) for theoretical variables.

Part Two gets down to the brass tacks of just how to conduct a piece of research. Chapter 7 provides a checklist of the basic steps often taken when executing an empirical research project. If you are actually doing a piece of research in conjunction with reading this book—as we very much hope you are—then you should certainly start by reading Chapter 7.

Other chapters in Part Two discuss crucial decisions in the research process and what to do once you have made them. Chapter 8 deals with a crucial initial question—how to assess the potential value of a research project. Chap-

ter 9 considers a problem which comes up in almost all research—how to make the research project feasible by studying just some of the objects you are interested in (U.S. citizens, for example) rather than all of them, while seeing to it that your conclusions apply to everyone, not just those you have studied; that is, the chapter deals with sampling. Chapters 10 through 14 present different ways of gathering data—through experiments (Chapters 10 and 11), surveys, participant observation, and other nonexperimental ways of collecting your own data (Chapters 12 and 13), and by using data made available by others, including government data and newspapers (Chapter 14). Chapters 15 and 16 describe how to turn the data you have gathered into good indicators of the theoretical concepts you are interested in; Chapter 15 presents some principles of measurement, while Chapter 16 shows how scales and indexes are actually constructed. And Chapter 17 provides practical advice about handling the data you have collected.

The chapters in Part Three consider the obstacles that nature puts in the way of the fact seeker and that prevent one from getting valid answers quickly and easily with common sense alone. These include obstacles stemming from the human imperfections of the observer (Chapter 19), the complexities of those other people he or she is studying (Chapter 20), and the scarcity and inadequacies of the available evidence (Chapter 21). Special problems that arise in searching for causal relationships are discussed in Chapter 22. Chapter 23 considers what is often the master obstacle to research: cost. Ways of surmounting each obstacle to knowledge—the warp and woof of research method—are discussed in each chapter.

Part Four discusses what to do with your data once they are collected—how to analyze them and interpret them statistically (Chapters 24–28), how to use them to make predictions and to generalize (Chapter 29), and how to deal with a variety of statistical issues (Chapters 30–33). Chapter 34 discusses how to decide on a sample size; it properly belongs in

Part Two, but it had to follow Chapters 24–33. Chapter 35 discusses the crucial concept of causality in social science. Chapter 36, the epilogue, discusses in broad terms the powers and limitations of social science.

3. The Place of Statistics in the Study of Research Methods

Great research has been done by people with no formal knowledge of statistics. And a little study of statistics sometimes befuddles students into thinking that statistical principles are guides to research design and analysis. This mistaken belief only inhibits the exercise of sound research thinking. Kinsey put it this way:

> However satisfactory the standard deviations may be, no statistical treatment can put validity into generalizations which are based on data that were not reasonably accurate and complete to begin with. It is unfortunate that academic departments so often offer courses on the statistical manipulation of human material to students who have little understanding of the problems involved in securing the original data. . . . When training in these things replaces or at least precedes some of the college courses on the mathematical treatment of data, we shall come nearer to having a science of human behavior. (Kinsey et al., 1948: p. 35)

Nevertheless, a working knowledge of the basic ideas of statistics and probability helps clarify one's thinking and improves one's capacity to deal with practical problems and to understand the world. In fact, of course, statistics are all around us—from ballplayers' batting averages to the SAT scores used to predict the likelihood of succeeding in college to the index of leading economic indicators used to predict in what direction the U.S. economy will move. This book will show how statistics can help us make research decisions and understand the data we collect. Chapters 30 through 33 offer a new approach to statistics that may have special interest for students who are scared by sta-

tistics. This method substitutes "Monte Carlo" experiments for mathematical analysis. It also emphasizes the *reasoning* of statistics—the most important ideas in statistics, which are usually learned only informally. This method has now been shown experimentally to be unusually effective (Simon, Atkinson, and Shevokas, 1976).

4. Some General Remarks

A book about how to do research inevitably makes research sound difficult and treacherous. And this book gives special attention to the obstacles to knowledge that one faces in doing research, so as to help you recognize and overcome them.

But please don't let these obstacles cause you to lose heart. Sound and valuable research can be done even by ordinary undergraduates—general research that is worth publishing, and applied research that is of value to organizations and decision makers. All research has flaws, but the flaws need not be so grave as to invalidate the research, even if it is course-work research conducted with a small sample, no money, and limited time.

Furthermore, research can be enormously exciting and great fun. To find out something about the world that no one has ever known before is a rare thrill. And it is a thrill that almost anyone can experience who will start with a sensible idea, work enthusiastically and hard, and proceed with caution.

Though research can be great fun, we do not like to think of it as a game. Rather, we prefer to remember that sound research can make a valuable social contribution, improving the lives of individuals and communities and enriching our culture. Thinking of research as a game can lead researchers to focus only on the professional acceptance of their work and its influence on their careers, rather than on the social and intellectual benefits of the research. Of course we all want to get ahead in the world. But if we want *only* to get ahead, if our eye is on only the main chance professionally, then we will all be losers in the long run.

This book is a textbook. Though some of the ideas in it are new, most are not. Like other textbooks it constitutes a sort of folk wisdom; the folk are the teachers, colleagues, and students who have discussed research with us. Some of this wisdom seems never to have been collected or transcribed from the oral tradition. (For example, the phrase *ceteris paribus* must have a very high spoken frequency among social scientists, yet it does not appear in the index of a single one of the most popular books about research methods in the social sciences.) To collect and discuss this wisdom is the aim of this book.

AFTERTHOUGHT

David Reisman, author of *The Lonely Crowd* and teacher of a famous experimental general education course at Harvard, wrote:

> In the early years of the course, the staff and I had our greatest difficulty in persuading students to do small-scale pieces of empirical work for their term papers. They were used to working from books, and if they wanted to do some sort of historical or bibliographical study, we were agreeable. But what we wanted to overcome was was the diffidence of many students as to whether they themselves could make discoveries about America which would teach me something—something nobody had already discovered before them.

> Some students were naturally diffident about interviewing, and I do not blame them for that; I am too, and I have to make myself do interviews—knocking on a door, and fearing rebuff or interference from the television set or other family members, can be some of the most taxing work in sociology and polling. But more difficult to overcome was the students' belief that everything was already in the books, and the idea that they could possibly discover something that contradicted what an authority had said was a disturbing notion.

Part One

The Process
of Social-Science
Research

The Language of Research: Definitions and Validity

1. Operational Definitions

A stranger driving a car with California license plates stops you on the street in Urbana, Illinois, and asks "Where is New York?" You, being a lyrical poet with a feeling for the spiritual side of life, tell him, "New York is in the land of the sea, the singers of mercantile songs, and rotten paintings. Why go there?"

The stranger looks annoyed and says, "Come on, buddy, quit the nonsense and tell me where New York is."

"On the East Coast, north of Washington, south of Boston," you answer. He looks bewildered, so you add: "Latitude 40° 40' North, longitude 73° 48' West."

He looks outraged. "Will you or won't you tell me what road to take?" he says. "How do I get there?"

What the man really wants is for you to say: "Continue down this street to the first stop sign, about a quarter of a mile. Turn right onto Highway 74 . . ." and so on.

Now you have satisfied him. You have provided *instructions* that he can follow. The instructions are unambiguous (you hope), and, if he follows your instructions exactly, he must arrive exactly where you and he agree he is trying to go—New York, in this case. You have told him what he needs to know—nothing more and nothing less. You have not told him to follow the road around curves, because he needs no instruction to do so. But you have told him which way to turn when he reaches the highway, because you have no reason to assume that he knows whether to go right or left at that point.

An important part of the language of science consists of *theoretical* or abstract concepts, such as "utility" in economics and "reinforcement" in psychology. Such terms are not very useful in *empirical* work, however, unless they can be tied to actual research operations. Just as with travel instructions, the language of em-

11

pirical scientific research is made up of instructions that are descriptions of sets of actions or *operations* (for instance, "turn right at the first street sign") that someone can follow accurately. Such instructions are called an "operational definition," or, more formally: "A definition is an operational definition to the extent that the definer (a) specifies the procedure (including materials used) for identifying or generating the definiendum and (b) finds high reliability in [consistency in application of] his definition" (*Dictionary of Social Science*, p. 476). A. Bachrach adds that "the operational definition of a dish . . . is its recipe" (1972: 74).

Here is an example: Assume that you are a psychologist and you wish to write to another psychologist to tell her what color stimulus card you used in an animal training experiment, so that she can duplicate ("replicate") the experiment. The word "green" alone might be dangerously imprecise. There are many shades and intensities of green, and your correspondent might choose a color that would lead to different experimental results.

You could ensure that she uses exactly the same color if you send her the stimulus card you actually used. Your operational definition would then be "Use the enclosed color card."

If it is impractical to send out samples, you could compare your stimulus card to an interior decorator's color chart, then write down the name and number of the matching color and the firm that puts out the color chart. Comparing the stimulus card against the color chart is the *operation* that *defines* the color in question.

Now some actual examples. Who is the "head" of a family? You might define that as "whoever is in charge." But being in charge is a rather abstract concept, and people might disagree about who is in charge in a particular family. The U.S. Bureau of the Census, which has collected information on heads of families for many years, needed a clear operational definition of "head of family," so that everyone collecting the information would follow the same procedures. So they *defined* the husband as the head of the family when both husband and wife were present. In recent years many people objected to what seemed to be an assumption that it was always the husband who was in charge, so the Census changed its procedure. In the 1980 *Statistical Abstract of the United States*, the term "head of family" was used to describe the first adult household member listed on the census questionnaire; this might be whoever answered the door to talk to the census taker, rather than the husband (U.S. Bureau of the Census, 1980: 3). (Beginning with the 1980 census, the term "head of family" was eliminated altogether; "householder" replaced it.) Although the official definition of head of family changed, it was perfectly clear to everyone, both before and after 1980, what the term meant, because the procedures for defining the head of family were spelled out precisely.

Psychologists have thought more deeply about operational definitions than have other social scientists, because psychology tries to connect what can be observed objectively to what is unobservable inside people's minds. An example is the concept "personal adjustment." Army Research Branch scientists in World War II wanted to study "how personal adjustment varied in the army." The key theoretical (hypothetical) term, "personal adjustment," was operationally defined this way:

> With respect to verbal behavior, it is assumed that, *on the average,* men who said that they were in good spirits, that they were more useful in the Army than as civilians, that they were satisfied with their Army jobs and status, and that in general they liked the Army, were better adjusted to the Army than men who were negative in several of these expressions. (Stouffer, et al., 1949, I, 83)

Notice the words "who said that they were good spirits." A questionnaire is an essential part of this particular operational definition. Men who answered the questions in one fashion are operationally defined as "well adjusted"; others are "ill adjusted," *by definition*.

Happiness is a concept related to personal adjustment but even more difficult to define satisfactorily. Happiness is perhaps as elusive a concept to define perfectly as it is to achieve. N. Bradburn tackles head-on the problem of operational definition: "One way to find out whether people are happy is to ask them. Respondents were asked to answer this question: 'Taking all things together, how would you say things are these days—would you say you are very happy, pretty happy, or not too happy?' " (1963: 2).

By contrast, creating satisfactory operational definitions is seldom a problem in economics, for the theoretical concept in economics often points clearly to the empirical variable that should be used. Of course even a concept like money is not automatically defined operationally; in some cases the economist includes savings deposits along with cash and checking accounts in the operational definition of money, in other cases not. And the concept economic backwardness bristles with such definitional problems as whether a country's present income level or its rate of growth is the more appropriate proxy. Furthermore, putting values on a country's output is a very tricky procedure that affects the relative backwardness of the country and makes one scholar ask "Is [backwardness] an operational term?" (Gerschenkron, 1965: 42). But seldom is the relationship between theoretical and empirical variables as arguable in economics as is the relationship between, say, the theoretical (hypothetical) concept of love and its operational definition.

Operational definitions are to be distinguished from *property* or *attribute* definitions, in which something is defined by saying what it *consists of*. For example, a crude attribute definition of a college might be: "An organization containing faculty and students, teaching a variety of subjects beyond the high-school level." An operational definition of university

might be "An organization found in *The World Almanac*'s listing of 'Colleges and Universities.' "

Operational definitions also differ sharply from dictionary definitions. A dictionary definition of "green" is "1a: of the color green (~ jade) b: having the color of growing fresh grass or of the emerald (~lawns)" (*Webster's Third New International Dictionary* [unabridged], 1971:996). The dictionary definition often gives synonyms, which help you translate the word you do not know into words you already know, or gives *examples* of the word that help you to learn how it is used. But for many words the dictionary definition could not *guide the actions* of one person to correspond exactly to what someone else wanted. A dictionary definition of "New York" would not be at all helpful to your friend who wants to drive there from Urbana. A dictionary definition of "apple strudel" will not guide your grandmother to make exactly the dish that you enjoy. A dictionary definition of "green" will not guide another experimenter to use exactly the same color you did. The dictionary definition of "consumer price index" will not tell you how to reproduce the consumer index used by the United States.

There have been heated philosophic arguments about operational definitions and their place in science.[1] The argument is brought out by e. e. cummings (1954:190).

(While you and i have lips and voices which
are kissing and to sing with
who cares if some oneeyed son of a bitch
invents an instrument to measure Spring with?)

In these lines, the poet catches the essence of empirical science, even though he denounces its effects. With ingenious empirical

1. What has been said so far does *not* reflect an allegiance to the philosophic position called "operationism." The substitute label "working definition" suggested by Selltiz et al. (1976: 43), avoids many unnecessary associations of the term "operational definition." But we shall stick to the common usage.

research designs and instruments, meteorologists actually do measure spring. But notice that the researcher must specify which readings on the instruments he or she will consider to denote spring. That specification is the operational definition.

Another side of the matter is given by Kruskal (1981), a statistician turned rhymemaker:

> "You'll care if some four-eyed bastard
> invents a better forceps for the resulting infant,
> or even if, by measuring Spring, the slob
> eventually figures out how to prolong it."

Cummings would have been disturbed if he had known that scientists also measure love—sometimes with the very kisses that he mentioned. "Love" can mean many things, of course, and the operations for measuring any facet of it are far from obvious. Consider, for example, measuring the amount of love between mother and child by the number of times the mother kisses the child. In this case, we certainly have established an operational definition of *something* when we specify counting the number of kisses. But few of us would believe that the number of kisses is a perfect and true index of the amount of "love"; in fact, there may be cases in which number of kisses and amount of love may be inversely related. But for some purposes it might be a *useful* index.

Dispute has arisen because some scientists have taken a position implying that love *is* the kiss count and that the word "love" can have no meaning apart from the description of an operation. Whether or not this general position is wise, a less extreme position is possible, that is, that hypothetical (or theoretical) concepts can certainly be useful in science (and in common language) even though they are not operationally defined. The very fact that one can have in mind a concept that is *not yet* defined operationally but toward which one reaches with an operational definition is proof that concepts can have meaning even though they are not operationally defined. For example, we

probably can have some meaningful conversation about happiness even though it is a many-sided and imprecise concept to us. And, when introducing an operational definition of happiness, we may talk about the concept in general terms. That general discussion is a "hypothetical" concept of happiness or, as Underwood calls it, a "literary definition" (1957: 54–55).[2]

When you come to execute a piece of empirical research, all the concepts in the research and all the important words used in the write-up *must* be defined in terms of operations. About this point there should be no argument: If, for example, you are to study love empirically, there must be *something* that you can count or measure that will stand for love; otherwise, you simply cannot do any empirical research.

What is the relationship between the operationally defined kiss count and love? Is there a *logical* relationship between the two? Does "love" mean something apart from a kiss count? Is "happiness" only the answer to a question on a questionnaire? Troublesome disagreement can be avoided by saying that the kiss count stands for love in at least a partial way and that the questionnaire answer is a partial proxy for happiness. We need not assert that the kiss count *is* love or that it is *all* there is to the concept of love. We can agree that there may be *other* measures that stand for other aspects of love, while still making good use of the operational definition. "Basically, an operational definition asserts only that a phenomenon has been reliably measured" (Underwood, 1957: 62). Whenever you complete the sentence "I measured it by . . . ," referring to a variable, you have provided an operational definition of the variable.

The key property of an operational definition is that it helps other researchers repeat exactly what one researcher has done. And getting the same results after following the same proce-

---

2. A concept may also form part of a deductive theory, even though it is not operationally defined. In that case we call it a "theoretical concept" or an "unobservable."

dures (replicability) gives credibility to the conclusions of scientific research. An operationally defined concept like a kiss count can never represent all aspects of a theoretical concept like "love," but one of the marks of a wise scientist is that he or she develops operationally defined concepts which are good "proxies" or "indicators" of the theoretical concepts— that is, capture as much of their essence as possible. How this is done is discussed below and in Chapters 15 and 16.

There is still another benefit from forcing yourself to operationalize your definitions: It can save you from getting trapped with concepts that are circular ("tautologous") and hence meaningless. Tautologies have too often afflicted science. For example, the key Darwinian concept of the survival of the fittest is often (if not always) a meaningless tautology. How does one decide whether the elephant or the mosquito is more fit to survive while both species are still alive? And if the dinosaurs (or the Assyrians) became extinct because of a change in environmental conditions, is saying that they were not fit to survive any different than simply saying they died? To avoid tautology—you know they were not fit to survive because they died—an operational definition of fitness is needed that you can use to predict in advance which species is more likely to survive.

2. Numbers and Operational Definitions

Now let us talk about some simple numbers.

"How far is it to New York?" the traveler asks you next. He is again annoyed when you answer, "a long way," because what is a long way to you might be a short way to him or vice versa. But just putting the distance into numbers is not enough. He will still be confused if you tell him "three short ways."

You might do a little better if you told him it was 3,382,000 cubits to New York—provided he has studied his Bible carefully. The Bible, however, is not clear about the length of a cubit, so describing the distance in cubits might still be confusing. And if the traveler has never read the Bible, he has even less information than if you said, "a long way."

"About 950 miles, or 860 miles on the old road if you want to go that way," is a very satisfactory answer. The traveler will know what you mean, and he will be able to figure how much time and how much gas it will take to get there.

Behind every numerical measurement lies an operational definition. A very precise interpretation of "three feet long" is "put three foot rulers end to end, and the distance in question is from one end of the foot rulers to the other." Many years ago, the operational definition of "three feet long" was cruder. It was "Put the heel of your left foot on a mark on the ground, put your right foot directly in front of your left foot, and then your left foot in front of your right foot. Then compare the thing you are measuring against the distance between the mark on the ground and the toe of your left foot."

To take another example, a department store may want to know your income when deciding whether to give you a credit card. For the store, "income" may simply mean your salary (that would be the operational definition). The way the Internal Revenue Service defines income for tax purposes is different; in fact, it may take many pages in a tax guide to explain how income is to be calculated—that is, to provide an operational definition of income from the IRS's point of view. All numerical measurements are ultimately based on ideas about what is to be measured combined with a set of procedures for actually doing the measuring— everything from the gross national product to SAT scores to the appraised value of a house (Zeller and Carmines, 1980: Chap. 1).

Still another example: Assume you must determine what proportion of the children in Lincoln County live on farms. How should you go about it? Your first impulse is to answer, "Go and look at all the farms." Or if you are slightly wiser you might say, "Look at a sample of the farms." But those are unsatisfactory answers, as we shall see.

For convenience in discussion let us narrow the problem to determining how many children live on just a *single* farm, say the old Carey place. You send a girl to look at it, and she comes back with the answer, "two children." But then you wonder—did she count *all* the children and *only* the children? You have never told her whom she should consider a child, that is, at what age a child stops being a child, and you have never told her whether to count infants as children. Now you must make those decisions. You send her out again, and she returns and says, "Well, there are two children playing on the road near the house but not on the farm land itself." Should you count them or not?

You never gave her a rule for deciding whether children live or do not live on a farm, whether to count children visiting on the farm or visiting away from the farm. Then you must instruct her about whether a particular place is to be considered a farm (does the land have to be farmed in order for the place to be a farm?) and so on. You must give her instructions that will cover almost every possible situation in which she may have doubt, plus the important general instruction to ask you for further instructions about any situation that the rules do not cover. Notice that each of your instructions tells her *how to perform an operation*. "Ask 'do you live here?' " is an instruction to perform the operation of asking. The operation to determine whether a farm is being farmed is not obvious; for example, does a small patch of vegetable garden make it a farm?

Other language need not always be as precise as the language of science. The glory of poetry and religious language often is that many meanings are possible, and the reader may find the meaning that satisfies one's own heart. Legal decisions are often purposely ambiguous; sometimes a judge writes a decision that will not bind future generations or reduce

their flexibility, using "words that trail rainbows but disguise his meaning," in Oliver Wendell Holmes' lovely description (Rosenfeld, 1962).

It is easier to be vague than to be specific or numerical, as you know if you have ever tried to evade a difficult examination question. Vague and empty language, which Barzun calls "hokum," may go undetected elsewhere, but it is fatal in research.

> Hokum is the counterfeit of true intellectual currency. It is words without meaning, verbal filler, artificial apples of knowledge. . . . Words should point to things, seen or unseen. But they can also be used to wrap up emptiness of heart and lack of thought. (Barzun, 1954: 25)

Locke long ago diagnosed the difficulty:

> . . . [H]e that shall well consider the errors and obscurity, the mistakes and confusion, that are spread in the world by an ill use of words, will find some reason to doubt whether language, as it has been employed, has contributed to the improvement or hindrance of knowledge amongst mankind. . . . This, I think I may at least say, that we should have a great many fewer disputes in the world, if words were taken for what they are, the signs of our ideas only, and not for things themselves. (Locke, 1956: 204)

As a test of precision, state your research procedure as a written set of instructions to a *layperson*. If the average person can follow your instructions and then return to you with the correct data you want to gather, then you have stated your research design well.

A class exercise dramatizes how difficult it is to write even the simplest set of instructions in unambiguous language. Students work in pairs. Each student leaves the classroom for five minutes and counts any set of objects in the rest of the building—perhaps the number of chandeliers on the first floor, the number of doors to the building, the number of stairs in the north staircase, or anything of which there is more than one. Then each student writes a set of instructions for his or her partner in hopes of leading the partner to count exactly the same things and to arrive at the same answer. The partners then exchange instructions and carry them out.

The results are often funny. One person counts five statues on the first floor; the partner counts none. Why? The instructions said "black statues," and the partner did not think the statues were exactly black. One person counts fifteen chandeliers on the first floor; the partner counts none. Why? What one partner called the first floor the other called the basement. One person counts eight staircases, and the partner counts two staircases. Why? One person counts the stairs between each floor as a staircase; the other counts the stairs from top floor to bottom floor as a staircase. And so it goes, showing how difficult it is to write *any* set of instructions, that is, an operational definition, that will really be satisfactory.

The language of empirical science has much similarity to the language that a witness is permitted to use in court: no hearsay, no speculation, what the witness himself observed and *only* what he or she observed. The empirical researcher must transform the vague, the unspecified, the abstract, into the specified and concrete, even though precision is hard work and all of us are lazy.

Trouble with scientific language also arises because of wrong notions about the relationship of words and things. Most people assume that, if there is a word, there is also a thing that corresponds to the word. If that were so, finding the right word would be a matter of searching through dictionaries and rule books until you found the right word for any thing or vice versa. This attitude is fostered by our laws and by the rules that parents must make for children as they are growing up. The state and city ordinances tell you, as they must, exactly what "speeding" is. And our immigration laws are precise about what makes a person "American." But, if you are doing a research study on speeding, the legal definition will probably not help you. Instead, you will have to make your own definition, a definition that is operational,

so that you can work with it and communicate it to others. And the definition must fit your particular research needs. And, if you are studying Mexican musicians, you will have to decide whether a pianist born and brought up in Russia but who now holds Mexican citizenship is a Mexican musician. The legal definition of "Mexican" will not suffice; nor can you use an operational definition that someone used in a study of Mexican exports.

The crucial idea is that *you must create your own definitions*—no one can do it for you. And the words do not have meaning—at least for the purpose of your study—until *you* give them meaning. As a practical matter one must try to use words in a manner that other people can understand. It is seldom sensible to coin words or to use familiar words in unfamiliar ways, and whenever possible you should use *exactly* the same operational definitions as previous writers in the field so that your work may be compared with theirs. But the definitions must fit *your* needs.

In applied research for clients, one often has trouble getting the client to be specific about what he wants to find out. If the client says, "Find out how to improve our advertising operation," the researcher cannot answer him *as a researcher*. (He may act in the role of consultant, but that is not research.) The researcher must find out whether the client wants to know the optimum *amount* of advertising or the best *type* of advertising, or what. The same is true in applied research for government agencies. It should be a *policy* decision whether the City of Los Angeles orders research done on how badly off is a minority group in housing, employment, or both, though the researcher may advise on which of the research projects would be most fruitful and feasible.

3. Validity and Reliability

Every piece of research aims to produce an answer to a scientific question. And it is reasonable to ask just *how good* an answer the research provides. Two concepts we use in judging how good the answer is are validity and reliability.

These concepts are most often used in judging particular parts of the research, especially the measurement of the variables we are interested in. A measurement (or definition or classification) is valid if it really classifies or measures what you want it to classify or measure. An I.Q. test is valid if it really does measure the future school success of students, because that is what it is intended to measure. A scale weighs validly if its weights agree with the commonly accepted weights of the Bureau of Standards in Washington. A pre-election Presidential poll is valid if it accurately picks the election winner. A count of the gold bars in Fort Knox is valid if it reveals how many bars "really" are there. (The best answer we can get might be off by $20 million in either direction, according to Morgenstern, 1963.) An operational definition of love is valid if all those people who fit it seem to the experts in the field to be in love.

There is no simple rule for deciding whether an operational definition is valid. Rather, the decision calls upon your judgment and scientific wisdom. Often a good test is whether you can persuade other scientists that the definition is valid. And of course the validity must depend upon the purpose of the study. For example, it is easy to make up a very reliable operational definition of "the faculty of the University of Illinois." You could use any of these definitions: the full professors listed in the staff directory; all assistant, associate, and full professors in the directory; all members of the faculty club; all buildings-and-grounds employees listed in the directory; or any other easily defined group. But if your purpose is to survey "faculty" opinion about an important campus issue, it is not so clear which definition to use. Should you include teaching assistants? research associates? retired professors? and so

on. A bad choice will give you an invalid definition. But what is the criterion of validity? The most valid definition in this case probably includes *those people whom your listener or reader will have in mind when you tell him what the faculty opinion is*.

Often there are several possible ways to validate an operational definition, and the validating method is best that gets "closest" to what the definition is intended to define or measure. One can think of a hierarchy among various validating methods. For example, no one would disagree that the *ultimate* validation of an I.Q. test is that it predicts well which students do well in school and which students do poorly. But another approach to validating an I.Q. test is to compare its results to those of well-established I.Q. tests. The latter validation is less powerful than the school-success validation, for it is less direct and therefore more subject to flaw; the well-established tests themselves may not be very valid. One method may be said to provide stronger validation than another method in a given situation; in another situation the relative validation power of the same two methods might be the reverse.

Entire studies as well as specific aspects of a study may be described as valid or invalid. For example, a study may be carried out with great precision, but the results may prove irrelevant to the question that motivated the work in the first place. For example, American I.Q. tests may be invalid for measuring the intellectual capacity of children in other cultures. Or a sample of prison convicts is probably invalid for study of the sex behavior of all Americans.

A study may also be invalid because its *internal* procedures are invalid. For example, a study of the effects of early stair-climbing training on a group of infants is invalid unless the results are compared with those from a group of infants who received no training. The results of such a "control group" will indeed reveal that the training has no long-run effect; the untrained group soon catches up with the trained group.

Reliability is an important element of validity. Reliability is roughly the same as *consistency* or *repeatability*. The concept applies to either operational definitions or to measuring devices. Unreliable results cause a study to be invalid. For example, if an intelligence test sometimes yields a high I.Q. score and sometimes a low I.Q. score for the same child, the results of the test are unreliable, and any study that employs the test is invalid.

A good operational definition is very reliable; that is, applying the definition produces the same result every time. And a weighing scale is reliable if it shows exactly the same reading every time a given iron bar is placed upon it. An I.Q. test is reliable if people get the same score when they are tested twice. Good operational definitions of "children," "live," and "farm" will lead *any* person to count the same number of children at a sample of dwelling places.

It is easy enough to check the reliability of a merchant's scale with repeated weighings of the same iron bar. But checking the reliability of an I.Q. test is more difficult. For example, most people do better the second time they take a given test. One of many ways to check the reliability of the I.Q. test is to split the test into two halves and examine whether the scores on the halves are similar.

An operational definition or measurement can be very reliable but still be invalid. For example, if the weighing scale always reads 10 per cent higher than a fair scale, the readings are no good. And if an I.Q. test has excellent split-half reliability but does not give higher scores to the students who later do better in school, the test is not useful. Another example: A thoroughly reliable operational definition for "love" is "Add the weights of a boy and a girl. If their combined weights total over 322 pounds, they will be said to be in love." But this measurement does not correspond at all to

the hypothetical concept of love you are trying to measure, and therefore it has no meaning. Chapters 6 and 15 describe the validation process and reliability in more detail.

4. Writing Scientific Reports

The "mere" writing up of results may strike you as a minor part of the research process. But do not skip this section; the subject is not trivial at all. The written description of research is a critical part of research itself. For example, in some kinds of research—especially experimental and survey tests of sharply stated hypotheses—you can often write up the report of the research before the data are collected, except for the actual results. This exercise helps you to think through a study and often uncovers difficulties in theory and design that would otherwise appear later and cause trouble.

If you write up the report early and if you write it up well, you have done much of the research job.

Research reports, and research proposals too, must follow the specifications that we have set forth for scientific language. Scientific communication must be *objective*, rather than *subjective*, in both the words and the concepts used. "Subjective" here means the thoughts that are inside one person's head and that are unavailable for checking by other people. "Objective" here means those statements that are *public* and checkable. ("Public knowledge" and "private knowledge" may be better terms respectively than "objective" and "subjective.")

We will not give you a set of step-by-step instructions on how to write up a research project. Such a set of procedures might force all your write-ups into that format whether or not it fits the needs of a particular project. And *no* format will fit *all* research. When preparing to write up a piece of research, read well-done pieces of research in your field, and choose as models one or more that resemble your project. Notice that no one format is used by all writers, even within a single restricted journal in a branch of psychology, say. There may be some very general similarities of format, but the organization of each report is tailored to the particular needs of each research project.

An important issue in many write-ups is how much to generalize from the data or how much to qualify the conclusions. Some researchers are supercautious about drawing inferences about their work or about hazarding the inferences in print. For example, to report a finding that men have more dreams of violence than women do but to claim that, because the sample all came from Illinois the results cannot therefore be generalized beyond Illinois, is ridiculous. Or, a biologist who finds that cigarette tars cause cancer in rats may refuse to suggest that cigarette tars may well have the same effect in humans. By so doing you may protect yourself from criticism, but you may also lessen the importance of your work by failing to make it relevant to researchers who are interested in cancer in humans. (Furthermore, there is an unattractive hypocrisy in such overcautiousness. We all know damn well that the only reason one studies the effect of cigarette smoking in rats is because of the possible implications for human beings.) Later, and particularly in the section on experiments, there is further discussion of when it is and when it is not reasonable to draw general inferences from samples.

On the other hand, the researcher also has an obligation to keep the reader from drawing unfounded inferences. Kinsey and his associates (1948) devoted much of their long explanation of method to limitations of data and method. But the officially appointed statisticians who reviewed the work (Cochran et al., 1953) gently chided them for not repeating the cautions regularly in the rest of the book so that the casual reader would not be misled.

Sometimes when you have a great many data you must decide how much to include in your report. Err on the side of reporting too much rather than too little, especially in appendixes. You can always cut out the excess.

A word about style in scientific writing. One of the purposes of the founding of the great Royal Society of London in 1660 was to encourage writers on scientific matters not to write special-pleading polemics full of loaded adjectives, but rather to use unemotional and unbiased language. This purpose is indeed admirable, but it has had some unintended and unfortunate consequences. For example, many scientists now refuse to write in the first person, which means that they must often forgo the active voice in their sentences. The passive voice often leads to tortured and ludicrous sentences that resemble a person's contortions when he or she tries to hide from a spotlight; the movement is not graceful. Furthermore, if a writer is artificially restricted from using such linguistic constructions as "I," there are fewer options and fewer tools available, and precision must diminish.

Scientific caution and the desire to avoid criticism also make scientific writing more complicated and sap its vigor and pleasantness. But, when we must make a choice, it is unhappily true that vigor and stylistic grace are the less important of the virtues.

5. Communicating with Yourself

Being precise, specific, and concrete in communicating *with yourself* is also important. To fail to make detailed plans is unwittingly to make important decisions by postponing or ignoring them. Not deciding may mean not doing, and what is not done now may not be possible at a later stage.

Specify as much as you can in advance. Draw up the tables for which you wish to collect data; you will be surprised how hard it is to do this, a sure tip-off that your thinking is too vague. When possible, it is wise to write up the research report prior to collecting data as an aid to good design planning. We cannot overemphasize the importance of doing these and similar exercises *early* in your research work.

Your self-communication is improved by subjecting yourself to the same discipline and requiring the same precision as for communication with someone else. Make liberal use of pencil and paper. Write down what you think you are thinking. You will constantly be surprised at how this method helps to clarify your thinking.

> . . . [V]ery often, a problem seemed settled, everything fixed and clear, till I began to write down a short preliminary sketch of my results. And only then, did I see the enormous deficiencies, which would show me where lay new problems, and lead me on to new work. In fact, I spent a few months between my first and second expeditions, and over a year between that and the subsequent one, in going over all my material, and making parts of it almost ready for publication each time, though each time I knew I would have to rewrite it. . . . I have written up an outline of the Kula institution at least half a dozen times while in the field and in the intervals between my expeditions. Each time, new problems and difficulties presented themselves. (Malinowski, 1961: 13)

It also helps to ask and answer such questions as "What do I really want to know?" and "What am I really trying to find out?" Returning to these fundamentals when you get stuck often clears up confusions like magic.

Your jottings in the course of the work serve as a better record of your research than your memory does. For example, when you make a decision to exclude or include a subject or datum in the sample, write down why. Later you will need this note when you write up the research. Write down all the other observations of what you see, and note what you did and why you did it. These notes are like the laboratory notebook that is of such crucial importance to natural scientists.

6. Honesty in Scientific Reporting

Scientific research is a human enterprise. And the individual researcher often has a stake in obtaining some particular outcome from the research—because the particular outcome will confirm his theory, or will be consistent with her ideological biases, or will be sensational and make him famous, or whatever. In this as in all other situations where there are interests at stake, there is pressure to produce the desired outcome, whether or not it can be found in the data.

Some scientific dishonesty[3] is flagrant, as in the example of Cyril Burt, the leading British psychologist of his time. His findings apparently showed that the intelligence of blacks, women, and lower-class Englishmen is lower than that of whites, men, and the British middle class. These findings have had a great influence on psychologists, on the lay public, and on social policy. A few years after Burt's death in 1971, unlikely coincidences were found in the data that led to the discovery of many other discrepancies, and to the judgment that his findings are scientifically worthless. Burt's motive apparently was that he wished to support his personal beliefs about the intelligence of various groups.

Another famous example is that of Piltdown man, the supposed remains of a prehistoric human that was concocted of modified modern remains in 1908 and not exposed until 1953.

Some other well-known recent examples from outside the social sciences include the following:

> Item: A scientist at the Sloane-Kettering Institute painted dark patches on white mice to make his colleagues believe he had perfected a way to make skin grafts between nontwins.

> Item: The Food and Drug Administration charged a major pharmaceutical manufacturer,

---

3. The following paragraphs are based on Rensberger (1977); see also Hunt (1981).

G. D. Searle & Company, with falsifying the scientific data upon which claims of the safety of two drugs and an artificial sweetener were based. Searle's research methods, according to an F.D.A. report, were so careless that reliable scientific conclusions could not be derived from them.

Item: A promising student at Harvard University reported experiments showing that something in the blood of one animal can be injected into another, transferring immunity to certain foreign substances. No other research group was able to reproduce the striking results. The line of research was abandoned amid publicly voiced suspicions that the test animals had been tampered with.

Item: A Pennsylvania State University chemist said that he had evidence that the sex scents of insects vary according to what the bugs eat. If true, his "finding" would destroy a major new avenue of research on safe pest controls. His university touted the results loudly. However, the chemist's co-workers examined the same data and repeated the experiments and found no evidence for the claim. The chemist said that he still believed in his theory and would repeat his experiments. (Rensberger, 1977: 1)

You are not likely to be tempted to commit such out-and-out major frauds. Your temptation may come when your data show a reasonably consistent picture, in accord with the outcome you desire, and then some fragment of conflicting evidence crops up—perhaps an experiment with a few rats of a different strain, or a sample of data from a census prior to the one you have been working on, or an analysis using a different mathematical form that you have assumed to be less appropriate than the line of analysis you have chosen. Or the conflicting evidence may be results contained in a forgotten article in an obscure journal by an unknown author that you just happen to come across.

Then the temptation is simply to convene a short conference with yourself, in which all sides of your mind arrive at a consensus that it would be scientifically appropriate to ignore the additional and conflicting evidence on the grounds that it really is not relevant. We doubt that any practicing empirical researcher is so saintly that such a thought has never crossed his or her mind. Our informal interviewing reveals that nine out of ten researchers admit it, and the tenth is a damned liar. Even Gregor Mendel, the founder of modern genetics, is now thought not just to have contemplated touching up the data, but actually to have falsified them to make them fit his theory—though the theory was in fact correct.

The prevalence of the problem is suggested by this observation:

Last spring a graduate student at Iowa State University required data of a particular kind in order to carry out a study for his master's thesis. In order to obtain these data he wrote to 37 authors whose journal articles appeared in APA journals between 1959 and 1961. Of these authors, 33 replied. Twenty-two of these reported the data misplaced, lost, or inadvertently destroyed. Two of the remaining 11 offered their data on the conditions that they be notified of our intended use of their data, and stated that they have control of anything that we would publish involving these data. . . . We met the former condition but refused the latter for those two authors since we felt the raw data from published research should be made public upon request when possible and economically feasible. Thus raw data from 9 authors were obtained. From these 9 authors, 11 analyses were obtained. Four of these were not analyzed by us since they were made available several months after our request. Of the remaining 7 studies, 3 involved gross errors. One involved an analysis of variance on transformed data where the transformation was clearly inappropriate. Another analysis contained a gross computational error so that several *F* ratios near one were reported to be highly significant. The third analysis incorrectly reported insignificant results due to the use of an inappropriate error term. . . . (Wolins, 1962: 657)

Doctoring the data can ruin your reputation and destroy your career. In addition, every instance of a scientist's dishonesty that becomes known damages the reputation of the scientific enterprise and makes it more difficult for all scientists to gain the support they need to do their work. And remember that unexpected, even seemingly incorrect, results can lead to a positive outcome; some of the world's great discoveries have come from researchers who took apparently conflicting data seriously and pursued the discrepancy, rather than sweeping it under the rug, thereby leading to great new findings.

7. Summary

Theoretical scientific discussions must be converted into operationally defined terms when empirical research is performed. One key test of an operational definition is whether readers and subsequent researchers will know exactly what empirical operations you performed, so that these operations can be repeated precisely. This is the test of *reliability*.

A good operational definition must also refer closely to the theoretical concept you are interested in; a reliable but irrelevant operational definition is not *valid* and hence worthless. A good operational definition also has little error in measurement.

More generally, an empirical study is valid if it yields a reliable answer to the question to which it is addressed, that is, if the research purpose is well met.

Good scientific communication claims neither too much nor too little for the findings of a study. Good scientific writing is clear and vigorous, but relatively objective and unemotional.

EXERCISES

1. An operational definition should suit the purposes of the particular study in which it is to be used. Briefly describe a research project in which each of the following terms might be used, and then create a satisfactory operational definition of the term: "learning"; "part-time job"; "religious rite"; "aggressiveness"; "personal income"; "vacation"; "memory"; "war"; "bartender"; "most popular man on your college campus"; "money" (be careful not to stop with just currency); "tribal loyalty"; "vocational education"; "Negro."

2. Work out an operational definition for the concept "United States resident" for use in a census in this country. Do the same for an underdeveloped African country. Pay special attention to whether a person lives there on the date of the census and whether that person ordinarily lives there. Explain the reasons for your operational definitions in terms of the purposes of the censuses.

3. Find five examples of good operational definitions in your major field of interest. Then find five examples of poor operational definitions. Tell why they are good or bad.

4. You want to explore the relationship between the amount of attention mothers give to infants and the extent to which one-year-old babies love their mothers. Define "attention" and "love."

5. You want to test the hypothesis that the introduction of universal literacy into underdeveloped countries leads to rapid social and economic development. Define "introduction" and "development."

6. Read the following quotation. How would you go about constructing operational definitions of the 15 major types of headaches?

Heady with victory over gravity, tooth decay and the atom, laboratory science appears to be gearing up for an assault on mankind's oldest ailment—the headache.

The first report from the battlefront by the Ad Hoc Committee of the Classification of Headache of the National Institute of Neurological Diseases and Blindness lists 15 major types of headache, from migraines to cranial neuralgias. (Champaign-Urbana *Courier,* January 26, 1964, p. 33)

ADDITIONAL READING

On operational definitions, see Underwood (1957: Chap. 3). Also see Selltiz et al. (1976: 42–44).

On the writing of research reports, especially in sociology, see Whitney (1950: Chap. 16) and Selltiz et al. (1957: Chap. 15); for business and economics, see Berenson and Colton (1971).

Useful notes on research procedure and information about papers, libraries, and so on, may be found in Bart and Frankel (1979), especially for sociologists.

To improve your prose, see *The Elements of Style* by Strunk and White, a clear and pleasant summary of the important rules for good writing.

Basic Concepts of Research

1. Variables in General

Variables and parameters are the final forms in which you work with scientific terms and concepts. Therefore, the words "variable" and "parameter"—along with "function"—are the most common words in most scientific discussions.

A variable is not just "some quantity that varies." A variable is a quantity *in which you are interested* that varies in the course of the research or that has different values for different samples in your study. Everything changes sooner or later. But a variable is a factor whose change or difference you study.

Perhaps giving specific examples of "variables" will help.[1] Amount of rain is probably a

variable to a meteorologist studying precipitation but not to an astronomer who is studying stars—though the rain may be annoying to the astronomer because it makes the stars invisible. Rain is not likely to be a variable to a biologist studying lung cancer. But rain *might* have something to do with air pollution, which might have something to do with lung cancer, in which case rain would indeed become a variable to the biologist. Temperature and humidity are probably not variables for a psychologist studying intelligence in Chicago school children, but they might well be variables to an anthropologist or economist studying the cultural or economic development of primitive peoples.

The researchers choose their variables on the basis of their interests and their ideas

---

1. Some social scientists use "relevant variable" as "variable" is used here. We think it is less confusing, however, to consider that irrelevant variables are not variables at all.

about what would be especially important or valuable to investigate. For example, it is entirely a decision of the researcher to study the effects of broken homes on juvenile delinquency rather than the relationship between neurosis and juvenile delinquency. Both choices may be good ones, and the choice is not forced by the nature of reality. Of course, the good researcher does not choose variables at random or casually; rather he or she chooses them with extreme care, for such choices are crucial ones. Poorly chosen variables yield useless results.

2. The Dependent Variable

The dependent variable (actually there may be several dependent variables, but that is unusual) is that quantity or aspect of nature whose *change or different states* the researcher wants to understand or explain or predict.[2] In cause-and-effect investigations, the effect variable is the dependent variable. If you wish to investigate whether there is any relationship between the mother's smoking cigarettes and the weight of the baby, then cigarette smoking is an independent variable.

3. The Independent Variable

The best definition of an independent variable is a variable *whose effect upon the dependent variable you are trying to understand*. There may be several independent variables. You may simultaneously investigate the effect of the mother's cigarette smoking, the mother's exercise, parents' weights, and other variables upon the weight of the baby.

In some kinds of research one cannot label the variables as dependent and independent. In descriptive studies, you may only wish to show how a population is distributed on some

2. The terms "explain" and "predict," as well as the related terms "causality," "function," and "scientific law," are distinguished and defined in Chapter 35. For the time being, these words are used in a crude sense corresponding to everyday usage.

variables; the U.S. Census tells, for example, how many people live in each county in the United States. But in studies dealing with complex processes and many variables, a variable may be independent in one part of the study and dependent in another part. When trying to analyze the determinants of economic success, for instance, one may first use education as an independent variable to predict income level, and then treat education as a dependent variable predicted by such variables as father's occupation, in order to map the multistage process leading to success.

4. Parameters

The concept of parameter is tricky. A parameter is a quantity that has some importance to a study but that remains *unchanged* in the course of the study. This is why some people say frivolously that a parameter is a variable that does not vary.

To illustrate, Figure 3.1 shows the hypothetical relationship between the price of scallions and the quantity of scallions that people buy in a given year.

The triangles represent the quantities sold during periods when various prices prevailed. The straight line is drawn among the triangles as close to as many of them as possible (though there are several ways to do it). The assumption is that each of the triangles may be somewhat in error and that the line represents a better guess than any given observation of how much would be sold at a given price, because the line is based on the information contained in *all* the observed triangles. One might draw curved lines of various shapes also, depending on one's general knowledge of the scallion market, but a straight line is particularly easy to work with.

In algebraic terms, the formula for a straight line is y equals a plus bx. Or, in the example at hand, $q = a + bp$, where q is the quantity of scallions sold and p the price of scallions and where a and b are measured from the diagram or estimated statistically. The algebraic con-

FIGURE 3.1 Hypothetical Relationship Between the Price and Production of Scallions

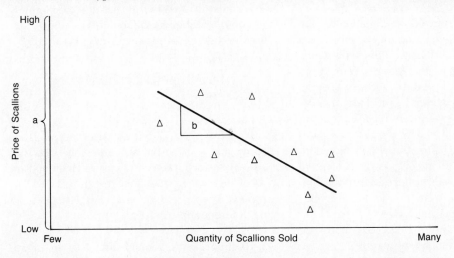

stants *a* and *b* are *parameters* for the scallion market and are assumed to stay the same no matter what the price of scallions is. With the help of the parameters, you can predict how many scallions will be sold for any price you pick.

Of course, the parameters may change. In another country or another decade, more or fewer scallions might be sold at any given price than the line in Figure 3.1 indicates. But, *for the particular set of circumstances you are working with*, *a* and *b* are assumed to be constant, and that is why parameters are called "constant variables."

A parameter is a property of a whole universe[3] and *not* only of the sample you observe. The term "statistic" is applied to the sample's counterpart of the parameter. For example, if you poll a sample of Kansas voters and find that 56 percent expect to vote Democratic in the next election, that figure is a statistic. On the basis of the sample you might *estimate* that 56 percent of *all* voters expect to vote Democratic, but your estimate of the parameter based on the statistic could be in error. The

actual percentage of all voters who expect to vote Democratic is the parameter.

5. The Functional Form

The mathematical-logical concept of function is very different from the anthropological-sociological concept of the same name (see Merton, 1968: Chap. 1). In the mathematical-logical sense with which we are concerned here, to say that "*y* is a function of *x*" means only that the magnitude of *y* *depends upon* the magnitude of *x*. The statement implies that *y* is the dependent variable and *x* (or several *x*'s) the independent variable(s).

Functional relationships are written in algebraic notation, for example, $y = f(x_1, x_2, x_3)$ if there are three independent variables. This algebra is to be read "*y* is a function of x_1, x_2, and x_3" or "*y* depends upon x_1, x_2, and x_3" or "*y* is the dependent variable whose values (magnitudes) depend upon the values (magnitudes) of x_1, x_2, and x_3."

Another letter, perhaps *g* or *h*, could replace *f*, just as *w* or *z* might be used instead of *x*; the choice of letters is quite arbitrary.

In the scallion example, (quantity of scallions produced) = *f* (price of scallions) is translated

---

3. See page 30 for a discussion of the meaning of the term "population" or its synonym in research terminology, "universe."

as "the quantity of scallions produced depends upon (is a function of) the price of scallions."

The causal direction of the functional relationship—that is, which variable is put on the left side as the dependent variable, and which is put on the right as the independent variable—is a decision that the researcher makes in light of his or her general knowledge of the subject matter. A given set of variables and data may sometimes be viewed one way, sometimes the other, and sometimes both ways together. For example, in some cases, the price of scallions is seen as the dependent variable, in some cases quantity is seen as the dependent variable, and in some cases—where there is thought to be mutual causation—both are dependent *and* independent variables. More about this later.

The concept and notation of a function are of enormous value in clarifying ideas. The concept is common in all sciences that have reached the stage of investigating relationships, especially cause-and-effect relationships. (But in types of research that really have no independent variables—especially descriptive research of the census type—the functional form is not appropriate or useful.) Algebraic notation is not necessary to express the functional notion that something depends on something else. As we have seen, this idea can be expressed in words alone by simply indicating which are the dependent and independent variables, and many teachers argue that algebraic notation only confuses the student. We are convinced, however, that the exercise of expressing variables in algebraic functional notation is very useful, even if one goes no further with mathematical analysis.

6. Assumption, Theory, Deduction, Hypothesis, Fact, and Law

Assumption, theory, deduction, hypothesis, fact, and law are commonly used concepts in science, though they are often confused with one another. Their definitions and the relationships among them can best be brought out in the context of a concrete case in economics, the most effective user among the social sciences of a deductive theoretical apparatus.

A. EXAMPLE 1: INTEREST RATES AND GEOGRAPHY

Problem and Fact.   It is an observed *fact* that savings-and-loan interest rates on deposits were higher on the West Coast than on the East Coast or in the Midwest in 1977. The *problem* is to predict what would happen to this difference in the future.

Assumptions.   We *assume* first that investors will choose the highest available rate of return among investments that have equal risks, that is, that investors are "rational" in this respect. (Notice that this assumption does *not* imply that human beings are generally rational rather than irrational or that all investors will act rationally. Every economist knows that humans are often irrational, just as many free-falling objects, such as leaves and balloons, do not obey the law of gravity. Rather, this assumption is an "abstraction" or an "ideal type," as Weber, 1974: 89, 110, called it.) Second, we *assume* that there are information flows in the real estate market. (In most problems, the economist goes further and assumes *perfect* information.) Third, we *assume* that there are no barriers to moving money from one part of the United States to another. (This assumption would not be made for movement among countries in an international trade problem.)

An assumption is any statement in this form: "If *w* holds true—and I assume that it does—then *z* will happen." There are many types of assumptions. One important distinction is between abstract assumptions that are part of the entire theoretical apparatus, of which we have given three examples, and assumptions that are specific to the case under discussion, such as the *ceteris paribus* clause—which means, in this case, that no unusual force is operating to confuse the situation (see Machlup, 1955, and Melitz, 1965).

Deduction. We then *deduce* that interest rates—savings-and-loan interest rates in this case—will be the same in all parts of the United States. Given the assumptions, this *deduction* can be made as formally as any deduction in geometry. But of course the deduction holds true only *if* the assumptions are well chosen—just as a calculation that uses the formula for a square to determine the area of a plot of land will be correct only if the plot of land has the shape of a square.

The test of a deduction—and of the theory within which it takes place—is that *all* scientists in a given field must be able to agree that the deduction is valid *if* the assumptions are well chosen. A deduction is only an exercise in logic, just as is the arithmetic statement that $3 \times 15 = 45$.

Theory. If there are well-established assumptions in a field, and if there is an apparatus that permits such a deduction as we have made, then one may talk about a body of theory. If so, a speculative statement (conjecture) must be related to this whole body of theory if it is to be called "theoretical." In other fields, any conjecture or deduction from general experience is called theory. More about this in Chapter 5.

Hypothesis. We then translate the deduction into a *hypothesis* or *conjecture* that can be tested empirically. In this case, the hypothesis is that interest rates for the same type of deposit will *become* more nearly equal in various parts of the country as time passes. The reasoning is that there must have been some unusual and sudden conditions that created a temporary imbalance among parts of the country. By deduction, the rates will be equal if there is not some continuing reason why they should be unequal, and we assume that there

is no such continuing force. Therefore, the interest rates can be expected to become more equal. This is the hypothesis to be tested empirically.

Not all hypotheses are deduced from theories, though most of them rest on facts and assumptions. One might look around and hypothesize that tall girls get married earlier than short girls. This is indeed a scientific hypothesis, but it comes directly from observation and unformalized intuition rather than as a deduction from a body of theory. And a hypothesis is not the same as a theory, though many writers use the two terms almost interchangeably (for example, Friedman, 1953: 3–46). A hypothesis (conjecture) is a single statement that attempts to explain or predict a single phenomenon, whereas a theory is an entire system of thought that refers to many phenomena and whose parts can be related to one another in deductive logical form.

An unfortunate confusion in usage pervades this book and others, however. We often talk about "theoretical concepts" when we really mean "hypothetical concepts." For example, when discussing an investigation into people's *happiness*, we called the vague and undefined concept *happiness* a theoretical concept—even though it is not part of any theory—to distinguish it from the *empirical* concept (in this case, people's answers to a questionnaire) that will *stand for* the hypothetical concept. But in view of existing practice, to stick to the better usage would only be confusing here. Furthermore, the terms "empirical concept" and "empirical variable" are both used, though they are synonymous, which adds further confusion.[4]

Law. If many empirical tests of the hypothesis confirm it, the generalization might be called a *law*, provided that the finding is sufficiently important. Even if our hypothesis were

4. Sociologists commonly use a slightly different lingo. This book's "empirical variable" is their "indicator," and this book's "hypothetical concept" is just plain "concept" to them.

to be confirmed empirically, it is insufficiently important to be called a "law."

7. Universe and Sample

A universe (or population) is some group of people or objects in which you are interested. A universe can be finite and well-defined— "everyone registered to vote in Cleveland" for example—or it may be infinite or hypothetical—"all students who will graduate from college in 2010 and thereafter."

A sample is some *subgroup* of the universe. The purpose of studying a sample is to make some generalization about the universe. The major reason for taking *only* a sample, rather than studying the entire universe, is *cost*, which is discussed in more detail in Chapter 23; studying the entire universe is almost always prohibitively expensive.

There are many kinds of samples, of which the random sample is a very important type. A sample is random if every member of the universe stands the same chance[5] of being included in it. (Read this definition again, and make sure you understand it.) Groups chosen on the basis of the researcher's judgment about their similarity or typicality are another type of sample. Sampling validity and efficiency will be discussed at length in Chapter 9.

8. The Ideal Causal-Study Design

Much—but not all—of social science is the investigation of causal relationships. Therefore, let us consider what is involved in establishing a causal relationship between some dependent variable y and a particular independent variable x. This section is a preview of much that follows about research design.

Determining a causal relationship would ideally be done as follows: The value of the dependent variable y that is observed for any

5. More precisely, the sampling *process* is random if every member of the universe has a *known* chance of being included in the sample.

given subject in the study depends on three elements: first, what the subject was like before it was acted upon by the independent variable; second, the particular level (value or strength or variety) of the independent variable's action upon the subject during the study period; and, third, the particular values of all other variables that act upon the subject during the study period, both those in which you may be interested and those that are just interferences. To put it in algebraic notation (which you may skip if you like but which we believe will help you and should not scare you at all):

$$y_i = f(x_{i,\,1},\, x_{i,\,2} \ldots x_{i,\,n};\, v_{i,\,1},\, v_{i,\,2} \ldots v_{i,\,n};\, z_{i,\,1},\, z_{i,\,2},\, \ldots z_{i,\,n}).$$

In this equation y_i is the observed value of the dependent variable for subject i; $x_{i,\,1}$ is the value of the independent variable x_1 that subject i is exposed to during the study; $x_{i,\,2} \ldots x_{i,\,n}$ are other variables in which you may be interested that act upon the subject i during the study period but that we shall ignore now; $v_{i,\,1},\, v_{i,\,2} \ldots v_{i,\,n}$ are the influences that acted upon the particular subject i and formed him or her before the study began; and $z_{i,\,1},\, z_{i,\,2} \ldots z_{i,\,n}$ are other influences that may affect the outcome of the research (that is, may affect the observed y for a given subject) but which you are *not* interested in. The z's will be called "interfering" or "confounding" variables or, in some contexts, "parameters." (The definitions of all these terms vary somewhat among the people who use them and the situations in which the terms are used.)

For example, consider a study of the effect of the amount of protein in children's diets upon their ability to learn, as indicated by their ability to memorize nonsense syllables. The symbol y_i represents child i's score on a memory test. The symbol $v_{i,\,1}$ represents the intelligence of her parents, $v_{i,\,2}$ the quality of her schooling, and so on for other v's. The symbol $x_{i,\,1}$ is the independent variable, the amount of protein in child i's diet. The symbol $z_{i,\,1}$ might represent the amount of exercise the child gets during the study period; $z_{i,2}$ might represent the time of the day the memory test is given; $z_{i,3}$ might represent which tester examines and grades the child; and so on for the many other possible z's.

The ideal study is one in which two (or more) groups of subjects, each made up of subjects with exactly the same v qualities, are subjected to two (or more) different levels of independent variable x_i, *ceteris paribus*, that is, while all the other z influences are kept exactly the same for all the subjects in the study. In the example above, it could mean that, say, two identical groups of children (that is, each group containing children with exactly the same personal-background qualities [v] as those in the other group) would have two different amounts of protein in their diets. All would be tested for memory at the same time of day, all would get the same amount of exercise, and so on.

Now we must ask how the researcher can meet these requirements for the ideal study of causal relationship. *First,* how can the personal-background variables be made equal in the two groups? If you can conduct a controlled experiment, this problem in achieving *ceteris paribus* may be solved perfectly, at least in principle, by calling upon the device of *randomization of the assignment of subjects to treatments*. If you were working with rats instead of children (and testing their memories with a device more appropriate to rats than nonsense-syllable learning), you could start with a large collection of rats and could randomly choose which rats would get the high-protein diet and which the low-protein diet. This could be done by giving each rat a number and then assigning the high-protein diet to the first half of the numbers pulled from a hat. If the sample groups were large enough, all the relevant background characteristics (v's) would then be distributed fairly evenly between the high-protein and low-protein groups (the proof of this is the statistical principle known as the "law of large numbers"). This is why the ran-

domization of subjects is a powerful weapon and a crucial principle in carrying out valid studies of causal relationships.

For several reasons a researcher may not be able to achieve this ideal in equating personal-background characteristics. First, the group of subjects may be too small in number for the law of large numbers to guarantee a decent split of the various characteristics among the two groups. In that case, you may try to *match* the groups by assigning subjects that exhibit the characteristics you deem relevant to the two groups as equally as possible. Effective matching of experimental groups is not easy to achieve, as we shall see later.

A *second* force that may prevent random assignment of subjects to groups is that the researcher may not have the power to arrange a controlled experiment; that is, it may just be impossible for you to assign people to groups and then subject the groups to experimental treatment—as may well be the case with protein diets and children. One possible (but treacherous) device is to match subjects *after the fact*, that is, to find apparently similar people who *already* have been subjected to one or another of the treatments and then compare them on the y variable. This device will be discussed at length later.

Now we proceed to the part of the causal study that is usually *hardest* to do well, the handling of the interfering variables (z's) that influence the subjects starting at the time when x_1, the independent variable of interest, begins to act, that is, after the study period begins. The first point to remember is that *each z variable must be taken care of separately and explicitly by the researcher*. This situation is unlike the one with the personal-background variables, in which—if experimentation and random assignment of subjects are possible—you can take care of all of them at one fell swoop by assigning subjects randomly to the experimental groups. In the present instance, if you do *not* properly take care of some important z your research may be ruined.

One way to take care of any z variable is to make it a *parameter*, that is, to "hold it constant" and make it the same for all subjects in all experimental groups. In the protein-memory example, amount of sleep might affect the subjects' performances. This factor can be held constant by putting all the subjects in both experimental groups to sleep at the same time and waking them all at the same time. But some variables cannot be held constant in this fashion; in every piece of research there are several such variables. For example, one might want all the children to eat their meals at the same time of day, to have their memories tested at the same time of day, and to have their memories tested by the same examiner. But suppose that it is physically impossible for each child to begin eating at the same moment because of limited feeding facilities, and some children must wait for others to be tested before it is their turn. And unless there is only one examiner, the children must somehow be divided among different examiners. For any one of these variables that cannot be held constant, an effective alternative is to arrange it so that the members of each experimental group are affected *randomly* by the variable. For example, it should be a matter of a coin toss or dice throw whether each child in each group eats on the early or the late shift. Also the order in which the children are tested, and by which examiner, should be arranged with random drawings. These random arrangements will—if the groups are large enough—accomplish much the same result as holding the variables constant, by ensuring that *on the average* the two groups will be affected reasonably equally by each of the z variables. This device may be termed "randomization of interfering variables to avoid confounding" or just "randomization." When the researcher cannot control these variables experimentally, however, difficulties arise.

Earlier we said that there is no automatic way to achieve *ceteris paribus* and to handle *all* the nonrelevant variables, even if one has complete experimental control. The reason should now be clear. The experimenter must be able at least to *identify* each nonrelevant variable that might influence the results so that she can try to hold it constant or randomize its effect; no blanket mechanism handles *all* these nonrelevant variables. And no one's imagination is active enough to think of *all* the possible interfering (confounding) variables. Furthermore, no one's resources are great enough to be able to deal with every possible interfering variable that has even a slight likelihood of being important.

9. Ceteris Paribus[6]

Theoreticians can ignore the *ceteris paribus* problem, or simply salute it. But to arrange affairs so that other things *are* reasonably equal is perhaps the hardest and most important struggle that the empirical researcher must face.

One of the outstanding characteristics of the social sciences is that the subject matter is not static, not fixed, not immutable. In classical physics or chemistry you can usually be confident that what happens today will also happen tomorrow, that what happens in the East will happen in the West, and that what happens to the contents of one test tube will happen again to those of the next test tube. The chemist or physicist seldom needs to worry that a sample of matter perversely jumped into the hand to be studied just *because* it is different from other samples of matter. But exactly these things occur in social science studies all the time. All such occurrences are "departures

6. *Ceteris paribus* is Latin for "other things being equal."

We reduce to inaction all other forces by the phrase "other things being equal": we do not suppose that they are inert, but for the time we ignore their activity. This scientific device is a great deal older than science: it is the method by which, consciously or unconsciously, sensible men have dealt from time immemorial with every difficult problem of ordinary life. (Marshall, 1961: xiv) from" or "breaches of " *ceteris paribus*. All of them are conditions that the social scientist must overcome in order to "hold everything else constant."

Here are two glaring examples of breaches of *ceteris paribus* that vitiate comparisons:

SAT Scores Show 300-Point Variation Across U.S.

> Students' average Scholastic Aptitude Test scores vary by as much as 300 points from state to state, according to a new survey. . . . Each half of the test is scored on a scale of 200 to 800. The highest average score was in Iowa, where 1,300 seniors . . . scored 515 on verbal and 566 on math for a combined score of 1081.
>
> The lowest average scores were in South Carolina—374 verbal, 406 math, 780 combined. . . . (Nashville *Tennessean*, November 2, 1981, p. 12)

One might think that the main cause of this difference is a difference in education or intellectual abilities among high school students in different states. However,

> the main reason for the differences is that relatively few students took the college entrance examination in the states with the highest scores, according to College Board officials. . . . Robert Cameron, the College Board's executive director of research and development said, "The Iowa students taking the test are (probably) going to competitive colleges such as the University of Chicago, Stanford, (and) the Ivies." Most students in Iowa and other Midwest states take the rival exam offered by the American College Testing program of Iowa City. (Connell, 1981)

That is, only three percent of Iowa seniors took the test, and many of these were probably among the best students in the state. In South Carolina, 48 percent of seniors took the test, including many more average and even below-average students. Naturally the more highly selected group of students made higher scores.

> We hear of a museum in a certain Eastern city that was proud of its amazing attendance record. Recently a little stone building was erected nearby. Next year attendance at the museum mysteriously fell off by 100,000. What was the

little stone building? A comfort station. (Wallis and Roberts, 1966: 160)

The enormity of these *ceteris paribus* breaches make it likely that the researcher will find them out and remedy them. More dangerous are the subtle influences that can ruin the research, like those Pavlov described:

> The environment of the animal, even when shut up by itself in a room, is perpetually changing. Footfalls of a passer-by, chance conversations in neighboring rooms, slamming of a door or vibration from a passing van, street-cries, even shadows cast through the windows into the room, any of these casual uncontrolled stimuli falling upon the receptors of the dog set up a disturbance in the cerebral hemispheres and vitiate the experiments. To get over all these disturbing factors a special laboratory was built at the Institute of Experimental Medicine in Petrograd, the funds being provided by a keen and public-spirited Moscow businessman. The primary task was the protection of the dogs from uncontrolled extraneous stimuli, and this was effected by surrounding the building with an isolating trench and employing other special structural devices.
>
> Inside the building all the research rooms (four to each floor) were isolated from one another by a cross-shaped corridor; the top and ground floors, where these rooms were situated, were separated by an intermediate floor. Each research room was carefully partitioned by the use of soundproof materials into two compartments—one for the animal, the other for the experimenter. For stimulating the animal, and for registering the corresponding reflex response, electrical methods or pneumatic transmission were used. By means of these arrangements it was possible to get something of that stability of environmental conditions so essential to the carrying out of a successful experiment (1966: 109)

The point of the *ceteris paribus* idea is that it is not sensible to compare a sample of apples to a sample of oranges if you are trying to find out the effect of two kinds of fertilizer. How would you ever know whether the apples had an especially good season *because* of fertilizer A, or because it was a good season for apples and not for oranges? Analogously, people in Rochester may differ from people in Syracuse, for many reasons. To compare their reactions to different advertisements is to compare the effects on apples and oranges. All other things in Syracuse are not equal to all other things in Rochester, and therefore the simple comparison is flawed.

Of course, it is true that we can *never* get all the other things equal. Even the people *within* Rochester are not exactly like one another, and no two apples in a basket are perfectly alike. The only way that we could get everything *perfectly* equal would be to try the different fertilizers on the *same* tree or to try the different advertisements on the same person. Even then all else would not be equal because a person is not the same person after being exposed to the first advertisement, and the tree is not the same in two successive growing seasons.

We must resign ourselves to the fact that we shall never get all the other things *exactly* equal. Instead, our job is to get other things *as nearly equal as possible* or at least equal *enough* so that we can proceed with the research without hindrance by unexpected and unknown inequalities in the conditions surrounding the research.

10. Summary

This chapter introduces basic concepts in research.

A *variable* is a factor in which you are interested that varies in the course of the research. The *dependent* variable is the quantity whose variation you wish to explain or predict or understand. *Independent* variables are forces whose effect upon the dependent variables you wish to evaluate.

The term *parameter* has two quite different meanings. In one meaning it is a quantity that may affect the research but that you wish to keep immobilized and unchanged throughout the study. In another meaning a parameter is a property of a universe, in contrast to a *statistic*, which is an estimate of the parameter obtained from a sample.

The *functional form* $y = f(x)$ is the basic logical structure of all cause-and-effect research.

Assumption, theory, deduction, hypothesis, fact, and *law* are often-confusing elements of the meld of theoretical and empirical research. Their meaning and use differ from one social science to another.

A *sample* is a group selected from the *universe (population)* for the purpose of describing the population. *Randomly drawn* samples have great advantages but sometimes they are not practical; sometimes matched or judgmental samples are more appropriate.

The ideal design for the study of cause and effect compares the effect of different independent variables upon the dependent variable in randomly chosen sample groups. Irrelevant factors must be controlled to prevent them from ruining the study; that is, there must be no important breaches of *ceteris paribus*.

EXERCISES

1. Give an example of a quantity that is a variable to one researcher but not a variable to another researcher, though it is part of the "environment" of the second researcher's study.
2. Illustrate the concept of parameter in a context other than economic demand analysis.
3. Illustrate the relationship of the concepts of statistic and parameter for a given universe.
4. Express the essence of any three scientific studies in the functional form $y = f(x_1, x_2 \ldots)$. Or, if you have dug in your heels and resist accepting the algebraic functional

form, write down the dependent and independent variables for the three studies. (That is, we are asking you to write down the dependent and independent variables for the three studies in an explicit fashion.)

5. Suppose you want to study the market value of houses in your neighborhood. Your method is to ask your neighbors how much they paid for their houses. One family bought their house in 1967 for $20,000; another bought their house in 1981 for $60,000. What breaches of *ceteris paribus* conditions might stop you from concluding that the second house was worth three times as much as the first? Think of three other examples in which lack of attention to *ceteris paribus* conditions could cause you to come to incorrect conclusions.

Types of Empirical Research $\boxed{4}$

1. Introduction

Students of psychology often think that experimental investigation of cause-and-effect relationships in human or animal behavior constitutes the whole of social-science research. Many students of economics think that the statistical investigation of the past relationship between price and the amount of commodities sold is the only way to do empirical investigation in economics. Some students of anthropology believe that only participant-observers learn anything worthwhile about the social world we live in. Psychoanalysts sometimes act as if no one can claim to understand anything about human behavior without subjecting it to clinical analysis in depth. Students of market research sometimes think that all research involves finding the relationship between particular personal and social characteristics and purchasing behavior. And the other disciplines have pet methods too.

Each of these beliefs has some basis in fact.[1] But one of the main themes of this book is that there are many types of empirical research and that each may be proper for a particular scientific researcher tackling a particular question. "Mere" description by an anthropologist may seem terribly primitive to a psychophysicist, but a wise psychophysicist may sometimes use a simple descriptive technique to a good advantage. Conversely, an anthropologist who has an imaginative approach to the subject may one day engage in a simple laboratory experi-

1. The best way to define the various social-scientific disciplines may well be in terms of their characteristic methods, whereas it seems to us that the natural sciences tend to cluster around substantive problems.

ment to test a theory. One should not let one's discipline determine the choice of method; rather, one should fit the method to the problem.

The task of this chapter is to distinguish among and describe the various types of research *problems,* to help you understand the research possibilities of the research question you select. In order to choose the appropriate research *methods,* one must understand the nature of the research question (see Chapter 18) and also the *obstacles to getting knowledge* to answer the question.

This chapter may seem unsatisfying to you because it introduces a great many topics without discussing them thoroughly. More detailed discussion comes later. The purpose of this chapter is primarily *orientation,* to provide a wide overview of the types of work done in social science.

2. Case-Study Descriptive Research

In the beginning, there is description. When one does not know anything at all about a problem, one must understand it in a *general* way before beginning to make specific inquiries about specific aspects of the subject. For example, the early explorer in a new land writes a general description of the appearance of the country, its geography, climate, people, flora, fauna, and much else. Sea captains and missionaries wrote such descriptions of many exotic lands, though too often their reports were anecdotal and shallow. The early explorer chooses to describe what he or she thinks is important and interesting, without any rigid rules of scientific evidence. This first description is important because it serves to focus subsequent studies. Geologists later come to study the peculiar stone formations mentioned in the explorer's report. And anthropologists rush to study with great objectivity the extraordinary patterns of mating with foreigners only hinted at therein.

Detailed, descriptive case studies are usually the jumping-off point for the study of new areas in the social sciences (and are described in more detail in Chapter 13). Freud's case history "Observation 1—Miss Anna O." and similar histories of other patients laid the foundation for modern clinical and personality psychologies. Since Freud's original descriptive explorations, there have appeared many other types of studies of the original theories, including observational and questionnaire surveys and experiments. As Freud put it, "the true beginning of scientific activity consists . . . in describing phenomena and [only] then in proceeding to group, classify and correlate them . . ." (Kaplan, 1964: 78).

Much anthropological research is descriptive, deliberately setting out to create a rounded picture of an entire culture or some broad aspect of it. In economics the industry case study continues to be done long after economics has left its infancy, though in contemporary industry studies, the economist uses sophisticated theories and statistical techniques of description that encompass the other types of research we shall discuss. (This fact shows the difficulty of classifying types of research. We shall also find descriptive research done within frameworks of classification, cause-and-effect, and other methods.)

A business consultant generally begins work with a general description of the situation. But the "operations research" person often skips this stage, immediately narrows down the problem, and tackles it as a more "advanced" type of research. Sometimes this early narrowing-down is successful, but sometimes it causes the operations researcher to miss the essence of the problem.

Some scientists regard descriptive research as only an early stage of research. There is some value to this point of view. Descriptive research does not create laws and conclusions that apply beyond the subject matter described. Rather, it provides *clues* for subsequent research to pin down and generalize.

Nevertheless, we think it is unsound to see

descriptive research as only a stage. First, a piece of descriptive research can be of important scientific value for itself, even though it cannot be generalized; a study of the aluminum industry, for example, can provide information valuable for such purposes as antitrust evaluations, even though the findings do not apply to all other industries. And, second, the stage view implies that we know what the later stages of research are. We do not think there is solid evidence for such an evolutionary view of science.

The importance of deciding upon and defining the variables in a research study was emphasized in the previous chapter. But a descriptive study often does not have a set of clearly delineated dependent and independent variables. It has the goal of trying to describe whatever is important in a situation, without limiting the focus in advance to a small number of well-defined variables, which is what distinguishes case-study descriptive research from other types. (There are case studies that are guided by specific theories and that focus on a small number of variables, but they are not the exploratory type of research described here; see, for example, Lipset, Trow, and Coleman, 1956).

Students should not *automatically* shy away from descriptive research. Professors often tout students off descriptive projects, however, because they are harder to do well and easier to do atrociously than are other types of research. Descriptive research does not reveal sloppy and brainless work as glaringly as do more "rigorous" types of research. For this reason, other types of research usually make better training exercises than does descriptive research.

Path-breaking descriptive research, such as that of Freud, is especially difficult because one starts with empty hands—few guideposts, no standards, sketchy intellectual framework. The researcher's main resources are whatever concepts he or she can borrow from other areas, plus prior experience, common sense, and ability to observe and think carefully. Such researchers must create their own classifications and their own guideposts. They must decide what to look at and what to ignore, what to record and what not to record, which clues to follow up and which to drop, what is important and what is valueless. The early descriptive researcher has great freedom, but such great freedom can be terrifying. Once a tradition of descriptive research is established in a field, however, as is now the case in anthropology, there are standards and concepts that subsequent researchers can use.

3. Classification Research

Classification is the process of *sorting out* a collection of people or objects and of developing a set of *categories* among which you divide the collection. No sooner does the scientist see several different examples of a given phenomenon than he or she begins to say, "This one is like that one and both are different from that other bunch." Then the scientist coins common names for those examples that are like one another. The sorting out may come first and the construction of categories (called "taxonomy") afterward, or the order can be reversed (*a priori* classification). Classification as an end in itself is the subject of this section. More frequently classification is a step in some other type of research.

Bacon was an early "imperialist" in the history of science. He viewed all science as within the domain of his favorite scientific method—classification. Of course, there is more to science than classification, yet much advance in all the sciences has come from developments in classification. Linnaeus' eighteenth-century scheme for classifying the entire plant world helped reveal the family relationships of the various species. Mendeleev's nineteenth-century periodic table of the elements stimulated work in chemistry and physics, including the discovery of new elements. And for a long time medical research meant little but classification of diseases by their symptoms. Even now classification is important in the advancement of medicine.

PHOBIAS IN BRITONS FALL INTO 130 TYPES

A half million Britons are afraid of things ranging from blood to barbershops, with some even afraid of being afraid. . . . Britain's phobia victims suffer from at least 130 different types of irrational fear. . . .

The . . . British Medical Association and the National Association for Mental Health said that one of the largest groups was the agoraphobics—people afraid of open spaces. They number 100,000, many of them women fearful of leaving their own homes. . . .

Fear of spiders, matches, green leaves, pictures of ships in distress, birds and feathers, cats, dogs, mice, frogs, toads, wasps, snakes, blood and thunder were among disabilities haunting people. (*New York Times,* Oct. 14, 1969, p. 13)

Important classification research is found in all the social sciences. Political scientists and economists classify government attempts to change people's behavior as "regulation strategies" if they require people to act a certain way or be punished, or as "incentive strategies" if they reward people for acting a certain way (Balch, 1980). The American Psychiatric Association spends vast effort to improve the classification of mental disorders for diagnosis and treatment. Sociologists classify social protest movements. Political scientists since Aristotle have classified various forms of government. Economists classify markets, pricing schemes, and devices used as barriers to entering markets.

The two basic tasks in classification work are: (1) constructing the categories and (2) assigning each observation to the appropriate category (or several categories if the classification is "multidimensional," as when people are simultaneously classified by sex, age, and earnings). "Numerical taxonomy" (see Sneath and Sokal, 1963) is the name of a recent statistical approach to classification that can help systematize the process of making classifications; the

technique of "blockmodeling" may be useful as well (White, Boorman, and Breiger, 1976).

What is classification research good for? Here are five uses of a classification scheme:

A classification enables one to deal routinely with individual cases. After a doctor has decided that a patient has smallpox, the treatment is almost automatic. And the authors of an obesity classification report that it has aided them in diagnosing patients for treatment. Without a classification scheme a doctor would have to do an impossible amount of study on each patient before selecting a treatment; the classification scheme enables him or her to take advantage of the accumulated store of medical knowledge about which treatments aid which diseases.

A classification aids summarization. A political scientist trying to describe politics in many countries may simply describe each country, one after the other. But if he finds that countries with only one political party are very similar to each other, as are countries with two parties, and countries with more than two, while one-party states are very different from those with two parties and both are different from multiparty states, then he may conclude that he can easily summarize the politics of all countries by talking about just the three types. This would be much easier (and much easier to understand and remember) than descriptions of each country separately. Similarly, once psychiatrists classify patients as "manic-depressive" or "schizophrenic," a researcher can summarize the prevalence of different types of mental illness in various countries.

A classification makes other scientists aware of differences among the categories. Whether the categories be species of plants, types of headaches, or varieties of monopolies, classification often leads the other scientists to understand and explain the differences. For example, after Freud classified the various defense mechanisms, it was natural to inquire into why some people repress, others rationalize, still others project, and so on.

The classification may contain within itself the explanation of phenomena. If the category description says that a person suffering from familial obesity "usually leads a sedentary existence," it suggests a reason why the person is fat. The explanation may have been unintentional on the part of the classifier, but such explanations are a frequent valuable by-product of classification.

A classification clarifies one's understanding. Remember how many times you have gotten into an argument that seemed futile and then you (or even the other fellow!) said: "Let's make a distinction between the zilches and the squilches. What you say may be true of the zilches, but it certainly isn't true of the squilches." You may find that the argument has suddenly evaporated and that the two of you agree. (This fifth point is really a summary of the previous four points.)

But the process of putting people or things into categories also has a drawback. One inevitably loses some information. For example, assume you have collected "open-ended" free interviews about racial integration. In order to handle the data quantitatively, you classify ("code") the interviews into those for or against integration. You thereby lose all the *shadings* of opinions voiced by the interviewees and the richness and variety of their comments. But, unless you classify in this manner, you cannot handle the people in groups. (Later, however, we shall see how some of the other information can be saved and used simultaneously by *cross-classification*—classification on several dimensions at the same time.)

The loss of individuality in a classification scheme is the basis of a persistent attack on social science. The critic says, "How can you talk as if any two different people in your survey were exactly the same?" or "How can you lump together wholesalers in Vermont and wholesalers in Louisiana when they serve very different markets?" The real question is whether the items are *similar enough* for your purposes; if so, the classification is fruitful. Mineral oil and coffee is the appropriate antidote whether a child who swallows furniture polish lives in Vermont or in Louisiana. In that instance the difference in geography does not matter at all. (But for other purposes the difference in geography is indeed crucial.)

People who refuse to ignore the differences among individuals may avoid erroneous generalizations. But they may also avoid any generalizations at all, which makes science impossible. (Some people criticize classification from a sincere desire for deeper truth; some, to thwart the efforts of others, use anecdotal evidence and exceptional occurrences to throw sand in the gears of scientific conceptualization.)

Classification research is different from other types of research in that one does not usually go out and collect new data for a classification study. Rather one is likely to work with *existing* data, sorting it into a classification that makes sense of it. Therefore, classification research tends to follow after descriptive research in the sequence of scientific stages.

As for the concept of variable in classification research, the classification scheme itself can be viewed as one massive variable *or* as a set of variables, for it is a set of distinctions among a set of related phenomena. But the variable or variables are not "dependent" or "independent," at least until employed in other research. For example, if one wanted to determine whether women are more prone to familial obesity than are men, the obesity classification would be a *dependent* variable; obesity type = f(sex). Or if an economist were to investigate how the presence of monopoly affects economic development, the market classification into monopoly or other forms would be an *independent* variable; rate of economic development = *f*(type of market form).

Every collection can be classified in many different ways. For example, we trust that you will not take too seriously the scheme by which research problems are classified in this chapter; one could slice up the research salami in many different ways, some of them more careful and systematic than the classification we use here. Our object is to illustrate for you the variety of problems within scientific research, in contrast to the view that all science can be boiled down to a single sort of problem, and the classification scheme is intended to do this and only this; if it does, it is a good one, and if not, it is not.

4. Measurement and Estimation

Measurement research differs from case-study description by focusing on one or a few dimensions, rather than many, and by measuring them systematically and in great detail, rather than in a rough and ad hoc way.

Measurement research seeks to establish the magnitude or size of a phenomenon on one or more of its dimensions: its weight, height, speed, intelligence, number of members, or what have you. Learning to measure important phenomena—the speed of light, the charge of an electron—has been a crucial part of the advance of all sciences.

Much of social science research has been devoted to developing ways to measure the important phenomena of social life—for example, the gross national product, intelligence, attitudes, status, and political activity. Among the things social scientists have wanted to know are: the total amount of something (the gross national product is a kind of measure of the total amount of economic activity in the country); the central value (such as a measure of average intelligence); proportions (such as the proportion of the population likely to become men-

tally ill); the distribution by various categories (such as the distribution of income by occupation); and the amount of variability (such as how much population density varies by blocks within a city). Much effort has gone into the development of *social indicators,* such as measures of household composition, crime rates, or income, which would enable us to describe our society and how it changes over time (DeNeufville, 1975).

Deciding *what to measure* and how to draw the definitional boundary lines around the quantity to be measured—translating the theoretical (hypothetical) concept into empirical terms—is a crucial decision in measurement research. For example, an economist trying to measure the gross national product must decide whether to try to include receipts from illegal activity in the measure. Similarly, when one wants to estimate the cost to General Motors of producing another hundred thousand automobiles, should one include any of the salaries of the top management in the measurement? The cost accountant will always say "yes," but for some decisions the better answer is "no," as, for example, when General Motors must calculate its costs in connection with a potential sale to a fleet owner of a batch of already-produced trucks.

5. Comparison

Most empirical research in psychology, sociology, marketing research, education, anthropology, political science, and other social sciences employs comparisons, usually as part of an attempt to establish cause and effect. The comparison may be of something against nothing; for example, an hour's tutoring may be compared against no tutoring to see whether the tutoring raises grades.

Let us consider some further examples. We compare the nation's preferences between two people by means of a presidential election. Market researchers use television ratings to compare the number of listeners that two television shows attract. Psychologists compare the efficiency of teaching machines with the efficiency of conventional classroom instruction. In their interpretation of their data Kinsey and his associates (1948) frequently compare the behavior of men with that of women, that of young people with that of old people, and so on. Cultural anthropologists sometimes compare two cultures to discover differences and similarities. And social anthropologists sometimes compare the kinship systems, say, in a great many different cultures.

Comparison and measurement have much in common. In fact, you can have an enjoyable time arguing that comparison is really a subtype of measurement or, conversely, that measurement is really a subtype of comparison. The key difference between comparison and measurement is that measurement is against a *known standard*. The standard may be a man's foot or a carob bean or a platinum-iridium meterstick. But the standard is assumed to be *commonly known*, and its common acceptance gives the standard its value as a standard.

Comparison research, on the other hand, compares two or more entities with one another. In a comparison we are interested in the *relative* measurement of *two or more* phenomena, whereas in measurement problems we are interested only in *one* event relative to a standard quantity. When the psychologist compares two methods of teaching children to read, he or she is interested in finding the *faster* method, not in learning how long either one takes in absolute time. When a network compares the ratings of two television shows, its usual purpose is to identify the *more popular* show. An election seeks to establish which candidate is *preferred* to the other candidates. The difference between comparison and measurement is illuminated by the different types of adjectives used, "fast" versus "faster," the absolute versus the comparative.

We often use comparisons because we want to describe entities as best we can but have not been able to establish a measurement standard (or cannot even imagine how we would do so). Thus, for example, we can compare the strength of two voters' attachments to the Democratic party, finding that one has a strong sense of identification with the party, and the other a weak sense of identification. Though we cannot measure the strength of identification on an absolute scale, the comparative measure has proven valuable in many studies (Hamblin, 1974; Kruskal and Wish, 1978). Similarly, we can compare the social status of families or occupations and thereby learn much about what society values, even though we cannot measure exactly how much status any particular family or occupation has (Treiman, 1977; Nock and Rossi, 1978). Comparisons are so important in the social sciences that major quantitative techniques have been developed to help make them as useful and precise as possible (Kruskal and Wish, 1978).

Comparisons are usually made on one *dimension* at a time. We might say that one reading-instruction method teaches children *faster* but that the other method requires *less teacher attention*. These dimensions of speed and amount of teacher attention are chosen for comparison because the researcher believes them to be interesting, or important for practical or theoretical reasons, or relevant in some other way.

Comparisons may be made on more than one dimension by *combining the ratings* on several dimensions into a single index. Sometimes this combining is part of the research job, as when one uses several items on a single test. But sometimes it goes beyond the research job. If a school system gives a reading-instruction method two points for excellence in speed of teaching and one point for amount of teacher attention, the over-all comparison must depend on the value judgments of the school board about the importance of teaching speed and teacher attention; these value judgments are the source of the point values.

In the natural sciences and increasingly in the social sciences as they become more mature, comparison studies often give way to measurement as absolute scales are refined and measurement techniques improved. Long ago a foot racer would race only against another runner, and the better and poorer runners would be established by comparison. Now a runner also races against a clock and achieves a time record.

Even with our excellent contemporary timepieces, however, a time record does not always contain as much or more information than does a comparative result. A woman may prove she is a very fast runner by beating other fast runners, even though the recorded time is slow, because the race is held on a slow track and against the wind. Comparative times of race horses on different tracks and against different competition are widely recognized by racing buffs as inconclusive evidence in handicapping a race.

A comparison may be quantitative like "20 percent faster than . . . ," but often the results cannot be expressed any more precisely than "more" or "less" or "equal to." With two paintings you are not likely to go further than asking whether a person likes one of them *better* (although you *might* get more precision by asking whether the interviewee likes painting A "much more than" or "a little more than" painting B).

6. Research That Tries to Find Relationships

The types of research we have discussed in previous sections—description, classification, measurement, and comparison—are intended to reveal what phenomena *are;* more broadly, all of these approaches are descriptive. Description and measurement studies describe many or a few aspects of one event or one set of events taken as a single entity. Comparisons describe two (or several) things or groups with reference to each other, and classification stud-

ies create devices for more accurate and meaningful descriptions.

Now we shall discuss the first of two types of situations in which we ask how events are *related* to one another. The second type, focusing on cause-and-effect, is really a subclass of the first.

A few examples should make clear the nature of relationship problems: How well are I.Q. test scores related to future success in school? That is, how well do I.Q. scores *predict* future school success? How well does the behavior of groundhogs on Groundhog Day predict the end of winter? How closely related are income and other indexes of social class? Do rises and falls in the economy follow rises and falls in the stock market?

We shall defer until the next chapter consideration of such problems as whether smoking *causes* lung cancer and whether stock-market movements *cause* movements in the economy. Some of the ticklish philosophical arguments involved will be dealt with in Chapter 36.

An investigation into whether there is a relationship between two occurrences or variables is an attempt to find out whether two (or more) phenomena are part of the *same scheme of things*, that is, whether they are closely associated with each other in nature's cobweb. The cobweb analogy is instructive. If two particles are entrapped close to each other in a cobweb, and if one of them moves, the other will move in close agreement with it. But if the particles are much farther from each other, movement in one will not be *as closely* accompanied by movement in the other. Furthermore, notice that movement in particle A and in particle B can be related even if neither A nor B but rather C initiates the motion.

Of course it is true that everything is related to everything else to *some* extent. If you drop a stone to the ground in Illinois, theoretically there will be an impact in Chile, Ghana, and every other part of the world. But the impact in Chile is so slight that we can ignore it, and no instrument will be sensitive enough to record it. In a psychological context, it is surely true that if some environmental factor causes a change in one aspect of a personality, all other aspects of the personality will be affected to some degree. And if some economic shock in Guatemala causes an inflation in the quetzal, there will be *some* related movement in the value of the dollar. Nevertheless, relationships like those in the examples given are so insignificant that we ignore them. We shall confine our interest to *important* relationships between events, relationships that *matter*. And of course relationships must be large enough to be detected by the crude instruments at our disposal. (An atomic explosion or earthquake in Chile can probably be detected in Illinois, though the fall of a stone cannot.)

There are several types of relationships that are not the simple cause-and-effect relationships. Among them are these:

A *third* phenomenon, C, may cause *both* A and B, accounting for the apparent relationship between them. Yet A and B vary together, and we therefore say that there is a relationship between them; to illustrate, tax changes will affect both the stock market and gross national product.

Or A may cause B (or B may cause A), but we may not be able to establish which causes which. Nevertheless, we may be able to establish the extent of the relationship between them. Do you do well in a course because you like the course, or vice versa? Probably both are true. Does a young boy fall in love because a girl asks him to go steady, or vice versa?

Or it may be that A is a partial cause of B and B is a partial cause of A. One such type of interrelationship is "feedback." I hit you, which causes you to hit me. The blow to me is feedback from my blow to you. The going-steady and doing-well-in-course examples might also be examples of feedback.

There can be great value in knowing what relationships exist even if we do not know their nature in terms of cause and effect. Here are some of the uses to which such knowledge can be put:

First, one phenomenon may be used as a *predictor* of another phenomenon of interest. The "index of leading economic indicators" calculated and reported by the U.S. government every month seems to predict what will happen in the economy during the next few months. The flight of birds close overhead may usually predict rain, even though the flying birds do not cause the rain; when we see the birds, we put up the shutters to avoid being drenched by the oncoming rain.

Second, one phenomenon may serve as a proxy measurement of the other. An advertising researcher may believe that the amount of readership of advertisements in magazines is closely related to the effect of the advertisement in creating sales. If the situation makes it difficult or impossible to measure the *sales* effect of the advertisement directly, the researcher may then measure the amount of *readership* the advertisement gets and use this measurement as an indirect *index* of the sales the advertisement produces.

Third, the relationship between two proxy measurements may be of interest. In the previous paragraph, we discussed the relationship between sales—which is really what the advertiser is interested in—and readership, which the advertiser might wish to use as a proxy index of sales. But the advertiser might also be interested in the relationship between two separate proxy indexes of sales—perhaps readership and the number of coupons that are clipped and returned.

Neither readership nor coupon response is the "real" cause or the "real" effect of sales. But an investigation of the relationship between the two indexes can tell the advertiser whether the firm can reasonably assume that *both* indexes can stand for the same thing. If readership varies with sales, and coupon response varies with readership, the advertiser can expect coupon response to vary with sales.

TABLE 4.1.   Income and Party Choice

| Income | Percent voting for: | | Subtotals |
	Republicans	Democrats	
Below $20,000	Cell A = 35 34%	Cell B = 68 66%	103
Above $20,000	Cell C = 47 48%	Cell D = 50 52%	97
Subtotals	82	118	200 (100%)

Educators and educational researchers often look at the relationship of one aptitude test to another aptitude test. If both tests give high and low scores to the same people, then the test that is cheaper and simpler to administer can be used. Similarly, if the Dow-Jones Index of thirty industrial stocks is closely related to the composite of all industrial stocks on the New York Stock Exchange, there is no need to compute the more complete index.

Intelligence tests pose a curious question about indexes. Should we say that a score on an I.Q. test *is* intelligence? This seems to be what people mean when they say "He has a high I.Q." Alternatively, we can think of an I.Q. score as simply a somewhat inaccurate *index* of capabilities that bring about success in the future. For most purposes, it does not matter which way we think of the I.Q. But confusion becomes apparent when we begin to say about someone "He is very bright even though his test scores don't show it." If we interpret the I.Q. score as the *same thing* as intelligence, then the statement would make no sense.

The strategy of research in looking for a relationship is to examine the *patterns of variations* in the two phenomena you seek to relate. If A generally goes up when B goes up, then A and B are related to some extent. Or, for that matter, if A generally goes *down* when B goes up, they are also related but inversely.

A basic way to examine the variations and test for the presence of a relationship is to arrange the data in some form like a table or a graph.[2] For example, if we want to find out whether or not there is a relationship between a man's income and which political party he votes for in a small town, we might record the data from our sample of 200 in this way, in a two-row, two-column ("two-by-two") table, as in Table 4.1.

The table shows that 34 percent of those earning below $20,000 voted Republican, while 48 percent of those earning above $20,000 did. If all the observed people had fallen into cells A and D, it would be obvious that there is a relationship. Similarly, if A and B had equal numbers of people and if C and D also had equal numbers of people, then it would be equally obvious that there is *not* a relationship. But in the social sciences we are rarely so lucky as to have such clear-cut results. Almost invariably the data will show a mixed pattern like that in the table. We therefore have some difficulty in deciding whether there is or is not a relationship between income and political party and, if a relationship does exist, how "strong" it is.

Casting tables into percentages often clarifies whether there is a relationship. In this case, the cells show what percentage of people at each income level voted for each party. If there were no relationship between income and political party, the percentages in cells A and C would be equal, as would the percentages in cells B and D. That the percentages are

2. Consult Zeisel (1968) and Ehrenberg (1975) for a clear discussion of how to arrange data in tables and graphs.

not equal suggests a relationship between income and political party, though we must check later whether such a pattern might be caused by chance, and how strong the relationship is (see Part Four).

The question of which percentages should be computed always arises in a table like this. The way the table is now, it shows how people with different incomes voted. But the percentages could also be calculated to show what percentage of Republicans and what percentage of Democrats had incomes above and below $20,000. Or the percentages could be calculated as the percentage of the total number of voters (200) in each cell. How you compute the percentages in the table depends upon what you want to know. Whether there is a relationship, however, is something you will discover no matter how you compute them.

7. Finding Causes and Effects

As we have mentioned, cause-and-effect relationships are a subclass of scientific relationships in general. Deciding whether to call a particular relationship between two variables, say A and B, a "causal" relationship is sometimes a straightforward matter. If the observed relationship is the result of an *experiment*, there is usually little argument about saying that an observed relationship is a causal relationship, implying that the artificially manipulated independent variable is the cause and the dependent variable whose change is observed the effect. Indeed, one of the best ways to reduce confusion about whether an observed nonexperimental relationship is causal is to subject it to experiment.

As we shall see in more detail later, however, an experimental relationship may *not* deserve to be called a "causal" relationship, usually because there is something wrong with the way that the experimenter has "specified" the independent variable. Consider, for example, the fabled gentlemen who got experimentally drunk on bourbon and soda on Monday night,

Scotch and soda on Tuesday night, and brandy and soda on Wednesday night—and stayed sober Thursday night by drinking nothing. With a vast inductive leap of scientific imagination, they treated their experience as an empirical demonstration that soda, the common element each evening, was the cause of the inebriated state they had experienced.

Observed relationships that do *not* spring from controlled experiments are much harder to characterize as causal or noncausal (see Chapter 35 for a detailed discussion). Various practical devices can, however, assist in safe classification of a relationship as causal. Here is one such device: If you observe a relationship between A and B and if you can establish that A did not cause B, the *likelihood* that B caused A is then greater. For example, years in which the corn price is high are followed by years in which large amounts of corn are grown. We can be quite sure that the high price is not caused by the large supplies because the high price occurs in the *previous years;* causes usually (but *not always!;* see the postscript to Chapter 35) precede the effects. (But this relationship *by itself* is not sufficient to establish causality from B to A; C might cause both.)

Another device that increases confidence that a relationship is causal is cross-classification analysis with tables. If you try out many of the most likely additional variables in a cross-classification and if the original observed relationship between your variables is not affected, you have made a more convincing case that your observed relationship is causal. Examples of cross-classification are given in Chapters 24 and 25.

Some *scientists* react to the difficulties of establishing cause and effect by withdrawing into their shells and refusing to say that the relationships they find are anything more than correlations. (Sometimes this is a safety play to avoid possible criticism, as with some scientists' findings of relationships between smoking and lung cancer.) But *decision makers* cannot avoid making judgments about cause and effect, even if they wish to weasel out of it. If smoking does not *cause* cancer, there is no point in trying to stop people from smoking. If the stock market does not *cause* changes in the economy, there is not much point in trying to control the action of the stock market as an aid to controlling the economy. Therefore, it is often the decision makers who frame research problems narrowly in terms of cause and effect. What causes juvenile delinquency? How can I increase the readership of my furniture advertisements? How does a longer school year affect a child's education? Do television dramas cause violence in children? The decision maker wants to know what to change so that he can achieve the effect he wants.

The decision whether to call a relationship "causal" is indeed a delicate matter. Statistical techniques alone cannot guarantee that an observed nonexperimental relationship is causal. Nor can statistics or other formal reasoning methods guarantee that even an experimental relationship is causal. Statistics would not reveal the flaw in the reasoning that soda causes inebriation. The only protection that the researcher can give himself is to *saturate himself* in the complicated and detailed richness of the phenomenon he is working on. An hour's elbow bending and casual talk about liquor at a neighborhood bar will save you forever from believing that soda is the active ingredient.

8. Mapping Structures

This last type of research problem will be discussed only briefly. Examples include finding the kinship structure of a group, that is, who is related to whom in what ways; determining the structure of an unwritten language; and mapping an economy. Structure (or system) mapping is a sort of description, but it is more highly organized than ordinary description. It is a good deal like putting together a jigsaw puzzle; first, one tries to find a second piece to fit a given piece, then a third piece to fit the first two, and so on until the whole system falls

into place. Unlike exploratory descriptions, structure mapping begins with a conceptual structure that the investigator tries to fill in. One knows in advance what one is looking for; for example, the linguist tackles an unknown language knowing that it must have phonemes, morphemes, nouns, verbs, and so on. His or her job is to identify the various members of the classes and the relationships among them. To put it another way, the structure mapper starts off knowing the generalities of the language; his or her job is to fill in the specifics.

Taken as a whole, structure mapping encompasses many other types of research, especially classification and comparison—for example, comparing two words that sound similar to see whether a speaker of the language distinguishes between them. Mapping a system is a sequence of trial, observation of the result, deduction of a new hypothesis, trial of the new hypothesis, and so forth.

Structure mapping is important in economics. For example, an input-output analysis is a map of the flows of materials to and from each segment of an economy—where nails from nail factories go and where raw materials for nails come from. In sociology, the mapping of relationships among friends has shown how friendship choices are related to occupational background (Laumann, 1973), and the mapping of relationships among scientists helps us understand how scientific fields grow and develop (Breiger, 1976).

Deduction usually plays a large part in structure mapping. For example, when the linguist identifies one word as a noun and then hears another word used directly after the noun, he deduces that the second word is not a noun also, because one noun seldom follows another. And in economic input-output analysis one can deduce useful facts about the inputs of nails to various industries if one knows the total output of the nail industry.

The work of structure mapping re-enacts in microcosm the activities of the various disciplines *taken as wholes*. Whole series of studies follow the same pattern as do the individual steps in structure mapping. An example is a series of related animal experiments in the psychology of learning. The studies form a sequence of experiments, observations, deductions, further hypotheses, and so on. The difference is that in psychology the unit of work is defined as a single experiment, whereas in kinship studies or field linguistics the unit is defined as the mapping of the entire system.

9. Evaluation Research

Evaluation research is *not* another sort of research different from the types of research described above—despite some recent claims to the contrary. Fad, fashion, and catchwordism run wild in science, just as elsewhere in society, especially when money is to be made by being "with it." And with recent demands by the holders of grant pursestrings that social science be "relevant" and "responsive to current social needs," there emerged the label "evaluation research," which seems super relevant and responsive.

Every comparison study in the history of the study of learning is an "evaluation" of one method of learning or teaching compared to another. Every economic study of the effect of a minimum-wage law on employment and earnings of poor people is evaluation research, evaluating the effect of such legislation. Every medical and anthropological study tracing the impact of Western culture on an isolated tribe's physical and mental hygiene is evaluation research. In short, many comparison, measurement, and cause-and-effect studies yield explicit evaluations, and many of the rest yield implicit evaluations; there does not exist a distinct kind of research known as evaluation research.

Much research could be made much more valuable, however, if the researcher would aim to produce results yielding clear-cut evaluations that can be used to improve social judg-ments. But this is a distinction between (a) sound, well-designed research and (b) ill-conceived, sloppy work, rather than between "evaluation research" and other research.

In concluding this chapter, we want to repeat that there *are* several ways to attack research problems and that, furthermore, there *ought* to be. Unfortunately, too many scientists in various disciplines assume that their approach is all there is and all there should be to scientific research. Some economists think and act as if deduction and statistical analysis of time series is the beginning and end of social science. Some psychologists claim that all scientific research is and should be a process of testing hypotheses by experiments. The danger of such narrow claims is that they lead to stereotyped choices of research methods, which blind the researcher and cut down his or her effectiveness.

It seems to us that the demand that *all* research be thrust into any one mold, hypothesis testing for instance, is an example of a common and destructive tendency in science—overstating the merits or generality of a theory or method, or "intellectual imperialism" as we choose to call it. This imperialism results in bitter arguments about this theory *or* that theory, rather than agreement that each theory (and method) may do some jobs better than the other theory (or method).

The purpose of this discussion of the various types of research problems has been to lead you to ask yourself: "What type of research problem is the question that I am trying to investigate? Into which class does it fall?" This approach helps one to understand the nature of a research problem and how to go about it.

10. Summary

Each social-science discipline uses some method almost to the exclusion of others. For example, psychology specializes in experiments, sociology in surveys, and economics in statistical analysis of government-produced data. However, other methods sometimes can be more appropriate. The task of this chapter is to describe the various types of empirical research so that you may think of them when you need them.

Descriptive research is especially called for when a field is first opening, to define the problems and to produce clues to follow up with further research.

Classification research makes distinctions among the phenomena under investigation. This may lead to causal explanations of the differences among the phenomena or of the relationships among them. Or the classification may serve as a map of the territory to orient subsequent researchers.

Measurement (estimation) research is a quantitative, and therefore more precise, form of descriptive research, but it is usually less flexible and rich in variety than is qualitative descriptive research. The most common measurements are: counting, central value, proportion, distribution, and variability.

Comparison research is done to find out which alternative is bigger, faster, or perhaps better.

Relationship research attempts to determine whether there is an association between two phenomena. This may be to aid prediction, or to determine whether one variable can be used as a proxy for the other, or it may be a prelude to determining a causal relationship.

Cause-and-effect research can be done with experiments or surveys; best of all is a combination of methods, together with good judgment. Cause-and-effect research attempts to go beyond the existence of an association to determine if one of the variables can plausibly be said to cause the other.

Structure mapping is research that investigates an entire structure, whether it be a kinship group or an economic system. It encompasses other sorts of research as well.

EXERCISES

1. Within one given field, for example, psychology, economics, or anthropology, find examples of each of the seven types of research—description, classification, measurement and estimation, comparison, search for relationships, cause-and-effect, and mapping structures. Some rummaging around in the literature will be necessary to find all seven types.
2. If the class is doing individual research projects, classify each student's project by type of research.
3. Read through the first five *empirical* articles in a professional journal or in a book of readings of empirical research, and classify the studies by type of research.
4. Show how a particular distribution of data would be summarized one way for one purpose and another way for another purpose.

ADDITIONAL READING

On exploratory and descriptive studies, see Selltiz et al. (1976, Chap. 4).

For fascinating firsthand accounts of participant-observation studies, see Riley and Nelson (1974).

Descriptive research in anthropology—that is, field methods—is covered well in T. Williams' (1967) short pamphlet.

The relationship between qualitative and quantitative research and some relationships among different types of research are discussed in Merton et al. (1979).

On evaluation research, including its use for policy purposes, see Struening and Guttentag (1975).

Tanur et al. (1972) contains a wide variety of studies showing how quantitative statistical methods can be used for measurement, estimation, comparison studies, and the finding of relationships. Though the book's subject is statistics, no previous knowledge of statistics is required, and the studies are a pleasure and a joy to read. They cover a wide variety of areas from anthropology to business, and from pure to applied research. The studies include both the social sciences and the biological sciences, and some natural sciences as well. Very highly recommended.

Theory, Model, Hypothesis, and Empirical Research

5

The purpose of this chapter is to throw some light on the confusing relationships among theory, theorizing, models, hypotheses, and empirical research.

The aim of all research—theoretical and empirical—is to get new knowledge. But we can distinguish among quite different types of knowledge that one may be seeking. One may seek better understanding of the social world, that is, a better explanation of some human phenomenon such as racial discrimination or psychological depression. Or one may seek to find the best way to deal with a given class of situations, say, economic recession or drug abuse. Or one may seek to evaluate the effects of a program, say, school busing or psychotherapeutic treatment. There is some—but only some—connection between this variety of aims and the nature of various research problems described in the previous chapter.

The roles of theory and empirical research, and the relationships between them, differ with the types of knowledge one seeks. Here are a few examples to illustrate possible relationships between theory and empirical research:

(1) An urban planner may want to know whether the prospective dwellers in a new area will support a shopping mall. This is a simple empirical question, and theory will probably not play much of a role in answering it. (2) Malthus deduced from basic principles of economic theory the hypothesis (conjecture) that additional births cause the standard of living to fall. For many years that deduction was regarded as an accurate description of the relationship between births and the standard of living; few people saw any need for empirical research to see if the description was correct. (3) In recent years researchers have used Malthus' hypothesis to guide their research, examining the data on birth rates and standards of living for various countries to see if the relationship between birth rates and economic growth was as Malthus predicted. Their work combines theory and research, using theory to guide the empirical research, and the results of the research to modify the theory where nec-

essary. Their aim was not to challenge the body of economic theory from which Malthus' deduction was drawn. When the data turned out not to support Malthus' theorizing, however, three possible conclusions were suggested: Either Malthusian theory was insufficient and must be improved, or the data and data analysis were not appropriate for testing the theory, or both.

1. What Is Theory?

Empirical research was easy to define (see page 3). But theory is harder to nail down, partly because the concept has very different meanings in different disciplines and even at different moments in particular disciplines. In fields such as economics and physics, where there are well-established assumptions and an apparatus for making systematic deductions, then there is said to be a *body of theory*. The theory must cover a substantial portion of the material in a field or subfield, and it must be *systematically organized*, or else one should not say that there is a body of theory in a discipline. To put it another way, there is no theory unless it is a *body of theory*.[1]

The deductions from the theory need not be *correct* for the theory to claim the title of "theory," but people are less likely to honor the claim of a theory that often produces crack-brained hypotheses.

Another requirement of a body of theory is that the same assumptions and the same type of deductive apparatus must be used for many of the problems in the field. One could work out a set of assumptions from which one could deduce *any* single hypothesis. But such a set of assumptions would not be enough to constitute a theory; a set of assumptions must support not just the one hypothesis but many other hypotheses also. The assumptions that make up microeconomics, for example, underlie an enormous body of economic analysis.

In other fields where phenomena cover a wider range of behavior than does economics—sociology, psychology, and anthropology among them—it has not yet been possible to develop an integrated body of propositions, which most writers accept as the basic underpinning for the field as a whole. In such fields the term "theory" has a looser meaning; it often refers to a loosely organized collection of hypotheses (rather than a logical, deductive system of assumptions and propositions), and sometimes is even used to refer to almost any speculative thinking offered as an explanation for some phenomena.

The key element of theory is that it *abstracts* a few characteristics of reality in an attempt to isolate and describe its central features. The rational profit-making firm in economic theory is such an abstraction. Everyone knows that no organization is perfectly rational or perfectly single-minded in the pursuit of a single goal. But the microeconomic theory which is built upon this abstraction, together with other abstractions such as perfect competition and complete information, is useful and hence is retained and used despite the fact that the theory departs from complete realism when it abstracts and focuses on a few key elements.

Another example of such theoretical abstraction comes from research on fertility. Obviously there are a great many influences that determine whether a family (or community) has more or fewer children. To describe fully in all its richness even one family's process of making a birth decision would require much time and many words. But theories employed by both sociologist-demographers and economist-demographers will lead them to focus on education as a potential determinant of fertil-

---

1. W. Letwin (1975) makes this argument very forcefully in his discussion of theory in economics; G. Homans makes a similar point about sociological theory (1964: 11–12). And this point of view is well accepted in the physical sciences. Unfortunately, however, it is far from universal among social scientists; many social scientists continue to use the terms "theory" and "hypothesis" interchangeably. Such usage leaves no room for the important distinction between statements that are logically related to other statements within a deductive system, and statements that are not.

ity, and they in fact discover that more education among women is the strongest and most reliable factor associated with lower fertility.

Once the role played by education is known, the researchers' attention is likely to turn to discovering what other factors influence fertility. To some extent the choice of additional variables will depend upon the researchers' background—economists are more likely to focus on economic factors such as family income, while sociologists might consider religious beliefs. When it comes to choosing variables to focus on, theory can be wise, or foolish and wrong-headed. The test is whether the elements of the theory yield hypotheses that are important, reasonable, and relevant to one's interests. This is not the same as being right or wrong, however—some wise thinking can turn out to be wrong on the facts, yet the theorizing was worthwhile because it led us to learn something of value that we did not know before.

2. Models, Theory, and Hypotheses

Some disciplines and parts of disciplines are not ready to build an all-embracing body of theory, or they may call "theory" what is actually only a rather vague, loosely connected set of ideas about their subject matter. But imaginative scientists may draw on the available ideas to put together sets of abstract propositions relevant to one corner of a field or to a few related phenomena, and may deduce some hypotheses from the propositions. An explicit set of propositions based on a theory is often called a *model* in the social sciences; sometimes the model will be in the form of a set of equations which hypothesize that some variables are related to others in particular ways (as in economists' models of the national economy; see Kaplan, 1964: Chap. 7).

A model is like a minitheory. It has the same basic nature as a theory because it focuses on a few elements abstracted from all of reality. Sometimes the terms "model" and "theory" are actually used interchangeably. Often, however, the term "model" is used by social scientists to mean a set of explicit propositions based on the vague "theories" available to them; the extra explicitness or clarity of the model make it easier to see if its hypotheses are consistent with relevant data.

3. Two Views of Theory and of Science in General

There are two views of the universe that lead to two views about theorizing—and of science in general. One may view the world as a system having inherent order, and the task of the scientist being the discovery of the "true" propositions and relationships in that system. For example, one may think that the speed with which a body falls due to gravity is one of the inherent characteristics of our world, and if we diligently seek after such characteristics we can discover them all and then have a complete understanding of the universe. To put this view another way, at the beginning the universe was created or evolved according to a set of equations, and it is our job to discern the equations.

The other view—the one which we find more helpful—is that the universe is not perfectly formless or chaotic—though it may once have been—but that the regularities and generalizations we discover result from our interests and perceptions as well as from the features of the world. That is, we invent and develop the relationships we find, rather than merely discovering them. For example, what shape is the earth? It is round and smooth to a firm that manufactures cheap globes, but is bumpy to a manufacturer of more expensive globes. To a surveyor or farmer, it is flat. Its circumference is greatest at the equator, for some persons. To an aviator, it is an unsmooth, unround set of upcropping mountains. And so on. The earth does not have one shape but many, and the relevant "model"—flat, round, bumpy—depends upon your needs and interests. No "model" of the earth captures all its features—because then it would not be an abstracted model, but the earth itself. As Georgescu-Roegen put it:

> [A]ctuality is a seamless whole we can slice . . . wherever we may please. And, Plato to the contrary, actuality has no joints to guide a carver. . . . Only our particular purpose in each case can guide us in drawing the boundary of a process. So, every scientist slices actuality in the way that suits best his own objective—an operation that cannot be performed without some intimate knowledge of the corresponding phenomenal domain. . . . (1970: 3)

Just so it is with the familial process of making decisions about whether to have another child; no single statistical model of it is *the* correct one. Rather, different models of the fertility decision will be appropriate for answering different scientific questions, and with respect to different scientific purposes.

4. The Relationship Between Theory and Empirical Research

Now we tackle the tangled relationship between theory and empirical research. In applied research the relationship between hypothesis (there is seldom anything that can be called theory) and empirical research is so close as to be obvious. Consider the research firm that polls the electorate to predict the winner of the presidential election. The relevant assumptions are mostly obvious: The election will really be held, the candidates will stay alive, and so on. No real theorizing is involved, the empirical research is the entire scientific task.

In "evaluation" research—such as an evaluation of whether busing affects the attainment and socialization of students—the empirical research also often seems to proceed without theory. But it is worth noting that the reason there is a busing phenomenon to investigate is because of the speculation some years back that school integration *would* affect students' attainments and socialization.

In "pure" research that seeks to explain the human world in general scientific terms, the relationship between theory and research is more complex. Theoretical speculation and empirical research are two approaches to the knowledge one seeks. The central task in using them together is to mold them and sharpen them so that both are addressing the same question, in such manner that their results can reasonably be compared. Then the use of two very different approaches together can be much more powerful than one approach alone. If the two approaches give the same answer, then one can feel much more secure with the conclusion than with only one approach. And if the two approaches do *not* yield the same answer, you are alerted that the matter is not so settled and straightforward as one approach alone would suggest. This is true for the combination of theory and empirical research just as it is for two separate empirical methods.

"Operationalization" of the theoretical concepts is the task of finding appropriate empirical proxies for the theoretical variables. "Conceptualization" is the complementary process of finding appropriate theoretical constructs for interesting empirical patterns that turn up. Operationalization and conceptualization work hand in hand as the research work progresses. Very often the researcher passes back and forth from conceptualization to operationalization, rather than the one-way flow from theory to empirical work envisioned by the philosophers of science.

A key link in the struggle to have the theoretical statements and the empirical work deal with the same phenomena is sound definition of the variables. On the theory side, there is no special technique except general clear thinking to help define terms clearly. But on the empirical side, the operational definition is a powerful tool in working toward definitions that all researchers can understand and that therefore can be compared against the theoretical terms.

An example of the connection of theory—assumption, deduction, and hypothesis—with empirical research whose purpose is to test the theory was given on page 28. Here is another example, again taken from economics:

A. EXAMPLE 1: ADVERTISING RATES IN NEWSPAPERS: FACTUAL PROBLEM

It is an observed fact that newspapers charge lower advertising rates to local retailers than to national advertisers. To explain why they do so is a research problem.

Assumptions. We *assume*, first, that sellers (newspaper owners, in this case) will charge that price to each group of people that will result in *maximum profit*. (This is the "economic maximizer" assumption, the same as the first assumption in the example on p. 28.)

Second, we *assume* that sellers *know* how groups of customers (retailers and national advertisers) react to various prices. (This is the "perfect knowledge" assumption, the same as the second assumption on p. 28.)

Deduction. We *deduce* that if one customer group is *less sensitive* to a price increase than is another group, it will be profitable to charge a higher price to the less sensitive customer. This can be shown with a standard logical chain of economic deduction.

Empirical Test. There are many possible ways to test this deduction empirically. One could, for example, try to find out whether local advertisers really are more sensitive to a price increase than are national advertisers. This could be investigated by examining the changes in the quantity of local and national advertising following individual price changes in a sample of newspapers. Or, one could relate the aggregate amounts of local and national advertising to the average prices of local and national advertising over a period of years. Or, one might persuade one or more newspapers to conduct controlled experiments with their advertising prices. All these methods examine changes in economic data, and then reason back to the beliefs and behavior of presumably rational decision makers.

Another approach is to directly examine the beliefs of the newspaper executives. This is the method we shall consider, with the hypothesis and related test as follows:

Hypothesis. We *hypothesize* that, if the deduction is correct, the newspaper publishers *believe* that national advertisers are less sensitive to price changes.

Research Method. The hypothesis can be tested by finding out what the newspaper advertisers believe about the relative sensitivity of local and national advertisers. A questionnaire study found that publishers do indeed believe that national advertisers are less sensitive to price changes and thus confirmed the hypothesis (J. Simon, 1965).

B. LOGIC AND THE CONNECTION BETWEEN THEORY AND EMPIRICAL WORK

Philosophers have devoted much effort to analyzing the logic of the scientific process. They have outlined how science begins with a theoretical framework, deduces propositions, and tests the propositions. Scientific publications tend to follow this format, which is also shown in the examples on page 28.

The actual development of a scientific project seldom follows this logic, however. Rather, you may begin with some data, get an idea out of the data, scratch around for some relevant theory, then test the theoretical deduction, find that the theoretical deduction is not confirmed, do some theorizing, get some more data, get new ideas, and on and on. Or the scenario may begin with a casual observation in everyday life, move on to data or to theory, and so forth.

The point is that the route to valuable scientific results tends to be circuitous, unprogrammed, nonlogical, intuitive, repetitious, frustrating, surprising, and hence exciting, as Hasburg's map (Figure 5.1) illustrates.

A last point about the connections between theory and empirical research: They go both

FIGURE 5.1

Source: Ernest Harburg. Reprinted by permission.

ways. Just as theory supports empirical research, there also can be no science without empirical research to serve as a bridge between scientific thought and reality, as the source of speculation and as a *test* of hypotheses. Empirical work and hypothesizing shade into one another. When you look out the window, observe rain, and announce "It's raining outside," you are extrapolating that it is raining all around the house and not just outside one window. Empirical and theoretical statements form a continuum.

> . . . [N]o observation is purely empirical—that is, free of any ideational element—as no theory (in science, at any rate) is purely ideational . . . the terms of even the barest description carry us beyond the here-and-now, if only because they must be capable of more than one utterance to have a usage. When I say, "This object is red," I am inescapably relating the present occasion to others in which "red" is properly used. . . . When we see that someone is pleased or angry, we are relying on a whole framework of ideas about cultural patterns in the expression of emotion, just as we understand what is said not just on the basis of what we hear but also in terms of a whole grammar somehow brought to the hearing. (Kaplan, 1964: 58—59)

The relationship of theory to research is discussed from a related point of view in the following chapter.

5. Summary

The relationship between theory and empirical research differs from situation to situation. Seldom does the pattern follow the philosophical-logical model beginning with a body of theoretical axioms and proceeding through deduction to empirical testing. Rather, the process may begin at any point—data, curiosity about an observation in daily life, or theoretical deduction—and then it flows back and forth in a web of ideas and empirical testing and theoretical development.

The place of theory differs from discipline to discipline. In some fields the body of theory is strong and well-integrated, whereas in other fields the best that one can hope for is a modest model to guide empirical study. Applied work tends to proceed without theory as such, but rather on the bases of hunches and guesses relevant to a practical need for tested information.

ADDITIONAL READING FOR CHAPTER 5

The topics covered in this chapter are the subject of frequent discussion and analysis by social scientists; see Selltiz et al. (1976, Chap. 2); Merton (1968); Stinchcombe (1968); Blalock (1979; 1982).

Kaplan's *The Conduct of Inquiry* is an excellent treatise on the philosophical basis of social research, and especially the relationship of theory to empirical research.

Kuhn's theory of the development of science has been very influential recently, though somewhat controversial. It is worth getting acquainted with.

Choosing Appropriate Proxies for Theoretical Variables

When the research project begins with abstract theory, you must find one or more reasonable empirical proxies (indicators) for the theoretical variables. Even when the research is "applied" rather than "pure," you must be sure that your empirical variables lend themselves well to the empirical work. This chapter discusses how to choose empirical variables. It follows naturally from the discussion in the previous chapter of the relationship of theory to empirical research and expands on it.

When the theoretical structure is well-defined, the theoretical variable may be confined to a single dimension. But in fields in which the researcher works less with a well-structured theory and more with free-ranging imagination, the theoretical variable is likely to be multidimensional. Lazarsfeld describes this part of the transition from theoretical to empirical variables:

Imagery. The flow of thought and analysis and work which ends up with a measuring instrument usually begins with something which might be called imagery. Out of the analyst's immersion in all the detail of a theoretical problem, he creates a rather vague image or construct. The creative act may begin with the perception of many disparate phenomena as having some underlying characteristic in common. Or the investigator may have observed certain regularities and is trying to account for them. In any case, the concept, when first created, is some vaguely conceived entity that makes the observed relations meaningful.

Suppose we want to study industrial firms. We naturally want to measure the management of the firm. What do we mean by management and managers? Is every foreman a manager? Somewhere the notion of management was started, within a man's writing or a man's experience. Someone noticed that, under the same conditions, sometimes a factory is well run and sometimes it is not well run. Something was being done to make men and materials more productive. This "something" was called management, and ever since students of industrial organization have tried to make this notion more concrete and precise.

The same process happens in other fields. By now the development of intelligence tests has become a large industry. But the beginning of the idea of intelligence was that, if you look at little boys, some strike you as being alert and interesting and others as dull and uninteresting. This kind of general impression starts the wheels rolling for a measurement problem.

Concept Specification. The next step is to take this original imagery and divide it into components. The concept is specified by an elaborate discussion of the phenomena out of which it emerged. We develop "aspects," "components," "dimensions," or similar specifications. They are sometimes derived logically from the over-all concept, or one aspect is deduced from another, or empirically observed correlations between them are reported. The concept is shown to consist of a complex combination of phenomena, rather than a simple and directly observable item.

Suppose you want to know if a production team is efficient. You have a beginning notion of efficiency. Somebody comes and says, "What do you really mean? Who are more efficient—those who work quickly and make a lot of mistakes, so that you have many rejections, or those who work slowly but make very few rejects?" You might answer, depending on the product, "Come to think of it, I really mean those who work slowly and make few mistakes." But do you want them to work so slowly that there are no rejects in ten years? That would not be good either. In the end you divide the notion of efficiency into components such as speed, good product, careful handling of the machines—and suddenly you have what measurement theory calls a set of dimensions. (Lazarsfeld in Brodbeck, 1968: 610–611)

Now let us return to one-dimensional variables; further discussion of multidimensional variables is in Chapter 16.

There are several stages in the process of moving from a speculative question about the world to the beginning of the actual empirical work. The first necessary step is to transform the original question into the functional form $y = f(x_1, x_2 \ldots)$. Then you must translate the *hypothetical* (theoretical) variables (concepts) as they appear in your functional form into *empirical* variables ("indicators") that you can work with. The philosophical relationship between hypothetical and empirical variables has already been discussed (Chapter 2). Now we can get down to the actual process of choosing ("specifying") appropriate empirical variables.

The choice of appropriate variables is perhaps the most important decision that the researcher must make. It is at this stage that one finally pins down the vague interest and turns it into concrete operational research: the process by which one moves from "I want to find out how people feel about. . . ." to a researchable statement. Like every other decision in the research process, the choice of variables must depend on just what it is you want to find out and why you want to find it out.

Sometimes the general research question immediately suggests the empirical variables. For example, when one asks about the effect of prosperity on whether Democrats or Republicans win presidential elections, one can easily decide how to measure whether a person is a Democrat or a Republican, though the measure of prosperity is not so obvious (Bloom and Price, 1975). If one asks whether people drink more liquor in summer or winter, it is easy to decide that the Federal Alcohol and Tobacco Tax Unit data are appropriate. But, even in such simple cases, definition of the variables is not automatic and requires some judgment. Are beer and wine counted as liquor? And what about illegal moonshine?

In most research projects, however, one cannot simply plunge in and start measuring an obvious approximation to the theoretical (hypothetical) variables of interest, for one of two reasons: Direct data on the hypothetical (theoretical) variable may not be available, or the hypothetical variable may be a vague concept like love, happiness, welfare, or conformity, none of which immediately suggests empirical counterparts. To put it another way, one cannot find an empirical counterpart about which almost everyone will agree that it really "means" the same thing as the hypothetical variable. Yet in both cases *some* empirical measurement must be done, and it must be done in some way that has meaning. In either case one must create a "proxy" (or "surrogate")—a variable that is different from but stands for the phenomenon in which one is interested. The trick is to create good proxies, proxies that reveal something about the "real" variable in which one is interested.

Better than any single proxy are *several different proxies*. If you use several proxies, and if the results agree, you will reduce doubt about whether you have captured the theoretical variable in your empirical variables. Equally important is that several proxies allow you to draw a more general conclusion from your empirical work, and to map out the domain within which your theoretical proposition does and does not hold.

1. Dependent Variables Whose Referents Are Clearly Defined

This section deals with the type of problem Pogo faces forthrightly in Figure 6.1. Walt Kelly is kidding—but not entirely. When television was young, an engineer in the Dayton, Ohio, Water Department discovered that when the commercials came on the water pressure dropped as people went to kitchens and bathrooms. This measurement of program and commercial popularity is known in research folklore as the "Dayton Water Survey."

Archimedes provided a nice illustration of the substitution of an easily measurable quantity for a quantity that is harder to measure. Archimedes sought to measure the *areas* of various geometrical shapes. But could he do that empirically? It would require cutting up a shape into tiny squares and counting the squares, which would be tedious, to say nothing of difficulties with incomplete squares with curved edges. Archimedes then hit on substituting a process of weighing figures drawn on material of uniform thickness; weight provided

a good and handy proxy for area (Mason, 1962: 51). The same old dodge is still used for estimating the area under curves in, say, radioactivity studies in biology.

Shortly we discuss such unobservable concepts as beliefs, attitudes, and preferences. First, we deal with concepts that are measurable *in principle* but not *in practice*. That is, we are talking here about concepts for which we have satisfactory operational definitions but for which we cannot carry out the operations. One can develop quite satisfactory operational definitions of a competitor's advertising expenditures, of China's rice crop, or of a jury's deliberations, even though one is blocked from actually carrying out the operations. On the other hand, there can be no satisfactory operational definitions of such inner states as beliefs and preferences, except in terms of the behavioral proxies that one creates for them.[1]

There are two ways to justify the measurement of a given variable as a proxy for another variable that is clearly defined but cannot itself be measured. The first is to demonstrate an *empirical association* between the proxy and the hard-to-measure variable. The second is to demonstrate a *logical link* with a chain of reasoning between the proxy and the conceptual variable. A combination of the two methods is best. Each of the two ways will be illustrated here.

Many examples of pure empirical proxies can be found in aptitude and vocational testing. One testing organization asks the subjects to write as many words as they can, any words at all, in a one-minute period. A person who gets a high score is said to have an aptitude for those jobs that require high creativity. This prediction is based on the supposed fact that people who are successful in creative vocations

1. One might argue that there is no difference between hypothetical (theoretical) concepts for which we have no operational definitions, except in terms of proxies, and concepts for which we have operational definitions that cannot be carried out. If you do not find the distinction useful, ignore it

FIGURE 6.1

Source: *Pogo*, November 26, 1963, by Walt Kelly; © 1963 Walt Kelly.

score higher on this test than do other people. One might be able to find some logical rationale for such a relationship, but basically it is a purely empirical link; if people who are successful in creative jobs were found to score low on this test, a low score would then be accepted as a predictor of success in creative jobs. Vocational tests that predict job performance have been used by major corporations for years when hiring or promoting employees. Because the tests provide a way to evaluate employees fairly and objectively, their use has been encouraged in recent years by the courts in equal employment opportunity cases (Schlei and Grossman, 1976: 66–73).

Many of the projective tests used by clinical psychologists—such as the Rorschach ink-blot test and the Thematic Apperception Test, as well as such personality batteries as the Minnesota Multiphasic Personality Inventory—are "validated" in a purely empirical way. Those responses or "profiles" that are found among people known to be manic-depressive rather than schizophrenic, say, or neurotic rather than psychotic, are then used as "indicators" to predict whether a given person is of one type or another.

In most of the social sciences, the relationship between a proxy and a defined but hard-to-measure conceptual variable is through a *chain of reasoning*. For example, Warburton (1932) made a fascinating determination of how much liquor was drunk in the United States during Prohibition. The usual measurements of liquor consumption—tax receipts—were not available, so he made the following estimates:

1. Amounts used of various possible *ingredients* of liquor (corn sugar; corn syrup and corn starch, corn meal; corn, rye, and other grains; malt syrup; fruits and vegetables), plus estimated amounts of industrial alcohol, medicinal alcohol, and smuggled alcohol
2. *Death rates* from alcoholic diseases
3. Number of *arrests* for drunkenness

He then combined these three types of estimate in one grand estimate. The relationship between each of the three estimates and actual consumption could not be directly validated empirically, except perhaps by a survey, and it was too late for that. Warburton's only validation of each of these estimates, and therefore of his combined estimate, was his *reasoning* about the link between drinking and the sources of production, death rates, and arrest rates.

It is sometimes possible to study an invisible phenomenon by finding something visible that is logically linked to it. A famous example in the physical sciences is observation of the Brownian movement of invisible molecules by the use of the "cloud chamber." In this device the molecules become attached to droplets of oil that are of visible size, and the motion of the molecules can then be inferred from the observed motion of the oil droplets.

Business researchers have used many ingenious methods—some ethical, some not so ethical—to obtain sales information that their competitors do not disclose. Retailers who want to know a competitor's sales volume can count the number of customers who enter the competitor's store and then multiply by the estimated size and number of purchases. (Sometimes a retailer takes the more direct method of having agents watch the cash registers in the competitor's store for five minutes at a time and then projecting overall estimates from that sample evidence.) Measuring competitive sales by consumer-purchase panels and by store inventories is a large and flourishing business for many commercial firms.

Information about a competitor's advertising budget is normally obtained by keeping a count of the number and sizes of the competitor's advertisements in all advertising media that the competitor is known to use. Commercial firms and trade associations perform this service for many types of firms in many industries. But the counts are never quite complete. Each firm therefore adjusts its estimate of a competitor's budget by comparing the amount the outside agency estimates for the firm's own expenditures against the firm's own *actual* expenditures, which might be 30 percent to 90 percent greater, and it then makes the appropriate adjustment in the reported figures for its competitor.

Military intelligence officers commonly estimate unavailable magnitudes from what can be observed. Content analysis is frequently used for this purpose. For example, we are told that in World War II the Allies in England counted and measured the numbers of various types of songs played on various European radio stations as an index of changes in German troop concentrations, and deduced from the serial numbers of captured weapons the extent of German war production.

To learn about unobserved or unobservable human behavior, we must usually depend upon the *subject's statements about his or her behavior* as proxies for the behavior itself. But we must always worry about how good a proxy "verbal behavior" is for actual behavior. The most common way of finding out how people spend their time, for example, is to ask them questions in a survey about how much time they spend working, traveling, doing housework, and so on. But it turns out that their reports are not very accurate. For one thing, they tend to exaggerate the amount of time spent in socially approved activities, such as working for voluntary organizations. Reports of time use in daily diaries are much more accurate (Robinson, 1977: 9). Many studies, therefore, devote considerable resources to checking on the reliability and validity of verbal statements about behavior.

Laboratory experimentation sometimes provides reasonable proxies when subject matter is not accessible. Researchers at the University of Chicago who wished to study the workings of the jury system were denied access to actual jury deliberations for ethical-legal reasons. (After they had obtained permission from one judge to monitor a jury room, a member of Congress became so indignant that he called for a full congressional investigation, even though the cases were minor and the judge and lawyers all had given their permission.) To overcome this obstacle experiments were set up with the cooperation of courts in which people currently on the jury list listened to *recorded mock trials*.

The problem of estimating the characteristics of a group of people *that does not yet exist* illustrates the difference between hypothetical variables that are *conceptually* vague—such as attitudes and beliefs—and those that *in principle* are not vague. How can a university administration estimate what kind of housing the students twenty-five years hence will want when those students have not even been born yet? There is no difficulty in constructing a perfectly satisfactory operational definition of the body of students twenty-five years from now, but the operation obviously cannot be carried out. (A sensible approximation may be to assume that present-day students are like future students.)

Whenever possible, you should try to validate your empirical variable by comparing it directly with the variable that is of ultimate interest to you. For example, one of the authors once developed a method to help marines improve their performance with the .45 caliber pistol. The teaching device was a series of holes in a sheet of metal into which the shooter placed a rod in the barrel of his pistol. The shooter's task was to pull the trigger when the gun was aimed at the target, at which time the rod was within the hole. If he jerked the gun off the target, an electric circuit would ring a buzzer. This method did improve the marines' skills in dry-firing in the laboratory, and it seemed reasonable that skill on the live-ammunition range would also be improved. But would improvement actually show up on the firing range? That would be the ultimate validation. Unfortunately the author was transferred before he could compare the empirical dependent variable (performance in the laboratory) with the variable of ultimate interest (performance on the target range).

Generally, the greater the similarity between the proxy and the actual variable, the better the proxy. For example, if you want to find out whether a small child thinks that a dollar bill is worth more than 100 pennies, you will probably do better to ask "Which one do you want for your birthday?" than to ask "Which one is bigger?" or "Which one is worth more?" The Schwerin firm exploits this principle in measuring the effect of advertising. Before and after showing commercials to special movie audiences, Schwerin holds a lottery and offers people their choice of various brands of merchandise if they win. Choice when one may actually receive the merchandise is a more realistic measure of preference than asking "Which brand do you prefer?"

The extent to which attitudes are reasonable proxies for behavior must also be considered carefully. For example, it is common to reason that a woman who says she hates blacks is more likely to discriminate than is a woman who says she likes blacks. Maybe so, but maybe not. But it is surely foolish to pay *no* attention to attitudes and to argue that attitudes are always a worthless measure. For example, it was found in World War II that, among soldiers who had never been in battle, those who said they were confident of their skill in battle, less fearful of getting hurt, and aggressive toward the enemy did indeed perform better in battle later on (Kendall and Lazarsfeld, 1950). And, the more positive a woman's attitudes toward female labor-force participation, the more likely she is to get a paying job (Waite, 1978).

Just *how* good a proxy an attitude is depends on the situation. Advertisers have had to be sophisticated about this point. For example, consider just a *few* of the possible measurements that relate to the selling power of a magazine advertisement: the number of copies of the magazine sold, the number of people who look at the magazine, the number who look at a particular page, the number who notice the adver-

tisement, the number who read part of the advertisement, the number who remember the advertisement, the number who exhibit more favorable *attitudes* after seeing the advertisement, the number of people who remember selling points about the product, the increase in the number of people who say they *want* the product, the number of people who try out the product, and, finally, the number of people who actually become purchasers.[2] The closer the measurement is to actual purchasing, the better the proxy should be. On the other hand, closer proxies—including actual sales—are often much harder to measure, and therefore a compromise is usually struck. Under the best of conditions the proxy is also validated empirically.

In some situations one selects an empirical variable that is related to the variable of final interest only by a long chain of reasoning. As an illustration, Haire (1950) wanted to find out why women did not buy instant coffee. That question is reasonably specific, but it is still a long way from being specific enough to define a piece of research. What Haire had to do next was to specify a set of dependent and independent variables and a functional relationship that he could study empirically.

What he actually did was to conduct an experiment in which he submitted two shopping lists to two groups of women. On the shopping list he gave to group A were many items of food plus "Nescafé instant coffee." On the shopping list for group B were all the same items except that "Maxwell House coffee (Drip Ground)" replaced "Nescafe instant coffee." Haire then asked the women in his groups to say what kind of woman they thought had made out the shopping list. Twenty-four of the twenty-five women in group A, whose list included instant coffee, gave such judgments as "lazy housekeeper." Only two of fifty in group B, whose list included regular coffee, said the woman was a lazy housekeeper.

---

2. See Madow et al. (1961: 41 ff.), for a similar discussion of types of television-audience measurement.

The functional form of Haire's research design was "Judgment about shopping-list maker is a function of whether instant or regular coffee is on the shopping list." But his original purpose was to find out why women do not themselves buy instant coffee. It seems reasonable, then, to ask what the connection is between Haire's original question and the functional form he actually used.

The connection between the basic question of the research and the actual variables and functional form is a *chain of reasoning*. Haire assumed that women could not or would not give the real reasons that they themselves did not buy instant coffee. He further assumed that they might "project" their real reasons onto other people. Therefore, the chain of reasoning was as follows: First, if a woman thinks that she herself is lazy when she buys instant coffee, she will say that *another* woman who buys instant coffee is lazy; second, if a woman thinks herself lazy when she buys instant coffee, she will not buy instant coffee. Haire therefore assumed that if women did judge instant-coffee buyers lazy, he would have evidence that belief in the laziness of instant-coffee buyers really does inhibit purchase. And that is indeed what he found. (Haire then buttressed these findings by a supplementary investigation of which women did buy instant coffee, and, indeed, the women who did *not* say that other instant-coffee users were lazy tended to buy instant coffee themselves.)

A variable that is a good proxy at one time may not be a good proxy years later. Studies that repeated Haire's 1940s experiment in the 1960s and 1970s did not obtain the results he did, probably because of a shift in attitudes toward instant coffee (Arndt, 1973).

2. Dependent Variables Whose Referents Are Not Clearly Defined

We have just discussed empirical variables as proxies for concepts that are clearly defined but *impractical* to measure. Now we shall discuss proxies for variables that are not clearly

defined or are *impossible* to measure. Empirical validation of these proxies is not possible; often logical validation is not possible either. These proxies differ from Warburton's example, for in *principle* he might have validated his estimates by taking surveys of how much people drank during Prohibition.

The intelligence test is an interesting example because it illustrates both types of uses of proxies. If the I.Q. test is interpreted as a *prediction of future school success*, it illustrates the first type, because it can be validated by comparing I.Q. scores with later school grades; a high correlation convinces us that the I.Q. test is a good proxy.

If we interpret performance on an I.Q. test as an empirical proxy for a hypothetical notion of general intelligence, however, that is another matter. Then the performance is supposed to represent something that is an inner mental condition or process, and no empirical or logical validation is possible. This becomes clear when we consider *artificial* intelligence, the kind manifested by computers. Computers can now play chess better than all but 5 percent of American tournament chess players, solve increasingly complex physics and mathematics problems, and recognize visual stimuli. Some computer scientists aim "to build a computer that, by its output, simply could not be distinguished from a mind" (Bernstein, 1981: 92). But would that mean it was "intelligent" in the same way a person is? "It is not entirely clear what would settle the debate," Bernstein says. "Even if a humanoid machine were built, many people would certainly argue that it did not really understand what it was doing, and that it was only simulating intelligence, while the real thing lay beyond it and would always lie beyond it."

There is also a close relationship between choosing proxies for vague variables and choosing measurements, as this story illustrates:

GROOMING CODE: SISTER TURNS "FINGER-MAN"

Ferndale, Mich., Feb. 20 (AP)—Too bushy or not too bushy? That is the question at St. James

Catholic High School in this Detroit suburb. Sister Mary Aurilla, school principal, has devised a simple test to answer the question of whether the hair styles worn by the 200 girl students are too bushy. She pushes her index finger into the girl's hair. If her finger tip touches the girl's head and the knuckle doesn't show above the hairdo, then it's too bushy. Girls who fail the finger test are sent home to rearrange the situation. (Champaign-Urbana *Courier*, February 21, 1965)

If bushiness of hair is understood to refer only to the *single dimension of* thickness, then we can view the finger test as a *measurement*. But, if bushiness could mean *other* characteristics in addition to thickness, then the finger test is a one-dimensional proxy chosen to stand for the more complex hypothetical (conceptual) variable.

When your hypothetical variable is vague, you must bull ahead and say "This empirical variable is what I shall call. . . ." When Wilensky wanted an empirical variable to stand for the development of the welfare state—a very general concept—he chose to look at social security expenditures because they "form a more or less coherent package and tend to move together" (1975: 3). Similarly, when Gamson (1975) pondered how to tell when a social protest group had won new advantages for itself, he decided simply to accept the conclusions of historians or the group itself. In both Wilensky's study and Gamson's, other empirical proxies for theoretical variables could have been chosen, but based on their experience, knowledge of the alternatives, and practical considerations, Wilensky and Gamson chose the particular proxies they did.

One can validate this type of variable only with *judgment*. The variable has been well chosen if other scientists are willing to accept that the empirical variable gets at the hypothetical variable. Not all empirical variables are well enough chosen to overcome this obstacle, and indeed some proxies are downright foolish. To measure mother love by how often a mother cuddles a child might or might not be satisfactory. To measure mother love by how

much the mother *says* she loves a child would probably be worth little or nothing. In the cartoon in Figure 6.2, Garry Trudeau makes fun of those who act as if it were easy to find an empirical proxy for an important but vague variable—"public opinion," or "the will of the people."

One must not forget the distinction between the proxy and the "real" variable. For example, running away from home might be a good indicator of unhappiness in adolescents. But one should not therefore think that anyone who runs away from home *is* unhappy. To show such a relationship, a researcher would first have to show an empirical link between running away and *other* indicators that are generally accepted signs of unhappiness.

Can one ever observe the "real" variable directly? Consider again being inside a building and wanting to know whether it is raining outside so that you can decide what you should wear. You are likely to look out the window to see whether you can see raindrops falling. Are you then observing the "real" variable, or are you observing only a proxy variable? Common sense says that you are observing the real variable, as it is the rain itself that you are looking at. But what you observe will depend upon the time of the day and other conditions that affect your vision, so that what you observe is not *just* the real variable. Perhaps what you observe can better be described as the visual impression of the raindrops seen from a distance under certain visual conditions.

Deciding whether you are observing the "real" variable is not likely to be a problem. You will be on safe ground if you describe your observed variable as a close or not-so-close proxy for the phenomenon in which you are interested. If you think that what you are observing is the "real" variable, you might state that there is complete identity between the proxy and the phenomenon you are studying.

Sometimes several research techniques can be strung together to form a logical chain between a proxy and an ill-defined variable. In a library study we conducted, for example, we

FIGURE 6.2

Source: *Doonesbury,* August 13, 1978, by G. B. Trudeau. Copyright 1978, G.B. Trudeau. Reprinted with permission of Universal Press Syndicate. All rights reserved.

wished to determine the relationship between the scholarly value of given books and the rates of their withdrawal from the library (Fussler and Simon, 1961). Therefore, we first investigated the withdrawal of books from the library by studying withdrawal records. Then we investigated the relationship between book use within the library and withdrawals from the library by a questionnaire survey of the unrecorded use of books. Then we related recorded book use to the ultimate value of books, with the aid of judgments by a panel of expert scholars in various fields. Given that validating chain of reasoning, we could reasonably accept the rate of withdrawal of a book as a proxy of its value in the succeeding work.

Students of human emotions often validate by comparing several different proxies. If there

is high agreement among them, faith in one or all of them is increased. One may also decide that the proxy that best agrees with all the others is the *best* proxy among them. For example, if we want to measure how happy people are, we might ask them these questions, each of which, we think, tells something about how happy a person is:

1. In general, how satisfying do you find the way you're spending your life these days? Would you call it *completely* satisfying, *pretty* satisfying, or *not very* satisfying?
2. Taking all things together, how would you say things are these days—would you say you're *very* happy, *pretty* happy, or *not too* happy these days?
3. Here is a picture of a ladder. At the bot-

tom of the ladder is the worst life you might reasonably expect to have. At the top is the best life you might expect to have. Of course, life from week to week falls somewhere in between. Where was your life *most of the time during the past year?* (Scale: ladder with nine rungs extending from "Best life I could expect to have" to "Worst life I could expect to have") (Andrews and Withey, 1967: 66–70)

If the answers that people give to the three questions are highly correlated, our confidence is increased that singly or together these questions are indeed measuring happiness. (Chapter 16 discusses the combination of separate proxies in composite *indexes*.)

The branch of economics called "welfare economics" offers a particularly interesting and thorny problem of relating the proxy to the theoretical variable. Most economists agree that the aim of welfare economics is to study the effects of various arrangements on the "welfare" of groups of people, and "welfare" is generally taken to be a synonym for "happiness" (Boulding, 1952). But *the amount of goods and services* (purchasing power) is always the proxy used in welfare economics; studies in welfare economics commonly consider what happens to the goods and income of a community under various conditions. Anyone with a grain of wisdom knows that money is not all there is to happiness, however. And quite obviously a particular good does not have the same happiness value for all people. Here is the perennial stumbling block of "interpersonal comparisons": How can we tell the amount of happiness that a loaf of bread will give a poor person compared to the happiness it will give to a rich person?

Some economists have given up on the idea of validating welfare economics by empirical or logical methods. They feel that the reader must *intuitively* accept the "objective function" relationship between goods and happiness if he

is to accept welfare economics. Others simply deny that they are talking about happiness and restrict their discussion to *material* welfare. But then welfare economics loses its claim to speak of the ultimate human concern, and it can become arid and without content.

The situation may not be as bad as it seems; some empirical validation may be possible. "Happiness" has been investigated successfully under various other sets of conditions, and there is no *a priori* reason why it is not possible to relate happiness to various economic conditions also. In fact, happiness seems to be positively related to people's incomes (see J. Simon, 1974).[3]

Empirical investigation of the qualities of art is not dissimilar to welfare economics in this respect. In both cases the dependent variable is ephemeral and subjective. Anyone can simply *state* that a particular novel or painting is "better" than another novel or painting without needing any definition or proxy for "better." But to make a *scientific* study of what makes one novel or play better than another, an objective empirical variable is necessary. It is not difficult to find *some* objective empirical variables; for example, the number of copies the novel sells, and the price paid for the painting, may appeal to many businesspeople as excellent proxies for excellence of art. Or one might compare how much two novels or two plays move people by measuring various physiological changes associated with emotion—perhaps respiration or sweating—with devices similar to the lie detector. But we doubt that in the near or distant future *any* objective proxy will satisfy critics and artists as a "true" or "self-evident" measure of the value of art. Instead they are wont to say that to measure art is to measure the unmeasurable. (However, content analysis, discussed in Chapter 14, might reveal

3. Earlier it was noted that economics has relatively little difficulty in validating its variables, however, precisely because they *can* usually be expressed in single-dimension variables such as dollars or tons of steel.

that "good" adventure stories use higher proportions of active verbs than do less exciting
adventure stories.)

3. Choosing Independent Variables

Most of the proxies discussed in the previous
section have stood for *dependent* variables. But
difficulties also exist in choosing appropriate
independent variables. For example, if you
want to investigate the effect of training on the
performance of a rat running through a maze,
you must first specify exactly what you mean
by "training," and then you must train the rats
in exactly that way.

This is a good place to say again that the
questions in a questionnaire survey can have a
major influence on what answers mean. To exaggerate the point, if you were trying to measure the dependent variable "degree of liking of
Ronald Reagan," it would make quite a difference whether an interviewer says "Do you like
that great American Ronald Reagan?" or "Do
you like that traitor Ronald Reagan?"

In contrast to specifying dependent variables, choosing independent variables often
permits performance of an objective test to see
which variable is better. The researcher can
often try out two or more independent variables to see which one works best in "explaining" the dependent variable or which one is
more closely correlated with the dependent
variable. For example, an economist who is
studying the demand for autos and other goods
may have a choice between using family income or family expenditures in a given year as
a variable; the two may differ because families
may save some income or spend some savings.
The economist may have theoretical reasons
for preferring expenditures, say, but he probably will try out both variables to see which
gives the best results.

Another problem is *how many* independent
variables to use at one time; this problem
mostly afflicts the economists and sociologists
in their nonexperimental research. We do not

really know how to answer this question; at
best the answer is complex and not well understood. In crude terms, one keeps on adding
more variables to a cross-classification or other
multivariate scheme as long as they improve
the explanation appreciably. However, one
must avoid adding variables that are *not* relevant, because adding them introduces error;
this is another difficult and little-understood
problem. And sometimes a new theory will
help explain a dependent variable better using
fewer, but different, variables than before
(Hamblin, 1974).

The choice of variables is a cousin to classification; in the latter you specify the *dimensions* or *attitudes* (and the *categories* of those
dimensions) on which you will measure the
events or species or groups of people in which
you are interested. Classification is discussed
in Chapter 15, as are the related matters of
scaling and *measurement*.

Making sure that the supposed variables are
not *tautologies*—and therefore not usable in
empirical research—is a last obstacle in choosing variables. For example, Freud's pleasure-
pain principle is a tautology as it is usually
stated. If one says that a person does what is
pleasurable to him and that he does not do
what is painful, then *everything* he does is
pleasurable by *definition*. And, if so, there is
no way of empirically distinguishing pleasurable from painful actions or of using pleasure-
pain as an empirical variable. Darwin's evolution principle also is often stated as a tautology.

4. Choosing a Level of Aggregation

The world is like a cobweb, we suggested before. Because every filament is ultimately related to every other filament, a movement of
any filament will finally be reflected by every
other filament. Nevertheless, some filaments
are closer to or farther from others, and there
will be stronger or weaker association between
them. Also, a movement in a given filament y
might be caused by the movement in filament

x, where the movement is initiated; or the movements in both *x* and *y* might be reflecting movement initiated at *z* (the "third factor").[4]

Now we must consider a more complex view of the world. Consider the question of why people buy automobiles. Just a few strands of this question are shown in Figure 6.3.

The four different *purchase* rectangles represent four different "levels of aggregation." A given scientist might—and some do—try to explain any one of the following:

1. *Total* purchases (or changes in total purchases)
2. Purchases by particular *groups,* like northerners or blacks or Catholics (or *comparisons* between groups, northerners versus southerners, for example)
3. Purchases by *households,* expressed as probabilities
4. Purchases by *individuals*

Economists are mostly interested in total purchases; sometimes they think about the group or individual level of aggregation but primarily as a means for understanding and predicting total purchases. Anthropologists are also mostly interested in total purchases. Sociologists are more likely to be interested in the group level of aggregation. Psychologists are mostly interested in individual purchases. Market researchers are interested in individual purchases when they study advertising appeals related to auto styles, for example; but they work at the group level of aggregation when they study where to locate dealers and where to advertise, and at the level of total demand for autos when they advise on how many cars to produce. Most of the market researcher's attention is actually devoted to a level of aggre-

gation not even shown in the diagram—individual purchase of particular *brands* of cars.

These points should be considered when deciding at which level of aggregation to work: First, what level of aggregation are you *interested* in? That is, for which level of aggregation do you want to make decisions—for example, the individual or the nation? Or what body of data do you want to explain? If you want to study the causal relationship running from per capita income to literacy or the correlation between per capita income and suicide rates, you want data for individuals and not groups. But you might want to study the relationship between *national* income and literacy if you are interested in the extent to which a high national income produces literacy. The level of aggregation in which you are interested is often influenced by the discipline within which you work, but you should not *blindly* adopt the level of aggregation usually used in your discipline.

Second, which level of aggregation is it *feasible* to study? Sometimes data are not available at the desired level of aggregation. For example, people interested in politics (including politicians) have long wanted to know why voters choose one party over another. Before techniques for conducting good surveys were developed, the only way to investigate this was at a high level of aggregation, looking at data on states, congressional districts, or the country as a whole. The data seemed to show that election outcomes were related to the economic situation, and most people assumed this was because voters were "voting their pocketbooks," with those who were doing well voting for the incumbent party and those who were doing badly voting against it. Recent data on individuals shows, however, that people are not as self-centered as previously believed. The state of the economy in general is more important to them when deciding how to vote than is their own economic situation (Kinder and Kiewiet, 1979).

Sometimes one must make an extra effort to

4. The scientist's problem is that the connections among filaments do not always seem obvious or sensible. "During World War II, the production of optical instruments was temporarily greatly hampered by a shortage of babies' diapers. The reason was that diapers were an excellent polishing material for lenses" (Morgenstern, 1963: 133).

FIGURE 6.3 Some Possible Variables and Levels of Aggregation for Use in Analysis of Auto Purchasing

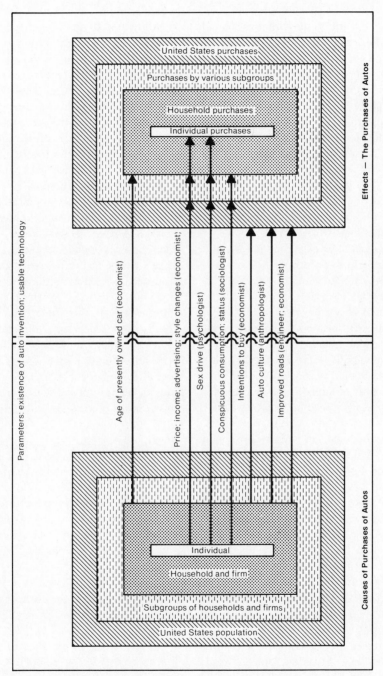

Note: The assignment of concepts in this diagram to particular fields may be misleading, especially in these years of the 1980s when the social sciences seem to be breaking down the partitions among them.

study the subgroups separately so as not to be misled by the aggregate. This is especially true when comparing two or more aggregates that are composed of different proportions of subgroups. For example, the crude death rate among U.S. blacks (that is, the proportion of deaths in a year to total population of U.S. blacks) is lower than the crude death rate for U.S. whites, but the life expectancy at birth for whites is higher than for blacks, as of 1978 (U.S. Bureau of the Census, 1980). The explanation is that a larger proportion of whites are in the older age brackets, due to lower mortality and lower fertility in the past. In such a situation one must disaggregate and compare the mortality rates for each age group in order to compare blacks and whites fairly.

Third, sometimes it is easier to understand the whole than to understand all its parts and the relationships among them. For example, it will be much easier and more accurate to determine the effect of a price rise on auto sales by studying the relationship of *total* auto sales in past years when different prices prevailed than to try to understand the motivations and psychological reactions to a price rise of individuals who might or might not purchase autos. It is particularly sensible to work at the higher level of aggregation (total purchases, rather than individuals, in this case) when there are *many* different motivations and psychological influences that bear importantly upon the individual's response (in this case, response to the price rise).

Sometimes, however, the whole does not equal the sum of the parts, in which case one cannot reason from the parts to the whole, or vice versa. One reason that the whole may behave differently from the parts is that there may be *interaction* among the parts. An example is Niebuhr's argument about "moral man and immoral society"; one cannot ascertain the likelihood of a country's starting a war from data on the amount of conflict and hostility among neighbors within the country. Keynes' thrift paradox is another example; societies whose citizens save a lot may thereby grow poor instead of rich.[5]

Experience and careful thought, then, are the only aids to making correct decisions about levels of aggregation. Often the wisdom of your field will be a good guide but not always; for example, an economist can sometimes do better by abandoning the usual economist's level of aggregation—total demand—and working at the level of individuals (Katona, 1960) or subgroups (Morgan, 1954). Similarly, a psychologist can often best answer a psychological question by working with groups of people rather than with individuals.

Some people have thought that the lowest level of aggregation must always be best. This view is called "reductionism." The argument against reductionism is mostly not a matter of logic, except to the degree that, because there is always *some* possible lower level of aggregation, *no* level really meets the reductionist requirement. In this view, psychology is more "basic" than sociology, biology is more basic than psychology, chemistry is more fundamental than biology, and so on. It is a simple empirical fact of the history of science, however, that in many cases it has proved more fruitful to work at higher levels of aggregation.

5. Choosing a Level of Explanation

There are many, many variables that one might say are causes of auto purchases. Just a few of these variables are shown in Figure 6.3. The question is, which of these variables should one choose when investigating the causes of auto purchasing? Deciding among

---

5. Another technical reason that the whole may not equal the sum of its parts is known as the "aggregation problem" in economics. The *demand functions* of individual consumers, say, do not sum in any simple way to the demand function for the economy as a whole. The problem is particularly acute in economics because the basic deductive theory concerns individuals, but the data and policy decisions concern higher levels of aggregation, such as the nation.

possible alternatives is the central task in specifying variables.

This section deals not with how to *think up* variables, but rather with how to *decide among* variables, that is, how to choose which variables to include and exclude among those you do think up. We assume that you have already completed the thinking-up stage, which you should summarize this way:

auto purchasing $= f$ (the invention of autos, the auto culture, per capita income, income of individual, age of present car, price of autos, style changes of cars, desire for sex mastery, desire to consume conspicuously, desire for high status, stated intentions to buy a car, condition of roads . . .).

This equation is simply an all-inclusive listing of factors that you think might influence purchasing. Writing down the functional form is a crucial step in jogging your imagination and clearing your mind. You may find it easier to write symbols instead of words (for example, S = auto sales), but we find it safer to stick to words at the very beginning.

When you decide at which level of aggregation you will work, some variables will be excluded. For example, the sex drives of the country as a whole do not vary much from year to year, though individuals may change and there may be a difference among individuals. Therefore, sex drives are not a useful variable in explaining the variation in auto purchases from year to year. On the other hand, if you are working at the level of individual purchases, the existence of our automobile culture will not help much as a variable, for all individual subjects are part of the culture. The same is true of price and the individual. But there is not an *automatic* relationship between the level of aggregation on the right side and the level of abstraction on the left side. For example, intention to buy is an individual-level variable, but it can be used to predict total purchases. You must think your way through this maze, variable by variable.

Your discipline may supply some guidance on which variables to include on the causal side. For example, social status is a "sociological variable." But on occasion economists and psychologists have also found it useful.

There are also causal relationships among some of the variables on the causal side. If a relationship between two independent variables is very strong, it is not sensible to use both variables because their effects will overlap strongly.

The key point is that no one level of explanation is *inherently* superior to other levels of explanation. Consider also the example of mental illness and the many levels at which it is fruitful to investigate it. Biologists and physicians have studied the physiology and pharmacology of mental illness, and they have discovered valuable physical and chemical treatments. Psychologists think about mental disease as a functional disorder that results from a person's early learning and life experience, and they study how to retrain the individual psychologically. Sociologists and social psychologists have studied the various types of home life and environment that lead to mental disease, and perhaps this work teaches us how to reduce mental illness by reducing the conditions under which it arises. Economists have not paid much attention to mental illness, but if they did they would assess its economic effect upon the community and then study the costs of various programs to reduce mental illness; such studies might be valuable (see Fein, 1958).

Each of these levels of investigation and explanation of mental illness can be valuable, and we benefit if each person—psychologist, sociologist, or biologist—tackles the problem with those theories and methods that he or she knows best.

Causation of automobile accidents is still another example. As Figure 6.4 shows, there are many factors that may be considered causal variables or conditions for an accident. The variables that an investigator chooses to study depend upon his or her discipline and his or her ability to manipulate particular aspects of the situation. Engineers can manipulate the design of highway and car; therefore they study how various designs affect the accident rate. Educational psychologists study methods of teaching auto safety. And so on. There is potential value in studying many of the listed variables that enter at various points in the causal chain.

Variation in birth rates offers a last example of a phenomenon that can sensibly be studied at many levels of explanation. Aside from bio-

FIGURE 6.4   The Story of an Accident

Source: "Framework for Assessment of Cause of Automobile Accidents," pp. 442–3, by J. Stannard Baker, in *The Language of Social Research*, edited by Lazarsfeld and Rosenberg; copyright © 1955 by The Free Press of Glencoe, a division of The Macmillan Company.

logical facts, why do some families have more children than do others? At the psychological level, the effects of personal inadequacy, "ego-centered interest in children," and liking for children have been examined. Such social-psychological variables as marital adjustment, conformity to group patterns, and doubling-up of families have been investigated. Sociological variables have included religion, nationality, adherence to traditions, social class, education, and their associated values. Variables with an anthropological flavor include the sacred values of a culture, the extent of structural cohesion and authority in a culture, and the extent of

How and Why It Happened

One day Joe was late and wanted to make up time.	**Hurry**	
That night Joe was going faster than usual.	Speed	
There was a slight mist falling.	Weather	
He did not slow for the curve.	Neglect to reduce speed	Mediate Causes Combination of
As he started to take the curve, Joe felt the car lean sharply and begin to slide.	Flat, sharp curve	
He realized he was going too fast.	← POINT OF SURPRISE	
So Joe stepped on the brake to slow down.	Braking on curve	
The car slid off the pavement.	← POINT OF NO ESCAPE	

. . . . Direct Cause

It ran off the shoulder.	← KEY EVENT		
And lunged into the shallow ditch where it came to a stop.	← FINAL POSITION		Result
The car was not damaged.	None	Cause of DAMAGE	
But Joe scratched his left arm on the broken window handle. He thought nothing of it but stopped a little bleeding with his handkerchief.	Sharp broken part of car	Cause of INJURY	
Joe's arm finally swelled. He had a fever. When he got a doctor, it was too late. Infection set in. Joe died.	Infection	Cause of DEATH	

social disorganization. And, of course, economic variables, including per capita income, laws governing inheritance of land, business cycles, and tax laws subsidizing or penalizing large families, have long been considered relevant to birth rates. Some of these sets of variables have proved more fruitful than have others, but each level of explanation has certainly been worth the investigation (Bane, 1976; Moore and Hofferth, 1979).

6. Constructing a Path-of-Causation Diagram

Once you have selected your variables and chosen a level of explanation, you will want to think about the causal relationships among the variables.

A path diagram is a formal but simple device that can help you sort out lines of causal influence. The path diagram may also be the prelude to the scheme of statistical analysis called "path analysis." Either way, the diagram can be enormously helpful in clarifying your thinking.

The path diagram is nothing more than a series of arrows that connect variables in a fashion that you believe (based on your thinking, what you have read, etc.) describes the flow of causal influence among them. For example, assume that you wish to understand how some factors influence the incomes of American men. Everyone believes that occupation and education affect income, so you draw them as in Figure 6.5. The arrow leading from one variable to another means you think the first causes the second; the "+" with regard to son's education and occupation means you think the relationships are positive—the more education and the higher the status of the occupation, the higher the income.

Then you wonder whether family background might affect a person's income. There are a number of possibilities. Having a well-educated father in a good job might help someone get a good education himself and might help him get into a high-status occupation; thus, there are arrows with plus signs from father's education and occupation to son's education and occupation. Does family background have a direct influence on one's income, or only on one's education and occupation (and thus indirectly on one's income)? You might think not, in which case you would draw no arrows from father's education and occupation to son's income (as in Figure 6.5); later, with data, you can see if your guess is right.

You might also think that some relationships could be important, but might not be very sure. Thus, for example, you might believe that well-educated fathers are likely to have relatively few children, and that sons with relatively few brothers and sisters are likely to get more education (possibly because families with fewer children will find it easier to pay for college for those children they have). Thus, you have an arrow with a minus sign and a question mark running from father's education to number of siblings, and from number of siblings to son's education—your speculation about the

FIGURE 6.5   The Determinants of Income—A Path Diagram

nature of the relationships and your degree of confidence in what you think.

Constructing such a diagram clarifies your thinking by: (1) getting you to be explicit about what variables you think are important causes of what you are interested in; (2) making you decide what you really think about the relationships among the variables (including, in some instances, about a lack of relationship). Such an exercise can serve as the basis for a statistical *model* of the process leading to income attainment, and you can then use path analysis (described in Chapter 27) to see how well the model conforms to reality.

7. Summary

Theoretical variables must be made operational if empirical research is to take place. The choice of empirical proxies to represent the theoretical (hypothetical) variables of interest is crucial. The empirical variables must be both observable and relevant.

In some cases the choice of proxy may be straightforward because the hypothetical variable is clearly defined (for example, the number of people watching the Olympics on television). In other cases the theoretical variable may be vague and abstract (for example, happiness).

The ingredients in making a wise choice of proxy are the usual ones: research, imagination, experience, and good judgment. Choosing independent variables wisely requires that the investigator understand the material and have sound hunches about the causes of the phenomenon being studied.

An important decision is the level of aggregation of the dependent variable. Should one work with individuals, or small groups, or large groups? If possible, it is best to work at *several* levels of aggregation to see whether the results corroborate each other.

The independent variables may also be considered at various levels of explanation. To some extent the choice depends upon your discipline and point of view, but the choice also should be illuminated by general scientific intuition.

To help provide an overall picture of how all the variables are related to each other, it may be helpful to literally draw a picture—a path diagram in which arrows are drawn from independent variables to dependent variables, with the absence of an arrow suggesting that the variables are believed to be unrelated to each other.

EXERCISES

1. Give examples from your field of five dependent variables for which direct data cannot be obtained but whose conceptual referents (hypothetical variables) are clearly defined.
2. Suggest proxies for the variables you gave in Exercise 1.
3. Give examples from your field of five hypothetical (theoretical) variables that are vague and not clearly defined.
4. Suggest proxies for the variables you gave in Exercise 3.
5. Give a realistic example of how a slight difference in a question might have a large effect on the result.
6. Give an example of a research situation in which one must decide at what level of explanation to work.
7. Give an example from your field in which the researcher would come up with an erroneous conclusion (the opposite from the right conclusion) by working at the wrong

level of aggregation, that is, an example in which the whole does not equal the simple sum of the parts.

8. Select a dependent variable and a group of independent variables that you think explain the dependent variable. Draw a path diagram in which you show how you think all the variables are related to each other. Give reasons for putting arrows connecting some variables and not others.

ADDITIONAL READING

Carmines and Zeller's book (1980) discusses some of the problems in dealing with variables whose referents are not clearly defined.

Andrews and Withey's book, *Social Indicators of Well-Being* (1976), is an excellent study of an important but difficult-to-define variable.

Mosteller and Tukey (1977), and Blalock (1972; 1979), discuss the intricacies involved in choosing variables, levels of aggregation, and levels of explanation.

Part Two

Research Decisions and Procedures

The Steps in an Empirical Research Study

1. Finding a Good Research Problem
2. Ask "What Do I Want to Find Out?"
3. Establish the Purpose of the Project
4. Determine the Value of the Research
5. Saturate Yourself in the Problem
6. Formalize the Problem
7. Choose Empirical Variables
8. Calculate the Benefits of Accuracy and the Costs of Error
9. Determine the Most Important Research Obstacles
10. Choose Methods
11. Check the Ethics of Your Proposed Research and Method
12. Prepare a Detailed Design of the Method
13. Collect the Data
14. Analyze the Data
15. Write Up the Research Work
16. Summary

How do you start a research project? What do you do first and second and next after that? These are the pressing questions to the novice in research. The aim of this chapter is to tell you how to get started on your research work, step by step.

The procedures described will be loose and unspecific because of our emphasis on the diversity of research types and methods. Once you have reached the point of deciding on the actual method you will use, however, you may wish to examine the specific procedures recommended in books devoted to the problems of research in particular fields.[1] Remember, nevertheless, that any given procedure is not a sacred order that must be obeyed but is rather a series of steps that has often been found useful in a *particular* field.

The following broad discussion of approaching a research problem is intended mainly as a checklist for doing research. It may also be val-

1. That is, for economics and business, Ferber and Verdoorn (1962, Chap. 2); for education and social psychology, Whitney (1950, Chap. 5); for marketing research, Lorie and Roberts (1951, Chap. 3); for sociology, Selltiz et al. (1976: 12–14).

uable as a checklist in analyzing the research reports done by others. If you are able to ask and answer these questions about someone else's research, you know what the other person did and how well he did it.

The steps given here look neatly ordered. In practice, one goes back and forth from one aspect of the research process to another, sometimes with the feeling of getting nowhere. Harburg's map on page 56 dramatizes the variety of paths one may follow in the search for knowledge.

Step 1. Finding a Good Research Problem

This book is about research methods. But the best chosen methods and the fanciest, most rigorous and sophisticated techniques are worthless unless the problem is important. It behooves you, therefore, to invest time, energy, and thought into finding an *important* topic for research. (How to decide which problems are important is discussed in Chapter 8.)

But more. Even if the topic is important, you won't get far unless you are interested in it. So you must try to find a subject that will keep you interested.

We can divide the sources for research ideas into five categories: (1) The scientific literature; (2) fields of your general interest; (3) recognition of social problems; (4) ideas suggested by others; and (5) data collected by you for other purposes. Let us consider them one by one.

1. Scientific articles and books often provide ideas for research. Sometimes the authors themselves suggest important questions they would like to answer but have not been able to. Book reviews often point out gaps in an author's evidence or some questions he or she failed to answer. Or you may not be satisfied with a book or article; for example, you might want to know whether an article's conclusions about men are also true of women, or if times are changing so rapidly that former research conclusions are out of date.

2. You may have a strong interest in Appa-

lachia, or gymnastics, or cooking, or unemployment. If so, you may have run across questions to which you could find no answer. One such question can point to a topic that will interest you.

3. Social problems are perhaps the best source of important ideas. For example, the rampant unemployment of the 1930s stimulated Keynes to write his world-shaking book. More likely for a beginner, you may be aware of a local problem such as how to inform students of available health services; perhaps there is an interesting and useful project for you in experimenting with various communications methods to determine which works best. Managers of nonprofit and business enterprises often have problems that need study, and are delighted to work with you.

4. Instructors often have ideas that they are happy to suggest to you. Don't feel bashful about asking, and ask several instructors, so you can have a better chance to choose one that interests you. The best instructors to ask are those who have done a lot of empirical research themselves.

5. An infrequent but important source of research ideas for the professional investigator is the data that the investigator is studying for another purpose. In the course of examining or analyzing a set of data the investigator may notice an unexpected pattern, or a discrepancy from the standard pattern, or simply an interesting observation. This process of unexpected happy discovery of a new scientific lead was labeled "serendipity" by Merton, and the name stuck.

By its nature, you do not *choose* to stumble across new ideas by serendipity. But you can increase the probability of such a "lucky" event by reading widely, thinking freely, and spending much time with large masses of data.

Step 2. Ask "What Do I Want to Find Out?"

No matter what type of problem you want to work on and no matter what methods you will

FIGURE 7.1

Source: *Ziggy*, December 8, 1978, by Tom Wilson. Copyright 1978, Universal Press Syndicate. Reprinted with permission. All rights reserved.

eventually use, your empirical work *must* begin with a careful consideration of the research *problem*. You must find out what it is that you are trying to find out. You must ask: What information am I trying to obtain? What is the exact question to which I seek an answer?

It is hard work to specify an intellectual problem exactly. It is much easier to wave your hands in the air and say something vague to yourself or to other people about how "I'm interested in getting some answers about juvenile delinquency." What answers? To what questions? Do you want to know how many juvenile delinquents there are? Or whether parents' incomes affect the rate of juvenile delinquency? Or whether juvenile delinquents enjoy their delinquency? Or what?

And each of those questions is still too vague. If it is the effect of parents' incomes on juvenile delinquency that interests you, do you want to find out whether low income causes increased delinquency? Or whether parents with high incomes can use their money to buy their children out of jams? Or whether children in different income groups are delinquent in different ways? Or what?

Conformity is another example. Eminent social observers—including psychologists, psychoanalysts, and sociologists—hand down to anyone who will listen pronouncements that Americans have become more conformist in the twentieth century.[2] Interesting, but is it true? Before anyone can really know, the question must be made more specific. Do Americans join more organizations than they used to? Do we dress and talk more alike than we used to? Is there less variety in our political opinions? There may be great disagreement over *which* specific question or combination of questions is appropriate; one must choose here which operational definitions will stand for theoretical concepts. But there can be no disagreement that if casual observations about conformity are to be proved or disproved, *some* specific operational questions must be substituted for the unspecified term "conformity."

Economists have trouble with such problems as whether people are "better off" in one economic system or another and in developed or underdeveloped countries. They usually duck these matters by claiming that they are interested only in *economic* welfare and that economic welfare is measured by per capita income, and that is that. Do you think that this attitude is reasonable?

Making a research problem specific robs it of its conversational glamor. But you must do it if you want to be a successful hard-nosed empirical researcher.

Making a problem specific is difficult for the

2. "Eventually, he [the industrial worker] is under the influence of our whole cultural apparatus, the advertisements, movies, television, newspapers, just as everybody else, and can hardly escape being driven into conformity, although perhaps more slowly than other sectors of the population. What holds true for the industrial worker holds true also for the farmer." (Fromm, 1955: 163).

same reason that creating specific operational definitions of scientific terms is difficult. You must *make up the rules yourself*, rather than find out what someone else has in mind. Research is not the same as answering examination questions; it is more like constructing the questions.

Zen Buddhism offers a clue to why specifying research problems is so hard. Read this description of a fictional incident from West's *The Ambassador:*

> Sometimes he would lay before me, as a subject of meditation, one of those apparently meaningless propositions which are *kōan*.
>
> The one which he proposed to me, and to which he returned always with mild persistence was this:
>
> "What will you do when they ask you to kill the cuckoo?"
>
> My first reply was a challenge to Musō to define the terms of the proposition. Who, for example, were they? What was the cuckoo, and why should I be asked to kill it?
>
> Musō smiled and refused the challenge. "You, Amberleysan, *you* must tell *me* what I mean." (West, 1965: 17).

There are no boundary lines or classifications in nature, and *you* must draw such definitional lines around the part of nature you want to study.[3]

How to *find* problems on which to work is not discussed here; it is primarily a matter of scientific imagination and insight.[4] The re-

search questions that you uncover will depend on your interests, on the gaps in empirical knowledge in the field in which you are working, on what your bosses want to know, and so forth. These and many other factors will determine how, in moments of inspiration, you finish this sentence: "Gee, wouldn't it be interesting to find out . . . ?"

It is helpful to consider *which general type* a research problem is. Is it an attempt to establish a comparison? to find a cause or an effect? to measure the dimensions of something? Chapter 4 classifies research questions and discusses the types.

Step 3. Establish the Purpose of the Project

Why do you want to know the answers to the research question you are asking? How will the information be used and by whom? The purpose and the destination of the knowledge can be important in deciding how to carry out the research. The U.S. Bureau of the Census uses methods of collecting data that are different from those used by commercial research organizations because the purposes of the two kinds of research are different, although the subject matter may be the same. Compare how you investigate whether it is raining before going on a picnic to the way in which the U.S. Weather Service collects information for farmers to use in deciding when to plant. Television ratings also exemplify how a technical choice depends upon purpose. Such ratings generally measure the number of *households* in which the television sets are tuned to various programs. The household, rather than the individual, is the purchasing unit, and the sponsors who pay for the ratings are interested in purchasing. An educational television station, however, is more interested in which *individuals* watch given shows than in which households.

Your purpose may also determine whether you can use information already gathered by

3. The analogy between Zen and science goes further. Zen works to wipe out the conventional categories of everyday life so that one may see the world with fresh eyes. And the good scientist refuses to accept conventional ways of classifying the world and its relationships. As the imagination transcends the old categories. it moves on to new ways of perceiving the world. The end points of Zen and science are completely different, however. The scientist must eventually convert his or her vision into objective concepts so that they can be communicated to others and enter into the body of science, whereas the Zen adept's vision remains his or her own.

4. For discussion of this aspect of research, see Young (1977); Bachrach (1972); Cannon (1965); Beveridge (1960, especially Chaps. 5 and 6); Mills (1959: 200–201, 211–217).

other researchers. For a picnic decision, you can use the Weather Service report. But if you farm in a section of the country that has its own precipitation peculiarities not reported by the Weather Service, you may have to collect your own rainfall data. Another example: Educational television stations sometimes feel it necessary to collect their own data on viewing, even when commercial ratings on their stations are available to them.

Step 4. Determine the Value of the Research

Perhaps you have several ideas for research projects. You want to invest your time and energy in the work that will be *most* valuable according to whatever is the relevant measure of value. For example, understanding the economy of the United States is more valuable than understanding the economy of Kankakee, Illinois. And depression is a more important psychological problem than is fear of stuffed pandas. Chapter 8 is devoted to methods of comparing the various candidates for your attention.

Step 5. Saturate Yourself in the Problem

It is important to have a wide and deep understanding of the background of your study, especially in research to determine relationships of cause and effect. Notice how Benedict saturated herself in her materials at the beginning of an anthropological project:

> . . . [D]uring the period when she was doing the research that led to *The Chrysanthemum and the Sword* . . . she did not evolve her ideas "mystically" from her inner consciousness, but worked very systematically. She saturated herself in Japanese materials of a carefully selected variety: literature, art, projective tests, interviews, etc. After she thought she had detected some highest common factors or least common denominators that constituted, so to speak, implicit premises cutting across bodies of culture content that were

quite different, she then wrote down some hypotheses as to what she should find—and should not find—in as yet unexamined data if her initial formulations were correct. She then sought out fresh materials drawn from the same categories and validated, rejected, or reformulated her initial hypotheses and made at least one more trial run. Most American social psychologists, to be sure, would have been appalled at one aspect of her procedure. I once asked her: "But *how many* new novels, for instance, do you think you must read and analyze before you stop?" She told me plainly that this was a silly question. (Lerner, 1959: 261)

And Whyte's experience in "street corner society" taught him the importance of saturating oneself in the situation:

> The ideas that we have in research are only in part a logical product growing out of a careful weighing of evidence. We do not generally think problems through in a straight line. Often we have the experience of being immersed in a mass of confusing data. We study the data carefully, bringing all our powers of logical analysis to bear upon them. We come up with an idea or two. But still the data do not fall in any coherent pattern. Then we go on living with the data—and with the people—until perhaps some chance occurrence casts a totally different light upon the data, and we begin to see a pattern that we have not seen before. This pattern is not purely an artistic creation. Once we think we see it, we must re-examine our notes and perhaps set out to gather new data in order to determine whether the pattern adequately represents the life we are observing or is simply a product of our imagination. (Whyte, 1961: 279–280)

Here is an example of how one can get fooled by lack of knowledge of a situation: As a well-known sociologist and one of us were driving down a U.S. turnpike, we saw several groups of U.S. army trucks traveling in convoy. No truck was going faster than the fifty-five-mile-per-hour speed limit. We were both impressed. She commented that she would never have expected to see such discipline in, say, Italy or Israel, and in fact such discipline is surprising in the United States, too. Then we stopped for coffee, and in the men's room one of us saw one of the army drivers. He was asked, "How come none of you guys ever goes faster than fifty-five?" "That's easy," he said, "there's a mechanical governor on the trucks' transmissions that will not permit more than fifty-five." Without that chance encounter we might have told the story of the U.S. army discipline many times and even worked out a neat social theory to fit this nonfact, just as we do too often in science.

Step 6. Formalize the Problem

After you have steeped yourself in the actual situation that you will study (if that is possible) and in all the other relevant materials, written and otherwise, it is time to develop some theoretical structure for the research project (see Berger and Kellner). In studies which lend themselves to causal explanation, you can create some structure by reducing your questions to functional language. To put it symbolically, you frame the research as a functional relationship in the form $y = f(x_1, x_2, x_3 \ldots)$. That is, you designate which will be the dependent and which the independent variables. This is not the final stage of specificity; that comes when one finally decides how to *measure* the variables, a matter discussed in Chapter 6.[5] But the translation of the question into a functional form is a giant stride in the empirical research.

Sometimes the translation into a functional relationship is a simple matter of finding empirical "proxies" to stand for the theoretical concepts and of deciding which variable to consider dependent and which to consider independent. For example, perhaps you have narrowed your area of interest to the point at which you ask "What is the relationship of scallion prices to sales of scallions?" One way—but only one way, and others are possible—to translate your question into functional language is to hypothesize that "quantity of scallions sold = f (price of scallions)." Notice that you could also have formulated the functional relationship as "price of scallions = q (quantity of scallions sold)," if you were primarily interested in explaining changes in price rather than in explaining changes in the amount sold.[6] In either instance, you would still have to specify the actual operational definitions of your variables, for "price" and "quantity" can mean different things, and each can be measured in different ways.

Now let us consider an example in which it is more difficult to translate the original question into the specific form required for empirical research. Your original vague interest is in "finding out what a single person's life is like." An all-encompassing study of all aspects of singles' lives is obviously impossible; therefore, you first narrow the question to "Are singles more or less happy than are married people?" You must now reduce your question to functional language. Implicit in the form of the question "Are singles more or less happy than married people?" is the more specific question "Is there a connection between a person's marital status and his or her state of happiness?" Therefore, you write the function "happiness of people = f (marital status)." This function expresses a question that you will then test with empirical data: Is there a relationship of the sort represented in the equation? Later you must go further and state the variables in terms that suggest how the variables will be *measured*.

The more complex the question, the more difficult it is to choose satisfactory variables. Breaking down the issue into several parts is often helpful. One often comes to realize that

5. The final stage of specificity also requires that the *form* of the functional relationship be specified; that is, whether a graph of the variables would be a straight line or a curve of one sort or another. The most common functional form is the straight line, which is implicit in most simple correlation studies. One can avoid choosing a functional form only if one limits the study to classification.

6. In some cases you might simultaneously investigate *both* these functional forms. But such sophisticated matters need not concern us now.

there are two or more questions. When the questions are separated, the tangle sometimes disappears magically.

A further important step toward developing a structure for your investigation of causal relationships is to diagram the interrelations among the variables, as in the path diagram in Figure 6.5.

Step 7. Choose Empirical Variables

It is at this stage that the talkers are separated from the fact-getters; it is the stage at which interesting ideas are transformed into empirical research probems.

One of the important functions of teachers is to exhort students to narrow down the problem to manageable size, so that they will finish within a reasonable length of time. Such a narrowing-down goes hand in hand with thinking through the problem to the point at which the variables are stated in *operational terms*. The struggle to specify variables that can be investigated empirically often forces the researcher to narrow the problem to a sensible size.

Perhaps the necessity of formalizing and narrowing down the question does not apply with such force to those researchers who embark on descriptive research in totally new areas of investigation. But successful descriptive research requires great competence and is usually done by people who break this rule of narrowing-down only with calculated forethought.

Let's go back to the study of whether singles or married people are happier. The measurement of marital status is fairly easy, but the measurement of happiness is obviously a thorny matter. Some aspects of happiness have been successfully measured with questionnaires (Andrews and Withey, 1976) and you decide to do so also. Therefore, you write "people's answers to questions about happiness $= f$ (marital status)."

But the variables have not yet been specified completely, because operational definitions have not been formulated. For example, what are the exact questions whose answers will be considered the measures of happiness? Nor has it been decided *at what level of aggregation* the variables will be measured, that is, whether you will deal with group averages of marital status, income, happiness, and so forth, or will work with the data on individuals (discussed in Chapter 6).

A good test of whether the problem and variables are specified sufficiently will be to ask whether or not another researcher could take your statement of the variables and probably arrive at much the same outcome as you would if you finished the research project yourself.

An advantage of research that *tests a theory* is that the theory often suggests a precise hypothesis that can be tested empirically on neatly defined variables. But hypotheses that are not deduced from a body of well-knit theory seldom come in such precise form.

Making clear which universe you want to understand and which universe is practical to work with will help you to reduce the problem to a functional relationship. This decision affects all subsequent decisions about research design. For example, a veterinary researcher interested in the growth of animals in response to hormone injections probably will proceed differently from a researcher whose ultimate interest is the mental growth of humans and who experiments with hormone injections in animals as an intermediate research device.

It is perfectly legitimate to confine your interest to a subuniverse. Kinsey studied only white males at first. But do not confine yourself to a subuniverse that is of no interest in itself simply because it would be troublesome to gather data on the larger universe.[7] One re-

---

7. "Universe" and "subuniverse" are relative terms. Every universe can be viewed as part of some larger universe. We use the term "subuniverse" to apply only to a unit that is not of ultimate interest but is part of the universe that is. Also one person's subuniverse is another one's universe; one sex researcher might be interested in only white midwestern males, though most people would be more interested in statements about all U.S. males.

viewer took Kinsey and his associates to task severely on this point:

> The point is simply this: unless one is interested only in the 5,940 women in Kinsey's sample, which of course nobody is . . . then the reader must be able to project the found percentages against *some* kind of meaningful population. Indeed, what on earth is a measurement from a total sample good for, unless it is "more or less representative" of some meaningful population? (Zeisel, 1953: 520)

On the other hand, one does not always have to take a random sample of the entire universe in order to generalize with some confidence, as we shall see when we discuss sampling. This is particularly true if you are trying to generalize about a *process* rather than about a population, and if you can find some evidence leading you to believe that the process operates the same way in other samples as it does in yours. Thernstrom, for example, wanted to learn how family background has affected occupational success in the United States over the last 100 years. He was able to do a detailed study only of Boston, hardly the whole United States. But comparisons of various sorts between Boston and other cities convinced him that the process he was interested in operated the same way in the other cities as it did in Boston (1973, Chap. 9).

The topic of choosing empirical variables has only been introduced here; the next chapter describes it in detail.

Step 8. Calculate the Benefits of Accuracy and the Costs of Error

What is at stake in the research? One must make explicit what depends on the results and their accuracy. Estimating the costs of various amounts of error in the conclusions or, conversely, the value of the research at various levels of accuracy is especially difficult in pure research. At least some comparisons are possible, however. For example, we know now, and probably scientists knew even when the first measurements were made, that a 10 percent error in the estimate of the speed of light and

a 10 percent error in unemployment statistics are more serious than a 10 percent error in the estimated speed of quarterhorses at a state fair in Montana.

One of the most promising developments in research methods in recent decades has been the theory of the value of information—which information, and how much of it, is of economic value. For example, is it worth drilling a test oil well before the main drilling, or is it a better bet to proceed directly to the main drilling? The answer depends on the chances of hitting oil with a test and with a main drilling, the costs of the test and the main drilling, and the likely profit from the well.

The estimate of the value of accuracy will affect how one goes about the research and especially how extensive a sample one takes. Correct determination of the winner in the race for the presidency of the United States is important enough so that every single person who wants to vote is polled on election day—a very expensive survey, indeed. But, to choose the fireworks for a town's Independence Day celebration, the mayor may sensibly begin and end the poll with his own child and the child next door.

Step 9. Determine the Most Important Research Obstacles

The answers to most research questions are not immediately obvious. The patterns of nature and social life are often obscure. Nature seems to throw stumbling blocks—disruptions, deceptions, long distances, high costs, and so on—under the feet of the scientific inquirer. Of course, it is foolish to think that there is an evil genius who foils the investigator, though some scientists offer explanations that would almost imply the presence of such an evil genius.[8] At this stage of the research, you must

---

8. To credit the possibility that smoking does not cause health damage but rather that smokers are genetically more predisposed to a whole host of different diseases is almost to believe in a genetic component that has such an evil genius. See J. Simon (1966c) or Brownlee (1965).

think ahead and take stock of the obstacles to be overcome. Only after you have spotted them can you develop a sensible procedure for your research. For example, people often do not like to talk about such behavior as sexual practices, illegal acts, or family violence, and when they talk, they may not tell the truth. Or different persons have different views of what has happened—husbands and wives may report differently about who makes certain decisions, for instance. Faced with such difficulties, researchers have developed new methods that form an important part of their work (Huber and Spitze, 1981; Gelles and Straus, 1979).

Step 10. Choose Methods

Once the important obstacles have been identified, you should select the methods that will surmount the obstacles most efficiently and effectively. Consider *all* the various research methods and combinations of them. This is the time to ask, How shall I gather the information I need?

> Rather than disputing about what is "the" best method, behavioral scientists, it seems to me, should examine dispassionately the advantages and disadvantages of every established technique in terms of the relevant situation and the specific questions that are being asked. . . . (Lerner, 1959: 259)

For a problem in social psychology one might evaluate the potential of an experiment against that of a survey. For a study of the economics of two-seller competition, one might compare a laboratory experiment with a field investigation of two-seller markets. For a problem in market research or sociology one might compare personal interviews with mail interviews. In public health one might compare a questionnaire survey with an examination of hospital records, as in the design of smoking-and-health studies.

Real-estate appraisers use many methods. A house is a house, it would seem, but, depending upon the circumstances and the informa-

tion available, an appraiser may value the house mostly on the basis of its past selling prices, by comparison with the selling prices of other houses sold recently in the neighborhood, or by summing the values of such aspects of the house as value of the land, number of rooms, and age. The final appraisal probably takes more than one of these methods into account.

Advertising-effectiveness researchers have an especially wide armamentarium, and it takes good judgment to pick the method that will yield much information at little expense. Among the methods are experimental, survey, and panel measurements of sales; readership scores; lotteries in special theaters that show commercials; attitude surveys; and many more. The history of advertising research illustrates the value of a wide knowledge of methods. But the neglect of sales-evaluation methods also illustrates the ill effects of narrow knowledge. Such neglect occurred because most advertising researchers were trained as psychologists or sociologists and never learned the methods for sales evaluation that are common in the training of economists.

To illustrate the process of considering the merits of various methods, imagine that we want to find out how sensitive the consumption of liquor in the United States is to changes in the general price of liquor, so that we can predict the effect of a liquor-tax increase. If the price goes up, people will drink *somewhat* less liquor, but we want to know how *much* less. If the price goes up 10 percent, will people drink 1 percent less, 5 percent less, 10 percent less, 20 percent less?

It is reasonable, when one wants to know something about people, to think of *asking* them. But people do not tell the full truth about their consumption of liquor, and, furthermore, they probably cannot predict their responses to a price change very well. Therefore, we must turn to other methods.

Experimenting with the average price of all types of liquor in a liquor store might give clear-cut and reliable results. It would, however, be difficult to obtain the cooperation of a liquor store for such an experiment. More important, other stores nearby would maintain the old prices, and many people would simply shop elsewhere at the old prices, which would ruin the experiment for our purposes.

We might analyze the sales of liquor in the nation as a whole over a period of years. Indeed, this method was used fairly successfully in England and Sweden (Stone, 1952; Prest, 1949; Malmquist, 1948). But it suffers from the lack of variation in the price of liquor, and the variation is hard to measure in a nation as a whole. Without variations in price we cannot measure the effect of price on consumption. We might compare consumption in countries in which liquor prices differ. A working solution was to compare consumption (actually, sales) before and after *tax changes* caused across-the-board price increases in various states in the United States (J. Simon, 1966a).

At some time one should consider whether or not the question can best be answered through *pure deduction*. Some ancient philosophers believed that they could deduce the answer to *any* question, and they looked down their noses at empirical research. Better to discuss with other wise men how many teeth are in a horse's mouth than to examine the dental equipment of a real live hayburner. Such a narrow attitude is foolish. But there are many situations in which deduction is more appropriate than any empirical method. For example, whether or not trading stamps raise food prices can probably be answered more correctly with deduction alone than with empirical studies, given the poor data that are available. Similarly, we shall see that our reasoning about the effect of population growth on economic development is more impressive than is the scanty empirical evidence.

Here is a brief checklist for evaluating alternative research methods:

First, how *relevant* will the results be? An experiment often can promise clear-cut reliable results, but they may not generalize to the universe in which you are interested. For example, animal experiments with tobacco tars are relatively easy to run, but who is to say that tobacco tars affect human beings in the same way as rats?

Second, how *clear* and *unmuddied* will the results be? Questionnaire surveys of smoking and health are certainly relevant, but they are muddied by many facets of human psychology and biology that cannot be held constant in the survey. In other words, one must consider whether the method avoids the obstacles to knowledge of the problem.

Third, how much will the method *cost?* The high cost of personal-interview attitude surveys is one of their chief drawbacks, and it often forces substitution of another method or abandonment of the project.

Fourth, how *accurate* is the method? Some methods are more accurate than are others, aside from the matter of cost. In other cases, one must estimate the accuracy of the method at various cost levels, for example, at various sample sizes.

Fifth, how *long* will the method take to produce results? Longitudinal studies of the development of children require observing the *same children* at each stage of their lives. Can you afford to wait so long for results, or will some other technique produce acceptable results in less time?

Sixth, are the necessary personnel and equipment available?

Seventh, is the method ethically acceptable (see Chapter 36)?

Once again, you must avoid limiting yourself to a narrow choice of methods. Too many researchers are stereotyped in their research behavior, following Kaplan's Law of the Instrument: "Give a small boy a hammer, and he will find that everything he encounters needs pounding." However, if you discover a new technique, seeing how widely the technique can be applied is often fruitful.

Several methods together may provide better and cheaper answers than any single method can. For instance, a cheap burglar alarm and a cheap safe together may constitute much better burglar protection than either a first-class alarm or a first-class safe. Two blankets, each with many moth holes in it, will keep you warmer than one good blanket. A postcard survey to thousands of people, in conjunction with a handful of intensive interviews, may better reveal how people feel about an election than will either method alone. And, in judging whether smoking is injurious to health, the Surgeon General's committee considered the results of animal experiments plus clinical and autopsy studies plus statistical analysis of surveys of the mortality rates of smokers and nonsmokers:

> Each of these three lines of evidence was evaluated and then considered together in drawing conclusions. The Committee was aware that the mere establishment of a statistical association between the use of tobacco and a disease is not enough. The causal significance of the use of tobacco in relation to the disease is the crucial question. For such judgments all three lines of evidence are essential. . . . (U.S. Public Health Service, 1964: 27–28)

The virtue of complementary techniques is that one is not subject to the same defects as are the others.

Experiments and surveys complement each other well, especially when the surveys are detailed. The combination of those two methods has been the convincing factor in the cigarette-and-lung-cancer issue. Kluckhohn noted the value of a combination of methods in his anthropological work:

> Even when the questions being asked are of the same general nature, different methods may complement each other. During my years of work with Navaho children, I sometimes envied my colleagues in psychology who could bring their subjects into an experimental room where noise and other distractions were eliminated, temperature and other variables perfectly controlled, etc. Nevertheless, I reflected, my psychological colleagues saw the children they were

studying for a few hours a week at most and had to depend for an account of what went on the rest of the week upon an interview with the mother or, possibly, both parents. In contrast, my co-workers and I were able to live with a Navaho family in their one-room hut for virtually twenty-four hours a day. Not many family secrets can be concealed for more than a short period under those circumstances. What the psychologists learned, they learned—admittedly—in a more rigorous way. Our knowledge, however, was richer, more ramified, and pertinent to behavior in ordinary daily life settings. (Lerner, 1959: 260)

Among the striking resemblances between military intelligence and empirical scientific research is that both profit from the use of multiple methods. Thousands of years ago the Chinese military writer, Sun Tzu, pointed out that ". . . the master of intelligence will employ all five kinds of agents simultaneously [native, inside, double, expendable, and living]" (Dulles, 1965: 14).

Of course, there are also many situations in which you will do best to devote all your resources to a single best method. A first-class safe *or* a first-class burglar alarm *may* be better than a combination of the inferior safe and inferior alarm.

Step 11. Check the Ethics of Your Proposed Research and Method

Sometimes enthusiasm and zeal can lead you to a course of research that is not ethically acceptable, simply because you do not stop long enough to ask the question, "Is this ethical?" So do stop and think.

The ethical issues involved in studying human beings are many and complex; some will be dealt with in more detail later (Section 5 of Chapter 36). Your main concern, of course, is whether your proposed research can harm anyone. All ethical social scientists agree that it is "unconditionally unethical" (Riecken and Boruch, 1978: 520) to do research in which the harm done outweighs the advantages to be gained, and most question whether it is appropriate to do research that does any harm at all, except under the most unusual circumstances. People may be harmed in various ways in social research—in psychology experiments involving potentially dangerous physical tests; in surveys that ask for information about illegal activities for which respondents could be prosecuted if their answers were not kept confidential; possibly even in social psychological research in which people are lied to or made to feel ashamed or embarrassed (Gamson, Fireman, and Rytina, 1982; Riecken and Boruch, 1978). Increasing concern about these issues has led in recent years to increasing regulation of research by universities and the federal government.

Therefore, you must think about whether your research could harm anyone, and if the answer is yes, change your plans. And you must in any case be sure that your subjects know the nature of the project they are involved in ("informed consent") and that information you collect from individuals is kept confidential.

Step 12. Prepare a Detailed Design of the Method

Chapters 9 through 14 describe the rudiments of design for the major types of methods. Here we offer only a handful of aphorisms and snippets of wisdom.

First, think at length, think in detail, think about everything *before* collecting data. This advice must begin to sound like a broken record, but it is worth the repetition. Time and money spent collecting data before you have done all the thinking possible will be expensive in the short and long run. But of course the future cannot be foreseen perfectly, especially in exploratory research.

Pretests are an important aid to planning. Run little pretests of method, materials, assistants, and everything else, as long as you can

do it cheaply. The researcher should stay close to the work at this stage of the game, rather than delegating tasks to assistants. If you will be using a questionnaire, try out the questions on friends or on people in the street. Do not worry that your friends are not a random sample. If the questionnaire is designed for Hottentot infants, your friends' reactions may be meaningless. But in most situations *any* interviewees will reveal whether the questions are unintelligible or anger the interviewees, whether two questions elicit identical answers, and so forth.

If you will be running an experiment, have someone play the experimenter while you are the subject; a person never really understands an experiment until he or she has served as a subject for it. And start off with crude equipment. Do not spend a lot of time and money building finished equipment before you have tried out crude models.

Run pretest after pretest as you continue to make improvements in the method. But, if pretests are very expensive, it may pay to shoot the works the first time—after you have thought the problem through as far as possible.

Pretest the data-record sheets. A well-constructed data sheet is a great help; a poor data sheet can be an awful nuisance. Whenever possible, design your data sheets so that they facilitate later transcriptions, either human coding or machine processing.

Second, be aware that many decisions made at the design stage inevitably contain an element of guesswork. If you knew exactly how everything would turn out, there would be no need to do the research—you would not be doing anything new. Because any piece of research involves doing something new, there is no rule book to tell you what decisions to make when a question arises about sampling, interviewing, variable selection, and so on. One must often rely on informed judgment, good advice, and the occasional hunch about how things will turn out.

The basic requirement for making sound decisions is a good set of *reasons*. Often this requirement means setting up reasonable criteria for decisions. The novice often has trouble making decisions where there are no hard-and-fast rules. The worst pitfall is to make an arbitrary decision *without recognizing* that it is arbitrary and that other alternatives should be considered. The next worst pitfall is to freeze into paralysis in the face of the alternatives, unable to make a decision because there is no "scientific answer" or because the answer cannot be found anywhere in textbooks on research.

Third, draw up in outline the tables and charts that you expect your data to fill. This procedure forces you to think out the details of the research design. Writing the names of the variables across the top and down the side of the tables and charts makes you state the variables explicitly. Ask yourself: "What numbers do I want my study to produce?" For example, in a comparison study write down the comparisons you would like to make at the conclusion of your research. If you are studying the election process and you want to evaluate the effects of age, sex, and religion on voting, you might end up comparing such groups as "Catholic, male, age twenty-one to twenty-five" with "Jewish, male, age twenty-one to twenty-five." Each of these groups should then constitute a *cell* of your table. A working table with such cells might look like Table 7.1.

The best argument for the value of this exercise is the resistance that you feel as you try to draw up the charts and tables. After you try it, you will recognize why this exercise has such power to prevent mistakes and omissions in your study.

Draw up a separate table for each relationship, each comparison, and each measurement that you hope your study will produce. Do not try to cram everything into one master table. And the captions on the blank tables and charts *must be specific*. That is what the exercise is for—to get you to be *specific* about the details of your proposed design and your objectives. However, you should not become so wedded to your preliminary tables that you are blind to other relationships that you may discover in the course of examining your data. These preliminary tables are only a helpful prod to think-

TABLE 7.1 Sample Working Table

| | Percentage Voting Democrat | | |
	Age 21–25	Age 26–35	Age etc.
Catholic			
Male	? %	? %	etc.
Female	? %	etc.	etc.
Protestant			
Male	? %	etc.	etc.
Female	? %	etc.	etc.
Jewish			
Male	? %	etc.	etc.
Female	? %	etc.	etc.

ing, not a contract that you are obligated to fulfill.

Step 13. Collect the Data

There is little of a general nature to say about the process of collecting data, except that you should exercise *care* in what you do. Sloppiness, especially sloppiness in maintaining data and in recording just what is done at each step, can lead to disaster—the necessity for repeating your work, or scientific error and loss of reputation. See Chapter 17 for detailed discussion of this stage.

Collecting data takes much longer than you think it will. We have never known anyone to do his or her first research project without being surprised at the number of unexpected and time-consuming snags. The simplest study bristles with minor problems in data collection; no wonder complex projects can become a life's work.

The great quantity of detail can offer an unexpected temptation. As a student, you try hard to finish school projects so that you can receive course credit and a degree; details that delay you are annoyances. But professors who do research under their own direction do not have such externally imposed deadlines to pressure them. Often academics lose themselves in the detailed busy work of a research project because it is comfortable and relatively undemanding. Instead of looking for shortcuts so that they can finish and move on to other work, they sometimes take a larger-than-necessary sample or submerge themselves in doing interviews or experimentation themselves or in coding their data. The work is pleasant, it provides the satisfaction of accomplishing a day's work each day, and the researcher avoids the hard work and decision making involved in writing up the findings and setting up another piece of research. Such professors are using the busy work of research as an escape. (Of course, such practice is not unique to professors. Many people in other lines of work—

often those people who refer to themselves as "perfectionists"—fall into the same trap.)

Step 14. Analyze the Data

Chapters 24 through 27 discuss data analysis in considerable detail.

Step 15. Write Up the Research Work

In Chapter 2, pages 19–20, there is a discussion of writing up research, the final stage of the work.

The foregoing list of steps for doing research adds up to a good checklist for evaluating and criticizing research done by others:

1. First ask *what* the researcher is trying to find out.
2. Then ask *why* he or she wants the knowledge.
3. Judge the *value* of the research.
4. Specify exactly *which variables* the researcher uses, if he or she does not provide an explicit equation.

16. Summary

This chapter lists and describes the main steps in carrying out a research project. This list is also useful in evaluating and criticizing the research of others. Of course such a list does not fit all research situations, but in the main it does apply. The steps are:

1. Find a good research problem.
2. Ask "What do I want to find out?" First you must decide what problem you are interested in. Then you must answer this central research question clearly, and keep it in mind as you make decisions throughout the project.
3. Establish the purpose of the project. Similar research questions can be asked for very different purposes. And you must refer back to your purpose if you

are to make sound decisions about variables, data collection, and analysis.

4. Formalize the problem. If the study is to be causal, this is best done by identifying the independent and dependent variables to the form $y = f(x_1, x_2, x_3 ...)$, and by drawing a path diagram of the causal interrelationships.

5. Determine the value of the research. Ask yourself, "Is this research, in my judgment, likely be of greater relative value than other research alternatives?"

6. Saturate yourself in the problem. Learn the background. Steep yourself in the situation. Range widely for the relevant facts. Only thus can you wisely decide which factors are likely to be important in your research situation.

7. Choose empirical variables. Select operational proxies for the theoretical (hypothetical) concepts that you wish to investigate.

8. Calculate the benefits of accuracy and the costs of error. What is at stake in the research? What is the value to researcher and institution and society of reducing the likely error by using more expensive methods on a larger sample? The answer points toward a rational choice of a sample size and sometimes helps you choose among alternative techniques.

9. Determine the most important obstacles you will face in your research. What difficulties will there be in getting an answer to your research question? Ruminate on these obstacles in advance and make them explicit.

10. Choose methods. Design your research so as to overcome the main obstacles to knowledge that you face, keeping in mind the constraint of the master obstacle: cost. Choose your methods from the wide variety of techniques in use in the social sciences, rather than limiting your choice to the conventional method of your subfield. Prefer a combination of two or more methods over a single method.

11. Prepare a detailed design of the method. Leave nothing vague or unspecified. Run preliminary tests. And prepare the tables and charts you will later fill with data.

12. Check the ethics of your proposed research and method.

13. Collect the data—carefully.

14. Analyze the data—sensibly and imaginatively.

15. Write up the research work.

AFTERTHOUGHT

In that first lecture I asked the rhetorical question who is man, the artist? and answered it by saying: He is the unspoiled core of everyman, before he is choked by schooling, training, conditioning, until the artist-within shrivels up and is forgotten. Even in the artist who is professionally trained to be consciously "creative" this unspoiled core shrivels up in the rush toward a "personal style," in the heat of competition to be "in." (1973: x)

These words of Frederick Franck are as true for the scientist as for the artist.

EXERCISES

1. Refer to the example of the vagueness of statements on increasing conformity on page 83. Think of another frequent statement about society or human nature that is vague and not easily provable. Give some appropriate ways to make this statement specific, so that it can be tested empirically.

2. Give an example of similar data being collected in different ways for different purposes.
3. How would you measure "friendliness"? "aggressiveness in business"?
4. What are the obstacles to studying the ways in which income influences happiness? to finding out whether a particular advertising campaign for beer is more or less effective than the previous campaign was?
5. Describe a study, and then prepare a working table to show the data that should be produced to fulfill the purpose of the study.

ADDITIONAL READING

On the steps in social research, see Selltiz et al. (1976: 12–14).

Bachrach (1972) provides a short and readable introduction to psychological research, telling what the researcher is up against and how the researcher goes about it.

A breezy but informative introduction to social research is that of Agnew and Pyke (1969).

Hammond's book (1964) contains a variety of firsthand descriptions of how some eminent authors did important pieces of research in a variety of fields.

On selecting a research problem, see Selltiz et al. (1976, Chap. 3) and Sjoberg and Nett (1968, Chap. 5).

On ethical issues in research, see Cook (Chapter 7 in Selltiz et al., 1976); Reynolds (1979); and Warwick (1980). A provocative discussion of ethics and research by a researcher involved in a highly publicized ethical controversy is that by Milgram (1974).

A fundamental theme of this book is that when quite different research methods produce the same result, the conclusion is all the stronger; and when studies using different methods disagree, it is a clue to retest until the discrepancy can be reconciled. A first-rate article on reconciling the results from experimental and survey studies is that of Hovland.

How to Assess the Potential Value of Research Projects

1. Evaluating the Inputs Required for a Research Project
2. Estimating the Value of Research Projects
3. Summary

To notice an important problem for study that others have not seen is the mark of a path-breaking scientist. In Zuckerman's interviews with U.S. Nobel winners, "Almost to a man they lay great emphasis on the importance of problem-finding, not only problem solving" (Merton, 1968: 60). And beginners in research think it difficult to find *any* research problem for a course or thesis; after you leave school and begin a career in social science, however, you quickly become aware of a great variety of possible projects competing for your time. To a professor or to a researcher in industry or government, the question becomes: *Which one* of the many questions that I might work on would be best? The subject of this chapter is how to choose among possible subjects for research so as to obtain the greatest long-term benefit.

The choice among "pure" research problems is more difficult than among applied problems, as we shall see, so let us talk about the pure-research decision first. One's first impulse is to say that the scientist should work on the "most important" of the research problems that are competing for his or her attention. But how does one decide which is most important? And

should one work on the most important problem even if it is expected to take twenty years, whereas a matter only slightly less important would take only one year or one month?

Whether pure or applied research is in question, the decision about which of several problems to study empirically is much like the businessperson's decision about which new business opportunities to invest capital in. In both science and business the solution is to estimate what the benefit-cost ratio (value of output/value of input) promises to be for each of the possible alternatives and then to choose the alternative for which the ratio is highest. Some academics find it repugnant to frame the problem in these "commercial" terms, but if they will examine the basis of their own decisions, it boils down to the same thing. From a philosophical point of view Kaplan argues that "These and similar questions cannot be put aside as extralogical, 'merely practical' in import. They arise, whether or not they have been explicitly formulated, in every actual context of inquiry . . ." (Kaplan, 1964: 252; see his pp. 250–254 for further discussion of this and related points).

The businessperson's estimates of this ratio

are easier to make than are the scientist's. Both are uncertain about how large the outputs and inputs will be, but at least the businessperson can measure cost inputs and profit outputs in the common unit of dollars. It is much more difficult to find measuring rods for the skill and energy the researcher puts into the study and for the value of the knowledge that may come out of the study.

Some scientists say that research need not have any practical effect or social benefit. Nevertheless, Einstein, whose work was as "pure" as anyone could wish, felt this way about the matter: "The concern for man and his destiny must always be the chief interest of all technical effort. Never forget it among your diagrams and equations" (Snow, 1967: 51).

1. Evaluating the Inputs Required for a Research Project

The inputs to a study are of two sorts: first, the time and energy required of the *researcher* and, second, the money costs to the funding foundation or commercial employer or non-profit client.

A responsible researcher should calculate the cost of the inputs required by a given study from his or her own point of view *and* from the point of view of the organization that is the source of funds. For pure research one should assume the organizational point of view to be that of the society as a whole.

It is not easy to estimate the time and energy a study will require. The more experienced one is, the more accurate the estimate of the snags and obstacles that will be met and of the resources required to overcome them, just as an experienced building contractor can estimate the time and cost of putting up a building better than a novice.

Any study takes much longer than a novice expects. Sometimes when you read of someone else's work, a project that took a full year seems as if it should not have required more than a couple of weeks. And indeed, if the

same person were to do the work over again, he or she might well be able to finish in a couple of weeks. But if you or we or anyone else were to try to repeat the work—even with the report to follow—it might require two or three months. And, if we had to start from scratch, as that person did, without knowing which path would turn out to be worthwhile and which mistakes to avoid, we would soon find out why the research took a full year. Usually one makes several false starts before developing a satisfactory method, and that takes time.

The time needed to do empirical work varies greatly among researchers. Just as in other trades, there are good research craftsmen and poor research craftsmen, and the difference in their efficiencies can be enormous. The poor research craftsman often takes ten or twenty times as long as the good one does because he or she lacks a nose for shortcuts; gets hung up on insignificant details; lacks competence in dealing with materials, people, and machines; and does not know when to consider the empirical work complete.

Beware of hidden costs. On first thought, for example, it may seem almost costless to add another question to an interview schedule. But remember to take into account the additional money cost of editing the results of that question and of keypunching it, and—perhaps most important—the time cost to you when you feel you must analyze the results from that question because you have collected the data.

The following qualities make a good research craftsman: experience, which as we know comes only after it is most needed; ingenuity, resourcefulness, and imagination; and an attitude that keeps a person's eyes open for better and quicker methods. You can acquire the last by forcing yourself to look around regularly for better and quicker methods, but many people prefer not to take their eyes off the trees to see the forest; it is worth training yourself to keep your eyes open for better methods.

The time a project takes also depends upon the funds available for assistance. Up to a point, the more assistance one can afford, the more quickly the work will go. But, curiously, beyond a certain point *too much* available money can slow down a project. The project director finds himself spending much time hiring workers, checking time slips, and answering questions about exceptions in the work. Often results that are almost as accurate can be obtained with a smaller sample that requires fewer helpers or even with a shortcut method such as using published data instead of creating raw data. In any case, remember that many hands do not always make quick work.

Responsible researchers try to develop research methods that require a minimum of money. For example, they take a sample rather than measuring a whole universe. They use telephone interviews rather than personal interviews if the former are feasible. They mechanize the job of data processing efficiently. Amazing cost reduction can sometimes be achieved by a touch of resourcefulness. In general, responsible scientists do not treat outside funds as costless to themselves and therefore to be spent casually. Not all scientists rate top grades in this respect.

2. Estimating the Value of Research Projects

Here are the relevant benefits to researchers themselves from a research project.

1. Their own pleasure and enjoyment. Some kinds of research will be more fun than others, depending on your own likes. Some anthropologists enjoy field work with primitive tribes; others cannot stomach it.

2. Short-term professional benefits. The immediate professional payoff may depend upon the moment's fashion in one's academic discipline or upon the needs of the business firm or government bureau. The benefit to you also depends upon the competence of the study, although competence in a researcher is less obvious than it is in a basketball player. And the benefits may depend upon your situation—for example, if you are a student or young scientist you may feel the need to show results quickly, whereas an older researcher may feel less hurried to produce results.

3. Long-term professional benefits. If all's right with the world, the long-run professional benefits will be in proportion to the intrinsic importance of the research, as measured by the influence of the research on a body of thought or on the magnitude of decisions affected by the study.[1]

As an example, an outstanding anthropologist might compare the value of two studies this way. A study of culture 1 would probably require a year, and its probable results would affect perhaps four pages of a basic textbook. A study of culture 2 would probably require twice as much time, and its probable results would affect perhaps five pages of a basic textbook. The output of the first study is four pages per year but for the second only two and a half pages a year, which makes the first a better investment (provided that there are other comparable studies for the researcher to do when the first is complete). Such a calculation may seem too calculating, but pure scientists undoubtedly do such figuring implicitly when deciding what to do next.[2]

A study's potential influence on scientific thought is hard to gauge. Here are some guidelines to help you judge. First, empirical studies that test important theories are themselves important. A study testing part of Keynes' theory about economic growth would be more important than a study testing a the-

---

1. There is considerable controversy about how closely scientific recognition is related to scientific achievement (Cole, 1979; Reskin, 1980; Zuckerman, 1977). Injustices occur, but universities are probably more objective in hiring and rewarding scientists than most other institutions are with regard to their employees.

2. Footnotes and references to a person's work are another quantitative measure of productivity value frequently used to measure eminence. And even the purest in heart find themselves counting their own footnotes occasionally. The Science Citation Index and the Social Science Citation Index provide systematic and comprehensive information on the references to scientists' work.

ory about what kinds of automobile accessories consumers are likely to prefer.

Second, the more surprising and unexpected the result of a study, the more valuable is the study—assuming that the surprise does not arise from faulty procedure. As information theory points out, a man who hollers to you "Your house is on fire" is usually telling you something more valuble than if he hollers "Your house is not on fire." Studies that showed traditional farmers in underdeveloped countries to be responsive to new ideas and to money incentives were more valuable because the opposite was generally assumed to be true and would have been no surprise (Schultz, 1965: Chap. 2). Studies that showed that quality of education did not seem to be strongly related to student achievement stimulated much more controversy than studies that showed the opposite would have (Aaron, 1978: Chap. 3).

Third, results that offer the possibility of useful action are more valuable than results that close off the possibility. In the previous example, the finding that traditional farmers are responsive to money incentives opens the door to modernizing a country's agriculture by making it worthwhile for the farmers to change their behavior.

Fourth, the wider the application and the more universal the conclusions drawn from the study, the more important the study is. All research is done on *some* limited collection of people or animals or objects or organizations. For example, an economist might learn that, when a Nigerian family has sufficient money income, it buys first a refrigerator and later a washing machine, rather than vice versa. The implicit side conditions of this study are that the subjects live in Nigeria in the 1960s. The study would have more importance if there were reason to think that the same pattern holds in many countries in any decade.

Studies of occupational status offer another example. When social scientists discovered at the end of the 1940s that Americans tended to agree with each other about the relative status of different occupations, the finding was of mild interest. When they discovered that people in other industrialized countries agreed with Americans in their rankings, that was more interesting, because it implied that the rankings might be the product of something general to industrialized societies, not just peculiar to the United States. And when they discovered that the rankings seemed to be shared by people all over the world, the findings were seen as extremely important, and led to major theoretical work trying to explain them (Treiman, 1977).

The generality of the results is also one of the criteria that distinguish between pure and applied research. For example, consider an experiment showing that an argument that includes both the pros and cons of smoking is more efficient in preventing smoking than is an argument that recognizes only the negative side of smoking. If this experiment were done solely to find out how to prevent smoking and if there were no reason to believe that the finding would also hold true for other persuasive situations, then the experiment would be applied research. But, if the purpose of the experiment were to investigate persuasive arguments *generally* and if the antismoking campaign were chosen only as a representative example, then the experiment is closer to pure research.

An industrial psychologist might decide between two potential studies in this fashion. Study 1 promises to improve job satisfaction in the baseball-glove industry, which employs x people. Study 2, requiring no more time, would improve job satisfaction an equal amount per person in the steel industry, which employs $10x$ people. Obviously the findings of study 2 would have more generality and therefore more value. Or an educational psychologist might consider doing a study to improve the reading speed of brain-damaged children or a study to improve the reading speed of culturally backward children. The latter study would affect more children and would therefore be more general.

The purest test of generality is the number of theories a given study would affect or the number of prior empirical studies that would appear in a different light after the work is complete. But this is difficult to illustrate in the short compass of space available here.

Fifth, the human importance of a study affects its value. More people suffer from baldness than from leukemia, but the latter is studied more because it is more serious.[3] Similarly, a clinical-psychology study that promises to reduce the anxieties in adolescents' first dates has less value than does a study that promises a way to bring psychotics back to reality.

Sixth, empirical studies that are *intellectually connected* with the rest of a field have greater value than do those that are not connected. By "connected"[4] we mean that a study is related to contemporary arguments and open questions in a particular science or that it extends or contradicts work that has already been done. For example, a study that measures the extent to which two kinds of behavior are similar or widely different in identical twins separated at birth is solidly connected with *several* fields, because it throws light on several open questions. Such a study tells the physiological psychologists about the extent to which behavior is biologically determined; it tells the learning and educational psychologists about the extent to which various types of behavior may be learned; and it helps the sociologist understand the impact of social interaction upon human behavior patterns.

The main shortcoming of many an "operations-research" study in applied science is that often it yields nothing but the answer to one specific operating problem. Examples on which one of us has worked include investiga-

tions of which advertisement for a particular product will be most productive, and of how many library books should be in open stacks and how many should be in less-expensive storage units. Solving such problems may certainly be important enough to justify the research work. But the work does not carry much interest for other scientists, for it throws no light on problems in which they are interested (except by accident or because new methods are discovered). That is, these operations-research examples are not connected strongly with the body of any scientific field.

Of course, some of the most valuable studies do not fit into the existing structures of the disciplines at the time the studies are done. Rather the discipline moves to meet them. But the *possibility* that sometime in the future the study will be connected into the body of a discipline is important. There must be a chance that a bridge will be created between the existing body of knowledge in a science and a new discovery once the latter's importance is recognized. For example, the first studies of the concentration of economic power in the United States seemed to have no connection with the body of economics. But, as the importance of the topic has been recognized, and as growing numbers of studies of this sort have been done, the subject has become connected with the rest of economics, as well as creating its own work tradition, the study of industrial organization.

Seventh, studies whose results may contradict intuition and common sense, or that might run contrary to commonly accepted popular or scientific belief, are more valuable than studies whose results are likely to accord with what we already think. For example, A. Carey's study (1967) that called into question the widely accepted results of the Hawthorne study was more valuable than if that study had simply corroborated the Hawthorne results. A study that shows that the number of Mexicans illegally in the United States is much smaller than previously thought is of greater scientific value than the study corroborating prior belief. Ku-

3. This choice of scientists also illustrates that the most dollar-profitable studies are sometimes not preferred. A baldness study would be more rewarding commercially than would a leukemia cure. The structure of nonprofit research grants to scientists may, however, explain the situation.

4. See R. von Mises' *Positivism* (1951: Chap. 6) for an excellent simple explanation of the concept of connectedness and its importance in the context of scientific language.

mar's study (1973) that shows that we are gaining rather than losing agricultural land worldwide is particularly valuable because it calls into question a widely held belief.

Estimating the value and future influence of a given study is difficult even after the study is complete. Some men in the field may say "a landmark" and others "a potboiler." Twenty years later one can tell how much influence the study has had on subsequent research. It is educational to read through the older studies that have turned out to be important in any field for clues to what makes important studies important. Books of readings collect those studies for you.

If it is difficult to appraise a study's probable influence right after it is done, it is even harder to appraise it *before* it is done—because you then do not know what will turn out or whether anything at all will turn out.

So much for the likelihood that a study will be influential. What about the likelihood that a study will be *correct?* And how important is it that the results will be correct?

First, decide what is at stake. Kaplan discusses this problem in the context of how big a sample to take:

> What is the stake for which we are playing—that is, what will we do with our estimate when we have arrived at it, and what will it do for us in return? Is there always a winner, and how is he selected—that is, what defines the "best estimate" in this situation? Does the situation allow us to make more than one estimate—can any number of entries be submitted by each contestant? What is the cost of making an estimate—what box tops must accompany the entry? What price must be paid for an error, and how is an error defined? Is the price fixed, or does it vary with the size of the error? Can an error be corrected subsequently—are we playing touch-move or can a bad move be withdrawn? How will the prize be diminished by the range of the estimate made—do we win anything by estimating the length as lying between a thousandth of an inch and a thousand miles? How much will additional measurements cost? How long do we have to make up our minds? How much must be paid—

in appropriate units of utility—for the use of a computer and other resources, both human and otherwise, available to the scientific enterprise? . . .

> What must enter into such criteria is a specification of the costs of reaching a decision, and of the losses incurred when the decision is a mistaken one. Of particular importance is the relative cost of errors. . . . The scientist invests time and money in his experiments, and if his conclusions are erroneous, damage is likely to be done to society as well as to his own reputation. (Kaplan, 1964: 252, 253)

Estimating the danger of error is difficult. But for applied research it can be done (see Ferguson and LeVeen, 1981; Rossi, 1980; Aaron, 1978, for social problems, or Schlaifer, 1959, 1961, for business decisions). And even for pure research, one can arrive at *some* sensible decisions. For example, an error in the results of an influential experiment in nuclear radiation effect or in a study of whether the economy is expanding or contracting is more important than is an error of the same probability in a study of whether people at the picnic like hot dogs better than hamburgers. But it is hopeless to count the cost of not considering some yet-unthought-of alternative.

The *ratio* of the estimates of the outputs and inputs of a particular study should then be compared to the ratio of other alternative studies. The total output of a small-cost project need not be as high as the total output of a long and expensive project for the inexpensive study to be the better investment, because its ratio of output to input may be higher. Furthermore, short studies represent less risk to the beginner, who is more likely to start into blind alleys.

One of the characteristics of research is that you are uncertain about what you will learn from the study at the time you decide whether to do it. Therefore the evaluation of proposed research must take into account the probabilities you estimate for the various outcomes, as well as their costs and benefits.

In recent years huge strides have been made in quantifying the value of information for use in deciding whether to do research, and in choosing the size of sample to take. Here follows an illustration of such a calculation. Readers who are not familiar with the concept of *expected value*[5] might skip this illustration.[6] But we believe that the importance of this approach to research valuation is sufficiently great that the example is worth including despite its length and complexity:

The proposed research is an experiment, with incentive payments for nonpregnancy, to be conducted in a sample of Indian villages. The goal is to help reduce the birth rate in those less-developed countries with rapid population growth. In some villages, women would be offered sums ranging from $75 per year, for women in the highest-fertility category, downward to relatively small payments for women in low-fertility categories, for each year they had no children. In other villages, the entire payment schedule would be lower. And still other villages would serve as controls, in which no money incentives would be offered for not having babies.

The situation may be diagrammed as in Figure 8.1. If alternative 1 is chosen and the experiment is carried out, I guesstimate that there is a 50-50 chance that the experiment will yield "positive" results and will be interpreted by social planners and decision makers as indicating that the incentive program is successful in reducing births. And if the experiment *is* successful, I estimate that there is about a 50-50 chance (say, .499, to avoid confusion) that a full-scale program will then be embarked upon; *if* the experiment is *not* successful, I estimate that there is a 1-in-8 (.125) chance that an action program will be undertaken. If *no* experiment is undertaken, I estimate that there is a 1-in-4 chance that a full-scale action program will be undertaken.

Now for the consequences if an action program *is* carried out: If it is undertaken after a *positive* experiment, it is reasonable to believe that the program has a better likelihood of being successful

than would a program carried out after a negative experiment. This is, in fact, the meaning of the information yielded by any piece of research— that the research result can help predict the result of the program itself. The probabilities of program success after positive and negative experiments are roughly estimated by me to be .49 and .124 respectively. And the probability of a successful program (if it is undertaken) *in the absence of experimental information* is estimated to be .249. All this probabilistic structure is summarized in Figure 8.1.

Now let us estimate the economic effects of a successful program. Let us first estimate the number of *fewer* births there would be with a successful incentive action program than with no incentive program. A wild guess for illustrative purposes is that the birth rate would be lower by a fifth if this program is undertaken (and is successful) than if it is not. And let us say that each avoided birth is worth $100–$500 (say, $200) to the rest of the community in India.[7] Avoided births in the future are of less present value than are births now (because of the discounting phenomenon), but as a crude trade-off estimate, let us consider only the next five years' births, undiscounted. This quantity is one fifth of 5×20 million expected births, or 20 million births, each multiplied by $200. This gives a total of $4 billion, the benefit we shall count for a successful program. There are no important operating costs to an *unsuccessful* program, because the heart of the program is to give money, and if the program is unsuccessful, no money will change hands. Similarly, there are no important operating costs to a *successful* program. And since the funds paid as incentives are transfers from person to person, they really have little social cost and may be ignored here. The cost of the scientific work involved in the experiment itself might be a quarter or a third of a million dollars, vastly less than the half-billion-dollar expected payoff.

The decision about whether to conduct the experiment depends on a present-value computation of the two alternatives. Denote by W the economic welfare that will result if nothing is done about a no-pregnancy incentive program.

5. The expected value of an alternative is the sum of the net values of the events that may occur, multiplied by the probabilities that they will occur.

6. This example is drawn from J. Simon (1972).

7. For a summary of this literature, see Pohlman (1971).

FIGURE 8.1

$$V_{\text{Experiment}} = .5 \times .499 \times .49\ (W + \$.4 \\ \text{billion} - \$.25\ \text{million}) \\ + .5 \times .499 \times .51\ (W - \$.25 \\ \text{million}) \\ + .5 \times .501\ (W - \$.25\ \text{million}) \\ + .5 \times .125 \times .124\ (W + \$4 \\ \text{billion} - \$.25\ \text{million}) \\ + .5 \times .125 \times .876\ (W - \$.25 \\ \text{million}) \\ + .5 \times .875\ (W - \$.25\ \text{million}) \\ \sim \$.52\ \text{billion} + W$$

$$V_{\text{No experiment}} = .25 \times .249\ (W + \$4\ \text{billion}) \\ + .25 \times .751\ (W) \\ + .75\ (W) \\ \sim \$.25\ \text{billion} + W$$

The V for the experiment alternative is higher, and hence it appears to make sense to undertake the experiment. It is also worth noting that if we perform a "sensitivity test"—changing some of the assumed probabilities and payoffs and observing the resultant changes in V—the experiment continues to make sense even with considerably less "favorable" assumptions. (J. Simon, 1972)

Of course this analysis is very much simplified and ignores many important factors. Furthermore, the probabilities are only guesstimates. But its value is that it clarifies the issues at stake and provokes us to argue about what is important and what is not.

Even though the foregoing valuation techniques are useful, the process of judging whether it is worthwhile to do a study remains largely a fine art: "It is perhaps the most precious art of the scientist to develop almost a sixth sense, based on deep knowledge of his whole field, that can tell him which researches are likely to be promising and which are not" (Price, 1961: 73). The Nobel Prize winners "uniformly express the strong conviction that what matters most in their work is a developing sense of taste, of judgment, in seizing upon problems that are of fundamental importance" (Merton, 1968: 60).

As a practical matter, the advice of one's elders in science is worth most to students in the choice of problems for term papers and theses. It seems to us that the last and most important gift a professor should make to a student is a subject for a thesis that is likely to turn out well—together with an assessment of the likely costs and benefits of various approaches to the problem, and perhaps some references to readily available data.

3. Summary

The professional researcher always faces the problem of having more alternative research possibilities than he or she can carry out with the time (and money) available. A wise choice among the possibilities is much like a business' or society's choice of investments: Which ones offer the highest potential return for the invested time and money?

Like other investments, the choice of research projects has two fundamental elements: (a) an estimate of the inputs necessary for the project, and their costs; and (b) an estimate of the project's likely output, and its value. The latter is the more difficult, but you should at least try to estimate the value of the output of the project even when doing the purest of pure research.

Those projects should be chosen that promise the highest benefit/cost ratio, taking risk and uncertainty into account.

EXERCISES

1. Select at random six articles reporting empirical research in your field, and randomly divide them into three pairs. Assess the relative value of the members of each pair, making explicit judgments based on criteria discussed in this chapter.
2. Consider in each pair the study that you adjudge on an overall basis to be less valuable. Assume that it took only half as long to do as the better study did. Now which study in each pair represents the better investment of a researcher's time?
3. Consider in each pair the study that you judge on an overall basis to be the more valuable. Think of at least one way to improve each of the more valuable ones. Try to calculate approximately how much each improvement would cost in time and money. Decide whether the value of the research would be improved enough to warrant the extra cost.

ADDITIONAL READING

Tull and Hawkins (1967, Chap. 3) explain clearly how one goes about figuring the value and cost of information, using examples from marketing research that may serve as models for all of social-scientific research.

The National Science Foundation *Guide to Programs* (1981) describes the criteria used by a major government agency to assess the potential value of research projects, and provides examples of the types of research supported in the physical, biological, and social sciences.

Granovetter discusses how he was able to carry out a study of how people find jobs almost entirely by himself and with little money (1976, 141–152).

Sampling

1. Sampling: The Problem of Representativeness

Suppose you want to learn some characteristic of a large group of people—say, what young people expect marriage to be like, what Americans of voting age think of the president, or how worried professional people are about losing their jobs. The obvious way to get the desired information would be to find all of the appropriate people—all young people, all Americans of voting age, all professional people—and to interview them. Unfortunately, that is impossible, because you could not afford the time and expense required to interview them all.

Fortunately, it is not necessary to get information on every person (or group, organization, government, etc.) in which you are interested to draw valid conclusions about a population. You can take a sample, getting data on *some* people and drawing conclusions about the whole group. If your conclusions are to be valid, however, the sample should be *representative* of the population. This means, essentially, that the sample should resemble the population with regard to the characteristics you are interested in—almost as if the sample were a miniature version of the population. If the sample resembles the population very closely (except for being smaller, of course), then you can be confident that conclusions you draw about the characteristics of the sample will also be applicable to the population.[1]

As a practical matter, of course, the only way to see whether a sample resembles a population is to compare the two; but if we could get information about the population, we would not need to sample in the first place. What researchers have done over the years is develop *procedures* for drawing samples that ensure that the average sample will resemble the population quite closely. The most commonly used

1. "Representativeness" is actually a difficult concept to define in a completely satisfactory way; Kruskal and Mosteller (1981) discuss some of the ways in which the term has been used.

procedures involve random sampling, which will be discussed in Section 2. Before discussing how to get a representative sample, however, it is important to show what can happen when conclusions are based on samples that are not representative; the results can be embarrassing.

The most celebrated fiasco caused by a biased sample and its misinterpretation was the *Literary Digest* polling debacle before the 1936 presidential election. The magazine's news stories convey the flavor of the event.

August 22, 1936

The *Digest* PRESIDENTIAL POLL IS ON!

Famous Forecasting Machine Is Thrown Into Gear for 1936

The 1936 nation-wide *Literary Digest* Presidential Poll has begun.

Unruffled by the tumult and shouting of the hottest political race in twenty years, more than 1,000 trained workers have swung into their accustomed jobs. While Chairmen Farley and Hamilton noisily claim "at least forty-two States," and while the man in the streets sighs "I wish I knew," the *Digest's* smooth-running machine moves with the swift precision of thirty years' experience to reduce guesswork to hard facts.

This week, 500 pens scratched out more than a quarter of a million addresses a day. Every day, in a great room high above motor-ribboned Fourth Avenue, in New York, 400 workers deftly slid a million pieces of printed matter—enough to pave forty city blocks—into the addressed envelopes. Every hour, in the *Digest's* own Post Office Substation, three chattering postage metering machines sealed and stamped white oblongs; skilled postal employees flipped them into bulging mail-sacks; fleet *Digest* trucks sped them to express mail-trains. Once again, the *Digest* was asking more than ten million voters—one out of four, representing every county in the United States—*to settle November's election in October*.

Next week, the first answers from those ten million will begin the incoming tide of marked ballots, to be *triple-checked*, verified, *five times*

cross-classified and totaled. When the last figure has been totted and checked, if past experience is a criterion, the country will know *to within a fraction of 1 per cent* the actual popular vote of forty millions.

As in former years, the *Digest* Poll will be marked by three distinctions:

Impartiality—A half century's reputation as the oldest and greatest news magazine in the world precludes any thought of bias; the *Digest* has no stake in the outcome. . . . Accuracy—The Poll represents thirty years' constant evolution and perfection. Based on the "commercial sampling" methods used for more than a century by publishing houses to push book sales, the present mailing list is drawn from every telephone book in the United States, from the rosters of clubs and associations, from city directories, lists of registered voters, classified mail-order and occupational data.

October 31, 1936

LANDON, 1,293,669; ROOSEVELT, 972,897

Final Returns in the *Digest's* Poll of Ten Million Voters

Well, the great battle of the ballots in the Poll of ten million voters, scattered throughout the forty-eight States of the Union, is now finished.

These figures are exactly as received from more than one in every five voters polled in our country—they are neither weighted, adjusted nor interpreted. . . .

November 14, 1936

WHAT WENT WRONG WITH THE POLLS?

None of Straw Votes Got Exactly the Right Answer—Why?

In 1920, 1924, 1928 and 1932, *The Literary Digest* Polls were right. Not only right in the sense that they showed the winner; they forecast the *actual popular vote* with such a small percentage of error (less than 1 per cent in 1932) that newspapers and individuals everywhere heaped such phrases as "uncannily accurate" and "amazingly right" upon us.

Four years ago, when the Poll was running his way, our very good friend Jim Farley was saying that "no sane person could escape the implication" of a sampling "so fairly and correctly conducted."

Well, this year we used precisely the same method that had scored four bull's-eyes in four previous tries. And we were far from correct. Why? We ask that question in all sincerity, because *we want to know*.

The *Literary Digest* prediction was not just wrong—it was so *grossly* wrong that it is given credit for the magazine's going out of business not long thereafter.

The most obvious conclusion from this case is that a huge sample is no protection against error. The *Literary Digest* repeatedly trumpeted that its sample was 10 million, one voter in every four, which is very impressive to the layperson. But with a sample of only 10,000 the results would have been practically identical. And a well-selected sample of 10,000 or less might have obtained the correct results with good accuracy.

Gallup has the right to say what went wrong with the *Literary Digest* poll, because he made a correct analysis *before* the election:

> The reasons the *Digest* poll went wrong in 1936 are obvious to anyone who understands modern polling methods. *The Literary Digest* sent out its ballots by mail and, for the most part, to people whose names were listed in telephone directories or to lists of automobile owners. From the point of view of cross section this was a major error, because it limited the sample largely to the upper half of the voting population, as judged on an economic basis. Roughly 40 per cent of all homes in the United States had telephones and some 55 per cent of all families owned automobiles. These two groups, which largely overlap, constitute roughly the upper half or upper three-fifths, economically, of the voting population.
>
> *The Literary Digest* in previous straw vote polls had sent post card ballots to the same groups, but the *Digest* did not reckon with two factors in 1936—the division of votes along income lines which began with Roosevelt's administration in

1932, and the substantial increase in the voting population which took place between 1932 and 1936. These new voters came predominantly from the poorest levels—from income groups which favored Roosevelt.

> The *Digest* not only failed to select a proper cross section, but the means by which the magazine reached voters—mail ballots—also helped to introduce error into the findings.
>
> Persons most likely to return mail ballots are those in the higher income and educational levels, and, conversely, those least likely to return their ballots represent the lowest income and educational levels. So, even if the *Literary Digest* had actually used lists of voters throughout the country as they did in a few cities, instead of names selected from telephone books and automobile lists, post card ballots would still have been responsible for a substantial error in the *Digest*'s findings.
>
> The fact that the *Digest* was using faulty methods was obvious long before the election revealed them. As early as July 14, 1936, two months before the *Digest* even began sending out its ballots, the American Institute [Gallup's organization] . . . predicted almost exactly the *Digest*'s final figure and described in detail exactly what was wrong with the *Digest*'s procedures. (Gallup, 1948: 73–75)

There were two major reasons why the *Literary Digest* poll was wrong. First, the *Literary Digest* was interested in the political preferences of a group of people defined one way—by eligibility to vote—but it sent ballots to a group of people defined a different way—by telephone or automobile ownership. The *sampling frame* (see the formal definition below) of telephone or automobile owners did not represent the population of interest, eligible voters, because many voters did not own automobiles or telephones (and of course, some who did would not have been eligible to vote). Second, the ballots were not even representative of the sampling frame because only the most interested or highly motivated people would take the trouble to return the ballots.

Polling organizations and social scientists

learned a lot from the 1936 *Literary Digest* debacle, but people still reach unsound conclusions from research on nonrepresentative samples.

IT'S A RETURN TO TRADITION FOR MANY YOUNG MARRIEDS, DESPITE WOMEN'S MOVEMENT

Engaged Couples Pleased with Traditional Roles

New York—Despite the women's movement and a more flexible attitude toward the role of the sexes in recent years, many young people now getting married have highly traditional views of what to expect from a spouse and how they should act themselves.

Young women automatically assume they will have to take over most household tasks regardless of their own careers . . . they worry that their husband-to-be will beat them in a fit of rage or drunkenness.

The young men doubt their intended wife's ability to handle money intelligently . . . they automatically act in a dominant way rather than as an equal partner, often pushing their own interests and activities on her. (Brooks, 1981: 64.)

The headline and the beginning of the article make you think that couples are generally quite traditional, and that the women's movement has had little impact. Then, however, the article describes the people from whom this information had been gathered: 40 percent from the St. Paul–Minneapolis area, with the rest from the Midwest and the Mountain states; most with some college education; all contemplating a Roman Catholic wedding ceremony. Thus, the sample contained few Protestants or Jews, no one from either coast, and few with only a high school education. Perhaps these left-out people are pleased with traditional roles, too. But the survey provides no information on them. The headline about "engaged couples" is misleading because it does not describe the majority of couples in the United States.

The value of a conclusion depends on two aspects of the data-gathering process: (1) the relationship between the population sampled —the sampling frame—and the population the researcher is interested in; and (2) the representativeness of the sample within the sampling frame. This chapter presents an intuitive introduction to the basic ideas of sampling and sampling frame. This introduction should enable you to draw a sound sample for most scientific and applied purposes. It describes what is involved in drawing a random sample, discusses how some of the practical problems in drawing such samples are dealt with, and considers the circumstances in which a wise scientist might decide to work with a nonrandom sample. But the drawing of samples for major surveys such as a national census is a highly technical matter demanding calculations not taught here. If you should contemplate doing a large-scale and costly sampling operation, by all means call upon the services of a professional statistician, and do so *before* you get started.

2. Universe, Sample, and Sampling Frame

A *sample* is the collection of observations for which you have data with which you are going to work. Almost any set of observations for which you have data constitutes a sample.

For every sample there must also be a universe "behind" it. But "universe" is harder to define, partly because it is often an *imaginary* concept. A *universe* (or *population*) is the collection of things or people *from which you want to say that your sample was taken*.[2] A universe can be finite and well defined—"all live holders of the Congressional Medal of Honor," "all presidents of major universities," "all billion-dollar corporations in the United States." Of course, these finite universes may not be easy to pin down; for instance, what is

2. "Universe" and "population" are perfect synonyms in scientific research. We choose to use "universe" because it seems to have fewer confusing associations.

a "major university"? And these universes may contain some elements that are difficult to find; for instance, some Congressional Medal winners may have left the country, and there may not be any public records on some billion-dollar corporations.

Infinite universes are harder to understand, and it is often difficult to decide which universe is appropriate for a given purpose. For example, if you are studying a sample of schizophrenics, what is the universe from which the sample comes? Depending on your purposes, the appropriate universe might be all schizophrenics now alive, or it might be all schizophrenics who might *ever* live. The latter concept of the universe of schizophrenics is *imaginary* because some of the universe does not exist. And it is *infinite* because it goes on forever.

Not everyone likes this definition of "universe." Others prefer to think of a universe, not as the collection of people or things that you *want* to say your sample was taken from, but as the collection that the sample was *actually* taken from. This latter view equates the universe to the "sampling frame," which is always finite and existent. There is an analogy here to hypothetical and empirical variables; in our view one actually deals with an empirical variable that stands for a hypothetical variable that may itself be difficult to pin down; the other view ignores the hypothetical variable completely when it refuses to deal with imaginary universes. The definition of "universe" offered here is simply the most practical, in our opinion.

A. RANDOM SAMPLING BASICS

Terminology right and wrong: The term *random* refers to the *process* by which a sample is chosen from a universe; the term does *not* refer to a given sample. It may be correct to say that a sample was "randomly chosen," but it is not correct to say that "the sample is random." In the long run and on the average, a random-sampling process produces representative samples, but a given single sample is not likely to be perfectly representative, and hence it is not strictly correct and may be misleading to call a given sample "random." However, like others we often slothfully use the term "random sample," and we hope you will mentally correct this error when you see it.

A randomly chosen sample is a *fair* sample, in the sense that every member of the universe has an *equal* chance of being included. If you put every name in the phone book on a separate index card and put all the cards in a huge bin, mix the cards up, and then pick a hundred of them out of the bin, the sample of a hundred will have been randomly chosen if you mixed up the cards well enough. Not all samples are random. A *biased* sample is one that is *not* drawn randomly and that therefore does not represent all parts of the universe. The sample is said to be biased in favor of any member of the universe who has more than a fair (or equal) chance of being picked for the sample. If the sample is biased in favor of some members, it must be biased against others. For example, if the index cards with names from the phone book were made up in alphabetical order and were put in the bin that way (with the A's on the bottom, the M's in the middle, and the Z's on top, presumably), and a sample was picked from among the cards on the top, the sample would be biased against people with names beginning with letters that come early in the alphabet (if the names were being picked to award prizes in a raffle, Burstein would be upset, but Simon might not be). Survey samples are biased against people living on the top floors of walk-up buildings in poor neighborhoods, because interviewers sometimes write down "not home" without even going there.

Whether a sample is randomly chosen, unbiased, and fair is not always obvious. If you have a very large sample, you may be able to test whether it was drawn randomly by examining whether any event, or pattern of events, appears more often than it would occur by chance. In addition, you can examine the sampling procedure itself very carefully to see if every element of it seems fair. But if you have a small sample, you are bound to observe patterns of events that appear to be very unusual but that easily could occur, for example, six heads, or head-tail-head-tail-head-tail, in six coin tosses. So for a small sample your only assurance that the sampling process is random must come from careful inspection of the details of the sampling procedure rather than from the sample itself.

There are two important aspects of obtaining an unbiased sample: taking a sample at random from the sampling frame, and selecting a sampling frame that is appropriate for the population in which you are interested.

B. TAKING A SAMPLE RANDOMLY FROM THE SAMPLING FRAME

In theory taking a sample randomly is perfectly easy: Just put all the members of the universe into a hat, shake them well, and take out those to be included in the sample, one by one—either "replacing" the sampled members or not, depending upon the situation (an important decision, which is discussed in Chapters 30–31). Each individual then would have exactly the same chance of getting into the sample. This procedure yields what is known as a *simple* random sample.

But practical difficulties arise in attempting to achieve this theoretical ideal. The first obstacle is that no good sampling frame may be available. A *sampling frame* is the empirical representation of the theoretical universe in which you are interested. For example, if your universe is black students at the University of Illinois, a complete list of such students would constitute an excellent sampling frame. But no such list existed until recently, and therefore it would have taken much work and energy to create a good sampling frame.

Another obstacle is that the members of the universe to be studied can themselves seldom

be placed into a hat and shuffled. The people in the United States cannot be placed physically into a vessel and mixed well. Instead, one must work with *symbols* that represent these people—their names and the data about them—on paper, rather than in person. Considerable accuracy may be lost in the process of transforming a group of people into a list of symbols.

Even after you have reduced the physical units to symbols on paper, the technique is still not straightforward and automatic. The telephone book may list the names of all telephone subscribers, but you do not want to go to the trouble of cutting apart all the names, one by one, and throwing them into a hat. In practice, you work out some sort of a rule that will help you draw a sample at random directly from the phone book, say, without cutting and shaking.

Some such rules are bad, some good. The rule to take the first hundred names beginning on a randomly drawn page of the phone book would probably be a bad rule for most purposes, even though the sample is random because every person has the same probability of falling into the sample. Certain national origins and religions are heavily concentrated in some first-letter groups, Z, for instance, and Y. Therefore, your sample will not be *representative*, even though it will be random. Such a procedure violates a basic rule of all sampling, both random and nonrandom: ". . . we want a . . . sample that has a wide representation of experiences" (Klein, 1965: 4).

A better rule would be to take every fiftieth name, every 125th name, or every "*nth*" name, with *n* standing for the interval necessary to obtain as many names as you need. By this method—yielding a *systematic* random sample rather than a "simple" random sample—you ensure that before the sample is drawn each part of the list has an equal chance of falling into your sample and that no one part of the list will be represented more heavily than will any other. But systematic samples may also have dangers. Taking every tenth house on a street might give you every corner house, and people who live in corner houses are different, at least in income, from the other people on the block. Nevertheless, unless you have some special reason to distrust the systematic every-*n*th sample from the phone book, it probably yields a good random and representative sample.[3]

Another kind of rule that would be a little slower but would avoid the danger of a systematic sample is to select one name randomly from each page, by selecting a random number for each page from a random-number table and then measuring with a ruler instead of actually counting names one by one.

Another danger-free procedure is to pick a page number at random and then a number for a name from that page at random, until you have a large enough sample. But this simple random sampling would be very slow and probably would yield only a slightly more random sample than would systematically taking every *n*th name.

A random-digit table is a great help in taking random samples. The random-digit table is the record of a process like spinning a ten-sided die again and again and again. Instead of spinning the die, you just proceed along a row or down a column (or in a hopscotch pattern if you like) of the random-digit table (see page 375 in Chapter 31). If you want to draw numbers between 0 and 999 instead of between 0 and 9, take groups of three-digit numbers. If you want only numbers between 0 and 63, say, simply ignore any numbers you hit between 64 and 99 and move on to the next pair.

Extreme vigilance is the only guarantee against departures from randomness. As Huff puts it, "The operation of a poll comes down in the end to a running battle against sources of bias . . ." (1954: 22). And in sampling, as in everything else in research, every technique

depends at some point on your experience, general knowledge, and judgment. For example, it is only your judgment that leads you to *reason* that the systematic sample of the phone book is better for your purposes than taking the first hundred names on the first page.

C. SELECTING THE APPROPRIATE SAMPLING FRAME

Selecting the appropriate sampling frame is like aiming your camera lens at what you really want to photograph. If you want to sample telephone subscribers for the telephone company, the telephone book is a fine sampling frame because it is an almost perfect representation of the population in which you are interested. (But it is not *perfect*. Some names in the phone book represent people who have moved away, some new subscribers are not yet listed, some people have unlisted phones, and some people have several listings. No sampling frame can ever be a perfect representation of the population. Even the Census misses some people—millions of them, especially young black males, as follow-up checks have revealed; Miller et al., 1972.)

If you want to sample the population for a voting study, however, the telephone book may not be a good sampling frame. Some registered voters do not have phones, and they are likely to be lower-income people who have different voting patterns from other registered voters. If you are sampling in a community where almost everyone has a phone, the sampling bias will be tiny, and you can usually ignore it. But, if only a small proportion of the community has phones, the bias in a sample from the telephone book can be enormous.

Demographers have used tombstones as a sampling frame in making estimates of the ages at which people died many centuries ago. But there are drawbacks, the most important of which is that the younger the person was when she died, the less likely she was to have accumulated enough wealth so that her heirs could afford to purchase a tombstone. Furthermore,

---

3. If a systematic random sample is to be used, it always makes sense to use two or more systematic subsamples that have different randomly chosen starting places, rather than a *single* systematic sample twice as large.

infants were usually buried without any stones. Therefore a sample of tombstones yields a biased estimate of the age distribution at death.

The choice of sampling frame for personal interviews is full of problems.

> The obvious thing is to start with a list of everybody and go after names chosen from it at random; but that is too expensive. So you go into the streets—and bias your sample against stay-at-homes. You go from door to door by day—and miss most of the employed people. You switch to evening interviews—and neglect the movie-goers and night-clubbers. (Huff, 1954: 22)

The secret of success in choosing a sampling frame is: *Fit the sampling frame to your purpose.* You must be careful to *include all* people you are interested in, *and* to exclude people not relevant for your purposes. For example, if Rolls Royce wants to gather market information about a change in design, the appropriate sampling frame includes only those people in the income class of present buyers, that is, the rich. But if Rolls Royce were to consider a big price cut to expand their market, then the appropriate sampling frame to learn about the effect of the price drop would include middle-income people. Similarly, if you wish to relate differences in diet to the incidence of stomach cancer, you must include in your sampling frame people with a wide variety of diets— maybe people from all over the country or even all around the world, who eat very different kinds of food. You are not likely to learn very much from a study of soldiers in the U.S. Army, all of whom eat much the same food.

If you keep in mind the purpose for which you are taking the sample, you will be alert in the choice of sampling frame to potential biases that might prejudice your investigation.

Earlier we mentioned that an important sampling-frame problem in telephone sampling is that many homes have unlisted or new phones—as many as 40 per cent in the largest metropolitan areas (Sudman, 1976: 65), and 20 per cent for the country as a whole (Cooper,

1964: 45; Glasser and Metzger, 1972: 60). One may circumvent this problem by random-digit dialing, which takes advantage of the fact that telephone numbers are concentrated within certain blocks of numbers. An efficient method is: (a) Select a systematic sample of telephone numbers from the telephone book; (b) Strike out the last three digits of each telephone listing selected; (c) Select a three-digit number from a table of random numbers, and append that to the shortened listings selected from the phone book. About half the numbers you obtain in this manner should be usable, and the resulting sample is randomly selected (Sudman, 1976: 65).

3. Efficiency in Random Sampling

You have a selected a sampling frame; now you must select a sample. When choosing a sample, one's goal is typically to obtain the greatest amount of information of the greatest accuracy at the least cost. One crucial measure of accuracy is the amount of *sampling error,* which is the discrepancy between the results one obtains from a given sample and the results one would attain from a study of all the members of the relevant universe. Sampling error occurs because, while a random sample is likely to be highly similar to the universe from which it is drawn, it is unlikely to be identical (in miniature, of course). A fair coin flipped over and over will come up heads half the time and tails half the time, over the long run; but we would not be surprised if in some sample of ten tosses it came up heads six times. The difference between the proportion of heads in the sample and the proportion one would get in the long run may be viewed as the sampling error for that particular sample.

A major advantage of random sampling, or any other kind of *probability* sampling in which the likelihood of being included in the sample is known, is that the amount of likely sampling error can be calculated in advance. This fact enables us to determine the trade-off between accuracy (in terms of sampling error) and cost of obtaining a sample. For example, the average sampling error for a given sample size, using a particular sampling method, tends to be halved each time you quadruple the sample; that is, quadrupling the sample reduces the likely inaccuracy by about half, rather than to a fourth of what it was. Here are some approaches used to get representative samples while keeping costs within bounds.

A. SYSTEMATIC SAMPLING

A systematic sample is one in which every *n*th member is chosen from a list or other array of the universe. Taking every tenth house on the street produces a systematic sample, as does taking every twenty-seventh card in a card file. A systematic sampling process is *random* because, if the starting point is chosen randomly (that is, if whichever of the first ten houses or whichever of the first twenty-seven cards in the file the sample begins with is selected by random drawing), each member of the universe has an equal chance of falling into the sample; each house then has a one-tenth chance or each card a one twenty-seventh chance of being sampled.

The convenience of a systematic sample is obvious. Think how much easier it is to take, say, the twelfth name, or the twelfth and seventeenth names, on each page of a telephone book than to take differently numbered names from various pages and to jump around from page to page, some of which would contain many sampled names and others none.

But an even greater benefit of a systematic sample is its gain in precision over a simple random-sampling process. Systematic sampling helps spread the sample evenly over the universe with respect to the dimension on which you are sampling systematically. For example, with simple random sampling the names in the phone book starting with any given letter—say "B"—will almost surely be somewhat overrepresented or underrepresented just by

chance. But with systematic sampling the number of names selected starting with "B" will be in the same proportion as "B" names are in the universe.

There is the danger in choosing a systematic sample of hitting a *cycle*, such as corner houses on the street. A corner house is usually more expensive and therefore has more affluent occupants than do other houses on the block. But in practice cycles seldom cause difficulty.

Once more, drawing two or more "interpenetrating" samples—that is, two or more systematic subsamples started at randomly chosen spots—is always superior to taking a systematic sample with a single starting place. Not only does this procedure reduce the danger of an unrepresentative start like corner houses, but it also permits quick inspection to see how much sampling error there is by simply comparing the means of the subsamples. The extra cost of this useful procedure is practically nil.

A systematic sample can also be a convenient device in carrying out the sampling technique we shall mention next, stratified sampling.

B. STRATIFIED SAMPLING

Stratified sampling is used primarily to reduce the cost of attaining a given level of accuracy in estimating the means and other parameters of populations.[4] The key idea in stratified sampling is that already-existing knowledge is used "to divide the population into groups such that the elements within each group are more alike than are the elements in the population as a whole" (Hansen et al., 1953: 40). In this way the researcher can reduce the chance of obtaining atypical samples. This idea can best be brought out with an example. Imagine that you want to estimate the average family income in a given town. On the basis of a previous survey as well as from visual observation, you are

---

4. For a very clear and simple explanation of stratified sampling, see Hansen et al. (1953: 40–48).

quite sure that the four equal-sized quarters of the town differ considerably in family income, NW (Northwest) being highest, followed by SW, SE, and NE in that order. If you take a small "unstratified" sample of only forty families, you might get fifteen families in NW, fourteen in SW, six in SE, and five in NE. That sample would probably give a mean income considerably higher than the mean that you would obtain if you included every family in the town. Or you might wind up with fifteen families in NE and a *lower* mean sample income than the average of the town as a whole. But compare this unstratified sample against a sample that is "stratified" to take ten families from each quarter. The stratified sample is likely to be closer to the "actual" mean than the unstratified sample, for it has equal numbers of families in the high- and low-income quarters. (But the stratified sample *could* be further away from the actual if the unstratified sample happened to include the lower-income families in the high-income quarters and the stratified sample happened to include an atypical bunch of families.)

To repeat, the greater accuracy of the stratified sample derives from the fact that it cannot obtain a disproportionate number of units in the high- or low-income quarters of the town. *This makes it impossible to obtain many of the more nontypical samples that might be obtained by a simple unstratified random sample.* But each family has the same chance of being picked as every other family in the stratified sample, which is the same probability as in the unstratified sample. Therefore, the stratified sample is thoroughly random. If your original information is wrong, however, and the four quarters of the town do not differ in mean income, nothing is lost by the stratification. The results will be just as good as an unstratified sample, though they will be no better if the basis of the stratification (the prior knowledge about mean incomes in each quarter of the town) is wrong.

Stratified sampling only improves the representativeness of the sample with respect to the variable on which you stratify and with respect to other variables closely associated with it. For example, if income is not closely associated with interest in music, then stratification by average income will not improve the sampling efficiency with respect to musical interest. (Income, however, is closely associated with many other social-science variables.)

In actual practice the stratification groups (the quarters of the town, in this case) are not exactly the same size, and the sample therefore takes the same *proportion* of units from each group, which means that each unit in the universe still has the same probability of being chosen. And, of course, each unit (family, in this case) within each group (quarter of town) is drawn by a random process, completing the requirements for a random sample—that each unit have the same (or known) chance of being picked for the sample.

Another use of stratified sampling is in estimating the means (or other parameters) of two or more *subgroups* within the population. Assume that you want to study the smoking habits of cigarette and pipe smokers. If you want equally accurate estimates for the two groups, you need equal numbers of cigarette smokers and pipe smokers in the sample. But, if you take a random sample of all people, you will surely get many nonsmokers, many cigarette smokers, and a few pipe smokers. For any given random-sample size, then, you would either be getting more accuracy than you needed for cigarette smokers or less accuracy than you needed for pipe smokers.

In such a situation, stratified sampling is a device that allows you to achieve more nearly equal accuracy for the different "strata" (cigarette and pipe smokers can each be considered a stratum) at the same total cost; or, put another way, stratified sampling enables you to achieve the same accuracy for the pipe smokers while decreasing the total cost.

It is fairly obvious that you should try to get approximately the same number of cigarette and pipe smokers into the sample; that is, you want to avoid spending money to obtain unnecessary cigarette smokers. For this purpose, you may *sample in different proportions* in the two strata. If you know *in advance* that there are approximately seven times as many cigarette smokers as pipe smokers, and, if you need to sample one in every 10,000 pipe smokers to get a subsample of the necessary accuracy, you must sample one in every 70,000 cigarette smokers ($7 \times 10,000 = 70,000$) to get a subsample of the same size and equal accuracy.

To carry out a program of stratified sampling, you must know something in advance about the relative proportions of pipe and cigarette smokers, of course. But it is reasonably easy to develop good estimates of those proportions with tiny pretests. And, if your estimates are off, no bias will be introduced, though the cost will be somewhat higher than with better estimates of the proportional sizes of the strata.

Sometimes it is necessary to take a 100 percent sample of some subgroups, and the samples may still be too small. For example, if you wished to find out the characteristics of *women* who smoke pipes, you might have to include in your sample every single woman who smoked a pipe.

A major difficulty with stratified sampling is identification of the people who belong in each stratum. If you are taking a sample of library books, it is easy enough to proceed through a card file taking every hundredth book in English and every fifth book in French; there is no difficulty in distinguishing the language a book is in, unless it is an esoteric language. But if you want to take a street-corner sample of every hundredth person who earns more than $10,000 and every tenth person who earns less than $10,000, it is not so easy to pick out people in the right proportions. And, indeed, your sample can be badly biased if you fail to include many well-dressed people who earn less than $10,000 in your sample. More rigorous identification procedures are obviously necessary. For this reason, samples are often stratified in terms of characteristics which are both obvious and believed to be important,

such as race, sex, or location of residence. Sometimes screening is used to identify people who belong in each stratum.

Remember that a stratified sample is a randomly drawn sample, even though all people do *not* have the same chance of falling into the sample, because the full definition of a randomly chosen sample is that each member *either* has an equal chance of falling into the sample *or* it is *known* what chance each member has of falling into the sample, so that the unequal chance can be allowed for. As long as it is known that individual pipe smokers have seven times as great a chance of falling into the sample as did cigarette smokers, we can make appropriate allowances. Bias enters only when various members have an *unknown* chance of falling into the sample, or no chance at all. No adjustment is necessary as long as you make separate estimates for the separate strata. If you are estimating the characteristic in the *universe as a whole*, however, *you cannot simply add together all your observations*. Instead, you must weight the different strata in the proportions in which they occur in the universe. This is *crucial;* to fail to weight stratified samples is to commit an elementary but not uncommon blunder. In the example given, to estimate the smoking habits of the population as a whole, you must weight the evidence of each cigarette smoker in your sample seven times as heavily as that of each pipe smoker in your sample, because of your stratifying plan, which gave each pipe smoker a seven-times better chance of getting into your sample.

C. CLUSTER SAMPLING

Cluster sampling is another device to collect more information at lower cost. It works by decreasing the transportation time and costs of interviewers. Assume that you are making a survey to determine the number of people of each religion in a community. You obviously get *less information* by questioning five members of the same family than if you question five members of *different* families. All five members of the same family are likely to have the same religious affiliation, and therefore you know very little more after asking all five than after asking only one and multiplying his answer by five. Of course, you might find *some* differences within families, but you would be spending a lot of interviewing time to find them. *But* it is much *quicker and cheaper* to ask a question about religious affiliation of five people in one house than to go to five separate houses and ask five separate people.

Cluster sampling is a technique that takes advantage of the *decrease in cost per interview* that comes from collecting data on several subjects in the *same physical location*, compared to the cost of traveling from place to place and collecting data on one subject in each place. If the decrease in cost per interview is to result in a real gain, however, there must not be an excessive decrease in the information produced per subject, as there is, for example, when members of the same family are asked about religious affiliation.

The trick is to work out a sampling system in which you can collect considerable data in each collection area but in which there is little homogeneity (large heterogeneity) among the subjects in each area. For example, there will be less similarity in answers about religious affiliation if you ask five people standing in a grocery-store line than if you ask five people in the same house. There will be greater similarity in the answers from the five people in the grocery line, however, than there would be for five people chosen completely randomly from the community at large, because people from the same neighborhood shop at the same grocery store, and people in the same neighborhood have a tendency toward similar religious affiliations. A cluster-sampling design that samples ten people at random in each of fifty randomly chosen towns (500 interviewees) might give higher accuracy at lower cost than sampling one person at random in each of 200 randomly chosen towns (200 interviewees).

Keep in mind that there is no gain in using a cluster-sampling design unless your subjects are originally spread over a wide geographic area, requiring high costs in transportation and time for interviewers.

The purpose of the foregoing discussions of stratified and cluster sampling is to teach you the basic ideas of these sampling strategies, but they do not tell you much about the *mechanics* of the strategies. If you undertake a large-scale study that might benefit from the use of either technique, call upon a sampling expert for help.

Cluster sampling yields the sometimes useful side benefit of enabling you to make estimates for the units from which the clusters have been drawn. For example, Kagan, Cartwright, Friedman, and Wheeler (1978) wanted to investigate how economic change, politics, and other factors have affected legal change, as manifested in the actions of state supreme courts. They could have drawn a random sample of cases decided by the supreme courts of all fifty states. Instead, they divided the states into five clusters and selected states within clusters, for a total of only sixteen states. As a result, they could analyze more cases from each state, enough so that they could draw conclusions about particular types of states as well as about the United States as a whole.

D. SEQUENTIAL SAMPLING

Sequential sampling is another device to reduce sampling costs. Like stratified sampling, it seeks to avoid gathering data that are unnecessary for the level of accuracy you want. Sequential sampling works by *examining the evidence as it comes in* and stopping data collection when enough data are in.

There is no point in examining a sample of 1,000 if a sample of 100 will provide the necessary accuracy. But often it is not possible to guess in advance whether a sample of approximately 100 or 1,000 will be necessary because of lack of knowledge of what the data will be like. Sequential sampling is a device for overcoming this difficulty.

For example, assume that you are the president of a neighborhood political organization and that you want to know whether a majority of your group will approve a gift to you of a golden gavel. You might start down the membership list, call your members on the phone, and ask their opinions. If the first ten members split five and five in their reactions, you may wisely decide that you will have to take a complete poll. But if the first ten people you call are all against it, you can easily decide that a majority of the members is against it and stop your calling right then (provided, of course, that the first ten people were a random sample of your membership and that the name list was not biased!). This is an example of sequential sampling.

Sequential sampling allows you to make a fresh decision from time to time about whether you have collected enough data or need to collect more data. This technique can save you from taking a much bigger sample than you really need. There is further discussion of sequential sampling in Chapter 34.[5]

More generally, doing a series of small studies rather than one huge study allows you to learn from your mistakes and to improve your methods.

E. SCREENING IN SAMPLING

Some studies require a sample of personal interviews with relatively rare individuals—people that have been to Africa, or blind people, or sociologists, or families with four sons. Sending interviewers to a random sample of all homes would be expensive and wasteful because no interview can be obtained in most visits.

You may sometimes circumvent this difficulty by obtaining a list of the rare persons, say, the list of members of the American Sociological Association. But there is no list of families with four sons. In such a case, you may do a screening sample by telephone or mail, asking whether that family has four sons, or a blind person, or whatever. The positive answers then constitute a sampling frame for the personal interview.

If screening is impossible, a relatively large sample is necessary. If you are interested in the amounts of inheritances passed from one generation to another, a few relatively rare big inheritances make a big difference in the total. A small sample will yield very unreliable, unstable results because of the low probability of getting a big inheritance in any one small sample. Another example: If you are interested in discovering what sort of people are likely to have heart attacks as they grow older and want to interview the same people repeatedly over a period of years, you obviously cannot screen people in advance. For cases such as these, when you are interested in relatively rare events but have no lists of the people involved and cannot screen, a large sample is necessary. Small or even medium-sized samples will yield unreliable results because of the low probability of finding a meaningful number of rare individuals in a given sample.

4. Nonrandom Samples

If you want to measure some characteristic of an entire population, you must not ignore *any part* of the population. You must make sure to count in all types of people, in the same proportions[6] in which they constitute the population. This is most obvious in political polling. To sample only in the East, say, or only among men or among Protestants would be *erroneous*.

Only a random-sampling process can guarantee you that the sample *approaches* a fair picture of some characteristic of the universe, though how closely depends on the size of the sample, and any *given* sample might be very odd. Despite this very desirable property of random (probability) samples, a wise scientist does not always decide to take a probability

5. Some caution is required in fixing the sample size by proceeding in several steps. In some cases there may be danger of bias. See Hansen et al. (1953: 79).

6. Or unequal but *known* proportions.

sample. The practical conditions may be such that you cannot obtain a randomly drawn sample at reasonable cost or even at all. Or there may be no need for a probability sample. Let us take the former case first.

As an example in which a nonrandom sample may be better because of cost, consider the case in which we want to find out whether or not people remember the past as happier than the present. A probability sample of the entire United States or world is too expensive. But the cheapest and most convenient sample—college students—might yield a very misleading answer; it might well be true that the felt relationship between adulthood and earlier years is different from, say, the relationship between middle age and the previous periods.

One way to handle this problem is to obtain as many different kinds of easy-to-obtain samples as possible: a parent-teacher association, a retirement club, an immigrant ethnic organization, a minor-league baseball team, a local plasterers' union, a group of waitresses at a restaurant, and so on. If in *each* of these groups people say that they were happier in prior years than at present, an excellent generalization is that people remember the past as happier than the present. The key to effective use of this strategy is to obtain as *varied* a collection of groups (or individuals) in your sample as possible.

Such a collection of diverse groups might be very cheap to obtain for group interviewing. A very much larger sample can be obtained, compared to a probability sample, in which group-administered questionnaires cannot be given.

Durkheim, in his famous study of the causes of suicide, used the device of replicating a study in order to strengthen his proof:

> . . . [T]he original finding is re-examined in different groups of subjects—for example, the excess of military over civilian suicides is confirmed for eight different countries of Europe. Durkheim further replicates this finding within the Austro-Hungarian Empire; the military-civilian difference persists in the various military areas. (Selvin, 1965: 122)

The people studied in social psychology experiments are rarely random samples of a population, but instead are usually college students, who are very different from the bulk of the population in age, educational level, and other characteristics. To get around this, social psychologists often try to repeat their studies with many different kinds of groups. When Milgram studied obedience, for example, he found that his subjects were willing to punish a person who did poorly on a test if the experimenter told them to; a high proportion of the time, they were even willing to cause the test-takers considerable physical pain by giving them electric shocks. (The shocks were not real, but the subjects thought they were.) At first, skeptics doubted that the findings described people at large, but rather only students at Yale College. Milgram therefore repeated the experiment again and again, studying the behavior of professionals, white-collar workers, factory workers, unemployed persons, and others. Eventually, the studies were replicated in other parts of the United States and other countries. The fact that the results were similar in all the experiments helped convince people that they were valid, even though none of the individual samples was random (Milgram, 1974: 170–171).

The matched sample is another example of the use of nonrandom groups. In comparison studies, the researcher prefers to compare two or more groups of subjects that are randomly drawn from the same sampling frame and then treated differently in the experiment. But sometimes it is not possible to make up groups of randomly selected subjects. A political candidate, for example, cannot set up groups of random subjects drawn from the same population on which to test two different political platforms. She may therefore find two cities that are very similar and compare the results in one city with those in the other.

The danger that bias will distort results of a

matched-group experiment is very great, however. In one view, "The value of [matching] has been greatly oversold and it is more often a source of mistaken inference than a help to valid inference" (Campbell and Stanley, 1963: 6). Geographical differences are a frequent obstacle. But worst is the distortion that arises when the independent and dependent variables are confounded, as we shall see in Chapter 22 when we compare people who went to Harvard Business School with people who *seem* equal in all respects except that they did not go to Harvard Business School.

Another situation in which random sampling is not necessarily best is that in which almost any group of individuals can be regarded as a sufficiently fair sample of the population with respect to the characteristics under study.

Though people who live in different places differ in many ways, not every piece of research must take a countrywide or worldwide probability sample. This is most likely to happen when you are studying characteristics that have a biological basis or a strong psychophysical component. In such experiments the researcher hopes to find characteristics that apply to *all* people, and therefore it makes no difference which specific people are studied. Thus, for example, scientists who want to discover how people think and solve problems, so that they can improve the problem-solving capacities of computers, sometimes use very few subjects.

Lazarsfeld and his associates made a similar argument for their choice of Erie County, Pennsylvania, as the place in which to conduct their election study:

Erie County in 1940 was small, reasonably prosperous, peopled with a homogeneous, friendly group of native Americans engaged about equally in agricultural and industrial work . . . it was not the "typical American county" but for the purposes of this study it did not need to be. We were not interested in *how* people voted but in *why* they voted as they did. We did not want to predict the outcome of the election but to dis-

cover certain processes underlying opinion formation and political behavior. (Lazarsfeld et al., 1948: 10)

For similar reasons, as shown in Table 9.1, Peoria, Illinois, has been the site of a great many marketing experiments with new products. But be very careful when you dismiss the possibility of geographical differences. Geography can show up as an important variable even in many biological investigations: In the study of smoking and lung cancer, for example, one might have to consider that the extent of pollution varies from place to place and that such variation might affect lung cancer rates.

Extreme caution and good judgment are necessary in any nonrandom sampling. For example, it may even matter whether auditory or visual experiments are run on individuals of one particular age group. Even when investigating "universal" phenomena, the researcher should try to take at least a part of the sample from individuals who vary in age, residence, and so forth, as a check that the phenomenon is indeed universal.

Quota sampling is a very important nonrandom sampling method. It may come as a surprise to you that almost all election polls (for instance, those of Gallup) and most other nationwide opinion polls use quota samples, rather than samples chosen on a probability basis. Quota sampling has a superficial resemblance to stratified random sampling. The stratification example given in our discussion would be a quota sample if the town were again divided into the four quarters and one interviewer were sent to each with instructions to interview ten "typical" families about whether they expected to buy a car this year or to vote Democratic. The crucial difference between stratified and quota samples, however, is that the "typical" families chosen by the interviewer for the latter are not likely to be chosen at random; he may avoid homes where there are ferocious-looking dogs, for example. Each family in the universe thus does *not* have the same chance of being chosen, and

TABLE 9.1　Profile of a Test Market—Peoria, Illinois, 1971

	Metro. Peoria	Total U.S.A.
Population:		
Male	49.2%	49.2%
Female	50.8%	50.8%
Children under 18 yrs. of age	35.5%	35.8%
Age Brackets:		
Under 5 years	11.5%	11.3%
5–19 yrs.	26.6%	27.2%
20–34 yrs.	19.1%	18.7%
35–44 yrs.	13.1%	13.4%
45–64 yrs.	20.4%	20.1%
65 & over	9.3%	9.3%
Employment:		
Employed males	53.1%	49.2%
Employed females	21.8%	23.2%
Unemployed males	46.9%	50.8%
Unemployed females	78.2%	76.8%
By occupation:		
Business & professional	9.6%	11.2%
Salaried & semiprofessional	7.8%	8.4%
Skilled	63.7%	59.6%
Unskilled	18.9%	20.8%
Median family income	$5,998	$5,660
Median school years		
(males, 25 yrs. & over)	10.2 yrs.	10.6 yrs.
Median age (total population)	29.4 yrs.	30.3 yrs.

SOURCE: *Advertising Age,* November 1, 1971, p. 147.

therefore the researcher cannot use statistical theory to estimate the accuracy of his results, as he can with a random sample.

The quotas are likely to be specified very closely, unlike the strata in stratified sampling. The interviewers are instructed to obtain interviews with fixed numbers of people in each of such categories as age group, color, income bracket, and religion; the proportions for each category are chosen to mirror the proportions in the population at large. Quotas must also be specified for working women, and for interviews done on the weekends and in the evening; unless special attention is given to these hard-to-obtain interviews, serious bias may re-

sult. The idea is that, if all the subgroups are given the appropriate amount of representation, the overall sample should then correctly represent the universe. And so it would be if the interviewers managed to choose people *within* each subgroup in a fairly random manner and the survey managed to sample each group in proportion to its actual size. But the survey may obtain too large or too small a proportion of people with little education, for example.

Quota samples are usually cheaper than are random samples of the same size. Some of them yield results of excellent accuracy, but poor construction has led to very inaccurate results in some cases. The excellence of the quota sample depends almost entirely on the skill of the researcher.[7]

Snowball sampling is a method used when members of a universe cannot easily be located by random sampling or by screening, and where the members of a universe know other members of the universe. Each member of the universe who is located is asked for names and addresses of other members. The snowball method has been used, for example, to create a sample of drug users, and to study friendship groups and elites. But the method does not work with blind persons, because they have a low propensity to know each other.

An important bias in snowball sampling is that the more others who know a given person as, for example, a drug user, the more likely the person is to be found in the sample. And drug users who are known as such to many other people may be quite atypical of drug users. (For more information see Sudman, 1976, pp. 210–211; Biernacki and Waldorf, 1981).

5. Summary

A sample is a device used to learn about a universe (population) without the expense of studying each member of the universe. A sample is well-chosen if it accurately describes what it seeks to describe, with reasonable efficiency.

Samples can be chosen by random selection or with human judgments. Random selection can depend on the support of probability theory to establish its likely accuracy whereas judgmental sampling cannot, but sometimes judgmental sampling's other advantages outweigh this.

Simple random sampling requires a list of the elements of the universe. Selection of the list—the sampling frame—can be a delicate matter requiring good judgment. From this list a selection is taken with some mechanical technique that seems random; choosing numbers from a table of random numbers is simple and sure if it is feasible, and if a nearly complete list of the universe is available.

Systematic sampling selects every nth element in an ordering of the elements of the universe. It may be easier to execute and can be statistically more efficient than a simple random sample. Its only drawback is the possibility that there may be some cycle in the data that systematically affects the nth element, but this danger is usually easy to avoid.

Stratified sampling can improve sampling efficiency by explicitly taking subsamples of fixed size within the important different sections of the universe, proportional to their representation in the universe. This improves the representativeness of a sample of any given size.

Cluster sampling takes several observations in each geographic area. This saves time and money. But each single observation in cluster sampling provides less information than in random sampling. On balance, cluster sampling may or may not be efficient, depending on the distance and time required to travel from one observation to the next.

In *sequential sampling* you continue taking observations until you have achieved the necessary accuracy. This method is in contrast with the procedure of fixing the sample size in advance. Sequential sampling is always preferable when it is feasible, but sometimes it is not practical.

Nonrandom samples cannot guarantee the likelihood of any given level of accuracy, as can randomly drawn samples. But sometimes samples cannot be drawn randomly, either because one cannot run a controlled experiment on humans, or because a randomly drawn sample is too expensive. A matched-group sample may

7. For empirical studies of the accuracy of quota samples, see Stephan and McCarthy (1963: Chaps. 7, 8). For detailed analysis of quota sampling in voting polls, see Mosteller et al.

be appropriate, but there is always the danger that the matched groups are not similar in some important respect. And a representative-group sample may not really be representative of the universe. Quota sampling is an important technique in public-opinion sampling, but requires remarkable judgment and great experience to carry out well.

EXERCISES

1. The public broadcasting system station in Champaign-Urbana takes a survey of the contributors to the station to determine their listening preferences. How might this choice of sampling frame influence the choice of programming? How might this choice of sampling frame influence the musical offerings available to people who like classical music, including both contributors and noncontributors?

2. How would you estimate how many people in the United States, in which categories, are not counted by regular census interviewers?

3. The Internal Revenue Service cannot afford to audit the tax return of every taxpayer, so it audits a sample of returns. If the IRS wanted to get a maximum amount of extra taxes from every return audited, how would you design a sample for the IRS?

4. Recent well-known studies of American sexual behavior, such as The Hite Report (1976) and The Cosmo Report (Wolfe, 1981), are based on data from questionnaires sent in by people who find them included in magazines, such as *Cosmopolitan* or *Penthouse*. What is the sampling frame for such studies? Of which group are the returned questionnaires representative? Could the books be said to describe the sexual behavior of American men and women in general?

5. Suppose you want to study the impact of serious illness on people's careers, and are especially interested in finding out whether illness affects blacks differently from whites. Describe at least two different ways to design an appropriate sample.

6. Assume you prepared a list of a sample of people in a midwestern city of 80,000 people, which you considered an excellent random sample of the population, and that you interviewed the people on the list about their voting intentions in a coming election. Several months later another researcher wants to do a market-research study on the entire population of the town. Can he use your old list? Is it or is it not a random sample?

7. Varsity football players at state universities receive lower grades than does the average student. Is this fact a good indication that high athletic ability goes with low scholastic ability in American boys?

8. To show how difficult it is to achieve randomness, have each person in the class pick a number between 0 and 9, and write it down. Then do it again, and a third time, and several more. What patterns do you see? Might they indicate a departure from randomness? (But beware of finding false patterns; see Chapter 33).

9. How would you compile a random sample of students of Chinese extraction at a university that keeps no records of ethnic background?

10. Specify a purpose for which the telephone book is *not* a good sampling frame.

11. Give an example in which stratified sampling would be a relatively inexpensive way to attain a given level of accuracy. Is there any case in which stratified sampling would be *more* expensive?

12. Show how an estimate can be unbiased, even though sampling units have different chances of getting into the sample. (Hint: Remember that probabilities can be *known* even if they are *different*.)

13. Give an example in which cluster sampling provides more accuracy for a given cost than does simple random sampling.
14. Give an example in which sequential sampling is feasible and helpful.
15. Give an example in which matching samples is an appropriate sampling technique.

ADDITIONAL READING

There are many good readings on sampling. Williams (1978) provides an excellent non-technical introduction, including a step-by-step guide to designing your own survey. For practical guidance in all aspects of sampling, see Sudman (1976). Hansen et al. (1953) give an excellent general discussion, with their Chapter 1 providing a remarkably clear exposition of the relationship between sample size and accuracy. Stephan and McCarthy (1963, Chap. 1–11) offer an easily readable classic treatment, especially about sampling of attitudes for public opinion surveys. A good description of the sampling process in market research may be found in Chapters 9 and 10 of Boyd, Westfall, and Stasch (1977). On the Bayesian and information-value approach to sampling, see Green and Tull (1975, Chap. 7).

About the sampling frame, see Deming (1960, Chap. 3). This book also contains excellent discussion on the theory of sampling and of other topics in sampling. The examples are drawn largely from business, but because of their emphasis on the value of information and the cost of error, they are very instructive to people in other areas as well. Above all, this is a practical book.

Groves and Kahn (1979) provide a comprehensive guide to the mechanics, costs, and benefits of interviewing by phone.

Kish (1965) is probably the classic complete treatment of sampling, both simple and complex, especially sampling for surveys.

Kruskal and Mosteller (1981) provide many examples of how *not* to do sampling.

Abramson (1983, Chap. 2) presents an interesting short history of survey research and a discussion of the advantages and disadvantages of different types of sampling.

Experiments: Pro, Con, and How to Do Them

1. The Distinction Between Experiment and Survey

An experiment and a survey are alternative methods of getting knowledge about the relationships between (or among) variables, most especially about the *causal* relationships between variables.

The crux of the *experiment* is that the investigator *intentionally manipulates* one or more of the independent variables (x_1, x_2 . . .), thus exposing various groups of subjects to the different variables (or to different amounts of the independent variables), and then observes the changes in the dependent variables (y_1, y_2 . . .). Members of experimental groups are usually selected randomly, which further ensures that observed differences among groups really reflect differences in the independent variables. The ideal design was discussed on pages 30–32.

A *survey* gathers data about variables *as they are found in the world*. The survey can *observe behavior*, as for example whether people are athletes, whether they smoke, whether the money supply is high in some years, and whether there is prosperity in those years. The survey can also collect data on what people *say;* for example, researchers can ask people of various backgrounds for whom they will vote or how much liquor they drink. The important distinction between the survey and the experiment is that the survey takes the world as it comes, without trying to alter it, whereas the experiment systematically alters some aspects of the world in order to see what changes follow. For example, a mother might want to learn which food causes her baby's rash. She might keep a diary of what foods the baby eats each day and whether he has a rash that day and the next day; that would be nonexperimental observation. Or she could systematically vary the foods that she gives the baby each day, trying first one food alone and then another food alone, noting the days on which the rash occurs; that would be an experiment.

This chapter is about research into relationships and focuses on experiments; it is therefore not concerned with description, measurement, or classification research, all of which must usually be done with the survey method. For example, you cannot find out how many people there are in the United States through a laboratory experiment; you must go out and count them. You cannot determine how many people will vote Republican in the next election with any laboratory procedures, nor can you use experimentation; you must take a poll.[1]

The first purpose of this and the following chapters is to teach you what you need to know about methods in order to choose the appropriate method for a given situation. Details of execution of each method are given only secondary treatment; references are supplied to technical works on each method.

In those situations in which it is possible to experiment with the real-life variables *within the actual real-life situations* in which you are interested, the experiment is *always* a more desirable means of investigating relationships than the survey. The real-life experiment is more desirable because it permits much more certain inference of a causal connection between two variables than does a survey. For example, it may be possible to observe from a survey that, when government spending is high, gross national product is high too. But the relationship might be obscured by a hidden third factor, perhaps the quantity of money in circulation, and gross national product might be unrelated to government spending except through the same other variable. You would have much stronger grounds for belief in their causal connection if you could (randomly) manipulate government spending to be low or high in various years and then see whether GNP is also low or high in corresponding years. Only then would you know that it is government spending that affects

GNP; the randomness of the decision that government spending be high or low in any given year would preclude some other variable from being the cause of both spending and GNP being high and low together; only *you the experimenter* would then be responsible for variations in spending and not some other variable.

For another example, without an experiment we must always recognize a possibility, though not necessarily a high probability (J. Simon, 1966c), that some constitutional (genetic) factor predisposes smokers both to become smokers *and* to die of cancer, heart disease, and other "smoking-caused" diseases. An experiment could reduce the probability by having a random sample of people become smokers or nonsmokers so that (with a big enough sample) there would be no possible relationship between any special genetic factor and both smoking and cancer; *you* would be the only cause of their starting to smoke.

One cannot ethically conduct such experiments on smoking, and it is seldom feasible to experiment with government spending. But in many real-life situations experimentation is quite possible. For example, if you want to find out which of two methods of teaching reading to first-grade children is better, you can set up a controlled experiment in the real-life situation by trying the two different systems in randomly selected classrooms. It is a real-life experiment because the methods are tried out under *exactly the same conditions* in which they would actually be put to work. (Remember, however, that even an apparently real-life experiment can be fouled up. For example, a group of students who know that they are being taught by an experimental system might learn faster for just that reason.)

But wait a minute: Be slow to conclude that an experiment is impossible. For years economists and sociologists have been interested in the effect of taxes on work and family behavior. They were sure that it was impossible to conduct an experiment in which some people's tax

1. Stouffer (1950) offers a useful schema of the differences between experiments and nonexperimental studies.

rates were different from others'. Then some brash soul decided to press for an experiment anyway. The result was the famous and invaluable set of negative-income-tax experiments of the 1960s and 1970s, where randomly selected people were given large income supplements, and their work and family behavior was then observed. The findings that the income supplements did *not* have a very negative effect on how much people work but *did* seem to increase the divorce rate in families getting the money had a major impact on congressional debates on welfare policy (Hannan, Tuma, and Groeneveld, 1978).

Similarly, two advertising campaigns can sometimes be studied in a real-life experiment by beaming them to different cities. Medicines are also always tested in real-life experiments before they are released for general use, but only after non–real-life experiments indicate that the real-life experiments probably will not be dangerous.

Whenever real-life experiments are feasible, they are preferable to survey methods. (By "feasible" we mean ethically, physically, and financially possible.) The principle of experimenting when possible seems obvious in the late twentieth century. But until perhaps a hundred or two hundred years ago, it just did not occur to people to learn about the world by running scientific experiments, that is, by systematically altering some aspects of the world and then observing other aspects to see how they were affected. And, in most parts of the world today, among those people who have not had modern educations, the idea of experimentation is still mostly unknown. Of course, people have always learned about good cooking by informal experiments with various recipes. But, when it came to learning how the world ticks, scholars just did not consider trying to gain knowledge by experimentation or, more generally, by any empirical methods. Many people thought Galileo was rather radical when he proposed actually going up to the top of a tall building and dropping objects of different weights to find out whether heavy objects fall faster than light ones, rather than just sitting around and talking about it.

Though a real-life experiment is preferable when feasible, sometimes it is impossible to experiment. Then the investigator must choose between two alternatives: observation of the real-life situation as it unfolds, that is, taking a survey and trying to assess the relationships among the variables, despite the obstacles to doing so; or experimentation with a laboratory imitation of the real-life situation, that is, testing the effects of smoking on rats instead of on humans or subjecting models instead of real buildings to earthquakes. In order to make this choice wisely, you must understand the strengths and weaknesses, advantages and disadvantages of the two methods.

2. The Steps in Experimenting

The beginner always wants a checklist of the steps he or she should take. You want to know what to do first, what to do second, and so on. Often it is dangerous to satisfy this request, because you may come to think that there really is some "correct" order of procedure; the danger is that you may forget that the procedure for each piece of research must be tailored especially to that research situation—that is, that the procedure should depend on what you want to know, what you already know, and what kind of researcher you are. If you keep in mind, however, that the following checklist is not rigid but is rather a suggested procedure that often fits what people do in experimental work, then it may be safe to put this checklist in your hands.

Let us assume that you have already worked your way through the general steps described in Chapter 7 and that you have arrived at the point of deciding that an experiment will be more effective and appropriate than a survey in providing the knowledge you want. (But, before you make that decision final, read pages

133–136 on the advantages and disadvantages of experiments and surveys.)

STEP 1: CHOOSE APPROPRIATE VARIABLES

Decide which observable variables will represent the "real" (hypothetical or theoretical) variables in which you are interested. For example, a gymnasium-test score may stand for (be a proxy for) physical fitness as a dependent variable; you are then saying that a score on the gymnasium test is a good measurement of what you mean when you talk about physical fitness in an experiment on fitness-training methods. Or some paragraphs in a foreign language that students read and then are quizzed about may be your measurement of reading comprehension in the language and serve as a dependent variable in an experiment on teaching foreign languages to students. Or, if you want to experiment with how people behave in risk situations, you might give them tiny sums of money and observe how they bet them in a laboratory game. The small sums of money stand for larger sums of money, and the laboratory betting stands for betting behavior in real-life situations.

Variables must have two properties: First, they must be measurable. Physical fitness *per se* is not measurable because it is not operationally defined. You define it operationally by letting something else that is measurable—a gym test, for instance—stand for it. Note that setting up an operational definition really is a matter of letting a measurable empirical magnitude stand for the hypothetical variable in which you are interested. Second, your proxy variable must be a *good* proxy, a "valid indicator"; that is, it must have a reasonable and sensible relationship to your hypothetical variable. Height would not be a good proxy for physical fitness, we think you will agree. Selecting appropriate measurable variables is very difficult indeed, and doing a good job of it demands clear thinking and imagination. We discussed the matter in Chapter 6. As has already been noted, it is often wise to observe the effects of several variables in a single experiment.

Deciding *how many* variables with which to experiment is also an important decision. The number of possible variables is limitless, but your time and funds are very much limited. Furthermore, for technical reasons difficult to explain here, there must be more subjects in the experiment than there are variables, preferably lots more, lest the results turn out to be meaningless.[2] Therefore, you must set up priorities among the variables, so that you can vary the most important of them experimentally and hold the others constant. The general logic of the cost and value of research, as described in Chapter 8, should be your guide.

STEP 2: CHOOSE TREATMENT LEVELS

Choose appropriate *levels* at which to test the independent variables. Often the choice is based on plain good sense and is forced by the situation. For example, if a school psychologist wants to see whether longer or shorter reading periods will result in quicker reading advancement, the school will not compare five-hour and five-minute periods with the present sixty-minute periods; rather, the psychologist will choose levels of perhaps thirty minutes and ninety minutes to compare with the present sixty-minute period. The first principle, then, is to vary the stimuli at such levels as are of *practical interest* in the real-life situation. This point is illustrated in Mauldin's cartoon about marijuana research (Figure 10.1). Often one of the levels will be a *control group*, which receives the standard treatment or no treatment at all. The control group provides a base

2. This point is very difficult to explain in simple terms. An analogy may help. No *one* number can establish the location of a point on a flat piece of paper; both length and width measurements are required. In a box, which has three dimensions—length, width, and height—*three* measurements are necessary. And, if you can imagine a four-dimensional space or an *n*-dimensional space, it would require four or *n* measurements respectively to establish the location of a single point.

FIGURE 10.1

Source: From *The Champaign/Urbana Gazette*, August 10, 1976. Reprinted by permission.

against which to measure the experimental groups.

The second principle is to vary the stimuli in big enough jumps so that you obtain measurable results. The psychologist will not compare sixty-one-minute and fifty-nine-minute reading periods with the present sixty-minute period, for no observable difference is likely to result. Similarly, if General Motors wants to experiment with a price decrease, it will not simply decrease the price of each car a dollar. An example related to this second principle comes from a survey rather than an experiment, a survey of the effects of strategic bombing on German morale in World War II. The first comparison, between groups of people exposed to 6,000 tons and 30,000 tons of bombs dropped, respectively, showed *no difference* in the morale of the two groups. This peculiarity was explained when a group exposed to only 500 pounds of bombs showed higher morale (Hyman, 1955: 184–185).

A third principle in choosing levels of independent variables is to choose *enough* levels of variation so that you will not be fooled by a curvilinear relationship. For example, reading advancement might be related to length of reading period in the fashion shown in Figure 10.2. If you experiment only with levels A and E, you will never find out that the best level is C. Therefore, it pays to experiment at several levels that are quite spread out—like A, B, C, D, and E in the figure. The cost of running treatments constrains you from running experiments at a very large number of levels, however.

STEP 3: DETERMINE SAMPLE SIZE

Decide what to do about sample size. Almost always you should begin by taking a small pretest sample that will give you some intuitive feeling for how big a sample you will need and that will also provide necessary data for the estimates of sample size described in Chapter 34. And, whenever possible, plan to take your sample on a sequential basis, gradually increasing the sample until it is large enough, rather than making a firm decision before you begin (Chapter 9). This sequential procedure is impossible in many types of research situations, however.

STEP 4: CHOOSE A SAMPLE

Select a sample of subjects for your experiment. The sample should be appropriately unbiased, and it should be drawn from a universe that is a reasonable and sensible representation of the universe in which you are interested.

STEP 5: CONTROL THE EXPERIMENTAL CONDITIONS

Plan the details of the experiment so that the *conditions* are correct. In every experiment there are many factors that can influence the outcome but that you do not want to vary experimentally; they are the *parameters*. You must arrange them to suit your purposes and so that they remain constant during the experiment. For example, if you are conducting psychophysical experiments on how hearing is affected by motivation, you will want your experimental room to be soundproof. Absolute quiet is one of the parameters of the experiment. Not only must you arrange for a soundproof room, but you must also make sure that, during your experiment, the building will not

FIGURE 10.2   Length of Training Periods

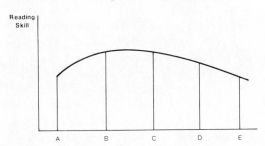

be remodeled with jackhammers and other heavy machinery whose noise will penetrate the soundproofing. Pavlov went to great lengths to create experimental conditions that would not disturb the conditioning process in his dogs.

Those conditions that cannot be held *physically* constant must be made to meet the test of *ceteris paribus* in other ways. Gamson, Fireman, and Rytina (1982) wanted to find out how small groups would respond to an unethical request. To hold conditions constant for every group, the experimenters followed a detailed script that gave the same instructions in the same way to each group. They even tried to be sure that the experimenter, after giving his instructions to the group, left the room equally quickly every time. Some experimenters even gave instructions to subjects in a short movie rather than in person so that the instructions would be presented in exactly the same way every time. Holding conditions constant is nothing but common sense, of course, but such matters are not always so obvious, and violation of *ceteris paribus* conditions causes many experiments to fail.

STEP 6: DIVIDE SUBJECTS INTO GROUPS

Divide the subjects into one or more experimental groups and (usually) a control group. The number of experimental groups depends upon how many different stimuli you want to test or on how many different levels of the independent variable you want to test. Whenever possible, divide subjects into the two groups *randomly;* this is your basic guarantee that the results of the experiment will mean something. Sometimes, however, it is not possible to make up randomized groups. For example, if you are test-marketing an advertising campaign and can afford to test the campaign in only four cities, you would probably arrange the cities so that you considered the groups *well matched.* Matching can be very treacherous, however, because you may set up the

groups in some way that merely seems convenient to you but that may really bear a relationship to the variables and may thus confound the experiment.

STEP 7: PLAN THE "EXPERIMENTAL DESIGN"

We have placed "experimental design" in quotation marks to indicate that the term has a special meaning in experimentation, apart from the basic plan of the experiment. The phrase refers to the *statistical* scheme by which the variables are related to one another, and the scheme is chosen in such a way as to obtain the greatest validity and efficiency from the experiment. For example, there are many designs in which you vary more than one variable at a time. (See Chapter 11; it is not true that in an experiment you can safely vary only one variable at a time.) Various experimental designs are discussed at length in Chapter 11.

STEP 8: PRETEST AND REVISE

Conduct a pretest, and then revise your procedure in light of what you learn from the pretest. Run another pretest. Revise again. And so on until your experimental procedure is pat and airtight. Then run the actual experiment.

The pretest period is a particularly good time to discuss your work with your fellow students and staff members. Advice you receive now, while you still have time to change your plans, is more valuable than advice received later, when it may be too late. Show them a brief write-up of what you are doing and of your preliminary results. You may be reluctant to show your work to others, out of embarrassment, from a reluctance to bother them, or from worry that you will look bad if they see your errors. Many people will be glad to help, though, and will understand that you are showing them a preliminary product rather than final results. They may be pleased that you consider their advice worth asking for. You should recognize that they are doing you one of the greatest favors possible when they give you the benefit of their attention, experience, and critical imagination.

STEP 9: ANALYZE THE DATA

Analyze and interpret your data and draw appropriate conclusions from the data, perhaps with the aid of statistics (Chapters 24–28 and 30–33). This stage is not as large a part of the whole job in an experiment as it is in a survey, because much of your analysis is really built into the experiment as you set it up.

3. Advantages of Experiments

A. ESTABLISHING DIRECTION OF CAUSALITY

The most important advantage of the experiment is that the relationship that you *actually observe* is clear in its causal direction. ("Actually observe" is italicized to emphasize that, if your variables are not good proxies for the hypothetical variables in which you are really interested, the experiment will not be meaningful.) In an experiment it is you, the experimenter, who manipulates the independent variables. If you observe variations in the dependent variable, they must therefore be caused by the variations in the independent variable and not by some other force that is affecting both the independent and dependent variables at the same time. This property of the experiment makes it possible to talk confidently about one aspect of causation. (But your independent variable may not be what you think it is, which may fool you about what is causing the change in the dependent variable.)

B. COST

The absolute cost of a laboratory experiment can often be low compared to that of alternative research methods. For example, an adver-

tiser can pretest the effects of two advertising campaigns in a laboratory situation with a very few people, whereas a field experiment or survey would require the advertiser to carry out actual advertising campaigns in expensive field tests. For another example, an engineer can make a structural analysis of a building's strength by constructing two-foot models in the laboratory, instead of constructing real buildings experimentally or making exhaustive studies of actual buildings that collapse.

C. CONVENIENCE

An experiment can be run whenever you like, to suit your convenience. If you are going to create a mock riot experimentally, you can pick your time and place so that you will have observers and equipment ready to observe the results. Real riots happen at unexpected times and in unexpected places, which is one reason we know so little about riots.

D. ADJUSTABILITY OF VARIABLES AND PARAMETERS

Unlike a survey, an experiment permits you to arrange the parameters and vary the variables in whatever fashion you desire, to look for whatever effects interest you. If you are studying the causes of riots, you can vary the temperature in the place where the riot will occur to see whether people respond more vigorously when it is hot. In real riots, however, you must take the temperature as it comes.

In an experimental study of families, Reiss (1981) was able to control how much family members could communicate with each other while trying to solve problems—sorting cards and doing puzzles—he gave them. He was therefore able to show that a family's communication patterns strongly affect its problem-solving capacity.

An experiment often allows you to investigate extremes of the independent variable that are not found in everyday life. It is only in an experiment that you can observe a person who has been awake for four days straight, who has been sleeping only fifteen minutes every four hours, or who has been subjected first to absolute quiet and then to enormous noise. But Festinger argues that, in social psychology:

> It is extremely difficult to create in the laboratory forces strong enough for results to be measurable. In the most excellently done laboratory experiment, the strength to which different variables can be produced is extremely weak compared to the strength with which these variables exist and operate in real-life situations. (Festinger, 1971: 141)

This is not only because experiments are difficult to do, but because "many dangers are present in their execution" (Festinger, 1971: 141). This comment makes sense when one reflects on the sort of phenomena that social psychologists deal with: race riots, conflict, love, and prejudice.

In experimentation you can systematically refine the relationship you are investigating. Perhaps you have been told by an Indian villager that a particular root has wonderful properties for reducing the blood pressure and tranquilizing excited patients. First you can experiment with samples of the root material. If it works, you probably will want to know exactly what it is in the root that has this medicinal effect. Therefore, your next move might be to experiment with the *juice* from the root. If the juice alone works without the fiber of the root, then next you might try various constituents of the juice. And so on until you have "isolated" the "active principle." Similarly, when Milgram (1974) studied whether people would administer electric shocks as punishment for doing poorly in a task, he began by conducting the experiments at a prestigious institution, Yale University, having men supposedly shock victims whom they could not see (no shocks were actually administered, but the men thought there were). As the experiments proceeded, Milgram changed the conditions by moving to a less prestigious location (an office

in downtown Bridgeport, Connecticut), by having women administer the shocks, and by bringing the victims closer to the person (supposedly) administering the shocks. Through altering and refining the experiment, Milgram was able, step by step, to learn about the circumstances in which people would stand up and refuse to cooperate in administering what seemed to be severe punishment.

E. REPLICATION

One occurrence is seldom enough to convince you that what you think happened really happened. For example (as noted on pp. 240–242), observers vary from time to time in what they observe. By repeating ("replicating") an experiment, you can obtain an average result; your conclusion is then not based on a single observation that might be unusually high or unusually low. Replication is one of the most useful tools in obtaining valid results, which is why classic experiments are often repeated, sometimes under slightly different circumstances, to ensure that it was not just an idiosyncrasy of the environment that caused the original results.

Study of the jury system was long hampered by the one-time nature of trials.[3] Furthermore, the particulars of cases differ greatly. Therefore, it was formerly difficult to investigate how juries react to various types of cases. In the experimental-jury paradigm invented by Strodtbeck, the experimenter *repeats* the same recorded trial to many juries and thereby obtains a sample of workable size (R. Simon, 1967).

F. UNRAVELING MULTIVARIABLE CAUSATION

If two independent variables are closely related in the world outside the laboratory, a survey cannot easily determine which of them

---

3. It might be interesting, however, to study trials that *are* repeated because of hung juries and higher-court reversals.

causes variation in the dependent variable. Because the laboratory experiment holds some factors constant as it varies others and then vice versa, the experimenter can track down the extent to which each is responsible for change in the dependent variable. (Of course, there are some cases in which it is only the *combination* or *interaction* of the two variables that will cause changes in the dependent variable; experimental designs that vary both variables simultaneously will reveal such interaction, however.)

4. Disadvantages of Experiments

The neatness of an experiment is very appealing, especially when the investigator is frustrated by the annoying shortcomings of survey data. Stouffer, who, more than any other one man, was responsible for *The American Soldier,* once wrote, "I would trade a half dozen Army-wide surveys on attitudes toward officers for one good controlled experiment" (1950: 211). But, if pressed, Stouffer would surely have qualified that statement, for the disadvantages of experiments can also be grave.

A. LACK OF "REALITY"

The most important disadvantage of the laboratory experiment (but not of the real-life field experiment, of course) is that you can never be sure that the analogy between the experiment and the real world really holds. In other words, there is always some risk involved in generalizing from what happens in the laboratory to what happens in the real world. Smoking causes cancer in laboratory experiments on rats, but is it correct to reason that the same thing happens with humans? (Chapter 35 discusses the grounds for safe generalizations.)

The riskiness of a generalization from a laboratory experiment depends on how well you specify your variables. Obviously it makes more sense to generalize about the effects of smoking from a laboratory experiment in which

apes smoke tobacco than from a laboratory experiment in which fish are exposed to the smoke from corn silk. On the other hand, much important theoretical work takes place in experiments with very "unrealistic" materials, because more realistic materials are too complicated to allow us to get a simple picture of what happens. From studies with unrealistic nonsense syllables, Ebbinghaus (1913) learned much about the learning process that he could not have with such complex subject matter as texts on Shakespeare or physics. It is much harder to run a "clean" experiment with Shakespeare or physics as the materials to be learned, because the subjects' prior knowledge complicates the experiment greatly.

B. UNREPRESENTATIVE SAMPLES

Another danger in drawing conclusions about the universe of interest from the laboratory experiment is that the subjects on whom the experiment is run in the laboratory may be very unlike the people in the real world about whom you wish to draw conclusions. Often it is difficult to persuade a fair sample of the universe to come into the laboratory. Consider these examples: First, economists try to experiment in the laboratory to find out how competing big businesses behave under certain competitive circumstances. But, because it is not possible to lure the presidents of, say, General Motors, Ford, and Chrysler into the laboratory for the experiment, the researchers study the behavior of *students* who are playing a business game. Can one generalize from the students' behavior to that of real executives? Second, a researcher wanted to experiment with the reactions of jurors to a mock trial after they had been given sensational or unsensational newspaper clippings about the trial, to find out the effect of newspaper publicity on the course of justice. But a disproportionate number of the people who agreed to take part in the experiment were from the middle and professional classes. In that study, the unrepresentative sample probably did not affect the direction of the outcome (R. Simon, 1966). In another study, however, the same experimenter found it necessary (and possible) to draw subjects from actual jury pools with the assistance of the courts, which ensured representative samples (R. Simon, 1967). Third, a market research firm runs experiments on people invited by postcard to come to free movies. During the movies, commercials are tested. But people who come to free movies in the afternoon are not necessarily typical of the people who might be exposed to the same commercials on television—which is what the advertisers are really interested in. Fourth, in their study of how people respond to authority, Gamson, Fireman, and Rytina (1982) wanted to be sure not to study only students, because they were afraid students' attitudes toward authority might be different from other people's attitudes; they therefore took special care to get all kinds of people in their sample.

What is important, of course, is that the subjects be representative *on the characteristics relevant to the experiment*. Pavlov's dogs were not representative of all dogs with respect to size, color, thickness of coat, and so forth, but there was no reason to think that any of those characteristics would affect the outcome of the type of experiment he was doing. Similarly, Ebbinghaus' sample was not representative with respect to his education, intelligence, or nationality, but these characteristics did not make him atypical in his *memory*. In a study of smoking, it would probably not matter if the sample were representative of different religious groups, because there is little reason to expect religion to affect how smoke changes breathing capacity. In an experiment on reducing anti-Semitism, however, it would be a good idea to include people from different religious backgrounds in the sample.

C. EXPENSE

Low cost was listed as one of the possible advantages of the experimental method. But some experiments may be very costly indeed, more costly than other research methods. Some structural testing may require fifty-foot models rather than two-foot models, and fifty-foot models may be expensive to build. A market test of a new product may cost as much as a quarter million dollars. It may be too expensive to gather together as many subjects as are necessary for the conditions of a real riot. Or giving players in laboratory games real money to obtain the necessary realism may be too expensive for some economics experiments.

D. HAZARDOUS OUTCOMES

It may be impossible to experiment with some real-world situations. For example, it is too dangerous economically to run controlled experiments on the national economy. And most sex experiments are unethical or objectionable to good taste. Smoking experiments on human beings violate all civilized ethics. (But we let convicts volunteer for hazardous medical experiments!)

5. Summary

In an experiment the researcher purposely alters the environment in order to observe the effect of the experimentally altered conditions. This is in contrast to a survey, in which the researcher observes only what occurs naturally without researcher interference.

Where it is feasible, a real-life experiment is usually preferable to a survey, though the cost may be much greater. A laboratory experiment affords greater control than does a field survey, but it may lack realism.

A major advantage of an experiment is that it helps clarify the causal relationship among the variables.

The steps in running an experiment are as follows:

1. Decide on empirical proxies for the theoretical variables. The proxies must be measurable, and they must be relevant.
2. Choose treatment levels for the independent variables. The levels should

bracket the real-life levels you are interested in. There should be enough treatments to catch important differences between the polar treatments, but few enough so that the experiment is cost-efficient.

3. Determine sample size on the basis of the expected accuracies of various sizes of samples, and of their costs and benefits.

4. Choose a sample that is as representative of the universe of interest as you can make it.

5. Plan the experiment so that the important non-experimental conditions are well-controlled.

6. Randomly allocate subjects to the various experimental and control groups.

7. Decide on the experimental design, the arrangement of stimuli, groups, and observations.

8. Pretest your procedure, and then revise your plans in light of the pretest.

9. Analyze and interpret the data.

EXERCISES

1. One must often choose between a laboratory experiment and a survey. Give one example in which each is preferable, and state why.
2. Give an example of a phenomenon that might be influenced by ten or more variables, and list the variables. Now pick the three that would be most worth investigating in a laboratory experiment to determine what influences the phenomenon.
3. Illustrate how an experimenter could be fooled by:
   a. varying the independent variable over *too narrow* a range
   b. examining the relationship among the independent variables at *too few* values
4. Describe a study in which one might use an experiment that alters two or more variables at the same time.
5. Give examples from your field in which:
   a. field experimentation is not feasible
   b. laboratory experimentation unravels multivariable causation
   c. lack of reality of experiments is a serious problem
   d. representative samples are not necessary for experiments
   e. diaries are a useful technique
6. Many studies have examined the effects of smoking; some are experiments, analyzing the impact of tobacco on animals, and some are surveys, asking people about their smoking habits and their health, along with other factors. What could you learn about the effects of smoking on human health in a survey that you could not learn in an experiment? What could you learn in an experiment that you could not learn in a survey?

ADDITIONAL READING

Aronson and Carlsmith (1968) is an excellent introduction to experimentation. General references for experimental procedure are Underwood (1957) and Banks (1965). Campbell (1966) discusses the validity of experiments in social settings. Festinger (1953) discusses laboratory experiments in social psychology, including a discussion of the disadvantages and advantages of experiments.

Experiments with organizations are often thought to be difficult or impossible. Evan (1971) presents a collection of studies of such experiments, showing where they are feasible and citing the problems with them in the laboratory and in the field.

The strengths and weaknesses of much recent experimentation in sociology are discussed by Bonacich and Light (1978). Large-scale social experiments, many of them related to public policy, are analyzed by Riecken and Boruch (1978). Gamson, Fireman, and Rytina (1982) show what happens when social psychologists try to turn issues from the "real world" into the subject of laboratory experiments.

Designing Experiments

11

The key element in an experiment—as compared to other methods of getting knowledge—is the planned, researcher-induced alteration of the situation. The alteration is made for the purpose of producing useful and valid information. Some experiments, however, yield no valid information, and others lead to misleading conclusions. Sometimes this is unavoidable. But more often an experiment fails because the pattern of induced variation—called the "experimental design"—is flawed. The main subject of this chapter, then, is the design of experiments that will produce valid results.

A second subject of this chapter is how to design experiments so that you can get a given amount of information for a lower cost, or a greater amount of information for a given expenditure—that is, experimental efficiency.

1. Simple Uncontrolled Exploratory Experiments

We take the liberty of using a very personal example to illustrate this section. Back in 1964 one of us began to teach his classes in research methods the Monte Carlo method of handling statistics problems (see Chapters 30–33). The results apparently were excellent, and this seemed to be a worthwhile method. Furthermore, the method seemed to have great promise for teaching probability and statistics to high-school students.

To find out more, this material was taught for six hours to a math class in a local high school. This was an "experiment" in the original meaning of the word, because it was a *test*, an attempt. The usual conditions were altered by teaching new material, and the results were observed. The high-school students quickly learned to handle both easy and difficult questions that would stump people with many more hours of conventional training in probability and statistics. And the students (and their instructor) enjoyed the experience very much.

One might conclude on the basis of this experiment (together with the previous experience with graduate students) that the Monte Carlo method of doing statistics should be taught in high schools and colleges, together with—or in preference to—conventional analytic methods. But others were not ready to reach the same conclusion on the basis of this experience. They said that the experiment did not prove the efficacy of the method because of at least two loopholes: (1) The good results might have been due to this one teacher's interest and enthusiasm, and might not occur with other teachers; (2) There was no proof that these excellent high-school students in University High School might not have learned as much if taught conventionally.

Let's consider the second objection. To put it technically, this objection is that the experiment lacks internal validity; that is, what we say happened was not proven. The claim was that the students learned more than they would if taught conventionally. The evidence for this was the result in class *compared to* general experience with other students. That is, the implicit experimental design was as shown in Table 11.1.

Others did not accept this design as valid, because they would not accept the implicit

comparison to a hypothetical matched group. And this objection has great merit. The tendency of an experimenter to see what he wants to see in a hypothetical comparison is overwhelming. That is, this experimental design is uncontrolled; it has no control group against which to validly compare the experimental group.

An experiment is not necessarily valueless because it is uncontrolled, however. *In the early stages of a study, it is often most efficient to proceed without any controls at all.* A controlled experiment demands that you work with a narrow set of variables, and at the beginning you do not know which variables might be most important and which ranges of the variables to try out. Therefore, you should not rush headlong to the stage of the controlled experiment.

When one first has an idea, one must explore in a loose and casual fashion to make a rough check on the idea and to get more ideas. It is important, however, that this exploratory uncontrolled knowledge-gathering experiment be offered not as proof, but as the exploration that it really is.

Another example: Consider the crucial world problem of people's aversion to new foods. Technology is now available to manufacture "new proteins" (the scarcest part of the diet for most poor people and the most important) at quite low costs and in abundance (Meier, 1966: Chap. 2). These new proteins include food yeast, fish flour, algae, processed peanuts, cottonseed meal, soy beans, and leaves. The pro-

TABLE 11.1   Uncontrolled Experimental Design (University High Experiment)

Stage 1: Choose Groups	Stage 2: Observe Subjects	Stage 3: Experimental Treatment	Stage 4: Observe Subjects
S (selected group, one class in U. High School)	(No formal observation)	X (experimental treatment, my teaching)	O (final exam and informal feedback)
MA (matched hypothetical)	(No observation)	(No treatment)	(no observation)

teins can be made to taste like the foods that people ordinarily eat, or they can be made tasteless. But it is not easy to persuade people to use these foods even when they and their children are suffering from terrible protein deficiencies.

Assume that our problem is to persuade people in a particular West African country to purchase and feed a particular new protein—a combination of processed soy bean and cottonseed, say—to their children. (ProNutro in South Africa and Incaparina in Guatemala have demonstrated that it *can* be done and with commercial success; see Belden et al., 1964). It is reasonable to try out various combinations of food tastes and ways of changing people's preferences. At this early stage of the game, it would be unwise to run neat well-controlled experiments comparing, say, finely ground and coarsely ground protein or introduction of the food through tribal chiefs or through parents of small children. At this stage of massive ignorance, it would be wise to try out a great many available forms of the new protein, using a wide variety of communication techniques, to a large number of groups of people without worrying about precise controls, for it would take much too long to try out all the possible variations in well-controlled experiments. Rather, we might send packages of various foods to Peace Corps volunteers all over the country and ask them to distribute the foods. Wherever acceptance is reported we could investigate further. Only after such a series of rough trial-and-error stages should we be ready to run controlled experiments to distinguish which are best among the somewhat successful foods and communications techniques.

2. Before-and-After Experiments

Let us leave the Monte Carlo study for a moment and consider another type of uncontrolled experiment, the pretest-experiment-posttest design. In this experimental design, one compares the subjects' behavior before and after the experimental treatment. This design is frequently used in educational and psychotherapeutic research. For example, patients suffering from depression are given a course of therapy, and any change in their mental state is attributed to the therapy. The design for this experiment is as shown in Table 11.2.

The possible defect of this before-and-after design is, of course, that the change in behavior might have occurred anyway, without the experimental treatment. Depressives tend to get well with or without treatment. And children tend to learn all kinds of things with the passage of time, with or without experimental educational intervention. Furthermore, people may do better in the second test than on the first just because they have greater test experience. Hence the difference in results before and after the experimental treatment cannot safely be attributed to the experimental treatment in this uncontrolled experiment.

3. Matched-Groups Design

Now let us return to the uncontrolled Monte Carlo teaching experiment. The obvious remedy for the lack of internal validity in this case would be to conduct a controlled experiment on two classes, one class taught conventionally and the other taught using the Monte Carlo method. This scheme was therefore planned,

TABLE 11.2   Before-and-After Design

Stage 1: Choose Groups	Stage 2: Observe Subjects	Stage 3: Experimental Treatment	Stage 4: Observe Subjects
S (a group of patients suffering from depression)	O (measure extent of depression)	X (therapy)	O (measure extent of depression)

with another person to teach both classes (so as to handle the objection that the results depend upon the teacher; more about that later). The design was to teach a class at University High and another similar class of excellent math students at a local high school. That is, this is a matched-groups design. Our intention was to compare the mathematic aptitude scores of the two groups before the experiment, teach the Monte Carlo method to the less-talented group (if a difference was observed), and afterward, to compare (1) the achievements of the two groups, and (2) the changes in knowledge of each group from before to after. The design would be as seen in Table 11.3.

As happens too often, practical difficulties arose and the matched group was not obtained from the local school. Hence, only the one group (in University High) was taught by Monte Carlo methods. The results were successful in the teacher's judgment; this increased the *external* validity of the two experiments together, by showing that the good results originally obtained did not depend on a single teacher. That is, the second experiment made the result somewhat more *general*, and generality of the results to other groups and conditions is the test of external validity (more on this to come). But without the matched group, the results were little more valid "internally" than was the first experiment alone. And the design of the second experiment could not be justified as being exploratory, because the exploration had already been done.[1]

1. Because so many students' work slides into this sort of situation, it is worth quoting Campbell and Stanley on the topic (1963: 7): "It seems well-nigh unethical at the present time to allow, as theses or dissertations in education, case studies of this nature (i.e., involving a single group observed at one time only). 'Standardized' tests in such case studies provide only very limited help, since the rival sources of difference other than X [the experimental treatment] are so numerous as to render the 'standard' reference group almost useless as a 'control group.' On the same grounds, the many uncontrolled sources of difference between a present case study and potential future ones which might be compared with it are so numerous as to make justification in terms of providing a bench mark for future studies also hopeless."

Let us consider the meaning of the results if the matched-groups design *had* been carried through. If the Monte Carlo group recorded higher test scores *in spite of* beginning with lower aptitude scores, that would have been strong evidence for the Monte Carlo's methods-effectiveness—but it would not have been *overwhelming* or *conclusive* evidence. In fact, one can *never* obtain conclusive evidence. Rather, one can only build a stronger and stronger case for one alternative as compared to another.

An important loophole in the matched-groups experiment is that the two groups may not really be similar. And even the lower math-aptitude scores of the Monte Carlo group might not resolve this question, because their aptitude for *probability and statistics* might have been higher. Or the time of the day at which they were taught might have been more propitious. Or some other subtle difference between the matched groups might have been responsible for the Monte Carlo group doing better.

What design would be better than matched groups? Probably no design could have been better *for that stage of the work*. We shall shortly discuss designs that yield more valid conclusions, but these more powerful designs require more and different resources than were then available. And such extensive designs became more appropriate only after additional evidence had accumulated that the Monte Carlo method is indeed promising.

4. Simple Randomized-Groups Design

The only way to ensure that the groups in an experiment are truly similar is by selecting the members of the groups by random sampling, as discussed in Chapter 9. Both mathematical logic and overwhelming empirical evidence prove that if two groups are chosen by a truly random selection process from a given population, then as the groups become larger in size they approach average equality in all their

TABLE 11.3 Matched-Groups Experimental Design

Stage 1: Choose Groups	Stage 2: Observe Subjects	Stage 3: Experimental Treatment	Stage 4: Observe Subjects
M_1 (selected group, one class in U. High School)	O (test math aptitude)	X_1 (conventional teaching)	O (final exam and informal feedback)
M_2 (matched group)	O (test math aptitude)	X_2 (Monte Carlo teaching)	O (final exam and informal feedback)

characteristics. Of course, two random samples of one person each might be quite unequal, but two random samples of 100 or 1,000 or 10,000 individuals will approach equality in their means and other measures of all their characteristics.

Two separate experiments were run on this simple randomized-groups experimental design by Simon, Atkinson, and Shevokas (1976). In both cases, separate sections of the same course were taught by Monte Carlo and by conventional methods. The students were assigned to the sections randomly, although some students requested one section or the other because of class conflicts; this latter element is a breach of strict randomization, but in the judgment of the experimenters—and some such judgment always comes into play somewhere—the breach was not serious. (As a further check, the students' math aptitude scores were compared, and were found to be similar in the various sections in both experiments.)

The experiment of design with randomly chosen groups—a "true" experimental design —is as shown in Table 11.4.

The simple randomized-groups design controls all sorts of threats to internal validity. That is, this design assures you that if you repeat the same experiment under the same conditions with subjects drawn from the same population, you will reach the same conclusion, subject only to the variation of sampling error.

A frequently used variation of the simple randomized-groups design was actually used by Shevokas and Atkinson. They wanted to know what effects the Monte Carlo and conventional methods would have upon students' attitudes toward mathematics. Therefore, the actual design included an attitude test given both before and after the probability-and-statistics instruction. On the one hand, this design, which allows comparison of changes, is very powerful statistically. On the other hand,

TABLE 11.4 Simple Randomized-Groups Design

Stage 1: Choose Groups	Stage 2: Observe Subjects	Stage 3: Experimental Treatment	Stage 4: Observe Subjects
R_1 (randomly chosen group)	O_a (observe math aptitudes and math interests)	X_1 (Monte Carlo instruction)	O_b (final exam and test of math interests)
R_2 (randomly chosen group)	O_a (observe math aptitudes and math interests)	X_2 (conventional instruction)	O_b (final exam and test of math interests)

there is a chance that the attitude test might influence the students' learning in some subtle way. That is, the attitude pretest might have a positive effect on students' learning by one method, and a negative effect on the other method. To put it another way, the results of the achievement-test comparison might be different with or without an attitude test. Therefore, when drawing conclusions about the effects of the two methods on achievement, one must keep in mind all the special conditions of the experiment—the age of the students and the kind of instructor, for example, *and* the presence of the pretest.

This brings us to the *external* validity of experiments such as these. The randomized-groups experimental design assures us that we will obtain similar results if the experiment is repeated with similar people under similar conditions. But what about *different kinds of people under different conditions?* That is, to what extent can we generalize from Shevokas' and Atkinson's experiments the conclusion that the Monte Carlo method produces more learning and better attitudes?

There is no systematic technical device for increasing external validity the way randomization improves internal validity. That is, as Hume (1758) taught us long ago (and as discussed in Chapter 35) generalization of results to different kinds of persons and conditions is not a matter of logical deduction but rather of cumulative evidence and sound judgment.

These three aspects of generalizing the Monte Carlo experiments immediately come to mind: (1) Will the Monte Carlo method do better than the analytic method with all sorts of students–bright and slow, old and young, English- and non–English-speaking? More generally, this is the matter of *generalization to other groups*. (2) Will the Monte Carlo method perform relatively better when taught by teachers who are not especially interested in it? More generally, this is the matter of *generalization to other experimental treatments*. (3) Are the results affected by the testing and other special aspects of the experimental situation?

There will never be a totally conclusive positive answer. But if many experiments are done by different teachers, with different sorts of students under a variety of conditions, using a variety of tests, and if most of the experiments show the Monte Carlo experiments to be relatively better, it will be reasonable to conclude that except under special conditions, it is indeed a better method and ought to be used in teaching statistics.

5. Some Additional One-Variable Designs

In psychological research one often is interested in whether an experimental treatment has any effect at all, compared to no treatment. The standard design for this situation measures the dependent variable for the experimental group both before and after the experimental treatment. Similar measurements are made for the control group, which receives no experimental treatment but which is selected randomly from the same population as the experimental group. This design may be diagrammed as in Table 11.5. The main comparison is between $(O_{1a}-O_{1b})$ and $(O_{2a}-O_{2b})$; that is, the size of the before-and-after differences for the two groups.

This design is very efficient statistically because one can compare *each subject's* before-and-after measurements, which holds consistent the original differences among persons. This quality makes the design very desirable. However, there is always the chance that the pretest measurement influences the extent to which the experimental treatment affects the subjects.

As a check on the effect of pretesting, one can use a design with *four* randomly-chosen groups, two of which are measured twice, and two of which are measured only at the end of the experiment. Comparison among these four groups reveals the effect of the experimental

TABLE 11.5 Simple Design to Test for Presence of Effects

Stage 1: Choose Groups	Stage 2: Observe Subjects	Stage 3: Experimental Treatment	Stage 4: Observe Subjects
R_1 (randomly selected group)	O_{1a} (measure)	X (treatment)	O_{1b} (measure)
R_2 (randomly selected group)	O_{2a} (measure)	——	O_{2b} (measure)

treatment with and without an accompanying pretest. This design may be diagrammed as in Table 11.6.

6. Multivariate Designs

The experiments discussed until now have all had a single experimental variable. In the statistics experiments, the variable is the teaching method, Monte Carlo or conventional. Of course, there have been other conditions that were not held constant in those experiments; for example, the hour of the classes differed among groups in the Shevokas and Atkinson experiments. But only the teaching-method variable was built into the design for systematic manipulation.

This section discusses designs in which *two or more* elements of the experimental situation are systematically altered.

The principle of *ceteris paribus* may at first seem to suggest that the experimenter can vary only one variable at a time, so as to hold all other conditions constant. But we shall see that the experimenter can often gain much by varying *several* variables at the same time in certain prescribed ways and still meet the requirements of *ceteris paribus*. The various designs used to study the effects of several variables simultaneously are called "factorial" designs (or "analysis of variance" designs, because a statistical device by that name is used to determine whether there are real differences between groups when the differences are too small for the answer to be obvious).

The biostatisticians (pre-eminently Fisher) have been especially ingenious in developing efficient experimental designs with which they can learn about the effects of various fertilizers, types of water, types of soil, types of seed, and so forth, with the fewest experimental plots.

There are several important and quite different reasons why one might wish to experiment with more than one variable at a time.

A. COST EFFICIENCY

You may be interested in the effects of two or more variables. Hence, you may experiment with them simultaneously in order to reduce

TABLE 11.6 Design for Control of Pretest Measurement Effect

Group	Observation	Treatment	Observation
R_1	O_{1a}	X_1	O_{1b}
R_2	O_{2a}	X_2	O_{2b}
R_3	——	X_1	O_{3b}
R_4	——	X_2	O_{4b}

the overall costs of experimentation while you gather given quantities of information. For example, a track coach might wish to investigate the popularly accepted coaching lore about the effects of (1) the interval between last heavy training, and (2) the presence or absence of sex activity on the day before a race. If you have 100 runners available for experimentation, you can simply split them randomly 50–50 on either the time-since-training variable or the sex-activity variable and get information only on that one variable. Or you can split the 100 runners into four groups of 25 runners as in Table 11.7.

With this design the researchers can compare two groups of 50 runners each on *both* the time-since-training and the sex-activity variables. Of course, the groups compared on time-since-training are *not* identical in all other ways, differing in sex activity. But the difference in sex activity is *known and controlled*, rather than being haphazard and uncontrolled. Hence, that difference is more likely to be a benefit than a detriment, for reasons to be discussed shortly. So in this design the coach gets more desired information from given resources by experimenting with two variables together rather than just one alone.

There is a wide variety of complex "factorial" designs to help you save money when experimenting with several variables, but that is an advanced topic that few will need to know.

B. GENERALITY AND EXTERNAL VALIDITY

Experimenting with two or more variables simultaneously can strengthen the external validity of an experiment by showing that the result occurs under diverse conditions (if it indeed does so). For example, we might have funds enough to support six comparisons of the Monte Carlo and conventional methods in high schools. We could (1) hire one teacher to teach twelve senior classes in one city, or (2) we could hire six teachers to teach two classes each, three comparisons in the senior year and three in the junior year, in six different communities. If all the comparisons are favorable for the Monte Carlo method, then we could assert that its success is not limited to one school year or one city or one teacher, but in fact is better under a wide variety of conditions. That is, this latter design increases the generality of the results at little or no additional cost. As Fisher, the master of experimental design, put it:

> There is a third advantage [of a factorial design] which, while less obvious than the former two [efficiency and comprehensiveness], has an important bearing upon the utility of the experimental results in their practical application. This is that any conclusion, such as that it is advantageous to increase the quantity of a given ingredient, has a wider inductive basis when inferred from an experiment in which the quantities of other ingredients have been varied, than it would have from any amount of experimentation, in which these had been kept strictly constant. The exact standardisation of experimental conditions, which is often thoughtlessly advocated as a panacea, always carries with it the real disadvantage that a highly standardised experiment supplies direct information only in respect of the narrow range of conditions achieved by standardisation. Standardisation, therefore, weakens

TABLE 11.7   Design with Two Independent Variables (Numbers of Subjects Shown in Cells)

		Training Interval	
		Short	**Long**
Sex on Day before Race?	**No**	25	25
	Yes	25	25

rather than strengthens our ground for inferring a like result, when, as is invariably the case in practice, these conditions are somewhat varied. (Fisher, 1971: 106).

C. INTERACTION EFFECTS

A phenomenon may depend upon two variables *working together*. This effect is called "interaction." More formally, interaction is present when the effect of one independent variable on the dependent variable *depends on* the values of one or more *other* independent variables. Interaction can best be investigated in experiments that vary more than one variable at a time.

For example, what about the effect of sex activity and recent training on running races? You could learn whether the two variables interact, rather than one or the other or both having separate effects, only if you experiment with both together. Thus, Box A of Table 11.8 shows the results of an experiment in which having recent training improves running time by five seconds, while sex activity has no effect. Box B shows the results when sex activity improves running time by three seconds, and

training interval has no effect. Box C shows the results of an experiment if both variables had an effect, but there is no interaction—a short training interval improves time by five seconds, sex activity improves it by three seconds, and both together add up to an improvement of eight seconds. Box D, however, shows interaction: Recent training helps by five seconds, sex activity helps by three seconds, but recent training and sex activity together help by twelve seconds; each variable enhances the effect of the other. Discovering this interaction effect of no recent training and much sex leads to a best-of-all alternative (but please don't generalize, or believe, this hypothetical example).

Similarly, if the statistics-teaching experiment were to be done in both junior and senior years with several teachers, it might show that the Monte Carlo method works better for juniors and worse for seniors. This could be an important piece of knowledge that would not appear if the experiments were done only with students in one year (a piece of information that would be lost and would only blur the overall results, if the experiment were done on both junior and senior students without plan-

TABLE 11.8   Illustrative Interactions in a Two-Independent-Variable Design (running time in seconds shown in cells)

		Interval Since Training	
		Short	Long
Sex on Day before Race?	Yes	45	50
	No	45	50

A

		Interval Since Training	
		Short	Long
	Yes	42	42
	No	45	35

B

		Interval Since Training	
		Short	Long
Sex on Day before Race?	Yes	45	50
	No	48	53

C

		Interval Since Training	
		Short	Long
	Yes	41	50
	No	48	53

D

ning and without checking the effect of the school-year variable). Searching for such interactive effects is an important function of a multivariate experimental design.

7. Experimental Designs to Study Delayed Effects

Implicit in the experimental designs previously described is that all the effects occur immediately. But sometimes the effects of the independent variables occur slowly and are spread out over time. Furthermore, one may want to know about the effects of *various amounts* of the stimulus given over time. This often is the case in medical research and in education and advertising. For example, Random House may wish to know the effects on the sales of the third edition of this book if it advertises in the fall of 1984, *or* if it advertises in fall 1984 *plus* spring 1985, *or* if it does not advertise at all.

The appropriate design experimentally treats the different samples different numbers of times (in separate time periods) and then observes the results *over several periods*. As an example of just one of the many possible designs, Table 11.9 shows that group S_1 (a sample of areas) receives advertisements in Fall 1984 and Spring 1985; S_2 (another group of areas) gets advertisements in Fall 1984, and S_3 gets no advertisements. The sales in all three groups of areas are measured not just in the advertising period but afterward as well, to see how much of the effect of the advertising continues into the future. This may be seen, for example, in the sales in Period III of groups S_2, and S_3, both of whom receive no advertising in Period II, though S_2 received advertising in Period I. And by comparison of S_2 sales in Periods II and III, one can determine how the effects of Period I's advertising "decays" over time in group S_2. Comparison of results for S_1 and S_2 will show how much effect the period II's advertising has *in addition* to the effect of advertising in Period I.

8. Simulation[2]

"Simulation" is an ambiguous label that refers to several research techniques. By one meaning any laboratory experiment is a simulation. For example, Ebbinghaus' experiment with the learning and retention of nonsense syllables can be called a simulation study of human learning processes. Laboratory experiments with physical models are also called simulation studies by some writers. An example is a laboratory wind-tunnel test of how model airplanes with various characteristics behave under various conditions. Or an engineer might want to know whether there is a chance that a new type of roof for an industrial building might fall in. Because it is impractical to build a full-sized roof and subject it to stress tests and because, for reasons that we shall discuss in the next section, the engineer may not be able to solve the problem with mathematics alone, he or she will often build a model building with a model roof, table-top size, and then study how much punishment the roof can absorb before it falls in. The Army Corps of Engineers built a scale model to simulate the behavior of tides and river currents in San Francisco Bay—all in a warehouse. These physical experiments are often run when the engineers know how to figure out the answer mathematically but the calculation is too complicated to do easily.

A second type of simulation study is the "game" study, in which people compete in laboratory games to simulate the way they compete in various aspects of real-life competition. Such games have been developed to simulate political relations (Guetzkow, 1962; Michener, Ginsberg, and Yuen, 1979); each player might be told that he is a country and that his goal is to make deals with other countries that will get him into the best power position. The re-

2. Guetzkow (1962) contains a variety of articles on aspects of simulation, a general bibliography (pp. 191–193), and bibiographies at the ends of individual articles. The article by Dawson offers a somewhat different scheme of classifying simulation studies than follows here.

TABLE 11.9   Illustrative Delayed-Effects Design

	Fall, 1984		Spring, 1985		Fall, 1984	
	Period I$_a$	**Period I$_b$**	**II$_a$**	**II$_b$**	**III$_a$**	**III$_b$**
S$_1$	X (advertise)	O (measure sales)	X	O	—	O
S$_2$	X	O	—	O	—	O
S$_3$	—	O	—	O	—	O

searcher then studies what kinds of deals the various countries make under various circumstances. The business games played by students at various business schools are another example. The students are given initial data about their products and the demand for them, their financial resources, and so on. The students then try out various price and marketing strategies to increase their shares of the market and their profits, usually at the expense of their competitors. Such business games might be considered a very complicated form of Monopoly in which the players have much more control of what happens and much less is left to chance and a roll of the dice. In the case of Monopoly, the purpose of the simulation might be to determine whether at game's end it is usual for one player to have all the wealth or whether the result is a standoff. The hallmark of this type of simulation experiment is that *people interact in the experiment*, usually in competition with one another.

Another type of laboratory experiment is that carried out by social psychologists studying "status organizing processes" (Humphreys and Berger, 1981). Berger and others have shown how people's beliefs about types of individuals—blacks versus whites, men versus women, and so on—affect how they work with them on laboratory tasks, leading to the recreation in the laboratory of the inequalities of the larger society. If men think women are less competent at performing a task, for example, the men will treat them as incompetent, even if there is no evidence that the particular women they are working with are any less competent than the men. Much of social psychology is based on knowledge gained from laboratory experiments.

Recently economists have also begun to use some mock-experimental evidence. To gain insight into the way that competing businessmen behave, games have been set up with the players in simulated business situations, and then their behavior has been observed (V. Smith, 1962). Games are also used by sociologists to find out how people in small groups interact with one another under various types of circumstances—under stress, for example.

A third type of simulation experiment is like the second, except that it is not played with real people but with a computer. The computer is given data about how each unit in the game is likely to act under various conditions, and then the whole thing is set into motion to see where it will come out. The most ambitious simulation of this type is that of Orcutt et al., (1961), in which data are put in about how the various units of the economy and society—for example, households and banks—are likely to buy, sell, and perform financial operations. Also put in are the relationships of these groups with one another. Then some starting "shock" is given to the system; for example, the banks are suddenly forced to raise interest rates. The computer then runs through the situations and interactions over and over again very rapidly, so that the researchers can see how things come out at the end of a long series of such situations. This approach can be used to "experiment" on a "model" of society without the risk of injuring real people, and many possible changes can be tried quickly and easily.

For example, we could program the computer to examine how various possible changes in the economy might affect other aspects of the economy, under a variety of assumptions about how the economy works, and then run the program many times. This type of simulation can be used to test the adequacy of models of the economy used by businesspeople and policy makers. But the value of a simulation depends entirely on the quality of the input data and relationships (Fair, 1979).

A simulation's main advantage is the obvious one: The simulation can be done when the real-life conditions cannot be experimented with. A simulation's grave danger also is obvious: The simulation may not resemble the real-life situation in one or more key elements. In an economist's market experiment, one must ask: Does the game resemble real life? Do the players act the way people in real-life situations act? Are the relationships programmed into the computer like those in the real world?

One difficulty in making the simulation realistic is giving the players motivations similar to those experienced in the real-life situations. For example, can a player who is told to play the role of the president of General Motors or the Chief of Staff of the Armed Forces, with billions of dollars or millions of lives at stake, reproduce the same motivations and feelings when playing for pennies or tin soldiers in a lab? Can a person who is given a blindfold and told to play the role of a blind person simulate the feelings of a person who is really blind and who cannot take off a blindfold at the end of the day? Another difficulty in making a simulation realistic arises from the complexity of social life. For example, how can the experiments simulate the conditions of bureaucratic complexity, or the complications of a real man-woman sexual relationship?

One may try to validate the simulation by comparing the results against other sorts of research. For example, if animal experiments with cigarette smoking jibe with nonexperimental survey data on humans' smoking, then both results are strengthened. In the case of computer experiments with households and banks, it is difficult to find other data to compare with. In such a case, it is helpful to check the accuracy of the input data about the behavior of the various units and about their relationships. "GIGO: Garbage In, Garbage Out." The input data must first be developed by the classical methods of empirical science—survey and experiment—before a simulation has anything to work with.

In some cases—such as a simulation of competition between two competing organizations (Simon, Puig, and Aschoff, 1973)—information neither on other studies nor the input variable may be available. In that case, the only validation method may be to check that the results make sense internally, and that they jibe with theory and general experience.

9. Summary

It makes sense to take the time and effort at the beginning of a study to create a good sampling or experimental design. This investment can pay off handsomely in the course of your work. The aim of the experimental design is to produce data from which you may derive sound conclusions, and to do so as efficiently as possible. Perhaps the most important element of the experimental design is that any differences in results shown among the various experimental and control groups should arise from differences among the stimuli given to the experimental groups rather than from differences in original composition among the groups. But it is often impractical to achieve the ideal in equalizing the groups—random selection—either because the research is at an early exploratory stage, or because of cost, or because of ethical considerations. The chapter discusses randomized-group designs as well as designs that may be appropriate where random assignment of subjects to groups, or random selection of groups, is not feasible.

Designs that vary more than one experimental element at the same time often have advantages over one-variable designs. Multivariate designs can be cheap, and they can produce more information and greater generality of conclusions by showing the effect of each variable under a variety of conditions of the other variables; they can also reveal interactions among variables.

A variety of designs can measure delayed effects; most important is to be aware of possible delayed effects and to build them into the design rather than to forget them.

A simulation can be a laboratory experiment, a gaming study, an experiment with a computer, or any other sort of manipulation of a model. The value of the simulation depends on the realism of the inputs.

EXERCISES

1. Suppose you saw a commercial on television in which an aspirin manufacturer says he did an experiment in which he proved that his aspirin cures most headaches: 75 per cent of people with headaches who took his brand of aspirin were better within six hours. How well does this experiment support the claim of aspirin effectiveness?

2. Assume that a prestigious university such as Harvard wanted to show that the education it provides its students is superior to the education students get at most other schools. With the cooperation of other schools, an experiment is carried out. Students admitted to Harvard and exposed to its classes (the "experimental treatment") are given the Graduate Record Examination before they graduate, and so are students at other schools, who are matched with the Harvard students in that they started college the same year. Harvard students do better. Does this show that Harvard provides a better education? Why or why not?

3. Imagine that doctors have developed a new type of heart surgery which they think is better than an old type and will save more lives. Before they can be sure the new surgery is an improvement, however, they must do an experiment to see how effective it is. Try to design an experiment which would show whether the new type of surgery is superior to the old one.

4. Give an example from your field in which the experimenter could reasonably expect to find interaction between two independent variables.

5. Design a simulation that could throw light on how the severity and certainty of punishment influences "white-collar" business crimes.

ADDITIONAL READING

Campbell and Stanley's monograph (1963) is an outstanding treatment of the subject of experimental validity. The first part of this chapter was inspired by their treatment of the subject. Aronson and Carlsmith (1968) also provide useful information on experimental design.

Wright and Hyman (1964–1967) discuss the special problems of experimentation in sociology.

Experimental designs, especially in psychology, are described at length by Wood (1974, Chap. 5–9). Other useful references concerning experimental design in psychology are Underwood and Shaughnessy (1975), Matheson (1978), and Kappel and Saufley (1980).

Boyd and Stasch (1977, Chap. 3) discuss experimental designs in the context of market research.

Hovland et al. (1949) is a classic experimental study in social psychology.

Nonexperimental Designs for Studying Relationships

An experiment has great advantages for studying relationships. But sometimes you cannot experiment, or choose not to. Then you must turn to examining data as nature throws them up to you.

There are two basic strategies for collecting naturally occurring data for the purpose of examining relationships. You may collect data on a *particular* person or group at a number of points in time, either by using data that have already been collected (such as that collected by the U.S. Census every ten years since 1790), or by planning a long-term study in which you will collect data at regular intervals for a number of months or years. This is often called "time series" data. Or you may collect data on *different* individuals or groups at the *same* time and compare them; this is "cross-sectional" data. It is also possible, of course (though often complicated), to collect data on many individuals or groups at a number of points in time—that is, collecting data on the same people or groups over and over again. This is a "panel" or "pooled cross-sectional

time-series" design. The essential ingredient to obtaining valid results with any of these strategies is that the independent variable(s) in which you are interested must have varied due to reasons unrelated to the nature of the sample periods or sample individuals. For example, perhaps you are interested in the relationship of income to suicide. You might compare income and suicide in (a) the various U.S. states, or (b) various years in the past in the United States. But it may be that there is some important element in people's makeup that is responsible for *both* low income and low suicide, say, education. This would vitiate both the time series and the cross-sectional approaches—unless you somehow allow for this and other factors that account for changes in the independent variable (income) and that are also related to the dependent variable (suicide). Chapter 22 discusses this obstacle to the use of these nonexperimental designs, and how to overcome it.

Though the time series and the cross section sometimes are alternative designs, by far the

153

most compelling conclusions emerge if you are able to use *both* the time series and the cross section, and if their results agree. If the results do *not* agree, this may be a clue to important underlying processes that it will pay to investigate. More about this in Section 4. In some cases, time series and cross sections may be conceptually similar and measure the same phenomenon. For example, one may use a time series and a cross section interchangeably to find out how much taller boys are at ten years of age than at five years of age. We can either measure a group of boys when they are five years old and measure them again when they are ten years of age, or we can measure two different groups of boys at the same time, one "cohort" of ten-year-olds and one "cohort" of five-year-olds. But in some cases time series and cross sections may capture quite different phenomena, as when political cross-sectional polls reveal a different relationship between income and political-party membership than do time-series data (Brunner and Leipelt, 1972).

We shall consider the nature of time series and cross sections in that order. Then we shall take up the special places of the two methods for studying processes that develop only over a period of time. Last, we shall discuss the panel method as a device for studying changes over time.

1. Time Series—The Long View

Using the time-series method has three major advantages. First, the historical record provides a set of varied observations of the phenomenon in question. That is, past periods constitute a bank of data. Second, and very important, knowing how events are ordered in time provides, as the Nobel Prize winner in economics, Herbert Simon, has written, "one of the most powerful means available to us for specifying the mechanisms operating in a system," because causation cannot work backward through time. "If we have variables measured at different points in time, then the earlier var-

iable may exert a causal influence on the later, but not the later on the earlier. Thus, if we had measures of IQ taken at the time schooling began and measures of verbal activity taken later, then IQ could affect verbal ability, but not verbal ability IQ" (1979: 72–73). Note that the earlier variable *may* cause the later; it might not. Knowing time order can help us learn what causes what, but just because one thing precedes another, there is no guarantee that it is the cause (see also Firebaugh, 1980b, and Chapter 22).

Third, the time series method can often be statistically efficient because the people being observed serve as their own *controls*. For a crude example, assume that you want to know whether people lose weight during the night. It is intuitively obvious that if you weigh a sample of people both night and morning and compare each person's night and morning weights, you can obtain the same accuracy with a smaller sample than if you were to weigh one group of people at night and another in the morning. If you weigh the same people twice, the extraneous variables are mostly held constant, whereas different morning and night samples may differ in many ways that require a large sample to "smooth out" the results.

The same principle holds if you compare the use of a sample of books in one year to the use of the *same books* five years later, if you compare the I.Q.s of a group of children at five years of age with the I.Q.s of the *same children* at ten years of age, or if you compare the sales in a group of supermarkets in January to the sales in the *same* supermarkets in February. In each case a much larger sample would be needed if you sampled *two different groups* of books, children, or supermarkets, because of the much greater *variability* that would be introduced.

There are also two major obstacles to the use of the time-series method. First, it is vulnerable to changes in general conditions that may be relevant to the phenomenon you want to study. For example, there have been steady increases in the average height of Americans from generation to generation, and therefore a comparison of the heights of people of different ages from different generations may be blurred by the long-term shifts.

As another example, researchers wanted to learn how the *age* of a book in a research library affects how much people read it, in order to know which books should be kept in expensive locations where people can find them easily. A card in the back of each book revealed how many times it had been used each year for the past fifty years. But fifty years ago there were many fewer people at universities who might have withdrawn *any* book, and therefore the most-read books fifty years ago were read much less than the most-read books now. This increase in university population distorts the picture to make it seem that the difference in the use of a given book now and when it was younger is much less than it really is. (That is, there are more potential readers now to offset the decline in interest.) There were also many fewer books to compete for attention fifty years ago. Though these two major changes affect the use of books in opposite directions, we have no reason to think that they cancel out. Either one of them could distort the picture badly.

In such a predicament the "cross-sectional" method can help. Instead of comparing the use of a given book when it was one year old with its use when it was fifty years old, it was possible to examine the use during *one year* of fifty-year-old books and of one-year-old books. We thus look for the effect of age but under the same conditions of equal numbers of university students and books in the library.

The second potential problem with the time series method is that the dependent variable may change in such a way that we may be misled about the direction or causes of change; this sort of problem can arise when change is very slow or when it reverses direction, for example.

Thus, if a researcher studies the effect of an independent variable on a dependent variable that reveals its change only slowly, he or she may find it tempting to conclude that "time" itself is causing the changes. But time itself works no changes; time is only a proxy for other processes that operate over time. For example, a prolonged period of smoking is apparently necessary to affect health, and the effects may become apparent late in the smoker's life—even if the person quits smoking. Or, even less pleasantly, syphilis contracted when young can cause a person to go mad many years later. In these examples of long time lag—or long "latency period"—between cause and effect, it is not *time itself* that produces the delayed effects but rather various series of biological changes that take place unobserved and in interaction with subsequent happenings.

The difference in the short-run and long-run purchase responses to price changes offers another example in which a time variable is a proxy for other changes. If the power company raises the price of electricity, you may do nothing immediately, but next time you buy a stove you may shift to gas.

Sometimes the long run actually *reverses* the short-run direction. For example, when a baby drinks from her mother's breast, she diminishes the milk supply for a while, but this activity stimulates an increase in production that results, several hours later, in a *larger* supply than if the baby had not suckled. These examples emphasize that it is crucial to choose the appropriate time period in which to look at the effect of the independent variable.

In some situations the independent variable takes effect gradually and *cumulatively*. A cigarette advertisement has some immediate effect in cigarette sales, but this year's advertising also has some effect next year, five years hence, and even twenty years hence, because an advertisement may create a brand loyalty that persists for many years. In the pre–World War II cigarette market, fully 80 to 85 per cent of the effect of a given year's advertising took place in the years after the year in which the advertising was run (Telser, 1962). The researcher must then find some way of summarizing the effect of a given year's advertising in *all* the following years together—not an easy task.

Sometimes the study of changes over time is really a *comparison of various stages*. For example, if a person wants to know how his weight is changing—perhaps as a result of a diet, or perhaps only as a result of aging—he wants to compare his weight this year with his weight last year. But such comparisons are bedeviled by time-related breaches of *ceteris paribus*. Researchers must separate the change caused by the internal processes of the material, which is what they are interested in, from the *environmental* change effects. Therefore, they must make sure that they work with appropriately chosen time periods. For example, the weight watcher must weigh himself consistently each day. It will not matter whether he weighs himself at the height or at the depth of the daily weight cycle, whether he weighs himself every morning or every night, as long as he is consistent. But, if he sometimes weighs himself in the morning and sometimes at night, the picture will be confused. Similarly, when a businessman wants to compare his sales from year to year to see whether the business is growing, he can safely compare the same month for two or more years, even though that month is an unusually high or an unusually low month in the yearly cycle.

Thus, in order to be confident about the results of time-series research, one must try to get enough observations, over a long enough period of time, to be fairly sure that long term trends and whatever cyclical effects there might be will both show up in the data. In addition, one has to think about whether general conditions may have changed so much during the observation period that they obscure or confuse the relationships the study is focusing on. Some ways of overcoming these problems will be discussed in Sections 4 and 5.

2. The Cross Section—The Wide View

The wide view has three advantages.

First, the overwhelming advantage of the wide view over the long view is that, because all observations are made at the same time, there is no problem of changes in conditions.

Second, data are often much easier to obtain for a wide view. If you want to find out how the price of a Honda motorcycle depreciates over the life of the motorcycle, you might not be able to obtain data for the prices that particular cycles sold for in previous years or even for the prices of *any* Hondas in previous years. But it would be easy to obtain price quotations on Hondas of all ages at the present moment.

Or, if you are a demographer, or an actuary working for a life-insurance company, and you wish to construct a "life table" that shows the proportions of a group of people who will die at various ages, it is impracticable to follow the course of a given group of people all their lives. Rather, you examine the proportions of various age groups that die in a given *year* and construct a "synthetic life table."

Again, even if it were decided to compare the use of the *same* books when they were one year old with the use now, when they are fifty years old, most libraries do not have records of the use of particular books that go back fifty years. In that case, unless one were willing to wait another fifty years, there would be no choice but to use the wide view and to compare the use of one-year-old books *this year* with fifty-year-old books *this year*.

Third, the wide view can be employed even when the subject matter can be observed only once. For example, you cannot shoot the same rifle cartridge twice in different rifles, to compare the accuracy of the rifles. Instead, you must compare the results of *two different samples* of cartridges. Similarly, asking a person her voting intention in a campaign may alter her subsequent behavior, in which case it will not be safe to ask her her intentions a second time. This danger is probably less with purchase panels, however; there is little theoretical or empirical reason to believe that membership in a panel will eventually bias a person toward brand A and against brand B.

The major disadvantage of the cross-sectional method is that there is likely to be considerable variation among the sampling units that has no connection with the variables of interest. Such variation does not bias the results, but it does require a larger sample size to achieve any given level of accuracy than if there were less irrelevant variation among the subjects.

For example, you might want to study the effect of liquor prices on liquor consumption, and you consider relating the price of liquor in various states to per capita consumption in the states. It is very difficult to study the effect of liquor prices in the United States *as a whole* because the level of liquor prices changes infrequently and raggedly. And one cannot experimentally raise or lower the prices of liquor in the country as a whole, or even in individual state or communities, just for the sake of research. The various states already have different price levels, however, because state legislatures have different revenue policies affecting liquor prices. But it is not possible simply to compare the consumption of liquor in various states that have various liquor prices, because there are differences in consumption from state to state, independent of price. For example, Table 12.1 shows that per capita liquor consumption can vary a great deal from state to state, even where the different states have the same prices.

There is an analogy between this disadvantage of the wide view and the major disadvantage of the long view. With the long view, conditions change over the length of the study; with the wide view, conditions are different over the width of the study. Such change may not matter if plenty of data are available at low cost. But sometimes there is not enough data available to compensate for this defect of the wide view. The variability in liquor consumption among the states from such other causes as religion is so great that a cross-sectional sample of perhaps 500 states would be necessary to obtain a reasonably reliable answer—and there are not that many states in the Union.

A solution (J. Simon, 1966a) was to study those instances in which the state changed its revenue policy (and hence the prices of liquor) on a given date and then to compare the consumption patterns *before and after* the price changes in each state separately. The difference between the before and after consumption could then be attributed to the price change. (And, to take account of possible differences *over time* in each state, Simon standardized by subtracting the changes in consumption over the same periods of time in states in which price remained the same from those in the price-change states. This device allowed for increases or decreases in consumption resulting from religious and cultural

TABLE 12.1

State	January 1962 Price Index (Seagrams 7 Crown)	Per Capita Liquor Consumption in 1961	Gallons of Liquor Consumed per $1 million of Income
Indiana	4.85	1.26	350
Massachusetts	4.85	2.76	681
Minnesota	4.85	2.22	613
New Mexico	4.85	1.75	506

SOURCE: *Liquor Handbook*, 1962.

changes, tension-level changes, and other society-wide effects.) This design really is a combination of the time-series and cross-section methods, being a cross-sectional sample of changes over time.

3. Causes of Differences in Results from Time-Series and Cross-Sectional Studies

Sometimes the results produced by time-series and cross-sectional studies differ greatly, producing apparent paradoxes. For example, within various industrialized countries most cross-sectional studies of the relationship between income and fertility show that lower-income families have more children. On the other hand, time-series studies over the period of a few business cycles show that the *higher* per capita income is, the *more* children people have. And to confuse things further, time-series studies over *long* periods of time—say 100 years—show drops in fertility as per capita income rises.

There are several reasons why the results from cross-sectional and time-series analyses may differ (Firebaugh, 1980b). First, variables omitted from the analysis may have different effects across units than over time. Suppose you wanted to study national levels of drunkenness, for example. You might have data on some factors related to alcohol consumption, such as religion and the price of liquor, but may have no data on some other factors, such as attitudes about drinking. In a study of trends in one country over time, attitudes may not change much, and may not be that important in explaining changes in drunkenness, in the context of all the other factors. In a study comparing countries cross-sectionally, however, attitudes about drunkenness could be an important part of national culture and an important part of the explanation of intercountry differences. The results of the two studies, therefore, could be quite different. As a researcher, then, your problem would be to decide

whether you are more interested in how drunkenness changes over time or in why it varies from country to country.

A second reason for differences in results is that a time-series study will show how changes take place from year to year, while a cross-sectional study may show the end result of a long period of change, looked at during a particular time. If a country invests a lot of money in new factories every year for a few years, the disposable income of the people may go down for a while because so much money is going into investment. But a cross-sectional study comparing countries twenty years later could show that the country which invested in factories wound up with a very high income, as the result of the investment in prior years.

In contrast, time-series and cross-sectional analyses may differ because the cross-sectional data are collected while major changes are going on and relationships among variables are changing. A cross-sectional study would allow you to analyze the change at one moment in great detail, but could not describe what the trends would be like.

Finally, another cause of discrepancy between time-series and cross-sectional results—as seen in studies of the relationship between fertility or suicide and income—is that the cross-sectional studies, and usually the time-series studies too, do not take proper account of the past effects of the relevant variables (income, in this case). The cross section includes data only on people's present incomes, but their past incomes also influence their present behavior, sometimes in ways that counteract the effects of present income. For example, higher-income families give their children more education, which may teach them to want, and how to achieve, smaller families. But the statistical natures of the short- and long-time series and the cross sections are quite different, and they are affected differently by the past. Therefore, one must be particularly thoughtful when choosing a wide-view or a long-view method whenever the past may still have influence on the present values of the dependent variable.

4. Designs for Studying Changes Over Time

People change. A few examples: First, the percentage results of a presidential election would be somewhat different if the election were held a month earlier or later. The results would even differ slightly if the election were a day earlier or later. (Even if during the campaign few people change their minds about which candidate they prefer, the proportion of people who are prepared to vote may well change.) Second, a question asked at the beginning of an interview may get a different answer than if it were asked at the end of the interview, either because of fatigue or because an earlier question may alter the interviewee's knowledge or attitude toward the subject of a later question. Third, at the end of the day chimpanzees may take longer to learn how to reach the banana than at the beginning, or they may learn more slowly during one season of the year than during another. Fourth, in 1890 practically no one smoked cigarettes. Fifty years later half the nation smoked cigarettes. These changes over time are breaches of *ceteris paribus* for studies that use several time periods as samples.[1]

We say that changes occur with time. True enough. But it is not time itself that brings the changes to pass; rather, various processes that occur over time bring change. If people were frozen in such a way as to slow all their bodily processes but not to kill them—as can be done with small cells and human sperm—the passage of time would have no effect. Rather, it is *fatigue* that affects the chimpanzee's perform-

ance late in the day. It might be growing annoyance that produces a different answer to a question late in an interview. It is changes in the world situation that alter the election-poll results over time. And it was a shift in tastes as well as improvements in tobacco and cigarette-making technology that caused the increase in United States cigarette consumption in the twentieth century. The word "time" itself is nothing but shorthand for other changes that occur.

Change over time comes in several varieties. A change can be a long-run trend; for example, we believe that the long-run change in our economy will be upward. Change can be cyclical: Each morning the chimpanzees' responses may be faster than in the evening. Or change can be totally unpredictable and without apparent regularity, as is the case with the interest rates on the bond market from day to day (Cootner, 1964). (If you *do* find regularities in the bond market that you can predict in advance, be sure to let us know immediately.) Any or all of these kinds of change over time can throw a monkey (chimp) wrench into your research.

Even if a change seems to occur over time—or along with some other change in condition—you often cannot be sure *which* of the other things is not being held constant and is therefore to blame.

For example, until 1982 scores on the Scholastic Aptitude Test (SAT) had declined fairly steadily for over ten years. Many things have been proposed to account for the decline, including declining school quality, excessive television, an increasing likelihood that poor students will take the test, increasing test difficulty, and poorer test-taking skills. At this point, none of the studies on this subject is conclusive because so many things have changed over time. Interpreting the studies requires good judgment and the guidance of theory if we are to separate the likely causes of the decline from unlikely ones.

---

1. Whether one can predict the future from the past depends on whether one can assume *ceteris paribus* from the observed period to the future. This issue is discussed in detail in Chapter 3.

The obvious way to study changes over time is to obtain a sample of the subject matter and actually to watch its change. Some famous studies have followed phenomena over a long time. Terman (1976), for example, tracked the growth patterns and maturity of a group of exceptional children for almost thirty years. Seltzer (1968) studied the health and habits of a group of Harvard undergraduates for many years after graduation. And economists have studied the course of some series of agricultural prices for hundreds of years.

But, there are many obstacles to the straightforward application of the long-view method—notably that, unless the data from the past already exist, few of us have the patience to wait around for slow-moving events to unfold themselves. There are, however, a number of ways of overcoming obstacles caused by the facts that we have neither data about the past nor enough time to wait around for a long process to unfold.

One way to find out what happened long ago is to *ask* people (though one must ask questions very carefully to reduce as much as possible inaccuracies caused by forgetfulness and other factors). For example, one of us wanted to find out how people's happiness changed when their family incomes changed, without waiting many years to collect the information. Therefore he employed questions of this sort:

Given your present knowledge of yourself and of other people, what proportion of Americans of your age and sex would you say are (were) happier than you are (were)?

A.   Less than 10% happier than you
B.   10–25%
C.   25–50%
D.   50–75%
E.   75–90%
F.   More than 90% happier than you

_____ At present
_____ When you were in early grammar school, grades 1 to 4

_____ When you were in grammar school, grades 5 to 8
_____ When you were in high school
_____ When you were age 17 to 22 (or in college)
_____ (Skip if under 29) When you were age 23 to 29
_____ (Skip if under 39) When you were age 30 to 39
_____ (Skip if under 49) When you were age 40 to 49
_____ (Skip if under 59) When you were age 50 to 59
_____ (Skip if under 69) When you were age 60 to 69

Sometimes one can surmount the obstacle of slow change by artificially speeding up time. Geneticists cannot wait around for the many years between generations of human beings; instead they study the genetics of fruit flies or other organisms that reproduce generations very quickly. In a year's time they can trace a genetic change through perhaps thirty successive generations of fruit flies.

Time may also be speeded up artificially with a combination of analytic and experimental devices. For example, earlier we noted that there are too few business cycles in recent U.S. history to provide economists with sufficient data for study. Another way to handle this situation is to make various assumptions about how typical individuals and institutions of various types in the economy behave—banks, families, steel companies, Federal Reserve Bank, and so forth—and then to "simulate" their interaction on a computer. Instead of taking three years, a business cycle can be run through the computer in minutes. Then the economist can examine what kind of business cycle results from a given set of assumptions, as outlined in Chapter 11.

For studies of child development, aging processes, and life histories, the method of *artificial cohorts* can be substituted for actual cohorts. For example, if one wanted to see how great an impact family background had on people's occupational success as they got older, one could study an actual cohort of people (that is, a group of people of about the same age) as they begin their careers, and follow them through their lives. But if one did not have the time or money to carry out such a study, one could interview a cross section of people of different ages, divide the sample up into age groups—artificial cohorts—and see how their present occupational success was related to family background. Or one could compare the activity rates of each of a group of one-month-old monkeys with a group of two-month-old monkeys on the same day, rather than beginning with a group of one-month old monkeys and then waiting a month to study them again.

Accounting for effects that are spread out over time can often be done effectively with statistical analysis of past data. But it is often preferable, where possible, to investigate such effects with experiments that permit observations in several successive periods.

5. The Panel

The panel is a special type of time-series technique; it measures some attributes of a *given sample* at several moments. But is differs from other long-view studies in two ways.

A first major difference between the panel and nonpanel long-view techniques is that the panel is much more efficient when you want to measure *changes* from period to period rather than the *absolute levels*. A campaign manager wants to know whether people are shifting toward his candidate, or the soap firm wants to know whether more people are shifting to its brand than away from it. The television executive wants to know whether one episode of a show is *better or worse* than another episode in terms of listenership. For such *comparative* problems the panel method offers great statistical efficiency; there is much less sampling error in the panel, because individuals can be compared to themselves at different moments

A panel is *not* the only way to obtain historical information, however. It is possible to take *separate samples* at various points in time instead of collecting data on the single panel sample. For example, if you want to know in *absolute* terms what proportion of the vote your candidate has at different times before the election, then it really does not matter, conceptually, whether you poll 1,000 people two months before the election and *another* 1,000 people one month before or whether you poll a 1,000-person panel twice. There may be *practical* differences between these two strategies, such as the possibility of spoiling the panel by polling them once. But there are not likely to be major cost differences between these two strategies (except perhaps higher costs in finding the same people twice). Similarly, separate samples give conceptually the same television ratings, but for some rating methods—especially those that require placing electronic meters in homes—it is enormously *cheaper* to use panels of the same people for repeated measurements.

A second—and perhaps more important—difference between the panel and nonpanel long-view methods is that the panel method can reveal much back-and-forth shifting of behavior that is otherwise hidden from view. This can have important implications for our understanding of social processes. Until the late 1960s, for example, poverty was considered to be a more or less permanent characteristic of individuals. Nearly every cross-sectional survey showed the same proportion of Americans living in poverty, and it was assumed that it was the same people in poverty each time. Aaron wrote:

> The only comprehensive statistics available during the 1960s were snapshots of the overall distribution of income. Following these data was like watching the grass grow. They showed almost no year-to-year change in the distribution of income. . . . As is so often the case, the characteristic of available data influenced perceptions

and descriptions. Poverty could be perceived as a relatively fixed state and the poor as an identifiable group because all surveys were cross-sectional snapshots rather than longitudinal moving pictures. Movement in and out of the poverty population, by implication, was difficult and infrequent. (1978: 17–18)

These shortcomings are now being remedied. Based on the first five years of the Panel Survey on Income Dynamics . . ., a major new study has shown that at the end of five years, fewer than half of the people in poverty in the first year remain in poverty.

Roughly one-third of those who are poor one year are not poor the next and were not poor the year before. The number of poor is stable because large flows in and out just about balance. . . . The view of poverty prevalent in the 1960s is distorted; a sizable fraction of the poor do not seem to be mired in that state. . . . In short, the simple snapshot of poverty that many people carelessly adopted a decade ago has become a complex moving picture. (1978: 36–37)

A panel study is not always feasible, however. One difficulty is that the events or thoughts may already be long past by the time the researcher begins. Occasionally this difficulty can be overcome by the use of retrospective questions, as illustrated in the question block on happiness in Section 4 of this chapter. Memory is not always reliable, however, and indeed one of the panel's major charms is that it avoids memory loss because questions are asked about contemporary behavior and thoughts.

Still another difficulty of the panel method is "mortality," the loss of respondents from wave to wave of interviewing. And there can also be statistically dangerous mixups in the identities of interviewees from wave to wave.

Another panel difficulty is that asking the panel questions may affect people's behavior. And sometimes the cost is high. Nevertheless, the panel can sometimes provide data that cannot be obtained in any other way.

6. Summary

When experimentation is not feasible, one turns to the data that occur without researcher interference. Two such basic research designs are the cross section and the time series.

Often cross-sectional and time-series analyses of the same phenomena will lead to the same conclusions, but sometimes they will not. Disagreements in results may come about because of differences between places or times not taken into account in the analyses, the length of time needed for changes to take place, and uncertainties about what factors cause what results.

Whenever possible, one should try to use *both* a cross section and a time series. If the results agree, the conclusions are strongly supported. If the results disagree, further analysis is needed to discover why; ultimately, you may get a better understanding of important social processes than if you had done only one type of analysis.

Many of the most important phenomena in social science unfold slowly over a period of years. Changes over time are not caused by abstract time itself but rather by various processes that occur over time. And such changes may be trends or cycles. In some cases you may grapple with changes over time by taking measurements appropriately spaced over the time period. In other cases you may be able to work at a given moment with samples of various ages. As usual, the appropriate tactic must depend on the purpose of the research.

As a substitute for observing the change over its full period, one may instead examine and compare at a given moment a cross section of people (the "wide view") who are at different stages of the unfolding of the phenomena. The wide view also protects against irrelevant but large changes in general social and economic conditions that always occur over long periods of time.

A very different situation is that in which the researcher wishes to know how people will behave when subjected to a single different condition found in different areas. But so much else also varies from place to place that a reasonable comparison cannot be made. As a substitute for the wide-view comparison, the researcher may turn to a long view from historical records of given people who were exposed to different treatments at different times in their lives.

The panel method offers the best advantages of the wide view and the long view combined, and hence it has enormous research power. It has great statistical efficiency because the same individuals can be compared with themselves at different times, hence reducing extraneous variability, and they can also be compared to each other. Panels require forethought and much organization, as well as expensive observation over the study period. But they are nevertheless the most appropriate method in many research situations.

EXERCISES

1. Give three examples in your field of use of the long-view approach.
2. Give three examples in your field of use of the wide-view approach (that is, the cross section).
3. Give an example of the use of the panel in your field and why it was preferred to other methods.
4. Give an example in which data are easier to obtain for a wide view than for a long view; give a contrary example.
5. Explain why the long-view technique used in one of the examples in Exercise 1 was preferable to the wide-view approach. Do the same for one example in Exercise 2, explaining why the wide-view was preferable to the long-view approach.
6. A university runs a high school for gifted students. You wonder whether the admission system is biased in favor of the children of parents who work in the school of education at the university. How would you determine whether such a bias shows in the composition of the student body? (Don't forget children whose parents don't work at the university but who are accepted at the university high school.)
7. How would you go about checking whether there is a bias in favor of brothers and sisters who are already at the university high school? That is, does a student with an older sibling have a better than average chance of being accepted?

ADDITIONAL READING

Firebaugh (1980b) discusses the differences between cross-sectional and time-series research, and the advantages of each.

Glenn (1974; 1977) discusses how to do studies taking separate samples at various points in time.

Zeisel (Chap. 10) gives a full but simple account of the panel method in public opinion and advertising research. Ferber and Verdoorn (1962: 267–277) discuss consumer-panel use in economics and business. They present a great deal of information on the time-series method and the cross-sectional approach. Markus (1979) shows how panel data are analyzed and interpreted.

Two of the best known panel studies are those of Morgan and Duncan (1979), which deals with the economic situation of families, and of Jennings and Niemi (1981), which considers how parents transmit attitudes to their children.

Tilly (1981) provides a fascinating description of what may be learned by bringing "time-series" analysis as customarily practiced by sociologists and economists together with the types of analysis carried out by historians. Special problems can arise in cross-cultural or cross-national analyses, where the differences between the units of analysis are tremendous, but such analyses can produce unusual insights into social life as well.

Armer and Grimshaw (1973) and Przeworski and Teune (1970) provide analyses of the promises and pitfalls of "comparative" research.

Surveys and Other Ways of Gathering Your Own Data

13

1. The Nature of Nonexperimental Research

Nonexperimental research, unlike experiments, gathers data about variables *as they are found naturally in the world*. The data for this type of research may already exist in the form of records such as the national census or the questionnaire data in the Roper Center repository (at Yale University in New Haven, Connecticut) that were collected in the past; or you may need to collect new data especially for your purposes. The logic of the nonexperimental approach is much the same either way.

This chapter considers research in which you collect data yourself, focusing on the method most often used to collect data on lots of people—the survey. The next chapter describes research in which you use data other people have already collected.

The term "nonexperimental research" is applied to two very different sorts of investigation. The first aims to learn about relationships between variables, especially causal relationships. Causal-analysis research is quite analogous to experimentation, with the single (but overwhelmingly important) difference that the independent variable(s) is not controlled and manipulated by the researcher. Instead the researcher seeks out groups of people that have *already* been exposed to different levels of the independent variable. For example, instead of subjecting randomly selected groups of people to different amounts of cigarette smoke, the researcher finds people who have smoked various numbers of cigarettes. Or a researcher who wants to study the effect of family income on juvenile delinquency does not choose various groups of families to receive various incomes; rather, he finds and assesses the amount of delinquency in families with different incomes.

The steps in pursuing causal-analysis research are much the same as those set forth for an experiment. Furthermore, the obstacles to studying causal relationships with nonexperimental research and the methods of overcoming these obstacles contribute much of the subject matter of this book. Therefore, we shall not pursue the matter further in this chapter, except to summarize the advantages and disadvantages of the nonexperimental method for causal analysis. After that, we shall focus on research that aims to provide quantitative *descriptions* of some aspects of a universe rather than to discover relationships.

2. Advantages of Nonexperimental Methods for Relationship Research

First, *with nonexperimental research you can get closer to the "real" hypothetical (theoretical) variables than with a laboratory experiment*. You can actually inspect the variables in their real-world setting; for instance, you can examine real cases of lung cancer and real movements of the economy without having to abstract from the real variables to a mock-up laboratory situation. This is the preeminent advantage over an experiment in those cases in which you want to investigate relationships but in which real-world experiments are impossible.

Second, nonexperimental research is often quite *cheap,* especially if you can use existing records and data. If data exist for the prices and amounts of onions sold each month for several years, using them to explore the relationship between price and quantity is obviously cheaper than setting up a laboratory situation in which people are given quantities of money and opportunities to purchase onions and other foods at varying onion prices.

Third, huge masses of data are often already available or can be culled from existing records—voter-registration lists, for example. This is a major statistical advantage, because the large samples provide high internal reliability. Such huge samples are seldom available in experimentation.

Fourth, nonexperimental research can yield a very rich understanding of people—both in breadth by collecting a wealth of information, and in depth by probing people's motives.

3. Disadvantages of Nonexperimental Methods for Relationship Research

The major disadvantages described here apply only to causal and noncausal *relationship* research and not to census-type research.

First, the crucial disadvantage of the nonexperimental method in causal analysis is the *lack of manipulation of the independent variable*. Because there is no "controlled" variation in the independent variable, it is always possible that the correlation between the independent variable and dependent variables is not "causal" (see Chapter 22). But is is a mistake to say that the results never show causation. Whether the results are causal depends on many things (see Chapter 35). One short example here: Changes in state liquor taxes are accompanied by changes in the prices of liquor. The effects of these changes in price on liquor consumption can be studied. The changes in consumption may reasonably be said to be caused by the changes in price because there is no likely connection between consumption and the moment when the legislators decide to raise the tax; the states act in much the same way that an experimenter would if he were randomly selecting when to raise taxes. There is no other likely relationship between the tax rise (and the price change) and the change in consumption, and therefore it is *reasonable* to say that the price change causes the change in liquor consumption.

To repeat the main point, nonexperimental research lacks the almost clinching proof of actually trying out the relationship by varying the independent variable to see whether it is indeed followed by changes in the dependent variable.

A second disadvantage of this approach is that *one cannot progressively investigate one aspect after another of the independent variable* to get closer to the "real" cause. One cannot first try out the cigarette, then the cigarette paper and the tobacco separately, and so forth until the ingredient that really causes cancer is isolated.

Third, *statistical devices are not always able to separate the effects of several independent variables* when there is multivariable causation, especially when two independent variables are themselves highly associated. For example, the same people tend to have high incomes and high education; therefore, it may be difficult to tell from survey results whether it is education or income that causes the purchase of books and "high class" magazines.

Our final comment on the choice of experimental or nonexperimental methods for causal analysis is old stuff to you by now. Several methods are better than one. If you can seek the knowledge you want with *both* types and if the results jibe reasonably well, you have a much stronger basis for belief in your results than if your conclusions were based on just one of the techniques.

4. Descriptive Surveys

Now let us discuss the method social scientists use most frequently to gather their own data— the *survey*. We will focus on descriptive surveys here, in contradistinction to causal research surveys. They are surveys whose purpose is to provide true quantitative descriptions of aspects of a universe of people or things.

Because the purpose of the descriptive survey is to obtain an accurate picture of the universe, *random sampling* is particularly important. If the sample is biased in some way, so that it does not cover an important segment of the universe, and if each segment is not sampled in proportion to the relative size of the segment, then the picture of the universe will be distorted and misleading (unless the nonproportional sampling is done purposely and with full knowledge). It is obvious that you cannot find out who will win the next election by asking only Republicans for whom they will vote; yet *The Literary Digest* did almost precisely that when it predicted that Landon would win in 1936. Usually the bias is more subtle, however, and therefore more dangerous. For example, a local civic association decided that it would survey what the people in one city think about the educational system, the work opportunities, and other aspects of the community. The survey was worked out in very nice detail with but one flaw: The sampling plan originally omitted all streets north of the tracks, where most blacks live, because the person running the survey thought that "it would be dangerous for student interviewers." Of course, it is just those blacks who would most likely be dissatisfied with the educational system and other city services. The bias introduced by not taking a random sample *must* have distorted the results to make the picture seem rosier than it is—though perhaps that was what the civic association really wanted.

There are several dimensions of classification that tell us something about the nature of a survey:

1. As already noted, a survey can aim to discover causal relationships or to create accurate quantitative descriptions of one or more aspects of a universe. All subsequent discussion applies only to descriptive surveys.

2. A survey can be a *complete census* of the universe, or it can be a *sample survey* of the universe in microcosm. The advantage of the complete census is accuracy; the advantage of the sample survey is lower cost.

3. A survey need not be a survey of people.

You can survey either *people* or *things*. The library study alluded to earlier surveyed the use of *books* in libraries. Or the survey can be of animals (how many cattle are there in Texas?) or of plants (how many acres of corn were planted in Illinois last year?). Most social-scientific surveys are of people, however. And one may survey *groups* as well as individuals. Families are the smallest groups commonly studied. The largest groups are nations; one can survey the nations of the world to discover their policies toward population control by sending questionnaires to the relevant bureaucrats in each nation. Voluntary organizations are forever surveying their local groups as, for example, when they ask for yearly reports on membership and activities undertaken throughout the year.

4. A survey can either *observe* or *ask questions*. All surveys of nonhuman material must use the observational method—at least until we find a horse that really does talk. But many surveys of human beings also observe behavior rather than asking questions, as, for example, when we count the passengers who ride buses, observe how many people buy a product at different price levels, or meter the number of television sets tuned to a given program.

5. One borderline technique between observing and questioning is to ask people to observe themselves (the diary technique). Another is to ask them what they have done in the past. Observation by the researcher, his or her assistants, or mechanical devices is generally preferable to self-observation, but often it is too costly or otherwise impractical, as, for example, in sex surveys. Self-observations can have severe limitations. Cantril found that only 86 per cent of people who were interviewed twice at a three-week interval gave the same answer both times about whether they owned a car, and only 87 per cent gave the same answer about how they voted in the 1940 presidential election (Cantril, 1977: 102–103). The diary technique can avoid such memory losses, but memory failure is not the only cause of the

type of discrepancy found in the second interviews.

Instruments enhance the power of the researcher to observe human behavior. One-way glass enables the psychologist to see without affecting the subject. Fingerprint paper enables the magazine researcher to count the number of people who thumb pages. Infrared dust on people's shoes leaves detectable traces where the subjects walk. The eye camera records eye movements of people as they walk through supermarkets. The camera and tape recorder are invaluable additions to the anthropologist's armamentarium, as Mead (1961) never ceases to remind us.[1] Instruments can also be used to observe physiological states such as blood pressure and galvanic skin response; they are useful in studying levels of emotional responses to various stimuli.

Often the choice between observing and questioning is a matter of convenience and feasibility. But sometimes the types of data that may be obtained by observing or questioning are very different. For example, people's answers to questions about how happy they are constitute one possible proxy for happiness. And observed rates of suicide and lynching constitute another possible proxy for happiness (actually for the opposite of happiness). But the concepts of happiness for which the proxies stand might be considerably different.

This book gives relatively little treatment to questionnaire surveys. There are several reasons for what may seem a cavalier neglect of the technique that constitutes so much of research in sociology and market research and social psychology. For one, the questionnaire survey is very well covered in an extensive literature. Furthermore, a special treatment of questionnaire surveys leads readers to think that questionnaire research has very special properties that make it entirely different from

---

1. Webb et al. (1966) have collected a great many of what they call "unobtrusive measures" or "oddball measures" of human behavior.

other kinds of research—which is not so. Also, we want to decrease the likelihood that students will rush blindly to use the questionnaire survey. It is not that we want to discourage its use when it really is appropriate, but too often people do questionnaire research just because they do not realize that there may indeed be much better methods for getting the knowledge they want.

6. Another way of classifying surveys is by the several types of information that they can obtain. A survey may obtain such *demographic data* as population, age, weight, income, and so forth. The U.S. Census is the major illustration of a demographic-data survey. But most other surveys collect some demographic data also, often to describe behavior and attitudes of different groups of people.

Demographic data have been collected as long as there have been governments; information about population and property has always been important to rulers so that they could levy and collect taxes. Toynbee (the uncle) quoted this interesting speech about a proposed English census survey, delivered in Parliament in 1753, by Mr. Thornton, Member for the City of York:

> I did not believe that there was any set of men, or indeed any individual of the human species, so presumptuous and so abandoned as to make the proposal we have just heard. . . . I hold this project [a census of population] to be totally subversive of the last remains of English liberty. . . . The new bill will direct the imposition of new taxes, and indeed the addition of a very few words will make it the most effective engine of rapacity and oppression which was ever used against an injured people. . . . Luckily this dire prediction has not come to pass. Moreover, an annual register of our people will acquaint our enemies abroad with our weakness. (Toynbee, 1884/1956: 7, 127)

Information about people's *behavior* may also be obtained by surveys. Knowledge of behavior is the goal of much of the behavioral sciences and all of economics; therefore, behavior

surveys are of obvious use. Furthermore, information about behavior may also be of interest to us if we are interested in what people *think*, because we can often infer attitudes and beliefs from people's behavior. The behaviorist psychologists go very far in saying that nothing *except* behavior can be meaningful data in psychology (and speech is therefore known as "verbal behavior"). This matter is discussed in a brief note at the end of the chapter.

People's *intentions about future behavior* can sometimes be ascertained by asking them what they plan to do in the future. Important economic data about consumers' intentions to buy durable goods and about businesspeople's intentions to invest in plant and equipment are regularly obtained by surveys of intentions. Naturally enough, people do not always do what they have earlier said they intended to do. How well the intentions jibe with the behavior depends on such factors as the length of time between the survey and the behavior and whether there are unusual occurrences (such as a recession) in between. To some extent the errors wash out; some people who intended do not do, and some who did not intend do.

The amount of *information* that people have about various aspects of the world is sometimes the subject of surveys. For government- or business-policy purposes, it may be important to know how many people know that a new recreation area has been opened or that all males must register for the draft or that the income tax has been changed or that Argonaut is now president of the United States. Gallup polls often seek this kind of information.

Opinions, attitudes, beliefs, and interests are often the subject of surveys. We lump all these categories together and call them *thoughts* or *mental contents* because the type of method that is used is quite similar for all of them. This is tricky knowledge to obtain because practically every obstacle enumerated in earlier chapters crops up.

As we have noted, sometimes we survey behavior as a means of inferring what people think. The converse is also true; sometimes we survey people's thoughts in order to learn something about their behavior. The justification given by many social psychologists for surveying attitudes about race relations is that we can infer something about people's behavior from their attitudes. Such inference is hazardous at best, as advertising research tells us with great authority; there is a very tenuous relationship between what people say about a product and their actual purchasing. There must be *some* relationship between the contents of people's minds and what they do, but the relationship is very often not straightforward. Part of the trouble is that there is no one-to-one relationship between what is in a person's mind and what that person tells an interviewer.

The reasons people give for their actions are still another subject of surveys: the surveys that ask "why?" Why did you buy a Ford this year? Why did you not go fishing in your neighbor's canoe? Why did you vote for Reagan?

Many surveys of other kinds are also intended to discover the causes of human behavior, but in some cases the simple question "why?" can unravel a complex matter with dispatch. This is especially true when one is inquiring into rational actions that are under conscious control, like asking a professor why she gives Jones "F" and Smith "A." The question of why is also very effective when one is trying to find out a set of social *rules;* for example, if you ask a Japanese why he takes off his shoes when he visits a house, the answer will probably be useful and accurate. But when investigating motivations that are less rational and that depend on a person's tastes, loyalties, and education, "why" questions are not so likely to produce useful answers. For example, think how confusing it would be if someone asked you why you bought the car you did. To start with, you would not know whether you were being asked why you bought *any* car or why

you bought this particular make of auto. And if the latter, you would have difficulty in conveying just why you bought a Ford.

7. Questionnaire surveys are classified by whether they are done *by mail, by telephone, or by personal interviewing. The mail survey* is generally cheapest, though sometimes telephone interviewing within a local area can rival it for cost. The main disadvantage of the mail survey is the difficulty of obtaining a satisfactory random sample because some people do not return the questionnaires. Furthermore, those people may well be very different and might give different answers from those people who do respond. (Nonresponse bias is discussed on pp. 265–269.) Sometimes it is possible to increase the response by mailing repeated questionnaires to people. And occasionally the types of information that you seek will not be in danger of bias from nonresponse; a trivial example would be a poll of a professional association's membership about whether the convention should be in New York or Baltimore; there is no reason to believe that the nonresponders would have different preferences from those of the people who do respond. But usually you must investigate the extent and nature of the bias with auxiliary techniques—perhaps with telephone or personal interviews of a sample of the nonresponders—so that you can allow for the bias by adjusting the results of the mail sample.

The rate of response to a mail questionnaire depends very much on who is sending it out, its subject, who receives it, and how easy it is to answer. The response rate can also be influenced by the cover letter sent with the questionnaire and by the inducements offered. Earlier one of us reported that a three-cent ballpoint pen doubled responses in a library study (Fussler and Simon, 1961). Another report, slightly unbelievable, indicates that 75 per cent of a ballpoint-pen group responded, whereas the control-group response was 18 per cent (Klein). Sometimes it is worthwhile to purchase people's answers by sending a nickel, dime, quarter, or even dollar with each questionnaire.

The U.S. Bureau of the Census has employed mail questionnaires as the primary method of collecting data on population and housing since the 1970 Census. A test produced a response rate of 83–89 per cent for the first mailing, and the Bureau hopes to do better in the future. The biggest problem is creating an accurate mailing list (S. Cohen, 1965: 22).

Telephone interviewing can be a remarkably efficient survey method. Until recently it was used only locally because of the cost of long-distance calls, though in some cases long-distance telephone interviewing was efficient. Recently the phone companies have made available various flat-rate plans under which unlimited long-distance calling is possible within wide areas; in some plans the state is the limit, in others the entire United States. These deals are in the process of giving telephone interviewing a vast new importance, we think. Telephone interviewing has been too little used in the past to replace personal interviewing, but now it must come into its own.

There is little difficulty with nonresponse in telephone interviewing, and therefore the sample obtained from a telephone survey is sufficiently random for many purposes. Furthermore, the sample can be taken sequentially; you just keep making more calls until your sample is big enough, which relieves you of having to decide in advance how large it must be. One snag is that the telephone book is not a very random sample; it excludes unlisted phones and people who have moved recently, which together total about 20 per cent of the total phones in service (Cooper, 1964: 45; Glassen and Metzger, 1972: 60). But random-dialing techniques have been developed that avoid this difficulty (Groves and Kahn, 1979).

The main disadvantages of the telephone interview are these: First, the interview must usually be short; unless you prearrange the interview, it is seldom practical to ask more than a handful of questions. Second, you cannot observe the subject visually; in personal interviews observation can reduce lying. However, people may not lie or exaggerate as much in a phone interview as in a personal interview because they are not as personally involved with the telephone interviewer. Third, some people do not have phones, but in some areas of the United States such high proportions of people have phones that the worst possible bias from this source cannot be very dangerous.

Personal interviews suffer only from the disadvantage of high cost in money and time. At 1982 costs, personal interviews of a sample of people chosen randomly throughout the United States may cost $75 or more *per interview*, even when carried out by organizations that already have staff facilities set up for interviewing. If you had to start from scratch, the cost would be even higher. Local interviews can be much cheaper, of course.

But personal interviews have some important advantages over mail and phone interviews, which is why they are used despite the high costs. The interview can be long, sometimes several hours; people often enjoy being interviewed. The interviewer can check some information with his or her own eyes, which may reduce exaggeration; for example, not many people who live in shacks dare report high incomes to interviewers in person. (However, the personal relationship with the interviewer leads some people to want to impress the interviewer.) Another major advantage of the personal interview as compared with the mail survey is that the interviewer can probe for further information, by asking "What do you mean by that?" and so on, and he or she can also explain questions that the subject cannot understand; the interviewer can even translate into a foreign language for a subject who does not speak English.

The choice among mail, telephone, and personal interviews is delicate and calls for good judgment on the part of the researcher. You must consider all the advantages and disadvantages of the various techniques (summarized in Table 13.1) *as they apply to your particular research project*. The trick is to balance the advantages against the disadvantages to arrive at the best possible technique for the expenditure of time and money (Groves and Kahn, 1979).

5. Questionnaire Construction

We have emphasized that there are lots of ways to get data other than by asking people

TABLE 13.1   Relative Merits of Principal Methods of Data Collection

Personal Interview	Mail	Telephone
	Advantages	
Most flexible means of obtaining data	Wider and more representative distribution of sample possible	Representative and wider distribution of sample possible
Identity of respondent known	No field staff	No field staff
Nonresponse generally very low	Cost per questionnaire relatively low	Cost per response relatively low
Distribution of sample controllable in all respects	People may be more frank on certain issues, e.g., sex	Control over interviewer bias easier; supervisor present essentially at interview
	No interviewer bias; answers in respondent's own words	Quick way of obtaining information
	Respondent can answer at leisure, has time to "think things over"	Nonresponse generally very low
	Certain segments of population more easily approachable	Callbacks simple and economical
	Disadvantages	
Likely to be most expensive of the three	Bias due to nonresponse often indeterminate	Interview period may have to be relatively short
Headaches of interviewer supervision and control	Control over questionnaire may be lost	Questions must be short and to the point; probes difficult to handle
Dangers of interviewer bias and cheating	Interpretation of omissions difficult	Certain types of questions cannot be used, e.g., thematic apperception
	Cost per return may be high if nonresponse very large	Nontelephone owners cannot be reached
	Certain questions, such as extensive probes, can not be asked	
	Only those interested in subject may reply	
	Not always clear who replies	
	Certain segments of population not approachable, e.g., illiterates	
	Likely to be slowest of all	

SOURCE: *Research Methods in Economics and Business,* p. 210, by Robert Ferber and P. J. Verdoorn; © The Macmillan Company 1962; reprinted by permission of The Macmillan Company.

directly. Nevertheless, this approach is used very frequently, so in this section and the next we provide some guidelines to two critical aspects of the data-gathering process: questionnaire construction and interviewing.

These are key elements in sound questionnaire construction:

1. Keep your study's purpose clearly in mind at all times. This will help ensure that you ask all the questions you want to ask, and leave out questions you do not need answers to.
2. Begin by jotting down the topics you want information about, without worrying about wording or logical order.
3. Number the topics in a logical order, using these principles:
   a. To the interviewee, the organization of the questionnaire should seem sensible and smooth-flowing.
   b. If some questions will affect the answers to others, put the influencing questions afterwards.
   c. If there are some questions (such as income) that you may not get answers to, and that may antagonize people, put them last.
   d. Put the least important questions near the end, in case they do not get answered.
4. Write first approximations of the questions. Use simple language, make each question as short as possible, and use other techniques of effective writing. Devising good questions takes experience and good judgment. Some of the specific obstacles you may encounter are discussed in Chapter 20. For more detailed guidance, see Payne (1951); Schuman and Presser (1981); Bradburn, Sudman et al. (1979).
5. Pretest the questionnaire by *personally* going out and asking the questions in an "open-ended" fashion—that is, without a list of answers among which the interviewee must choose. Talk to, say, ten friends and acquaintances (with whom you can feel comfortable) as well as a few members of the target population. Tape-record some of the interviews if you can.
6. Rewrite ambiguous questions, reorganize the questionnaire where necessary, throw out unnecessary or unsuccessful questions, convert some open-end to closed-end questions, and generally tighten up the questionnaire. Attend to the length of the questionnaire: Telephone interviews must be relatively short—and the shorter the interviews are, the cheaper and more effective they will be.
7. Write an introduction that will persuade potential interviewees to participate. If you just say, "Please answer this questionnaire," or "I need it for a course," many people will turn you down or throw away a mail questionnaire—and there is little reason for them not to. But if you tell people how their responses can help society or some particular group or themselves, or how the interview will be an interesting experience, you'll get much greater cooperation. In some cases, it will be best to pay people or give them presents for being willing to be interviewed.
8. Pretest again.
9. Improve the questionnaire again.
10. Go into the field for part of the interviews.
11. Check the preliminary results. If satisfactory, complete the work.

It is well to remember that no one ever becomes perfect at constructing questionnaires. Hanan Selvin, most helpful and generous sociologist-editor of this book and a man of great survey experience, confessed that on a 1974 survey of the faculty of his university, he forgot to ask the respondent's sex, and in 1975 he remembered sex but forgot to ask the respondent's race. There is no cure for such flaws except extensive pretesting. The experienced "pro" may get into trouble by figuring he or she is so good that pretesting can be skipped. Don't skip or skimp on pretesting; pretest again and again and again and. . . .

> As question worders we need to develop a critical attitude toward our own questions. We must check the tendency to accept the first wording that makes sense to us. We must subordinate any pride of authorship to this critical attitude and should try to substitute clarity for cleverness. Every objection that may be raised about the phrasing should be carefully considered, because that problem may occur many times over in the full-scale survey. If even a single test interview or comment from one of our associates implies any fault in the question, that fault should not be passed over. How many people in the final survey will stumble over the same obstacle?
>
> The tendency to take things for granted is not easy to correct, simply because it is such a common characteristic of us all. (Payne, 1951: 17)

There is a vast literature on the construction of appropriate questions and appropriate ways of asking questions (Schuman and Presser 1981; Payne, 1951; Bradburn, Sudman et al., 1979). Many examples show that small differences in the form of the question can make a big difference in the responses, as we saw earlier. The danger is greatest when one seeks to learn about people's attitudes and opinions. The form of the question is not as important when you ask for *factual information*. "What is the name of that traitor who is president?" may get practically the same responses as "Who is that great American who is president?" Sometimes researchers waste their own and other people's energy in nit-picking discussions about which is the best question to use to ask a person's age or whether to ask the question at the beginning or the end of the questionnaire schedule. The form of the question, however, can be enormously important in supposedly factual questions too, as this incident in the measurement of the labor force demonstrates:

> Prior to July 1945 a single question was used. It asked, *Was this person at work on a private or government job last week?* Beginning in that month, two questions were substituted. The first of these merely asked what the person's major activity was during the preceding week. If the major activity was something other than working, the enumerator then asked whether in addition the person did any work for pay or profit during the week.
>
> The upshot of this change in questions was that in the trial when both versions were used, the new questioning showed an increase of 1,400,000 employed persons over the old wording. About half of these additional workers had worked 35 or more hours during the week under consideration! (Payne, 1951: 11)

Payne argues that the critical issue in designing questions is "to make sure that the particular issue which the questioner has in mind is the particular issue on which the respondent gives his answers" (p. 9). Trying out your questions to see how they actually work in a pretest is equally important.

> If all the problems of question wording could be traced to a single source, their common origin would probably prove to be in taking too much for granted. We questioners assume that people know what we are talking about. We assume that they have some basis for testimony. We assume that they understand our questions. We assume that their answers are in the frame of reference we intend.
>
> Frequently our assumptions are not warranted. Respondents may never before have heard of the subject. They may confuse it with something else. They may have only vague ideas about it and no means for forming judgments. (Payne, 1951: 16)

The *scope* of a question is important. Economics has shunned question-and-answer explanations of economic behavior because, we believe, the few attempts by economists have used questions of too wide a scope. They have asked businesspersons "How do you set your prices for liquor?" They would do better to ask the narrower question "Why is your price for Bonny Scotch $32 a case?" or, even better, "By what percentage would sales rise if you raised the price of Bonny Scotch to $33?"

In general, writing good questions is an art that usually requires imagination and experience. But a favorite question comes from a college yearbook and is shown in Figure 13.1.

You can obtain some information by asking for it directly. But some information must be obtained by indirection. Income, for example, is a touchy topic, and it is usually asked about by showing the respondent a set of cards with different *ranges* of income, e.g. $10,000–$15,000, and the subject is asked to point to the appropriate income range.

On some topics people hesitate to make revelations about themselves but are willing to make statements about *other* people. It may be reasonable to assume that such statements are projections of one's views about oneself. For example, R. Simon and J. Simon wished to determine the likely effect of possible government subsidies and taxes on people's fertility behavior. People may believe that it is im-

FIGURE 13.1   Do You Drink?

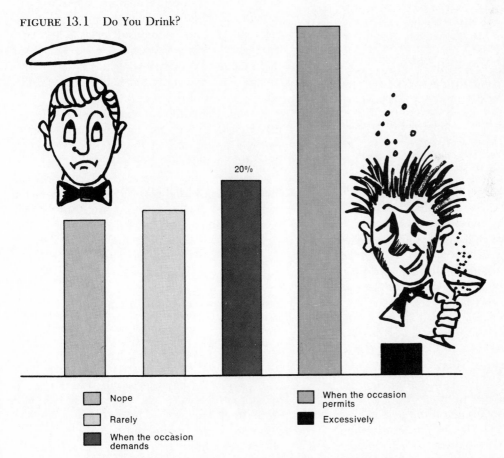

20%

Nope

Rarely

When the occasion demands

When the occasion permits

Excessively

Source: *Harvard Yearbook*, 1950; adapted by permission of Harvard Yearbook Publications, Inc.

moral or repulsive to have, or to not have, children for pay. They may resist placing a monetary value on unborn or already-born children. Therefore, people may not reply candidly to direct questions. Their verbal responses to direct questions may cover up their feelings, beliefs, and intentions about their likely behavior. For that reason, Simon and Simon asked both direct and projective questions. The projective questions were intended to ease the sense of repulsion or embarrassment and to allow people to describe their own feelings behind a facade of impersonality.

First respondents were asked:

> Please think for a moment about the average family in your neighborhood. How many children do most of the families in your neighborhood have before they stop having children?

Respondents were then asked:

> If the government were to give a monthly payment of $50—that is, $600 per year for each child after the second until that child is 18 years old— do you think the average family in your neighborhood would have more children than the (number answered in previous question) children they now have? (J. Simon and R. Simon, 1975: 586–587)

Unfortunately there is almost no information on how well projective questions really work, and under which conditions. Therefore, the result of a projective question must be buttressed with other sorts of information to support its standing as scientific evidence.

Even though you may do an excellent job in preparing the questionnaire, some questions will be more effective and easier to answer than others. It is useful to know which questions are superior, as an aid to evaluating your results. Twedt (personal correspondence) suggests you ask each interviewer to give two ratings to each question on the schedule, one for understanding and one for cooperation: "To the best of your memory, what percentage of the respondents *understand* the question, and

what percentage *cooperated* with truthful, considered answers?"

Another approach is to ask each respondent to indicate for each question how strongly held is the judgment or opinion given. This provides two ratings for each question, one for context and one for intensity. The intensity measure is then used to weight the influence of the substantive answer in the overall result.

6. Personal Interviewing

Interviewing has always been the main device for obtaining social, psychological, and economic information. And it will certainly continue to be important in the future despite the growth of self-administered questionnaires, self-reports, and automated data collection. Therefore, a few words especially dedicated to the practice of interviewing seem in order, though interviewing is touched upon in many other sections of the book.

Perhaps the most important element in good interviewing is that the interviewer not influence the response that the interviewee gives, by word or gesture or general demeanor, as discussed in this chapter. The interviewer must be friendly and pleasant so that the interviewee will be willing to cooperate. But the interviewer should not make the interviewee want to answer in such manner that he or she thinks will please the interviewer. And, the interviewer must not send out signals that will antagonize the interviewee into answering wrongly or perversely as an attempt to foul up the interviewer.

Toward the same end, the interviewee should not indicate in any way what answers the interviewer expects or wants to receive.

In addition to being pleasant and interested in the interviewee, the interviewer can increase the likelihood of obtaining cooperation if she or he dresses more-or-less like the interviewee, though not in a spectacular or "far out" manner.

A good interviewer must know the material thoroughly and follow instructions to the letter. Questions must be read exactly as they are written, in the order in which they are given, and the answers must be rendered faithfully, with as little interpretation as possible. All this requires study and practice before going into the field.

Sometimes interviewers are instructed to go beyond the written questions in order to "probe" for answers and underlying reasons. Good probing requires experience and tact.

The work of hired interviewers must be spot-checked by supervisors to ensure that the interviews were really done, and that the responses are those that the interviewee gave.

Some interviewers are much better than others (Sheatsley, 1967; Sudman, 1967: 108–153). Interviewers who have worked at the occupation for a long time are—on the whole—faster, more efficient, and more accurate than newer interviewers. This may be because the poorer interviewers leave the occupation, because people learn, or both.

Education and intelligence also are positively associated with the quality and quantity of work that interviewers produce. National Opinion Research Center's demographic profile of the best interviewer is a married, middle-aged woman, with some college education and previous interviewing experience.

Personality and motivation also are important factors in interviewer success. This includes self-confidence, a positive attitude toward interviewing, and the desire to do a good job—none of which is easy to measure, however, and most of which would make the person an effective employee in *any* position.

Even more important than screening potential interviewers before hiring them is to continually evaluate their performance after they have been hired. An attentive, close-watching supervisor is the basic check. Additionally, coders of the data can supply quantitative estimates of interviewer quality by recording in-

terviewer errors. This is the error-weighting system used by National Opinion Research Center:

Type of Error	Error Weight
1. Answer missing	3
2. Irrelevant or circular answer	3
3. Lack of sufficient detail	2
4. "Don't know" with no probe	2
5. Dangling probe	1
6. Multiple codes in error	1
7. Superfluous question asked.	1

(Sudman, 1967: 109)

7. The Steps in Executing a Survey

Step 1. Follow the procedures outlined in Chapter 7, to the point at which you are ready to decide on a method.

Step 2. Find out if the data you want to collect already exist in some published study or in one of the "data banks" of some major university research organizations. It is a shame to find out too late that you could have saved hours and dollars with a simple phone call or a letter. Sometimes the existing data are not exactly what you want; for example, the data published by the Internal Revenue Service do not contain fine breakdowns that would often be valuable, and people and firms are classified in categories that may not be ideal for your purposes. Nevertheless, it may be possible to adjust and interpolate the data to make it yield most of the information you want.

Step 3. From here on, it is assumed that you have *not* been able to find all the data you want in existing records but must collect some raw data yourself.[2] Your next step is to *define the*

2. In many studies, newly collected data is combined with old data in order to provide a more complete description (Hyman, 1972: Chap. 2).

universe that you want to sample or poll. The universe you work with might dictate whether you reach one conclusion or its opposite. For example, assume you want to know if there is any relationship between per capita income and radio ownership or between per capita income and the diets people choose. If you take a sample in a very homogeneous community like Park Forest, Illinois, you will find practically no differences. The range of income is very small, everyone owns a radio, and most people eat steak, drink milk, and eschew caviar. But, if the sample is taken in Chicago, which is more heterogeneous and has a wider income range than Park Forest has, there will be some people poor enough not to own radios, so that some relationship will appear between income and radio ownership. There will also appear to be some relationship between income and menu, for the lower-class black eats collard greens and side meat, and the hillbilly immigrant eats what she ate in the Ozarks. If the researcher wants to obtain a really high correlation, all she has to do is take a world-wide sample. Practically no one of low income in India has a radio.

A similar example exists for drinking behavior and religion. Just because the major religions in the United States do not differ significantly in their stands on drinking, one should not conclude that their point of view is common in all human groups. If the universe includes the Muslim countries, the results will be markedly different. Clearly the universe should be chosen for its relevance to the problem you are interested in and not for how strong a relationship it will yield.

Step 4. Next, decide on the *sampling procedure* you are going to use. This step includes deciding what list of people or other representation of the universe you will select from, the physical procedure you will use to select names (for instance, systematically by taking every nth name or randomly by selecting a random page and then a random name or going to every nth house), and then actually making up a list of people (or objects) to be sampled.

Step 5. Think out and decide on the procedure that you will actually use in *observing or questioning* your subjects. If you are gathering data with a questionnaire, preparation of the questionnaire is crucial. If you are using an observation survey, you must decide what pieces of behavior you will watch and count; this decision requires classification and definition. If you are studying the first stair-climbing behavior of babies, you must define what will count as climbing motions. If you have already prepared dummy tables, as we suggested on page 93, you will find them an enormous aid in the construction of the questionnaire or observation procedure.

Step 6. *Test* the questionnaire or the observation procedure in a preliminary run. Look for such things as confusion on the part of respondents about what questions mean and inability to answer within the categories you have provided. Then *revise* the questionnaire or observation procedure. Test again and revise until your procedure does the job it is supposed to do. It pays to iron out all possible difficulties at this stage rather than later.

Step 7. Collect your data.

Step 8. Analyze your data. This subject is covered in Chapters 24–26. Statistical analysis is usually a larger part of survey research—especially that seeking relationships—than of experimentation because the researcher must examine the effect of the variables *analytically* rather than by varying them physically as in an experiment.

Step 9. *Interpret* the data, and draw sound *conclusions*. Chapters 27–33 cover this work.

8. Participant Observation

If you want to study a complex situation about which little is known, then becoming personally involved in the situation—observing while participating—may be the best strategy. One tries to "record the ongoing experiences of those observed," and to "adopt the perspective of those studied by sharing in their day-to-day experiences" (Denzin, 1970a: 185) in order to understand the richness of individual and group experiences.

Participant-observers immerse themselves in a situation, and learn about it from all available sources of information—informal talks with members of the group being studied, reading letters and other documents, passively observing and listening while simply "hanging around" with the group, and so on. The key difference from other research methods is that participant-observers *participate with* and have some sort of role in the group, rather than maintaining a distance between themselves and the observed.

Research based on participant observation is likely to be exploratory. Richard Fenno, who spent years studying how members of Congress deal with people in their districts, has written:

> Someone doing this kind of research is quite likely to have no crystallized idea of what he or she is looking for or what questions to ask when he or she starts. Researchers typically become interested in some observable set of activities and decide to go have a firsthand look at them. They fully expect that an open-minded exposure to events in the milieu and to the perspectives of those with whom they interact will produce ideas that might never have occurred to them otherwise. (1978: 250)

Fenno describes how he followed members of Congress to their districts and watched what they did. He shows how his ideas about representatives changed during the research, and how he was impressed by how hard they work to keep in touch with their constituents, and

by how vulnerable to defeat they constantly feel.

Sometimes participant-observers try to answer previously formulated theoretical questions, while also raising new questions and providing new insights. For example, Elliot Liebow (1967) spent more than a year with a group of black streetcorner men in Washington, D.C. He hoped to see if the urban poor were part of a "culture of poverty," distinct from the culture of the middle class (as Oscar Lewis believed), or if their behavior could be explained, in ways readily understandable by the middle class, as being the result of the social, economic, and political circumstances in which they found themselves. His experiences convinced him that there is no deep-seated culture of poverty, but that the lives of those he studied would change dramatically if their economic circumstances and future prospects improved.

It is extremely difficult to observe well while participating in a manner that will aid observation. "Carving out a role" in the group is treacherous and presents difficult choices of tactics (Denzin, 1970a: 188). One must choose whether to hide one's purpose and pose as a regular member of the group—a tactic that raises ethical questions and creates technical difficulties for recording information. Or one can explain one's purpose and try to enlist cooperation. Should one try to use the same vocabulary as the people whom one is observing? How do you get yourself released from the insane asylum to which you have gotten yourself committed (Rosenham, 1973)?

If done well, participant-observer studies can provide rich and accurate descriptions of social life as well as ideas for further research. The great nineteenth-century economist Alfred Marshall said this well:

> The method of le Play's monumental *Les Ouvriers Europeens* is the *intensive* study of all the details of the domestic life of a few carefully chosen families. To work it well requires a rare com-

bination of judgment in selecting cases, and of insight and sympathy in interpreting them. At its best, it is best of all; but in ordinary hands it is likely to suggest more untrustworthy general conclusions, than those obtained by the *extensive* method of collecting more rapidly very numerous observations, reducing them as far as possible to statistical form, and obtaining broad averages in which inaccuracies and idiosyncrasies may be trusted to counteract one another to some extent. (Marshall, 1961: 116)

After the participant observation has been completed and the key elements of the situation have been identified, research methods that are less dependent on the researcher's personality can be employed. For example, after ideas about poverty were developed in participant-observation studies (such as Liebow's) and other kinds of research, large-scale income-maintenance experiments and surveys were carried out to determine more systematically how the poor would respond to changes in their incomes (Hannan, Tuma, and Groeneveld, 1978).

9. Expert Opinion

Sometimes a quick way to gather data is to gather expert opinion—the judgments and estimates made by people who have spent much of their lives working on a subject, gathering, organizing, and storing information.

Let us distinguish between the use of expert opinion as a source of *general guidance and clues* for getting started in the right direction on a particular topic, and its use as the *final data* on which you base your conclusion. General guidance from experts can be indispensable; one of us once began a study of race horses without soliciting the "expert" opinion of habitual bettors on which variables to study, and the study suffered. It would be total folly, however, to accept expert opinion as your final scientific conclusion on how to predict which horse will win a race. On the other hand, a court often relies upon the judgment of psychiatrists as to whether a person is insane (al-

though in many cases the jury has the final say). And for some purposes of social science, one might accept a psychiatrist's *judgment* that more patients recover from schizophrenia than from depression.

Experts can often provide information that would be more expensive or difficult to collect by other techniques, and experts can render judgments that require examination of an entire *context*, that is, taking into account an ill-defined total picture rather than a limited number of well-defined factors. An example is asking a psychologist to judge whether a patient is neurotic on the basis of his entire profile on a psychological test battery rather than on the basis of a single score. But Goldberg (1959), among others, has shown that simple statistical rules of thumb can make such predictions about as well as the experts.

Expert opinion is indispensable when the judgment involves *human values*. For one example, in the library study our ultimate interest was in creating a scheme that would keep the *most valuable* books in the central library (Fussler and Simon, 1961). We developed statistical rules of thumb to make the judgments, but the ultimate judgment of value had to be made by noted scholars in various fields; what they judge as valuable is valuable, by definition. Therefore, the best rule of thumb was one that agreed most closely with the expert judges. Another example is scholars' ratings of university graduate departments (Cartter, 1966). The scholars' opinions do not simply *stand for* some more objective measure of the quality of a graduate school; their judgments *are* the measure of values. If one believes that more objective data, like the amount of scholarly writing produced by a department, provide the final test of a school's value, one should then collect such information rather than asking for experts' opinions.

You may consult a single expert, or survey many experts. An elaborate way of drawing on multiple experts is the Delphi technique. After experts are asked for their opinions on some issue, often pertaining to future developments, the opinions are compiled and then circulated among the same group of experts, who may then respond to slightly different questions or refine their previous statements in light of what the other experts have said. The aim is to arrive systematically at some consensus. The technique has been used, for example, to have experts predict when breakthroughs in science and technology are likely to occur (Stewman and Lincoln, 1981).

It is not always easy to draw a sharp dividing line between what is expert opinion and what is first-hand data. In the example of asking psychiatrists about recovery rates from schizophrenia and depression, is a survey of psychoanalysts a survey of expert opinion or a survey of first-hand data? The analysts keep records, and a survey of such records—even informally through psychiatrists' judgments—is very much like gathering first-hand data in many other surveys.

Here are some points of difference between expert opinion and more formal scientific investigation: First, scientific method generally tries to minimize the human judgment involved in the data-gathering process; a meter reading is the ideal of scientific technique. But when you gather expert opinion, there is much room for human error to creep in, in the form of any of the obstacles to knowledge described in Chapter 19. In expert-opinion studies there is more opportunity for other people's minds to intervene between the researcher and his or her subject matter than with other techniques.

Second, ordinary scientific studies can be closely replicated, because the researcher specifies exactly how he or she obtained the data. In expert-opinion studies researchers can tell you how and what they asked the experts, but they cannot tell you exactly how the experts gathered the information that went into their judgments and estimates.

A sample of experts is probably better than a single expert, and a random sample of experts may be useful. But mere quantity is worthless unless the experts are expert. The statements of a million people about the size of your feet will be less accurate than the statement of the person who just sold you a pair of shoes.

Scientists are wary of conclusions based on expert opinion and perhaps for good reason. It is well to keep in mind that, as Samuel Johnson said centuries ago, "A compendium of gossip is still gossip." Nevertheless, expert opinion will always be an important source of guidance in science as well as in everyday living, and it can be an easy and cheap way to get an overall picture of knowledge in an area.

10. Summary

Nonexperimental research gathers data about a population and its characteristics. It observes the population as it exists, without altering it experimentally.

Surveys can gather data by observing or questioning; the data can be demographic characteristics or behavior or intentions or attitudes. Surveys can be done by mail, telephone, or in person; each method has advantages and drawbacks.

The main advantage of a survey over a laboratory experiment is its realism, and it may have a cost advantage over a field experiment. Its main disadvantages are: (1) its difficulty in establishing that two groups being compared are really similar, and (2) the difficulty of clarifying causation. The chapter lists the steps in executing a survey.

Another type of nonexperimental research is participant observation. It is often used in exploratory research or when the researcher wants to get the whole "feeling" of a social situation. The conclusions from participant-observation research may be less generalizable than the results from a survey.

Expert opinion can be useful, but data gathered from experts must be used as cautiously as any other kind.

EXERCISES

1. Give an example from your field in which doing participant observation would be preferable to doing a survey. Then give an example in which doing a survey would be better.
2. Give an example from your field in which doing an experiment would be preferable to doing a survey. Then give an example in which doing a survey would be better.
3. Give an example in which expert opinion can be gathered in such a way that the study is replicable and therefore public and checkable by others.
4. Give examples in which
   a. the higher cost of personal interviewing is warranted
   b. lower-cost mail or telephone interviews are more appropriate than personal interviews
   c. an experiment would be cheaper than a survey
   d. a survey would be cheaper than an experiment
   e. observation surveying is preferable to interview surveying
   f. interview surveying is preferable to observation surveying
5. Give examples of surveys that study
   a. behavior
   b. intentions
   c. people's information
   d. attitudes, opinions, beliefs, or interests
   e. reasons given for behavior

ADDITIONAL READING

Babbie (1973) is a readable general book on survey methods. Stephan and McCarthy (1963, Chaps. 12–22) include a wealth of useful ideas on the execution of sample surveys. Hyman (1955) is an excellent general work on surveys.

On questionnaire construction, see Selltiz et al. (1976, Chaps. 9, 10) and Kornhauser and Sheatsley (in Selltiz et al., pp. 542–62). Oppenheim (1966), Schuman and Presser (1981), and Bradburn, Sudman et al. (1979) are excellent on question writing. Questionnaires for use in market research are discussed well in Boyd and Stasch (1977, Chaps. 7 and 8). For examples of hypothetical question techniques, see Simon (1966b) and Rossi and Anderson (1982). Paul (1953) discusses limited-scope questions in anthropology.

On interviewing, see Bradburn, Sudman et al. (1979); Converse and Schuman (1974); Cantril (1971, Chaps. 1–4, especially 1 and 2); Parten (1950); Payne (1951); and almost every textbook in social-scientific and market research. Also see Gordon (1969); Kahn and Cannell (1967); Richardson et al. (1965); Cannell, Miller, and Oksenberg (1981).

Denzin (1970a, Chap. 6) describes the sociological interview from the "interactionist" perspective.

A good description of interviewing under difficult conditions is found in Ginsberg (1975, Chap. 3).

Sudman (1967) provides a lot of useful information on how to reduce the cost of surveys.

Groves and Kahn (1979) discuss the costs and benefits of telephone and personal interviewing.

Dillman (1978) provides a very detailed guide to carrying out mail and telephone surveys.

Useful works on participant observation and related approaches include Denzin (1970a and b); Bogdan and Taylor (1975); and Emerson (1981).

A readable description of his own adventures and those of other investigators, both in the United States and in Latin American contexts, is that of Glazer (1972).

Anthropologists give you the lowdown on participant observation, together with plenty of examples, in Frelich's book (1970). Note especially his introduction. A no-nonsense description of *Field Methods in the Study of Culture* is by T. Williams (1967).

For a discussion of "reasons why" analysis, see Zeisel (1968, Chaps. 6, 7, 8); Lorie and Roberts (1951, Chap. 17); and Lazarsfeld (1935).

Studies Using Other People's Data

14

1. Types of Data

Because gathering data can be costly and time-consuming, it is worthwhile to see if the data you seek have already been collected by someone else. A large proportion of the research done by sociologists, economists, political scientists, and increasingly, by anthropologists and historians, employs previously collected and publicly available data, either as the mainstay of the research or as ancillary data.

This chapter discusses types of data available, and describes, step by step, how to work with them. This is the process often called "secondary research."

There are three types of secondary data available, and each has its advantages and disadvantages. The first is data collected by the government or organizations from other organizations or individuals. Examples include the U.S. Census, which tries to collect information from every household in the country with the goal of accurately describing the entire population, income data collected by the Internal

Revenue Service, statistics on the use of national parks, and information collected by the Gallup poll. The organizations collecting these data will inform you how the data were collected, how valid and reliable they are, and what inaccuracies might exist. Such data are often available free or for a small fee. But such information is collected on some matters but not others; the U.S. Census, for example, gathers a lot of data on demographics but very little on attitudes.

Another source is data collected by people or organizations about their own activities: businesses' personnel records, hospital data on patients, and telephone company records of long-distance calls are examples. Studies of careers, churches, schools, police departments, and businesses have used such data (White, 1970; Dentler and Scott, 1981), whose major advantage is its uniqueness. The major problems are accuracy and secrecy. Because such data are not usually collected with research in mind (unlike census data, for example), less care may have been taken in collecting them, and it may be harder to find out how accurate the data are. In addition, the data you want may be held by a company or organization that wants to keep them secret and will not release them.

Still another source is data collected by non-scientific professional observers for their own purposes. Newspaper stories, diaries, and letters can all provide useful information about social and psychological processes. Novels sometimes describe social activities in distant times and places about which little other information is available. But because such data are not collected with scientific purposes in mind, their accuracy and generality must be considered especially carefully.

The greatest advantage of secondary analysis is low cost. The greatest disadvantage is that the data may not exactly suit your purposes because you were not in charge of collecting them. As always, you must use judgment in deciding which types of data to use for your study, keeping in mind that the best studies often use several different types of data.

2. Using Available Social and Economic Data

Here is a guide to using data that has already been collected by someone.

Step 1. Complete the steps described in Chapter 7.

Step 2. Find appropriate raw data. The library reference room is an excellent place to start, especially the many excellent works on governmental statistics in the United States and elsewhere (some are described at the end of this chapter). Another approach is to look through the basic compilations of available statistical data such as the *Statistical Abstract of the United States* and *Historical Statistics of the United States*. If you find data that are relevant to your problem, you can go back to the sources from which the data were compiled—

many of them nongovernmental sources, of course.

Librarians can give you good tips, especially the librarians in charge of special libraries. Other researchers who have already worked in the same field can offer help to you, as can articles on related topics. And eventually you yourself will learn where the basic data sources are—but by then you will be older than you are now.

Step 3. Check the accuracy of your data in every way you can think of. There is a common and dangerous tendency to simply accept published data as satisfactory. Like most everyone else, we too often succumb to this tendency and the easy rationalizations for it. But an acquaintance with Morgenstern's *On the Accuracy of Economic Observations* should be enough to at least frighten you about the hazards of not checking.

Step 4. Decide what your sample will be. The first sample decision concerns which *universe* you will study. If you wish to investigate the relationship of the population growth rate to the amount of education people get, will you study the poorer countries separately, or the richer countries separately, or both, or all of them together? You might decide on the poorer countries alone if that is what you are interested in; or you might restrict your study to the richer countries because no data are available for poorer countries. Unless there is some such special reason, however, it usually makes sense to study both. But if you think that there are structurally different processes occurring in the two sets of countries, it will make sense to treat them separately—though also considering them together, to see how the results differ from the separate-sample results. In brief, your theory, your interest, and the availability of data will dictate which universe and subuniverse to study.

The next sample decision often is about how

to define the sample. How, for example, should one define "poor country"? Should it be by per capita income, and if so, should the demarcation be $1,000 or $900 per year? Or, should the definition include such criteria as literacy and life expectancy?

Here we have a very definite rule for you to follow: When in doubt about the criteria for a sample, make separate analyses with each of the criteria, and then compare the results. If, as is likely, the results are much the same with each of the samples, you have resolved your doubt. And at the same time you have made your conclusions more "robust," in the trade jargon, because you have shown that results are not sensitive to minor changes in the sample. If, on the other hand, the results differ for the various criteria, this can be a clue to discoveries about the nature of the process that you are studying.

The same general point holds for many decisions in studies with social and economic data: When in doubt about which way to do it, do it both ways and compare the results. In these days of cheap computer time, this suggestion is practical and efficient.

Next, we must consider the sample-size decision. When working with social and economic data you will often use all of it that is available, especially if it is "macro data"—that is, data for aggregates such as states or countries, as compared to "micro data" for individuals. There will never be murder data or GNP data for so many countries, or for so many years for a single country, that you are constrained by cost to use less than the full universe of data available. But if you are working with micro data—such as the hand-written records from the 1880 U.S. Census—then you must draw a sample to make the project feasible. You will aim to increase the sample size only as long as the benefit of additional cases in the sample is worth their extra cost.

Sampling methods, and the sample-size decision are treated in Chapter 9 and Chapter 34 respectively.

Step 5. Adjusting the data. The data you have gathered will seldom exactly fit your research objectives. Experiments usually produce clean, orderly, relevant data, because what comes out is a product of what is put in and the researcher has considerable *control* of what goes in. Sometimes the experimenter disregards some observations because they are "obviously" in error—perhaps because an earthquake hit at the moment the observation was made—but, aside from such matters, little adjustment is usually done with experimental data.

In nonexperimental research the situation is different. The researcher must take what he can get and then patch it up and adjust it. This seems scholarly betrayal to researchers who do mostly experimentation. Yet the adjustment must be done and done well if nonexperimental research is to get anywhere at all. Here is an example of adjustments made to the sample in the Survey of Consumer Finances in order to render it suitable for economic analysis:

The sample included for analysis. In keeping with our previous comments about the difficulty both with the data and with their interpretation for spending units involved in some entrepreneurial activity, we decided to exclude from the sample farmers and those who owned a business.

In any survey, there are some interviews where a relevant item of information is not obtained, e.g., income, assets, or some component of saving. When, as in the Surveys of Consumer Finances, it is intended to publish data and relations pertaining to the nation as a whole, it is best to assign values to these cases by matching these spending units with others in the sample who are like them in as many respects as possible. The alternative would be to eliminate these interviews entirely, throwing away all the other information, and implicitly assigning them the mean sample values of all the variables (by reweighting the other interviews). However, for our purposes, where we are interested in detailed patterns of relationships and levels of significance, it seemed better to eliminate all these cases and any possibility of spurious relations resulting from the assignment procedure. Hence, we removed from the samples all cases where the amount of income, assets, or saving had been assigned. For the relevant tables we also eliminate the cases where such things as income change, occupation, etc., were not ascertained.

Finally, we made two other types of exclusion: First, we excluded a few cases where there seemed good reason to suspect the reliability of the information. For instance, we took out cases where saving was so large as to indicate a level of expenditure out of proportion with the general economic position of the spending unit. The latter cases usually involved some large transactions where all the money did not seem to be accounted for. Second, there were some cases where extreme saving behavior was clearly present, but it was so extreme and so unusual as to require a separate treatment. (Morgan, 1954: 98–99)

M. Friedman emphasizes the importance of wise adjustment of the data:

In seeking to make a science as "objective" as possible, our aim should be to formulate the rules explicitly in so far as possible and continually to widen the range of phenomena for which it is possible to do so. But, no matter how successful we may be in the attempt, there inevitably will remain room for judgment in applying the rules. Each occurrence has some features peculiarly its own, not covered by the explicit rules. The capacity to judge that these are or are not to be disregarded, that they should or should not affect what observable phenomena are to be identified with what entities in the model, is something that cannot be taught; it can be learned but only by experience and exposure in the "right" scientific atmosphere, not by rote. It is at this point that the "amateur" is separated from the "professional" in all sciences and that the thin line is drawn which distinguishes the "crackpot" from the scientist. (Friedman, 1953: 25)

And one more quotation—this time by a chemist—about this very sensitive issue, which illustrates once again that much of science is art and judgment:

THE REJECTION OF OBSERVATIONS

One of the most difficult decisions which an experimenter has to make is whether or not to reject a result which seems unreasonably discordant. Such results occur, because of accidents or mistakes (Sec. 9.1), with greater or less frequency depending on the skill and care of the investigator. If a mistake of addition is made, it is certainly not reasonable to expect the number obtained to tell very much about the quantity being observed. In particular the use of statistical techniques based on the normal law of error is hardly justified.

Sometimes the reason for a "wild" result is obvious. The operator may know what he did that caused it. These clear-cut cases are not important—if the operator makes a mistake which he knows will spoil the results, he should stop the measurement at that point, or at the least mark it irrevocably for discarding, even if it eventually should come out close to expectations.

On the other hand, the search for specific reasons for rejecting a result after the fact is highly dangerous. It is too easy to find an excuse and too likely that prejudice and emotion will enter. However, if the observer is willing—and strong-minded enough—rejections may be made by the rule that, if a given circumstance is once used to justify discarding a discordant result, the occurrence of the same circumstance must cause rejection whenever it happens and whatever the result.

It is important to look for causes of unusual results; many great discoveries have been made in this way. . . .

There is clearly no magic formula for the rejection of observations. Consideration of the difficulties involved is worthwhile if it leads to the attitude that it is important to be very careful to prevent mistakes and accidents.

With experiments requiring extremely good conditions of observation or extremely high sensitivity on the part of the operator, there is often a desire to disregard negative results on the grounds that conditions were not right or that the operator was not in the right mood. This is undoubtedly responsible for much pseudo science, psychic phenomena, and similar material.

If negative results are excluded from a chance sequence, a positive average will naturally result. It is easy to dismiss these cases as mere charlatanism or self-deception, but many educated people do accept such nonsense. (Wilson, 1952: 256–257)

One reason that adjustment of the data is so important in nonexperimental work is that the data may be limited. In physiology, chemistry, or experimental psychology, the researcher can repeat the experiment and obtain new data to check whether an observation really is a "sport" (an error of some sort) and should be thrown out of the study. But one cannot simply throw out one year's observation of gross national product. (Yet, that is just what is often done with war years!)

Definitional difficulties often lie at the root of discrepancies in the raw data. For example, look at the entries for the population of China in the years 1578, 1661, and 1749 in the "Returned in Census" column in Table 14.1.A. Usher explains these peculiarities to us:

. . . The returns were used as a basis for taxation, and the unit of enumeration has commonly been presumed to be the family. But some enumeration of individuals (mouths) was made as part of the return, and at some periods the return of "mouths" is held to be more trustworthy than that of families. The bias likely to develop from the system of taxation is minimized by the return of both taxable and nontaxable persons. The periods of greatest difficulty are the Sung and early Tsing dynasties. In the Sung period, the basis of enumeration of "mouths" was changed, and males alone were included. In the early reigns of the Tsing Dynasty only males of military age (16–60) were recorded. When adjustments have been made for these divergences of practice, the series of returns becomes essentially self-consistent and conforms to the expectations created by the history of the country. (See "Probable Total" column in Table 14.1; Usher, 1930/1956: 15)

TABLE 14.1   Population of China (in millions)

Year	Dynasty	Returned in Census	Probable Total
2	Han	59.5	71.0
156	Han	50.0	60.0
606	Tang	46.0	55.0
733	Tang	45.4	54.0
754	Tang	52.9	63.5
1080	Sung	33.3	79.0
1260	Yuen	53.6	65.0
1290	Yuen	58.8	70.5
1381	Ming	60.5	72.5
1393	Ming	58.6	70.1
1491	Ming	56.0	66.0
1578	Ming	63.5	75.0
1661	Tsing	21.0	105.0
1690	Tsing	20.3	101.5
1710	Tsing	23.3	116.5
1749	Tsing	177.4	177.4
1780	Tsing	276.6	276.6
1812	Tsing	360.4	360.4
1842	Tsing	413.0	413.0
1860	Tsing	260.0	?
1885	Tsing	377.6	377.6
1923	Tsing	414.0	414.0

SOURCE: "The History of Population and Settlement in Eurasia," p. 123, by Usher, in *The Geographical Review,* Vol 20 (January 1930).

Sometimes, however, one cannot discover *any* reasonable explanation for discrepancies in the raw data. This may be because the data sources are no more than someone's guesses, which are reprinted and passed along as gospel truth. What would you make of the population history of Japan from A.D. 589 to A.D. 1702, from the data in Table 14.2?

Sometimes you may adjust a set of data by *weighting* some data more heavily than others. For example, if you have yearly data on the incidence of mental disease and you want to investigate the relationship between mental

disease and religion, you might well pay more attention to the data of the last thirty years than to those from more than thirty years ago, because recent statistics on the incidence of mental illness are more accurate than those from further back. Many scientists are suspicious of such weighting on the grounds that it is subjective, and properly so, because the method and results of the study cannot be so easily checked by someone else. But *some* such subjective judgments are inevitably part of every study; the researcher has to designate *some* year as the first year he or she will in-

TABLE 14.2   Estimated Populations from the Early Times to the Middle of the Tokugawa Era

Date A.D.	Population	Authorities
589	3,931,151	*Shotoku Taishi Denki*
"	4,031,050	*Taishi Denki*
	4,988,842	*Taishiden*
610	4,990,000	*Jugan-iko;* Nishikawa-Korinsai, *Nihon Suidoko*
"	4,969,699*	Jurei Suzuki, *Kofutaii*
650–1150[2]	8,833,290*	M. Kimura
710–48[3]	5–6 millions*	G. Sawada
721	4,584,893	*Gyoki Bosatsu Gyojoki*
724–48	2 millions	*Gyoki Shikimoku*
"	4,508,551	*Ibid.,* Differently quoted
"	4,899,620	*Ibid.,* Differently quoted
"	8 millions	*Jugen-Iko* and Nishikawa, *op. cit.*
"	6,631,074	Arai-Hakuseki, *Oritakushiba no Ki*
736	8,631,770*	Ishihara
823	3,694,331*	Y. Yokoyama, *Nihon Denseishi*
859–922[4]	3,762,000*	*Ibid.*
901–22[5]	2 millions*	Hidenori Ino
923	1,128,167*	*Chirikyoku Zasshi*
986–1010[6]	22,083,325*	Hidenori Ino
990–1080[7]	4,416,650*	Yokoyama, *op. cit.*
c. 1155	24–25 millions*	Hidenori Ino
1185–1333[8]	9,750,000*	
1278–87[9]	4,984,828	*Kongyoku Satsuyoshu* and *Ruiju Meibutsuko*
1528	4,916,652	Bishop Shuntel, *Zakkishu*
1553	2,330,996*	*Chirikyoku Zasshi*
1582	4,994,808	Katori Bunsho
1573–91[10]	18 millions*	T. Yoshida, *Ishinshi Nachiko*
1673–83[11]	24 millions	Nishikawa, *op. cit.*
1688–1703[12]	26 millions*	Yoshida, *op. cit.*
1702	24,994,600*	*Chirikyoku Zasshi*

*Indicates estimates by present-day writers.

SOURCE: Ishii, 1957: p. 4

clude in this study and usually does so according to the adequacy of the data. The danger, of course, is that the reseacher will choose a cut-off date (or weighting scheme) that will prove the hypothesis he or she wants to prove. There really is not much defense against this fudging danger except making an explicit statement of why you did what you did.

Another fix-it operation is collecting more data to beef up an area where your data are too few. For example, in a study like Kinsey's (1948) you might find upon first inspection of the data in hand that too few men aged fifty-five to sixty-five, Roman Catholic, and members of the middle class have fallen into your sample, perhaps because there are very few people of this sort. If your sample is randomly selected, you can go out and obtain data on more people that meet these specifications; this move is particularly feasible if you are taking your sample in several sequential steps. (But you *must* remember to take account of these resamples when you make estimates for the universe as a whole; see Chapter 9 on stratified sampling for an explanation.)

A last step in the adjustment process is to examine the data to see if the results are reasonable. If the results are not reasonable, there may be an error. Novices laugh when they hear economists or psychologists say, "If the data don't agree with the theory, check the data." But, indeed, the data are often found to be in error when they disagree with the hypothesis. The stronger the theory, of course, the more likely you are to put your money on it when it quarrels with the data.

But watch out—danger ahead! If you recheck your data when they do not agree with your hypothesis and do *not* recheck the data when they *do* agree with the hypothesis, you are loading the dice in favor of getting data that agree with your hypothesis. The only solution is *always* to recheck your data.

Step 6. Estimate missing data. Sometimes you need a datum that is not available. You

then have two choices: Abandon the study, or estimate the datum. And if you cannot estimate the datum or if the datum represents too large a part of all the data in the study, then you *must* abandon the study.

There are many devices for estimation, all of them involving mostly common sense. In Chapter 21 we will find the example of estimating unavailable advertising expenditures for a given year by assuming that the ratio of 1983 expenditures to 1982 expenditures would be the same as the ratio of 1983 gross national product to 1982 gross national product. Another example of the same strategy is William Petty's 1687 estimate of the population of London, which took advantage of the fact that the authorities had burned the house of each person who died of the plague of 1666:

> The number of houses which were burnt Anno 1666, which by authentic report was 13,200; next, what proportion the people who died out of those houses bore to the whole, which I find . . . Anno 1666 to be almost 1/5, from whence I infer the whole housing of London Anno 1666 to have been 66 thousand; then finding the burials Anno 1666 to be to those of 1686 as 3 to 4, I pitch upon 88 thousand to be the number of housing Anno 1686. (Letwin, 1975: 143)

Interpolation and extrapolation are similar devices. If you have data for 1978 and 1980 but not for 1979, it may be reasonable to split the difference and *interpolate* for 1979. (But, if you have the average temperature for Chicago in May and October, do not estimate the average temperature for August by interpolation.) If you have the data for 1979 and 1980, it may be reasonable to *extrapolate* the trend into 1982. (But do not extrapolate the temperature trend for June, July, and August into September.)

Another trick is to *disaggregate*. It is often easier to estimate for individual parts of a whole and then to combine them for a better overall estimate than to estimate straight-off. For example, perhaps we want to estimate the gross revenue of a particular lunch counter for a year. We have no basis for a direct estimate.

But if we sit at the lunch counter for an hour we can count the number of customers in that period of time, estimate the average bill per customer, multiply by the number of hours a day the counter is open (adjusting for busy and slow hours), multiply by the number of stools in the lunch counter, adjust for the time the stool is not in use, and arrive at an estimate. As a matter of fact, we could even estimate the revenue from a single stool without ever going into the restaurant. This kind of disaggregated estimate is a mental sampling process, and it is likely to be closer to the actual figure than if we made a direct estimate for the entire lunch counter.

Another method of estimation would be to watch the cash register for ten minutes, total the receipts, then expand for the whole year.

Another illustration: How tall is the Empire State Building or the tallest building in your town? You know that each floor is eight to eleven feet high, and you can estimate the number of floors. Presto—an estimate.

Valuation estimates can often be improved by disaggregating. For example, when planning a week's riverboat-cruise vacation, one of us and his wife discussed whether to pay $40 extra for a private shower. The valuation seemed to make sense only after we divided by the number of showers we expected to take and estimated that each private shower would cost between $3 and $4. We could then say to ourselves, "Would I pay $3 to $4 extra to take a shower in the room rather than walk a few doors down the corridor?"

Sometimes it is difficult to get several people to agree about what is the most sensible estimate. Enthoven finds that, in government policy research, offering three estimates—high, low, and middle—can often bring agreement: "It is surprising how often reasonable men studying the same evidence can agree on three numbers where they cannot agree on one. In fact, one of the great benefits of this approach has been to eliminate much senseless quibbling over minor variations in numerical esti-

mates of very uncertain magnitudes" (Enthoven, 1963: 421).

Step 7. Use imputation as needed. Sometimes we need to quantify something but have no really satisfactory way of doing so. In calculating the national income, for example, some people think it makes sense to include the value of the work performed by women in the home. Unfortunately, since women are not usually paid for housework, it is hard to know what dollar value to place on it.

This and related problems must be solved by *imputation*, the process of estimating a quantity when there is little or no scientific rationale for the estimate. Morgenstern calls imputation (of value) "perhaps *the* classical problem of economic theory" (1963: 245). Imputation is also an important problem in other social sciences. We shall discuss two difficult kinds of imputation problems here: separating combined data into parts and allocating parts of a whole (see also Chapter 17).

A. SEPARATING COMBINED DATA

One of us wanted to determine the differences in state tax revenues from distilled spirits in the thirty-four states with private-enterprise liquor stores, compared to the sixteen states in which liquor stores are run by the states and "socialized" (J. Simon, 1966b). But in some states, like Hawaii, the data for beer and wine are lumped together with the data for distilled spirits, and we wanted the revenues for liquor only. Table 14.3 illustrates how the data are lumped together (as well as other complexities that an investigator must unravel if he wants to use such accounting data for scientific purposes).

In this case, as in many similar cases, the solution was to refer to states in which the revenues are separate and to assume that the *proportions* would be the same in the states that do not reckon the taxes separately.

TABLE 14.3   Liquor-Tax Revenues in Hawaii, 1961

	Number	Amount	
Permit fees			
38 liquor-tax permits at $2.50 (rounded)			$ 95.00
Taxes			
Wholesale		$3,508,524.00	
Retail		6,234.00	
Taxable use		14,742.00	
Total liquor-tax collections			$3,529,518.00
Miscellaneous income			39.00
Total state collections from alcoholic beverages			$3,529,652.00
Costs of collections (estimated)			7,259.00
Net state revenues			$3,522,393.00
Local collections (license fees)			
City and County of Honolulu	649	$ 339,619.00	
County of Maui	134	51,058.00	
County of Hawaii	176	64,379.00	
County of Kauai	83	30,174.00	
Total local collections		$ 485,230.00	
Costs of local collections (estimated)		24,900.00	
Net local collections			$ 460,330.00
Total net state and local revenues			$3,982,723.00

B. ALLOCATING PARTS OF A WHOLE

This type of imputation is truly separating the inseparable. For example, how would you decide how much the husband is responsible for the popularity of a given couple and how much the wife is? One tactic would be to investigate the popularity of the husband and the wife in the social relations that they conduct separately. But they may go everywhere together. Furthermore, their popularity or lack of it may stem from how they behave *as a couple*, which may be quite different from how they behave separately; that is, there may be an *interaction effect*.

In the case of this married couple, it may be *meaningless* to impute responsibility for popularity to the husband or the wife. In such cases, you should refuse to try to separate the inseparable. Indeed, if you are studying married couples *qua* couples, there is probably no reason even to try to establish separate responsibility for the popularity of the couple.

In some other cases, however, the problem simply cannot be ducked. The allocation of overhead costs in the U.S. Post Office offers a classic case. Congress sets postal rates for different classes of mail and takes into account the costs of handling the various classes of mail. But how much of the cost of constructing and maintaining the post office building should be charged to first-class mail, how much to second-class mail, and so on?

One answer is obviously wrong. It would make no sense to charge *each* class of mail as much as it would cost if there were no other classes of mail. If so, the sum of the allocations would be much larger than the actual total cost. Nor is there any particular justification for allocating the costs in proportion to the number of pieces of each class of mail or to the other costs for each class of mail—although these are the answers that accountants would probably offer.

Because there is no agreed-upon or scientific rationale for apportioning these costs, the arguments rage, and the pressure groups scream. The answer is at best a matter of philosophy, judgment, and determination of ultimate purpose. To indicate just one possible line of reasoning, if we assume that the United States *must* have first-class mail and if the other classes of mail are merely riders on the coattails of first-class mail, then it might be sensible to charge to first-class mail *all* the overhead costs for facilities that are used jointly by all the classes of mail. On the other hand, if the object were for the government to make as much profit as possible, the prices would be set purely in terms of what the customers would pay, and no allocation of joint overhead costs would be necessary. If the object is to allocate the costs "most fairly," then the government would probably have to have a national referendum.

This ends the list of steps that are particularly relevant to studies working with publicly available macro data and micro data. Then you proceed to anlyze the data, using the care discussed in Chapter 17 and the analytic methods discussed in Chapters 24–28.

3. Content Analysis

Very often the data used in real-world studies comes in "packaged" form—for example, you may use statistics provided by the Bureau of the Census, or the answers people give to multiple-choice questions on a public opinion poll. Often, however, the data you might want are not available as a package, or such data might be inappropriate. For instance, you might want to know whether it is true, as some have claimed, that the courts are more sympathetic to blacks who complain of employment discrimination than they are to white women who do the same. Unfortunately, nobody routinely collects the kind of information on court cases that would enable you to answer the question. Or you might want to learn how people view the American political system and what they think should be done about its problems. In such a case, finding their responses to alternatives posed by interviewers might not tell you much about how they view the world.

To get an answer to the question about the courts, it would make sense to read cases dealing with discrimination against blacks and women, and see how they came out. To find out how people view politics, it might make sense to ask them very general questions, and then record their answers while they just told you what they thought and felt. This kind of thing is done all the time. Lawyers and law professors read court cases, focusing on those they believe are especially important, and draw conclusions about trends. Newspaper reporters are always talking to citizens and figuring out what is on people's minds.

The problem with these approaches is that they are not systematic; the results depend heavily on the selection of cases and the intuitions of those doing the analyses. The *systematic* analysis of written or oral material is called *content analysis;* it is a way of quantifying what people write and say by *coding* the material according to *explicit instructions*, categorizing the ideas expressed and counting how often certain things are said. To some people, content analysis is an attempt to quantify the unquantifiable. It is true that an intuitive reading of a document or the sensitive interpretation of an interview may uncover subtleties that no coder following a set of rules could. But the kind of knowledge to be gained from the systematic content analysis of large amounts of material can be invaluable.

The first step in a content analysis is selecting the material to be analyzed—a set of court decisions, transcripts of interviews, a collection of newspaper stories, and so on. Typically the researcher then reads some of the material and develops a preliminary coding scheme, a set of rules for describing what the material says. The most important decisions in content analysis involve the choice of categories, which must accurately represent the ideas or concepts that you want to measure. (Chapter 15 discusses the issue under the general rubric of "classification.") In considering court cases, for example, the analysis might focus on the nature of the case (whether it is civil or criminal, for example), who the parties are (businesses, individuals, government officials, etc.), who wins, and so on. Two or more coders will then test the coding rules, coding material and modifying the rules to make them clearer and to resolve unforeseen problems, until the point is reached at which two coders, analyzing the same material, agree almost all the time on how it is to be coded; this makes the procedure replicable and the data reliable. All the material can then be coded, and the data used in subsequent analyses, often in combination with data of other types.

Early examples of formal content analysis were provided by military-intelligence agencies in World War II. Enemy newspapers and radio stations were monitored exhaustively, and counts were made of various kinds of references to transportation, obituaries, and so forth. Variations in the numbers of such references from week to week often signified troop movements or other changes that were clues to the intentions and actions of the enemy.

One of the more adventurous uses of content analysis is D. McClelland's study of the historical relationship between the motivation to achieve among the members of a society and the economic development of the society. He and his associates have measured the frequency of "achievement imagery" in the popular literature of the society at various periods and have related these frequencies to economic indicators. For example, Figure 14.1 shows the close correspondence (with a time lag of about fifty years) between the content-analysis data and coal imports into London from 1550 to 1850. When one considers the multitude of obstacles present in such an investigation, the closeness of the correspondence is startling, and it reassures us that empirical research in social science need not be hamstrung by the less-than-perfect conditions under which we must work.

Content analysis has become an increasingly popular technique in recent years. Data from newspapers has been used to study the impact of political protest in the United States and Europe (Jenkins and Perrow, 1977; Tilly, 1978, has an excellent methodological appendix). The decisions made by state supreme courts have been analyzed to show how the law changes as the result of industrialization, urbanization, and other factors (Freidman et al., 1981). Bills introduced in Congress have been examined to show how congressional ideas about how to deal with social problems have changed over the years (Burstein and MacLeod, 1980). Even novels and works of art can be systematically analyzed. Griswold (1981) analyzed a random sample of 130 novels published in the United States between 1876 and 1910 to consider how important aspects of the national literature—including social concerns, plots, and kinds of protagonists—were affected by the imperatives of novelistic conventions, the copyright laws, characteristics of the authors, and other factors (see also Kroeber, 1948: 500–501). Unstructured interviews can be analyzed as well; Neuman (1981) analyzed depth interviews to find out how political sophistication is related to such factors as education and conservatism.

Content analysis is very laborious, but computer systems have been developed to speed and refine it. Both the original material and the results of the analysis can be stored for ready access (see, for example, Tilly, 1978).

4. Deductive Reasoning

Deductive reasoning is not a way of gathering data; rather, it is a way of *thinking about* theory, data, and how they are related. Deductive reasoning can be so important in helping you decide what data to obtain and how to interpret it, however, that we thought we should say something about it here.

The principle of the deductive method for obtaining knowledge is using *logic* to show that, *if* A is true and *if* B is a true, then *under some specified conditions* one can safely say that C is true. Deduction need not be this sim-

FIGURE 14.1   Average *n* Achievement Levels in English Literature (1550–1800) Compared with Rates of Gain in Coal Imports at London 50 Years Later

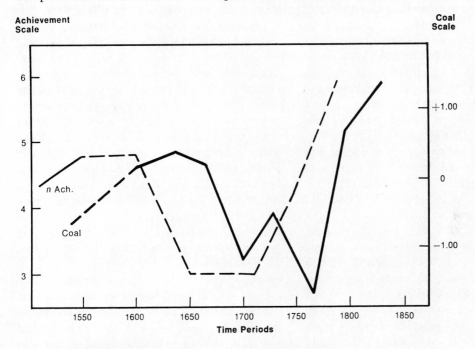

n Ach. = Mean number of achievement images per 100 lines.

Coal = Coal imports at London as deviations from expected in standard-deviation units.

Source: "Need for Achievement and English Industrial Growth," p. 19, Norman M. Bradburn and David E. Berlew, in *Economic Development and Cultural Change* (October 1961); reprinted by permission of The University of Chicago Press.

ple. The chains of reasoning can be long, complex, and probabilistic, but the same principle holds—the conclusions are based on logic.

Consider this example: You want to know whether it is raining outside. Your previous experience tells you that, if people are holding open umbrellas over their heads, it is raining; this observation is premise A. Premise B is what you see from your window—that almost everyone who is carrying an umbrella has it open. You deduce your conclusion C, that it is indeed raining outside.

Notice that whether your conclusion C is correct depends on the correctness (truth) of your premises. If you are in a country where people hold umbrellas over them to keep the sun off, then premise A is wrong in that case, and your conclusion will probably be in error. Similarly, if your eyes deceive you about whether people are holding open umbrellas, then premise B is incorrect, and your conclusion will probably be incorrect too.

In one sense, there is nothing "new" in the conclusion C; all the information contained in the conclusion is already contained in the premises. Nevertheless, deduction helps us understand the world about us because it shows us the connections among bits of information we already have. Like all mathematical analysis, deduction is a device for discovery of the truths that lie concealed within a set of statements.

In the case of the umbrellas and the rain, the deductive method might or might not be more effective than an empirical investigation. The empirical method of going outside and extending an upturned palm has the advantage of rendering you safe from most false premises. (But notice that the premise that water coming down from above is rain *might* be incorrect; someone might be spraying a hose out a window. In a way, all knowledge is deduced, and all knowledge depends on various premises.) The advantages of the deductive method in this case is that you do not have to go outside and get wet to obtain an answer.

We use deduction all the time as a helpful device. You might have followed this line of thought this morning: Classes meet Monday to Friday; today is Monday; therefore classes meet today. And off you go to class on the basis of your deduction, without telephoning to check that classes are indeed meeting.

Deduction can be an extremely useful method for improving our understanding of the world, particularly in two situations. The first is where we believe we know the *logic* of some phenomenon, but have little *information* about it. Thus, scientists deduced a great deal about nuclear fission, on the basis of their prior knowledge about physics, long before they were able to run actual fission experiments. Their deductions helped guide the experiments, making them much more efficient than pure trial-and-error procedures would have been; the deductions also warned the scientists to be careful, lest they accidentally blow up their laboratories.

The second situation where deduction is especially useful is where we have some information about something, but cannot make much sense out of it. For example, in the 1950s and 1960s, many Americans thought that the Republicans and Democrats had very similar party platforms. According to the ideas people had about politics at the time, however,

parties were supposed to disagree very strongly. The similarities didn't make sense, and, in fact, seemed bad for democracy, because the voters did not seem to have much of a choice at election time. Some deductive political scientists, particularly Anthony Downs, put the similarity between the parties in a new light. He showed that the *parties* might agree about what they wanted because most *voters* agreed about what they wanted, at least on some issues; in trying to do what the public wanted, both parties came to agree with the public and with each other. The deductions helped explain why the parties might agree, and even showed how the agreements might be a good thing in a democratic country.

Notice that we call deduction a "method of getting *knowledge*," in the same way that we have talked about various empirical methods of getting knowledge. In one sense an empirically established fact has more claim to be called "knowledge" than does a conclusion arrived at deductively, because whenever a deduction and an empirically established fact collide, the deduction must give way: The empirical demonstration is the ultimate test. As someone has said, many a beautiful theory has been slain by an ugly fact. For example, nineteenth-century economists, like twentieth-century ones, wanted very badly to explain why each period of economic prosperity was followed by a depression. W. Stanley Jevons, the famous British economist, deduced that the business cycle was caused by *sunspots*. Business cycles, he thought, had a duration of 10.46 years, and sunspots had a cycle of 10.45 years. He thought that sunspots caused weather cycles, which caused rain cycles, which caused crop cycles, which caused business cycles (Heilbroner, 1968: 375). There was a certain logic to this, but a problem arose: New data showed that the sunpot cycles were longer than previously believed and they did not coincide with business cycles. A new theory of the business cycle had to be sought.

The contest between deduction and empirical knowledge is not always so easily settled, however. Often the empirical fact is not so clear-cut because the empirical measurement is uncertain, and in that case a strong deductive argument may be more persuasive. This may be particularly true when policy decisions must be made immediately on the basis of available knowledge, or where people concerned about an issue disagree strongly about premises.

As an example of the former, the effect of population growth on economic development is one area where we put more stock in deduction than in empirical evidence. Easterlin sums up the latter: "On the whole, then, simple empirical comparisons between economic and population growth rates are inconclusive. Cases (nations) of high per capita income growth are associated with both high and low population growth" (Easterlin, 1967: 107). But the empirical analyses are extremely weak, for many reasons. And the theoretical reasons to believe that increased population causes lower income are very strong. Therefore, most scientists advocate population control as a means of speeding economic development, and many nations—not able to wait for more conclusive evidence—follow this recommendation, on the basis of deduction and without definitive empirical support.

Sometimes different people interested in the same phenomenon try to explain it on the basis of very different premises and, consequently, arrive at different explanations. Where the data are less than conclusive, both sides are likely to continue relying on their deductions. A good example involves the question of why managers and supervisors usually make much more money than the people they supervise. On the basis of their theoretical premises, most economists conclude that managers make more money because they contribute more to their businesses and are rewarded accordingly. Some sociologists and economists believe, however, that managers are paid more because they have more power than ordinary workers

and use the power to take more income than they deserve. There is some evidence on both sides of this question, but none of it is conclusive (see Wright, 1979; Keyfitz, 1981). As a result, people on neither side can be persuaded to change their minds. It is in a situation like this, which is quite common in the sciences, that effort must be put into collecting the empirical data that could resolve the disagreement.

Note that "deduction" is not the same as "theory." Theory is an interlaced body of existing systematic knowledge, and it is important just because it is a *source* of premises for deduction (see discussion in Chapter 3).

We may end this section with the usual admonition: Do not ignore deduction when it is useful, but do not limit yourself to its use and neglect other methods.

5. Summary

Often the data you need to do research will already have been collected by someone else, so you can save yourself a lot of time and trouble when starting research projects by seeing if the data you need are already available. Probably the best type of data, if it suits your purposes, are data collected by others for research. Such data will often have been collected very carefully, and more important, there will often be information available on how the data were collected and how valid and reliable they are likely to be. Data collected for other purposes can be useful too, but you must always be very thorough in checking to see that they are accurate.

The advantage of using other people's data is its low cost. The disadvantage is that you do not control the research design and data collection process as you would if you ran an experiment or did your own survey. You must therefore think very carefully about the data before using them; you have to be concerned about the universe and sample, adjusting the data you have, estimating data that are missing, and assessing the quality of everything you use.

When data do not come "prepackaged," content analysis can be used to turn all kinds of written and oral communications into quantified data. Content analysis can be a lot of work, but it can be used to create data that could not be generated in any other way.

Deductive reasoning can be a useful tool in research. It can help you decide what data you need and how to interpret the data you have.

EXERCISES

1. List five simple research projects for which you think you could rely on publicly available data. Then list five for which you think you would have to collect your own data and five for which you are not sure whether or not you would have to collect your own data. Try to find out if there is publicly available data appropriate for those projects that you are unsure about.
2. Find a recent issue of the *Statistical Abstract of the United States.* Look up a table in it that you find interesting. Read in the *Statistical Abstract* and the sources it refers to about how the data were collected and adjusted, and how missing data was dealt with. Do you agree with the decisions that were made about the data? Why or why not?
3. A professor uses one bedroom of her house for a study, in which she writes books. What cost should she impute for the space when she deducts her expenses for income tax?
4. Estimate the number of students who take basic courses in psychology and political science in the United States each year. Include night schools and irregular students. State how you built up your estimates.
5. Make some reasonable quantitative estimate of the comparative value to you of any two courses you might take next semester.
6. Suppose someone said that newspapers pay too much attention to crime and not enough to more positive subjects. You decide to see if newspaper coverage reflects the crime rate, going up when the rate goes up and down when the rate goes down. How would you find this out?

ADDITIONAL READING

There are many sources of information about publicly available data. In fact, many universities now have libraries of data, just as they have libraries of books, with indexes of available data.

One of the biggest compilers of data in the world is the U.S. government. Guides to U.S. government data include the *American Statistics Index* and the *Congressional Information Service Annual* (Congressional Information Service). Wasserman and O'Brien (1980) provide an index to many kinds of available data, including U.S. and foreign data on social, economic, educational, and other subjects. Data on foreign countries is found in the publications of the United Nations (such as *UNESCO Statistical Yearbook*) and the Organization for Economic Cooperation and Development.

Probably the biggest source of social science data in the United States is the Inter-university Consortium for Political and Social Research located at the University of Michigan. Information about its holdings is available at many libraries. Some of the most important public opinion poll data available is described in Converse et al. (1980). Data from hundreds of polls conducted by the Gallup organization are available too (Hastings and Southwick, 1974). Many of the data sources discuss the quality of the data and how they were collected.

Interesting discussions of content analysis and using the data collected that way are Janowitz (1976); Neuman (1981); and Snyder and Kelly (1977).

Abrams (1966) provides a good and simple example of how deductive reasoning may be used to improve our understanding of social processes.

Some Principles of Measurement 15

1. Introduction
2. Classification
3. Scales
4. Reliability
5. Validity
6. Summary

1. Introduction

Classification and measurement as types of *research problems* were discussed in Chapter 4; that is, classification and measurement were discussed as *goals in themselves* in some research situations. In research that seeks causal or noncausal relationships and in purely descriptive research, however, classification and measurement are the *means* by which the research proceeds.

Once the variables are chosen for any piece of research, the researcher must decide how to separate the variables into different values; that is, he or she must "scale" the variables. If the researcher scales a variable *qualitatively*, that is, without numerical relationships, then he or she is *classifying* the categories of the variable. If the researcher scales a value *quantitatively*, that is, if there are numerical relationships among the categories, then the variable will be a *measurement* scale. Examples to

illustrate this distinction will be found later in this chapter.

Five important issues are common to both classifying and measuring: first, choosing the *dimensions* to scale or measure (practically synonymous with choosing variables); second, deciding *which categories* to use in the scales or which *type* of scale; third, *defining* the categories and drawing their boundary lines; fourth, making sure that the measures you develop are *reliable*, that is, that the same procedures will produce just about the same measurements every time; and fifth, seeing to it that the measures are *valid*, that is, that they represent what they are supposed to.

This chapter will consider each of these issues in turn. The next chapter will provide examples of different types of measurements and will suggest some steps to take when measuring in the social sciences.

2. Classification

This chapter is about *how* to classify and measure and not about the *nature* of classification. Nevertheless, it is worth devoting a very few words to the nature of the process.

When you classify a group of people or a set of objects, you are putting people into a set of pigeonhole categories that have different names.[1] The names of the categories have no special scientific significance, though the names may be chosen for convenience; for example, Linneaus' two-name system for plants, replacing long and unwieldy names, was convenient and perhaps aided biologists' imaginations in understanding new connections among categories, though the names have no *intrinsic* meaning.

When you place a group of people in a single category, you are asserting that everyone in that category will be treated as similar and that people in different categories will be treated differently in the course of your study. When you classify people by nationality, you will, in your subsequent use of the data, treat all Americans as the same but as different from Chileans, Taiwanese, and other groups. These statements of similarity and difference are only a device to help you to handle the data scientifically, of course, and they say nothing about whether people are "really" equal or unequal, morally or otherwise.

Coding different things or people into the same category inevitably loses some of the information you have about them: Categorization is like converting a color photograph into black and white.

For example, you may have collected some open-ended (unstructured) interviews about people's feelings toward racial integration. In order to handle the data more easily, you

might classify (code) each interviewee as either "for" or "against" integration. You thereby lose all the shadings of opinion voiced by the subjects and all the richness and variety of their comments. But, unless you classify the subjects in *some* manner, you will not be able to summarize the data or manipulate them in other objective ways. (Of course, it is possible to classify on *several* dimensions at the same time, so that some more information can be saved and used simultaneously.)

Loss of individuality in observations grouped together in categories is the basis for a persistent attack on science. People say, "How can you treat a moderate and a radical as if they were exactly the same in your survey?" or "Why do you lump together wholesalers in Vermont and wholesalers in Louisiana when they serve very different markets?" The real question, however, is not whether the items that you lump together are different in some ways, but rather whether they are similar *for your purposes*. If they are, your classification is perfectly satisfactory. The same antidote is appropriate for a child who swallows cleaning fluid in Vermont or in Louisiana. The dimensions for the classification scheme should be chosen to *fit one's purpose*. You should choose a dimension (variable) for your study that you believe is either of interest in itself or is likely to be helpful in understanding another variable. For example, the U.S. Bureau of Labor Statistics wants to know the situation of labor in the economy. It therefore designates employment-unemployment as a dimension on which it is useful to classify people. When B.L.S. finds out how many people are in each of the categories "employed" and "unemployed," it has developed valuable information for its purposes.

A social psychologist might choose the dimension of employment for entirely different reasons—to help *explain* crimes of violence, perhaps. Counting how many people convicted of crimes of violence were in the categories

---

1. The pigeonholes can also be given identification *numbers* like the numbers on football players or railroad cars. But those numbers usually have little real significance, a point we shall touch on again in the section on measuring.

"employed" and "unemployed" might help to explain why crimes of violence occur or help to predict when and where crimes of violence will take place.

If you are studying only an Amish community in Pennsylvania, the religion dimension will not be useful as a classification. (But Amishness will be a *parameter* of your study.) In most sociological studies in the United States, you *would* use a Protestant-Catholic-Jew dimension. On the other hand, in most countries of the world, you would need additional categories for a religion dimension. And, of course, in many types of studies—of nutrition, say—religion may not be a useful dimension at all. (It might be, though, that an investigator would notice that religion does, indeed, make a difference in the food intake of people and might then decide to include it in the classification.)

There is no metaphysical all-purpose classification for everything in the world, though some philosophers have spent their lives trying to create one. An illustration of the variety of classification schemes for different purposes is the fact that different types of libraries find different classification schemes best for their various purposes.

Machlup provides an example and a discussion of the rationale of economic classification when discussing oligopoly (competition among a small number of firms):

> Hardly any generalizations could be made about the "economic consequences of oligopoly" or about the "causes of oligopoly" unless we first separate different types or kinds of oligopoly. In other words, a classification of oligopoly is needed.
>
> Of course, an indefinite number of features or conditions could be named as conceivable bases for classification. The problem arises what to select in order to obtain a classification useful for purposes of economic analysis. Distinctions should be made whenever one finds differences suspected of "making a difference" sufficiently important within the chosen frame of reference. It is probably generally agreed that selling prices, output volumes, selling efforts, product qualities are among the major variables considered relevant for our purposes. Hence, the distinctions made in a classification of oligopoly may relate to differences likely to affect these major variables. It will also be agreed that the question of the sources of monopoly power and of the conditions responsible for oligopolistic situations is significant. Hence, a classification may be based on distinctions of the causes of oligopoly. . . .
>
> [N]o single classification [of oligopoly] could possibly serve all purposes. Cross-classification may sometimes be helpful, although the number of possible combinations might become overwhelming. On the other hand, a problem under investigation may be aided by one classification while others are irrelevant. For example, those interested in public policy formation may find it important to know whether an existing big-firm oligopoly is based on definite real-cost advantages or rather on the exploitation of institutional privileges or on the use of coercive or oppressive practices. But they may not in the least be interested in the symmetry or asymmetry of the leadership aspirations of the firms in question. A cross-classification according to leadership and collusion, however, may be significant. For there may be important differences in the effects of collusion without leadership, leadership without [a high degree of] collusion, and collusion enforced by leadership. (Machlup, 1951–1952: 160)

More than one dimension is necessary if more than one dimension helps to distinguish various groups or to predict their behavior. But there is no use in having two dimensions if both classify all occurrences in the same way. For example, if all candidates for the baseball team who throw hard *also* throw far and vice versa, either throwing hard or throwing far will be sufficient.

Constructing an appropriate classification scheme is not as simple as it seems, and it requires imagination. A textbook, for example, is largely a classification of knowledge in a particular field. For example, a feature of this book is the classification of obstacles to research in Chapters 18–23. A classification scheme may be previously chosen by theory or by the direction of your interest, as we have discussed in previous sections on the choices of variables and proxies. But dimensions may also be selected by trial and error, especially in classification research in which the classification scheme is itself the goal of the research.

One usually constructs an empirical classification with several sequences of trial and error, followed by examination of how well the classification works. For example, think how you have arranged the books on your bookshelf. On an ad hoc basis, you have placed those books together that seem to *belong* together. You may have begun with some *a priori* elements in the scheme like separation of natural sciences, social sciences, and humanities. But beyond that you probably had no special scheme in mind, and you shuffled and rearranged until the arrangement seemed to make sense. Later on, as you lived with the classification, you may have changed the arrangement as you noticed that some books were used at the same time or that you could find some books more easily if they were nearer psychology than sociology, for example.[2]

Some of the choosing of categories can be done *after* the data are collected; you can still decide to group several categories together in fewer categories. But the crucial classification work takes place at the design stage. For example, you must decide whether to include the category of "partially employed," in addition to "employed" and "unemployed," and whether to code all subjects into one or the other major category. You must decide whether to classify countries as "highly developed" and "underdeveloped" on the basis of

per capita income, to add intermediate categories, or simply to use the continuous variable of per capita income. How sensibly you choose the categories and the dividing lines will determine how useful the variable will be to you. When constructing a classification scheme, you must be very flexible in accepting new categories (and dimensions) and throwing away existing categories (and dimensions).

If the categories are expressed in words, the scaled variable is often called "qualitative" or "discontinuous." But it is possible to go from words to numbers or vice versa, though the process is not symmetrical. For example, if you have the heights of the people in your sample in feet and inches, you can arbitrarily choose to call everyone over five feet, ten inches "tall" and everyone under that height "short." In this way you have converted "quantitative" data into "qualitative" verbal categories. The numerical cut-off points for the categories should be those that are most useful for you. The New York police force may establish a cut-off height of five feet, eight inches for policemen because it believes that five feet, eight inches is a better cut-off point for its purposes than six feet or five feet, three inches, taking into account its need for tall policemen as well as the potential supply of candidates for the job.

Sometimes it is helpful to think of each possible numerical measurement as a category in itself. At first, it seems that there is an infinite number of numerical categories, because, for example, the heights of any two people will differ by at least some infinitesimal amount and no two are exactly the same. But, when you record the heights, you must record in feet and inches, which means that anyone between five feet and six feet tall can fall into only one of twelve categories at most. Of course, if you used a finer scale—calibrated in sixteenths of an inch, perhaps—there would then be more and smaller categories. But there will always be *some* limit on how small the categories can get, for your measuring instrument will cease to distinguish at *some* degree of fineness; there

2. It is an interesting reflection of U.S. national character that, unlike most other library classification schemes, the Library of Congress system is entirely without theory and is based solely on the pragmatic judgment of which books will be likely to be *used* together. This totally empirical approach may well be the most successful way to deal with the insoluble problem in library classification: that books can be arranged *physically* on only one dimension, even though a *logical* classification would require many dimensions.

must always be some point at which the categories are discrete and not continuous.[3] (Notice that it is the *categories* that are discrete, *not* the people's *heights*. It does not make much sense to discuss whether people's heights are continuous or discontinuous, for the argument could be decided only by measurement, which *must* be discontinuous.)

Conversely, it is possible to go from verbal categories to numerical categories. If you have data on people's reactions to a political event, you can designate "like" as 3, "neutral" as 2, and "dislike" as 1. This technique is handy for many purposes, and it must be used whenever you transfer your data to cards or magnetic tape for automatic data processing. But you *must* remember that, just because you have designated "like" as 3 and "dislike" as 1, it does not mean that "like" is three times as great as "dislike," that three "dislikes" equal one "like," or that "like" is as far above "neutral" as "neutral" is above "dislike." You could have picked *any* numbers—01, 07, and 44, for example, instead of 1, 2, and 3. Unless *you* have decided beforehand, on the basis of some other evidence, that the categories bear some special numerical relationship to one another, you cannot assume any numerical relationship among them. But, if you do decide that two "likes" shall equal one "neutral," then you *can* add them and subtract them at will. Remember, though, that the final answer is dependent upon the numbers that *you* assigned. (Inexperienced or cynical researchers sometimes fool themselves or others by rigging the numbers

that they assign so that the outcome is what they want it to be. The Olympic Games provide a lovely example. The United States [unofficially] wants to count 5-3-1 for first, second, and third places; by that scorekeeping it beats the Soviet Union. The Soviet Union counts points 3-2-1 instead, and with that system *it* wins. Who is right? Nobody can be called "right" until we have other reasons to help us judge which system of counting makes more sense.)

After you choose dimensions and categories, you must operationally define the categories. For example, if you decide that the proportion of umbrellas in use will be your measure of the extent to which it is raining, you must decide whether parasols count as umbrellas. And will a newspaper over the head be counted as an umbrella? Is an open umbrella carried over the shoulder to be counted as an open umbrella?

You must define your categories so that most of your observations will fit into one or another category without too much doubt or arbitrariness in the process. The classification of humans by sex has the useful property that it is easy to designate most human beings as man or woman, though there will be some exceptions who are not easily classifiable.

Different definitions of "employed" and "unemployed" cause argument and confusion. For example, the National Industrial Conference Board estimated unemployment for November 1935 at 9,177,000, whereas the Labor Research Association estimated it at 17,029,000. This enormous difference came from the definition of "unemployed"; the Labor Research Association included farm unemployment and unemployment among professionals, whereas the N.I.C.B. did not. Also for 1935, the U.S. Chamber of Commerce estimated unemployment at a snappy 4 million, but sampling techniques may help to explain this low estimate (J. Cohen, 1938: 664). In 1949 Soviet official Georgi Malenkov could still estimate United States unemployment at 14 million—using good American data—whereas the U.S. Bureau

3. As Morgenstern forcefully points out, measurement that is too fine runs the great danger of deluding people into thinking that the data are much more accurate than they really are. Morgenstern quotes Wiener that "economics is a one or two digit science," which implies that any numbers that do not round off to one or two digits are misleading. An example is the history of the 1929 potato crop statistic: "First it was raised 2 million bushels, then lowered 30 million, then lowered another million, then boosted 5 million, and recently raised another million. It now stands at 333,392,000. Disregarding the 0's the only digit remaining of the six given in the original estimate is the first, the figure 3!" (Morgenstern, 1963: 116)

of the Census was estimating only 4 million unemployed. Malenkov simply classified as "unemployed" anyone who worked "less than full time" (Wallis and Roberts, 1966: 90–91).

Crime statistics sometimes take frightening leaps because the classification scheme has been changed (or because the recording of crimes has been improved). This has also been true of medical statistics; for example, better medical knowledge and practice led to more accurate diagnosis of lung cancer as a cause of death and decreased the number of mistaken diagnoses of tuberculosis and other diseases (U.S. Public Health Service, 1964: 127–141).

Here is the sort of definitional decision that must be made in categorizing employment status: If a woman worked twenty-two hours each week during the last month, should you mark her down as "employed" or "unemployed"? Your first reaction might be that the categories were not well selected and that there should be a category of "partly employed," perhaps. Or you might suggest that people should be categorized separately for 0-10 hours, 11-20, 21-30, and so forth. But for *some* purposes, at least, the simple dichotomous classification "employed-unemployed" is useful, especially as a simple index for laypersons to watch in the newspapers. So you must classify the woman who worked twenty-two hours one way or the other. Definitional decisions take up much of an empirical researcher's attention. Only the theorist can blithely ignore their existence.

Another example: Should the work that people do at home be counted as employment? Our usual practice is not to consider full-time homemakers as part of the labor force. This decision causes certain problems, as is illustrated by the story of the two Englishwomen who hired each other to do housework, then fired each other at the end of six months, in order to collect unemployment benefits.

Defining categories is a progressive process. As tough instances come along, you sit down and relate them to your final purpose and then amend your definitions to cover them. In establishing these criteria the important things to remember are as follows: First, have a *reason* for your decision; second, relate the decision to your ultimate purpose; and, third, refer back to your theory for guidance, if you are working with the aid of a strong theory. You must sometimes also throw in a touch of arbitrary reasoning. There will be some observations for which you are at a total loss how to decide, and you feel as if you could do as well by flipping a coin. Don't. Make yourself *select* one category or the other; that selection will probably be better than a random decision. One would hope, however, that such near toss-ups form only a small part of your sample.

3. Scales

Most of what is true of classifying is true of measuring, for measurement is a type of classification. (Or, if you prefer, classification may be considered a type of measurement, as we shall see.)

The main difference between classification and measurement is that measurement uses *numbers for computational purposes*. (Numbers can also be used simply as labels for categories, but this is still classification by numbers; labeling does not take advantage of the important properties of the number system.) Measurement is better than classification when it is feasible, because when you can measure objects or people on a variable, you can say in what way they differ, and by *how much*. Thus, you can classify a baby as "little" and an adult as "big," and this would tell you something about them. But you learn more about them when you can say that the baby is twenty-two inches tall and weighs nine pounds, and the adult is five feet, ten inches tall and weighs 160 pounds. Measurement allows you to give more precise meaning to "little" and "big"; more generally, measurement makes it possible to describe objects precisely and compare them to each other accurately and objectively.

A. THE NATURE OF MEASUREMENT

Stevens (1959: 25) gives a succinct definition of measurement: "Measurement is the assignment of numerals to events or objects according to rule." This is an important definition and worth pondering. It emphasizes the centrality of numbers in measurement. And it directs our attention toward the various rules that we may use in measuring.

A scale is the operational rule that one uses in a measurement. It is no coincidence that in English the measurement instrument for length is called a ruler. Our discussion of measurement is largely a discussion of which sets of rules—scales—are best for which kinds of situations.

There are many difficult philosophical arguments about measuring and scaling. The philosophical position that we shall take is the pragmatic one that whatever helps a researcher get on with the business of producing useful knowledge is sound measurement, and whatever in measurement hinders a researcher or causes a researcher to produce trivial though impressive-looking work is unsound.

In the physical and biological sciences, measurement is largely a matter of finding satisfactory *physical instruments* to measure the phenomenon one is interested in—the amount of oxygen on Mars, the speed of transmission of nerve impulses, the number of defects in an airplane wing.

The electron microscope and the radio telescope are polar examples of such technological advances. But instruments also can help in the social sciences. For example, because psychologists wanted to measure how active animals are under various conditions, they developed running wheels and treadmills that would automatically measure activity. Similarly, timed quick-exposure projectors make possible well-controlled experiments on learning speeds. And anthropologists measure the age of artifacts with the carbon-14 technique.

In problems that involve counting, simple arithmetic provides all the necessary scales and categories. But it is sobering to remember that this apparently simple mental machinery was not always with us. The number system probably originated with the desire of cattle owners to know how many cattle they owned and to keep track of their herds or flocks (Dantzig, 1967: 20–21). Counting the solidiers in an army was another early problem in cardinal measurement. The early rulers of Madagascar counted their army by marching one man at a time through a narrow mountain pass and dropping one pebble in a pile for each man who passed (Dantzig, p. 28). The inventions of numerals and early mathematics were extraordinary advances. But even after they existed, the crudeness of scales kept measurement inaccurate, as Heilbroner points out:

> . . . [T]he early merchant had to settle his accounts by weight of metal, and when a shekel was equal to so many grains from the middle of an ear of wheat and the carat of gold equal to the weight of a carob bean, there were problems enough to tax the skill of a modern arbitrager. (Heilbroner, 1956: 42)

Social scientists, also, seek better devices to learn about actual events and behavior. For example, estimating the number of houses in a country can be done by census enumerators, airborne photography, infrared photography, and so on. Or the student of communications who wants to know which pages of a magazine are read can use fingerprint powder. These "nonreactive" measures are appropriate when we are interested in what is outside of people's minds. But when we are interested in the contents or processes of people's minds, we must ask people to respond (react) to stimuli presented to them. It is the peculiar problems involved in constructing scales to measure the contents of people's minds that make scaling an important special topic in social science.

Please notice that the mere presence of a human being in a scientific measurement situation is not the source of our interest in scal-

FIGURE 15.1 Measurement in the Soviet Union

Source: © 1976/1969 by the New York Times Company. Reprinted by permission.

ing. If we want to know how hot a room is, and if a person reads a thermometer and records the result, human response is not central; we could replace the person with an automatically read thermometer. But if we ask the person, "How hot do you feel?" under a variety of conditions of temperature and stress, the person's responses are central in our interest. In the latter case we are interested in getting variations in reactions within or among persons as we change conditions, whereas in the former case of thermometer reading we are interested in *avoiding* variations in human responses.

B. STRENGTHS OF SCALES

Various scales can be assessed according to their "strength" or "power"—both vague words referring to the amount of formal infor-

mation contained in the scale. Following Stevens (1959) we distinguish four types of scale—nominal, ordinal, interval, and ratio.

Stevens considers classification to be a type of measurement–a *nominal* scale—because a number can be assigned to any given classification just as numbers are given to football players or chicken houses. But the numbers then mean no more than do any other names, for instance, "schizophrenia" or "prosperity" or "traditionalism." The number may be useful, but it is unnecessary, and we therefore do not consider classification a type of measurement.

An *ordinal* scale is exemplified by the street numbers on houses. If Jack lives at 1105 South Busey, you live at 1111, and Bill lives at 1115, we know that you live *between* Bill and Jack. Notice that this ordinal scale contains *more information* than does classification. If Bill wears

11 on his football jersey, Jim wears 13, and Jack wears 15, you know nothing more about Bill or Jim or Jack than if they wore any other numbers (although their numbers may tell you that all are quarterbacks).

Another ordinal example is the Mohs scale of hardness of minerals. F. Mohs worked out a system by which a given mineral would be rated for hardness *by comparison* with other minerals. Harder stones scratch softer stones, and any given stone is given a rating between a stone it can scratch and one that can scratch it. Note that one stone cannot be said to be twice as hard as some other stone. A stone can be said only to be harder than, softer than, or equal in hardness to another stone. At best, then, stones can only be put in an *order* of hardness, and this sort of scale is therefore called an *ordinal* scale.

Attitude and opinion scales are classic examples of ordinal scales. Here, for example, is an illustration of a brand-attitude scale:

> Listed below [Table 15.1] are several brands of each of two household products. For EACH brand place an "X" in the one box which best indicates how much you dislike or like that brand. The more you dislike it, the smaller the number you should give it. The more you like it, the bigger the number you should give it. There are no right or wrong answers. Only your opinion counts. (Abrams, 1966: 193)

A virtue of ordinal scales is that people can often make an accurate judgment about one thing *compared to another*, even when they cannot make an accurate *absolute* judgment. People can often say whether they like this painting better than that one, even though they cannot say how much they like either one. To illustrate the accuracy of comparative judgments, you can often tell whether a child has a fever—that is, when the child's temperature is two or three degrees above normal—by touching the child's face to yours and comparing whether her skin is warmer than yours. But you would be hard-put to say whether the temperature outside is 40° or 55° F, or whether a piece of metal is 130° or 150° F.

An *interval* scale contains even more information than does an ordinal scale. Unless all the lots on the block are the same size, we cannot tell *how far apart* our three houses are by just knowing the house numbers. But if the number on each house represented its *distance* in yards or rods from the bottom of the street, the house numbers would indeed tell us exactly how far apart any two houses are. This type of system is called an *interval scale* because the *interval* between 1 and 2 is equal to the interval between 2 and 3, 3 and 4, or 1105 and 1106. The intervals between numbers on an *ordinal* scale do not have this meaning at all.

TABLE 15.1

Products	Dislike Completely 1	Dislike Somewhat 2	Dislike a Little 3	Neither Like Nor Dislike 4	Like a Little 5	Like Somewhat 6	Like Completely 7
Toothpaste							
Brand A	—	—	—	—	—	—	—
Brand B	—	—	—	—	—	—	—
Brand C	—	—	—	—	—	—	—
Scouring cleanser							
Brand D	—	—	—	—	—	—	—
Brand E	—	—	—	—	—	—	—
Brand F	—	—	—	—	—	—	—

The example of the house numbers contains an additional kind of information that makes it a *ratio* scale. Ten yards contain twice as many one-yard segments as do five yards, and we can say that the ratio of ten yards to five yards is two to one. We cannot say, however, that 100° F. is *twice as hot* as 50° F., and therefore the Fahrenheit scale is only an interval scale and not a ratio scale. If this statement is not clear to you, reflect on the fact that 50° F. = 10° C. and that 100° F. = 38° C. Very clearly 38° C. is not twice as hot as 10° C. Interval and ratio scales are often known together as *cardinal* scales.

The most common uses of cardinal scales in the social sciences are in *counting*—counting people of various kinds, counting sums of money, counting the number of units of behavior, and so on. For example, Ebbinghaus grew dissatisfied with simply classifying people according to *whether* they could remember a given series of nonsense syllables, for he could not then distinguish among *degrees* of memory. Therefore, he tested each subject several times and counted the proportion of times each person correctly remembered the series. Such an approach gave him a cardinal scale to work with (Ebbinghaus, 1913: 9).

We can illustrate the relationships among these sorts of scales with a single example: You are shown three sculptures. You label them 1, 2, and 3 respectively, thereby creating a nominal scale. You decide that you like 2 better than 3 and 3 better than 1, a nice consistency; your preferences now form an ordinal scale. You decide that you would pay $200 more for 2 than 3, $100 more for 3 than for 1, and $300 more for 2 than for 1; those willing-to-pay numbers form an interval scale. If you now go one step further and say you're willing to pay $1,300 for 2, $1,100 for 3, and $1,000 for 1, those numbers form a ratio scale. Of course once you have the ratio-scale information in hand you could also go the other way; you could then form an ordinal scale by dropping the dollar figures.

Types of scales differ in the amount of information they provide. Ratio scales provide the most information, followed by interval scales, ordinal scales, and nominal scales. Using the type of scale with the most information is usually preferable, if you have a choice. And many of the statistical techniques that will be described later work best with ratio or interval scales, though there are no hard and fast rules about this. It is not always easy to develop interval or ratio scales—in fact, sometimes it is impossible—but it is usually desirable.

This might be a good place to mention again that measurement is operational definition. To say "stick is long" does not suggest any operation, explicitly or implicitly, and therefore the length of the stick is not well-defined and has not been measured. But to say "stick is same length as my arm" or "stick is longer than my arm" or "stick is two times as long as my arm" is to state implicitly that the relevant operation is a comparison of the stick with my arm; when someone has performed the operation of that comparison, he or she can know exactly what length of stick one is talking about. "A man's arm" may be a somewhat ambiguous measure, and that is why we have the platinum-iridium meter stick in the U.S. Bureau of Standards, where it is kept at a carefully regulated temperature, so that we have an almost-perfect ultimate standard against which we can measure things.

4. Reliability

When linking an abstract concept to empirical variables, you must attend to both *reliability* and *validity*. Reliability is essentially repeatability—a measurement procedure is highly reliable if it comes up with the same result in the same circumstances time after time, even when employed by different people. Thus, for example, if several nurses measure a patient's blood pressure and they all get the same reading, the procedure is reliable. Similarly, if there are several ways of measuring the crime rate—examining police reports, asking people how often they were crime victims, and examining insurance company records, say— and all the results agree closely, the measures are reliable. Low reliability—getting different results on different measurements—implies that there is random error in the measurement process. Obviously an unreliable measure is not very useful—there is little meaning if, when you "measure" a person's I.Q, the scores on different tests are 75, 150, 84, and 116.

One way to determine the reliability of a scale or measure is to see if the results of a measurement procedure are stable over time (Zeller and Carmines, 1980, Chap. 3) If you have a person answer questions designed to see if he is high or low in self-esteem, and his score today is exactly the same as it was last week, the reliability of the self-esteem scale would be 1.00, or perfect. Many factors can interfere with repeatability: moods, fatigue, mistakenly marking one answer when another is meant, and so on.

Another way to assess reliability is to measure the same concept in several different ways—to use *multiple indicators*—and see if the results are the same. When Entwisle and Doering (1981: 298–299) measured mothers' feelings about their husband's participation in the birth of their babies, they asked six questions—how the wife thought her husband felt during labor, how he felt during delivery, how they felt about their husband's presence during labor, how they felt about their husband's presence during delivery, what their husbands did to help during labor, and what they did to help during delivery. Because answers to all six questions were close—husbands were generally seen as very helpful and enthusiastic on *all* questions, or unhelpful and unenthusiastic on all, or in the middle on all—the six questions were seen as getting at aspects of the same concept, and the total score for all six questions may be considered a reliable index of husband's participation.

The only way to check on reliability is to have more than one measure—either multiple indicators at one time or the same indicator at different times. Without having more than one measure (or information about reliability from previous studies), there is no way to tell if the results of a study are trustworthy or just the result of errors in measurement.

5. Validity

Reliability is *necessary* for adequate measurement, but not *sufficient*. An adequate measure must also be *valid*—that is, it must measure what it is supposed to. A thermometer that always reads three degress too high provides a reliable indication of temperature, but not a valid one. Similarly, if you want to measure mathematical *talent*, but give a test of mathematical *knowledge*, you might not have a valid test of talent (though you could have a valid test of knowledge). Three ways to assess whether what you observe and measure is a satisfactory representation of your abstract concept are *content* validity, *criterion-related* validity, and *construct* validity (Zeller and Carmines, 1980: Chap. 4).

Content or "face" validity is simplest. You use logic, common sense, and previous work to specify which variables represent an abstract concept, and then select specific items. For instance, you might decide that a valid test of arithmetical ability should include items dealing with addition, subtraction, multiplication, and division. After that decision, you would choose the specific problems of each type for the test. Because the test of validity is entirely a matter of judgment in this approach, there can be great disagreement about whether a scale is valid.

Criterion-related validity is established by gauging the strength of the relationship between a scale and another variable—the criterion—to which it *should be* related if it is valid. For example, admissions committees at medical schools use the Medical College Admissions Test to predict success in medical school; they prefer to admit people with high scores because they believe those are the people most likely to do well. If there is indeed a strong relationship between the MCAT score and medical school grades, then the MCAT may be said to have high criterion-related validity; it is related to something it should be related to. Sometimes, however, no adequate criterion is available. For a measure of complex concepts like self-esteem or democracy, it is difficult, if not impossible, to decide what criterion could be used to validate the scale.

Construct validity is established if a scale measuring an abstract concept is related to *other scales* measuring other concepts in ways it should be, according to *theory*. Thus, you start with a set of concepts and some hypotheses about how they are related, then develop scales representing the concepts, and finally relate the scales to each other. Results consistent with what was expected indicate that the scales are valid.

Suppose you want to learn what makes people happy. To begin creating a "happiness scale," you might ask people about how happy they are with specific aspects of their lives, and then sum the individual scores. If the scale is reliable, you could determine its construct validity by relating it to other putative aspects of happiness, such as health, social status, stable family situation, and so on. If, as you might predict, healthier, higher-status people in stable families say they are happier than poorer, sicker people in less stable families do, the happiness scale would have construct validity (see how Andrews and Withey, 1976, deal with "well-being").

Construct validity is most desirable because it is based on theory. But evidence for or against validity has meaning only in a particular theoretical context. If your scale is related to others as predicted, that is evidence in favor of its validity. But if the scale is *not* related to others as predicted, either it is not valid, *or* there are problems with the theory or the measurements. At some point, you inevitably wind up using common sense to decide just how valid a scale is. The next chapter shows how to construct scales.

6. Summary

Classification and measurement are crucial technical operations in research procedure. The theorist may ignore these operations, but the excellence of empirical work depends on one's skill in carrying them out.

Measurement and classification link abstract concepts to empirical variables. Classification puts people or objects into categories in such a way that those in the same category are similar in ways important for your research, and different from those in other categories. Measurement puts people or objects into categories which are *quantifiable,* so that they can be described accurately in ways amenable to arithmetic or statistical calculation. The three basic rules for creating scales are these: a scale should contain as much information as possible (hence a ratio scale is better than an ordinal scale); the measurement procedure should be as reliable as possible; and the measurement procedure should lead to valid results. As always, the most important rule is that these research decisions should be made with regard to one's underlying purpose in conducting the research.

EXERCISES

1. Show how information is lost when classifying observations in some research study.
2. Give two research examples in which the subject's sex is an important dimension for classification and two examples in which it is not.

3. For what purpose might two categories of political party in the United States be enough, and for what purposes might more categories be necessary?
4. Give an example from research in your field in which definition of categories presents a major difficulty.
5. Show an example of use in your field of each of the following:
   a. an ordinal scale
   b. an interval scale
   c. a ratio scale
6. Suggest a reliable way to gauge the popularity of the president of the United States. What would be an unreliable way?
7. Suppose you want to develop a scale measuring people's self-esteem. How could you attain reliability?
8. Pick a concept that is important in your field. Develop a way to measure it, and then show how you could assess the content validity, criterion-related validity, and construct validity of your scale.

ADDITIONAL READING

For excellent discussions of the philosophy of measurement, see Kaplan (1964: 171–98); Coombs (1953); and Torgerson (1958).

On some problems and methods of measurement, see Selltiz et al. (1976, Chap. 6); Carmines and Zeller (1980); Zeller and Carmines (1980); Sullivan and Feldman (1979); and Blalock (1974).

Andrews and Withey (1976, Chap. 6) provide an especially interesting example of assessing reliability and validity in their analyses of measures of feelings of well-being.

Constructing Scales and Indexes

16

1. Introduction
2. What to Measure
3. How to Measure
4. Data Reduction, Including Factor Analysis
5. Summary

1. Introduction

The term "scale" is one of the most confusing in social science, because of the many ways it is used. Some discussion of "scale" and related terms and concepts is therefore in order.

First let us distinguish "dimension" and "scale." The concept of dimension belongs to the realm of theory. It refers to an aspect or *characteristic* of the phenomenon that you are interested in; for example, happiness or intelligence or productivity. The terms "dimension" and "theoretical component" are often used synonymously.

An "indicator," or "empirical variable," is an empirical tool—a proxy for the theoretical dimension—used to capture and represent a theoretical dimension. For example, one question in a series of questions about a person's self-judgment of his or her happiness might constitute an operational proxy for happiness. Or one might use the suicide rate as a proxy for the relative happiness of given groups of people. The term "scale" is frequently used as a synonym for "indicator" or "proxy."

If the indicator contains several elements—for example, a happiness scale consisting of several related questions—each question is called an "item." Each item may be thought of as an ordinary variable, and a scale can be composed of two or more simple variables; for example, a baseball player's ability may be scaled based on one point for running ability, one point for throwing ability, and two points for hitting strength.

"Index" is another word for an empirical variable or set of empirical variables used as proxies for an abstract concept (the difference between "index" and "scale" is partly a matter of usage—an economist is likely to say "index" where a psychologist would say "scale"). Indexes are often constructed so that seemingly different things can be added up and described in a single number. For example, a newspaper headline said "1964 Crops Near Record in Illinois." But how can one decide easily whether the crop in one year is better than the crop the year before? Perhaps the wheat crop was better but the corn crop worse, the sorghum crop a little worse, the apple crop better, and so on. On what basis do you decide whether the crop as a whole was better or worse? From the point of view of farmers as a whole, the simple cash value of the crops is a good index. But from a wider point of view this index is insufficient, for prices go up when crops are poor. Therefore an *index* is needed that takes into account the amount of each type of crop and weights each of them. And, indeed, the U.S. Department of Agriculture has just such an index, which allows it to say that the "all crops production index as of September 1, 1976, is at 118 percent of the 1967 index used as a standard, down from last year's 122 percent." (AP, September 11, 1976, from Champaign-Urbana's *News Gazette*, p. 1)

How do the judges decide who wins a boxing match? Unless one fighter knocks out the other fighter, the judges must take into account several different factors: aggressiveness, number of blows struck, and strength of blows struck, among others. And there must be *some* system to weight the different factors; for instance, number of blows struck is more important than is aggressiveness. The system of weights, and the overall result, is an *index number*. The index number for boxing differs from country to country, and who wins may depend upon the particular system in use.

Wages are another example. How much did wages go up last year? Janitors' wages went up 9 percent, but professors' wages went up 7 percent. Even if the whole world were composed of only janitors and professors, it would not make sense simply to split the difference, because there are more janitors than there are professors.

The stock market indexes illustrate that conclusions may depend on how the index is constructed. On a particular day the Dow-Jones Index may go down while the Standard & Poor Index is going up.

Dealing with the index-number problem reaches a peak of frustration when you must decide whether a group of people *taken as a whole* is better or worse off following some social change. A few people may suffer "greatly," and a lot of people may benefit "slightly." But we have no Benthamic "felicific calculus" with which to figure out whether the *total* of human happiness has increased or decreased.

Four things to be concerned about when trying to construct scales and indexes are: picking items to use (or deciding what to measure); deciding how to measure them; weighting them; and figuring out how to put them together in a valid and reliable index (or scale).

We take published indexes for granted. We forget not only how arbitrary and chancy they are but also how difficult and time-consuming they are to create. All of us think we know which supermarket is the most expensive in town and which is the least expensive. But the price-ranking of a supermarket is based on thousands of different articles. It took a researcher 300 skilled labor-hours to figure out the price ranking of just eight supermarkets in a shopping area (Holdren, 1960: 68).

2. What to Measure

The first principle in making indexes is to choose items for the index that are representative of the universe whose movement you want to measure. If you are constructing an index of consumer prices, you cannot measure the price changes in *all* items customers buy, so you take a sample. You might include bread, washing machines, ballpoint pens, men's underwear, and so on.

What can you do if you want to measure something as general as "quality of life"? Andrews and Withey found, "The notion of measuring quality of life could include the measurement of practically anything of interest to anybody. And, no doubt, everybody could find arguments supporting the selection of whichever set of indicators happened to be his choice" (1976: 6). To avoid seeming arbitrary or having to measure anything and everything, they did a pilot study and found that people divided up their lives into distinguishable parts, such as marriage, health, friends, job, religion. By being sure to ask questions about quality of life in each separate area, Andrews and Withey could be quite sure they were not leaving anything important out of their index.

3. How to Measure

Some abstract concepts are easily linked to variables that are simple to define and measure. The concept of length is readily translated into certain operations with a yardstick. Some social science concepts are like this; when a government agency wants to measure the number of births in a city during a year, the relevant variables—births, city, year—are very clear-cut.

Often, however, measurement is more complicated. Sometimes a concept must be measured as a combination of many variables; we might know how to measure each one, but not how to put them together. An example would be the Consumer Price Index; it is easy to find out the price of any product, but difficult to combine the prices in a way showing how all prices move together (does a change in the price of shoelaces count for as much as a change in the price of milk?). Even worse, sometimes the variables themselves may be difficult to measure. How can one measure "perceptions of well-being" or "intelligence" or other mental activities? Here we consider how to measure variables. The next section deals with putting them together.

Some of the most important work on scaling has been done by people interested in mental activities, because such activity can never be measured directly; proxy measures are always needed. Among the types of mental activity that have been measured are perception, cognition, intention, values, attitudes, and mental capacities.

The psychophysicists took the lead in scaling human responses when they began work on how different stimuli are *perceived* by a person. For example, how is a person's capacity to discriminate between two tones affected by the loudness of the sound? Scales invented in the nineteenth century are still in use today.

One scale of perception, Weber's, repeatedly presents two stimuli to the observer and measures the proportion of the trials in which the person can correctly identify the stimuli. For example, we may present a sound of a given loudness to the subject and then present a series of sounds of other loudnesses (and also the reference sound at appropriate intervals). After each test sound we ask the subject whether it is louder or softer than the reference sound. Then for each test sound's loudness we compute the proportion of trials that the subject got right. The difference between reference and test sounds that is large enough to produce some given proportion of correct responses—say, 75 per cent, because 50 per cent correct is expected purely by chance—is called the "just noticeable difference." The proportions correct for the various loudness differences is a scale that measures accuracy of perception as a function of the differences.

Scales to measure *cognition* (knowledge) are straightforward: One asks the subject, "How many people would you guess live in China?" The resulting data can be compared to the actual figure, and then the distribution of answers can be plotted among individuals.

Scales that measure *intentions* are of great importance to all research that aims to change people's behavior. An example is applied research into the effects of marketing variables, such as advertising and price, on people's purchases; intentions to purchase consumer durables are used as a reasonably close proxy for actual future purchases, both by commercial firms and by economic analysts when forecasting the near future of the national economy.

Sometimes simple questions about what

people intend to do—"Will you buy a car with an airbag?"—can obtain accurate answers directly. In other situations people cannot or will not tell accurately what they will do. If so, one may (a) use composite scales that contain several relevant questions which work from various points of view, to study both the pattern and the number of responses saying yes and no (more about composite questions later); or (b) substitute other sorts of scales for the intention scale; attitude and preference scales are frequent substitutes, which will be discussed later.

Many kinds of research seek to measure attitudes. This is usually quite difficult because people have trouble expressing these tendencies or are reluctant to do so. Prejudice research is an example; it is hard for any of us to really know our own attitudes toward other racial and religious groups, and we are often reluctant to tell other people about such attitudes.

I.Q. and other tests of *mental capacity* involve challenging problems of measurement and scaling. Which test items indicate the ability you wish to measure? Which set of items taken together makes up a useful mental scale? In which order should the items be given? Which items stand for which abilities? These issues have led to a large and important body of scaling knowledge called psychometrics, which is too specialized to pursue here.

Note that some research focuses on differences between *stimuli* and some on differences in *responses*. Psychophysical research focuses on how differences among graded stimuli affect the respondent. The experimenter may present a variety of sounds to a single subject to determine how differences in stimulus intensity are perceived. That is, in stimulus-oriented scaling the researcher is interested in differences among responses *by the same subject to variation among stimuli*.

Some research aims to find how various responses to the *same* stimuli are distributed among a group of people. For example, what

proportion of the public wants the town to float a bond issue to improve the schools? What proportions within the groups of Catholics, Protestants, and Jews believe that blacks are naturally superior to whites in athletics? Which segments of the public will be quickest to buy a new health food? Is there a difference among racial groups in ability to distinguish sound intensity? This is research that studies similarities and differences among people and their responses, rather than similarities and differences among stimulus objects and situations.

There are numerous types of scales for the study of attitudes, opinions, beliefs, and other mental states. They range from ad hoc scales made up specially for single purposes to generalized instruments such as the semantic differential. Which scale, containing which categories, is best depends wholly on the purpose of the study and the general situation.

The intervals on a scale may simply be numbers from 0 to 1, or −5 to +5, or 1 to 10, or any other pair of numbers that serve as poles. The respondent then indicates how far he or she is from each pole. Poles may be "approve" and "disapprove," "happy" and "unhappy," or whatever. Within the poles numerical intervals can be marked, or there may simply be a line on which the respondent makes a mark. The intervals on the scale also may be specific categories that seem to form a continuum. It is desirable that the items in such a specific-category scale be arranged in a reasonable order, and that they measure the same dimension.

In addition, the categories should represent all the variation in possible responses that would be meaningful to most people. There is probably something wrong with a seven-category scale, for instance, if everybody's response fits into only one or two categories.

Andrews and Withey found, for example, that if you want to gauge how satisfied people are with different aspects of their lives, you can't just ask them how satisfied they are, on a scale ranging from very satisfied to very dissatisfied, even though that might seem like the obvious thing to do. Most people respond that they are quite satisfied, a term that seems to cover a wide range of feelings. To get people to express themselves more fully, Andrews and Withey developed the "Delighted–Terrible Scale (Figure 16.1); using this scale produced a wider range of responses (1976: 18–19). (The scale has seven categories, and no more, because people don't generally make finer distinctions than that.)

It is often worthwhile to try out several different scales to see which one works best. Figure 16.2, for instance, provides three examples of scales devised to assess attitudes about scouring cleanser. While you may have to make up a scale for your purposes, it is often worthwhile to see if a potentially useful scale has already been developed and tested. If it has, you may save yourself some work and avoid the risk of developing a defective scale. Heise showed that using the same scales—the "semantic differential"—over and over led to the important conclusion that "humans of all kinds react to stimuli of all kinds according to three different dimensions of response: *evaluation* (good versus bad); *potency* (strong versus

weak); and *activity* (lively versus still)" (1979: 14).

4. Data Reduction, Including Factor Analysis

Once we have our measures, we have to weight them and combine them into scales or indexes. Indexes are made the way all of us implicitly make daily decisions. Consider, for example, the situation of a fellow like Arrowsmith, who has decided to marry one of two women but has not yet decided which one. Sheila is more beautiful, has more money, and cooks better, but Victoria is more intelligent and dances better. How is a man to decide? He might make up a scoreboard like this:

	Sheila	**Victoria**
Beauty	10	5
Cooking	2	0
Intelligence	3	10
Dancing	1	2
Money	5	3
Wife index	21	20

FIGURE 16.1 The Delighted–Terrible Scale: Categories Used for Assessing Affective Evaluations

I feel:

7	6	5	4	3	2	1
Delighted	Pleased	Mostly satisfied	Mixed (about equally satisfied and dissatisfied)	Mostly dissatisfied	Unhappy	Terrible

A Neutral (neither satisfied nor dissatisfied)

B I never thought about it

C Does not apply to me

Source: Andrews and Withey, 1976: 18.

FIGURE 16.2   Examples of Rating Scales Used in Marketing Research

(a)

7 Very Gentle
6 Somewhat Gentle
5 Slightly Gentle
4 Neither Gentle nor Harsh
3 Slightly Harsh
2 Somewhat Harsh
1 Very Harsh

(b)

_____ I definitely agree with the statement
_____ I generally agree with the statement
_____ I moderately agree with the statement
_____ I moderately disagree with the statement
_____ I generally disagree with the statement
_____ I definitely disagree with the statement

(c)

Definitely Would Buy

May or May Not Buy

Definitely Would Not Buy

13 12 11 10 9 8 7 6 5 4 3 2 1

Source: Green and Tull, *Research for Marketing Decisions*, 3rd. ed., © 1975, p. 180. Adapted by permission of Prentice-Hall, Inc., Englewood Cliffs, New Jersey.

Notice that the fellow is giving more weight to beauty, intelligence, and money than to cooking and dancing. Implicitly he is saying that beauty, intelligence, and money are more important than cooking and dancing. The sum of each woman's scores in the five "unaddable" dimensions is her wife index.

For a woman trying to make up a husband index, another complication would be added if she *does not know* exactly how each man stacks up on one or more dimensions. Let's say she knows that Arthur is well off and his money is important to her, so she weights it twice as much as intelligence (and handsomeness). She *thinks* Michael may have money, and if he does, he has twice as much as Arthur has.[1] She figures the odds are 25 to 75 that Michael does have the money. The score card is then as follows:

| | *Arthur* | | | | *Michael* | | |
	Points	Odds	Weighted Sum		Points	Odds	Weighted Sum
Handsomeness	10 ×	1	= 10		5 ×	1	= 5
Cooking	2 ×	1	= 2		0 ×	1	= 0
Intelligence	3 ×	1	= 3		10 ×	1	= 10
Dancing	1 ×	1	= 1		2 ×	1	= 2
Money	20 ×	1	= 20		40 ×	.25	= 10
Husband index			36				27

1. We are assuming that twice as much money is twice as desirable, which it usually is not; see Galanter (1959: 54–55) for a discussion of weighting.

This kind of scheme is a formal explicit representation of much of our everyday decision-making process; we would frequently make better decisions if we made explicit scorecards. This is the nature of indexes and the weighting of the components of indexes with "subjective probability" estimates of the odds.

Scales *can* consist of a single item—for example, asking about which tone is louder, which chocolate is preferred, in which order one ranks racial groups by liking, and which candidates one intends to vote for.

Simple single-item scales may not be adequate, however. Therefore, one may employ a multi-item composite scale. Such a scale may contain more information and be more reliable (remember from Chapter 15 that reliability cannot be ascertained unless more than one item is used to measure something).

Choosing items for a composite scale is critical. You should be concerned about four things. First, use the *right* items—those that represent the dimension you are interested in, and no other. Second, include *enough* items to distinguish among all the important gradations of a dimension and to check reliability; the emphasis here is on thinking of lots of items. Third, decide whether every item is supposed to represent the entire dimension you are interested in, or if the items are supposed to vary in "difficulty," each representing just part of the dimension. Fourth, keep costs down by excluding superfluous items that provide no extra information; use only the items you really need.

There are many ways to choose items. The choice can be made with unaided judgment, or a panel of expert judges can be used. Often preferred, however, are methods that make it possible to assess how well a set of items "hangs together," that is, whether it contributes significantly to the reliable measurement of a well-defined concept.

There are basically two ways in which items can "hang together." The first is where each of your items reflects the underlying dimension

roughly equally well. An example would be a "political liberalism" scale, in which each item asked how liberal a person was—for example, on a scale from 1 ("very conservative") to 7 ("very liberal") with regard to a number of issues, perhaps prayer in public schools, the equal rights amendment, spending on Medicaid, and eliminating tax loopholes that favor business. Someone creating such a scale would probably expect that a person who was "very liberal" on one item would be very liberal on the others, and a person who was very conservative on one would also be very conservative on the others. Thus, the dimension ranges from "very liberal" to "very conservative," each item contains the entire range, and, if the scale is reliable, all the items will be highly correlated with each other. In fact, the correlations can be used to calculate the reliability of the scale; then items improving reliability can be included, and those detracting from reliability can be excluded. You can keep trying to construct a scale in different ways until you find the one that is most reliable (Bohrnstedt, 1969).

The simplest type of composite scale presents several items to the respondent and considers a sum of the responses to the items to be the scale score. Likert scales, which present statements with five possible responses from "strongly approve" to "strongly disapprove," are commonly used in summed scales with numbers attached ranging from, say, $+2$ to -2. The score is the simple sum.

The second way in which a scale can "hang together" is for each item to represent a particular place on the scale (rather than the entire range) and for the different items to go together in predictable ways. For example, a ten-item I.Q. test could be constructed so that the items are ordered from easy to hard; that is, the test would be reliable if no person would answer a "hard" question correctly after missing an "easier" question. Or a "hawkishness index" of congressional voting could be created, in which a bill (or a vote for a bill) at one end of the dimension would represent a very unaggressive American foreign policy, then, as one moved along the dimension there would be bills calling for an increasingly aggressive policy, with the most "hawkish" at the far end (Burstein, 1978a).

One approach to constructing scales that hang together in this way is Guttman scaling. The Guttman Scalogram is a method for investigating whether the items make up a *cumulative* scale; that is, whether the questions are arranged so that a person who, say, answers no to Question Four after answering yes to Question Three will also answer no to all questions after Question Four. The underlying idea in the scalogram is to arrange the items in order of their "strengths" so that the step at which the respondent changes from one answer to the other is an index of the degree of the person's attitude.

There are many ways of constructing scales, some simple and some complex. Some scales have been validated through long and varied experience; others are constructed just for a particular study, and relatively little is known about how reliable and valid they are (see D. Miller, 1977; Lodge, 1981). Before constructing a scale, it can be useful to see what sorts have been developed by people doing similar kinds of research. Fight against becoming bewitched by the formal machinery of scale construction. A complex composite technique can produce useful knowledge only if its basic principle is sound for the particular situation.

Factor analysis is a technique used to investigate the relationship between theoretical dimensions and empirical variables, and to construct scales; it is used widely in psychology, sociology, political science, and other social sciences. Factor analysis is used to *reduce a large number of items to a smaller, more manageable number of scales;* it shows which items should be used in which scales and how they should be weighted (Zeller and Carmines, 1980; Kim and Mueller, 1978a and b). It is a technique that must be used *very* carefully, because the results can always be used to create scales, even when they are nonsensical (Gould, 1981). Used carefully, however, and along with a big dose of common sense, the technique can be helpful.

Factor analysis was developed to help construct good indicators of abstract concepts. The first concern was dimensionality. Does an abstract concept refer to one type of thing or several? That is, is it unidimensional or multidimensional? Thus, if "intelligence" is unidimensional, there would be a kind of "general" intelligence—a person intelligent in mathematics would be intelligent in biology, English, and psychology as well. If there were different kinds of "intelligence" in each area— that is, if someone could be intelligent in biology but not in art, or in English but not in accounting—then it is probably not useful to discuss intelligence in general, as if it were unidimensional. Instead, we would talk about different kinds of intelligence, or different dimensions—mathematical intelligence, verbal intelligence, and so on. Each type of *measured* intelligence would be a *factor* corresponding to a theoretical *dimension*.

To discover how many factors are in a set of items, factor analysis examines the correlations among the items. Though there are many varieties of factor analysis, a basic concept is that items that are highly correlated with each other will be part of the same factor, and items that are correlated weakly or not at all will be on different factors.

The high correlation among items on the same factor leads to the second contribution of factor analysis—reliability. As discussed above, high correlations among items in a scale is taken as evidence that the scale is reliable.

Finally, and most basically, factor analysis is concerned with the validity of translating an abstract concept into particular indicators. It is never possible to be sure about the validity of indicators (as discussed above), but it is widely accepted that *if* the factors discovered prove to match the concepts that the researcher began with (in number and content) and the factors are reliable, that is positive evidence of validity.

As a practical matter, factor analysis is used by researchers to discover how a large number of items may be condensed into a small number of reliable scales, making analysis easier (because there will be few scales instead of many items). For example, some political scientists and sociologists who study democracy have thought it might consist of two theoretical dimensions: popular sovereignty, involving the power to replace governments through elections, and political liberties, including free speech and a free press. A factor analysis has shown, however, that the different aspects of democracy form just one factor, so it will often be possible and useful to construct a single "democracy index" to describe a country's government (Bollen and Grandjean, 1981).

Other techniques for scaling and data reduction are treated in Chapter 28.

There are many ways to create scales. But— relax. Don't let the huge number of possible scaling methods paralyze you with fear. The results you get are not likely to be *very* sensitive to which scale you use. And if you try two rather different scales and the results agree, you can feel reassured that you are not likely to be badly in error.

Sometimes the full power of sophisticated complex scaling techniques is necessary and helpful. But such situations are not likely to confront you in your early research work.

5. Summary

"Scaling" is a term applied to a variety of measurement techniques. Many ingenious scaling methods have been developed to measure social and psychological phenomena. The choice of the appropriate scaling devices requires artistry, good sense, and knowledge of the underlying reality.

Three things to be concerned about when trying to construct scales and indexes are: deciding what to measure, which involves being very clear about what you want to study and not leaving any aspect out; deciding how to measure, which includes thinking about strengths of scales, scale categories, and types of scales; and data reduction, which involves using lots of information to construct scales that satisfactorily represent the concepts you had in mind when you started.

Composite scaling devices can help you squeeze information out of data. But the more clear-cut the problem and the better your data, the simpler the techniques you require. And if the data collection was poor in meaning and execution, no amount of fancy techniques will avail.

EXERCISES

1. Pick out an important but general concept in your field (for example, in economics, it might be "income"; in social psychology, "alienation"; in sociology "status"). Develop a list of empirical indicators of the concept. How would you measure them? How would you decide which ones to use in a study? How would you construct a scale representing your general concept?

2. Suppose you wanted to find out how satisfied students were with their college or university. Develop a way to measure the level of satisfaction. How could you tell if you have developed a good way to measure it or not?

3. Evaluate the cost of eating at four campus eating places, including a college cafeteria. This evaluation requires creating a food index. Then ask a sample of students to rate the eating places in order of cost, and compare what the students think to what your index shows.

ADDITIONAL READING

An excellent general discussion of scaling is in Selltiz et al. (1976, Chap. 12).

Edwards' short book (1957) is an excellent text on the special topic of attitude scaling. Summers (1970) and Blalock (1974, 1982) also provide much useful information about attitude scales.

On scaling procedures in market research, with special attention given to psychometric techniques, see Green and Tull (1975, Chap. 6).

On factor analysis, see Kim and Mueller (1978a and b) and Zeller and Carmines (1980).

On the details of many scales and how to construct them, see D. Miller (1977) and Lodge (1981).

Data Handling, Adjusting, and Summarizing $\boxed{17}$

Let us pick up the task at the completion of pretesting. Your study design is all set—at least until further modification. Now you must actually collect the data, work them into shape for interpretation, and analyze them. This chapter discusses the process from data collection until you begin the analysis.

1. Data Collection and How to Avoid Disaster

No part of the process of data collection and data handling is safe from human error. Many of the systematic sources of error from observers will be discussed in Chapter 19. But just plain mistakes can creep in anywhere, like the night air. For example, mistakes are made in writing down the data, in transferring them from data sheets to punched cards, tape, or disk (human errors though; the machines are nearly fool-proof), labeling the results, and so on.

Unsound decisions about classification and measurement are another major source of error in the data-collection process. Deciding on the exceptional cases and other trivia of the data-collection process is irritating and demanding work.

These decisions about exceptions—many of which occur in the coding of questionnaires, for example—are the soft underbelly of any research project. One of the weakest links in social science is that, when someone reads a published report of a piece of research, he or she cannot know how wisely or unwisely these decisions have been made. Yet a study can arrive at quite incorrect results if they are made poorly.

The only remedies for the human errors in the data-collection process are eternal vigilance, spot rechecking, checking the data against your intuition, and more checking.

2. Errors in Automatic Data Processing

You should have at least an onlooker's understanding of what computers can do. You should understand how a card, tape, or disk serves as a repository of information and how to get information onto and off it. Whether you should program your own work is another question. It may be most efficient to use the services of people who make their livings working with computers. As computers have become more complex, however, they have also become easier to use; you can now learn all the necessary skills of basic programming for social-science research in just a few days.

Whether you do all the work yourself or someone else does it for you, here are some specific pieces of advice for the data-handling process (do not attempt to do the first four steps until you have some acquaintance with data-processing procedures and equipment).

First, "clean" (check) the data thoroughly. You should clean to see whether any data appear in columns that should be blank on all cards (or in all records on a tape or disk), in which case you have probably spotted a record on which all the columns have been shifted to the right or left. Clean to see that there are no punches other than the ones that your code allows for, column by column. And so on.

Second, spot-check your data both at the raw stage and at the card stage to see if there are glaring errors. A good way to check is to "print out" all the data and run your eye down the various columns.

Third, check a random sample of the data for minor errors. The number of errors you find will enable you to estimate how many errors there are in the data as a whole. This is a type of quality-control check.

Fourth, at each stage at which you multiply, divide, or otherwise transform your data, print out the results of the transformations and check each calculation. Only experienced researchers can appreciate how many ways there are for transformations to go wrong, mostly through wrong instructions to the programmer or wrong programming. The former director of one of the important computer laboratories swears that the amount of error that takes place in data processing is enormous, danger-

ous, and mostly unknown to anyone even after the results appear in print.[1]

All this checking and rechecking may seem excessive. But small accidents in data handling have sometimes led to major errors in conclusions. For example, in his "The Case of the *Missing-Values* Card, and Other Mysteries," Firebaugh claims that another researcher left out an instruction to the computer about how to handle cases where data was missing, and that this error led to erroneous conclusions about the relationship between government involvement in the economy and economic inequality within nations. "I retraced his study, from first datum to last beta coefficient," Firebaugh writes. " . . . circumstantial evidence indicates that a missing-values card was missing in [the] computer program . . . [and the] finding that government involvement reduces inequality apparently is based entirely on an error in the analysis . . . " (Firebaugh, 1980: 137–39).

Fifth, never throw away any original data until five years after you are absolutely sure they have already been useless for ten years; that is, do not ever throw away the data. Especially do not throw away original data if you have transformed them into a more refined form. Transformations (for example, averaging) are often not reversible; sometimes you cannot get back to your original data from the transformed data.

Sixth, if data on other dimensions that just *might* be relevant sometime are available in the data-collection process at only slight extra cost, collect them (but don't go hog wild and swamp yourself with useless data).

Seventh, if your data have idiosyncrasies because of the particular nature of your study, try to collect them in such a way that the idiosyncrasies will not hamstring their use in some future study.

Eighth, keep careful, well-organized records of every step in the data collection, transfor-

1. A. Hoggatt, in conversation.

mation, and storage process. Dates, locations, and explanations of what was done should be recorded in detail. Parts of your data may wind up being useless to others, and even to you, if you cannot explain, even months or years after originally using the data, exactly what you did with them and why.

Ninth, do everything possible in duplicate. Have duplicates of your data, your records of data collection and processing, and so on. Real tragedies have occurred when months of work were lost because a programmer error caused the computer to erase a data set or an airline lost luggage containing crucial work records.

After your first close-up experience with the actual workings of a research project, you may be horrified at the inaccuracies and possible errors in the process. This is especially likely to happen after you conduct your first personal interview in a lower-class home, where you quickly find out how much judgment is required of the interviewer. The coding process can also frighten one into thinking that all research must be worthless. This reaction is similar to the one you experience when you first go into the kitchen of a first-class restaurant: You swear never to eat out again. Still, the number of food poisonings is smaller than the appearances lead you to expect. (But there is no more *excuse* for a sloppy research project than for a restaurant's filthy kitchen—and both *can* be dangerous.)

3. Imputing Value in the Absence of Standards

Sometimes your concern will not be with error creeping into the recording and processing of data you already have, but rather with getting any data in the first place. There will be times when there is no empirical source for data but the data are vitally needed; then you must somehow make the *most sensible estimate*. Base your estimate on any evidence you can adduce.

For example, consider the problem that

arises when a university tries to put a value on a piece of its own land—something it *must* do if it is to make wise decisions about where to place which of its buildings. Land for a proposed library site in the middle of the campus obviously has great value, and that value is an important component of the total cost of the building. But what value should be imputed? Only one thing is sure: To impute *zero* value for the land because you have no firm basis for estimation is folly, though this exact course might be suggested by an old-fashioned accountant. (Yet some big companies such as Union Carbide still do carry "good will"—the value of their organization and trade name—on their accounting books at $1.)

For a university, the best estimate of land value might be the cost of similar land as estimated by real estate brokers, if the university had to go out and buy. The most sensible estimate is a delicate piece of judgment in which the skills of the scientist and the knowledge of experienced people (in this case, the economist and the real estate broker) must be combined. Lately there has arisen a body of logical theory—called "Bayesian statistical decision theory"—that provides guidelines for systematically combining such estimates with your other data.

Imputed values can be tested only by judgment. There is no scientific test of the fairness and soundness of an imputed value, and indeed a jury is often required to render a judgment:

LAND PRICE SET BY JURY

A circuit court jury late Tuesday night returned a verdict of $64,500 for land required by the University of Illinois for the $14.3 million Center for the Performing Arts.

The verdict is the second in the series of condemnation suits by the university to acquire the site bounded by Goodwin Avenue, Gregory Place, Illinois Street, and Oregon Street. The property involved in the latest suit is owned by Albert and Beatrice Gregerson.

The University had appraised the property at between $52,000 and $55,000, and the defendants at between $74,000 and $78,000. (Champaign-Urbana *Courier*, March 25, 1965, p. 3)

The importance of sound imputation is seen in the magnitude of the decisions that are affected. Imputed value judgments of alternative school curricula, not any empirical scientific tests, are the basis of France's nationwide school curriculum decisions. And the imputed "shadow prices" that government agencies pay each other for goods influence the entire makeup of the Soviet economy. (How does the U.S.S.R. decide what price for truck engines the engine factory should charge the truck factory? General Motors has this problem too. One of the possible bases for the Soviet price is the amount the engines sell for in free-world markets. The existence of automatic self-regulating prices, rather than imputed prices, is a key difference between socialism and capitalism.)

4. Standardizing the Data

Once you have collected your data and begun to process them, you will discover that much of what you are doing involves *comparison*—of one person to another, one country to another, one variable to another, and so on. For the comparisons to be useful, the various pieces of data must be made comparable; you must *standardize* the data.

Lack of comparability in data is a fertile source of fallacies and lies based on statistical presentation. Often the fallacious implication is not intended to deceive people, but people are deceived nevertheless. For example, the National Safety Council reports that two-thirds of the people killed in automobiles are traveling forty miles an hour or under. But does that figure tell you anything about whether it is safer to travel under or over forty miles per hour? It does not. It would be much more illuminating to know the chances of being killed *per mile*

driven at speeds under and over forty miles an hour.

Huff gives us the story of the roadside merchant who, when asked how he could sell his rabbit-meat sandwiches so cheaply, replied: "Well, I have to put in some horse meat too. But I mix 'em fifty-fifty: one horse, one rabbit" (Huff, 1954: 114).

Two newspapers, one for and one against Roosevelt's New Deal, carried these two headlines and stories in the same week, differing in the mode of standardizing:

ELECTRIC OUTPUT IN SEASONAL RISE

Electric power production for the week ended May 28 rose substantially above the total of the previous week. . . .

POWER OUTPUT OFF 10.6% FROM 1937 FIGURES

The production of electricity in the United States in the week ended May 28 was 1,973,000,000 kilowatt hours, a drop of 10.6 per cent from the 1937 week according to the Edison Electric Institute. (cited in J. Cohen, 1938: 659)

Another example is the comparison of countries for wealth. The yearly income of India is greater than that of Luxembourg or Holland. But on a per capita basis Luxembourg and Holland are wealthier than India.

But *how* a set of data should be standardized is never obvious. Like every other decision in empirical research, this decision must be made with reference to the purpose of the research. Assume, for example, that you want to compare the average male of two countries for physical strength, as measured by how much weight he can carry for a mile. Should you make a straightforward comparison, man for man, or should you calculate the amount of weight carried *relative to the body weight* of each man? Standardizing men by their own weight is common practice in many of the Olympic games and in collegiate wrestling, boxing, and judo (but not in running and swimming). Or perhaps you should standardize by the amount of food they eat or by any of a dozen types of standardizing measurements.

The decision must be made with reference to the *universe of interest* that you are trying to investigate. If you want to know how much human male *lifting power* is available in a country, for the purpose of evaluating its labor resources, you would not want to standardize at all. But, if you want to know about the physical *condition* of the men in the various countries and about their "prowess" as we usually think about it, you would standardize by weight, age, and other dimensions.

In experimentation the *control group* is a standardizing device. The control group constitutes a base-line standard against which to compare the experimentally treated group. The key idea is that the experimental group, which is randomly chosen from the same universe as is the control group, would show the same results as the control group *if it had not been treated experimentally*.

Almost every national economic statistic must be standardized. Here is a description of one:

> The US Department of Commerce has developed a new analytical tool to measure economic growth in regions, states, and countries. Its study shows what the "normal" change in the number of workers in an area would have been if its economic conditions had been parallel to the nation's between 1940 and 1960. The difference between actual employment change and "normal" employment change measures the amount by which an area rate exceeded or lagged behind the national rate. This measure is then cross-classified according to the type of industry in the area, and the rates of growth for its industries are compared with the national rates to obtain a measure of relative growth potential.
>
> As an example of employment shift between 1950 and 1960, jobs in Scranton, Pennsylvania, would have increased by over 9,700 if that city had grown at the "normal" rate. Actually Scranton had a decline of over 8,400 jobs. In effect, this was a net loss of over 18,100 jobs. The study

found that the two fastest-growing regions were the Ft. Lauderdale, Florida area, and Anaheim-Santa Ana-Garden Grove, California. These had job gains between 1950 and 1960 of 249 percent and 201 percent, respectively, of their total 1950 employment. The three areas which lost the most jobs were those of Jersey City, New Jersey; Erie, Pennsylvania; and St. Joseph, Missouri, which experienced declines during the decade of over 24 percent each. (*Illinois Business Review,* April 1966, p. 9)

Another common standardizing device for demographic and economic national statistics is the *base year,* in which each year's (or month's) amount is expressed as a percentage of the first or other base year. The deflated dollar is a very useful standardizing device in economic statistics; its purpose is to standardize the *values* of amounts of money earned or paid in years when the values of the dollar were different.

Here is an example of how lack of standardization can turn the world topsy-turvy:

> Many an American youth believed that his life was to be cut off prematurely when the government called him to the colors in 1917 to fight for his country. The fact was that he was really in less danger while fighting for the land that bore him than he was while engaged in his peaceful vocations. Fifty-three thousand-three hundred American soliders were killed or died of wounds during the nineteen months of our participation in the War, victims of every refinement of modern slaughter; yet during that same period 132,000 persons were killed at home in the performance of the tasks of peace. (*New York Herald Tribune,* January 2, 1927, in Cohen, p. 666)

The *proportion* or *ratio* is a useful device for standardizing data. Its sole purpose is to indicate the *relative sizes* of two quantities to be compared. The percentage is a special kind of proportion; it is a standardization device, for two percentages can immediately be compared to see which is bigger, whereas 22/73 and 18/67 cannot be compared until they themselves have been standardized. All of us have used percentages all our lives, and it is hard to imagine how we would get along without this device. But the percentage is deceptively simple, and it takes a lot of hard thinking to decide which percentage to compute.

Taking out trends is often a necessary standardizing device. Later we will see that, if the relationship between auto sales and auto prices is plotted for several decades, it appears as if the two variables go together, leading to the inference that higher prices cause higher sales. Actually, it is the *trends* of higher prices and higher auto sales over the years that confuse the picture. One way to clarify the matter is to consider the *difference from year to year* in sales and prices, which serves to remove some of the effects of trends (of some kinds).

5. Avoiding the Hazards of Hired Help

Other people are not as smart as you are. Even worse, they have only the faintest glimmering of what you are trying to do in your research. And worst of all—though it is perfectly understandable, of course—is that other people do not *care* about your research nearly as much as you do: The performance you get from people depends on their motivations.

These considerations suggest that you should try as hard as possible to (a) involve your assistants in the work, and give them a personal stake in the output; and (b) watch over them with as much vigilance as possible, and tell them that you will check on their work, as, for example, telling interviewers that there will be follow-ups on a randomly selected portion of the interviews. Furthermore, be supercareful about which tasks and responsibility you delegate to assistants. Of course, you are not ready to employ assistants yet, but soon you may be. Even more important, this section may lead you to see the potential hazards in research from a different and sobering point of view, both as a producer and consumer of research.

The dilemma is clear: The principal investi-gator cannot make all the hundreds, thousands, even tens of thousands of nonroutine decisions about data collection in a major study, but delegation is dangerous. And just because it is so irritating, time-consuming, and demanding, you are tempted to leave the decisions to your assistants. But you must not yield to this temptation. You must ride herd on the data-collection process at all points, and you must make all extraroutine decisions yourself until you have trained an assistant and checked his or her ability. Even thereafter you must check periodically to ensure that he or she has not strayed. In this periodic checking look for *big* blunders. Check the big items. See if everything looks *approximately* right. If it does not, find out why.

The only possible solution is a managerial solution: Find capable assistants, train them well, and check on them constantly. To be afraid to delegate is to doom yourself to research projects so small that you can do them with your bare hands and to a scientific output a fraction of what it might otherwise be. But to delegate unwisely is to waste all the work that you do.

As a first step in the training of any assistants, have them read, sign, notarize, and swear on their great-grandmother's grave that they will follow the instructions listed here. Even following instructions will not guarantee that errors will not occur. But the instructions will give you justification for great righteous anger and outrage when you bawl out your assistant for noncompliance. And *that* may have some effect.

INSTRUCTIONS TO RESEARCH ASSISTANTS (AND TO YOURSELF)

1. When doing a new task, carry out only a small part of the work and then check with your supervisor that the method is correct.
2. Keep a precise and detailed record of exactly how you handle each nonroutine decision.

3. Handle no exceptions without consulting your supervisor.
4. Figure the number of significant digits correctly; if in doubt, ask the supervisor.
5. Perform all computations on paper, with a calculator, not in your head.
6. Throw away nothing—not work sheets, not computations, not unusable data—nothing.
7. Label everything—all data sheets, all work sheets, everything.
8. Indicate the source of each piece of data and computation, whether from published sources or from your own original data.

Roth described several instances in which he and other graduate students cut corners when working on research projects. The lapses increased with time on the project, as the workers came to think that they could cheat without affecting the study's results.

> When a researcher hires others to do the collecting and processing tasks of his research plan, we often assume that these assistants fit the "dedicated scientist" ideal and will lend their efforts to the successful conduct of the over-all study by carrying out their assigned tasks to the best of their ability. As suggested by my examples, I doubt that hired assistants usually behave this way when they are junior grade scholars themselves. It becomes more doubtful yet when they are even further removed from scholarly tradition and from the direct control of the research directors (e.g., part-time survey interviewers).
>
> It seems to me that we can develop a more accurate expectation of the contribution of the hired research worker who is required to work according to somebody else's plan by applying another model which has been worked out in some detail by sociologists—namely, the work behavior of the hired hand in a production organization. . . .
>
> [W]orkers made the job easier by loafing when the piece rate did not pay well. They were careful not to go over their informal "quotas" on piece rate jobs because the rate would be cut and

their work would be harder. They faked time sheets so that their actual productive abilities would not be known to management. They cut corners on prescribed job procedures to make the work easier and/or more lucrative even though this sometimes meant that numerous products had to be scrapped. (Roth, 1966: 191–92)

Between us—but don't tell your assistant or ours—the errors an assistant does make will sometimes not be very dangerous if they are made *randomly,* in which case they tend to cancel out. This is likely to be true of purely arithmetical errors. For example, in a study of the effects of liquor prices on liquor sales in various states, a clerk made errors, many of them serious, in the calculation of every single one of the state price changes, but correct recalculation arrived at almost the same *median* estimate as did the calculation that contained the errors. On the other hand, even random measurement errors reduce the apparent association between two variables.

If there is any *systematic* bias, however, errors of any kind may damage your study. For example, if interviewers systematically overestimate the values of the homes of whites and underestimate those of blacks, the data on value of homes will be worse than useless for many. Even purely arithmetical errors can be affected by bias; the Internal Revenue Service finds that a large proportion of mistakes in the arithmetic of tax returns are in favor of the taxpayer rather than of the government. And errors in birth records show girls as boys more often than the reverse, and girl babies are more often left out entirely (Wallis and Roberts, 1966: 95). Whether the error is damaging depends on the purpose of your study.

6. About Computers and You

A few years ago you might, in some pieces of social science research, have had a reasonable choice between using a computer and doing without it. Nowadays the choice exists less often; few studies can reasonably be done without the computer's help in statistically testing and characterizing causal relationships. Therefore, you might as well resign yourself to getting acquainted with a computer. But cheer up—you are very likely to find that the computer is a lot less formidable to control than you may now think, and it can be a most helpful friend. Furthermore, wherever you eventually work—for a railroad or an accounting firm or a retail business or in scientific research—you are likely to make good use of the knowledge of computers that you pick up now. So getting acquainted with computers now is likely to be an excellent investment even if you never do another piece of scientific research.

A choice that you *will* face in processing your data by computer is whether to gain a fairly general command of what the computer can do for you, or instead to find someone who will prepare for you the most specific recipe of how to get the computer to execute only the task you need done in this study and nothing else. The latter may (or may not) be cheaper in hours right now than the former. But it has the drawback that you will not be getting any return in later general knowledge of the computer. Furthermore, you run the risk that your consultant will not understand why you need to do what you want to do, and therefore may give you the wrong recipe for your purpose.

A further choice that will face you is whether to give your instructions to the computer on cards or through an interactive terminal. Once again, use of the terminal requires some extra learning. But the use of terminals is spreading fast throughout our society, and hence you are very likely to make good use later of your investment in mastering the terminal now. (Lest you take fright that the "investment" time is larger than it is, we think that three or four days of reading and experimentation will be sufficient to enable you to use a terminal and the canned programs that will serve to process almost all social science data.)

The information that you feed to the computer is of four general types: (1) identification

and billing information; (2) indication about which subprogram you wish to use; (3) instruction about the tasks you want the subprogram to perform; and (4) your research data. Here are a few words about each of these four sorts of input information:

A. IDENTIFICATION (SIGN-ON) AND BILLING INFORMATION

This block of information is usually nothing more than your ID number or name, a secret password to ensure that only you can use your allocation of computer time, and the number of your account. Giving the computer this information should be a breeze, nothing more than mechanical reproduction of your own data. Yet it often is an infuriating experience until you master it. You may not find out about some petty detail such as putting in a slash-mark. Or your billing information has not been properly sent to, or processed by, the computer accounting office. Until the identification works the first time for you, you will face the frustration and agony of wasting time. But once you master it—and your instructor may well help you get through this with no hassle at all—you will not have to worry about it again.

(Key idea: For many operations the computer demands absolute accuracy, a discipline that you seldom run up against in your everyday life, except when you try to turn a lock with a key that fits the slot but is the wrong key. A missing or misplaced period in a computer program can do you in until you learn the discipline. On the other hand, once you learn to speak the computer's precise language, the computer is more reliable and diligent than any other agent in your life.)

B. CHOICE OF SUBPROGRAM

Some subprograms such as FORTRAN or BASIC are for general programming; you will not need them unless you get into writing your own programs. Other subprograms include SPSS or BMD, which are "canned" programs for use in the social and biological sciences. To use these subprograms you give a specified command to your computer such as "GRAB, SPSS", and then indicate the specific operations you want done, such as CORRELATION. The rules are found in a manual for the particular subprogram that you buy in a bookstore or obtain from your computer operator. (Incidentally, the SPSS manual, by Nie et al., 1975, is about the handiest compilation of information on statistical procedure that we have yet seen.) There is nothing inherently complex about this procedure, and certainly nothing mathematical. What is required is that you read carefully, ask for advice when you get stuck, and not lose your patience when you make a few mistakes. We strongly recommend the SPSS program for your use in most social science studies.

C. DATA INPUT

Somewhere—either at the very beginning, or after the choice of subprogram—you must tell the program the exact details of the set of data that you will be putting in next, that is, where on cards, tape, or disk your variables are.

The next part of your program consists of inputting the records of your actual raw data, either on cards, tape, or disk, through a terminal, or through other means of access. Your data must conform to a fixed pattern in order to be read intelligibly.

D. EDITING PROGRAM

If you use a terminal—as we hope you will—you will need to learn one more piece of business, the program to edit your program. This consists of operations such as substitution of one word for another, deletion of a line, up-and-down spacing, and so on. The editing program is like a very clever typewriter that helps you correct mistakes very flexibly. Learning to use an editing program reasonably well should take you between three and five hours of reading and practice.

7. Summary

This chapter discusses the process of collecting and processing data. These are administrative tasks, calling on the skills of personnel supervision, attention to everyday detail, constant checking for mechanical and human error, and deciding what to do about the innumerable out-of-the-ordinary situations that arise.

Imputing values in the absence of standards and standardizing data are necessary tasks that call for considerable judgment. Both require not only wisdom but honesty with yourself to avoid the natural tendency to juggle the data so that they show what you expect or want them to show.

Standardizing the data is crucial to the reasonable comparison of groups. The trick is to find a basis of comparison that controls for the main differences among groups that are not themselves the subject of your interest.

Computers seem intimidating at first, but it takes only a few days to learn basic computer skills, and they are likely to prove useful in many areas of life as well as in your courses.

EXERCISES

1. Is there a single most appropriate index for comparing the relative safety of airplane and auto travel? Give one or more indexes along with the purpose(s) for which it is most appropriate.
2. Estimate the number of single men aged seventeen to twenty-five who had no dates in your town or city last Saturday night.
3. Estimate the total market value of all the clothes being worn at this moment by people in your town or city.

4. What standardization devices are used in measuring I.Q.? What standardization devices are reasonable when measuring I.Q.s of boys and girls who grow up in "culturally disadvantaged" homes?

ADDITIONAL READING

Mitchell (1951, Chap. 3) presents an excellent discussion of data standardization and related topics in the context of economic data.

See Tintner (1965) for a technical discussion of index numbers.

On data processing, see Selltiz et al. (1976, Chap. 13).

Schlaifer (1959: 2–13 and Chap. 2) provides a very good discussion of how to combine probabilities and values to arrive at rational decisions.

Goodman (1955: 277–81) demonstrates this approach in the context of social policy decisions.

The Census Bureau data error, described as the "Case of the Indians and the Teenage Widows," by Coale and Stephan (1962), is worth the reading. On index numbers, we recommend Suits (1963, Chap. 9).

The SPSS (*Statistical Package for the Social Sciences*) manual (Nie et al., 1975) provides an excellent introduction to computer data processing. Most computer centers have manuals and short courses which describe what is needed to run computer programs at their particular location.

Sonquist and Dunkelberg (1977) provide an excellent guide to editing, coding, checking, and preparing data for computer analysis.

Part Three

The Obstacles to Social-Science Knowledge and Ways to Overcome Them

The Concept of Obstacles in the Search for Empirical Knowledge

18

1. The Concept of Obstacles to Knowledge
2. A General Approach to Surmounting Obstacles
3. Summary

1. The Concept of Obstacles to Knowledge

After the researcher has specified the question that he or she wants the research to answer, all he or she has to do is to go out and get the facts. But knowledge can be tricky to obtain, and common-sense knowledge-gathering methods may not be sufficiently powerful. There are often many *obstacles* that prevent you from getting accurate knowledge easily. When we say there are obstacles, we mean that the world is big, complex, numerous, expensive, and tiring to try to understand, not least because human nature is so complex. The resulting complications, as well as the large numbers and vastness of nature that demand time and money, are indeed obstacles to your finding out what you want to find out.

To put it another way, the flaws that occur in other people's research, and for which you criticize them, result from the obstacles that the researchers did not succeed in overcoming. The concept of obstacles to knowledge is perhaps the most important single concept in this book.

In the several years that I have been teaching research design to first-year graduate students no single problem has caused me more persistent anguish than that of trying to organize research errors into a meaningful pattern. I would like (as I think anyone would like) to have a scheme of presentation which is logical and at the same time exhaustive of these research errors. It might be useful too to have a checklist of known errors so that in designing an experiment we could go through and see if we have successfully avoided such errors. (Underwood, 1957: 89)

The aim of Part Three of this book is to provide such a presentation and classification of obstacles to knowledge and of research errors, as well as to offer methods of overcoming these obstacles. The purpose of this chapter is to introduce the general concept of obstacles to knowledge and to lay the groundwork for the discussions of particular types of obstacles in the chapters that follow.

Examples of obstacles to knowledge are easy to come by. Major obstacles usually exist even for research problems that seem straightforward, as these examples show: How many people in the United States are over six feet tall? You could measure every one of the more than 230 million Americans, but the *cost* of doing so is a major obstacle, an obstacle that you can surmount by *sampling*. Next, how hot is the surface of Jupiter? Touch your hand to Jupiter, or hold a thermometer to it. Until you can do so it is necessary to find a method of measuring temperature at *long distance*. Third, what does the Kremlin plan to do about the Middle East? You could ask the Russian Premier, of course. But there is at least a tiny chance that he will not answer your question or will not answer it truthfully. No one has yet developed a satisfactory scientific method to overcome this obstacle. Fourth, how do Americans feel about Thanksgiving? You can ask one or a dozen Americans. But you must find a method to ensure that the people you ask are typical. Fifth, and perhaps most important of all, who will win tomorrow's game between the White Sox and the Tigers? You can easily find out who won yesterday's game. But yesterday does not repeat itself perfectly; there is *variability* in day-to-day scoring. You might look to see who won most of the games between them last year. But team personnel changes from year to year. The obstacles are indeed great.

Sometimes it seems as if nature—and particularly the human aspect of nature that is the realm of social science—diabolically throws sand in the researcher's eyes and leads him or her to wrong conclusions. Not so. "God is subtle but not malicious," Einstein is reported to have said. If nature did indeed try to fool and foil you, your task would be a lot more difficult even than it is.[1] Subjects who lie purposely to deceive you and communities of people who deceive you purposely are unusual exceptions to this generalization.

Our aim in emphasizing the obstacles to knowledge is not to discourage you or make you feel that the game of research is very hard to play well. Rather, we want to convey that overcoming the obstacles is the very essence of the game of research. If there were no difficult obstacles to knowledge, there would be no need for research or for skilled researchers. The obstacles are the challenge, the spice that makes the game fascinating.

Ebbinghaus began his study of the learning process by setting forth the two major obstacles that prevent easy application of natural-science method:

> In the first place, how are we to keep even approximately constant the bewildering mass of causal conditions which, in so far as they are of mental nature, almost completely elude our control, and which, moreover, are subject to endless and incessant change? In the second place, by what possible means are we to measure numerically the mental processes which flit by so quickly and which on introspection are so hard to analyse? (Ebbinghaus, 1913: 7–8)

The most infamous example of an unsurmounted obstacle was the *Literary Digest* presidential poll of 1936. The poll failed disastrously because it did not overcome the obstacle of bias in its sampling procedure; it simply did not succeed in getting a representative sample of the voters.

Whenever two or more studies of the same question arrive at different answers, one or both of the researchers has failed to surmount some important obstacles. On page 197 there is an example of various researchers who set out to determine why supervisors earn more than the people they supervise. They reach very different conclusions because important obstacles to knowledge are not overcome in their studies.

Unsurmounted obstacles sometimes go undetected for a long time in pure research. But

---

1. Those who still believe that genetic factors might be responsible for diseases caused by smoking *and* for smoking behavior implicitly believe in a nature that goes to remarkable ends to confuse scientists (Brown, 1963).

in commercial research, competition among various firms can be highly effective in revealing errors caused by unsurmounted obstacles. Consider this story from the trade press:

STUDIES YIELD CONTRASTING DATA FOR MAGAZINES

Some SRDS Totals Are Markedly Higher Than Politz's or Simmons'

New York, Aug. 10—SRDS-Data Inc. has released new total audience figures for 27 magazines included in its Consumer/Audience Profile, thereby providing a comparison with figures previously reported by Alfred Politz and W. R. Simmons & Associates.

In some cases the Data Inc. numbers jibe with those from the other two researchers. But for some publications, Data Inc. audience totals range up to 41% higher than Simmons' and 14% greater than Politz's.

Simmons, for example, projected a total audience (of persons age 18 or older) of 10,957,000 for *Woman's Day*, whereas Data Inc. reported 15,543,000, or 41% more and Politz found 13,310,000, or 22% more than did the Simmons organization. . . .

Several factors may account for the different audience totals found by the three researchers: (1) different probability samples; (2) different methodologies in conducting interviews and projecting the figures nationally; (3) not all researchers were in the field at the same time—thereby possibly introducing an audience "seasonality" factor. (*Advertising Age*, August 16, 1965, p. 66)

2. A General Approach to Surmounting Obstacles

One must learn how to recognize in advance the various obstacles and know how to surmount each of them efficiently. In this third part of the book, we shall discuss the various obstacles one by one, and in conjunction with each obstacle we shall discuss research tactics to overcome it.

Of course, you cannot spot *all* obstacles in advance. Unexpected obstacles always crop up as you get deeper into your research work, and then you must retreat a bit and modify your method. The entire research process is a cycle of obstacles, methods, new obstacles, modified methods, and so on.

Government intelligence work generally, and spying in particular, resembles research in being a matter of first identifying the obstacles and then finding the appropriate methods to overcome them. "Clandestine intelligence collection is chiefly a matter of circumventing obstacles in order to reach an objective" (Dulles, 1965: 58).[2]

Some types of knowledge are harder to obtain than are others. It is probably true that the *wider* the scope of the knowledge, the more difficult it is to obtain. It is easy for you to state what magazine *you* read yesterday, although your memory may be faulty. It is a bit harder for your spouse to determine exactly what magazine you read yesterday, and it is decidedly more difficult for a stranger to find out what you read. It is hardest of all for a stranger to find out what magazines *each and every* American or the "typical American" read yesterday.

Newspaper reporters usually have no trouble finding out such facts about a riot as what time it started, how much damage it caused, and how many police officers were on the scene. They have much more trouble in determining "public opinion" about the riot. The difficulties in finding out who started the riot are so great that a reporter who does so successfully may earn a Pulitzer Prize. And the underlying causes of the riot pose a question that bristles with obstacles. After the exhaustive McCone report and innumerable other

---

2. Stigler tells us that "business is the collection of devices for circumventing barriers to profits" (Stigler, 1952: 435). The business of science is knowledge, and the business of business is profit.

studies the causes of the 1965 Watts riots are still not clearly known (Governor's Commission, 1965).

This seems an appropriate moment to remind you that *no* empirical knowledge will ever be absolutely perfect and certain—not even your own name. Perhaps there was a case of mistaken identity at birth.

Some obstacles are more likely to appear in some disciplines than in others. But, as with the temperate-zone doctor who occasionally spots a case of tropical disease, a wide acquaintance even with the obstacles that are infrequently found in your area may make the difference between your being a routinely skilled or a really gifted diagnostician of research obstacles.

Skill in recognizing and overcoming research difficulties is a matter of special importance for the statistically trained researcher. (Nonstatisticians may skip the following sentences.) Each assumption that underlies a statistical test is really an assumption that certain obstacles are not present in sufficient degree to invalidate the test or estimating technique. For example, interrelationship among the independent variables is, as we shall see, a common and tricky obstacle, but the assumption that *no* interrelationship exists is necessary for the use of many statistical techniques. If the statistician rushes ahead and applies a statistical technique when the assumptions do not hold or when he or she has not found some way of rendering the obstacle harmless, the statistical conclusions may fall into serious error. And indeed, not only are statistical techniques often misapplied in this way, but the way the results are stated often obscures the fact that basic assumptions are not valid. Such reports can easily mislead the unwary or less sophisticated reader.

Remembering that there are no standard solutions for obstacles can reduce your frustration and anxiety in designing research. It just is not possible to compile a handbook of research solutions in the style of medical reference books, which indicate one or more specific treatments for each particular disease that you diagnose. Furthermore, as in medicine, there are in research some afflictions that are incurable. For example, survey researchers asking people about things that have happened in the past will never be able to completely overcome the fact that people forget.

One helpful tactic is to compare the results of a study to the results of other studies. Another is to compare a second source of data; for example, use hospital records to verify patient reports about treatment. But different studies often suffer from the same defect, and it is often not possible to obtain additional data.

Some obstacles are particularly prevalent in certain social sciences. But, to a surprising degree, most obstacles are found in all the social sciences. Consider economics. Most economists seldom come face to face with the obstacle that people of whom they ask questions may lie to them or rationalize their answers. But that is because most economists work with data gathered by other people—and at *some* point in the data-gathering process *someone* faced these obstacles. For example, a labor economist might work with U.S. Bureau of Labor Statistics unemployment data and take the data at face value, without taking into account that the raw data came from a questionnaire survey of a sample of families, some of whom might have lied, rationalized, or done other human things that present obstacles to getting knowledge. Similarly, almost all the price data that economists work with are or were collected by surveys and question asking and are subject to all the obstacles inherent in that process.

The best general approach to overcoming obstacles to knowledge is to employ two or more *very different* research methods. No single method can overcome all the important obstacles. But different sorts of methods overcome different sorts of obstacles, and together their strengths can cover each other's weaknesses, provided that the results agree. Emphasis on the joint use of two or more empirical methods, together with theoretical speculation, is a basic theme of this book, a strategy called "triangulation" by Denzin.

Please do not allow your awareness of the obstacles to knowledge faced by empirical research to focus you only on the flaws of the research of others, or to conclude that all data and research results are worthless because none can be perfect. Minor flaws need not invalidate research. And if the researcher has a good basic idea and a basically sound research approach, even a good many minor flaws and a small scale of research will not invalidate the research results.

Although the term "obstacle" does not sound attractive, we think we should not complain that knowledge is not perfectly easy to get, just as we should not lament the existence of the phenomenon of friction on earth. To repeat, the obstacles to knowledge are what make the achievement of knowledge interesting. Also, they provide livelihoods for social scientists who sweat for knowledge in universities, government agencies, and business; it is because there are obstacles to knowledge that people will pay to obtain it.

And now, on to the obstacles themselves.

3. Summary

Some factual knowledge about the world comes easily. But the task of empirical social science is to produce the knowledge that cannot be obtained simply and easily by casual observation.

There is a wide variety of obstacles that prevent easy acquisition of reliable knowledge. Sometimes these obstacles keep people from attempting to gather the information; sometimes the obstacles cause information-gathering to yield wrong conclusions.

One of the main tasks of the skilled researcher is to construct the research design in such manner as to overcome these obstacles successfully and efficiently. The battle against nature's complexities is hard and never-ending. But this battle is the bread and butter of the empirical social scientist, and it may be won with diligence and ingenuity.

EXERCISES

1. Discuss how each of the three factors listed on page 237 might have accounted for the differences in readership figures for *Woman's Day* estimated by Politz, Simmons, and Data Inc.
2. What are the obstacles to a reporter's finding out who started a riot?

ADDITIONAL READING

Obstacles to research are usually discussed in the context of errors and fallacies. See Mead (1963: 45–48) on anthropology; Saiger (1960) on medicine; Morgenstern (1953: 13–70) on economics; Campbell and Stanley (1963) on psychological experiments; Tanur (1981) and Cannell, Miller, and Oksenberg (1981) on surveys; Gould (1981) on biology. Kruskal (1981), Blalock (1972, 1979), and Cohen and Nagel (1962: 316–323) are general references that discuss errors and fallacies in social science research. Morgenstern's *On the Accuracy of Economic Observation* (1963) is a frightening compendium of information on the state of such affairs in economics.

Obstacles Created by the Humanness of the Observer

19

This is the first of the group of chapters cataloguing the specific obstacles to knowledge and the tactics by which the obstacles may be surmounted. The obstacles described in *this* chapter all arise because the *observer* is a human being rather than a machine. Indeed, if a way could be found to replace the observer with a machine, these obstacles would often be surmounted; that is why data-gathering instruments are used.

To put it another way, obstacles that must be overcome arise because research workers are as complicated as their subjects. This chapter and following ones offer examples of each different obstacle and of methods for overcoming it. You will best understand the nature of the obstacles, however, if you create your own examples from your work and reading.

1. Observer Variability

This obstacle arises from the observer's most human quality—imperfect physical and mental faculties. We are not now talking of bias, which is a *systematic* tendency to deviate from the "true" value in one direction. Rather, we mean the inability of a given observer to *repeat* an observation again and again in exactly the same way with exactly the same result.

Observer variability occurs even when it would seem easy to be objective. For example, in library-science research it is sometimes necessary to decide whether two similar works by an author are two different works or two editions of the same work. Even an experienced observer will decide differently about the same pair of books from one day to the next. In other words, there will be variability (dispersion) in the observer's judgment from time to time.

In the physical sciences too—especially in the early stages of a physical discipline—observer variability is an important obstacle. For example, a human laboratory assistant does not read a thermometer perfectly. One important reason is that on repeated trials the observer looks at the thermometer from slightly different angles, giving slightly different readings. The difficulty is compounded if the observer cannot get close to the thermometer, as, for example, when he reads it from inside a window. Many other minor influences also cause variability and prevent precision.

As the natural sciences progressed and as more accurate instrument readings were needed, ingenious researchers developed such ways of surmounting variability in instrument reading as the following:

1. Repeat the observation, and take an average of the observed values. If the observer-variability errors are unrelated to (independent of) one another, the average of the observations is likely to be closer to the actual value than is a single observation.
2. Reduce the variation in the viewing angle with a mechanical device that holds the chin of the observer in a fixed place and thus fixes the location of his or her eye. Placing a mirror behind the needle is another common device to increase precision in reading instruments.
3. Read and record electronically, and print the reading automatically. But electronics has not completely licked this obstacle. Variability in observing stars is a major difficulty in astronomy, for example.

The social scientist controls observer variability with similar tactics. Whenever possible, observations are repeated and averaged to cancel out random variation. And, analogous to the use of the chin bar in reading thermometers, the social scientist often *reduces the scope* of the observations. For example, if a field worker is to gather data on family income, she can be instructed to determine only *how many* cars are owned, *how many* rooms the house contains, and the occupation of the breadwinner. This list leaves less scope for judgment than would a general instruction to estimate the income level. (Narrowing the scope of judgment may also be considered a step toward operationalizing the definitions the observer works with.)

Reducing scope is a device to restrict the observer to gathering knowledge that he or she can obtain reliably. Earlier we said that it is easier to state accurately what magazine you yourself read yesterday than to find out what a stranger read or what the average person read. This decreasing accuracy parallels the continuum of confidence you can place in an observer. You rely heavily, for example, on her statement of how she herself will vote. You may place considerable credence in her statement of how her husband will vote. You do not have much confidence in her casual statement about how her neighbors will vote. And you are politely skeptical about her prediction of how her state will go in the next election.

Here are two general principles about observer accuracy and the scope of observation: First, the sharper and more measurable the categories, the more accurate the judgments. An observer who estimates the year of a respondent's car will be more accurate about its *age* than if he judges it to be simply "old" or "new." And a judgment of "old" or "new" will be more accurate if he specifies a cut-off point, say three years old. On the other hand, it is a waste to ask for more categories of accuracy than are needed. Second, the less the observer must summarize, the more accurate the observations will be. The observer will be more accurate in judging the intelligence of a single person than in judging the average intelligence of a whole group of people.

Learning from experience usually reduces observer variability. Professors often take advantage of this process when they grade exams by reading several exam books and giving only tentative grades before beginning to grade in earnest—and then regrading the exams that were read first. Kinsey required a *full year* of practice from his interviewers before he would accept their data. The Kinsey interviewers, however, needed such an extraordinarily long training period because they had to exercise a great deal of judgment.

Mechanical and electronic devices can occasionally be employed in the social sciences to reduce observer variability. For example, College Board Examinations are graded and totaled mostly electronically. Of course, instruments cannot make observations and measurements that require judgment. In educational examinations, this limitation sometimes means ignoring some kinds of complexities in responses and not measuring some kinds of abilities. (In English composition, however, College Board Examinations are graded by judges, and several independent judges provide a consensus.) Tape recorders and cameras are frequently used in anthropology to produce a permanent record that can be reviewed repeatedly, either by the observer or by other people, in order to check on and reduce the extent of variability (Mead, 1963). And the experimental psychologist uses many gadgets to reduce observer variability—running wheels to measure animal activity, water and food meters to measure intake, and timers of all kinds to ensure exact timing of stimuli.

2. Observer Bias

The tall fellow records a lower temperature than the short fellow because the tall fellow looks down at the thermometer. This innocent propensity to take a lower reading that inheres in the tall fellow we shall call by the ugly name "bias." In scientific usage, "bias" is merely a tendency to observe the phenomenon in a manner that differs from the "true" observation in some *consistent* fashion.

But usually there is no way to determine the "true" value, especially before the study is complete. Therefore, we assume that *every* observer may be biased in one direction or the other. Our job is to minimize each observer's bias and allow for what remains.

Most biases in the social sciences are *social*. Social-scientific topics and situations stir up and involve the observer's beliefs, emotions, and other mental baggage. For example,

sportswriters lament the fate of the noble boxer Battling Siki, who underestimated the problem of observer bias; he fought Mike McTigue for the light-heavyweight championship in Dublin on St. Patrick's Day 1923 and lost by a decision. (No kidding!)

Observer bias was noticed early in the history of social science, for example, in Rice's 1929 study of the causes of destitution. Comparing the results obtained from poverty-stricken respondents by two different interviewers, he discovered that one interviewer's cases showed overindulgence in alcohol as the most common cause of destitution, while the other interviewer found social and economic conditions to be the most frequent causes. The first interviewer was a prohibitionist, the second a socialist (Cannell, Miller, and Oksenberg, 1981: 390). In the "Priscilla's Pop" cartoon in Figure 19.1 the interviewer's feminist bias seems to be affecting her survey slightly.

Observer bias creeps in no matter how careful you are. Many scientists have had an experience like this one: One of us had an idea that professors who had taken their Ph.D. degrees from universities with lesser reputations would be more productive than would colleagues *serving on the same faculty* who had taken their Ph.D. degrees from schools with higher reputations. He therefore began to match up pairs of professors on given faculties who had taken their Ph.D. degrees from different schools in the same year, intending to compare productivity. But he soon found that his desire that his idea be confirmed was causing him to match pairs that would show the results he wanted to see, thereby invalidating the work.

Anthropology has suffered worst and longest from observer bias. Modern anthropologists regard most early anthropological accounts by sea captains and missionaries as almost useless, simply because the authors' perceptions were so warped by their own cultural background. Their bias was often that all non-Europeans were heathen, savage, primitive, and without law or social organization. Even so astute a so-

FIGURE 19.1

Source: *Priscilla's Pop*, November 6, 1966, by Al Vermeer: © 1966 by NEA, Inc.; reprinted by permission of Newspaper Enterprise Association (or NEA).

cial scientist as Malthus fell afoul of this problem:

> The prelude to love in this country [New South Wales] is violence, and of the most brutal nature. The savage selects his intended wife from the women of a different tribe, generally one at enmity with his own. He steals upon her in the absence of her protectors, and having first stupefied her with blows of a club, or wooden sword, on the head, back, and shoulders, every one of which is followed by a stream of blood, he drags her through the woods by one arm, regardless of the stones and broken pieces of trees that may lie in his route, and anxious only to convey his prize in safety to his own party. The woman thus treated becomes his wife, is incorporated into the tribe to which he belongs, and but seldom quits him for another. The outrage is not resented by the relations of the female, who only retaliate by a similar outrage when it is in their power. (Malthus, 1963: 15–16)

Overcoming the obstacle of observer bias in physical problems like thermometer reading is reasonably easy. The simplest tactic is to obtain readings from several observers and to calculate their mean value, on the assumption that their biases will cancel out. (Remember, however, ten blind people see no more clearly than does one blind person.)

The tactics used to reduce variability *within* observers also reduce variability from bias *among* observers. In the thermometer case, such tactics might include careful instructions, devices that put the tall and short men's chins on the same bar, and automatic reading with instruments. Most observer bias in the social sciences is not dealt with so easily, however. (This is one reason why the design of research procedures is often more challenging in the social sciences than in the natural sciences.) Here are some tactics that prove helpful.

First, train observers very carefully. In a famous study of racial bias, Allport (1954) found that many whites who were shown a picture of a white man and a black man later said that the black was holding a razor, even though it was the white who really held the razor in the picture. The better trained the observers, the less likely they are to make such biased observations. Careful training is the keystone of modern anthropological method.

Second, specify the observer's task as closely as possible, to reduce the area of discretion within which bias may operate. As with observer variability, an observer's bias in estimating family income can be controlled by having him count the age and number of cars owned or the number of rooms in the house.

Third, require observers to refer frequently to detailed instructions. This requirement is a sort of training, for it forces observers to retrain themselves by constantly rereading their instructions. It also reduces their area of discretion by reducing the chance that they will drift away from their instructions.

Fourth, require immediate and detailed reporting whenever possible. Anthropologists try to record their field notes every day, to minimize the chance that their memories will play biasing tricks upon them. Police officers are also trained to take on-the-spot notes, to prevent bias and inaccuracy from creeping in, and courts give special attention to such notes (Ginsberg, 1975: Chap. 3; Howell, 1973: 376–78).

Fifth, mechanical devices like the camera and the tape recorder can sometimes reduce the discretion of the field observer. The permanent record can be checked later against the observer's observations, to evaluate bias. This technique has been used extensively in anthropology, market research, and social psychology. The coming of recording devices drastically altered the working habits of anthropologists (Mead, 1963: 55–56).

Sixth, have several observers observe the same phenomena, and compare their observations. Note that often all observers must observe at the same time, because, for example, an interviewee may answer differently or not at all in a second interview. Complete duplication is usually too expensive, especially in interview studies; in fact, the cost of interviewing is the basic limitation on the size of the study. Comparing the data from several observers to establish their individual biases is usually feasible only on a small part of the study; those biases can then be taken into account when the rest of their data are analyzed. Such a comparison can also test whether the observers have been trained well enough to squeeze their biases out of them. An example is a study in which two well-trained psycholinguists counted the number of pauses of various kinds in a recorded speech. Both of them practiced and compared their counts until these practice counts agreed with each other (Maclay and Osgood, 1959). Then each could observe individually without fear of undue bias creeping in. It is often wise to select observers who differ on relevant dimensions, for example, foreign-born and native-born, old and young, white and black, and so on.

This technique of comparing ratings among observers, and of averaging the ratings among observers if the ratings differ, can be especially powerful when the observers themselves are part of the situation and therefore have strong emotional reactions that affect their judgments. For example, the average judgment among a sample of several enlisted men is likely to provide a less biased rating of an officer than will that of just one enlisted man (Selvin, 1960: 31–33); averaging samples of students and patients is likely to provide "better" judgments of teachers and doctors, respectively, than are judgments by just one student and one patient.

The previous examples show how observers can inject bias into what they hear and see and also into their judgments of what they hear and see. But bias can also come from the way that the researchers themselves *affect* the human subjects, as we shall see shortly.

3. Cheating by Interviewers

Interviewers have found many ways to avoid their assigned duties (Roth, 1966). Some of these deviations are not larcenous; for example, the interviewer may merely skip an interview because the house does not look pleasant from outside. But some of the deviations are pure theft; the interviewer may fill out the questionnaire schedules in an armchair at home, and, worst of all, may do it with such skill that the answers are hard to distinguish from the real thing without some independent check. (An experienced survey analyst claims, however, that, even though he cannot detect one phony interview, he can tell when a whole group has been falsified by examining the pattern of dispersion among the answers. We hope he is right.)

Prevention and detection of interviewer cheating require a detective's imagination and resourcefulness. Here are some frequently used techniques.

First, the study supervisor may check to see whether the interviewer really carried out the interview by contacting some or all of the subjects by telephone or postcard. This tactic is not feasible if the respondents are guaranteed anonymity, but is proper if they are just told their answers will be kept confidential.

Second, examination of the answers and analysis of their internal consistency can reveal cheating; this is dramatized in Figure 19.2.

Finally, some researchers claim to have developed special cheat-catcher questions, but they are kept as trade secrets (Gallup, 1976: 97–100; Groves and Kahn, 1979: Chap. 6–7).

If you detect cheating, *find out how much cheating there is,* and report it in your write-up, even though unsophisticated readers of your study or critics with vested interests may seize upon this report as a means of damning the study. In an example of this procedure, Evans (1959) found no important personality differences between Ford owners and Chevrolet owners. Commercial motivation researchers raised a howl because this finding threatened their livelihoods, and one of the motivation researchers seized upon Evans' report that one of his interviewers had cheated—which Evans

FIGURE 19.2

"Our computer analysis of your consumer interviews shows you chickened-out after the second question, Ralph."

Source: Reprinted from *Marketing News* published by the American Marketing Association. June 4, 1976, p. 11. Used with permission.

had allowed for by discarding those data—to discredit the study. But sophisticated readers gained confidence from his report because they were reassured that there was no unreported but worrisome cheating.

4. Observer-Caused Effects

The researcher's efforts to study a phenomenon *always* affect the phenomenon and change it. The observer is inevitably a part of the same environment as is the phenomenon he or she is studying. Therefore, the observer, like all other aspects of the environment, must influence the phenomenon. Sometimes the effect is so slight that it may be ignored, as is usually the case in the physical sciences. For example, the act of measuring the time it takes a ball bearing to roll down an incline affects the ball in some infinitesimal way; there is gravitational attraction between the observer's eyeballs as they roll in her head and the ball bearing as it rolls down the incline, but the attraction is too small to measure. On the other hand, a chemist's breath may well affect a reaction he is running.

The observer effect in medical examinations straddles the physical and social sciences. Studies of the relationship between lack of human companionship and heart disease have found, for example, that "a nurse's hand can slow a patient's pounding pulse; the simple routine of pulse-taking often calms arrhythmic heartbeats" (Bernikow, 1982: 26).

More generally, there is the possibility that *every* sort of observation method, whether or not it involves a human observer, may importantly influence the behavior of the subject matter. The most general remedy for this obstacle is to make the observation procedure as "unobtrusive" as possible (see Webb et al., 1966). This topic will be discussed in more generality on page 280.

The danger of observer-caused effects is that the researcher may not realize that they are operating and affecting the results. In Pavlov's case:

> It was thought at the beginning of our research that it would be sufficient simply to isolate the experimenter in the research chamber with the dog on its stand, and to refuse admission to anyone else during the course of an experiment. But this precaution was found to be wholly inadequate, since the experimenter, however still he might try to be, was himself a constant source of a large number of stimuli. His slightest movements—blinking of the eyelids or movement of the eyes, posture, respiration, and so on—all acted as stimuli which, falling upon the dog, were sufficient to vitiate the experiments by making exact interpretation of the results extremely difficult. In order to exclude this undue influence on the part of the experimenter as far as possible, he had to be stationed outside the room in which the dog was placed. . . . (Pavlov, 1966: 108–109)

The consequences may be especially serious where observer-caused effects combine with observer bias. For example, the early I.Q. testers were interested in showing that psychology could be a science. They also were often also convinced that I.Q. was an inherited characteristic, and that native-born Americans were smarter than other people, especially immigrants from southern and eastern Europe and blacks. Their first major opportunity to test lots of people's I.Q.s came during World War I, when they were allowed to test thousands of U.S. army recruits. Could the test conditions have affected the results?

> Many recruits could not see or hear the examiner; some had never taken a test before or even held a pencil. Many did not understand the instructions and were completely befuddled. Those who did comprehend could complete only a small part of most tests in the allotted time. Meanwhile, if anxiety and confusion had not already reached levels sufficiently high to invalidate the results, the orderlies continually marched about, pointing to individual recruits and ordering them to hurry in voices loud enough, as specifically mandated, to convey the message generally. Add to this the blatant cultural biases . . . and the more subtle biases directed against those who could not write numbers or who had little experience in writing anything at all, and what do you have but a shambles . . .
>
> [The testers] acknowledged several times that a high frequency of zeros reflected poor explanation, not stupidity of the recruits . . . Yet, when given an opportunity to correct this bias by ignoring or properly redistributing the zero scores, [the] statisticians did just the opposite. They ex-

acted a double penalty by demoting most zero scores to a negative range. (Gould, 1981: 211, 212, 216, 217)

As Spencer pointed out long ago (1912: 66–67), observer-caused effects make trouble in the social sciences because human beings are both the subject of study *and* the observers. The consequent *interaction* between subject and observer must have consequences. We humans spend large parts of our lives learning to pick up and act upon subtle cues given us by people with whom we are in contact. Therefore, even very subtle behavior of the observer can affect the study results. For example, the inflection and tone of voice in which an interviewer asks a question can produce one response or another. A serious charge against the Kinsey study was that the subjects told the interviewers what they thought the interviewers wanted to hear or what they thought would shock the interviewers. But Kinsey's cross-checking techniques satisfied the official reviewers that error from this source was not great (Cochran et al., 1953).

One might argue that in history, economics, or political science there are no observer-caused effects because the research generally takes place after the events are complete. Brutus killed Caesar, no matter what the historian says about it now. But might not Brutus' act have been affected by how Brutus thought that future historians might interpret and judge what he did? Furthermore, Brutus' behavior was probably influenced by bystanders, who were really the observers of the event and the sources of the accounts that historians use. And in economics the course of economic events is clearly affected by the kind of *records* that are kept, which are the raw material for the economist later. Someone has argued that Germany was more injured in World War II by unsatisfactory national accounting than by its oil shortage.

We shall consider five kinds of observer-caused effects in social science: first, interviewer effects on interviewees; second, effects of publicity about study findings; third, time-sequence and repetition effects; fourth, placebo effects; and fifth, experimenter effects.

A. EFFECTS OF INTERVIEWERS UPON INTERVIEWEES

Interviewers' biased perceptions of interviewees and their responses can cause trouble, as we saw earlier. But, even if the interviewer is perfectly unbiased, the interviewee may be affected by him or her. In both instances, the nature of the observer or his or her action affects the observation and creates an obstacle. When the observer actually causes change in the phenomenon he or she is studying, we call the change an "observer-caused effect." But if only what the observer *sees and hears* is affected, we call it "bias." Some people may not care to make the distinction between the two difficulties.

. . . [A] whole series of studies shows that survey results for specialized attitudes are affected by the disparities or similarities in the group membership of interviewer and respondent. For example, in two NORC surveys samples of Christian respondents in New York City were asked whether Jews in America had too much influence in the business world. Among those who were interviewed by Christian interviewers, 50 percent said the Jews had too much influence, but among those interviewed by Jewish interviewers, only 22 percent said so. In another survey in which respondents were asked whether they agreed with the statement "Prison is too good for sex criminals; they should be publicly whipped or worse," among women respondents who were interviewed by men interviewers 61 percent agreed with this statement; whereas when women were interviewed by women interviewers, only 49 percent agreed. It would seem either that women are less bloodthirsty when they are in the company of their own species or, put more precisely, that they feel more compelled to give the conventional and sanctioned attitude to a male interviewer. In another survey, in which one group of Negroes was interviewed by white interviewers and an equivalent group by Negro interviewers, similar effects were observed. For example, when asked whether the Army is unfair to Negroes, 35 percent of those interviewed by Negroes said "Yes," but only 11 percent of those interviewed by whites were willing to express this critical attitude. It is well documented that responses vary with the disparity between interviewer's and respondent's sex, class, color, religion, and other group-membership factors. And the systematic direction of these effects is such that one would not attribute them to mere unreliability but to the way in which the respondent alters his behavior in accordance with the kind of person who speaks to him. (Hyman, 1954: 517–518)

Techniques for overcoming this obstacle are much the same as the techniques for surmounting observer bias. For example, observer bias in questionnaire surveys is often reduced by handing the subject a written question list. Construction of unbiased questions is a similar problem that we shall discuss later.

The participant-observer method in anthropology is fraught with the difficulty of observer-caused effects, and it is not easy for the researcher to decide how to act. Whyte experienced these difficulties in an Italian ghetto in New England:

I had to face the question of how far I was to immerse myself in the life of the district. I bumped into that problem one evening as I was walking down the street with the Nortons. Trying to enter into the spirit of the small talk, I cut loose with a string of obscenities and profanity. The walk came to a momentry halt as they all stopped to look at me in surpise. Doc shook his head and said: "Bill, you're not supposed to talk like that. That doesn't sound like you."

I tried to explain that I was only using terms that were common on the street corner. Doc insisted, however, that I was different and that they wanted me to be that way. . . .

While I sought to avoid influencing individuals or groups, I tried to be helpful in the way a friend is expected to help in Cornerville. When

one of the boys had to go downtown on an errand and wanted company, I went along with him. When somebody was trying to get a job and had to write a letter about himself, I helped him to compose it, and so on. This sort of behavior presented no problem, but, when it came to the matter of handling money, it was not at all clear just how I should behave. Of course, I sought to spend money on my friends just as they did on me. But what about lending money? It is expected in such a district that a man will help out his friends whenever he can, and often the help needed is financial. I lent money on several occasions, but I always felt uneasy about it. Naturally, a man appreciates it at the time you lend him the money, but how does he feel later when the time has come to pay, and he is not able to do so? Perhaps he is embarrassed and tries to avoid your company. On such occasions I tried to reassure the individual and tell him that I knew he did not have it just then and that I was not worried about it. Or I even told him to forget about the debt altogether. But that did not wipe it off the books; the uneasiness remained. I learned that it is possible to do a favor for a friend and cause a strain in the relationship in the process. (Whyte, 1961: 304–305)

And Malinowski, an early developer of the participant-observer method, pointed out:

. . . [I]f, like a trader or a missionary or an official he [the anthropologist] enters into active relations with the native, if he has to transform or influence or make use of him, this makes a real, unbiased, impartial observation impossible, and precludes all-round sincerity, at least in the case of the missionaries and officials. (Malinowski, 1961: 18)

B. THE "PUBLICITY" OR "DISCLOSURE OF RESULTS" EFFECT

The public announcement of presidential pre-election polls may affect the election. On the one hand, a poll result might persuade some people that it is a waste of time to throw away their votes on a candidate who is going to lose, and such a reaction might aid a candidate whom the poll shows to be ahead. This is an example of a "self-fulfilling prophecy" (Merton, 1968: 179–95). Politicians believe in this poll effect, judging by their screams at election time. Lazarsfeld and his associates (1948: 107–108) did demonstrate that there is some "bandwagon effect"—people voting for the candidate they expect to win; poll publicity could affect such expectations.

But a poll might help a candidate who is shown to be losing narrowly, by stirring his or her partisans to rise to the emergency. Perhaps such a self-*defeating* prophecy helped to elect Truman in the 1948 presidential election; the polls showed him slightly behind Dewey. The only evidence on actual election effects that we have seen is that voters who do not vote in the morning may be led not to vote at all by news reports of early election returns (Fuchs, 1965).

A forecast of economic inflation may magnify the inflation or even create an inflation that would not have occurred otherwise. People who hear the inflation forecast rush out to make purchases before prices rise. These purchases then actually cause prices to rise. For a contrary example, a forecast of low corn prices may discourage some farmers from planting corn, which may in turn *raise* the price of corn above the level it would have reached without the forecast.

Unlike most other research obstacles, publicity effects can easily be prevented by researchers. All they have to do is refrain from disclosing the results until events have run their course.

Some studies are done expressly to influence the outcome of the event. The study results are then publicized, withheld, or distorted for tactical reasons. Such use of research is one government weapon against economic recession or inflation. If people are told that prices are coming down, they may refrain from buying and wait for the lower prices. The fall in purchasing may then drive down the prices and curb the inflation (Gallup, 1976: 31–41).

This phenomenon resembles "feedback," which is discussed on page 290. True feedback, however, does not involve the observer but only the subject; something that the subjects themselves do affects their own subsequent behavior.

C. SEQUENCE AND REPETITION EFFECTS

One observation sometimes influences the next observation. The farmer cannot afford to break open each egg he sells to see if it is fresh; the next person to examine the egg would then surely find it worthless. Observations that require breaking the egg or the light bulb or the clay pigeon are called "destructive testing," for obvious reasons, and they are one form of repetition effect in which what you do at one time affects the subsequent state of affairs.

Here is an anonymous wag's illustration: You step on a man's toe and then apologize. He accepts your apology graciously. If you then repeat the experiment and step on his toe again, his second response may not be the same as his first.

Sequence effects (also called "position" effects) are a frequent obstacle in psychological studies of learning. We know that the first and most recent stimuli will often be remembered best. For example, if you ask a subject to memorize a list of nonsense syllables, the middle syllables will not get a fair shake. Therefore, if you want to compare the memorization speed of one type of nonsense syllable with the memorization speed of another type of nonsense syllable, you must somehow overcome this obstacle.

A standard technique for avoiding sequence effects is to *vary the sequence* in which the stimuli are presented to different subjects. If there are only three stimuli, one group of subjects may be given stimuli ABC in that order, whereas other groups receive the stimuli in orders BCA, CAB, CBA, ACB, and BAC. The design is "balanced"; that is, each stimulus has an equal chance to be first, second, or third, and the average scores for the stimuli can be compared directly. In other cases in which every stimulus does not have an equal chance, one can determine how much worse the middle (and perhaps last) stimuli did and then make appropriate adjustments. When there are many different stimuli, one can present them to subjects in random order.

Repetition effects are particularly important in panel studies and in any research in which subjects are observed or questioned more than once. Sometimes the subjects are not affected by repetition; there is some evidence that on consumer buying panels the subjects do not "wear out" very rapidly (Sandage, 1956; Sobol, 1959). But some studies of politics have shown that asking people about their political attitudes can change them, as in the case of a woman who "asked her husband to give her a 'crash' course on politics" when she became part of a study (Jennings and Niemi, 1981: 14).

As an example of the repetition effect, let us consider these data on the rate of recall for advertisements of a group of women who were interviewed several times:

RECALL AVERAGE

First interview	19.1
Second interview	24.9

"Respondents were not told on the first interview that they would be contacted again. Yet their interest in advertising was heightened . . . and their retention of commercial messages in the magazine was vastly improved" (Politz, 1964: 7).

In studies in which there is danger of subjects' being sensitized by earlier observations, the first step is to establish whether there really is a sensitization effect. The simplest way to do so is to compare the second responses of one group against responses of a similar group that has not received a first treatment. In panels, compare a particular set of responses of prior members of the panel with parallel responses from newly recruited panel members. If there is no difference, then you can assume that sensitization is not taking place, and you can accept the panel data at face value (Sudman, 1966).

If significant sensitization does occur, you must forgo the repeat-interview or panel technique and employ some other method instead, or figure out how to take the sensitization into account.

D. PLACEBO EFFECTS

Long ago physicians observed that giving a patient a pill—*any* pill, even if it contained only sugar—would often alleviate the symptoms of many diseases. The effect is not limited to those ailments usually regarded as psychosomatic. It includes angina pectoris, which is a type of heart disease; *any* new remedy seems to have the power to alleviate angina symptoms for six or eight months. This is the "placebo effect"; the fake medication is called a "placebo."

Sometimes the fake medication really affects the patient physically. Other times the patient only *thinks* he is getting better and reports the alleviation of symptoms to the doctor even though his underlying condition does not change. This can confuse the investigation of worthless drugs. When medical researchers experiment with the chemical effects of a drug, they must allow for the possible placebo effect, in order not to confuse the two.

The placebo effect brings home to us that medical research is in many ways a social science. It shares many obstacles to knowledge with other social sciences, and it therefore uses many of the same research methods, which is why examples from medical research are included in this book.

One way to avoid the placebo effect is to give the medication without the patient's knowing that he is receiving it—dissolving it in food, perhaps, or mixing it with some other medication that the patient already takes routinely.

The "double blind" experimental design is another method. In the first period group A receives a placebo that looks and tastes like the experimental medicine, and in the second period group A is switched to the real medication. Group B starts with the medication and then is switched to the sugar pill. Neither the doctor nor the patient knows who is getting the placebo; hence the name "double blind." Not only does this design prevent the patient from being affected psychologically, but it also prevents the doctor from reading the symptoms he or she expects to see. The amount of the placebo effect is then subtracted from the medication effect. One can then infer that any observed differences between the medication effect and the placebo effect may be accounted for by the medication.

E.   EXPERIMENTER EFFECTS

The famous Hawthorne effect is another illustration of how researchers can unwittingly obscure the effect of the variable in which they are interested. A group headed by Mayo (Roethlisburger and Dickson, 1949; Madge, 1962: Chap. 6) working at the Hawthorne plant of Western Electric set out to determine the effects of variations in the intensity of light and working hours on the productivity of a group of women factory workers. To their surprise, they found that *everything* they tried—even worse lighting—seemed to increase productivity. Then an explanation dawned on the researchers: The increases in productivity were apparently (but perhaps not actually) caused by the *attention* paid to the workers as subjects of research.[1]

1. Here is a digression on the history of social science that carries an important warning. For almost five decades the Hawthorne findings have exerted a powerful effect both on the social sciences—actually creating a whole new research tradition—and on American industrial relations. In 1978 Franke and Kaul made a persuasive attack upon the Hawthorne work as a whole, arguing that its conclusions in no way follow from the actual data and that the work falls into error because it fails to conform to elementary canons of scientific procedure. And they note that similar questions were raised shortly after the first Hawthorne reports appeared but were ignored by most social scientists (see also A. Carey, 1967). These charges have not been rebutted, which—together with the strong evidence he and others have offered—suggests that the Hawthorne study conclusions are unfounded in fact. Yet they continue to be taught and quoted. (We can usefully continue to refer to Hawthorne effects here, however, whether or not they really exist in industry.)

The Hawthorne experimenter-attention effect—the subjects' performing better (or worse) so as to please (or displease) the experimenter—is only one of many influences that the experimenter can unwittingly have on the subjects in the experiment. An equally prominent problem is that the subjects may find out what behavior the experimenter expects of them, and then perform as expected (see Rosenthal, 1966). This phenomenon is important both for its effects on research and its effects in operating situations such as the classroom.

An example of expectancy effect in an operating situation is an experiment where teachers were told that certain children "would show unusual academic development" during the school year, though the children so designated were actually chosen at random. Then the children were tested at the end of the year. The effect of the teachers' expectancies can be seen in the results for grades 1 and 2 in Table 19.1.

The expectancies of an experimenter can be transmitted subtly, sometimes so subtly that they are difficult to detect. The story of Clever Hans, the horse who could do arithmetic, brings out the point:

> Clever Hans . . . was the horse of Mr. von Osten, a German mathematics teacher. By means of tapping his foot, Hans was able to add, subtract, multiply, and divide. Hans could spell, read, and solve problems of musical harmony.
>
> Mr. von Osten . . . did not profit from his animal's talent, nor did it seem at all likely that he was attempting to perpetrate a fraud. He swore he did not cue the animal, and he permitted other people to question and test the horse even without his being present. Pfungst and his famous colleague, Stumpf, undertook a program of systematic research to discover the secret of Hans' talents. Among the first discoveries made was that if the horse could not see the questioner, Hans was not clever at all. Similarly, if the questioner did not himself know the answer to the question, Hans could not answer it either. Still, Hans was able to answer Pfungst's questions as long as the investigator was present and visible. Pfungst reasoned that the questioner might in some way be signaling to Hans when to

TABLE 19.1   Teacher Expectancy Effects: Gain in IQ of Experimental over Control Groups (after eight months)

		Initial Ability Level		
Grades	**Higher**	**Average**	**Lower**	**Weighted Means**
1	+11.2	+9.6	+24.8	+15.4
2	+18.2	−2.9	+6.1	+9.5
3	−4.3	+9.1	−6.3	−0.0
4	0.0	+0.2	+9.0	+3.4
5	−0.5	Not obtained	+1.2	−0.0
6	−1.3	+1.2	−0.5	−0.7

Source: Rosenthal, 1966: 411

begin and when to stop tapping his hoof. A forward inclination of the head of the questioner would start Hans tapping, Pfungst observed. He tried then to incline his head forward without asking a question and discovered that this was sufficient to start Hans' tapping. As the experimenter straightened up, Hans would stop tapping. Pfungst then tried to get Hans to stop tapping by using very slight upward motions of the head. He found that even the raising of his eyebrows was sufficient. Even the dilation of the questioner's nostrils was a cue for Hans to stop tapping.

For some experiments, Pfungst discovered that auditory cues functioned additively with visual cues. When the experimenter was silent, Hans was able to respond correctly 31 percent of the time in picking one of many placards with different words written on it, or cloths of different colors. When auditory cues were added, Hans responded correctly 56 percent of the time.

Pfungst himself then played the part of Hans, tapping out responses to questions with his hand. Of 25 questioners, 23 unwittingly cued Pfungst as to when to stop tapping in order to give a correct response. None of the questioners (males and females of all ages and occupations) knew the intent of the experiment. When errors occurred, they were usually only a single tap from being correct. The subjects of this study, including an experienced psychologist, were unable to discover that they were unintentionally emitting cues.

Hans' amazing talents, talents rapidly acquired too by Pfungst, serve to illustrate further the power of the self-fulfilling prophecy. Hans' questioners, even skeptical ones, expected Hans to give the correct answers to their queries. Their expectation was reflected in their unwitting signal to Hans that the time had come for him to stop his tapping. The signal cued Hans to stop, and the questioner's expectation became the reason for Hans' being, once again, correct. . . . (Rosenthal, 1966: 137–138, after Pfungst)

There are a variety of strategies for reducing the danger of experimenter effects, as summarized in Table 19.2. But sometimes it is difficult to overcome this obstacle. In the Hawthorne case, for example, researchers might have varied the intensity of the light without the workers' perceiving that they were the subjects of an experiment. But it would have been next to impossible to vary the hours in the work day without the workers' realizing that they were being singled out for special attention. Some other techniques are therefore required.

One way of allowing for observer interference when you cannot prevent it is to vary the amounts and kinds of experimenter behavior, holding all else constant, as suggested in strategy 8 in Table 19.2. At Hawthorne the observers might have varied the amount of time they spent with the workers and whether they acted friendly or unfriendly toward the workers under well-controlled conditions. If such variations on the part of the observer produced *no* differences, then it would be safe to say that

TABLE 19.2   Strategies for the Control of Experimenter Expectancy Effects

1. Increasing the number of experimenters:
     Decreases learning of influence techniques
     Helps to maintain "blindness"
     Minimizes effects of early data returns
     Increases generality of results
     Randomizes expectancies . . .
     Permits statistical correction of expectancy effects
2. Observing the behavior of experimenters:
     Sometimes reduces expectancy effects . . .
     Facilitates greater standardization of experimenter behavior
3. Analyzing experiments for order effects:
     Permits inference about changes in experimenter behavior
4. Analyzing experiments for computational errors:
     Permits inference about expectancy effects
5. Developing training procedures:
     Permits prediction of expectancy effects
6. Maintaining "blind" contact:
     Minimizes expectancy efforts [by avoiding feedback from experimenters and subjects]
7. Minimizing experimenter-subject contact [by using screens and automated data-collection systems]
8. Giving different expectancies to various experimenters:
     Permits assessment of expectancy effects

Source: Adapted from Rosenthal, 1966: 402–404

the observer is not an important source of variation. As a further control, it is possible to bring the observer into a situation in which nothing else is changed from normal and then measure whether his presence alone would cause any difference. This is like giving one group no pill at all and the other group a placebo, to estimate the effect of the placebo alone.

5. Summary

Observers of human behavior are themselves human, and hence are subject to human errors. These human errors are one of the main obstacles that the researcher must overcome.

Humans vary from moment to moment in how they observe even the same phenomenon. This variability must be controlled as well as possible with instrumentation, instructions, and training. Variability *among* observers may be tackled in similar manner.

Observers often bring their own biases to their work. These biases must be made to affect the observations as little as possible, and what effect does occur should be evaluated and allowed for.

Cheating by observers is a problem to be tackled with checkups and detective work.

Among the conditions that might be altered to influence experiementer expectancies are: descriptions of the subjects (e.g., as fast learners or slow learners); descriptions of the effectiveness of the experimental variable; and expectations of results predicted by the theory (Rosenthal, 1966: 404).

Now that you have read through this first of the chapters on the obstacles to knowledge and the devices for surmounting them, you have perhaps concluded that the tactics for overcoming obstacles in research are merely common sense. True. But the study of *other people's* common-sense learning, as embodied in this and other books on the subject, can save you time, money, and heartbreak.

EXERCISES

1. Give examples, from actual research in your field, of these obstacles:
   a. Observer variability
   b. Observer bias
   c. Observer-caused effect on subjects
   d. Publicity effects
   e. Sequence or repetition effect
   f. Hawthorne (placebo) effect
2. Suggest methods to surmount each of the obstacles in the examples you have given in Exercise 1.

ADDITIONAL READING

Observational methods and problems are discussed by Bickman (Chapter 8 in Selltiz et al., 1976).

Webb et al. (1966) detail a great many strategies, with accompanying examples, in the use of devices to study people without their knowledge and without interfering with their behavior.

Denzin describes the sociological interview from the "interactionist" perspective (1970a, Chap. 6).

The basic work on interviewer effects and selection of interviewers is Hyman (1954). See also Parten (1950) and Payne (1951) on this topic, as well as Hyman (1950: 519–523); Freeman and Butler (1976); Bridge et al. (1977); and Sudman et al. (1977).

Rosenthal (1966) is the classic work on experimenter effects in behavioral research.

For an excellent examination of how biases and expectations can ruin the work of even the most respected scientists, see Gould (1981).

Complexities and Intractability of the Human Mind

20

The obstacles to knowledge that are discussed in this chapter are both the bane and the joy of social-science researchers—especially of the social scientists who work with questionnaires. These obstacles are the salt of their work; they give it the unique flavor that sets it apart from other scientific work. The chemist or astronomer never faces these obstacles. When one studies people, one must face the fact that they may be ignorant, forgetful, dishonest, over-eager to please, and unconscious of their true motivations. This chapter describes some of the things social scientists do to overcome these obstacles to accurate knowledge about the social world.[1]

1. There is an excellent and voluminous literature on these matters, and you should read extensively in it if you plan to do work in social psychology, economic-data collection, market research, anthropology, or related areas (e.g., Ferber and Wales, 1963; Hyman, 1954).

1. Lack of Knowledge by the Subject

You cannot accurately report much of your own behavior. In some cases this is because you do not pay attention to the behavior. For example, if you were asked exactly how many pages you had actually opened a particular magazine to, you would have trouble answering accurately ten minutes later even if you were prompted by being shown all its pages one by one. (One researcher overcame this obstacle by putting little dabs of light glue between each pair of pages of magazines, then examining the copies to see how many glue seals had been broken.)

Another example is the number of television commercials you actually watch, compared to how many you switch stations to avoid or how many you tune out by leaving the room or attending to something else. One's self-report is not likely to be accurate about this behavior. Steiner (1966) attacked this problem by having observers surreptitiously watch other members of their families during commercials.

Still another form of this obstacle arises in obtaining data on the *combined* behavior of various people. Even if I know how many pages of a magazine I read, I do not know how many other people have read how many pages of the same copy, even if it is my family's copy. Or I may know that I found my job with the help of information provided by a friend, but will not know where my friend got *his* information (Granovetter, 1976).

Businesspersons' lack of knowledge of their own behavior is an interesting example. Two economists asked businesspersons how they set prices, and many replied that they added fixed markups to their costs (Hall and Hitch, 1939). But other analyses that assume prices are set according to what the market will bear explain actual prices better than do the businesspersons. Apparently they fail to recognize when they make adjustments to meet competition and otherwise maximize their profits. One can, however, ask different kinds of questions of the businesspersons. A used-car dealer may be able to tell you very intelligently and accurately why he set a price of $2,000 on a particular two-year-old Chevrolet even if he cannot tell you how he sets prices *in general*. Still another way is to infer his procedure from his answers to various relevant facts. One of us asked newspaper executives what they thought their sales to two classes of customers would have been if their prices had been 10 per cent lower or 10 per cent higher. Their answers explained satisfactorily why one class of customers was charged more than the other (J. Simon, 1965).

An anthropologist must ask "natives" the kinds of questions that the natives can answer knowledgeably, as Malinowski points out:

> Exactly as a humble member of any modern institution, whether it be the state, or the church, or the army, is *of* it and *in* it, but has no vision of the resulting integral action of the whole, still less could furnish any account of its organization,

so it would be futile to attempt questioning a native in abstract, sociological terms. . . .

> Though we cannot ask a native about abstract, general rules, we can always enquire how a given case would be treated. Thus for instance, in asking how they would treat crime, or punish it, it would be vain to put to a native a sweeping question such as, "How do you treat and punish a criminal?" for even words could not be found to express it in native, or in pidgin. But an imaginary case, or still better, a real occurrence, will stimulate a native to express his opinion and to supply plentiful information. (Malinowski, 1961: 11–12)

Sometimes one group of respondents can answer with more knowledge and accuracy than another group. World War II questioning showed that men who had not yet been in battle were most afraid of air attack, whereas men who had been into battle most feared 88 mm. artillery. To rely more heavily upon the answers of combat veterans seems sensible because their knowledge is greater (Stouffer et al., 1949, Vol. II: 235).

2. The Fallibility of Memory

One of the ways that we can learn about human behavior is to ask people how they have acted or what has happened in the past. But it is not news that people sometimes forget things. If you intend to use the products of people's memories as data, you must guard against the inaccuracy of their memories.

Kinsey recognized that his subjects might have forgotten what they had done in the past, at what age they had first done it, and how often. To estimate the importance of memory loss he checked up on subsamples of interviewees' memories by various devices. One of these important devices he called "take and retake." Subjects in the take-retake group were asked for their sexual history and then were interviewed again many months later. The two interviews were then compared to see how well the subjects' later statements checked against their earlier statements (Kinsey et al., 1948, 1965).

Kinsey and others arrived at these conclusions: First, people are more likely to remember important events than unimportant events. Second, people are more likely to remember events that have happened recently than events that happened in the more distant past; people forget details even of events that were very important at the time, as when older married couples have to think a minute before they can remember the date or even the year they were married. Third, memories about behavior tend to be much more reliable than memories about attitudes; a couple's memories of where they went on their honeymoon is much more likely to be accurate than their memory of how they felt about each other or of what they hoped for the future. Finally, *types* of behavior are remembered better than *frequency* of behavior, and *timing* of behavior is remembered least.

Ingenuity can offset memory loss. For example, if you want detailed biographical data such as job histories, you may aid recall by reminding people of major events that took place in the years you are asking about (Hoinville and Jowell, 1978: Chap. 3).

Another method of reducing memory loss is to have subjects keep *diaries* of their behavior, so that no remembering is necessary—a common practice in television-viewing research and in market research. No consumer would be likely to remember after a week just what products he had bought the week before and how much of each. But if you get him to write down his purchases *immediately after* he makes them, memory loss can be negligible.

Mechanical devices are sometimes useful. The Nielsen Audimeter is a mechanical device that automatically records when a television set is on and when it is off. And Lazarsfeld and Stanton developed a "program analyzer" with which a person registered his likes and dislikes of various parts of radio programs by pressing buttons. (Stanton was president of CBS, and we wished he would have put a program analyzer in *our* houses.)

In some cases you can circumvent people's bad memories by referring to existing records. For example, Coleman, Katz, and Menzel (1966) gathered information on drug prescriptions by checking pharmacy records.

The type of forgetting euphemistically called "confusion" is a bugaboo of readership research. Show a person a magazine, for example, and ask him whether he has read it. He may say yes even though he has *not* read it. Actually, memory (or other faculties) plays tricks on people, and they confuse what you show them with something else that they have seen. To overcome this confusion, one group of people is shown a dummy magazine that has never been printed. The proportion that says yes to having read this "placebo" is subtracted from the proportion that says yes to having read the real magazine.

Percentage who say they read actual magazine	42%
Percentage who say they read dummy magazine	12%
Percentage estimated to have read actual magazine	30%

Here is a general precept for dealing with memory loss: It is always good practice to reduce the time period between the event to be remembered and the interview to the shortest possible interval.

Perhaps the simplest memory obstacle to overcome is increasing *fatigue* in the subject. For example, in readership surveys, the interviewer shows the subject page after page of a magazine and asks whether the subject has seen the page. Toward the end of the interview the subject is tired and therefore less likely to remember an article or advertisement. If the interviewer always started at the front of a magazine and worked toward the back, the pages at the back would always be tested on tired people and would therefore be underrated. Readership surveys overcome this difficulty by starting at different places in the magazine with different respondents. In this way, pages at the front, middle, and back have equal opportunities with fresh and fatigued subjects. "Other things" are not equal for any *individual* subject. But for the group taken as a whole, all other things are indeed roughly equal for front, back, and middle advertisements and articles.

3. Cover-Up and Deception

There are some factors that people do not want to reveal to strangers (even to intimate friends, or *especially* to intimate friends) because of embarrassment, guilt, shame, or other social motives. The subject may therefore deny, exaggerate, minimize, or otherwise knowingly operate upon the truth to shape it into a form that he or she feels is more acceptable. Barry Goldwater believed that this obstacle was operating strongly in preelection polls in 1964:

> Senator Goldwater's own polls show that President Johnson has a large lead over him. Sources close to Mr. Goldwater said last week he believes that if his position in the polls does not improve he will be politically dead.
>
> But the Senator is also said to believe that "subtle impulses," many of which the voters will not discuss candidly with pollsters or with any other questioners, are at work among voters this year and could bring him victory Nov. 3. (*New York Times*, September 4, 1964, p. 2E)

Observation can sometimes operate as a check and prevent misinformation, as, for example, when the subject claims a level of income quite inconsistent with her home or job. Or the researcher can build into the interview internal checks that get at the truth in several different ways and therefore show up inconsistent answers. The take-retake technique can also be used to check on how much cover-up is operating; as cross-examining lawyers know, falsehood can be revealed by discrepant answers to repeated questions when the subject forgets the original lie.

Sometimes one can check on the accuracy of a survey by checking the accuracy of some accessible part of it. For example, a survey of people's gambling compared the amounts people said they wagered in legal racetrack betting with the actual amounts wagered at tracks. The rather good agreement between these two figures suggests that people might also report accurately on illegal gambling (though of course there is greater reason to cover up the latter).

The intuition of a highly trained interviewer can often distinguish truth from falsity. Kinsey's interviewers, for example, were trained to recognize and use the vocabulary of prostitutes in order to elicit responses that would help them to judge whether a woman was really a prostitute. Kinsey relied heavily upon this sort of ability in his interviews. But each of the Kinsey interviewers had a full year's training in these skills. There are few interviewing staffs that can be so well trained and upon whose intuitive capacity it would be sensible to depend to any great extent.

Sometimes people will try to mislead an investigator, not because they are embarrassed by a question, but because they want to prevent the investigator from knowing the truth for their own purposes. Deception is especially bad because all the usual scientific weapons—random sampling, for example—fail to help. The subject plays against you like an opponent in a game and holds many of the winning cards.

There are many wonderful stories of deception by so-called "primitive" tribesmen who tell whoppers about their sex lives to anthropologists and then chortle among themselves at the stupidity of the "civilized" scientist who could believe such nonsense. These reports may be apocryphal; nevertheless, they are instructive.

Tax data are always subject to deception.

> . . . [W]hen in 1711 a census was taken in China in connexion with the poll tax and military ser-

vice, the total arrived at was 28 millions, but . . . when some years later another census was taken with a view to certain measures for the relief of distress, the total arrived at was 103 millions. (Carr-Saunders, 1925: A2)

Kinsey's interviewers sometimes heard remarkable lies. Some businesses make a point of releasing false data about their operations, in order to mislead their competitors. Other companies have gone to great lengths to prevent their competitors from gaining useful marketing information. The Federal Trade Commission record in the Clorox case documented instances in which Procter & Gamble concentrated unusual amounts of merchandising effort in markets in which their competitors were testing new marketing techniques, in order to muddle up their competitors' research (Federal Trade Commission, 1963). In another instance, one magazine sent out vast quantities of free magazines in the weeks that a major readership survey was going on so that the apparent circulation of that magazine would be inflated relative to its competitors.

Deception by national governments to frustrate the intelligence-gathering services of other nations is standard practice. Some acts of deception—feeding wrong information to enemy agents, for example—are very direct. But nations also plant false stories in their own newspapers to throw enemy content analysis off the scent. Nations have falsified national budgets, gold reserves, and production figures: "It is reported that in Russia in the early 1930s the central statistical authorities had worked out 'lie coefficients' with which to correct the statistical reports according to regions, industries, etc." (Morgenstern, 1963: 20–21).

There is no simple prescription for dealing with deception. Most important is to be alert to the possibility of deception; research is no place for a sweet belief in the goodness of human nature. Aside from caution and skepticism, your best bet is to make independent checks of the evidence. Kinsey compared answers given by husbands and wives and by pairs of people who could provide information about each other, to determine the extent of deception. His basic technique to overcome deception was the free interview and the trained intuition of his interviewers, who could spot much deception and refuse to be taken in by it.

If deception cannot be avoided or minimized, you may have to shift to working with other subject matter that is less subject to this obstacle. There is no point in doing research that will be wrong because you were fooled while acting in good faith.

4. Trying to Please the Observer

People like to please other people, and subjects in research studies are no exceptions. Interviewees often answer questions the way that they think the interviewer would like them to answer. And subjects in experiments often act the way they think the observer wants them to act. This is very nice of them, but such genial behavior has a ruinous result unless the researcher does something about it.

For example, when a sample of people were asked, "Would you say that most men are better suited emotionally for politics than are most women, that men and women are equally suited, or that women are better suited than men in this area?", 38.3 per cent said they thought men are better suited (Schuman and Presser, 1981: 221). But when another sample was asked: "Do you agree or disagree with this statement: 'Most men are better suited emotionally for politics than are most women,'" 48.2 per cent said men are better suited. Such distortion affects not only the distribution of answers to a particular question, but also the statistical relationships between that and other variables.

In questionnaire surveys, asking the questions in an impartial way that does not reveal the interviewer's prejudices can help to overcome the obstacle of subjects' trying to please the interviewer.

5. Rationalization and Repression

In the section on cover-up, we discussed conscious distortion of the truth. Freud convinced us, however, that much lies in the human mind that either comes into consciousness as a subconscious distortion of reality or else does not come into consciousness at all because it is repressed.

> [W]hen a group of men who had said that they wanted to avoid serving in the Infantry were asked why, only 8 per cent said that this was because the Infantry "sees too much combat" or because "Its casualty rate is too high." The great majority indicated such reasons as "I don't think I'm physically qualified for it," "It would not give me a chance to do the kind of work I can do best," and "It would not give me training for a better job after the war." The analysts felt that, in a number of cases at least, such responses were rationalizations of the "true" motive—desire to avoid danger. In an effort to determine the extent of such rationalizations, they studied the relationship between reluctance to serve in the Infantry or in overseas combat units and reported worries about battle injuries. They discovered that there was a marked relationship: the great majority of those who said that they worried often about battle injury—79 per cent to be exact—wanted to avoid both the Infantry and overseas combat service. This is in contrast to 37 per cent of those saying that they never worried. Frequently a set of interlocking questions of this type permits an intrinsic check on evasions, and their analysis leads to more convincing results. (Kendall and Lazarsfeld, 1950: 172)

Digging out the real beliefs and reasons for behavior may involve the use of one or more of the variegated ingenious processes that psychologists have developed. (A full description of this armory of techniques for outwitting the unconscious may be found in Selltiz et al., 1976: Chap. 8).

6. A Brief Note on Behaviorism

The workings of the human mind are hidden from view. How, then, can we study a person's attitudes, desires, beliefs? One way to learn about mental processes is to assume that a person can really observe his or her own mental processes and report them accurately. This technique uses the subject as an instrument of the researcher to see what the researcher cannot see, a technique that was the basis of the introspectionist school of psychology.

Many psychologists became dissatisfied with using introspective reports by subjects because of the many kinds of distortion and inaccuracy found in them. They turned to observing the *behavior* of subjects and inferring mental processes from it. The behavioral psychologist measures whether a person is hungry, for example, by whether she eats, rather than by her statement that she is hungry. This technique has great advantages of *precision* because we can establish with great accuracy whether eating takes place, whereas we cannot verify objectively whether she is "really" hungry. Furthermore, this technique has the bonus advantage that it allows us to study the hunger of animals, whom we cannot ask for verbal reports.

The behaviorist technique consists of watching outward behavior that can readily be observed and then assuming that the behavior is related to the inner states that are not visible for study. The advantages and disadvantages of behaviorism in psychology and related disciplines are a matter of hot dispute. It is certain that there are research situations in which observing behavior is the best possible approach. An advertiser, for example, is supremely interested in whether people really buy his product; information on purchases is more valuable than any reports of such mental processes as attitudes, feelings, beliefs. On the other hand, watching behavior provides far too little information to a psychiatrist who is trying to diagnose a case, though a good psychiatrist will make the most of behavioral evidence too. What *is* very clear is that, although studying behavior may *often* be the best way to infer knowledge about how people's minds work, it is *not always* the best method for doing so.

7. Summary

The complexity of human responses is both the source of our interest as social scientists, and an obstacle to learning about people and their behavior.

The main human-response obstacles that the researcher must contend with are: (1) lack of knowledge by subjects about what they do and why they do it, (2) fallibility of people's memory about their past behavior, (3) covering up of information that subjects think shameful or do not want to reveal, or deceiving the observer about behavior, attitudes, and motives, (4) trying to say and do things that will please the observer, and (5) rationalization and repression.

For each of these human-complexity obstacles there is a wide variety of techniques to help you overcome them. Many of these techniques are described in this chapter of the book. Others are learned with research experience.

EXERCISES

1. Give examples from research in your field to illustrate the following obstacles:
   a.   Lack of knowledge by the subject
   b.   Fallibility of subject's memory
   c.   Cover-up by the subject
   d.   Deception
   e.   Trying to please the observer
   f.   Rationalization or repression
2. Suggest methods of surmounting the obstacles you described in Exercise 1.
3. How would you determine how willing people would be to will their body parts (such as kidneys or eyes) to organ banks in return for monetary payments?

ADDITIONAL READING

Tanur (1981: 592–603) and Alwin (1977) provide a good summary of possible sources of error in surveys. McCallister and Fischer (1978) discuss how some of the obstacles described in this chapter were overcome in a study of people's networks of friends and acquaintances. Mangione, Hingson, and Barrett (1982) discuss strategies for collecting data on sensitive subjects.

Obstacles to Obtaining Adequate Subject Matter

21

If a social scientist is to arrive at sound conclusions, he must have good statistical data in sufficient quantities, good subjects for laboratory experiments, or good respondents for surveys. Computer people have a pungent phrase to describe what happens when a researcher uses poor data input: "GIGO—garbage in, garbage out." This chapter deals with the obstacles to achieving good data—the obstacles of too much and too little data, biased data, and various types of inadequate data.

1. Bias in the Sample

This interchange between George Bernard Shaw and Frank Harris illustrates the problem of bias in obtaining a fair sample of subject matter for observation:

> *Shaw:* The first thing we ask a servant for is a testimonial to honesty, sobriety and industry; for

we soon find out that these are the scarce things, and that geniuses and clever people are as common as rats.

> *Harris:* The English paste in Shaw; genius is about the rarest thing on earth whereas the necessary quantum of "honesty, sobriety and industry" is beaten by life into nine humans out of ten.

> *Shaw:* If so, it is the tenth who comes my way. (Harris, n.d., p. 358)

Like Shaw and Harris, researchers want to set forth a true description of an entire universe. Shaw and Harris did not go beyond their casual impressions for information about the universe of interest. In the social sciences, however, we often study the universe by taking samples from it. Taking a sample is something like looking at a distant scene through a telescope. The image of the universe that you obtain from the sample will be a true image if your sample represents the entire population. But, if some of the population escapes your sample, the image that you see may be distorted, just as the image of a distant scene will be distorted if your telescope does not cover the whole scene. A sample in which all of the population is not represented or is not represented fairly—without the researcher's knowledge—is called a "biased sample." (But do not leap to the conclusion that all biased samples are *bad* samples. "Bias" is a descriptive title, not a value judgment.)

Sampling bias is one of the two causes of a sample's not being a truthful image[1] of the universe with respect to the characteristic in which you are interested. In technical terms, sampling bias is one of the two sources of difference between the sample estimate and the population parameter. The other cause is *sampling error*, the difference between the sample and the universe that results from the workings of chance; for instance, just by chance the results of ten coin flips might be three heads or five heads or seven heads. Sampling bias and error are discussed in detail in Chapters 9, 30, and 33.

Whether a sample is biased depends upon *which universe you want to describe*. If a newspaper reporter wants to determine the voting intentions of a city's poulation, a sample made up of the people at a local bar is likely to be biased. But if a reporter wants to get the reaction of bar patrons to a rise in liquor prices, a sample drawn from a local bar may be unbiased and perfectly appropriate. The danger, always, is that the biased sample may give you an image unlike the image of the universe that you would get if you studied each and every member of the population.

An example is the data that are collected by the American Newspaper Publishers Association on the amount of advertising in United States newspapers. The data cover only 389 daily papers in 146 cities. The cities that are covered are the *biggest* cities. This means, on one hand, that the data cover 60 per cent of all daily circulation but, on the other, that they distort the picture by omitting more than 1,300 smaller newspapers. (Samples are often *purposely* distorted by the researcher, however, for reasons of efficiency. Such a practice requires that the researcher know where the distortion is *and* that no part of the universe be omitted *completely*.)

Only randomly drawn samples (probability samples) can offer a *guarantee* against bias. But it is not always easy to draw a random sample even if you understand exactly what you are doing. Expense and energy often rule out true probability samples, and the researcher may compromise on the closest he or she can get to a probability sample within the allotted budget of time and energy.

The most frequent compromise with randomness in the social sciences is the use of college students as the sampled universe when the researcher really would like to study the universe of all people or when the entire United States is the "target universe." So many psychological and sociological studies have been limited to college students that some critics of the social sciences claim that we have no general psychology or sociology, but only a psychology and a sociology of American college students, and that we therefore have no psychological or sociological knowledge of people in general.

Limiting a study to college students is not always bad. A psychologist who studies hunger contractions in the stomach or psychophysical functions like hearing and seeing usually need

1. The term "image" is picturesque but somewhat inaccurate. No sample is ever a perfect replica of the universe from which it is drawn, and in fact the sample can safely be very different from the universe in all characteristics other than those being studied. Furthermore, it would be rare for a sample and a universe to have *exactly* the same mean, say, just because of the workings of chance. To put it more correctly, an unbiased sample is one in which the estimates of the characteristics under study have "expected values" equal to the universe parameters.

not worry that college students are much different on those characteristics than are other people, just as Ebbinghaus and Pavlov did not require representative samples for their experiments to be valid. But a study of voting behavior or sexual behavior is surely biased if it is limited to college students but generalizes for all people.

Many studies of sex behavior had been done before Kinsey's, but almost all had been limited to college students, and therefore we really knew very little about the sex behavior of Americans in general until Kinsey came along. Kinsey's sampling certainly was not perfectly random or unbiased—for example, half the men in the male survey lived in Indiana, and the lower-income and less-educated classes were very much underrepresented—but Kinsey's study at least came much closer to obtaining a fair sample of the universe than did any previous work. (As a matter of fact, Kinsey's first survey was limited to white males in the United States; the second was limited to white females.)

The consulting statisticians who judged Kinsey's sampling techniques thought that Kinsey had gone far to get a fair sample. They still asked, however, that Kinsey take at least a small truly random sample to validate his other data and to serve as a conceptual bridge to the other data (Cochran et al., 1955).

The danger of sampling bias is not merely a theoretician's nitpick. In addition to the *Literary Digest* case, you have also seen the example on page 237 of the different results in estimates of magazine audiences obtained by three commercial services, all of whom were highly sophisticated and paid great attention to drawing fair samples. Some difference in estimates will occur because of the inevitable sampling error from small samples. But the differences in this case were so great that the three organizations *must* have drawn their samples in different ways, thereby introducing bias into the estimates.

2. Nonresponse: Unavailability of Some Part of the Universe

The preceding discussion of sample bias emphasized that if researchers wish to draw sound conclusions about a universe, they must study the whole universe or all its separate parts, although this investigation can be made with samples. If a study does not cover all parts of the universe, the researcher cannot draw conclusions about the entire universe. If you want to study women Ph.D.s, you must study those women who are not now teaching as well as those who are teaching, or you cannot describe the entire universe of women who have Ph.D.s. If you want to draw conclusions about newspapers, you must have information about small-town papers as well as about big-city papers.

One way to bias a sample is to draw it from the universe disproportionately and then not make allowances; the *Literary Digest* example is outstanding in this respect. Another major obstacle goes by the special name of "nonresponse bias." By this name we refer to all situations in which some part of the relevant universe (and therefore some portion of a sample drawn from that universe) is not available for study. For example, some people (more at the beginning of the study than later) would not allow themselves to be interviewed by Kinsey. And some people did not answer the questions of the researchers who studied the effects of smoking (U.S. Public Health Service, 1964: 113). Indeed, in practically every significant study of human beings there will be some people who refuse to cooperate. (Do not condemn people who refuse to cooperate. Sometimes they have a perfectly good reason, one of which may be that it is a nuisance.) In addition, some members of the sample cannot be reached to ask for their cooperation.

Critics of the Kinsey study delight in pointing out that all Kinsey's subjects were volunteers. It is common sense that people who are

FIGURE 21.1

"Is no wonder capitalist polls can't match ours for accuracy and dependability!...Imagine asking people instead of telling them!"

Source: From the *Wall Street Journal*. Reprinted by permission of Herbert Goldberg.

willing to volunteer their sex histories might well have different attitudes and sex histories than do people who are more reticent. And indeed, one study did show that people who are low in self-esteem are both more likely to refuse to volunteer for sex studies *and* more likely to have conventional sexual behavior (Maslow and Sakoda, 1955). Kinsey data, too, show that the average sex outlet is lower in groups from which Kinsey obtained 100 per cent response than in his basic samples. This finding does indicate that data from volunteers will lead to overestimates for the population as a whole. (But do not leap to conclusions about the overall validity of the Kinsey study until you have examined its methods *in toto;* see Kinsey et al., 1948: Chap. 3.)

Unlike the Kinsey study, smoking behavior is not a "hot" topic; smoking is not strongly tabooed in our society. Even so, there may be a biasing relationship between refusal to respond to questionnaires, on one hand, and smoking behavior and health, on the other. People in the hospital dying of lung cancer or other diseases may lack the energy to answer a questionnaire, and the absence of their responses will distort the total picture (U.S. Public Health Service, 1964: 113).

You are not *necessarily* in trouble just because some people refuse to cooperate. Noncooperators may cause no trouble under some circumstances. If you are sampling on a street corner to find out whether people prefer one type of chewy caramel to another type of chewy caramel, a passerby may refuse to try the caramel because she has just come from the dentist. Such a refusal is not likely to cause error (another example of the decisions one must make on the basis of common sense).

Sometimes so few data are available that the study is impossible. A poll of the president's cabinet on its like or dislike of the president's spouse is not likely to turn up many willing subjects.

Having *100 per cent* of the subjects is not necessary; missing just a few subjects is seldom fatal. For example, if you can obtain responses from 90 per cent of your sample in a preelection preference poll and if 65 per cent of your respondents prefer candidate A, you can be absolutely sure that candidate A would be preferred by the majority even if every single one of the unavailable subjects preferred candidate B. Unless you are trying to make a very subtle study, you need not worry much about error in estimating the universe as a whole if you can gain access to *nearly* all your subjects.

Whether the nonresponders can cause error depends on whether the *reason* for nonresponse or the characteristics of the nonrespondents are related in any way to the information that you seek to collect. Having just come from the dentist is probably unrelated to whether a person would prefer one or another flavor of caramel, though it causes nonresponse. But a surly unwillingness to express a political pref-

erence might well be related to which candidate the nonresponder will vote for. For example, if one of the candidates has expressed an aversion to pollsters, his followers may refuse to answer in much greater relative numbers than will followers of the other candidate.

Unless you have *very strong* reasons to believe otherwise, you should assume that the nonresponders do *not* come randomly from the population. Nonresponders tend to be elderly, poor, urban, and less educated. Rich people and particularly busy people (such as members of Congress) are often unwilling to be interviewed (Hoinville and Jowell, 1978: 137; Alba and Moore, 1982). Unfortunately, the causes for nonresponse are often related to the variables the researcher wants to know about. A student of crime may find the greatest nonresponse rates in those neighborhoods where there is the most crime, because people are afraid to open the door to the interviewer.

Sometimes people are willing to be interviewed but will not answer certain types of questions or questions on certain subjects, especially in telephone interviews (Groves and Kahn, 1979: 99); this is called "item" nonresponse. In the 1970 U.S. Census, over 20 per cent of families would not tell their income (Tanur, 1981: 599). If there are substantial nonresponse holes in your data, you must employ remedial tactics so that you can make reliable estimates for the universe as a whole. Some of the possible tactics will be described here.

First, you may *work harder to increase the number of subjects who will respond*. One way is to use a "stronger" technique. For example, personal interviewing is a stronger technique than is the mail questionnaire; fewer people will refuse to answer questions in person than when solicited by mail.

Another way to decrease the nonresponse rate is to increase the number of attempts to find the subjects and obtain cooperation. Interview surveys sometimes go back to "not at homes" as many as eleven times in hopes of finding them in. Or, if a person does not respond to a mail questionnaire, you might telephone to ask him to fill out the mail questionnaire. In desperate straits, you might ask a mutual friend to intercede and persuade the subject to cooperate if a single subject is crucial, as is sometimes the case in political-science studies.

When making these secondary attempts to increase your subject coverage, you must be careful not to change the subjects' answers by your further efforts. If you annoy subjects you may affect what they say; they may give you a wrong-headed answer just to get rid of you.

Sometimes you can increase the response by *persuading* potential respondents to answer. In some cases, you can persuade them to respond by asking them very nicely or by showing them how their responses will benefit themselves or others in the long run; this technique is the same one that advertising copywriters or salespeople use to persuade people to buy. You can do better than just saying "Please answer this questionnaire for me." A related tactic is to have someone important write them to ask for cooperation, on the stationery of a prestigious institution.

Another technique is to offer *gifts or payment* to the respondents. Psychological laboratories are accustomed to paying students by the hour for prolonged sessions. And market researchers often find that dimes, quarters, or dollars will do the trick. Members of consumer panels are usually paid in merchandise. It is often surprising how much effect a small inducement can have. In a library study we attached a ballpoint pen that cost three cents to every other short questionnaire put into books in the library stacks. Twice as many of the questionnaires that had had pens attached came back as did questionnaires that had not had pens attached. As always, one must balance the cost of the inducement against the gains. For example, you can increase the response by offering a small payment, and then you would not need to send out as many mail questionnaires.

A second way to deal with nonresponse is to *assume* that the subjects whom you cannot reach or who refuse to cooperate are similar to the people whose responses you do obtain. You can then estimate the entire universe on the basis of simple proportionality. Interpolation or extrapolation for periods of time about which we have no data is an example of such simple extensions of data. If we have data on gross national product for 1982 and 1983 and estimates of advertising expenditures for 1982 but not for 1983, we might estimate the 1983 advertising expenditures by this formula:

$$\frac{\text{GNP 1983}}{\text{GNP 1982}} = \frac{?}{\text{Advertising Expenditures 1982}}$$

If the assumption of simple proportionality is not justified, your estimate will be a bad one. In this example, it is possible that advertising expenditures decreased from 1982 to 1983, even though GNP increased. Your only weapon is good judgment and such supplementary checks as knowledge that advertising expenditures were a constant proportion of GNP in prior years. You have no *scientific* guarantee that the estimation is not wrong. In any case, you must make crystal-clear to your readers just how much of the universe was not accessible to you, the assumptions that you made in taking account of the nonresponders, and how much effect the nonresponders might have on your findings if they were radically different from the rest of your sample.

Third, if your nonresponse is substantial, it is always wise to make a secondary investigation to find out whether the nonresponders differ from your original sample and, if so, *how*. With this information in hand, you can make modifications that will improve your extensions of the original data—or decide to give up the study if the problem is insoluble. Kinsey used many ingenious devices to determine how and in what ways the volunteers were different from nonvolunteers. One technique was to obtain 100 per cent coverage of several groups, including all those members who had originally declined to volunteer but were willing to change their minds when strongly urged. Kinsey then compared the complete-coverage estimates against the estimates he *would* have made if he had only had the original volunteers available. The results were encouraging. The volunteers were not *sufficiently* different from the nonvolunteers to introduce *major* errors into the results. (This statement is oversimplified. For a full discussion of this and other devices used to check on nonresponse, see the early chapters of Kinsey et al., 1948).

Many different techniques have been used to surmount the nonresponse problem. The common ingredients are ingenuity and common sense (Tanur, 1981).

Nonresponse varies from place to place, group to group, and survey to survey. Federal government surveys tend to have nonresponse rates around 2–3 per cent, while typical national surveys have nonresponse rates of 25–35 per cent. The French and Israelis are more reluctant to participate in surveys than Americans (Tanur, 1981). For reasons no one quite understands, nonresponse rates are rising in many countries, leading to fears that if the trend continues, the validity of many studies will be threatened (Tanur, 1981: 600; also see Schuman and Presser, 1981: 331).

3. Inability to Experiment with the Subject Matter

Experimentation has strong advantages over nonexperimental methods for research that aims to determine causality and as a device for overcoming many obstacles to knowledge. But an experiment, either in real life or in a realistic laboratory setting, is not always possible. For example, it is not morally permissible for scientists to apply tobacco smoke to the lungs of nonsmokers to see whether cancer develops, which prevents them from making an absolutely airtight case that smoking causes cancer. (With some other human diseases, however,

our society has been willing to sanction experiments on such volunteers as convicts.)

If experimentation is impossible we must do the best we can with evidence that comes from observation of *natural variations* in the independent variables. Sometimes these variations occur under conditions that are almost as neat as those the investigator would arrange. These situations are called by a variety of names— "quasi experiments," "ex post facto experiments," "natural experiments." The important characteristic of such quasi experiments is that some force *clearly unrelated to the dependent variable* causes the variation in the independent variable.

Nature usually does not arrange its experiments as systematically as a researcher would, and therefore the evidence is harder to interpret. As in the case of smoking and health, however, the natural evidence is often all we can get. Some people already smoke, and we must extract what information we can from the evidence that we obtain from smokers by survey.

If a researcher were running an *experiment* on smoking, he or she would constitute the smoking and nonsmoking groups randomly, choosing people to smoke or not smoke by pulling their names out of a hat so that the only differences between the smoking and nonsmoking groups would be the chance of the lottery. In real life, however, the very fact that some people choose to smoke and others choose not to smoke suggests that there are some differences between the groups to start with. Those differences—rather than the cigarette smoke—might be responsible for the higher incidence of lung cancer and other life-shortening diseases in the cigarette-smoking group.

There are several ways to attack this obstacle to knowledge, none of them totally satisfactory. One way is to *simulate* the experiment you would like to do by running an experiment with people and conditions as similar as possible to the real-life conditions that you are interested in and cannot experiment with. This is an age-old device in the engineering sciences, in the form of mock-up experiments, which have been used in engineering ever since Leonardo da Vinci, and probably before, to determine the effects of various stresses. Using models, Leonardo experimented with pillars and beams of various sizes, and he developed basic structural formulas based on these experiments (Mason, 1962: 149). In the life sciences, one often experiments with animals in lieu of people on the assumption that what is true of animals is likely to be true of humans. If, indeed, cigarette smoke causes cancer in rats, then there is some reason to infer that the same effect may occur in humans. But we can never be sure. On the basis of other evidence about the similarity of rats and humans, we must decide how relevant the rat evidence will be in this case. To illustrate:

> *Moscow*, Oct. 10, 1964 (AP)—Soviet scientists have immunized animals against cancer virus, the official news agency Tass said Saturday in Moscow.
>
> It quoted Nikolai Blokhin, president of the Soviet Academy of Medical Sciences as saying, however, that it was too early to tell whether the discovery had any practical application for treating human cancer patients.

Psychologists simulate when, like Ebbinghaus, they run experiments with nonsense syllables to learn about more complex learning situations. And economists sometimes organize laboratory experiments to simulate firms and consumers buying and selling in markets.

Games are also used by sociologists to find out how people interact with one another under various types of circumstances. The results of such games can be provocative and can provide clues to understanding behavior. But again the crucial question remains: Does the game resemble real life?

The advantage of such simulation studies is that they make it possible to work with sets of data that are too complex to handle mathematically. But a simulation can never be any better

than the empirical data about individuals and relationships that are fed into it. Unfortunately, it is rare that one has very good data to use in such studies—even in advertising research, where there are mountains of existing data. Simulation is discussed at length on pages 148–150.

One use of cross-cultural study is to replace experiments. For example, the smoking-and-health researcher looks for two countries that seem alike in most respects, except that in one country cigarette smoking was fortuitously introduced much earlier than in the other. The health records of the two countries can then be compared. It is important to be sure, however, that there was not some special nonrandom reason that caused cigarettes to be introduced earlier in one country than in the other; such a reason might itself be the cause of differences in health in the countries.

Economists have had to develop many specialized statistical methods to use in lieu of experiments because so many aspects of national economies are not subject to experimentation. An economist cannot carry out a systematic and controlled program of experimentation with the various factors that may affect the business cycle in order to increase our understanding of what causes boom and bust. Instead, the only alternative (except for mock-experiment methods) is to interpret the data that history has made available, using those statistical techniques called "econometrics," which squeeze the maximum amount of information out of available data. Whether A causes B or vice versa, A and B cause each other, or A and B are causally unrelated is, however, a major difficulty in econometrics; it could be resolved easily if experimentation were possible. An after-the-fact analytic device is seldom as strong as an experiment in supporting a cause-and-effect argument. Nevertheless, if enough evidence of different kinds is available and if such an argument is constructed soundly, the conclusions can come very close to making an airtight case for the existence of a causal relationship. This sort of reasoning was the basis for the unanimous judgment of the Surgeon General's committee that smoking "causes" lung cancer and other diseases.

4. Flaws in Subject Matter and Unreliability of Data

The botanist is sometimes troubled by specimens that are rotten, aged, atypical, or otherwise flawed. The historian spends much time making do with unreliable or incomplete records because people in earlier centuries were not as conscientious about keeping records as we now are. The economist often faces the same difficulty as does the historian because the raw material of empirical economics is generally historical records—though often of the recent past.

Historians generally work with nonquantitative data and report their results in literary rather than statistical fashion. They can therefore bridge gaps in subject matter with intuition or imagination. Economists, however, must have some kind of numerical data with which to work, even if they must construct and patch together series of data with baling wire and chewing gum, as someone put it. Sociologists, too, are often at the mercy of those who have created the demographic data they work with.

None of us is astonished to hear that there are errors in survey data, even though the magnitude of the errors is often much greater than we would have guessed. Once you read Morgenstern's classic book *On the Accuracy of Economic Observations,* you will no longer be the trusting soul you once were. We think it is more surprising to learn that even the published results of laboratory experiments are far from totally reliable. For example, a reanalysis of the data from seven psychological experiments found gross errors in three of them (Wolins, 1962: 657).

The clear moral is that when you use data that have been collected by other researchers as your raw material, you must take careful precautions to check the accuracy of the data. "Students have to be brought up in an atmosphere of healthy distrust of the 'facts' put before them. They must also learn how terribly hard it is to get good data and to find out what really is 'a fact.'" (Morgenstern, 1963: 305). But all too often researchers close their eyes to this obstacle, assume that published data mean what they seem to mean, and use the data uncritically. Here is the primrose path, dangerous for you and for the consumers of your research results. A famous economist recently was publicly embarrassed by inadvertently using data that had minor errors in it. And consider the enormous differences between two publicly issued statistics about the same thing, the movement of gold from France to England (Ferraris, in Morgenstern, 1963: 139–140):

Gold Movement from France to Britain
(in millions of francs)

	According to French Export Statistics	According to British Import Statistics
1876–1880	41.5	94.4

Here are some tactics to help you avoid error.

Find out exactly how the raw data were collected. Study the data-collection methods critically to see whether they make sense and fit your needs. Take nothing on faith. Sometimes you will find incredible blunders that have gone undiscovered for a long time. If insufficient description of the data has been published, write to the author and find out how he did the work. Sometimes such correspondence startles you by revealing that some of the data that you assumed to be hard facts were really just estimates by the author. Printed data, like rumors, have the unfortunate property of gaining the appearance of reliability and respectability as they are successively quoted and go from hand to hand.

Whenever possible, cross-check available data against other sources of data. If you are working with gross national product estimates and if you also have series of employment data available to you, see if the two series bear a sensible relationship to each other. If no other data are available, at least check the data against rules of thumb and common sense. In the gold-movement example, Ferraris checked the British import statistic against the French export figure. The disparity alerted him to danger, even though he could not determine which figures were correct. For another example, a student of unemployment movements should consider the evidence from *both* the Bureau of Employment Statistics series *and* the Bureau of Labor Statistics' *Monthly Report of Labor Force*. For example, notice in Table 21.1 how the up-or-down directions of the two

series, as well as the absolute size of the estimates, have differed.

Still another example is the difference between the numbers of unpaid female family workers in agriculture, aged fourteen or over, in a U.S. Bureau of Labor Statistics regular monthly sample survey of the labor force and in a special follow-up survey, as shown in Table 21.2. Less than a quarter were counted in the regular survey.

A. Schlesinger, Jr., illustrates how a military historian and political analyst goes about cross-checking the available data:

The [New York] *Times* on Aug. 10 described "the latest intelligence reports" in Saigon as saying that the number of enemy troops in South Vietnam had increased 52,000 since Jan. 1 to a total of 282,000. Yet, "according to official figures," the enemy had suffered 31,571 killed in action in this period, and the infiltration estimate ranged from 35,000 as "definite" to 54,000 as "possible."

TABLE 21.1   Unemployment Series: Levels and Changes, 1946–1961 *(in millions)*

	Unemployment		Monthly Changes		% Difference in Series
	1	2	3	4	5
	Census-M.R.L.F.	B.E.S.	Census-M.R.L.F. Monthly Averages	B.E.S.	$\dfrac{\text{Col 2} - \text{Col 1}}{\text{Col 1}} \times 100$
1946	2.3	2.8			21.7
1947	2.4	1.8	0.1	−1.0	−25.0
1948	2.3	1.5	−0.1	−0.3	−34.8
1949	3.7	2.5	1.4	1.0	−32.4
1950	3.4	1.6	−0.3	−0.9	−52.9
1951	2.1	1.0	−1.3	−0.6	−52.4
1952	1.9	1.1	−0.2	0.1	−42.1
1953	1.9	1.1	0.0	0.0	−42.1
1954	3.6	2.0	1.7	0.9	−44.4
1955	2.9	1.4	−0.7	−0.6	−51.7
1956	2.8	1.3	−0.1	−0.1	−53.6
1957	2.9	1.6	0.1	0.3	−44.8
1958	4.7	2.8	1.8	1.2	−40.4
1959	3.8	1.9	−0.9	−0.9	−50.0
1960	3.9	2.1	0.1	0.2	−46.2
1961	4.8	2.5	0.9	0.4	−47.9

Source: *On the Accuracy of Economic Observations,* 2nd ed., p. 225, by Oskar Morgenstern; copyright © 1950, 1963 by Princeton University Press; reprinted by permission of Princeton University Press.

TABLE 21.2   Estimates of Distribution of Population in Households Containing a Farm Operator

	Thousands of female unpaid family workers in agriculture, ages 14+
Enumerated in the regular current survey	860[a]
Enumerated in the follow-up survey	3,770
Missed by the regular survey	2,910
Worked 1–17 hours in the survey week	1,600
Worked 18 hours or more	1,310

[a]Including 200 thousand reported in the survey as nonagricultural workers.

Source: Adapted from Ducoff and Bancroft, 1945, p. 208

The only way to reconcile these figures is to conclude that the Vietcong have picked up from 30,000 to 50,000 local recruits in this period. Since this seems unlikely—especially in view of our confidence in the decline of Vietcong morale—a safer guess is to question the wonderful precision of the statistics. Even the rather vital problem of how many North Vietnamese troops are in South Vietnam is swathed in mystery. *The [New York] Times* reported on Aug. 7: "About 40,000 North Vietnamese troops are believed by allied intelligence to be in the South." According to an Associated press dispatch from Saigon printed in *The Christian Science Monitor* of Aug. 15: "The South Vietnamese Government says 102,500 North Vietnamese combat troops and support battalions have infiltrated into South Vietnam.

"These figures are far in excess of United States intelligence estimates, which put the maximum number of North Vietnamese in the South at about 54,000."

But General Westmoreland told his Texas press conference on Aug. 14 that the enemy force included "about 110,000 main-force North Vietnamese regular army troops." Perhaps these statements are all reconcilable, but an apparent discrepancy of this magnitude on a question of such importance raises a twinge of doubt. (Schlesinger, 1966: 114)

Sometimes one can check reliability by comparing sets of *different* data that should bear a close resemblance to each other. For example, a bell would go off in the mind of the production manager of American Motors if he were presented with very different data on the numbers of auto *bodies* and auto *engines* produced in his factories; there are very few cars with more or less than one body and engine, and therefore the two numbers must bear a close resemblance to each other.

Check the internal reliability of your data. Make sure that the parts add to the totals and that there are no inexplicable large variations from period to period or group to group. Experienced researchers frequently can detect mistakes in their own and other people's raw data just by scanning them and searching out peculiar variations. In "The Case of the Indians and the Teen-Age Widows," Coale and Stephan describe how they noticed a few peculiar data in the 1950 Census of Population and how they tracked down the cause of the anomalies:

Our first clue was the discovery in the 1950 Census of Population of the United States of startling figures about the marital status of teen-agers. There we found a surprising number of widowed fourteen-year-old boys and, equally surprising, a decrease in the number of widowed teenage males at older ages. The numbers listed by the Census . . . were 1,670 at age 14; 1,475 at age 15; 1,175 at 16; 810 at 17; 905 at 18; and 630 at age 19. Not until age 22 does the listed number of widowers surpass those at 14. Male divorces also decrease in number as age increases, from 1,320 at age 14 to 575 at age 17. Smaller numbers of young female widows and divorcees are listed—565 widows and 215 divorcees at age 14. These strange figures, even though they appear in a very minor part of the carefully prepared and widely useful data presented in the Population Census, aroused our curiosity and set us to searching for an explanation. (Coale and Stephan, 1962: 338)

The explanation: In a tiny fraction of the IBM cards the key-punch operators had moved the data one column to the right, and some middle-aged males were thereby transformed into teen-agers. Further investigation turned up related errors that were not so obvious upon first inspection.

If errors like the teen-aged widowers manage to creep into the U.S. Census—which is a remarkably well-run data-gathering operation—errors are much *more* likely in any other data with which you are likely to work.

Checking the accuracy of the raw data does not eliminate all the likely obstacles. You may also hit snags because the available data have been *summarized* in ways that do not fit your purposes. For example, one of us wanted to estimate how much shorter is the life of the average smoker than the life of the average nonsmoker (four years by his rough estimate) and how many minutes less of life, per cigarette smoked, the smoker lives (about seven minutes. Do you have a light?) These estimates were hampered by a *lack of comparability* in existing data. One study categorized smokers as "less than 10 a day," "11 to 20," "21 to 39," and "40 or over," whereas another study reported data as "less than 5," "about ½ pack," "about 1 pack," about 1½ packs," and other studies used such categories as "20 to 34," "35 plus," and "more than 1 pack."

The appropriate tactic was the reverse of one used to overcome nonresponse—the "linear assumption." That is, he assumed that the numbers of smokers who smoke eleven, twelve,

thirteen, and so on to twenty cigarettes a day are roughly equal to one another, and then he split the data for "11 to 20" in such a way as to make them comparable with other data. Or in a case like this, one might have made a graph of the data and interpolated the missing points. This would provide only a crude approximation, but one has to do *something*. The only question is whether some other approximation would be better.

Another obstacle is that the existing data may lump several other categories together with the one category in which you are interested. If you study expenditures for liquor advertising, you will find that the figures reported for magazines lump together the expenditures for beer, wine, and liquor, whereas the data for newspapers cover the categories separately. Chapter 17 discusses this problem in more detail. In this case, you can bring other evidence to bear. If you have data showing that the split between liquor and beer plus wine in newspapers is twenty to eighty, you might assume that the same proportional split would hold for magazines.

The example of liquor advertising is a special case of the more general obstacle of raw data not being *defined* in a manner that is useful for your particular purpose. As an illustration, unemployment statistics are variously defined as the number of people who are listed on the unemployment rolls or as the difference between the total work force and the number of people *employed*. The estimates from these or other methods can differ very greatly (see Morgenstern, 1963: Chap. 13, for detailed discussion).

Another obstacle is that the data may be averages for groups, whereas you may need data for the individuals within the groups. In some cases, you can safely use the group averages to describe the individuals, but this approach can lead to what is called the "ecological fallacy." For example, you might want to study the relationship between income and literacy because, perhaps, you want to know how people's incomes will be affected if literacy is raised. If you compared the literacy rates and *per capita* incomes for Kuwait, Austria, and Israel, you might come to think that more literate people have lower incomes. The fallacy, of course, is that in Kuwait a very few people have all the money and most of the people are very poor. So, even though Kuwait is a rich *country*, most of its individual citizens are very poor. Looking only at these countries, high rates of literacy go with low *per capita* incomes. *Within* each country, however, literate people will have *higher* incomes than illiterate people by and large, and, if one raises literacy, one can safely count on raising *per capita* income also. This is one of those cases in which it is an error to consider the relationship between characteristics of countries to stand for the corresponding relationship between characteristics of individuals. Data are therefore needed for individuals and not countries. (In other cases, however, it may be that you are in trouble because you have data on individuals and you want to study the behavior of *groups*. The whole is not always a simple sum of the parts.)

Mechanical and computational errors sometimes introduce significant error into the data that are available to you. Computers are free of many of the errors of human computation, but they suffer from "rounding" error—that is, the computer performs all mathematics in terms of arithmetical operations, and at each stage it must round off. The computer carries the operations to many digits, but nevertheless these errors pile up as the computer does the millions of computations necessary for even simple problems, and you often find that the same calculations done by different computer methods yield somewhat different results.

5. Shortage of Subject Matter

Sometimes there is insufficient subject matter available to support solid conclusions. This obstacle is less likely to appear in experimental work because data can usually be generated in unlimited quantity, subject only to the restriction of cost and available funds (on this point see Chapter 23). But sometimes the subject matter for experimentation is limited too. For example, in the early stages of the nuclear physics of various particles, the amounts of matter available for experimentation were in short supply, as dramatized in the story of the Curies and their radium shortage.

You are most likely to face a shortage of subject matter when experimentation is not possible. Wars may be mercifully few from the point of view of humanity, but historians must sometimes catch themselves wishing there had been more wars of certain kinds so that they would have more material to work with. Similarly, business cycles are always few in number compared to the economist's need for data.

Lack of data sometimes comes as a surprise. For example, it is a shock to fledgling demographers to learn that the United States was for a long time among the most backward of the industrial nations in recording births; collection of birth statistics did not even begin until 1915; it was not until 1933 that birth data were available for the entire country (T. Smith, 1960: 284–285). And there were no national-income statistics (for example, gross national product) for the United States covering the years prior to the third decade of the twentieth century until Kuznets (1946) came along and partly remedied the deficiency by organizing the appropriate data.

There are many possible reasons for the non-existence or the shortage of data. In antiquity, figures on Greek and Roman commerce and population were seldom collected. But, even when they were collected and recorded, the records that have come down to us often lack the totals because the totals were at the corners or bottoms of the stone tablets—and those are the parts of the tablets most likely to be broken off over time (Jones, 1948: 2).

When you are faced with a shortage of data, first look for more data. But look in places that are not obvious, as well as in places that are. If you have too few business cycles to work with in United States history, you might try examining business cycles in those other countries whose economies bear at least some similarity to that of the United States. If you want to study how a ban on advertising affects liquor consumption and if only a few states in the United States have bans, hunt up cases of other countries that have banned liquor advertising. Historians often exhibit genius in finding data in out-of-the-way places.

Sometimes physical instruments can fill gaps in the historical record. Anthropology furnishes an example:

> Now in the field of the nonliterate cultures and cultural items, where dates are totally lacking, and where archaeology can hope in general to give us only relative time sequences, it is also interesting to know whether an institution goes back a thousand or ten thousand years, or is older or younger than another institution. But how shall we learn? Now and then some other science comes to our rescue: geology and palaeontology in remote prehistory, botany or tree-ring dendrochronology in a few particular situations. Such outside aids are, however, rare and unusual. In general, cultural anthropology has to help itself. (Kroeber, 1948: 541)

Since Kroeber wrote the above paragraph, however, atomic physics has come to the rescue. The carbon-14 method is often an enormous help in establishing dates. In many cases, it is a superior substitute for examination of tree-ring patterns.

Another way to squeeze out more information is to divide up the available units of subject matter into smaller units. Economists sometimes use data for three-month rather than full-year periods, to increase the number of available observations, even though the quarterly data are much less accurate than the yearly data. Another example comes from a study of simulated jury deliberations. An enormous number of expensive jury experiments would have been required to obtain a sample of *decisions* large enough for statistical needs.

The researcher therefore also collected data about the *individual judgments* of jurors prior to the deliberations, which yielded a sample twelve times as large as the number of jury decisions (R. Simon, 1967).

Though splitting up the data into smaller parcels may increase its information value in one respect, you will probably have to pay a price in diminishing its information value in some other respect—usually in the form of increased error in the smaller units. In the jury study, the researcher had to be careful to emphasize that individual jurors' judgments are not comparable to decisions made by the jury as a whole.

When all else fails, the skills of the statistician can often squeeze extra meaning out of small samples. Anyone can come to a sound conclusion with a sample of millions. But, as we shall see in Chapters 24–35, it takes skill and ingenuity to infer sound conclusions from samples of five, ten, or one hundred observations.

6. High Individual Variability in the Data

Your intuition will tell you that it is easier to compare the monthly salaries of two jobs when the salaries within each of the two vocations are similar. If three people working at job A earn $1,000; $1,100; and $1,200; whereas three people working at job B earn $822; $1,060; and $1,280; it is difficult to tell reliably whether there is any difference in the average salaries of the two jobs because there is so much variability. But if all three people on job A earn $1,080 and all three people on job B earn $1,140, it seems much clearer that there is a difference between the salaries of the two jobs.

High variability among the subjects is a frequent difficulty in experimental as well as in survey research. For example, suppose you wish to compare the safety of anaesthetics used in surgery. Because patients differ in age, health, sex, and number of complications, these factors must be taken into account to be sure that observed differences are due to differences among anaesthetics and not differences among patients (Moses and Mosteller, 1978).

High variability within the subject matter is one of the most important characteristics that sets the social sciences off from the physical sciences. Prenuclear physics and chemistry can be said to be almost determinate, because what happens once will happen again. (But do not forget that many facts about human nature are almost as sure as those in the natural sciences. We can predict with practically perfect accuracy that, if we fire a blank revolver in front of your nose, your eyes will blink in a "startle reflex." And luckily the chances are fantastically good that your next-door neighbor will not turn out to be a cannibal or a pathological killer.)

Several tactics other than those suggested in Figure 21.2 can help you to make satisfactory comparisons between groups, despite a high level of variability within the groups. Two of these tactics are described here.

A. INCREASE THE SAMPLE SIZE

Television programming can be considered (and is) an experiment to see which programs are more popular. Even a slight difference in popularity could be detected if you measured the tuning of every one of the millions of network listeners for each of the programs. Such a large sample is not feasible, and a Nielsen sample of 1,200 dwelling units (Madow et al., 1961: 127) is generally large enough to measure most differences with acceptable accuracy. If two programs were very close, taking a sample many times as large would help. But remember that if a terrifically large sample is required, the difference probably is not sufficiently important to warrant attention.

B. COMPARE EACH SUBJECT WITH HIMSELF OR HERSELF

This tactic can be very powerful in surmounting the obstacle of high individual variability.

Assume that you are a campaign manager and that you want to find out the effect of having your candidate give personal talks in small towns. You would face the difficulty of high variability within towns if you tried to compare towns the candidate had visited with towns he had not visited. But if you measured preferences for your candidate before and after his visits to some towns, the variability within the towns would not be so great a difficulty. You would need only to compare each town against itself and then to average the changes. Each town is said to be its own control in this type of design.[2]

Variability within groups often impels critics to claim that it is impossible to make any valid predictions for an *individual* in one group compared to an individual in another group. If a poll predicts that 80 per cent of one group will vote for candidate A, the critic asks, How can you predict that *any given* individual in that group will vote for candidate A?

It is certainly true that we can never make a prediction for an individual with perfect accuracy. *Any* prediction is only a *probability,* and, as a simple pragmatic matter, knowing the probabilities for the group as a whole helps us make a prediction for any individual within the group. The odds are four to one that a *randomly chosen individual* will vote for candidate A if the group she is in is 80 per cent for A. First-place teams in the major leagues sometimes lose games to last-place teams. But even the most naïve bettor will not take even odds that the last-place team will win a *particular game.* (The picture is different, of course, if you know something special about the particular vote or the particular teams—who the pitchers are, in the latter case.)

The more that we know about the various groups with which we can identify an individual, the better will be our prediction for the

2. The statistically trained reader will recognize that the analysis of variance is the appropriate general model for determining whether the "within" variance is satisfactorily small compared to the "between" variance.

FIGURE 21.2

"Sorry sir, I'm not going to open up seven locks and disconnect the burglar alarm just to tell you what shampoos I favor."

Source: GRIN AND BEAR IT by George Lichty. © Field Enterprises, Inc., 1964. Courtesy of Field Newspaper Syndicate.

individual. If we had known before the Kennedy-Nixon election that a particular voter was Catholic, we could have said that the odds were 60–40 that she would vote Democratic. If we had also known that she lived in New York City, our odds might have been 80–20, a stronger prediction. (Sometimes, however, the interaction of two such traits can drive the combined effect in the *other* direction.) In general, the more finely we can subclassify an individual, the better will be our prediction for him or her. The nature of predictions and how to make them are explored at greater length in Chapters 25, 26, and 29.

7. Too Much Subject Matter

An experienced researcher's first response to the obstacle of too much subject matter is "It should only happen to me." Subject matter is like diamonds: a scarce commodity of which you cannot believe that you could ever have too much. But it is possible to be buried in data, just as a person might be buried in a landslide of diamonds.

The data in the U.S. Census, for example, overwhelmed researchers in the late nineteenth century. It took seven years and hundreds of clerks to bring order to the 1880 data and to develop summarizing statistics. It was the difficulty of coping with that great mountain of census data that led Hollerith to invent a system of punched cards and machines that would read and sort the data electrically. Machines very similar to those original 1890 machines are perhaps the commonest automatic data-processing machines in use today, and they are the granddaddies of the more sophisticated machines that are also in existence now. Hollerith's firm grew into IBM—all because of the problem of too much data (Halacy, 1969: 2, 41).

Ironically, the very machines that were invented to sort huge piles of data can themselves create new obstacles of masses of data. Everyone who has worked with high-speed computers has suffered fright and frustration on receiving literally pounds of paper and hundreds of thousands of numbers as the output of a computer run, even though all that was really wanted was a single yes-or-no answer. Then the researcher is again faced with the necessity of boiling down and summarizing the output into some useful and manageable form.

Automatic data processing is one way to cope with too much data. Another tactic is to take a sample of the large masses of data. The sample should be large enough to be sufficiently accurate yet small enough to be worked on easily (Chapters 9 and 34 discuss sampling and sample sizes in more detail). If automatic data processing were not available, it would be necessary to take small samples from the mass of census data collected and make estimates for the country as a whole based on those samples.

Then why not collect census data for only a sample of the population? The answer is that data on the entire population can provide knowledge about *small subdivisions* of the population, as well as about the population as a whole. A small sample of the entire population would tell us with considerable accuracy how many people in the United States as a whole earn less than $5,000 per year. But a small sample of the United States population could not reveal accurately how many people in Elko County, Nevada, earn $5,000.[3]

For accounting purposes, most business firms collect complete financial data on their operations in preference to taking samples of the data. Accountants generally insist on reckoning to the last penny rather than making estimates based on samples, even though the Internal Revenue Service will settle for accounts rounded off to the nearest dollar.

8. Invisibility or Inaccessibility of Subject Matter

There are times when you want to study a phenomenon that you cannot see or that you cannot reach with your measuring instruments as directly as you would like. For example, the United States wants to know how successful China's harvest is, but China does not supply the data, and the United States cannot make an on-the-spot survey. Or a firm wants to know how much a competitor is spending for adver-

---

3. In fact, the U.S. Bureau of the Census does conduct some of its business with samples. The monthly Current Population Survey quizzes 35,000 people. And only two or three questions in the Decennial Census are asked of everyone; the rest are sampled.

tising. Or you want to know exactly what is said inside jury boxes, but the law will not permit you to record the deliberations. Then you must work with a less satisfactory proxy.

9. Interference with Subject Matter by Researcher

When you observe or measure a phenomenon, you inevitably affect it to some extent. At one extreme is the example of von Osten's horse (pages 252–253), where the phenomenon that is observed is entirely caused by the observer. At the other extreme are studies of economic and social history, which employ records of the past; the events of the past are already complete and are not influenced by the observer except in the sense that the *records* of the past may be altered by the historian's activity. Much of social research falls between these extremes—the influence that asking a question may have on a person's thinking; the influence that watching a child's play may have upon the playing; and the influence of governmental study of an industry's practices upon the practices.

Almost always you will wish to minimize the influence of the researcher on the subject matter. Therefore you should seek methods of observing and measuring that will have as little

effect as possible. The less the subjects notice the process of observing and measuring, the less they are likely to be influenced by it. Therefore, it makes sense to make your observations as "unobtrusive" as possible, to use the now-well-known phrase of Webb and his associates (1966). Their book compiles and discusses many such unobtrusive devices; in this book such devices are mentioned throughout, as the theme arises repeatedly in various contexts.

10. Summary

Data, good data, are the researcher's life blood. But you may find it difficult to obtain *any* data. Or you may be unable to experiment with your subjects for ethical or practical reasons. Or the data may be unreliable. Or the sample of data may be biased, rather than being a fair image of the universe that you wish to describe. Or you may even have so much subject matter that you are overwhelmed by it. Or . . . or . . . or . . . For each obstacle to getting good data there are solutions, partial solutions, or substitutes, many of them mentioned in this chapter. But the ultimate resource is your ingenuity and your creative faculty, building on your experience. Good luck.

EXERCISES

1. Give examples from research in your field to illustrate the following obstacles to obtaining knowledge:
   a. Bias in the sample
   b. Nonresponse or unavailability of some part of the universe
   c. Inability to experiment
   d. Flaws in the subject matter
   e. Shortage of subject matter
   f. Too much subject matter
   g. Invisibility or inaccessibility of subject matter
2. Suggest methods for surmounting the obstacles you described in Exercise 1.
3. Find two sets of comparable data from different origins and cross-check them. How reliable are they, as indicated by the cross check?
4. Show an internal-reliability check of some data.

ADDITIONAL READING

Statistical records, personal documents, and other publicly available data are discussed in Selltiz et al. (1976, Chap. 11). For a discussion of the use of "secondary data"—that is, data that are publicly available—in the context of business research, see Boyd and Stasch (1977, Chap. 5).

The most important repository of publicly available data in the social sciences is the Inter-University Consortium for Political and Social Research at the Institute for Social Research of the University of Michigan; your library probably has information about their holdings. Information about some sources of data may be found in Hastings and Southwick (1974), and Converse et al. (1980).

Webb et al. (1966) give a remarkable number of examples of ingenious ways to obtain subject matter when the task seems especially difficult. This is a book to jog your imagination when you are stymied for lack of ideas on how to get information to answer a research question.

A good summary of techniques to overcome nonresponse in interviewing may be found in Stephan and McCarthy (1963, Chap. 11). There is a useful short bibliography at the end of that chapter.

Moore (1947) is an excellent short treatment of errors in economic data.

A useful general discussion of labor-force statistics is Jaffe and Stewart (1951).

Selvin (1965) cogently discusses the ecological fallacy.

Sonquist and Dunkelberg (1977, Chap. 6) discuss how to detect and avoid errors while processing data.

Obstacles to the Search for Causal Relationships

22

1. Causation by a "Hidden Third Factor"
2. Multivariable Causation
3. Confounding the Dependent and Independent Variables
4. Feedback; Interaction Between Dependent and Independent Variables
5. Summary

The ideal design of a study that seeks to establish cause and effect was set forth in Chapter 2. But sometimes the distinction between studies that do and do not establish causal relationships is subtle, confusing, and ambiguous. Chapter 35 tries to sort out the philosophical tangle of such borderline cases. This chapter discusses the *empirical obstacles* in the way of determining whether a relationship is causal and focuses on how to *design* the study to avoid them successfully.

This chapter and Chapters 24, 25, and 35 all deal with the search for causes and effects. Here is the distribution of labor among the chapters: This chapter discusses the practical decisions that you must make at the planning stage of your study to ensure that it will permit you to draw causal conclusions. Chapters 24 and 25 discuss how to handle your data after they have been collected, in order to extract the most knowledge about the cause-and-effect relationships. Chapter 35 considers some of the more subtle problems that arise when you must decide whether to refer to an observed association as a cause-and-effect relationship.

One general piece of advice before we tackle the specific obstacles: Get to know all about the circumstances surrounding the causal relationship you seek to establish. Saturate yourself in the relevant facts. It is only in that way that you can protect yourself against the kinds of mistakes about causal relationships that young children make, for instance, thinking that the turning on of streetlights makes the sun go down.

Most of the obstacles to establishing causal relationships afflict nonexperimental research most sharply. Therefore, most of what we know about establishing causal relationships comes from sociologists, economists, and historians, rather than from experimental psychologists. But even if you can experiment with your subject matter, your problem is not automatically solved, as we shall see.

1. Causation by a "Hidden Third Factor"

This section takes up the possibility of coming to believe mistakenly that one variable is causally influential when another variable is

282

"really" the cause—the "hidden third factor" error, also called "spurious correlation" in sociology and social psychology. Sometimes this obstacle is included under the term "confounding" in experimental psychology (Underwood, 1957: 89–92); and, along with the obstacle of multivariable causation, it is called "specification error" in economics.

The classic example of the hidden-third-factor error in an experimental context is the case of the gentlemen who, after getting drunk successively on brandy and soda, whiskey and soda, and bourbon and soda, concluded that the soda caused their inebriation. Notice that their deduction was perfectly sound, given only that much evidence. Other knowledge of the world is necessary to set them straight.

The situation is diagrammed in Figure 22.1. The objective is to determine the cause of y, the dependent variable—inebriation, in this example—when a relationship (broken line) with an independent variable, x_1 (drinking soda), has been observed. The "real" cause is shown by the solid arrow from w (liquor) to y and the fact that drinking liquor is accompanied by drinking soda is shown by the line from w to x_1.

Another example is Mark Twain's cat who sat on a hot stove lid: "She will never again sit down on a hot stove lid; but also she will never sit down on a cold stove any more." Twain's recommendation has merit: "We would be careful to get out of an experience only the wisdom that is in it—and stop there."[1]

Such errors have occurred many times in the history of science, and sometimes the error has temporarily knocked a science off the track. In one famous experiment, a scientist found that rats exhibited unexpected learning behavior, y, when stimulated by a blast of air, x_1. The results turned psychological theory topsy-turvy. Later, it was found that the rats' unexpected behavior was "really" caused by a piercing sound, w, that accompanied the blast of air

from the experimenter's apparatus, a sound that affected them the way a squeaky piece of chalk affects many humans.

For another example, medical researchers for many years attempted to graft y, a vital part of one mammal, onto another mammal of the same species, but the operations always failed, despite the delicacy with which the surgeons performed the operations. The medical researchers then concluded that there were physiological and chemical reasons, x_1, preventing the success of such organ transplantations. Then along came a Russian scientist who claimed to have succeeded in sewing one dog's head onto the side of another dog—and both heads barked for months. It was because his surgical technique, w, was so good that infection did not occur and the operation succeeded. The previously assumed causes of the transplantation failure—antibodies, protein reactions, and so forth—were found not to be the real causes at all.[2]

Sometimes it does not matter whether you know which is the "real" cause. If an ingredient in cigarette smoke causes cancer but must *necessarily* always be part of cigarette smoke, it does not matter much whether we say that cigarette smoking, ingredient X, or still another ingredient in cigarette smoke causes lung cancer.

On the other hand, if there is any possibility that the real cause might ever be *separated* from the other variables that accompany it, then it makes a difference whether we refer to ingredient X or something else as the real cause, for future research may thus be influenced. (Incidentally, finding that tars are the real cause does not weaken the causal status of cigarette smoking but rather *strengthens* it.)

Chemists often can approach progressively closer to real causes. They can now show that the tars contained in cigarette smoke cause

1. Thanks to Chuck Linke for this quotation.

2. A friend, Stanley Friedman, could find no reference in the scientific literature to this event, which was originally reported in the newspapers, so probably it is phony. But the example is still illustrative.

FIGURE 22.1   The Hidden-Third Factor Error

some kinds of cancers in animals. Perhaps sometime soon they will be able to show that cigarettes without these factors will not cause cancer (but perhaps may still cause myriad other diseases). They will then have come closer to isolating the "real" cause of cancer.

Remember also how the Curies refined tons of ore and progressively identified many elements as irrelevant until they found that radium alone was "truly" responsible for the radioactive photographic-plate effect that Becquerel had observed with potassium-uranium salt. The chemist and physicist can refine a given sample until it is almost perfectly pure, until it contains practically nothing but one compound or element. It is the *purity* of the specimen that makes us feel that the real cause has been identified. Nevertheless, the chance *always* exists that it is some impurity in the sample or container—or something else in the environment—that is the real cause of the phenomenon.

The social scientist cannot refine his material with such satisfying progressive logic, but his best strategy is somewhat similar. He should vary every possible condition except that which he regards as the cause, to see whether the variations change the values of the dependent variable. In experimentation, one varies each of the controlled conditions systematically. In nonexperimental research, various types of cross-classification are tried to see whether any other variables seem to exhibit any causal influence (Zeisel, 1968: Chaps. 8, 9, especially p. 192).

Sometimes, however, the hidden factor is tied so tightly to the apparent cause that they cannot be separated. In questionnaire research

the possibility always exists that it is some special quirk in the form of the question that forces a particular type of answer, rather than the intended content of the question. But a question must be asked in *some* words, which means that some quirk is always possible. Asking the same question in two different forms offers some check on this problem.

2. Multivariable Causation

This section takes up an obstacle that often afflicts research studies in which you want to establish the effect of one, two, three, or n (n is the standard symbol for some large but unspecified number) particular independent variables on a dependent variable. The difficulty is that the various independent variables do not change independently of one another, at least in the world outside the laboratory. If you want to determine the effect of rainfall, x_1, on crop yield, y, you may have to take account of the fact that, when rainfall is heavy, temperature, x_2, tends to be lower than usual. Therefore, you will not be able to determine, without making some special arrangements, what the simple relationship between rainfall and crop yield is. In other words, the difficulty is to create *ceteris paribus* conditions.

Again it is helpful to diagram the situation (see Figure 22.2). The object in this case is *not* to find *which* variable explains the variations in y, as it was in the previous section. Rather, the purpose is to determine *whether or not*, and *how much*, a particular variable x_1 influences y. The obstacle is that, unless the researcher *also* takes account of x_2 (or also x_3, x_4, and so forth), he or she cannot determine the extent of the

FIGURE 22.2   Multivariable Causation

causal relationship between x_1 and y, because there is a relationship (though noncausal) between x_1 and x_2.

Another example: Particular departments in department stores spend more for advertising, x_1, during those months when they have especially interesting merchandise. How, then, can you determine the effect of advertising on sales, y? A change in sales might be partly or wholly caused by the excellence of the merchandise assortment, x_2, rather than by the advertising, or it might be caused by both.

Many wonderfully wrong conclusions can be drawn from unwise handling of multivariate problems. For example, auto prices, x, and auto sales, y, both rose from 1932 to 1956 (see Table 22.1). It is unwise, however, to conclude that higher prices cause higher auto sales *or* that high sales of cars cause high prices over a long period of time. When one takes account of such other variables as disposable income, x_2, stock of cars on the road, x_3, credit terms, x_4, and other variables, then the *lower* the price the more cars that are sold, a more sensible conclusion indeed. All the other independent variables are themselves related to price, which is why the simple relationship between price and sales is confusing.

The multivariable obstacle is not simply that many different factors affect the dependent variable. Of course it is true that, besides a lighted match, a cigarette, a hand to hold the match, and air in which to burn are required to cause a lighted cigarette. But the presence of air may generally be treated as a parameter (that is, a condition that does not change in the course of the study); if it does change, the change is not related to the striking of the match. But disposable income and the stock of cars on the road *cannot* sensibly be treated as parameters in a study of the relationship between prices and auto sales.

The nature of the multivariate obstacle, rather, is that the conditions of *ceteris paribus* do not hold. Other things are not equal when the rainfall is high or low, and therefore the differences in crop yield at high and low rainfall may not be attributed simply to the differences in rainfall. If there were no relationship between rainfall and temperature, then it *would* by safe simply to look at the relationship between rainfall and crop yield, for the effects of temperature would average out over the period of the study, and the *ceteris paribus* assumption would hold. The crucial issue in the multivariate problem is that there *is* a relationship between the independent variables x_1 and x_2.

Similarly, if department-store product quality tends to change as the amount of advertising changes, then the conditions of *ceteris paribus* do not hold, and the changes in sales may not be attributed simply to changes in advertising.

If you can *experiment* with the subject matter, you may be able to surmount the multivariate obstacle, because the nature of experiment ensures the conditions of *ceteris paribus*. If, instead of examining data on natural rainfall and crops, you artificially *control* the amount

TABLE 22.1

Year	Real Retail-Price Index, Passenger Automobiles	Real Disposable Income (Billions of 1947–1949 Dollars)	Stock of Cars January 1 (Millions)	Retail Sales, New Automobiles (Millions)
1932	126.5	83.4	18.7	1.10
1933	128.5	82.6	17.9	1.53
1934	128.5	90.9	18.9	1.93
1935	120.5	99.3	19.4	2.87
1936	117.0	111.6	20.1	3.51
1937	121.0	115.6	21.5	3.51
1938	133.8	109.0	22.3	1.96
1939	131.0	118.5	22.7	2.72
1940	134.3	127.0	23.2	3.46
1941	144.9	147.9	24.5	3.76
1949	186.6	184.9	30.6	4.87
1950	186.6	200.5	33.1	6.37
1951	181.5	203.7	35.7	5.09
1952	195.7	209.2	37.6	4.19
1953	188.2	218.7	39.3	5.78
1954	190.2	221.6	41.6	5.47
1955	196.6	236.3	43.0	7.20
1956	193.4	247.2	47.0	5.90

Source: "The Demand for New Automobiles in the United States," p. 279, by Daniel B. Suits, in *The Review of Economics and Statistics,* Vol. XL (August 1958).

of water that each crop plot receives, you can then vary the amount of water among the experimental plots in *random* fashion. If the amount of water varies randomly, you can then be sure that the temperature will not be associated with the amount of water that the plots receive. The temperature will indeed vary also. But, as there will be no *systematic* relationship between temperature and water, you can be sure that the high-water and low-water trials among the plots will *average* the same temperature. If they average the same temperature, then the conditions of *ceteris paribus* hold—for temperature, anyway. Any changes in crop yield may then be attributed solely to changes in water. This example is an application of the crucial device of *randomization* in experimentation.

Sometimes you can arrange to conduct an experiment, even though it does not seem possible to do so at first. A department store may be loath to vary its advertising expeditures randomly in order to isolate the effect of advertis-

ing from that of merchandise quality. But you may be able to convince the manager to vary the advertising level *slightly* from week to week, so that the experimental data may be obtained without causing an executive uproar or disturbing the store's basic promotional scheme very much.

If experimentation is truly not feasible, all may still not be lost. You may be able to isolate your independent variable by holding the other variable(s) constant *statistically* instead of experimentally. Cross-classification is one statistical device that accomplishes this purpose. A cross-classification allows you to look at the effect of different levels of your independent variable x_1 at the *same* level of the other independent variable x_2, which makes it possible for you to examine the effect of x_1 on y under conditions that approach *ceteris paribus*. For example, perhaps you want to learn the effect of sex on incidence of auto accidents. The simple tabulation in Table 22.2 apparently shows that women are safer drivers than men. But it

TABLE 22.2　Accident Rates of Male and Female Automobile Drivers

	Men %	Women %
Never had an accident while driving	58	68
Had at least one accident while driving	44	32
Total	100	100
(Number of cases)	(7,080)	(6,950)

SOURCE: *Say It With Figures*, 5th ed., p. 120, by Hans Zeisel; copyright 1947, 1950, 1957, 1968 by Harper & Row, Publishers, Incorporated; reprinted by permission of the publishers.

seems plausible that amount of driving might affect the picture. And a cross-classification does clarify the issue.

Table 22.3 shows that when distance driven is crudely controlled by dividing the sex groups into more than and less than 10,000 miles driven, there is no difference in accident rates. (Furthermore, one can guess from this crude cross-classification that men are *safer* drivers per mile driven, as follows: The distribution of the sexes by amount driven indicates that men drive more miles than women. This implies that *within* both the more-than- and the less-than-10,000-miles-driven groups, men drove more miles than women. If nevertheless the accident rates within distance groups are similar by sex, men have less accidents *per mile*. A finer subclassification would check on this guess.)

The regression is another statistical technique that helps to isolate the effect of the independent variable in which you are interested. The regression is actually something more than a refined type of cross-classification; it takes advantage of the *continuous* gradations in variables, rather than lumping them into a few categories, as does cross-classification. A regression uses the information from all the observations to smooth out the whole set of observations, rather than each observation by itself. These and other analytic devices to accomplish the same purpose will be discussed at greater length in Chapters 24 through 26.

A question may have sprung to your mind: How can one know when all the important variables have been taken care of? There is no fully satisfactory answer. The core of the matter is thorough knowledge of the complexities

TABLE 22.3　Automobile Accidents of Male and Female Drivers by Number of Miles Driven

	Male Drivers		Female Drivers	
	Drove More Than 10,000 Miles %	Drove 10,000 Miles or Less %	Drove More Than 10,000 Miles %	Drove 10,000 Miles or Less %
Had at least one accident while driving	52	25	52	25
Never had an accident while driving	48	75	48	75
Total	100	100	100	100
(Number of cases)	(5,010)	(2,070)	(1,915)	(5,035)

Source: *Say It With Figures*, 5th ed., p. 133, by Hans Zeisel, copyright 1947, 1950, 1957, 1968 by Harper & Row, Publishers, Incoporated; reprinted by permission of the publishers.

of that aspect of the real world that you are investigating, as well as extensive trials of the likeliest variables.

This chapter explains what to do about multivariable causation in planning your study; Chapters 24 through 27 take up what to do after you have your data in hand. It is now, at the planning stage, that you should take advantage of your flexibility to choose sound variables. At the design stage you should arrange to collect the data you will need for the cross-classification or the regression. If you are doing an experiment, you should at this stage ensure that all the relevant variables are being held constant. In the crop-yield study you would collect temperature, as well as rainfall and crop-yield, data; if you were experimenting, you would hold the temperature constant. In the department-store study, you would obtain data on excellence of merchandise assortment, as well as on advertising and sales. In political polling, you would collect data on income, age, geography, and anything else that might seem relevant.

You should also consider collecting data in more than one way, so that your results will bolster one another and increase the weight of total evidence. Animal experiments and human surveys on smoking support one another and strengthen the argument for the cause-and-effect relationship with cancer because each method holds constant a different set of the multiple variables.

3. Confounding the Dependent and Independent Variables

Do England's leaders come from Oxford and Cambridge because the instruction at those universities makes leaders? Or is it simply that the people who would be leaders anyway are sent to Oxford and Cambridge? This is a hard question to answer, partly because it is difficult to measure the extent to which a university graduate is a "leader" or "succeeds." Let us instead ask a similar question about a type of educational institution whose graduates' success

we can more easily measure—business schools; it seems fair to say that the salaries paid to businesspersons are a reasonable proxy for success. We ask, then, does Harvard Business School make good business people? Or do people who would be successful in business anyway go to Harvard Business School?

It will not suffice to compare the salaries earned by graduates of Harvard Business School with the salaries of a group of business people who went elsewhere to business school or who went to no graduate school at all. If the best prospects go to Harvard Business School, then their salaries will be higher, even if they gain nothing at all from Harvard Business School training.

Attempts to evaluate the effect of psychoanalysis run afoul of a similar obstacle. One cannot simply compare a group of neurotics who have undergone psychoanalysis with another group of neurotics who have had no psychoanalytic treatment. The group that has had psychoanalysis obviously consists of people different from those in the other group to start with, for they *chose* to undertake psychoanalytic treatment. Making such a choice might well indicate a desire to overcome the neurosis that would have resulted in improvement even without treatment. Indeed, there does not seem to be satisfactory evidence for the effectiveness of psychoanalysis.

Still another example is the comparison of life expectancy of people who take exercise with that of people who do not. There is always an important possibility that people exercise because they are healthy, rather than vice versa.

In all these cases we say that there is "confounding" (see Figure 22.3);[3] that is, *both* the independent variable, x_1, in whose effect we

---

3. "Confounding" is a word used mostly by psychologists, and they use it to refer to almost any experiment that suffers from insufficient controls or incomplete design (Underwood, 1957: 89–90). The definition and usage here are more restricted but still common. Statisticians also use the term when they *purposely* give up some information in order to reduce the size of the experiment.

FIGURE 22.3 Confounding of Variables

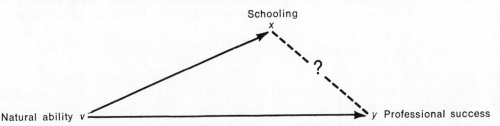

are interested (exercise, psychoanalysis, Harvard Business School training) *and* the dependent variable, *y* (success, mental health, physical health), may be caused by some other personal-background factor, *v* (brains and drive, natural healing processes, natural good health). The difference between confounding and the hidden third factor is that in the former we are *particularly* interested in whether the specific variable x_1 is a cause of *y*, whereas in the latter we concentrate on finding out *which* variable causes *y*. Confounding also differs from the multivariate obstacle; in the former confounding *v causes* x_1, whereas in the latter the relationship between x_1 and x_2 is *not* causal.

Notice the difference between this obstacle and the obstacle of nonresponse. If there is nonresponse, one cannot get data on one group of people that *may* be special. In confounding, the difficulty is that certain kinds of people *do not exist* or are not known to exist. The people who do not exist are people in every way exactly like those who go to Harvard Business School but who do not actually go to Harvard Business School.

It does not suffice simply to find a group of people who *seem* in every possible way like those who went to Harvard Business School or like those who underwent psychoanalysis or like those who took exercise but who did not *actually* do those things. They would still differ in one crucial way: whatever it was that kept them from going to Harvard Business School or taking exercise or psychoanalysis. That thing may well turn out to be the crucial difference between the groups.

To surmount the obstacle of possible confounding often requires exceptional effort and cost. The only way we can think of to measure fairly the effect of a Harvard Business School education would be to select *randomly* a group of young people who would otherwise not go to Harvard Business School—perhaps from among the entrants to the training programs of large business firms—send them to Harvard Business School, and then over a long period of years compare their careers with those of the rest of the group from which they were drawn randomly.[4]

In the investigation of the effect of exercise, it would be difficult to experiment with a group of people over a period long enough so that the exercise might be considered to make any difference. And, even if it weren't, it would be many years from the beginning of the experiment until the results were available.

Sometimes it is possible to carry out a *quasi experiment*. In the case of relating psychoanalysis to cure, there may be no psychoanalysts in some part of the country. Assuming that problems of geographical differences could be surmounted, one could compare the rate of recovery from neurosis where psychoanalytic treatment is available with that where there are no psychoanalysts. This design might be particularly useful in measuring the effects of

4. But difficulties never end. Glad pointed out, in a personal conversation with one of the authors, that even this experimental design is subject to an important flaw: People who return from the Harvard Business School program may progress more quickly simply because their superiors are impressed by the degrees, even if the training really has no value.

psychotherapeutic treatment on psychosis in mental hospitals.

4. Feedback; Interaction Between Dependent and Independent Variables

In this complicated world of ours, there are many situations in which A and B influence each other. We see this type of mutual influence in most human relationships: The more you love me, the more I love you, the more you love me. You step on my toe, I jab you with my elbow, you hit me on the nose. A change in demand for a product causes a change in the price, which causes a change in the supply of the product, which causes a change in the price, which causes a change in demand, on and on forever. Cause and effect bounce back and forth like a ping-pong ball or an echo in a canyon. This effect is called "feedback" or "mutual causation."

Feedback can be positive, in which case it increases the original effect, or it can be negative, in which case it tends to "dampen" the original effect. Jeremiah describes a feedback reaction involving the Children of Israel: "Thine own wickedness shall correct thee, and thy backslidings shall reprove thee" (Jeremiah 2:19).

The term "feedback" was invented by the radio engineers for circuits in which the output signal is "fed back," to be amplified again. The same idea has proved useful in the social sciences. For example, the basic Keynesian economic model can be shown in the schematic form that electronics engineers use. Figure 22.4 indicates that national income depends on investment and consumption and that consumption in turn depends on national income. There is mutual interaction between national income and consumption; the influence of each *feeds back* upon itself.[5]

5. The equations represented in the diagram are

National Income = Investment + Consumption $\quad Y = I + C$

Consumption = Constant Multiple × National Income
$$C = aY$$

Another example: In areas where liquor consumption is high, there are many stores that sell liquor. Does the existence of many stores lead to high consumption, as the prohibitionists believe, or vice versa? The influence is likely to run in both directions.

Still another example of mutual causation is the relationship between social status and choice of career. For example, doctors tend to claim that their own specialties have the highest social status among medical specialties. Do doctors choose these specialties because of the high social status, or do they "put a halo" on their own specialties to make themselves feel good? Probably both. When mutual causation exists, it is not easy to ascertain what causes what and to what extent. For example, advertising researchers want to know which advertising causes sales and how much. Starch (1961) and others have shown that a relationship exists between readership of magazine ads and purchase of the advertised products. Starch developed a system by which he purported to measure the *effect of the advertising* by measuring the difference between rates of sales to readers of the advertisement and to nonreaders of the advertisement. But, although people who read particular advertisements buy more of the products advertised in the ads, it is also true that people who buy particular products are more likely than other people to *read* the advertisements for those products *after* they have purchased the products (perhaps to reassure themselves that they have bought the right car or whatever). If so, to what extent can one say that reading advertisements causes the purchase of the products or that purchase of the products causes reading the ads?

There is no easy answer. Sometimes researchers dodge the issue by stating that they will restrict their interest to *establishing a relationship* between the variables, rather than trying to ascertain the amounts and directions of cause and effect. But in some cases, especially in research done to aid policy decisions, researchers cannot cop a plea that way. For ex-

FIGURE 22.4 An Example of Feedback

Source: *Mathematical Economics*, 2nd ed., p. 289, Allen, 1959. Reprinted by permission of Macmillan London and Basingstoke.

ample, we want to know if smoking causes cancer, not merely whether the two are related. Knowledge of a relationship is useful as a beginning, but knowledge of cause and effect is of ultimate interest here as it so often is elsewhere.

The problem of mutual causation is described in more precise detail on pages 339–341, and statistical methods of unraveling the lines of causation are introduced intuitively there.

5. Summary

Knowledge of causes and effects is all-important in building a social science. It is also crucial in situations where the aim is to make changes that will improve the quality of life. Causation can never be known in some absolute or ultimate sense. But we can get closer to a useful understanding of causal relationships with astute research.

There are several sorts of obstacles to a sound understanding of a causal relationship: (a) A third factor may account for both the hypothesized cause and effect. Systematic testing under a wide range of conditions can reduce the likelihood that such an unknown factor is causing confusion. (b) There may be several important variables jointly responsible for the phenomenon in question. Sound multivariate research, experimental or nonexperimental, can appraise the relative importance of the independent variables. (c) The line of causation may run from the hypothesized effect to the hypothesized cause. This is most easily checked by experimentation. (d) Both variables may influence each other, either simultaneously or sequentially.

Discerning the scheme of causation is a very general problem in social-science research. This chapter suggests some techniques. Others are found throughout the book.

EXERCISES

1. Give examples from research in your field to illustrate the following obstacles:
   a. Hidden third factor
   b. Multivariable causation
   c. Confounding the dependent and independent variables
   d. Feedback; interaction between independent and dependent variables
2. Suggest methods of clarifying the causal relationship in each example in Exercise I.

ADDITIONAL READING

There is an excellent simple exposition of cross-classification in Zeisel (1968).

The Master Obstacle: Cost

The cost of carrying out a piece of research is the most important obstacle that a researcher must overcome. This obstacle will face (or faze) you in one form or another in every single piece of empirical research you conduct. You must economize to do a satisfactory amount of good research, and your economies must be of money, energy, and time. Logically, this obstacle belongs at the head of the list. But the most logical order of presentation is not always the best pedagogical order, and therefore the discussion of cost as an obstacle has been deferred until now.

Cost is the *master* obstacle because almost all other obstacles can be overcome with large amounts of money and time. For example, if you were studying reading habits and if cost were no object, you could assign a full-time observer to watch and photograph every page that your subject reads or looks at, rather than depending on questions asked of the subject. Or you could reduce experimental bias by having many different experimenters rerun the ex-

periment. Reflection will convince you that most other obstacles could also be overcome with expenditures of money.

Cost is more than an obstacle, however; it is often the very factor that makes research necessary or useful. The information that comes from research often produces profit by reducing cost. Furthermore, scientific empirical research is a more efficient and therefore less costly method of getting knowledge than hit-or-miss methods of gathering knowledge. For example, it is cheaper to pretest a piece of advertising copy in a laboratory than to run an entire advertising campaign to find out whether the copy works well. There are several kinds of research decisions in which cost is a crucial factor; we shall now discuss them one by one.

1. Procedure to Produce Data for Study

Sometimes an investigator is limited to existing data; for example, one cannot go back and re-survey voting preferences before the election of 1936. And sometimes limited time requires the use of existing data; one cannot always wait for a survey or experiment to be executed and the data processed. Nevertheless, a researcher is often faced with a choice of whether to use existing data or to collect new data. The decision should be dictated by considerations of *cost and accuracy*. But lack of accuracy is itself a cost. To make this decision rationally, then, you must assess the cost that would result from lack of accuracy, as well as the cost of obtaining accuracy. The cost of the inaccuracy caused by flaws in existing data must be weighed against the cost of creating new data. What is most important is that you *make explicit* to yourself just how much you are spending to avoid the flaws in the existing data.

Another data-production choice is between experimentation and field survey. Sometimes a laboratory experiment is cheaper than a survey, but often a survey is cheaper. Again, you must balance the cost of the technique against the higher value of the information produced by the more expensive technique. (If the less expensive technique produces better data, your choice is made for you.)

Social scientists who do survey research must often decide among interviews conducted in person, over the telephone, and by mail questionnaire. In almost every case, the personal interview is more expensive, but sometimes the extra expense is necessary and justified. In surveys like Kinsey's in which subjects do not respond easily and straightforwardly, the skill of the interviewer in face-to-face encounter is necessary, especially when there are many questions to be asked. In contrast, the questions asked in surveys on smoking and health are few, easy to answer, and not likely to be touchy, so the mail questionnaire is quite satisfactory except for the problem of nonresponse. The expense of conducting hundreds of thousands of interviews for the smoking studies would have made those studies impossible.

Research on magazine readership has used all three interviewing techniques. The decisions in particular studies have been based on the exact nature of the information required plus the costs and revenues attached to the various accuracy levels. For example, a large consumer magazine can afford to spend more money on interviewing techniques than can a small trade magazine because positive information would mean a much greater gain in revenue for the large consumer magazine.

2. Sampling and Cost

In 1886 Booth sought to find out how many poor people there were in London, because the extent of poverty and misery was a subject for debate in the 1880s (just as the actual number of people in England had been a subject for debate a hundred years earlier) and because he wanted to find out what the causes of this poverty and misery were. Obviously he could not finance the gathering of such a monumental mass of data. Therefore, he turned to "the method of wholesale interviewing," as Beatrice Webb called it (Moser and Kalton, 1972: 19)—collecting information from school attendance officers, whose job it was to visit individual homes and children.

In the 1890s Rowntree felt that Booth's method was not sufficiently accurate, and he therefore employed interviewers to go to every wage-earning home. He worked in the city of York, however, which was much smaller than London.

It was an enormous advance in social research when in 1912 Bowley studied living conditions in Reading by means of a sample. Not only was a sample much cheaper than Rowntree's method, but with the smaller data-collection effort Bowley could take more care with such technical matters as nonresponse bias. Hence Bowley's results probably were more accurate than a 100 per cent sample would have produced.

The decisions on whether to sample, how to

sample, how large a sample to take, and what sampling method to use are basically cost decisions. If cost were no object, every study would take a very large per cent of the potential subject matter, because accuracy would then be greater and error smaller than in a smaller sample.

The presidential election in the United States is a 100 per cent sample (that is, not a sample) of all American people who want to vote. We do not know whether the nation goes to all this expense to prevent any trace of sampling error because its citizens do not know any better or because the election offers an important ritual of participation. (This 100 per cent sample does not guarantee a perfect survey, however; it was especially unsure in Boston when ballot-box stuffing and repeat voting were well-developed local arts.)

The U.S. Census attempted to be a 100 per cent sample for a long time. In recent censuses, however, some questions were asked of only one person in four, for example, and future censuses will probably go further with sampling. The preliminary reports issued by the U.S. Bureau of the Census for quick information dissemination are also products of a sampling process (but in this case the sample is a sample of the *data*, as distinguished from a sample of people).

3. Sample Size

We have said that the only reason for not taking a 100 per cent sample of the universe is cost. But how big *should* the sample be? The most common ways of choosing a sample size are to find out how big a sample is customary in similar research and to take as big a sample as the budget will allow. Both methods are logically fallacious, but the former contains some grains of practical wisdom. Observation of others' work can help the researcher to take advantage of their trial-and-error learning. For example, Kinsey spent much time in working out appropriate sample sizes, and, if you were

to carry on work similar to his, it might be reasonable to imitate his sample sizes.

Fitting your sample size to the available budget funds requires circular reasoning, because the budget has to be fixed on the basis of how large the sample size will be. Someone has to make an independent decision at *some* stage of the game.

The best general advice about sample size is to take a pretest sample that is small by *any* standard and then see whether you can observe any clear pattern of the sort you are looking for. You may find that even such a tiny sample is big enough. If not, the variation within your pretest sample will guide you in deciding how much larger a sample you are likely to need. Chapter 34 gives you detailed rational methods for deciding how large a sample to take.

4. How Many Variables to Investigate

There are always more variables that *might* be important than you have time and money to investigate. Therefore, you must decide which of the variables are promising enough to be worth the cost—a process of economics and good judgment. As Fisher put it:

> It is an essential characteristic of experimentation that it is carried out with limited resources, and an essential part of the subject of experimental design to ascertain how these should be best applied; or, in particular, to which causes of disturbance care should be given, and which *ought* to be deliberately ignored. (Fisher, 1971: 22)

For example, a wise advertising researcher does not bother to experiment with various shades of ink in a direct-mail advertisement; rather, she concentrates on such variables as the advertising message and the offer the advertisement makes. On the other hand, cancer researchers are willing to follow up leads that may seem very trivial at first because the problem is so important and because there are too few good leads of any kind.

There is not much that can be said about this

decision except that the researcher must *get into the habit* of asking whether an additional variable is sufficiently promising to justify its cost. There just are no scientific or automatic routines to aid in making such decisions.

5. Amount of Tolerable Bias

The Kinsey study made no attempt to achieve a random sample of the population of the United States, because the attempt would have been impossibly expensive. Furthermore, even if astronomical sums had been spent and a random sample had been *attempted,* the *departures* from randomness would still have been very large because of nonresponse. Kinsey's judgment on this matter was mostly approved later by the statistical review board of the American Statistical Association, though the statisticians did call for a small probability-sample test of just how much bias Kinsey's procedure injected into his study (Cochran et al., 1955). Other statisticians were less satisfied, however (Wallis, 1949); this is a matter of judgment on which there is room for competent professionals to disagree.

Cost also affected the geographic pattern of Kinsey's sampling. Half the subjects were from Indiana. But Kinsey judged that the expense of drawing more of his subjects from farther away would not be justified by the probable decrease in bias.

Bias and cost must also be balanced when deciding how much money and effort to spend on converting nonresponders into responders. Should the researcher call back twice? five times? eleven times? The decision must be based on the costs of calling back *and* the costs of inaccuracy caused by the bias.

6. Managerial Cost Efficiency in Research

Some researchers are crackerjack managers. They use the research money at their disposal as efficiently and conscientiously as if it came out of their own pockets. But too many researchers take no pride in cost efficiencies and ignore all reasonable procedures for calculating what should and should not be done.

Scientific accuracy and avoidance of error are important, but one can be too finicky about such things as not using existing data that may not be quite perfect for one's purposes, rather than collecting new data from scratch. Besides appealing to your sense of justice about other people's money, we suggest that economical practices may also be personally efficient for you and help you to accomplish a lot more work in your lifetime.

Having funds available to pay for help may expedite your work. But, beyond a certain level, *too much* money may slow you down by inducing you to magnify the size of your project to the point at which you must do large amounts of administrative and supervisory work. Or an excess of money may lead you to collect too much data and thereby slow down your analysis. Money and the help it buys are useful only if they do not prevent you from traveling light and fast.

Academic scientists sometimes forgo efficient shortcuts out of unnecessary prissiness. For example, market researchers have known for years that it is often cheaper in the long run to pay interviewees and panel members and that such payment can often be made without compromising the research. Yet we know of an academic researcher who put up a monumental battle against giving away a cheap pencil to induce people to answer a questionnaire. (A later test showed that the pencils far more than paid for themselves.)

A slight acquaintance with the basic notions of managerial economics can help a researcher, just as it can help any other administrator, to be more efficient. Consider, for example, a study situation in which you hand out one-question questionnaires in person at a huge convention. It pays to take a sample far larger than any sample size you might reasonably need because the *extra* cost of the extra questionnaires and their distribution is practically nil.

Perhaps this statement by a famous chemist will add weight to the argument:

> In designing a bridge, an engineer naturally chooses the most economical design which satisfies all the specifications, including the aesthetic requirements. In designing an elaborate experiment, questions of cost are all too frequently ignored completely. This is partly because of the great difficulty of making good estimates of the time required to carry out a given investigation, but it is also partly a traditional attitude that somehow science is above vulgar monetary considerations.
>
> With the increasing cost of research it becomes necessary to take economic factors into account, however difficult this may be. Certainly there is no excuse for doing a given job in an expensive way when it can be carried through equally effectively with less expenditure. It is much more difficult to decide whether a given project should be carried out at all, considering its probable cost. In applied research there sometimes exist fairly definite criteria, such as the possible monetary benefits of a successful research, coupled with a rough estimate of the chance of success.
>
> In pure science no estimate of monetary value is usually available or in fact desirable. Here cost still enters in deciding between alternative problems. Naturally this is not the only factor, but it is certainly wrong to disregard it altogether.
>
> Cost estimates should include not only direct expenditures for materials but also salaries and overhead, even if these are not directly charged to the project. (Wilson, 1952: 6)

Computers and modern data-processing technology have radically changed the economics of research. We mentioned earlier how simple IBM machines were developed to reduce the cost of the U.S. Census and speed up analysis. By now machines have reduced the cost of handling data to a point where many studies are possible that were out of the question before.

7. Summary

Cost is the master obstacle to getting empirical knowledge, because with enough expenditures of time and money almost all other obstacles can be overcome. Your task as a researcher is to devise sufficiently efficient ways of overcoming obstacles of all kinds so that with the time and money at your disposal, you can produce relatively large amounts of useful knowledge.

Sampling rather than studying the entire population is a basic cost-reducing tactic. Using available data is another. Also, one should use good judgment to avoid collecting unnecessary data on irrelevant variables, and not demand more accuracy than is required by the overall purpose of the research. And it is all-important to *care* about being a good manager of research resources, both because it will make you more productive and because you owe it to whoever—your institution, or society as a whole—is ultimately paying the bill.

EXERCISE

1. Give examples in which
    a. Experiment is cheaper than survey
    b. Survey is cheaper than experiment
    c. Sampling is not used at present but should be
    d. A slightly biased sample may be obtained at a much lower cost than an unbiased sample

ADDITIONAL READING

Fiedler (1978) provides a detailed guide to the practical aspects of field research, with considerable emphasis on costs; Sudman (1967) and Dillman (1978: 3–5, 68–72) describe the cost considerations involved in survey research.

Part Four

Extracting the Meaning of Data

Searching for Relationships and Characterizing Them

After data have been collected, they must be rearranged and fiddled with to make them yield up the information they contain. This is the process of analysis.

Many different processes in social-scientific research are called "analysis," and perhaps the most important job of this chapter is to distinguish among them. What type of analysis a researcher performs should depend on the type of research question that he or she seeks to answer, as well as on the method by which he or she collects the data and the sharpness with which the research question or hypothesis has been formulated.

Descriptive classification and measurement research call for processes that some writers do not call "analysis." There are no independent variables to relate to dependent variables. Rather, there is but one—or several—variable(s) whose relationships are not in question, as in a census or other measurement of multiple variables. The analysis begins with standardizing the data and separating it into convenient or interesting categories, and ends with summarizing statistics or with graphs or tables of the data. The appropriateness of the various

summarizing statistics for various types of research was discussed briefly in Chapter 4. Discussions and illustrations of the logic of tabular and graphic display can be found in almost any elementary statistics book or in Zeisel (1968, Part 1). Huff (1954, Chaps. 3, 5, 6, 9) shows how you and others can deceive people with tables and graphs.

A good descriptive analysis *shows* the important data in a form such that they will be clearly understood and their meaning grasped by the reader. For example, there should be a separate table or graph for each idea you are trying to communicate, rather than one enormous master compilation in which nothing is obvious.

The more complicated processes of analysis take place in causal- and non-causal-relationship research, in comparison research, and in prediction studies. This and Chapters 25–28 focus on the processes involved in analyzing causal relationships, which are the most difficult relationships to understand. The sequence of the discussion follows the sequence of steps set out in Chapter 7: searching for relationships; characterizing the forms of relationships if they seem to exist; testing statistically for the likelihood that the apparent relationships are not simply the result of chance; measuring the strength of relationships in scientific and/or policy terms; and constructing the web and paths of causation.

1. Searching for Relationships

Relationships that we find among variables help us to explain, understand, control, and predict. We *know more* about the world when we have established a relationship between variables. For example, we know that 51 per cent of American women were in the labor force in 1979, but after looking at Figure 24.1, which has information about labor force participation and two other variables, we better un-

derstand that 51 per cent. Figure 24.1 shows that there has been an upward trend, so that a woman is more likely to have a job now than she was thirty years ago. The figure also shows that women with school-age children are more likely to have jobs than women with younger children. Thus, with the aid of Figure 24.1, we not only know the present rate of labor force participation and its trend, but we can also predict that a woman with young children is less likely to work than a woman whose children are older (Cherlin, 1981: 51).

The investigator shuttles back and forth between two kinds of analytic activity when he or she seeks to determine causal and noncausal relationships. One is *getting ideas* about relationships, which the investigator then formulates as hypotheses. The other is *examining and testing* the hypotheses. We shall now con-

FIGURE 24.1   Labor force participation rates for married women with children, by age of children, 1948 to 1979.

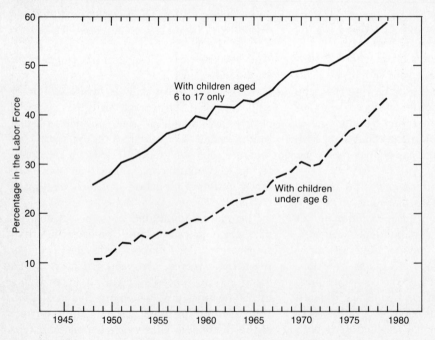

Sources: for 1948, 1960, and 1970, U.S. Bureau of Labor Statistics, *Handbook of Labor Statistics 1978*, bulletin 2000 (1979); for 1979, U.S. Bureau of Labor Statistics, "Multi-Earner Families Increase," Press Release no. USDL 79–747, Oct. 31, 1979.

sider these two activities with various kinds of data.

A. RELATIONSHIPS IN DATA CREATED ESPECIALLY FOR YOUR PURPOSES

Let's say that you are searching for relationships in a set of data that you yourself have produced by experiment or survey, data intended specifically to throw light upon the particular question in which you are interested. To begin, look at exploratory data analysis as detective work. A famous statistician has written: "Exploratory data analysis is detective work—numerical detective work—or counting detective work—or graphical detective work . . .

"A detective investigating a crime needs both tools and understanding. If he has no fingerprint powder, he will fail to find fingerprints on most surfaces. If he does not understand where the criminal is likely to have put his fingers, he will not look in the right places. Equally, the analyst of data needs both tools and understanding" (Tukey, 1977: 1).

Start by saturating yourself in the raw data. Look and look some more at the original data sheets and at the computer printouts of the data. You should look for any *regularities*. Ask yourself what *might* be interesting about the data. Look for simple facts, because the simple facts are the most important. Your knowledge of your discipline should tell you what facts and patterns are of importance in your discipline, and it is that knowledge that will guide your search.

Certainly you should be looking for *big* differences, especially in a comparison research problem, differences that will be apparent to simple eyeball inspection. Differences that require subtle statistical analysis are usually not so valuable.

Do your looking with pencil and paper in hand. Compute simple estimates for various variables—averages, totals, first-half-versus-second-half calculations, percentages, and so forth. Look at this raw material as if someone had given it to you as pieces cut with a jigsaw and you are to find the key to the puzzle.

Make crude tables and graphs. If you think you see a relationship between two variables, plot them on a graph. Not only will the graph give you an excellent view of whether there is a relationship, but it will also show you the *form* of the relationship. In addition, relationships may stand out in a graph as they never would in columns of numbers. As Tukey says, ". . . visual devices . . . show us the unexpected" (p. 27).

Watch a good researcher just after he or she has received the first batch of raw data from a piece of survey research. The data will probably be only a small installment on the total because he or she is anxious to get a first peek at them to see what they show. You will see the researcher poring over the data, sheet by sheet, back and forth, doodling quick crude simple statistics (totals, averages, medians, and so forth) on a pad. It is from such searching activity that new and interesting hypotheses spring.

When there is a huge mass of data and it has gone through various transformations, you must find some way of boiling down the computer output; no one can look for patterns in a stack of computer printouts a foot thick. One useful practice is to compute the simple correlations (a correlation coefficient is a common measure of the *association* of two variables) between each pair of variables you are working with,[1] and look through the set ("matrix") of correlation coefficients for each pair of variables on which you collected data. (Measurement of correlation is discussed in Chapters 26 and 33). Those variables that are correlated fairly strongly with the dependent variable

---

1. Some investigators condemn this practice because they are rightfully afraid that it leads to spurious correlations caused by chance. But, used with care and some delicacy, this practice need not necessarily lead to abuse—especially if the researcher demands that associations make sense before paying any attention to them and if he or she tests all such associations on fresh batches of data.

need to be considered further in the analysis, and those pairs of independent variables that are correlated with each other must be understood in relationship to each other.

B. INSPECTION OF DATA COLLECTED FOR OTHER PURPOSES

Selvin and Stuart (1966) aptly label it "data dredging" when the researcher looks in a set of data for ideas and relationships. This process is to be distinguished from first having a hypothesis and then collecting data to test the hypothesis. The data that you dredge may be data that you earlier collected for a particular purpose but that contain much more information than you used for the original investigation; or they may be data collected by government agencies for general purposes—the population census or the census of manufacturers, for instance, or data from public survey agencies like the Gallup and Roper polls, data on prices, freight-car movements, or amounts of employment advertising. This searching for new relationships in existing data is often called "secondary analysis" (Kendall and Lazarsfeld, 1950). The purpose of this section is to tell something about how to go about this secondary analysis.

The prepared mind—that is, one with a wide and thorough knowledge of the field under investigation—is a prerequisite for successful data dredging, just as it is for generating hypotheses from informal observation. This is why the job of searching for hypotheses cannot be routinized or given to computers. Some of our best friends are electronic computers, but reluctantly we must badmouth them: No computer can sort out your data for you. Once we had the idea that, if a researcher collected enough data on the stock market or the horse races, he could then shovel them into a computer, and the computer would find the useful relationships. But not so. The computer adds when you tell it to add, subtracts when you tell it to subtract, and correlates (for example) income with education when you tell it to do so.

But the computer has not the slightest capacity for guessing that the relationship between income and education means anything; nor does a mathematical statistician. That part of the job is strictly yours.

2. Characterizing the Form of a Relationship

Relationships can be of many varieties: positive (direct) or negative (inverse); and straight-line (linear) or curvilinear or oscillating. Complex statistical techniques often obscure the form of a relationship. Hence an invaluable first step when you are investigating the form of a relationship is to *graph* the data. For example, assume that you have data on the birth rate in Yemen for each of the past twenty years. Is the birth rate going up or down or staying the same? It is often surprisingly difficult to make a valid analysis. And a graph is an important first step in determining the nature of the association.

Graphs are generally limited to exhibiting the association between two variables, though a third variable can be shown by plotting two different sets of data on the same graph; for example, the relationship of age to weight can be shown separately for men and women in the same graph. Even when you think the relationship is multivariate, however, it can be illuminating to plot the dependent variable two-dimensionally against each independent variable.

One reason that a graph of the data is so important is that some kinds of association become visible that would not appear in other kinds of statistical analysis. For example, if you want to know whether women have been having fewer children recently than they used to, you might compare the number of children born to women who grew up during the first quarter of this century with the number born to those who grew up later. The averages would not look very different. But Figure 24.2 shows that just looking at averages would cause

FIGURE 24.2   Cohort total fertility rate for single-year birth cohorts, 1891 to 1950.

Source: Robert Heuser, *Fertility Tables for Birth Cohorts*, U.S. Department of Health Education and Welfare, 1976, pages 142–144 and U.S. National Center for Health Statistics, *Vital Statistics of the United States*, 1979, volume 1, pp. 43–44. Published by the Department of Health and Human Services, U.S. Government Printing Office, 1984.

you to miss some interesting and important information. Trends in number of children have reversed dramatically. The average woman born in 1890 or in the early 1930s had more than three children, whereas women born around 1950 will average less than two (Cherlin, 1981: 20).

The decision on whether to characterize data as an upward or downward straight line or as a curve of some sort must be a blend of judgment and a branch of mathematical statistics called "curve fitting." For example, in Figure 24.3 the American Council on Education drew a curve through the data of the experts' ratings of economics departments plotted against the amounts of scholarly publications produced by the economics departments. Would you care to

argue that a straight line or another shape of curve is not more sensible?

Analyzing the data in Figure 24.4, which plots the relationship between automobile speed and distance needed to stop, is more complex. If you assume that each of the observations was very certain and there was little or no error in measurement or variability in behavior from trial to trial, then it would be reasonable to assume that each point represents exactly what it shows on the graph, and therefore, you would leave the data as in Figure 24.4. However, if you believe that each point is affected by chance (as will usually be the case) or if you want to get a general picture of the data without worrying about every detail, you will want to "smooth" the curve. A modest

FIGURE 24.3   Relationship of Rated Quality of Graduate Faculty to Index of Publications, 71 Economics Departments

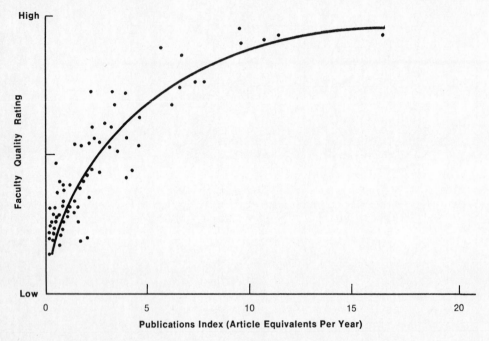

Source: *An Assessment of Quality in Graduate Education*, p. 80, by Allan Cartter, 1966; reprinted by permission of American Council on Education.

way to do so for the data shown in Figure 24.4 is to average small groups of adjacent observations. For instance, the "smoothed" stopping distance for a car traveling fifteen miles per hour might be the average distance for stops at fourteen, fifteen, and sixteen miles per hour, as in Figure 24.5. To smooth the curve even more, we can try more radical smoothing, using the averages of larger groups to eliminate the zigzags. We then get the picture in Figure 24.6 (see also Tukey, 1977: Chap. 7, for more on smoothing).

One might go even further and fit either a straight line or a curve to plotted data. (A curve might be especially appropriate if there is another observation at x in Figure 24.7.) Either a straight line or a curve uses *all* the data to throw light either on *all* the other data or on the kind of *overall* relationship that is assumed to hold between the variables.

There is more than one way to "fit" a line or curve to a set of data. For now let's limit the discussion to data that seem to fit a straight line rather than a curve, that is, "linear correlation." When you fit a line by eye-and-hand with a straightedge ruler—or better, with a black thread—your intuitive criterion seems to be simply to get the line "as close" to the observation points as possible. But how should one define "close"?

A reasonable criterion is to draw that line which minimizes the sum of the distances between the correlation line and the points; these minimum distances would be measured perpendicular to the correlation line, as seen in Figure 24.8. The usual criterion—chosen simply for mathematical convenience—is to select the line around which the sum of the *squared* differences between observations and the correlation line is minimum. One can select the

FIGURE 24.4   Relation of Speed of Automobile to Distance It Takes to Stop, as Shown by Individual Observations

Source: *Methods of Correlation and Regression Analysis*, p. 37, by Mordecai Ezekiel, 1930; reprinted by permission of John Wiley & Sons, Inc.

best-fitting line either by trial and error or by using the equivalent handy mathematical shortcuts.

3. Characterizing a Causal Relationship

The previous section concentrated on the relationship itself. Now we consider how to characterize the form of simple association when it is reasonable ·to assume that, if there is a relationship, one of the variables (x) causes the other (y). One frequently used way of doing this is called regression analysis.

Some associations should not be interpreted causally. For example, one would not suppose that either I.Q. or athletic ability is the cause of the other; rather, both may be caused by other common factors. Or, consider two hypothetical scales of violence on television, the

Bash and the Gore scales, constructed by different researchers. Each scale is set to run from 0 to 100 points. Both scales are used to rate 192 "action" programs. A graph of the results may show close association between the two scales, but clearly there is no causal relationship between the two scales.

Now let us consider the relationship of auto speed to distance required to stop. In an experiment where people are asked to drive at various speeds, it is clear that speed influences stopping distance rather than vice versa. The question we wish to answer is: At each particular speed x_1, what will be the stopping distance y_1? That is, we wish to predict a stopping distance conditional upon a particular speed, as accurately as possible. This implies that—if we assume a straight-line relationship between the variables—our aim is to find that line for which

FIGURE 24.5   Relation of Speed of Automobile to Distance It Takes to Stop, as Shown by Averages of Very Small Groups

Source: *Methods of Correlation and Regression Analysis,* p. 42, by Mordecai Ezekiel, 1930; reprinted by permission of John Wiley & Sons, Inc.

FIGURE 24.6   Relation of Speed of Automobile to Distance It Takes to Stop, as Shown by Averages of Small Groups

Source: *Methods of Correlation and Regression Analysis,* p. 45, by Mordecai Ezekiel, 1930; reprinted by permission of John Wiley & Sons, Inc.

FIGURE 24.7   Hypothetical Data for a Group of 15-Year Old Boys

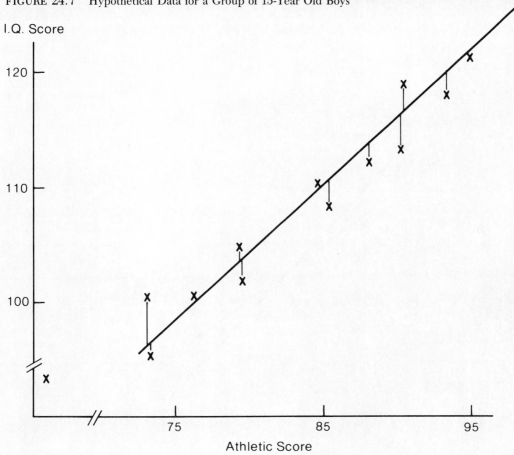

I.Q. Score

Athletic Score

the *vertical* deviations between observations and the regression line are as small as possible (as seen in Figure 24.7).

As with the correlation line discussed earlier, we could make the sum of the absolute deviations our criterion. But the standard criterion is the sum of the *squared* vertical deviations. (One could imagine situations where the sum of absolute deviations would be the more reasonable criteria, however.) The vertical distances that enter into the "sum of least squares" that we seek to minimize are shown in Figure 24.7.

The best-fitting regression line that minimizes the "sum of squares" can be found by a series of trial-and-error approximations, or commonly by mathematical formula with calculations performed on the computer. What is important is that you understand the "least squares" principle; not one in a thousand people who calculate regression lines with mathematical analysis on the computer could remember the mathematical derivation on the spot, and none needs to.

Curve-fitting by formula has some advantages over curve-fitting by eye, however.

1. Reliability. When data are clean and beautiful . . . , there is little problem about the fitting, but when we have a swarm of points with considerable varia-

FIGURE 24.8   Relationship Between Price and Production of Onions

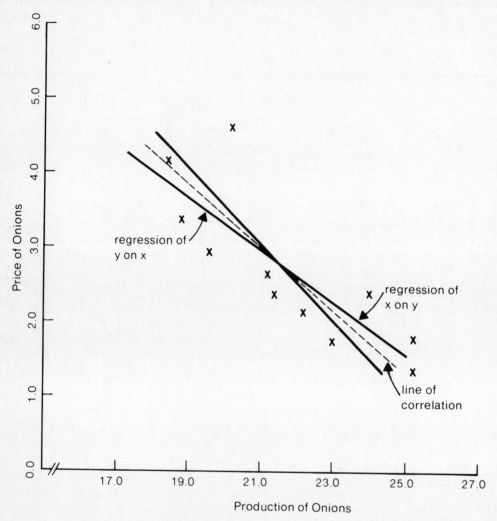

tion, our eye is not a sure guide in placing the line.

2. Objectivity. Scientists prize repeatable objective methods, because they fear that unconscious bias on the part of an observer may distort the results. [Curve fitting by formula will give the same results when repeated by other persons.]

3. Generalization. It is desirable to have a general method of curve-fitting that can be extended to new and more complicated situations. (Mosteller et al., 1970: 385–386)

Whenever there are two variables, one can compute *two* regression lines, since each variable can be *x* or *y*. In the early years of this century, social scientists were puzzled by the decision about which line to use, especially in economic studies of supply and demand. For example, if you have data for various years on the prices and quantities of onions sold, should price or quantity be the *y* variable? One response of economists was to calculate *both* regressions. If both are plotted on a single graph, this means finding one regression line that minimizes the sum of squared *vertical* de viations and another that minimizes the sum of squared *horizontal* deviations. These two regression lines may be seen in Figure 24.8.

Figure 24.8 allows us to see how the line of correlation relates to the regression lines: It bisects them. And that makes intuitive sense, because in correlation there is no implication of a directional relationship in *either* direction between the variables; it makes sense that this nondirectional line should lie halfway between the two causally directed regression lines.

The logic of curvilinear regression, as illustrated in Figure 24.3 is the same as that of linear regression. One may fit a curve either by the eye-and-hand method or with mathematical analysis and computers. The usual criterion of fit is still the same, however: to minimize the sum of squared vertical deviations from the regression line.

Often, however, it makes sense to transform a curvilinear relationship into a linear one. This can make the mathematical calculations simpler and ease understanding of the results. For example, Figure 24.3 shows that increasing publications from zero to five has a strong effect on the quality rating, but increasing the publications from ten to fifteen does not; each extra publication seems to make less of a difference. We can construct the graph so that the vertical scale shows differences in publications by *proportions* (rather than by equal *numbers*); doubling the number of publications from three to six might have about the same effect as doubling from six to twelve. If so, using the logarithm of the number of publications, rather than the number itself, would turn the curved line of Figure 24.3 into a straight line and make it easier to find the best regression line. Logarithmic and other kinds of transformations need not concern you now, though they are often used in economics and psychology.

4. Summary

Data analysis should begin with a close look at the data—examining individual variables, considering how pairs of variables relate to each other, and finally thinking about causal relationships. It is important to diagram the data to see the "big picture" as well as the details.

EXERCISES

1. List at least three (more if you can) observations you could make from Figure 24.1 other than the simple statement that women's labor force participation was higher in 1980 than in 1950.
2. Look at the diagrams dealing with automobile stopping distance (Figures 24.4–24.6). What can you learn from each figure that you could not learn from the other two? Might you ever want to smooth the data presented in Figure 24.2 on number of chidren? Why or why not?
3. Why is it a good idea to "eyeball" your data (examine the raw data themselves) before analyzing them mathematically or statistically? Why is it a good idea to use mathematical or statistical formulas to analyze the data after you have examined them, instead of just reporting the results of the eyeballing?

ADDITIONAL READING

Zeisel (1968), Ehrenberg (1975), Hartwig and Dearing (1979), and Tufte (1974) all provide interesting treatments of how to begin analyzing data, including discussions of how to use graphs and tables to make patterns in the data as clear as possible.

Tufte (1974); Chatterjee and Price (1977), and Ferber and Verdoorn (1962) provide simple step-by-step introductions to regression analysis that may be particularly useful to a beginner in this area. Almost every statistics book for business and economics contains a section on regression analysis.

Econometricians have developed a wealth of sophisticated regression techniques, which may be found in any elementary econometrics text. Two good texts are Johnston (1972) and Wonnacott and Wonnacott (1979).

Huff (1954) is an informative book about the analysis and misanalysis of social science data.

Rosenberg (1968) is a thorough detailed exposition of the principles of analyzing survey data.

A consumer's-eye-view of data analysis and the use of tables is found in Wallis and Roberts (1966: 270–279).

Testing and Refining Relationships $\boxed{25}$

Let's say that you have theorized, searched, and apparently found a relationship in your data between your dependent variable and one or more independent variables. Furthermore, you have investigated the form of the relationship and have characterized it as, say, linear. That is, a straight line fits the plot of the relationship as well or better than other forms.

There is still much more to be done. Usually (though not always) you would like to be able to say with some confidence whether the apparent relationship you have found can be regarded as causal. And you would like to learn if there is a more complex structure of causal relationships among the variables you are considering. This chapter presents methods of refining the relationships you have discovered. It also discusses how to decide how strong and important the relationships you find are.

Before you rush off to analyze and then write a book about the fascinating relationship you think you have found, you ought to check that the relationship actually exists and is not just an artifact of chance and sampling variation. Any column of random numbers *seems* to show a variety of patterns, and two adjacent columns of random numbers often reveal apparent relationships. Too often, researchers have wasted

vast efforts, and sometimes confused others and themselves, by building scientific explanations on patterns that were simply due to chance. To avoid this pitfall, we test relationships for statistical significance. This is the question that relationship testing seeks to answer: Is there, or is there not, an association between a particular pair of variables? Sometimes the answer is statistically obvious immediately. For example, Masserman (1944) observed that, when given a choice of milk with alcohol or without alcohol, only two of sixteen normal cats chose liquor, whereas ten of sixteen neurotic cats chose liquor. It was then reasonably obvious that the difference between two of sixteen and ten of the sixteen indicates a "real" association; that is, if he were to run the experiment over again, the neurotic cats almost surely would choose the liquor more often than the normal cats. Of course, the existence of an association would be even more conclusive if the results had been 20 of 160 versus 100 of 160, rather than 2 of 16 versus 10 of 16. But, even so, no further statistical proof of the association is necessary, and the analysis of Masserman's data is complete. All that is left for him to determine is that the experimental results are not an artifact of bad sampling or some other bias and then to say what the association between neurosis and alcohol *means*—a matter of theorizing that is beyond the scope of this book.

Sometimes it is not so obvious whether the apparent relationship is due to chance. Help in deciding may come from statistical tests (see Chapter 31). So far we have talked about testing for relationships in a bivariate context, that is, when only two variables enter into the analysis. Similar logic applies when you wish to test for a relationship between your dependent variable y and an independent variable x when one or more other independent variables need to be considered. Now we ask: Is there a relationship between x and y when other independent variables are allowed for?

1. Refining Observed Associations into Causal Relationships

The *association* (relationship) is the basic unit of any science that is past the early exploratory stage. It is all that the data can show directly—which is that two or more variables vary together. But we usually want to know more than that an association exists between two variables. We want to *infer* causes and their effects from relationships. We also would like to know more about the linkage between causes and their effects and under which conditions cause-and-effect relationships take place. The purpose of this section, then, is to describe briefly some devices for learning more about cause and effect than can be inferred from a given observed relationship.[1]

A. EXAMINING SPURIOUS CAUSAL RELATIONSHIPS

On page 283, we discussed the hidden-factor fallacy (spurious causal relationship), in which x does not cause y but in fact z causes the var-

1. This topic is discussed in much greater detail, at a simple level with illustrations, by Zeisel (1968, Part 2), by Kendall and Lazarsfeld (1950; an important original treatment and one of the great essays on the analysis of data), and by Hirschi and Selvin (1966) in comprehensive detail.

iation in both x and y. The problem, then, is to determine whether some hidden z accounts for an observed relationship between x and y.

In experimentation one tries to eliminate the possibility of a hidden factor by controlling all the conditions of the experiment except the independent variable(s). For example, when Gamson, Fireman, and Rytina (1982) wanted to find out if people differ in willingness to rebel against an authority figure who demanded they act unethically, they needed to ensure that the demands were the same for everyone. Therefore, the authority figure (who was part of the experiment) followed a detailed script so that every experimental trial would be the same.

In survey research, however, the researcher does not have the power to alter the conditions under which the data are collected. The best he or she can do is to try to hold conditions constant statistically. For example, Table 25.1 shows data on the relationship between candy eating and marital status, as reported by Zeisel (1968: 138).

There is clearly an association between the two variables. The difference between 75 per cent and 63 per cent, obtained from samples of 999 people and 2,010 people, is obviously not caused by chance; we need no statistical test to prove it. But what does this association *mean*? Candy eating clearly does not cause people to be single. The more sensible question is, Does being single cause people to eat more candy?

Now look carefully at Table 25.2.

We have controlled for *age* ("held age constant") by introducing it as a third variable in the cross-classification analysis. That is, we subdivide the married and unmarried groups by age and then note that there is *no difference*

TABLE 25.1   Percentage Who Eat Candy, by Marital Status

	Single	Married
Eat candy regularly	75%	63%
(Number of cases)	(999)	(2,010)

Source: *Say It With Figures*, rev. 5th ed., p. 138, by Hans Zeisel; copyright 1947, 1950, 1957, 1968 by Harper & Row, Publishers, Incorporated; reprinted by permission of the publishers.

TABLE 25.2   Percentage Who Eat Candy, by Age and Marital Status

	Married		Single	
	Up to 25 Years	**25 Years and Over**	**Up to 25 Years**	**25 Years and Over**
Eat candy regularly	81%	58%	79%	60%
(Number of cases)	(503)	(1,507)	(799)	(200)

Source: *Say It With Figures*, rev. 5th ed., p. 138, by Hans Zeisel; copyright 1947, 1950, 1957, 1968 by Harper & Row, Publishers, Incorporated; reprinted by permission of the publishers.

to speak of between the married and unmarried groups in either the "up to twenty-five years" or the "twenty-five years and over" category. In other words, when age is held constant, there is no longer a relationship between marital status and candy eating. Age was a hidden third factor.

Does this mean that age causes candy eating? Not necessarily. There may be further hidden factors that will remove the appearance of a causal relationship there also. Therefore, the investigator should try other likely variables to see if any of them removes the observed association.

Which variables should the investigator try? This is a crucial question, to which the answer will seem most unsatisfactory: The investigator chooses those variables that good sense, imagination, and professional knowledge suggest might be hidden third factors (and for which there is data available), often relying on theory and on the work of other researchers involved in controversies about the importance of particular variables—in other words, insight.

How *many* variables must you try before you can be satisfied that the observed association is indeed causal? The answer is the same: Only good sense can guide you. You can never try *all* the possible variables. Nor can you ever be *perfectly* sure that some hidden factor really does not exist. But, as you try more and more likely variables and the original relationship remains unchanged, you can be progressively surer that the observed relationship is really between cause and effect and is not spurious.

The candy example was worked using the cross-classification technique. But the technique of multiple regression (and occasionally discriminant analysis) is often better from many points of view when you wish to investigate the influences of more than one independent variable on the dependent variable y. The logic is the same as in simple regression except that instead of a line on a two-dimensional graph, one minimizes the sum of deviations from a multidimensional "hyperplane," for example, the deviations from a two-dimensional plane in three-dimensional space if there are two independent variables and one dependent variable. (When you think that two variables "interact" to cause a third—that is, when the impact of one depends on the level of another—cross-classification analysis could be superior. An example would be if marital status affected candy eating, but only among those over twenty-five years of age. Our theories often do not lead us to expect such relationships.)

When searching for a spurious causal relationship, the dependent variable y is regressed on the x variable and also on the z variable that you think might be the hidden cause of y's variation. If the coefficient of z is large whereas the coefficient of x is small—that is, if age is important and marital status is not, as in the candy-eating example—then you should conclude that marital status does not explain candy-eating behavior. (We will say more below on how to tell when a coefficient is large or small.)

B. EXAMINING FOR THE DIRECTION OF CAUSAL FLOW

The data of an observed relationship do not in themselves tell you what causes what. That became clear when we first looked at the simple relationship between candy eating and marital status: Without further information there was no way to decide whether candy eating caused marital status or vice versa (or neither caused the other, which is how it turned out). The further information we brought to bear was general knowledge (including time order) that made it unlikely that candy eating caused marital status (although candy might make people fat, which might keep them single).

On the other hand, the same uncertainty does *not* exist about the *direction* of the causal flow between age and candy eating. Age causes candy eating, not the reverse. We know this because, if candy eating caused one to be over or under twenty-five years of age (quite unlikely on general grounds!), the original relationship between marital status and candy eating would not have disappeared after age was introduced into the relationship. (This should become clear on reflection.)

There are, then, two complementary ways to determine in which direction causation flows between two variables: reasoning and general knowledge, on one hand, and introducing more variables, as already described, on the other.

Before leaving hidden-third-factor associations—remember that noncausal relationships can be useful as *predictive* indexes.

C. INVESTIGATING FOR CAUSAL INTERMEDIATES

The picture of the hidden-factor situation in Figure 22.1 was like this:

The cross-classification can reveal the existence of the links between w and y and between w and x, as in the candy eating example. But the *direction* of the causal flow is still not revealed by the data themselves. Instead, the appropriate diagram might be like this:

In other words, w could be an *intermediate* between x and y, rather than the cause of both x and y. If so, it is sensible to call *either x or w* the cause of y. But it is often useful to *understand* that w is an intermediate that links x and y.

The difficulty is that there is no way of telling *from the data themselves* whether the case involves a hidden factor or a causal intermediate. The flow of causality might "really" run

marital status ⟶ age ⟶ candy eating.

No analysis of the given data can show that this is not the appropriate interpretation.

The only way to distinguish between the hidden-third-factor case and the causal-intermediate case is on the basis of *further knowledge*. In this case, we have the knowledge that getting married cannot change one's age (unless one lies on the marriage certificate), and it is that knowledge and that knowledge only that convinces us that the age is a hidden third factor and not a causal intermediate between marital status and candy eating.

The time at which the various events take place is often sufficient additional knowledge with which to decide which "paradigm" is more appropriate.[2] For example, we know that agricultural operations take place in this order: fertilizing the soil, planting the seed, growth of

2. Kendall and Lazarsfeld (1950), Hirschi and Selvin (1966), and others want to make time order the basic and conclusive method of deciding the direction of causal flows, but we argue to the contrary in the postscript to Chapter 35.

the plant. Given that knowledge, we know that planting cannot be a hidden third factor that causes both fertilizing and harvesting.

D. EXAMINING FOR MULTIVARIATE CAUSATION

This type of causal analysis seeks to overcome the multivariable obstacle discussed in Chapter 22—that, if you take into account only one of two or more important independent variables, you will come to misleading conclusions. An example given was the relationship between auto prices and auto sales; only after income and stock of cars are taken into account does it correctly appear that higher prices cause fewer rather than more auto sales. Another example was that the single-independent-variable tabulation of accident rates by sex shows that a much smaller proportion of women drivers ever have accidents than do men.

Now we consider *how* to unravel multivariable causation. Table 22.3 shows further cross-classification of the accident-sex data. Now it appears that women are no safer drivers than are men. In another example, Table 25.3 shows the median salaries paid to economists with different amounts of education. If we exclude those with a Ph.D. degree, it appears that the more education an economist obtains the less money he or she will make. This situation seems quite improbable; general experience prompts one to look further into this association. But, in contrast to the hidden-factor case, a new variable (or variables) that will make the association between education and salary *spurious* is not sought. A sensible person

would guess that education will still have *some* causal effect on salary when other variables are taken into account. And so it turns out (see Table 25.4).

Table 25.4 cross-classifies by type of employer. *Within* each type of employment, amount of education and salary are *positively* associated. Together, amount of education and type of employment yield a better and more sensible cause-and-effect relationship than does either variable alone. (One proof that the explanation is better is that the range of salaries among amounts of education *within* each type of employment is greater than the simple range of salaries among amounts of education.)

This example is particularly interesting because the original relationship is *reversed;* the simple association shows an *inverse* relationship between education and salary, whereas the refined association is positive. This example shows the wisdom of further exploration into some negative or "zero" relationships, especially when the observed association does not make very good sense or fit well with theory.

If the number of observations is not very large, multiple regression is commonly used for this sort of work; the regression technique can often squeeze more information out of a limited number of observations than can cross-classification analysis.

As an example, let us consider extending into more dimensions the analysis of the strong relationship we know exists between education and income. We might hypothesize that income is the result—directly or indirectly—of occupation (higher-status occupations may have higher incomes), education (those with more schooling get better-paying jobs), experience (those with more experience may make more money), and family background (those from well-off families may do better than those who grew up in poor families). Figure 25.1a shows how we might diagram the possibility that all the variables have a strong direct effect on income. The arrows indicate direction of influ-

TABLE 25.3   Salaries of Economists at Different Education Levels, 1966

Degree	Median Reported Salary
Ph.D.	$13,500
Master's	12,000
Bachelor's	14,700
Less than bachelor's	16,500

TABLE 25.4   Salaries of Economists, by Degree and Type of
Employer, 1966

Degree; Type of Employer	Median Annual Salary
Educational institutions	
Ph.D. degree	$14,000
Master's degree	10,500
Bachelor's degree	11,900
Federal government	
Ph.D. degree	16,200
Master's degree	13,800
Bachelor's degree	13,400
Other governments	
Ph.D. degree	16,600
Master's degree	11,500
Bachelor's degree	12,000
Nonprofit organizations	
Ph.D. degree	18,500
Master's degree	14,000
Bachelor's degree	14,000
Industry–business	
Ph.D. degree	20,000
Master's degree	14,000
Bachelor's degree	15,000
Less than bachelor's degree	18,000
Self-employed	
Master's degree	18,000
Bachelor's degree	18,000

ence (causality); education and family background probably affect income, but an adult's income is not likely to affect his or her prior education or family background. The regression coefficients measure the impact of the independent variables on the dependent variable while taking the effects of the others into account. Statistically, we are answering questions such as the following: If two people have the same family background, the same education, and the same occupation, but different amounts of experience, will the amount of experience affect their incomes?

Figure 25.1b takes another step. If a coefficient in the equation for income shows a small effect, we can erase the arrow leading from its independent variable to income, indicating that there is probably no *direct* effect of the independent variable on income. But there may be an indirect effect. Family background might not affect income directly once the other factors are taken into account, but it might still affect, say, education, which in turn affects income. This we see in Figure 25.1c.

Qualitative variables such as sex and country of origin can also be handled within the framework of multiple regression with the device called "dummy variables." With this device you simply translate yes on a dimension into a 1, and no into 0. For sex, you can code those who are females as 1, and those who are not (males) as 0; then you proceed with the analysis just as with any other variable. The coefficient of the dummy variable for sex—and no-

FIGURE 25.1

(a)

(b)

(c)

tice that there is only *one* variable for the *two* sex categories—may then be interpreted as the mean difference on the dependent variable between males and females when all the other variables in the multiple regression are held constant.

When there are more than two qualitative categories on the dimension—for example, countries of origin—then the dummy-variable idea is ingeniously extended as follows: Assume that we are dealing with just three countries—Canada, the United States, and Mexico. We can first code as one variable whether or not a person is from Canada; the no's or 0s include people from the United States and Mexico. We then make a second variable doing the same for the United States, with people for both Canada and Mexico no. But—importantly—we do *not* also make a third variable

for Mexico, because anyone who is no for both Canada and the United States must be from Mexico. (This means that the third variable contains no new information; including such a variable will confuse the computer.)

2. Evaluating the Strength and Importance of Observed Relationships

A relationship between variables is usually worth attending to only if it is large enough to significantly increase our scientific understanding or if it helps make policy decisions. As a mail-order businessman put it when discussing tests of advertisements: Look for differences that scream, not differences that whisper. His point was that if you have two advertisements that differ little in their selling power, the difference is not worth attending to; rather, you should seek a new advertisement that is *much* better than the old one. The other side of the same coin is that finding a possible relationship to be small or nonexistent can be important if most people expect the relationship to be large. The Coleman Report on American education became famous because "The large differences between educational resources available to whites and those available to blacks and other minorities that everyone *knew* existed were not found. . . . What everyone knew to be true was *not* true. It was rather as if Coleman and his colleagues had just returned from the circumnavigation of a world everyone knew to be flat" (Aaron, 1978: 76).

The development of statistics to test whether differences and relationships exist *at all* has had an unfortunate side effect in this connection. Hypothesis-testing statistics tell people *whether* there is a difference (or relationship). They draw attention away from the *size* of the difference (or the strength of a relationship). The time has come to restore the balance: "The psychologist owes it to himself to determine not only whether an association exists between two variables—an association which may often be so small as to be trivial—but also to determine the probable magnitude of the association" (Dunnette, 1966: 350).

The size of a difference is obvious: If one type of fertilizer produces 120 bushels of corn per acre and another fertilizer produces 110 bushels at the same cost, the difference is ten bushels. Notice that here it is the *absolute* difference that is important—ten bushels—not the relative difference 10/110 or 10/120.

An example of the phony use of difference data occurred some years ago in the Great Tar Derby in cigarette advertising. *Reader's Digest* tested the quantity of tar in each brand of cigarette and found very slight differences among them. But *some* brand had to be lowest—which Old Golds was. The advertising for Old Golds immediately began to shout that Old Golds was "lowest in tars according to an im-

partial *Reader's Digest* test." This claim was true, but it was also meretricious and deceptive, for the difference between Old Golds and other brands really amounted to nothing. (A government agency eventually killed this Old Golds advertising, but not before the damage had been done.)

Evaluating the strength of a *relationship* is not so obvious. The best measure is usually the *accuracy of prediction* yielded by the relationship. If a particular entrance examination predicts with 80 per cent accuracy whether a student will succeed in or flunk out of a given institution and if, without the aid of the examination, you could predict with only 60 per cent accuracy (that is, if 60 per cent of all entering students do succeed), then the relationship between success and test score is big enough to be important. One way of thinking about this difference is in terms of its absolute size: With the examination 20 per cent of the students will be classified correctly who would otherwise be classified incorrectly. Another measure of the test's usefulness is that it improves prediction by $(80\%-60\%)/60\% = 33\%$. If another test predicts with 81 per cent accuracy, the difference between the two tests is too small to be important (though you certainly should use the 81 per cent accuracy test if there is no other difference between the two tests).

The strength of a *quantitative* relationship between two variables (in contrast to the yes-no relationship of the entrance test) may be measured by the improvement in capacity to correctly predict the dependent variable with the aid of the regression relationship, as compared to predictions made without it. Consider Figure 25.2. If one is to predict income from the distribution of people's incomes alone, the best prediction for a given individual is the mean of the group. The size of the deviations may be seen in the distances measured from each income point to the horizontal mean-income line. With the aid of the regression

FIGURE 25.2   One-Variable Versus Two-Variable Analysis (Hypothetical Data for People on a Block)

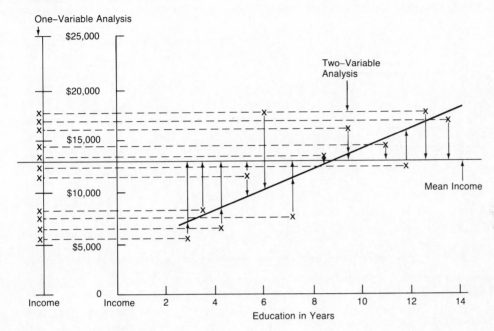

line, one can predict by using it instead of the mean-income line. It is clear from the measured deviations in Figure 25.2 that the differences between people's actual incomes and their predicted incomes are much smaller if one predicts on the basis of their education rather than on the basis of mean income alone.

The improvement in prediction that one obtains from a regression depends on two factors: (1) The steepness of the regression line, and (2) the variation remaining around the regression line. We see in hypothetical Figure 25.3a that even though education explains all of income, the regression analysis does not improve the accuracy of prediction very much because there is relatively little variation in income. In Figure 25.3c education aids prediction of income considerably because there is relatively much variation in income, and much (though not most) of the variation is explained by edu-

cation. In Figure 25.3b education explains income almost completely, and there is considerable variation in income; in this situation the regression analysis is most useful.

Now let us get a bit more precise. In the context of multiple regression—which is rapidly becoming the accepted mode of statistical analysis in the social sciences—you measure a relationship's policy importance (as distinguished from its scientific importance) with the unstandardized regression coefficient. The unstandardized coefficient tells you how many units of change you can expect in the dependent variable for a one-unit change in the independent variable, holding the other variables constant. For an example such as Figure 25.2 the regression tells you how many units of additional income one can expect from an additional year of education. This knowledge can be useful to an individual deciding about a ca-

FIGURE 25.3

reer, or to a country making a policy decision about how much to invest in an educational system.

Important points to notice: (1) The units in which the coefficient is measured depend on the units in which the variables are measured. If income is measured in units of hundreds of dollars, the coefficient will be a hundred times as large as if income is measured in single dollars. (2) The coefficient applies only to the par-

ticular place and moment for which the data are collected; the coefficient in the income-and-education example may well differ among places with different educational, social, and economic systems.

Usually the independent variables will correlate with each other (except in some experimental research). When the correlation between two (or more) independent variables is *very* high—as happens often with time-series data—the research may be afflicted with the dread disease known as multicollinearity (or just collinearity). Then one cannot freely talk about the effect of one independent variable on the dependent variable "controlling" for the effect of the other; because the two independent variables move in tandem, you cannot really "control" one as the other varies. A number of bad things then happen: the coefficients for the collinear variables may not make sense, even having the "wrong" sign; they will be hard to interpret; they will be unstable, varying greatly from one sample to another; and they may not even be accurate arithmetically, because multicollinearity causes problems for computers. For example, when one of us wanted to find out how changes in the incomes of blacks were affected by their education and by whites' prejudice, it turned out that measures of education and prejudice were almost perfectly correlated over time. It was therefore impossible to say how much of the improvement in blacks' incomes was due to their getting more education, and how much was due to the fact that whites were discriminating less (Burstein, 1979).

What can you do? If your goal is prediction rather than causal analysis, you can proceed blithely, because predictions are unaffected by multicollinearity. But if you are trying to understand the relative causal importance of the highly related variables, there is no good cure. You may be able to get more data and hope that the variables will be less highly correlated in the expanded set. If you have available a fairly large amount of data, you can break up your sample into two or more subsamples, and by examining how the coefficients vary, you may be able to get a better understanding of their relative importance. The use of "ridge regression" and other techniques too complex to present here may help. Usually, however, about all you can do is to drop all but one of the multicollinear variables from the equation; which to include and which to leave out is a matter of sound theoretical judgment and ex-

perience (a practical guide is Rao and Miller, 1971: 46–52; a sophisticated treatment is Belsley, Kuh, and Welsch, 1980).

3. The Tension Between Facts and Theory or Hypothesis

Sometimes the meeting of facts and hypothesis is a lovely wedding. The facts confirm the hypothesis, which in turn fits into the theory; the scientist is then as happy as a honeymooner.

Less happily, much of the time the facts that you observe do not sharply confirm your hypothesis. Often the situation is rather indeterminate, and you cannot tell whether the data do or do not support the hypothesis. In this case, you may collect more data to clarify the situation.

Even worse (as far as your state of mind goes, anyway), the data may slap your hypothesis smack in the face. And then you have some decisions to make. One possibility is to accept the facts as correct and the hypothesis as incorrect; this may not be a disaster, because the overturning of your hypothesis may itself be an important advance, as is often true in experimental psychology.

Another possibility is to modify your hypothesis so that it takes account of some conflicting facts but still points in the same general direction. For example, one of us thought he noticed an absence of Cadillacs among the cars in Yellowstone State Park, and hypothesized that rich people—as characterized by Cadillac ownership—do not go to national parks for vacations. Then he and his wife did a casual count of the proportion of Cadillacs they actually saw, and there were, indeed, Cadillacs to be seen, apparently contradicting his hypothesis. But then he thought he noticed that the Cadillacs were *old* ones. If so, he could salvage his hypothesis for the time being, by amending it to say that rich people, characterized by owning *new* Cadillacs, do not go to national parks.

Amending one's hypothesis can be a useful step. But it can also be a way of fooling oneself.

After excluding old Cadillacs from consideration, they again surveyed the cars and still noticed some new Cadillacs. But he thought he noticed that the new Cadillacs were *local*, from Montana. By excluding them as atypical, he might still save the hypothesis.

One could continue on this way for a long time, progressively modifying the hypothesis to remove discrepancies between it and the facts. But the final point will probably be either a confirmed hypothesis that is so narrow that it has practically no meaning, or a hypothesis that is confirmed for a small sample but that is specious and not true for a larger sample. More on this last point in the next chapter.

4. Summary

Sometimes the task of analysis is to sort out the relationships among a complex set of data, and sometimes to seek new hypotheses about relationships within a set of data. These tasks, in contrast to the analysis of simple relationships, are the subject of this chapter.

Ideas for new relationships may come from everyday experience, or from the body of theory, or from saturation in a body of data collected for other purposes. One must beware the danger that in any large body of data many apparent relationships may appear by chance.

Finding the meaningful relationships within a complex set of variables requires close study of them. Comparing cross-classifications and regressions that are run in several ways can often throw light on the causal network.

The goal of an analysis usually is to discover relationships that are sizable, improve predictive accuracy, and are causal. Sometimes finding little or no relationship between variables can be important, if the relationship is expected to be large.

EXERCISES

1. Suppose you have a regression equation in which the dependent variable is income, and the independent variables are education, occupation, experience, and family background. You find that the coefficient of the family background variable is close to zero. Does this mean that family background has no effect at all on income? Why or why not?
2. Find an example in the literature of a relationship that is statistically significant but too small to be useful or interesting.
3. Cities with high crime rates often have more police officers per capita than cities with low crime rates. Does this mean that having more police officers causes crime to increase? What might it mean instead? Draw figues like those in Sections 1c–d to describe your hypotheses.
4. Sometimes a relationship is large and helps you understand something, but has little relevance for behavior because nothing can be done to change the variable. An example is the relationship between rainfall and crop growth. Other times a relationship is large and influences behavior; knowing that there is a relationship between fertilizer use and crop growth leads farmers to use fertilizer. Think of another example of a relationship that is large but not likely to influence behavior and one of a relationship that is large and may influence behavior.
5. Give an example of a situation in which prediction is severely limited by major changes about which it is not sensible to assume *ceteris paribus*.

ADDITIONAL READING

S. Cole's description of causal analysis (1980, Chap. 2) includes some amusing examples.

Tufte's (1974) discussion of regression analysis is very good, particularly the material on improvements in prediction and the meaning of coefficients.

Chatterjee and Price (1977) show how to deal with many of the problems raised in this chapter.

Uses of Various Analytic Statistics

26

Statistics courses—this book, too—teach you how to calculate various analytic statistics such as measures of correlation and statistical significance, unstandardized and standardized regression coefficients, elasticities, path analysis, and so on. But learning *when and where* to use these analytic statistics usually comes only with painful blunders. This chapter offers some guidance to ease the bumps. We will consider the various statistics in the order in which you are likely to use them in a study of causal relationships, which is the commonest context for statistical exercises in the social sciences.

Please notice that our aim in this chapter is not to explain the individual statistics themselves; though a bit of explanation is necessary, the main task is to show the *order* in which the statistics can be best used, and the *relationships* of one to the other of them.

1. Simple Correlations

The first statistics that you should look at are the correlations between variables that you think may be causally related, either directly or indirectly. (You can obtain these correlations with every standard package of computer programs that you are likely to work with.) By convention, a correlation coefficient close to 1 or −1 means a strong relationship, in contrast to a correlation close to zero, which implies a weak relationship (see Chapters 25 and 33).

Theory tells you which variables' correlations you should look at first. But after you have followed whatever guidance your theory offers, you should then look for unexpected information in the data. To do so, you should seek variables that are strongly correlated with the variable that you wish to explain; the former are candidates to be independent variables in your subsequent analysis. A strong correlation between a pair of independent variables is a sign that they may be proxies for each other, or are sequentially related in some part of the causal chain.

How high a correlation is "strong"? This depends on the context. There is a joke that the tragedy in educational psychology is that no variables are related at all, whereas the tragedy in economics is that all variables are perfectly related. That is, correlations in educational psychology are often close to zero, because the data is often cross-sectional, including much uncontrolled variability among individuals, and educational approaches differ little in their effects. It is thus difficult to show that anything has much impact on the dependent variable. Correlations in economics, however, are often close to 1, because the data are often aggregate time series that move together. Here, everything may affect the dependent variable, and the coefficients often provide little help in understanding what is happening. A correlation of 0.6 might seem low to an economist and amazingly high to an educational psychologist. The point is that no general rule can be useful about meaningful sizes of correlation coefficients; for guidance, consult someone who is experienced with similar data.

2. Simple Linear Regression

Let's say that, for theoretical reasons backed up by your inspection of the correlation coefficients, there is only one plausible candidate to be your independent variable. Your next step is likely to be a "linear least squares bivariate regression." The "bivariate" means that only two variables are included, one dependent and one independent. The "least squares" means that the criterion used to fit the regression line to the observation is that the sum of the squared perpendicular distances from observations to the line of regression be as small as

possible; one could find such a least-squares line by trial and error, but everyone uses a short-cut mathematical algorithm that the computer executes for you. The "linear" means that the regression line is straight rather than logarithmic or some other curved shape.

If there is more than one candidate for independent variable, it is often wise to run bivariate regressions using each of these candidates as part of the overall process of unraveling the causal nexus; more about this in the discussion of path analysis.

3. Tests of Statistical Significance

Standard statistical computer programs calculate a variety of statistics, some automatically and some on special request; the "t ratio" usually comes whether you ask for it or not. This—and other "tests of statistical significance"—is an indication of how likely it is that a relationship that strong or stronger would be observed by chance in your sample, even though the "true" relationship in the population was zero (more on this in Chapter 33). Now—early in the analysis—you should consider an appropriate test of significance as a *filter* to separate useful variables from those that should be dropped. If the test shows that the observed relationship is not significantly different from zero, that will often be a sign to you to go no further empirically with this independent variable, *unless* theory predicted that the variable would have an effect—in which case the absence of statistical significance may be an important matter to report. Tests of significance in multivariate analyses as well as bivariate analyses may be thought of and used in the same way: as filters to screen out variables that are not likely to be worth considering further in the empirical analysis. (Theoretical and statistical considerations sometimes dictate that you continue to include in the regressions those variables you had expected to be important, however; they may prove to have effects not detected in the early analyses, and it may be important to show people the variables have no effect, if that is how the analysis turns out.)

Frequently—much too frequently—researchers simply report that a relationship or an independent variable has passed the test of significance, thereby confirming a hypothesis, and stop there. Common as it is, this is poor practice. It is all-important to go further and say *how much scientific or economic importance* the relationship has. A relationship that is merely statistically significant is simply not zero; it may nevertheless have little ability to explain the variation in the dependent variable or power to control it to a meaningful degree, and is therefore almost no discovery at all. (Indeed, the relationship between almost every pair of empirical, sociological, and economic variables will appear statistically significant if the sample is large enough.)

When you are examining the relationship between the dependent variable and many independent variables separately, you must remember that a few among a large number of such relationship tests will appear to be "significant," just by chance. Five significance tests out of 100 will appear to be "significant at the 5 per cent level" even when they are actually zero in the population, because that is one way of stating what the "5 per cent level" means—five times out of 100 the test will erroneously show the relationship to be significant.

What should you do if a relationship that you think is important is *not* strong enough to pass through the filter of the test of statistical significance? Classical statistical theory says that you should say "Begone" and banish the variable from your thinking, like a king with a recalcitrant subject. But in fact scientists do not, and most of the time probably should not, act that way. Rather, they are likely to check to see if there is an error somewhere, or if there is another empirical proxy for the same variable that may work better. Of course, to avoid falling into dangerous misconclusions you should

also check for errors—and equally diligently—in the variables that *do* work.

If the variable comes close but still fails to be reasonably significant statistically (notice that we have given no numbers here), then you may reasonably say that if the sample were larger, the variable might then appear to be statistically significant, and you might even enlarge the sample to see for yourself. But aside from that tactic, decency should impel you to have no further truck with variables that are not statistically significant.

4. The Proportion of Variance Explained (R^2)

If your regression passes the test of statistical significance, look next at the R^2, which is the square of the correlation coefficient (r) in the simple bivariate case. It measures the proportion of the total "variance" (a specifically defined measure of variation) in the dependent variable that the independent variable "explains." To put it (crudely) another way, the R^2 is an indicator of how much more accurately you could determine the value of the dependent variable with, compared to without, the help of the independent variable. But here a red-flag warning is needed: There are a variety of devices that can be (and too often are) used to boost the R^2 artificially, just to impress others that your findings are important; these devices an investigator learns too soon, and we need not list the malfeasances here. But if R^2 is used sensibly, with theoretically reasonable variables, the higher the R^2, the better your explanation. And the better the causal explanation, the nearer you are to the end of your task.

5. The Unstandardized Regression Coefficient

If a relationship is strong enough to pass a test of statistical significance, then you will often wish to know how much of an effect a given change in the independent variable will make in the dependent variable. If this is your concern, you should then examine the unstandardized regression coefficient, which is a statistic that tells you the practical implications of the relationship—for example, how big a change in the number of burglaries or autos sold that an increase of $1,000 in per capita income will make, or how much a person's earnings will increase for each additional year of education acquired. The unstandardized regression coefficient is especially relevant when you are interested in knowing the quantitative relationship for policy purposes (those focusing on scientific explanation are often more interested in R^2).

6. The Elasticity

Sometimes you want to know the quantitative relationship for policy purposes, but you want to know it *in general*, without having to worry about the units the variables are measured in.

For example, suppose you want to estimate the effect of a change in per capita income on burglaries or auto sales in any representative place, or any similar time, without specifying details of the time or place. One way to do this is to determine the *percentage change* in the dependent variable that you may expect for a given *percentage change*—usually one per cent—in the independent variables. That is, you can discuss change in terms of percentages rather than dollars, francs, or any other particular unit. This statistic—frequently used in economics but seldom elsewhere in the social sciences—is called an elasticity. It is immediately obtained when you measure variables in terms of logarithms, because the logarithm is a percentage-change concept. But an elasticity can also be computed from a linear or any other regression with a bit of arithmetic, keeping in mind that the elasticity is affected by the form of the relationship fitted.

For example, you might find that an increase in income of 1 per cent per person in a country causes an increase of 1/2 per cent in widget sales. And you might then speculate that the same will be true of other countries. You can examine this proposition—or even use it to predict, if you deem it wise—without needing any additional information, such as the value of the money units in the various countries, whereas such a conversion would be needed for the use of an unstandardized regression coefficient.

7. Multivariate Regressions: The Standardized Regression Coefficient (Beta), and Other Statistics

When there are interrelationships among the independent variables and the amount of data is limited, you are likely to employ multivariate methods to help you sort out the interrelationships, and to learn the effect of one or more independent variables with other independent variables "held constant" statistically. The multiple regression is the standard device used for this purpose in causal studies, when multiple cross-classification is not feasible due to lack of data.

The standardized regression coefficient (beta) is often used to assess the relative importance of the various independent variables in a multiple regression. Unlike the unstandardized coefficients, whose size depends on the arbitrary units of the independent variables— for example, whether a money variable is measured in dollars, cents, or rubles—the standardized coefficients are made comparable by expressing each observation on each variable as a proportion of a measure of its variation on that variable (the measure being the standard deviation). That is, each variable is transformed from the units in which it is originally measured into units of standard deviation. Each standardized variable can then be interpreted as a measure of the proportion of the total variation in the dependent variable that is explained by that independent variable.

The beta can be used—just as is the R^2 in a bivariate regression, and in fact it is numerically and conceptually the same as the R^2 in that case—as an index of the proportion of the variation in the independent variable that the particular dependent variable explains. In a multivariate regression the beta measures the proportion of the dependent variable's variation that a particular independent variable explains when the other variables in the regression are held constant statistically.

Betas are frequently used by sociologists, but almost never by economists—perhaps because economists are accustomed to talk theoretically of elasticities. Betas are used in a somewhat more complex fashion in path analysis, but we can defer that topic until later.

The unstandardized regression coefficient and the elasticity have much the same meaning in multivariate analysis as they do in bivariate regressions, except that in the multivariate context they are interpreted as showing their effects with the other variables allowed for.

8. Measures of Variance Explanation in Multiple Regression

In a multiple regression the R^2 measures the proportion of the variation (variance) in the dependent variable that *all* the independent variables account for *together*.

Often you will want to compare various models—various sets of independent variables—to see which model should be preferred. The R^2 for a regression with any given set of variables will always be lower than for a regression with the same set of variables *plus* any other variables. To allow for this automatic inflation of the R^2 with more variables, "adjusted R^2" measures that compensate for the number of variables are calculated by some computer programs for regression analysis. Whether such measures are available or not, keep in mind that it is not usually worthwhile to add a variable to your equation if the R^2 goes up by only a small amount.

9. Summary

Statistics courses usually teach you the nature of various statistics, but not when to use them. This chapter discusses what the various statistical tools can be used for, and especially about how their uses fit together. Correlations guide you in choosing variables for further analysis. Significance tests filter out variables that turn out not to matter. The proportion of the variance explained tells something about the overall scientific power of the regression. Unstandardized regression coefficients provide information for policy decisions. Standardized regression coefficients indicate the explanatory power of the independent variables. And the elasticity is a measure of covariation that is independent of the particular units of measurement in various settings.

EXERCISES

1. Think of a study in which you would use significance tests as a filter, eliminating variables not significantly related to the dependent variable from further consideration. Think of a case in which you would *not* ignore a variable just because its relationship with the dependent variable was not statistically significant.

2. Find a research report or article that describes the results of a regression analysis. Does the author use standardized coefficients? elasticities? unstandardized coeffi-

cients? Why do you think he or she made that choice? What can the author learn from the coefficient chosen, rather than from another type?

3. Why is a large R^2 generally better than a small R^2? Why should you not rely on R^2 alone to tell you how satisfactory your analysis is?

ADDITIONAL READING

Tufte (1974), and Chatterjee and Price (1977) provide examples of how to deal with some of the issues discussed in this chapter.

An Exposition
of Path Analysis

1. Why Path Analysis?

Suppose you want to explain a set of relationships—how people's incomes are affected by the amount of education they have, their occupations, their parents' education and occupations, and the number of brothers and sisters they have, for example. What will you do first?

A most valuable first step is to diagram the likely "paths" of causal connections among the variables. Drawing such a path diagram forces you to clarify your thoughts about the web of causal influences, thoughts that might otherwise remain in vague form. But later we also go further with path analysis, to show precisely how an initial set of variables influences other variables, and how both sets then affect the dependent variable.

Perhaps the most important function of the path-analytic scheme, however, is that it provides a rational system for organizing and reporting the results of a causal analysis. Typically, the investigator using public data finds that even a small handful of likely variables *can* be related in a very large number of ways. He or she needs guideposts to help decide which relationships to analyze, and in which order. Although the results of path analyses provide quantitative estimates of paths of causal influence, the major reason for doing a path analysis is usually to clarify your mental picture of the causal system and provide a way of organizing your work.

2. Steps in a Path Analysis

Our problem is to understand the determinants of a dependent variable. The variables and the correlations among them are the raw material for the explanation. Path analysis is a way to organize the analysis of a set of variables so that we can explain *how* the variables are related to each other. The steps are these: (1) *choosing variables* we think affect the dependent variable; (2) *developing hypotheses* about the causal relationships among those variables; (3) *drawing a picture* of the relationships—the "path diagram"; and (4) *using regression analysis* to show how each variable influences other variables and how strongly it affects them.

A. VARIABLES AND HYPOTHESES

Suppose you want to explain variance in people's incomes. The first step would be to decide which variables you think have influence; to keep things simple, let's say you decide that a person's income is affected only by years of education and the status of occupation. The next step is to think up hypotheses about how education and occupation might affect income. It is usually easy to think up several hypotheses about the relationships among even a small number of variables. For example, getting more education and getting into a higher-status occupation might both have a *direct* effect on income, independently of each other; that is, people with more education might tend to earn higher incomes than those with less, even when they are in the same occupation, and people in higher-status occupations might tend to earn more than those in lower-status occupations, even when they have the same amount of education. Alternatively, education might have an *indirect* rather than a direct effect on income; this would be the case, for example, if education affected occupational status, which in turn affected income, but education had no effect on income once occupation was taken into account ("controlled").

B. DRAWING A PICTURE OF THE RELATIONSHIPS

After you begin developing some hypotheses, you can keep them clear by drawing them in the form of a "path diagram" like Figure 27.1a. In the diagram, an arrowhead represents a hypothesis about causality. An arrow (or "path"— hence the name, "path analysis") pointing from education to occupation means that we hypothesize that a person's education has an impact on his occupation, but (since the arrow points only one way), his occupation has no impact on his education. The fact that there is no arrow connecting education and income means that you speculate that there is no direct relationship between education and income once oc-

cupation is taken into account (the second hypothesis above).

An alternative model, presented in the path diagram in Figure 27.1b, is one in which education is believed to affect income both indirectly, through education (as in Figure 27.1a), *and* directly as well. Other possible models include one in which education is believed to influence both occupation and income, but occupation is believed not to affect income (Figure 27.1c), and one in which education and occupation are related, but, while both are believed to cause income, neither is said to cause the other (Figure 27.1d). (That is what the two-headed arrow means—that the two variables are related but we are not interested in making any statements about cause. Variables connected by two-headed arrows are considered "exogenous" for purposes of the analysis, meaning that they are taken as given and are assumed not to be correlated with other variables not included in the model but related to the dependent variable.)

How do you decide which arrows to include and which way to point the arrowheads? This is a matter of theory and common sense, not statistics. Path analysis is a way of getting you to formalize your ideas so that they will be precise, testable, and easily communicated, but, as Duncan has written, "Your models can be no better than your ideas, even if trying to put your ideas in the form of models *may* (if yours is the kind of mind that works this way, but not otherwise) stimulate the flow of ideas" (1975: 151).

C. USING REGRESSION ANALYSIS

The path diagrams are pictures of hypotheses that show which variables are related to which other variables (having an arrow versus not having one), which causes which (the direction of the arrow), and which relationships are direct and which indirect. To test the hypotheses, you use regression analysis, regressing the dependent variable and the other

FIGURE 27.1

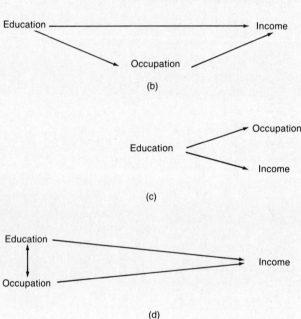

Education ⟶ Occupation ⟶ Income

(a)

Education ⟶ Income

Occupation

(b)

Occupation

Education

Income

(c)

Education

Occupation ⟶ Income

(d)

"endogenous" variables—those to be explained within the model, such as occupation in Figure 27.1a—on the exogenous variables and on the other endogenous variables believed to cause them. In most path analyses the models are assumed to be "recursive"; that is, two-way causation between endogenous variables is assumed to be so small that we can safely disregard it. The "path coefficients," which are measures of the strength of relationship put next to the arrows, are the *standardized regression coefficients* for the equations. Where a path coefficient is zero, we may eliminate the arrow from the path diagram and assume that there is no direct link between the independent variable and the dependent variable.

Thus, for the model in Figure 27.1a, income would be regressed on occupation and education, and occupation would be regressed on education. (You could just write out the equations and forget about the pictures, but the pictures make it a lot easier to keep track of what you are doing and explain the results.) To decide between the model in Figure 27.1a and that in 27.1b, you would regress income on occupation and education; if the coefficient for education were zero (or so very close to zero as to be not statistically significant), the diagram in Figure 27.1a is probably more consistent with reality than the model in Figure 27.1b, where there is an arrow directly from education to income.

When the set of relationships is complex enough so that you have some variables influencing another variable, which in turn influences others (as in Figures 27.1a and 27.1b, and, in more detail, below), you proceed as follows to get the clearest picture of the direct and indirect causal relationships: Look for endogenous variables—that is, variables that are to be explained within the model—that are not influenced by any other endogenous variables, and see how they are influenced by the exogenous variables (in a regression equation). Then look for an endogenous variable that is influenced by all the variables you have already considered, but which does not influence them, and regress it on the exogenous variables and the endogenous variable you have already analyzed. Then one by one, add the endogenous variables in the order in which they influence others but are not influenced by them until, finally, you get to the "ultimate" dependent variable. A more detailed example follows.

3. Doing a Path Analysis

Now let's get a little more realistic, and consider a model with more than three variables and some actual statistical results. Figure 27.2 presents a path diagram for a model in which sons' incomes are predicted by years of education, occupational status, father's education and occupation, and number of siblings. Note that much of the hard work has already been done in drawing the diagram; that is, Alwin and Hauser (1975) decided which variables were exogenous and which were endogenous, where the arrows were to be, and which way they were to point. There is no mechanical way to do this, though some of the choices are rather obvious (a father's occupational status can affect his son's education, but the reverse is not likely to occur).

We start work with our "model," repre-

FIGURE 27.2   Causal Diagram for a Linear Recursive Model

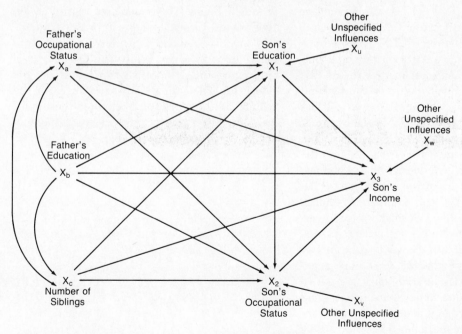

Source: Duane Alwin and Robert Hauser. "The Decomposition of Effects in Path Analysis." *American Sociological Review*, 40 (February 1975), 38.

TABLE 27.1   Coefficients of Variables in Standard Form in Reduced-Form and Structural Equations of a Model of Socioeconomic Achievement: Nonblack U.S. Men with Nonfarm Background in the Experienced Civilian Labor Force, Aged 35 to 44 in March 1962.

Predetermined Variable	Equation and dependent variable					
	(1)	(2)	(3)	(4)	(5)	(6)
	X_1	X_2	X_2	X_3	X_3	X_3
X_a	.2781	.2842	.1266	.1746	.0903	.0492
X_b	.1985	.1199	.0074	.1120	.0518	.0494
X_c	−.2053	−.1703	−.0540	−.0998	−.0376	−.0200
X_1			.5668		.3033	.1193
X_2						.3247

Note: See text for definition of symbols.

Source: Based on correlations in Duncan, Featherman, and Duncan, 1972: 38.

sented by the path diagram in Figure 27.2, which describes the hypothetical web of causation among the variables; the main concern is explaining the variance among sons' incomes (see Table 27.1 for a description of the sample; the example is taken from Alwin and Hauser, 1975, which in turn is derived from Duncan, Featherman, and Duncan, 1972: 34–45).

In the diagram, we see that X_1 (sons' education) influences sons' occupation (X_2) and sons' income (X_3) but is not influenced by them. This means that we probably want to understand what influences sons' education (because it has an impact on income), but we can ignore sons' occupation and income when doing so. We therefore regress sons' education (X_1) on the other variables we hypothesize may influence it, namely fathers' occupational status (X_a), fathers' education (X_b), and number of siblings (X_c), to learn the influences of these three variables from the resulting standardized regression coefficients (betas), shown in column 1 of Table 27.1 and in Figure 27.3. Fathers' occupational status and education have a positive effect on sons' education (as expected), and number of siblings has a negative effect (meaning that sons with more brothers and sisters tend not to get as far in school as those from smaller families).

Now we move on to use our new knowledge about sons' education (X_1) to explain sons' occupational status (X_2). First, we regress sons' occupational status on just fathers' occupational status (X_a), fathers' education (X_b), and number of siblings (X_c); the results are shown in column 2 and in Figure 27.4. Then we regress X_2 on those three variables and *also* on sons' education (X_1). These results are shown in column 3 and Figure 27.5. By comparing the results of the regression equation that included just the three original independent variables with the results of the equation including those plus sons' education, we increase our understanding of *how* the exogenous variables (X_a, X_b, X_c) af-

FIGURE 27.3

FIGURE 27.4

FIGURE 27.6

fect X_2. If they influence X_2 only because of their influence on X_1—that is, if all of their influence is *indirect*, then, when X_1 is added to the equation, their coefficients should fall to zero (moving from column 2 to column 3) because these path coefficients are measures of *direct* effect. If, however, the effect of the exogenous variables on X_2 is entirely direct and independent of X_1, then the coefficients would not change. The table shows that the coefficients of the exogenous variables do fall drastically. This suggests that father's education and occupation and son's number of siblings do affect son's income, but mostly *indirectly*, by affecting son's education, which in turn affects occupation and then income.

We can quantify these *indirect* paths from X_a, X_b and X_c to X_2 *through* X_1 by using an idea basic in path analysis: The indirect influence of

an antecedent variable (say, X_a) is measured as the coefficient of X_a in equations excluding all intermediate variables (such as X_1), *minus* the coefficient when the intermediate variable *is* in the regression. Here, the indirect effect of X_a on X_2 would be .2842 (as in column 2 of Table 27.1, for the equation *not* including X_1) minus .1266 (as in column 3 of the Table, for the equation *including* X_1), or .1576, as shown in Figure 27.6. We shall return to this idea later.

Now we can move on to use our new knowledge of X_1 and X_2 to explain X_3; this progressive onion-peeling is the distinctive aspect of path analysis, made possible by its recursive structure of no mutual influence. First we regress X_3 on the exogenous variables alone, with the results shown in column 4 of Table 27.1 and in Figure 27.7; we already see that none of them has a strong effect by itself. Then we

FIGURE 27.5

FIGURE 27.7

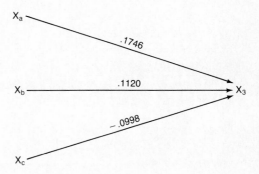

add X_1, and we see in column 5 and Figure 27.8 that the effects of the exogenous variables fall even further, while X_1's effect is reasonably large. Last, we add X_2 to the regression. We now see in column 6 and Figure 27.9 that sons' occupational status dominates the picture, X_1's residual effect is small, and the independent effect of the exogenous variables is virtually nonexistent.

So far the path diagram has given us a systematic procedure for our sequential regressions. But we also can go even further with a distinctive feature of the path analysis, decomposition of the total effect of an independent variable on the dependent variable into its direct effect and its indirect effect via other variables. We began this process earlier when we calculated the indirect effects of X_a, X_b, and X_c on X_2 through X_1 (Figure 27.6). Now let us proceed to calculate the indirect effects of the predetermined variables on X_3 through both X_1 and X_2, as summarized in Figure 27.10.

The *"total"* effect of, say, X_a on X_3 is its effect seen in column 4 and Figure 27.7 (beta = .1746) when only the exogenous variables are in the regression of X_3. ("Total" is in quotes to remind us that because we do not know the relationships among X_a, X_b, and X_c, we cannot attribute its so-called "total" effect uniquely to X_a). Its *direct* effect upon X_3, when X_1 and X_2 are also in the regression intermediating be-

FIGURE 27.9

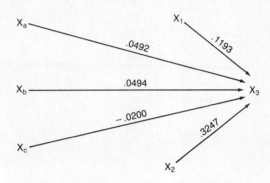

tween X_a and X_3, is .0492, as seen in column 6 and Figure 27.9.

The indirect effects of X_a via X_1 and X_2 may also be calculated with a bit more thinking. First, from the total effect (.1746) subtract the direct effect when X_1 (but not X_2) is allowed for (.0903 in column 5), to get .0843; this is the indirect effect through X_1. Now to get the indirect effect through X_2, we begin with the direct effect when X_1 (but not X_2) is allowed for (.0903), and from this subtract the direct effect when X_2 is also allowed for (.0492 in column 6 and Figure 27.9), leaving .0411 for the indirect effect through X_2. These calculations and the comparable calculations for the other variables, as shown in Table 27.2.

FIGURE 27.8

FIGURE 27.10

TABLE 27.2 Interpretations of Effects in a Model of Socioeconomic Achievement: Nonblack U.S. Men with Nonfarm Background in the Experienced Civilian Labor Force, Aged 35 to 44 in March 1962.

Dependent Variable	Predetermined Variable	Total Effect	Indirect Effects Via X_1	Indirect Effects Via X_2	Direct Effect
X_1	X_a	.2781	—	—	.2781
	X_b	.1985	—	—	.1985
	X_c	−.2053	—	—	−.2053
X_2	X_a	.2842	.1576	—	.1266
	X_b	.1199	.1125	—	.0074
	X_c	−.1703	−.1163	—	−.0540
	X_1	.5668	—	—	.5668
X_3	X_a	.1746	.0843	.0411	.0492
	X_b	.1120	.0602	.0024	.0494
	X_c	−.0998	−.0622	−.0176	−.0200
	X_1	.3033	—	.1840	.1193
	X_2	.3247	—	—	.3247

Note: See text for definitions of symbols. Data from Table 27.1

4. Summary

Path analysis is a program for analyzing causal relationships in a set of variables. It requires that a researcher spell out his or her hypotheses, and it provides a way to communicate them clearly in pictures as well as in equations, suggests how to test hypotheses, and provides a way to show how some variables influence others, both directly and indirectly. It is a useful way of organizing one's thinking when one can easily be overwhelmed by the number of ways even a small set of variables can be related to one another.

One begins a path analysis by choosing variables believed to affect the dependent variable and developing hypotheses about the causal relationships among the variables. The path diagram is a picture of the hypotheses. One then uses regression analysis to show how each variable influences other variables, and how strongly, beginning by analyzing the influences on the endogenous variables affected only by the exogenous variables, and gradually moving "forward" in the causal sequence until reaching the ultimate dependent variable.

EXERCISES

1. Think of a dependent variable in which you are interested and three independent variables that might explain it. How many *possible* causal models could there be with four variables? What *plausible* models can you think of, drawing on theory and common sense to develop hypotheses about causal ordering and the presence or absence of relationships? Draw path diagrams of three models you think are "best" and write the equations you would estimate to get the path coefficients.

2. Look back at Figure 27.1. Which model do you think is most plausible? Why? How would you use path analysis to see which model worked best?

3. What if you were interested in improving your grades and were trying to figure out what to do, and someone said, "That's easy. Grades depend on willingness to work hard, doing all the homework, going to class, native intelligence, taking easy courses, and getting to know the professor." How useful is this advice? Could you use path diagrams to help you think about what determines grades? How?

ADDITIONAL READING

Land (1968) and Duncan (1970, 1975) are very helpful in showing what can be learned from path analysis and related approaches.

Some Other Analytic Techniques

28

1. Investigation of Mutual Causation Between Dependent Variables
2. Multivariate Analysis of Qualitative Variables
3. Similarities and Dissimilarities Among Objects
4. Summary

The previous chapters described the most important and commonly used devices for thinking about and analyzing data. They enable you to handle most data you will run across, and most social scientists never use anything else. But you may run into situations in which none of the approaches described so far is appropriate. This chapter shows you that help is available. It focuses on techniques that are used often enough so that you should be aware of them.

1. Investigation of Mutual Causation Between Dependent Variables

Sometimes two variables in which you are interested probably affect each other. For example, we know that women in the labor force have fewer children than women not in the labor force. But what influences what? Does entering the labor force cause women to have fewer children? Are women with fewer children more likely to enter the labor force? Or both? And how strong are the causal influences? We are faced here with the difficult task of unraveling mutual causation.

If, in such a situation, we had data on successive very short time periods—month by month, for example—we could probably trace the effects back and forth relatively easily; the influences would not be perceived as simultaneous, and mutual causation would not be a difficult matter to resolve in simple ways.

Usually, however, we will not have data for very short time periods. Instead, we are likely to have data from a single survey on labor force participation and fertility at a particular time, so that we cannot readily learn much about mutual causation from information on these two variables alone. One might wonder why we cannot simply regress, say, women's labor force participation (WLFP hereafter) on fertility, or upon fertility plus women's education (ignoring other variables for simplicity) to learn the influence of fertility on WLFP, and then regress fertility on women's labor force participation (plus some other factors) to gauge the impact of WLFP on fertility. Intuitively, you may see that if WLFP causes fertility, and fertility causes WLFP, then some part of the WLFP you are using to explain fertility was *caused by* fertility, and you are basically using fertility to *explain itself* indirectly. Obviously, then, your estimate of the impact of WLFP will be larger than the "true" impact—your coefficient will be biased. More precisely, the factors that cause WLFP to be higher or lower in particular families, apart from the effects of fertility and education, are systematically related to fertility because of the feedback effect of WLFP on fertility.

To amplify this important but elusive point: Assume that WLFP is higher in some families just because jobs are more available in some communities than in others, a factor on which you have no data. But in those families in which WLFP is higher for this reason, fertility is then systematically lower because of the negative effect of WLFP upon fertility. This will be reflected in the coefficients of fertility in the sample regression, making it larger than would be shown by the "true" effect of fertility without this confusing feedback effect.

Let's try to see how this operates with a numerical example. Assume that adding an additional child would reduce the probability of a woman's being in the labor force by .2. Assume also that labor force participation reduces the average number of children by .4 children. Now assume that an industry moves to town, which increases the number of jobs open, and WLFP immediately goes up from say, .5 to .8. This would cause a reduction in the average number of children by $(.8 - .5)$ $(.4) = .12$ children per woman. But then the reduction in the number of children among those women will have a positive effect on their labor force participation in future years. (Being in the labor force is not a once-and-for-all decision.) These .12 fewer children in the average household will cause $(.12 \times .4) = .048$ greater WLFP. But in a single regression of fertility on WLFP in various communities, we will see not only the effect of the .12 fewer children from the .3 increased initial probability of working, but also the effect of the .048 greater WLFP due to the subsequent decline in fertility. And therefore the coefficient of WLFP would be "biased up-

ward," that is, it will show not only the effect of WLFP on fertility but also the effect of fertility on WLFP.

Various ways to get around this problem of mutual causation have been devised. The most common, easiest to understand, and perhaps the most general, is "two-stage least-squares" regression. The "least-squares" means that the regressions use the by-now-familiar principle of minimizing the sum of squared deviations from the regression lines. The "two-stage" means that two successive regressions are run, the first one in order to "purge" the second regression of the feedback effect. The key idea, as illustrated in the fertility-WLFP case, is as follows:

Women's education is clearly not affected by WLFP, because it is usually completed before a woman joins the labor force; that is, women's education can be considered exogenous in this context. (We can help make sure of this by limiting the analysis to women who are, say, 25 and over.) The amount of education a married woman has is a good predictor of whether she will be in the labor force, because it heavily influences the wage she can command; husband's income is another good predictor. Therefore, we first regress WLFP on woman's education alone and husband's income, and obtain an equation predicting WLFP as a function of education and husband's income.

Next we predict for each woman her likelihood of being in the labor force based on her years of education and her husband's income. And now—this is the key point—we use this *predicted* WLFP (and not the *actual* WLFP) as an independent variable in the fertility regression, along with other variables. This predicted WLFP is "purged" of the feedback effect of fertility on actual WLFP, because the variables used to predict it are not affected by fertility, and therefore the coefficient of the predicted WLFP is not biased. Of course, the relationship between predicted WLFP and fertility will not be as strong as the relationship between the actual WLFP and fertility, because there will be some random error in the predicted WLFP. But the size of the regression coefficient need not be affected too much by this sampling error if the sample is large enough—as it is, for example, in samples drawn from the U.S. Census.

The same device is used in reverse to learn how fertility affects WLFP. We first predict a woman's fertility on the basis of, say, her husband's education, religion, husband's income, and where she lives, and then we use this predicted fertility as a purged independent variable proxy for actual fertility. Its regression coefficient is an estimate of WLFP's effect on fertility, unbiased by the feedback effect of actual WLFP on actual fertility.

Having to run two equations to predict each dependent variable may seem rather complicated, but in fact the computations can be handled routinely in many computer programs. The difficult part is to think through how the analysis should be conducted, particularly deciding which variables to use to predict each dependent variable.

2. Multivariate Analysis of Qualitative Variables

Regression analysis is most appropriate when the variables are at least interval-scaled, and preferably ratio-scaled. We have already mentioned that when some of the independent variables are unordered categories, such as countries or different organizations people might belong to, each variable can be treated as a series of dummy variables scored 0,1, and those variables can be used in ordinary regression analysis (see Chapter 25). But what about when the *dependent* variable is categorical—for example, when we are interested in which brand of car people will buy—or when *all* the variables are categorical? When the dependent variable is categorical, you can use *discriminant function analysis*. When all the variables are categorical, you can use *log-linear analysis*.

A. DISCRIMINANT FUNCTION ANALYSIS

Often we want to know which *category* the observation will fit. Will it rain, snow, or be clear? Will a person vote for the Democrats, the Republicans, or stay home and not vote at all? Will a person buy a Ford, a Chevrolet, a Chyrsler, or a Toyota? Did a bone discovered by an anthropologist come from a chimpanzee, a human being, or some other kind of primate? We want to find a set of independent variables that enables us to predict well the outcome, and we want to describe how big an impact each variable has, controlling for the effects of all the others.

Where there are only two groups, the procedure is a simple variant on regression analysis. Suppose you want to know what distinguishes people who vote for the Democrats from those who vote for the Republicans (ignoring, for now, those who do not vote at all). You would score party choice as a 0,1 dummy dependent variable, and then regress that variable on independent variables you thought influenced party choice—maybe social class, religion, education, and degree of positive feeling for each candidate. Using the coefficients you get, you would then predict the score each person in your sample would get on the dependent variable. (We know that each would *actually* score either 0 or 1—Republican or Democrat—but, statistically, each person could come out anywhere in between.) Then we would find the *cutting point* between 0 and 1 that would provide the greatest accuracy of prediction. For example, it might be that all of the Democrats get a predicted score of .7 or more, and all of the Republicans get a score below .7. (There are some technical differences between these procedures and regression analysis, but they need not concern us.) This would mean that party choice could be predicted with perfect accuracy on the basis of the variables used—that is, you could discriminate perfectly between Republicans and Democrats.

More often, of course, you are not able to discriminate perfectly between the groups on the basis of the information available. It might be, for example, that 50 per cent of the Democrats get a predicted score—called the discriminant score—higher than .8, 90 per cent are higher than .7, and 100 per cent are higher than .5, while half the Republicans are below .4, 80 per cent are below .7, and 100 per cent are below .8. The analysis tells you which cutting point provides maximum separation between groups, so that the fewest errors of prediction would be made. In this case, the best cutting point might still be .7, but 10 per cent of the Democrats would be misclassified (because they scored below .7, like most Republicans), and so would 20 per cent of Republicans (because they scored above .7, like most Democrats). Nevertheless the analysis would provide the cutting point giving maximum accuracy of prediction, given the information available about all the people involved.

The situation becomes considerably more complicated when more than two groups are involved, but the basic idea is the same. Suppose you are a meteorologist wanting to predict tomorrow's precipitation (this example is taken from R. Miller, 1978). There are five possibilities: dry, a little rain, a little snow, rain, and snow. One way to make a prediction would be as follows: First, obtain information on local weather conditions associated with the five outcomes for lots of other times and places; possibly you think that barometric pressure, temperature, wind direction, and some other factors are relevant. Then calculate how to order the five outcomes in a way that provides the maximum separation among them along a dimension associated with the independent variables (as a practical matter, the computer will do the actual calculations, but you have to choose the variables and think about how they affect what you are interested in before telling the computer how to proceed). For example, say that the only independent variable is humidity. Then, if the outcomes are arranged along a dimension measuring humidity, it will probably turn out that when the humidity is below 20 per cent, it is likely to be dry; when the humidity is between 40 and 60 per cent, there is likely to be a little rain or a little snow; and when the humidity is over 80 per cent, there is likely to be a lot of rain or snow (maybe between 20 and 40 per cent humidity, there is a 50-50 chance of dry weather or a little precipitation, and between 60 and 80 per cent humidity, a 50-50 chance of a little precipitation or a lot). Then you determine which dimension works best (leads to the most accurate predictions) considering all the independent variables, and calculate the coefficients for all the variables on that dimension. Next you examine whether there is another dimension that helps in the prediction. For example, there could be a snowiness dimension predicting the type of precipitation to be expected—a high score might mean snow; a low score, rain; and a middle score, dry. For this dimension, too, the independent variables will have coefficients. There can be as many as $n-1$ dimensions in multiple discriminant function analysis (as it is called when there are more than two groups), where n is the number of groups, but usually most of the important information in the data will be contained in relatively few dimensions.

The coefficients based on weather in the past can be used for prediction. The meteorologist might say, for example, that based on present conditions, the most likely prediction for tomorrow is that there will be a little snow, with a 75 per cent probability that the prediction will be correct.

B. LOG-LINEAR ANALYSIS

Suppose you are interested in the odds that you will land in a particular type of occupation—a profession, for example. The simplest guess you could make about the odds, in the absence of any other information, would be that everyone has an equal chance of landing in any occupation. This is inadequate, however. First, you do not have an equal chance of getting into any type of occupation, because the numbers of jobs available are not equal. The average person is much more likely to become a skilled manual worker than a farmer because there are many more skilled manual workers than there are farmers. Second, not everyone has an equal chance of getting any particular job that is available; people whose parents had high-status jobs are more likely to get high-status jobs themselves than other people are.

The information needed to estimate the odds of getting into a particular type of occupation, given the jobs available and parental background, is presented in Table 28.1. Please notice that the dependent variable (son's job in the table) *and* the independent variable (father's job) are both categorical, or nominal, variables, so that ordinary regression analysis techniques are inappropriate. Here are some other examples where the independent and dependent variables are nominal: relating a person's neighborhood to the odds of his or her being the victim of certain types of crime; learning how occupation affects choice of hobbies; analyzing how ethnicity affects choice of political party.

Methods of analyzing tables like Table 28.1 lacked the power of regression analysis until the development of *log-linear analysis* (Knoke and Burke, 1980). The basic concepts in log-linear analysis are different kinds of "odds." The aim is to estimate the odds of being in one cell of a table rather than in other cells. The *marginal odds* are the odds for one particular variable; for example, the odds of being a farmer are low because so few people are farmers. The *conditional odds* are the odds of being in a particular category of a variable *given* that one is already in a particular category of another variable—for example, the odds of being a professional given that your father was a foreman in a factory. Conditional odds in a table are compared to each other in terms of

TABLE 28.1 Outflow from Father's Occupation to Son's Occupation, 1962 and 1973

Year and Father's Occupation	Son's Occupation (in percent)						
	Upper White-Collar	Lower White-Collar	Upper Manual	Lower Manual	Farm	Total	Row Percentage
1962:							
Upper white-collar	54	17	13	15	1	100%	17
Lower white-collar	46	20	14	18	2	100	8
Upper manual	28	13	28	30	1	100	19
Lower manual	20	12	22	44	2	100	27
Farm	16	7	19	36	22	100	29
Total	28	12	20	32	8	100	100%
1973:							
Upper white-collar	52	16	14	17	1	100%	18
Lower white-collar	42	20	15	22	1	100	9
Upper manual	30	13	27	29	1	100	21
Lower manual	23	12	24	40	1	100	29
Farm	18	8	23	36	15	100	23
Total	30	13	22	31	4	100	100%

Source: David Featherman, "Opportunities Are Expanding," *Society* 13 (1979):7. Published by permission of Transactions, Inc., from *Society*, vol. 13, no. 3. Copyright © 1979 by Transaction, Inc.

odds ratios, making it possible to calculate how strongly one's chances of landing in any particular cell are affected by the marginals and the other variables. (The approach is called log-linear analysis because one usually predicts the *logarithm* of the odds ratios as a *linear* function of other variables.) The procedures are very complicated computationally. (This is one of those techniques that might not have been invented, and certainly would not have been used very often, if it were not for high-speed computers.) But easy-to-use computer programs are available; the main thing to keep in mind for now is when log-linear analysis is appropriate and what the results tell you.

3. Similarities and Dissimilarities Among Objects

Most of the techniques discussed until now examine relationships among variables. There are times, however, when you wish to study objects such as persons, countries, companies, or species of animals to see how similar or different they are, what kinds of groups they form, or what patterns of relationships exist among them. Thus, for example, teachers can often teach better by separating a class into groups consisting of students who are at similar levels of achievement than by teaching the class all together. For economists, separating the countries of the world into more-developed and less-developed groups may help uncover relationships within the groups that are obscured when all countries are studied together. A marketer might want to know whether potential car buyers compare a new domestic small car to small foreign cars or to larger domestically produced cars.

Interest in objects rather than variables has arisen in almost every scientific discipline, from biology to archeology to psychology to economics, as well as in marketing and politics. Many different methods have been developed, some so complex that even the inventors do not completely understand them. We will focus on three methods: multidimensional scaling, blockmodelling, and cluster analysis.

A. MULTIDIMENSIONAL SCALING

Consider an airline mileage guide, a table with lists of cities down one side and across the top, with the air mileage between cities in the cells. You could estimate mileage figures from a map (the figures in the mileage guide are based on map distances, which are based in turn on actual physical distances), but the mileage guide is easier.

But what if you had to work backwards? That is, what if someone gave you mileages between cities in a country, and you had to draw a map of the country based on it? Analogously, sometimes we have information about the "social" or "psychological" distance between objects and would like to have a map showing how all the objects are related to each other.

Multidimensional scaling is a set of techniques enabling us to use information about "distances" between objects to create a picture of the whole set of objects in relation to each other. If we were to construct a map of the United States from a table of intercity distances, for example, multidimensional scaling would tell us, first, how many dimensions the simplest accurate map would have, and then would arrange the objects (points representing cities) so that it would look like a map. We would learn that for a large country, we could get a pretty fair map in two dimensions, but three would be needed for perfect accuracy (the earth is three-dimensional, after all). The points would be arrayed so that San Francisco would be at the opposite end from New York, and Chicago would be somewhere in between. An astronomical map of part of the galaxy would certainly require three dimensions, while a map of towns along a straight highway might require only one.

Here's a social science example. Suppose we want to draw a social, rather than a physical, map of the United States because we want to know which kinds of people are "close" to each other and which kinds are "distant." One might define "kinds of people" and "closeness" in different ways, but when Laumann (1973) became interested in this problem, he decided that it made sense to measure closeness in terms of choice of friends, and he focused on groups defined by occupation, ethnicity, and religion because those characteristics are important to many people. He therefore asked people about their own occupation, ethnicity, and religion, and also about the occupation, ethnicity, and religion of their best friends. If members of one group have a high proportion of their friends in another group, he defined the groups as close; in other words, the distance between groups was measured by the frequency of friendship ties between them. Thus, if lawyers tend to be friendly with doctors, but not with truck drivers, then lawyers would be close to doctors on the social map, and far from truck drivers. Similarly, if people of German background tend to be friends with people of Swedish background, but not with people of Italian background, Germans would be measured as close to Swedes but far from Italians.

This information about social distances was placed in matrices for ethnicity, occupation, and religion, and the social distances in the matrices were analyzed with a type of multidimensional scaling called smallest space analysis. The procedure makes no assumptions about how the different occupational, religious, or ethnic groups are related to each other, or about how many dimensions might be needed to describe all the relationships, which occupation is "higher" or "lower" than another, or whether people from some ethnic groups have a lot in common and others do not.

Two of Laumann's maps are found in Figures 28.1 and 28.2. The first shows how close different religious groups are to each other. Presbyterians, Lutherans, and Episcopalians are socially "close," in that people belonging to those denominations tend to be friends. They are less likely to be friendly with Baptists, however, and quite unlikely to be friendly with members of fundamentalist churches (there might be many reasons for this; the map shows only that it is so). Catholics are in the middle of the map, close to some Protestant groups

but not others, while Jews are a relatively self-contained group off to one side.

The second figure is an occupational map, which shows that occupation seems related to friendship choice. Manual workers seem to be on one side, close to each other and quite far from professionals, while people who work for themselves tend to associate with each other, as do people who work in bureaucratic settings for large corporations or government. The map shows that, however egalitarian Americans might be in ideology, they choose their friends from among people economically similar to themselves.

Multidimensional scaling has been used in many areas—to show the relationships among occupational groups (Featherman and Hauser, 1978: Chap. 2), test consumer sensitivity to differences among products (Schiffman, Reynolds, and Young, 1981), describe interlocks among major corporations (Levine, 1972), analyze perceptions of nations (Kruskal and Wish, 1978) and taste-test beers (Schiffman, Reynolds, and Young, 1981). Multidimensional scaling is useful when you desire to show the total configuration of a group of objects that can be related to each other by some kind of distance measure. As Schiffman, Reynolds, and Young state, "it is often easier and more informative to look at a picture of the data, than to look at the data themselves, particularly when the set of data is large. Stated simply, a picture is worth a thousand numbers!" (1981: 59).

B. BLOCKMODELLING

"It's not what you know, it's who you know," it is said. In fact, it's a bit of both (Granovetter, 1976), but the saying summarizes an important aspect of social life: Social networks affect people's lives. Through friends, acquaintances, and business associates, people find jobs, find help, obtain knowledge (Coleman, Katz, and Menzel, 1966; Breiger, 1976), and meet future spouses. Networks are important for organizations and countries, too. Ties among busi-

FIGURE 28.1   Graphic Portrayal of Proximity of Religious Groups, According to the Indexes of Dissimilarity of Friendship Choices

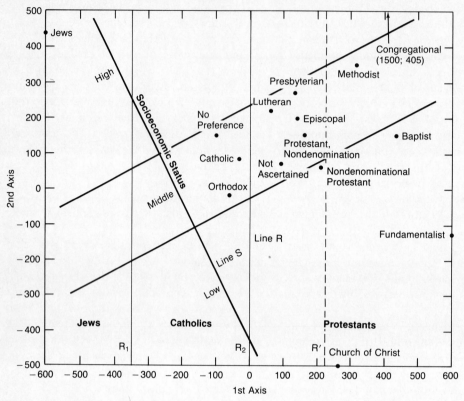

Coefficient of alienation = .180.

Source: Edward O. Laumann, *Bonds of Pluralism*. New York: John Wiley & Sons, Inc., 1973, p. 57. Copyright © 1973 by John Wiley & Sons, Inc.

nesses affect sales, networks of trade and alliances affect diplomacy and economic growth (Snyder and Kick, 1979), and communications patterns among military officers can affect the likelihood of there being a military coup. Blockmodelling is a way to study these networks.

In blockmodelling, you construct a matrix for each type of tie, with each object of analysis (each country, for example) having a row and a column of the matrix (like cities in a mileage guide). If a tie between two objects exists (if they trade with each other a lot, for example), then a 1 is entered in the matrix for the column of one country and the row of the other,

and a 0 otherwise. You will thus have a matrix of zeros and ones (intermediate values can be used, too, but that makes the analysis more complicated). Two objects are considered to be *structurally equivalent* when they have the same patterns of relationships (or nonrelationships) with all the other objects. Thus, for example, if country A had a big volume of trade with the United States, Britain, and France, but with no one else, and country B has the identical pattern, countries A and B are said to be structurally equivalent. With regard to another type of tie, however, such as mutual defense treaties, country A might have treaties with the same set of countries as country C,

FIGURE 28.2   Graphic Representation of the Two-space Solution for Indexes of Dissimilarity, Occupations of Friends

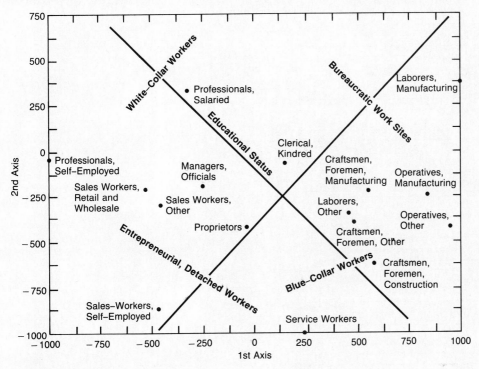

Coefficient of alienation = .122.

Source: Edward O. Laumann. *Bonds of Pluralism*. New York: John Wiley & Sons, Inc., 1973, p. 80. Copyright © 1973 by John Wiley & Sons, Inc.

but not the same set as country B; for this tie, countries A and C are equivalent.

Blockmodelling is a way of looking at a number of types of ties simultaneously and determining how objects should be grouped (or put into *blocks*) so that those within blocks are structurally equivalent in their relationships with other blocks. A group of scientists might form a block because they all cite certain other scientists but are not cited by them.

Use blockmodelling when there is reason to think that patterns of multiple networks among objects are important. Snyder and Kick, for example, found that countries could be grouped, on the basis of several kinds of ties among them, into three types, core, semiperiphery,

and periphery, with the location in international networks having a major effect on growth. Grouping countries, as they do, into three categories rather than the more customary two—developed and less developed—has important implications for the study of world economic development.

C. CLUSTER ANALYSIS

Cluster analysis takes a set of objects and gradually groups them, step by step, into larger and larger clusters based on their *similarities* on particular attributes (agglomerative clustering), or takes a large group of objects and gradually splits it up, step by step, into smaller

FIGURE 28.3   Clustering by Residential Integration: Peoria SMSA

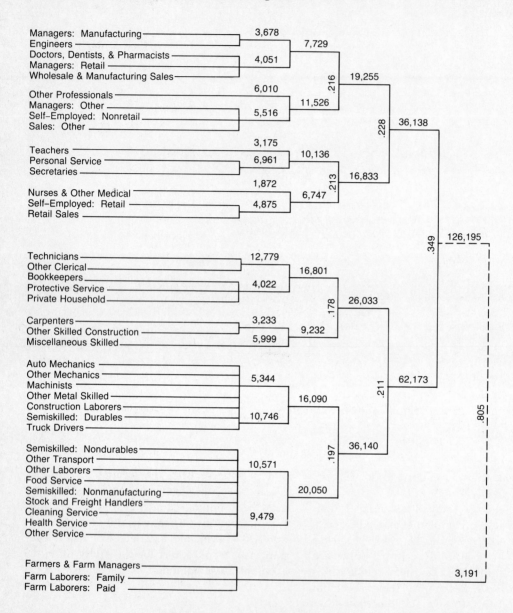

Horizontal figures indicate the number of people in each cluster; vertical figures indicate the segregation coefficient between the two clusters. The farm-nonfarm cluster was computed for the entire SMSA. All the remaining clustering was computed only for the urbanized portion of the SMSA. This explains why the total for the nonfarm cluster is larger than the sum of the totals for the working- and middle-class clusters.

Source: Reprinted from "The Occupational Composition of American Classes," *American Journal of Sociology*, 82 (January 1977), 800, by Reeve Vanneman, by permission of The University of Chicago Press. Copyright © 1977 by The University of Chicago Press.

groups divided by *differences* on particular attributes (divisive clustering).

Because no assumptions are made about how many larger or smaller groups will be found, cluster analysis can be a good way to find out how many groups "naturally" occur in a population without the researcher's having to make any arbitrary decisions about group boundaries. Thus, when Vanneman (1977) wanted to investigate the class structure of American society without relying solely on theoretical arguments or arbitrary judgments about how many classes there are, he used cluster analysis.

Vanneman wanted to know whether some kinds of upper-level manual workers are becoming "middle class," and whether, in contrast, some lower-level white-collar workers were basically "working class" in their life styles. He investigated where members of different occupations lived, because he judged that one criterion of shared class membership would be location. Given the way American cities are set up, people who live in the same areas can reasonably be said to be similar in class terms, and those who live far apart dissimilar in class. (This is not the only criterion for class membership, but it can be seen as a significant one.) Vanneman therefore used census data to derive measures of the extent to which occupational groups are residentially segregated from each other and then did a divisive cluster analysis. Vanneman's results are shown in Figure 28.3. As expected, the first big division is between farmers and urban residents. The next big division—shown by the solid black line near the right side of the page, which says .349 vertically—is between what Vanneman calls the working class and the middle class. All manual workers tend to live in the same neighborhoods, as do upper-level white-collar workers, but manual workers and upper-level white-collar workers tend to live far apart from each other. Vanneman found it especially interesting that certain lower-level white-collar groups, such as technicians and bookkeepers, tend to live in the same neighborhoods as manual workers, and not with upper-level white-collar workers. When Vanneman discovered the same grouping—manual plus lower-level white-collar versus upper-level white-collar—measuring differences between groups in still other ways, he concluded that a basic social division in American society occurs, not between manual and white-collar workers, but between upper-level white-collar workers and other urban workers. Though the results of no one study are definitive, this study using cluster analysis helps resolve an issue that had been the subject of endless argument but that could not readily be dealt with using many other techniques.

4. Summary

This chapter introduces a number of analytical techniques that are not used often but that can be invaluable under specific circumstances.

When you are interested in dependent variables that probably influence each other, two-stage least-squares estimates without bias the impact of each on the other, controlling for other variables. When you are analyzing data with a nominal dependent variable, discriminant analysis is appropriate. When all variables are nominal, log-linear analysis is often the appropriate technique.

Though research most often focuses on the relationships among variables, sometimes you wish to analyze relationships among objects. Multidimensional scaling can help when one wants a "picture" of the total configuration of relationships, blockmodelling can be used when one wants to analyze patterns of social networks, and cluster analysis can be used when one wants to put objects into groups.

Whatever the characteristics of your data, you can find an appropriate analysis technique. To do so, you have to think carefully about what kind of data you have before starting to analyze it, and you have to know how to find appropriate techniques.

EXERCISES

1. Suppose you wanted to learn why some married couples continue to stay married and live together, while others get separated, and some get divorced. If you thought that family income, number of children, religion, and age of the husband and wife affected the likely outcome, which statistical technique would you use to analyze your data? Why?
2. What if you wanted to learn how place of residence (neighborhood) in a city, race, social class, and marital status affected the odds of being robbed, assaulted, or burglarized. What technique would probably be most appropriate to analyze your data? Why?
3. If you were an automobile manufacturer trying to market a new car, you would want to know how potential buyers evaluate cars (is performance important? price? durability? size?) and how they might rate your new car relative to those already on the market. How could you use multidimensional scaling to help answer your questions?
4. Think of an example from your field where cluster analysis could be helpful.
5. Think of a research problem from your field where blockmodelling could be helpful.

ADDITIONAL READING

Mutual causation between dependent variables is dealt with by Duncan (1975) and Wonnacott and Wonnacott (1979). An early practical example, dealing with how friends affect each other's aspirations, is Duncan, Haller, and Portes (1968). Many universities have econometric software packages for doing the necessary calculations; an example is Peck (1981).

Discriminant function analysis is described in more detail in Cooley and Lohnes (1971) and in Morrison (1974). Easy-to-use computer programs are available in commonly used software packages such as SPSS (Nie et al., 1975).

Log-linear analysis is described in Knoke and Burke (1980); practical applications include Burstein (1978b) and Featherman and Hauser (1978, Chap. 2). A number of computer programs are widely available, including those in the BMDP package (Dixon, 1981).

Multidimensional scaling is described in Kruskal and Wish (1978); Schiffman, Reynolds, and Young (1981); Shepard, Romney, and Nerlove (1972); and Romney, Shepard, and Nerlove (1972). Romney, Shepard, and Nervlove, and Schiffman, Reynolds, and Young provide examples of many practical applications. Kruskal and Wish and Schiffman, Reynolds, and Young provide detailed information about the availability and use of the relevant computer programs.

Blockmodelling is described in White, Boorman, and Breiger (1976); Breiger (1976) and Snyder and Kick (1979) show how it can be used.

Cluster analysis is described by Bailey (1974); Vanneman (1977) shows how it can be used; some useful computer programs are found in the BMDP software package (Dixon, 1981), among other places.

Making Sound Predictions

29

1. Introduction
2. The Strategy of Prediction
3. Prediction, Science, and Judgment
4. Summary

1. Introduction

Readers may wonder whether prediction is a proper part of research, and therefore whether it belongs in this book. There are three reasons why we think that it makes sense to include a section on prediction here: First, the methods of research and prediction have a great deal in common. Second, even if prediction were not a proper part of research, understanding prediction helps us understand some important aspects of research. Third, in the long run, the aim of most research is to improve our capacity to predict what will happen in the future, unconditionally as well as conditional on our manipulations.

We all make predictions and act on them. And we believe that some people's predictions are better than other people's. This suggests that improvement in prediction is possible. The aim of this chapter is to help social scientists and others make sound predictions. The aim is *not* to throw more philosophical light on "the problem of induction," even though it will be necessary to explore the philosophic foundations in order to understand the process of predicting, and hence to improve it.

By "prediction" we mean a statement that someone makes concerning which he or she can have additional relevant evidence some time after making the statement that is not available when the statement is made.[1] The simplest case is sports. We predict that the University of Illinois will win the basketball game tonight; after the game, we will have information about the winner that we do not now have. Weather forecasting is another obvious example. And in social science, we may predict that there will be fewer riots next summer than last summer, or that GNP will rise by a smaller percentage this year than last year, or that copper, wheat, and oil will be decreasingly scarce in coming years.

---

1. We recognize that one may make predictions so far into the future that one will not be around to see the outcome. There are also other cases that this simple definition does not handle. But we do not think that these are great defects in the context of the discussion here.

The essence of the definition is that additional information is acquired after the statement is made, *not* that the event in question take place in the future. For example, we may predict that when the archaeologists dig deeper they will find out that Solomon kept camels as well as horses in his stables in Jerusalem, or that oil will be found under a house. In both cases, the physical presence of the camels and oil is the same before and after our statement, but the *investigation* will take place after our statement. Another example: You look at the data from a psychological experiment on learning and ask us to guess whether the well-fed or the ill-fed group learned faster. Our response is a prediction according to the definition of this chapter.

Prediction is a special type of generalization—a generalization from past to future. But unlike a generalization from a randomly drawn sample to the universe from which it was taken, prediction is *always* a leap of faith; there is no scientific guarantee that the sun will come up tomorrow. It is purely your judgment and knowledge of your subject that permits you to predict on the basis of prior experience that something will happen in the future.

A prediction is well founded if it is reasonable to assume that the past and the future belong to much the same universe, that is, if you can expect prior conditions to remain the same in the future. Predicting that next year's poll of architecture students about a military draft will yield much the same results as this year's is reasonable *if conditions do not change radically*. If the United States is attacked or there is peace on earth during the next year, this year's poll will probably not be a good predictor of next year's attitudes. The prediction that the sun will come up tomorrow morning is implicitly a statement that tomorrow morning comes from much the same universe as have all mornings in the past.

Sound predictions can be made even when changes in conditions will occur, if the changes are orderly and knowable. For example, one may predict that the amount of electric power used this year will be higher than the amount used in previous years. A shorthand way to justify such a prediction is that there has been an "upward trend" over many years. But the steady increase in power use is not a firm basis for prediction unless you know that the conditions creating the trend are also continuing. Thus, if you know that the number of generating stations, electrical appliances, and per capita income are increasing, while the price of electricity is not, you have a better basis for predicting an increase in this year's power use than if you just knew the trend. A prediction that the trend of electric power use in the 1920s would continue into the 1930s would have been wrong, because trends in income reversed due to the Depression.

The key point is that the past is never a guarantee of the future, and simple projection of past trends can be a treacherous basis for prediction. Extrapolating an observed trend into the future is safer when based on an *understanding* of the forces that underlie the process. Gaining such an understanding is more a matter of saturation in the situation than of scientific technique. Prediction shares this property with *all* generalizations from the known to the unknown.

Nevertheless, there is a distinction between prediction and explanation. Explanation is an attempt to make *sense* of a set of data, given the available information, whereas prediction need not *require* understanding. It is often reasonable to use mechanical rules to make predictions that would not be useful in an explanation; an example is the prediction that next year's crime rate will be about the same as this year's rate.

2. The Strategy of Prediction

Here is a series of steps to follow in making sound predictions. Of course, your actual steps will not be the same for every sort of prediction. You will have to choose your own procedure on the basis of judgment and wisdom. Yet we hope that the framework will be a useful one. The justification of these steps is presented mostly in the following section.

Before we discuss forecasting aggregate social phenomena, a word about predicting for a given person. The *best* prediction about a *single individual*, based on his or her membership in a particular group, is that the individual will be *average*. If all you know about a male baby is that he is American, your best prediction of his height is that he will be perhaps five feet nine inches. Similarly, if advertisement A makes 75 sales and advertisement B makes 60 sales, your best prediction for the future is that A will make 75/60 as many sales as B. But, if you have some *other* knowledge of the situation, you should alter your prediction to take account of it. For example, if you want to predict a male baby's adult height, there are two groups for reference: all males in the United States (or in the community) and his father (or parents). If his parents are six feet five inches and six feet two inches, should you predict that the boy's height will be six feet four inches or the five feet nine inches that is average for all men? In this case you probably would predict that the boy will be far taller than average, but perhaps not so tall as his parents. And you probably would make a similar prediction, though perhaps somewhat lower, if the baby boy with the tall parents is only average length at birth. A formal scheme for incorporating such further knowledge is called "decision theory," which most modern statistics books cover. This branch of statistical theory helps us to decide which is the best among several alternatives, based on predictions of the effects of the alternatives and of the *value* of the various effects.

A prediction can be made on the basis of a single observation. If you have no reason to believe that the single observation is unusually high or low, then the prediction should be the same as the observation. If you do have some such outside knowledge, however, you would modify your prediction accordingly. It is also legitimate and sensible to adjust predictions, even if you have large numbers of observations. Much of the difference between good and not-so-good election pollsters is apparently art and skill in adjusting their data. For example, Gallup is said to have reduced the weight given to Southern straw votes to three-fifths of the weight given to straw votes elsewhere in the 1960 prepresidential election polling. This was supposed to allow for the relatively light voting expected in the South.

Before you make a forecast for an important situation, we suggest you refer to Armstong's (1978) practical and delightful book. There you will find a host of useful suggestions about what is and what is not worth doing. Armstrong will undoubtedly disagree with the order of the suggested steps that now follow, but (aside from frequently referring you to his own book), we do not think he would add much to them.

STEP 1: PRECISELY STATE WHAT YOU WANT TO PREDICT.

Is it the U.S. crime rate in ten years that you want to predict? If so, perhaps trends reported in the FBI Major Crime Index might be a reasonable basis for prediction. Is it the future scarcity of raw materials that you want to predict? Then perhaps the future price per unit of copper or oil or wheat, relative to wages or to the average income or to the Consumer Price Index (or not adjusted at all for inflation) is the measure of scarcity that fits your needs.

Most important is that you somehow operationalize the subjects of your prediction, in accordance with the discussion in Chapter 2. Choose an indicator appropriate to the variable you wish to predict, one for which data are available.

STEP 2: DETERMINE THE PERIOD FOR WHICH YOU WISH TO FORECAST.

Crime or raw material scarcity for next week? Next year? Ten years from now? Thirty years from now? Or during a specific time, such as when the Republican National Convention will be held in your city?

The appropriate method for a prediction depends on the period in which you are interested. For example, if you want to predict how many people will be killed in auto crashes next year, simple extrapolation of the number killed this year would probably be best. If you want to predict how many will be killed in the year 2003, however, you would probably take into account design improvements that might make cars and highways safer, changes in the size of the population, and other fundamental factors. You might even consider the possibility that some entirely new mode of transportation will be invented in the meantime. (Imagine someone living in 1903 trying to predict the number of horse-related accidents just as automobiles were becoming popular.)

STEP 3: IF YOU ARE PREDICTING A FUTURE STATE OF AFFAIRS, BEGIN WITH THE PRESENT STATE AS YOUR BENCHMARK.

If you are predicting an individual's characteristics, start with the average for the group(s) you identify him or her with. Why? Because individuals similar in one way (group membership), are likely to be similar in other ways (the characteristics you are interested in). There must be some continuity, some nonindependence or similarity between contiguous events, if there is to be *any* better-than-chance predictability in this world. And because there often is some continuity, some nonindependence between contiguous events, the present is the most reasonable benchmark for a prediction, all else being equal. We will discuss this in more detail later.

STEP 4: DETERMINE HOW MUCH VARIABILITY THERE HAS BEEN DURING A PAST PERIOD EQUAL IN LENGTH TO THE AMOUNT OF TIME BETWEEN NOW AND YOUR PREDICTION DATE.

If there has been no variability at all, then your task has been simplified, though not ended. For example, if you want to know the likelihood that the state of Illinois will fulfill its pension promises even though it has not put the required amount aside, finding that all other states in similar situations *have* paid the pensions should reassure you. If you want to know the amount of liquor that people will drink ten years from now, and if liquor consumption per capita has changed very little from year to year in the past twenty years, then you can safely predict that consumption per person ten years will be what it is now.

If you have reason to think that a new factor likely to alter past patterns has entered the situation—a prohibition law, for example—then of course you will not predict that the future will resemble the past. Otherwise, however, lack of variability in the past suggests that the present status is your best prediction for the future.

It can be disastrous to assume wrongly there will be little variability. Based on the fertility rates of the 1930s, demographers predicted in 1947 that the U.S. population in 1970 would be 140 million; it turned out to be 205 million, much to the demographers' embarrassment. Fertility is much more volatile than many think it is.

STEP 5: LOOK FOR PRONOUNCED CYCLICAL EFFECTS.

Can you find a strong and obvious cyclical regularity in your data? Anyone who, in Illinois in August, predicts that the temperature outside will be the same six months hence as it is that day, is doomed to shiver. Plotting a few years' temperatures month-by-month on graph paper will correct this prediction.

Be very reluctant, however, to conclude that there is a cycle in the phenomenon you are interested in. Purely random fluctuations have a way of looking very much like cycles. We would hazard that nine times out of ten when people think they see a cycle—and bet on it—the cycle is pure illusion. Some statistical devices are available to help you decide if there is truly a cycle or cycles, but such devices should be used with extreme care.

STEP 6: EXAMINE THE LONG-TERM TRENDS.

See whether there has been a systematic long-run drift. The easiest way to do this is by comparing the averages of the more distant and more recent past periods—say, comparing liquor consumption in the 1960–70 decade with the 1970–80 decade. Plotting the data by year on graph paper is also a good way to examine for trends.

If you find that there has indeed been a trend during the relevant period, then it is often reasonable to extend that trend to make your prediction. But here you must exercise extreme caution. The biggest danger is projecting a short-term trend—an upswing in liquor consumption within the last three years, say—a long way into the future—say, consumption two decades from now. Rather, a gradual decrease in liquor consumption over the past two decades may be a safe basis for predicting a slight decrease next year compared to this one. One of the many sad examples of fallacious trend extension was the conclusion by individuals and governments that the raw material scarcity that appeared in 1973–74 would continue to get worse at the same rate indefinitely. This conclusion was very wasteful of social and personal resources.

Why is it reasonable to assume that a trend will continue? The short answer is that continuity is a basic feature—perhaps the *most* basic feature—of the world we live in.

The most important element in making sound predictions from trends is to grasp the long sweep of history. Obtain evidence from as far back in the past as you can, to ensure that what you think is a trend is really not just a blip in history. For example, notice in Figure 29.1 what different results you would get if you

FIGURE 29.1a   The Scarcity of Copper as Measured by Its Price Relative to Wages

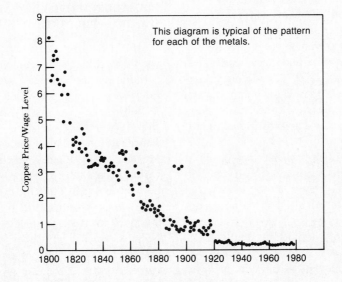

This diagram is typical of the pattern for each of the metals.

FIGURE 29.1b   The Scarcity of Copper as Measured by Its Price Relative to the Consumer Price Index

This diagram is typical of the pattern for each of the metals.

were to predict the course of future copper prices from 1970's evidence alone, rather than from the evidence going back to 1800.

If the pattern of the past is not consistent, you must decide which parts of the past to pay most attention to. It is generally reasonable to weight the recent past more heavily than the distant past, though never completely forgetting the distant past. You can study the effects of earlier periods on later ones and use the results for your weights. But this can be tricky.

There are many complex statistical devices that purport to help you make trend predictions. (For a discussion and very critical review, see Armstrong, 1978). But do not be deluded into believing that fancy mathematcial manipulations contain any forecasting power that is not otherwise available to the common-sense mind.

An example of an inappropriate use of mathematic manipulations for forecasting is seen in Figure 29.2, which shows a curve called a third-degree polynomial fitted to data on copper prices. This curve suggests that copper prices are increasing now. The simple long-term trends, however, suggest that prices are decreasing. It is irrelevant here that a third-de-

gree polynomial provides a better "fit" in statistical terms than does a curve that does not change direction. (Why was a third-degree polynomial chosen for this exercise? To make this kind of point about the misplaced accuracy of the fancy mathematical methods.)

STEP 7: FIND OTHER VARIABLES THAT GO TOGETHER (THOUGH NOT NECESSARILY CAUSALLY) WITH THE VARIABLES YOU WANT TO PREDICT.

If you have little or no data on a variable you want to predict, you may analyze change in a variable highly correlated with the one you are interested in, and for which data *are* available, to help make predictions, even if the relationship between the variables is not a causal one. There are no reliable data on the number of Mexican aliens illegally in the United States in various years. But there are data on the numbers of deaths of illegal Mexican aliens. Trends in deaths can be used to predict trends in living persons, though deaths do not cause live persons. And if you have known from demographic calculations what proportions of people die each year, you can predict the trend in

FIGURE 29.2

number of living persons even better. Another example is the amount of classified employment advertising, which may predict changes in the business cycle without causing those changes, any more than leaves falling from trees cause autumn.

How should you decide which purely predictive variables to use? Because you have—by definition—no causal relationships to guide you, you must rely on your intuition and your knowledge about what variables are correlated strongly with the one you want to predict.

STEP 8: FIND VARIABLES THAT CAUSE CHANGES IN YOUR VARIABLE OF INTEREST, AND PREDICT CHANGES IN THOSE VARIABLES AND THEN IN THE ASSOCIATED CHANGES IN YOUR VARIABLE OF INTEREST.

If you know how many bicycles will be sold—or better, how many will be in use in a given year—you have an aid to predicting sales of bi-

cycle tires, because very few bicycle tires are sold except to be used on bicycles. And perhaps the number of teen-agers, together with the income level, will predict the number of bicycles sold, because teen-agers buy many of the bikes sold, and income affects all purchases. Here we bring, for the first time, causal influences into our prediction process. Thus, if bicycle sales will be a major predictor of bicycle tire sales, then income and age distributions will be independent variables, and those variables themselves must be predicted. In practice this means that you work out a single predictive equation using as independent variables those that are relevant and available at any stage of the predictive game.

Remember, however, that there are important differences between a causal analysis and predictive work. In a causal study, for example, you need not be concerned about predicting the independent variables; rather, you are interested in understanding their influence. Yet such understanding will do one little good in predictive work if you cannot predict change as well. For example, we know that the money supply affects the business cycle. But you do not normally have much power to predict the money supply (unless you work at the Federal Reserve Bank) and hence cannot take advantage of this causal relationship even if you know what it is (though the officials of the Federal Reserve Bank *can* use this relationship to predict the effects of their manipulation of the supply of money).

In addition, in a causal study, you should not employ an independent variable that you have no theoretical reason to expect to influence the dependent variable, even if it somehow improves the "statistical fit" of your equations. But in predictive work you will use any variable that will significantly improve the accuracy of your predictions, even if its relationship with the dependent variable is not causal.

How should you decide which causal variables to include? By calling on your theoretical understanding of the phenomenon—that is, your full skill as a scientific investigator.

STEP 9: FOR VERY, VERY LONG-RANGE PREDICTIONS, CONSIDER FIRST WHETHER THERE ARE VERY LONG-RUN TRENDS IN THE PHENOMENA THAT WILL CONTINUE.

The very long-run trends in liquor consumption and in murder in the United States are downward. Unless you have some strong arguments against the continuation of those trends, they may be your best basis for predictions. But if you do have one or more strong reasons to believe that the bases for the previous long-run trends have changed, then you must attempt a wide-ranging forecast of what society will then be like, in light of the major technological and social changes that you expect will take place by then.

Much the same is true of any major social change. There is almost a qualitative difference between predicting the effect of a small change in a variable and predicting the effect of a large change. This is so, we believe, because it is reasonable to assume *ceteris paribus* for small changes, whereas large changes usually affect the entire structure of the environment in such a way as to render foolish an assumption of *ceteris paribus*. For example, in a town with twenty saloons, one might predict with reasonable certainty the effect of one more saloon on liquor consumption and on social habits. But the effect of a *hundred* more saloons seems much *less* predictable. A hundred more saloons would change the entire character of the town and might trigger a prohibitionist movement or a mass migration to or from the town.

H. Wold puts the matter this way:

> When it comes to [the effect of] deepgoing technological innovations such as the industrial revolution, or fundamental changes in the social system, such as the transition from feudal to bourgeois society, we are far above . . . the most attenuated relaxation of the *ceteris paribus* principle. We are then in the wide realm where scientific methods no longer suffice as a basis for forecasting. (Wold, 1966c: 37–38)[2]

An example is the issue of the "optimum population" for a country—whether the United States, say, would be better off with 50 million people, 300 million people, or 600 million people in the year 2000, or if the United States would have been better off in 1981 with 100 million or 400 million people, rather than its actual 230 million people. Theoretically, we can imagine what the United States might be like with a much larger or smaller population and no other major changes. Practically, however, radical changes in population would be associated with so many other changes that we could not predict what the implications would be. Fewer people imply more available natural resources per capita. But fewer people also imply fewer men in the military to prevent another country from appropriating the natural resources. Fewer people imply smaller mar-

2. The discussion in Chapter 36 of the limits of social science with respect to historical explanation is closely related.

kets for businesses to sell to, and therefore reduced stimulus to business investment. But many more people may mean reduced spending power per capita, especially for luxuries, and therefore reduced stimulus to business investment. Less business investment implies reduced per capita income in many cases, and so on.

The problem is not just that many things will change at the same time, but that we do not know they will interact and therefore how they will change.

A related example is the effect of various sizes of population on social organization. If there are very few people in a country and therefore few rules to prevent conflict among them, an increase in the number of people may well increase the amount of conflict. But if the population increase is very great, the increase in conflict may also lead to an increase in rules or in social cooperation that reduces conflict, *or* it may lead to a big conflict that kills off people and reduces the population.

The greater predictability of small changes explains the businessperson's willingness to try small changes in price and other variables, whereas he or she balks at large sudden changes. This concept also fits the United States' pragmatic and meliorist philosophy of government, which implies that the effect of major changes—that is, revolution—is treacherously hard to predict. The logic of this is, we think, that, as with the saloons, a *major* governmental change cannot occur in isolation. A major all-at-once alteration toward socialism, say, must affect not only economic variables but also the forms of justice, international policy, and so on.

3. Prediction, Science, and Judgment

Let us consider a homely example of prediction. You observe that the owner of the third house on the block owns a big new car. If you predict that the next-door neighbor in the fourth house also has a big new car, you will be right more often than if you guess that the neighbor has an average-size car. Furthermore, if you then observe that the fourth-house owner does have a big new car, a prediction that the fifth-house owner also has a big new car is more likely to be correct than if only the fourth house and *not* the third house had a big new car. That is, the high degree of similarity between the third and fourth house increases the chance of accuracy in a prediction that the fifth house would be like the fourth house.

The dimension on which one element is "next to" another need not be geographic. Frequently the relevant proximity is in time. The number of minutes of daylight tomorrow may be predicted on the basis of the number of minutes of daylight today and yesterday. A patient's mental state tomorrow may be predicted on the basis of her mental state today. And the speed it takes a rat to traverse a maze in trial 22 may be predicted on the basis of his elapsed time in trial 21.

Also, if two elements are similar on one dimension, they may be similar on another dimension as well. For example, if two students get the same score on an I.Q. test, one would predict that they would get the same grades in school. And if the same quantity of wheat is harvested in two given years, one would predict the same wheat price for the two years. (Remember, however, that they may not be similar to each other in ways that are important for your particular prediction or purpose, if the dimensions on which they are classified as the same are not relevant, as we shall see later.)

One may expand the concept of sameness a bit, still with simple examples. Consider trends, now. In some cases we do not assume that C will be the same as B but that, say, C will be proportionally as much larger than B as B is larger than A. So we now have two notions of sameness, the sameness of the elements and the sameness of the proportional differences between pairs of the elements.

An example of predicting on the basis of

such differences is found in crude or "naive" forecasts of gross national product. If GNP has been growing at the rate of 5 per cent per year in recent years, one may forecast that next year's GNP will be 5 per cent higher than the GNP recorded this year.

The reader may wonder, however, how one chooses *which* set of samenesses to use. How should we decide whether to forecast that GNP will be the same percentage (5 per cent) higher than last year, or the same amount ($100 billion) higher? That is, how do we decide "which curve to fit"? There are various technical devices for making such a choice. Most of them boil down to asking which curve would have given the best predictions if used in the past, with "best" being measured by some such criterion as the average difference between predicted and actual values.

It may also be useful to observe that elements are similar in more than one dimension, and therefore to make a prediction of one from the other, using the information from both dimensions. If you are told that two brothers are both five feet seven inches tall, and one is 150 pounds, it might be reasonable to predict that the other is 150 pounds, also. But if you are also told that both wear size 37 suits, you would have even more basis for a prediction that the second weighs 150 pounds. And if you are told that the first is five feet seven inches, size 37, and 150 pounds while the second is five feet seven inches and size 36, you could predict the weight of the second with more confidence than if you had only his height or suit size.

How do you determine which dimensions to use in the forecasting, and how to weigh the evidence? Multivariate analysis can help. So can judgment.

With the aforegoing as groundwork, we may now attack the problem of why and how better and worse forecasts are made. There are two major issues: (1) whether you have indentified the major relevant dimensions, and (2) whether you have information available for the major relevant dimensions other than the one you wish to predict. For a start let us consider a situation in which both these problems are minimal—the controlled experiment. Consider the experiment by Masserman (1944) in which a group of randomly selected cats were given a neurosis and another group were not; the neurotic group then chose to drink milk with alcohol, while the nonneurotic group did not. Though no two cats in any sample are exactly alike, the process of drawing random samples goes far to ensure that, taken as whole, the groups were very much alike in all aspects except whether or not they were given a neurosis. If you should now draw a third sample and give them neuroses, too, you could predict with high accuracy that most of them would choose milk with alcohol, rather than pure milk as did the nonneurotic cats. (The accuracy will always be less than perfect, both because something you do not know about could have affected one of the samples, and because of sampling error.)

When investigating the relationship between human neurosis and alcohol drinking, one cannot ethically experiment with people as with cats. This makes the job harder. However, you might select two groups of people that are matched on such dimensions as age, sex, and occupation, and then see whether those with neuroses drink more alcohol than those without neuroses. But if you then attempt to predict alcohol-drinking behavior on the basis of these dimensions, you might go far wrong because religious background might be very important, yet it was not included in the dimensions on which you originally matched. Of course, you can try very hard to match on as many dimensions as possible, but you can never match on all of them. And whether you have taken into account the most important dimensions can only be determined by judgment—which is the first reason why judgment is so crucial in good forecasting and prediction.

It follows that automatic projection of trends makes sense only when the causes of past levels of the dependent variable are many in number and each is so small that it cannot be identified, and that none of the biggest of them is subject to major discontinuous change. Such a case might be the increase in the divorce rate. But where the causes are few and relatively large—the rate of growth of your personal record collection, or current-period advertising as the cause of current-period sales for a one-shot mail-order business—automatic trend projection is (1) inferior to causal analysis, and (2) unwise if the major cause is subject to control and/or discontinuous change. For example, there is ample evidence that the best predictor of the level of the stock market as a whole tomorrow is the level today—unless you have some sort of inside information, in which case, it would be illegal for you to trade on it.

To clarify the relationship between the "naive" method, the causal method, and the social forecast method, let us imagine ourselves standing in 1880 trying to predict the number of horseshoes that will be sold in the future. If we want to predict the number of horseshoes that will be sold in the next week, the most reliable predictor—assuming that there is nothing special about the week—will be the number of horseshoes that were sold last week. If, on the other hand, we wish to predict the number of horseshoes that will be sold five years from now, then it might be reasonable to make a causal analysis of the relationships of income and the age distribution of the population to the number of horses, and thence from the number of horses to the number of horseshoes used per year. If, however, our horizon for forecasting were 50 or 100 years (that is, as of 1880), neither of these methods would be appropriate. Rather, it would make more sense to look around at the structure of the economy and of technology, notice the steam engine and its rise and the steamship and its rise, and guess that perhaps something will come along that will replace horsepower entirely.

Lest it seems easier to backcast with twenty-twenty hindsight than to forecast, let us look forward from now and imagine that a prediction about sales of automobile tires a hundred years from now ought to take into account totally new materials that automobiles might ride on—assuming there are automobiles—and perhaps that the wheel itself may be replaced by other methods of locomotion such as air cushions under land vehicles. Making such long-term predictions is extremely risky, but imagination *in combination with* the kinds of information and theory described above should make it possible to do better than you might expect.

4. Summary

Research and prediction are closely related. Often one of the aims of research is to improve our ability to predict some aspect of the future, and the safest basis for adequate prediction is an understanding of social processes that is likely to come from research.

Though prediction always involves uncertainty, there are ways to improve the accuracy of predictions, including being precise about what you want to predict, taking the past into account in a sensible—not a mechanical—manner, and finding variables consistently related to the variable you want to predict.

Prediction can be improved by careful curve-fitting and multivariate analysis. But good prediction, especially for the medium- and long-term, also depends on imagination and judgment formed through long experience with your subject.

In the space of one hundred and seventy-six years the Lower Mississippi has shortened itself two hundred and forty-two miles. That is an average of a trifle over one mile and a third per year. Therefore, any calm person, who is not blind or idiotic, can see that in the Old Oölitic Silurian Period, just a million years ago next November, the Lower Mississippi River was upward of one million three hundred thousand miles long, and stuck out over the Gulf of Mexico like a fishing-rod. And by the same token any person can see that seven hundred and forty-two years from now the Lower Mississippi will be only a mile and three-quarters long, and Cairo and New Orleans will have joined their streets together, and be plodding comfortably along under a single mayor and a mutual board of aldermen. There is something fascinating about science. One gets such wholesale returns of conjecture out of such a trifling investment of fact.

(Mark Twain, quoted in Armstrong, 1978: 165)

EXERCISES

1. Suppose your school had an important basketball game next week. How would you go about predicting the outcome? Suppose you wanted to predict the team's record for the season after next. How would you do that? What if you wanted to predict how well the team would do in ten years? What are the similarities and differences among the factors you take into account when trying to make the different predictions?

2. The Republicans won control of the U.S. Senate in 1980. Would you predict they will continue to control it? Why? Would being told that, before 1980, the Democrats had controlled the Senate continuously since 1955 change your prediction? Why or why not?

3. Choose an occupation and try to predict what the demand for new people in it will be next year, in five years, and in twenty years.

4. Why do you think it is relatively easy to predict how many Americans will marry next year but difficult to predict if any particular person will marry?

AFTERTHOUGHT

The Koran says: "God forbids only what is harmful and indecent." Among the forbidden things are the drinking of alcohol and the use of intoxicants, eating of pork, gambling, usury, sexual activity outside the bond of marriage, and attempting to divine the future.

Adapted from M.M. Siddiqui, *The Message of Islam*

ADDITIONAL READING

Armstrong's book (1978) is excellent as well as entertaining reading on forecasting. See also Lipset's essay (1979).

Inferential Statistics: Introduction

30

1. Types of Statistics

A statistic is a *number*.[1] There are two kinds of statistics, summarization (descriptive) statistics and inferential statistics. The most important summarization statistics are the total, average, range, distribution, and so forth. Those statistics are nothing new to you; you have been using them all your life, and they are discussed in detail in every elementary statistics text.

The second kind of statistics, inferential statistics, is the subject of this chapter and of statistics courses. Inferential statistics can be used for two purposes: to aid scientific *understanding*, by estimating the probability that a statement is or is not true, and to aid in making *sound decisions* by estimating which alternative among a range of possibilities is most de-

sirable. The latter type of statistical theory—"decision theory"—is a recent arrival (really a revival) on the intellectual scene but is beyond the scope of this book; it is well-treated by Raiffa (1968) and by Bross (1965) among others. This chapter will stick mostly to "hypothesis-testing theory," though there will be comfortably little mathematical theory in our discussion. In the previous chapter, we discussed the types of analysis in which hypothesis-testing statistics are useful. Now we get down to the brass tacks of how to use probability statistics.

2. The Nature and Meaning of Probability

What does the term "probability" mean? To say that an event has a high or low probability is simply to make a statement that forecasts the future. In practice, probability is stated as an arbitrary weight between 0 and 1, such that 0

---

1. A more conventional definition: "[S]tatistic: a summary value calculated from a sample of observations, usually but not necessarily as an estimator of some population parameter; a function of sample values" (Kendall and Buckland, 1957: 259).

means you estimate that there is no chance of the event happening, and 1 means you are sure it will happen. A probability estimate of .2 means that you think the chances are 1 in 5 (odds of 1 to 4) that the event will happen. A probability estimate of .2 indicates that you think there is twice as great a chance of the event happening as if you had estimated a probability of .1.

The idea of probability arises *when you are not sure* about something, that is, when you do not have enough information and therefore can only *guess*. For example, if someone asks you what your name is, you do not use the concept of probability to answer. To be sure, there is some chance that you do not know your own name, but for all practical purposes you can be quite sure of the answer. If someone asks you who will win tomorrow's ball game, however, there is a chance that you will be wrong, no matter what you say. Whenever the situation is such that there is a chance that you could be wrong, the concept of probability can help you.

A probability statement is always about the future. But one does not know what the likelihoods really are for future events, except in the case of a gambler playing black on an honest roulette wheel, or an insurance company issuing a policy on an event with which it has had a lot of experience, such as a life insurance policy. Therefore, we must make guesses about the likelihoods, using various common-sense gimmicks. All these gimmicks should be thought of as *proxies* for the actual probability. For example, if NASA Mission Control simulates what will probably happen if a valve aboard a space shuttle is turned, the result on the ground is not the *real* probability that it will happen in space, but rather a proxy for the real probability. If a manager looks at the last two Decembers' sales of radios, and on that basis guesses the likelihood that he will run out of stock if he orders 200 radios, then the last two years' experience is serving as a proxy for future experience. If a sales manager just "in-

tuits" that the odds are 3 to 1 (a probability of .75) that the main competitor will not meet a price cut, then all his past experience summed into his intuition is a proxy for the probability that it will really happen. Whether any proxy is a good or bad one depends on the wisdom of the person choosing the proxy and making the probability estimates.

The concept of probability helps you to answer the question: "What are the odds that . . .?"[2] The purpose of this discussion of probability statistics is to help you to become a *good bettor,* to help you make sound appraisals of true and untrue conclusions (or, in terms of decison theory, to help you to decide which alternatives you should bet on). The concept of probability is especially useful when one has a "sample" from a "universe" and wants to know the probability of various degrees of likeness between the sample and the universe. In other words, one wants to know the probability that the universe's average I.Q., for example, will not differ from the sample's average I.Q. by more than some arbitrarily chosen number of I.Q. points, say, ten points. A related question: What is the probability that a sample was taken from a given universe rather than from another universe, so that one can safely draw conclusions about the universe from the sample evidence?

What "is" probability? Various definitions of the term are useful in particular contexts (see Ayer, 1965; Schlaifer, 1961: Chap. 1; Leamer, 1978: 22–39). The rest of this chapter contains many examples of the use of probability, and as you work with them, you will develop a feeling for the concept. The following two defini-

---

2. A given probability may be expressed in terms of probability, odds, or chances, and we shall use all three terms to help familiarize you with them. If the chances are 1 in 10, the odds are 9 to 1, and the probability is .1. If the odds are 2 to 5, the chances are 5 in 7, and the probability is 5/7. If the odds are 99 to 1, the chances are 1 in 100, and the probability is .01. If the odds are 100 to 1, the chances are 1 in 101, and the probability is 1/101. "Likelihood" is a synonym for "probability."

tions (which are not always compatible) may be helpful to start you off:

1. The probability that an event will take place or that a statement is true can be said to correspond to the odds at which you would bet that the event will take place. (Notice a shortcoming of this definition: You might be willing to accept a $5 bet at 2 to 1 odds that your team will win the game, but you might be unwilling to bet $100 at the same odds.)

2. The probability of an event can be said to be the proportion of times that the event has taken place in the past, usually based on a long series of trials. Insurance companies, for example, use this type of definition when they estimate the probability that a thirty-five-year-old lettercarrier will die during a period for which he wants to buy an insurance policy. (Notice this shortcoming: Sometimes you must bet on events that have never or only infrequently taken place before, and so you cannot reasonably reckon the proportion of times they occurred one way or the other in the past.)

You have been using the concept of probability all your life, in practically every decision you have ever made and in every conclusion you have ever drawn. You place your blanket on the beach where there is a *low probability* of someone's kicking sand on you; you bet heavily on a poker hand when there is a *high probability* that you have the best hand; a hospital decides not to buy another ambulance when the administrator figures that there is a *low probability* that all the other ambulances will ever be in use at once.

How does one estimate a probability? First, let us consider how one can estimate an ordinary garden variety of probability, which is called an "unconditional" probability. Several ways to estimate an unconditional probability can be illustrated with an example from poker.[3]

3. We hope you are not offended by the references to gambling games in the discussion of statistics in this and other chapters. Not only was the theory of probability invented to answer questions about gambling games, but gambling games still provide the best examples.

What is the probability of drawing an even-numbered spade from a deck of poker cards?

The first possible source for an estimate of the probability of drawing an even-numbered spade is *experience*. If you have watched card games casually from time to time, you might guess at the proportion of times you have seen even-numbered spades appear, and you might guess "about 1 in 15" or "about 1 in 6" or something like that. (The actual probability is 6 to 52, of course.) You might make an estimate based on your experience if someone asked you the probability that two cards of the same denomination will turn up in the same hand of five cards dealt from a poker deck. General information and experience are also the source for estimating the probability that your team will win tomorrow, that war will break out next year, or that a United States astronaut will reach Mars before a Soviet cosmonaut. You simply put together all your relevant prior experience and knowledge and make a guess.

The second possible source of probability estimates is empirical scientific investigation with repeated trials of the phenomenon—called a "frequency series." In the case of the even-numbered spade, the empirical scientific procedure is to shuffle the cards, deal one, record whether the card is an even-numbered spade, replace the card, and repeat the steps a good many times. The proportion of times you observe an even-numbered spade come up is a probability estimate based on a frequency series. You might reasonably ask why we do not just *count* the number of even-numbered spades in the deck of fifty-two cards. No reason at all. But that procedure would not work if you wanted to estimate the probability of a batter getting a hit or a cigarette lighter lighting.

Observation of frequency series might help you to estimate the probability that a machine will turn out a defective part or that a child can memorize four nonsense syllables correctly in one attempt. You watch and record the results of repeated trials of exactly the same event.

There is no *logical* difference between the sort of probability that the life insurance company estimates on the basis of its "frequency series" of past death rates, and the salesman's seat-of-the-pants estimate of what the competitor will do. No frequency series can speak for itself in a perfectly objective manner. Many judgments go into compiling every frequency series, in deciding which frequency series to use for an estimate, and in choosing which part of the frequency series to use. For example, should the insurance company use only its records from last year, which will be too few to give as many data as one would like, or should it also use death records from years further back, when conditions were slightly different? In view of the necessarily subjective nature of probability estimates, the reader may prefer to talk about "degrees of belief" instead of probabilities. That's fine, just as long as it is understood that we operate with degrees of belief in exactly the same way as we operate with probabilities; the two terms are working synonyms.

(Of course, no two events are exactly the same. But under many circumstances they are *practically* the same, and science is interested only in such "practical" considerations.)

A third source of probability estimates is *counting the possibilities*. For example, by examination of an ordinary die one can determine that there are six different possible numbers that can come up. And one can then determine that the probability of getting a "1" or a "2", say is $\frac{2}{6}$, or $\frac{1}{3}$, because "1" and "2" are two of six possibilities. One can similarly determine that there are two possibilities of getting a "1" *plus* a "6" out of thirty-six possibilities when rolling two dice, a probability of $\frac{2}{36}$, or $\frac{1}{18}$.

Determining probabilities by counting has two requirements: that the *possibilities* all be known (and therefore limited) and few enough to be studied easily; and that the *probability* of each particular possibility be known. For example, it is known that the probabilities of all

sides of the die coming up are equal; that is, equal to $\frac{1}{6}$.

A fourth source of probability estimates is *mathematical calculation*. If one knows by other means that the probability of a spade is $\frac{1}{4}$ and the probability of an even-numbered card (Queen = "12") is $\frac{6}{13}$, one can then calculate that the probability of turning up an even-numbered spade is $\frac{6}{52}$ (that is, $\frac{1}{4} \times \frac{6}{13}$). If one knows that the probability of a spade is $\frac{1}{4}$ and the probability of a heart is $\frac{1}{4}$, then one can calculate that the probability of getting a heart *or* a spade is $\frac{1}{2}$ (that is, $\frac{1}{4} + \frac{1}{4}$). The point here is not the particular calculation procedures but rather that one can often calculate the desired probability on the basis of already known probabilities.

It is possible to estimate probabilities with mathematical calculation *only* if one knows *by other means* the probabilities of some related events. For example, there is no possible way of mathematically calculating that a child will memorize four nonsense syllables correctly in one attempt; empirical knowledge is necessary.

The mathematical theory of probability—with which we shall not deal here—concerns itself with developing ways to reckon complicated probabilities, for example, the probability that an even-numbered spade will come up in three out of the next seven cards followed by a red queen followed by an odd heart at least twice in the next five cards, and so forth. These complex calculations are of great importance—for example, no rocket would be put in orbit without many such calculations—but in the social sciences one can usually avoid them, at least while one is a beginner.

A. CONDITIONAL AND UNCONDITIONAL PROBABILITIES

Two kinds of probability statements must be distinguished, *conditional* and *unconditional*.

Let's use a football example to explain conditional and unconditional probabilities. In the

year this is being written, the University of
Iowa has an unpromising football team. Someone may nevertheless ask what chance the
team has of winning the postseason game at
the Rose Bowl, to which only the best team in
the University of Iowa's league is sent. One
may say that *if* by some miracle the University
of Iowa does get to the Rose Bowl, its chance
would be a bit less than 50-50—say, 40. That
is, the probability of its winning, *conditional*
on getting to the Rose Bowl, is .40. But the
chance of its getting to the Rose Bowl at all is
very low, perhaps .01. If so, the *unconditional*
probability of winning at the Rose Bowl is the
probability of its getting there multiplied by
the probability of winning *if* it gets there; that
is, .01 × .40 = .004. (It would be even better to
say that .004 is the probability of winning, conditional only on having a team, there being a
league, and so on, all of which seem almost
sure things.) Every probability is conditional
on many things—that war does not break out,
that the sun continues to rise, and so on. But
if all those unspecified conditions are very sure
and can be taken for granted, we talk of the
probability as unconditional.

A conditional probability is a statement that
the probability of an event is such-and-such *if*
something else is so-and-so; it is the "if" that
makes a probability statement conditional.
Now it is true that in *some* sense all probability
statements are conditional; for example, the
probability of an even-numbered spade is $\frac{6}{52}$ *if*
the deck is a poker deck and not necessarily if
it is a pinochle deck or a tarot deck. But we
ignore such conditions for most purposes.

Most of the use of probability in the social
sciences is *conditional* probability. All hypothesis-testing statistics are conditional probabilities.

The typical conditional-probability question
used in social-science statistics is: What is the
probability of obtaining sample S (by chance) *if*
the sample were taken from universe A? For
example, what is the probability of getting a

sample of five children with I.Q.s over 100 *by
chance* in a sample randomly chosen from the
universe of children whose average I.Q. is
100?

The first source of such conditional-probability statements is examination of the frequency
series generated by universes like the conditional universe. For example, assume that we
are considering a universe of children who average an I.Q. of 100. Write down "over 100"
and "under 100" respectively on several slips
of paper, put them into a hat, draw five slips
several times, and see how often the first five
slips drawn are all "over 100." This is the
Monte Carlo method of estimating probabilities.

The second source of such conditional-probability statements is mathematical calculation.
For example, if half the slips in the hat have
numbers under 100 and half over 100, the
probability of getting five in a row above 100 is
2^5; that is $2 \times 2 \times 2 \times 2 \times 2$. But, if you do not
know the proper mathematical formula, you
can come very close with the Monte Carlo
method, which is what you will learn here.

3. The Concept of Independent Events

A key concept in the use of probability and statistics is that of *independence* of two events.
Two events are said to be independent when
one of them does not seem to have any relation
to the other. If we flip a coin that we know
from other evidence is a fair coin and get a
head, the chances of then getting *another* head
are still 50-50 (one in two, or one to one). And,
if we flip a coin ten times and get heads the
first nine times, the probability of getting a
head on the tenth flip is *still* 50-50. This is why
the concept of independence is characterized
by the phrase "The coin has no memory." (Actually the matter is a bit more complicated. If
you had previously flipped the coin many
times and knew it to be a fair coin, then the

odds would still be 50-50, even after nine heads. But, if you had never seen the coin before, the run of nine heads might reasonably make you doubt that the coin was a fair one.)

Nevertheless, people commonly make the mistake of treating independent events as non-independent, perhaps from superstitious belief. Roulette gamblers say that the wheel is "due" to come up red. And sportswriters make a living out of interpreting various sequences of athletic events that occur by chance and talk of teams that are "due" to win because of the "law of averages." For example, if Rod Carew goes to bat four times without a hit, all of us (including trained statisticians who really know better) feel that Rod is "due" to get a hit and that the probability of his doing so is very high—higher, that is, than his season's average. The so-called law of averages implies no such thing, of course.

Not all events are independent, of course; far from it. A boy may telephone one of several girls chosen at random. But, if he calls the same girl *again* (or if he does *not* call her again), the second event is not likely to be independent of the first, and the probability of his calling her is *different* after he has gone out with her once than it was before he went out with her.

This observation suggests another way to look at the concept of independence. If the occurrence of the first event *does not change the probability* that the second event will occur, then the events are independent.

4. The Distinction Between "Probability Theory" and "Inferential Statistics"

The term "probability theory" refers to situations in which you know the nature of the system you are working with, and you wish to estimate the likelihood that the system will produce one or more *particular events*. For example, you can assume you know from the start the nature of a deck of bridge cards, and

you want to estimate, say, the likelihood that such a deck with thirteen spades among fifty-two cards will produce ten spades in the first thirteen cards dealt.

In contrast, the term "inferential statistics" refers to situations in which you do *not* know the nature of the system you are dealing with, and you want to *infer* the nature of the system from the evidence at hand. For example, someone may deal ten spades to you in the first thirteen cards, and you—not knowing what kind of deck it is—want to estimate how likely it is that the deck has only thirteen spades among the fifty-two cards, or if it has a larger proportion of spades.

To put it another way, in an inferential-statistics situation we want to determine one or more *statistics of the system;* the mean and the median are examples of such statistics that we wish to infer about an unknown system. In contrast, probability theory tells us about the likelihood of particular occurrences within systems whose statistics we already know.

Clearly, probability theory is relevant to situations such as gambling with cards or dice, where the physical nature of the system is known, and to such business situations as life insurance, where the overall probabilities of dying at each age are well known from a great deal of prior experience. (Business situations in which one does not know, but is prepared to assume, the structure of the situation can similarly be dealt with using probability theory.)

Inferential statistical thinking is particularly relevant for scientific investigations. In much of science the researcher tries to determine the nature of an unknown system from the evidence that he or she collects about it.

5. Translating Scientific Questions into Probabilistic and Statistical Questions

Science does not begin and end with statistics. Professional statisticians are quite humble about the importance of statistics. But taking a course or two in statistics has a way of going to a student's head, making him or her think that nothing can be proved without statistics and that anything can be proved if sophisticated statistics are used. This is the fallacy of "statistics is everything."

The fallacy of "statistics is nothing" is also dangerous, however. As Dunnette points out, researchers often disregard statistics because their *intuition* tells them that some conclusions *must* be so ". . . on the grounds that they are intrinsically good for humanity and that they need not, therefore, meet the usual standards demanded by scientific verification. . . . [Psychotherapy, for example] continues to survive in spite of a lack of evidence about its effectiveness" (1966: 346).

A social-scientific study begins with a general question about the nature of the social world. The scientist then transforms this question into a form that can be studied scientifically. The translation of general questions into scientific questions has been discussed earlier (Chapters 2, 5, and 6).

Let us suppose that, by this time, the researcher has not only translated his or her general question into a scientific question but has also *carried out* the scientific investigation as an experiment or survey. Suppose further that the data collected are not entirely clear-cut in support of firm conclusions. At this juncture, if he or she does not want to or cannot collect more data, the researcher may turn to inferential statistics for help.

The first step in using probability and statistics is to *translate the scientific question into a statistical question*. Once you know exactly what kind of probability-statistical question you want to ask—that is, exactly what probability you want to determine—the rest is relatively easy. The stage at which you are most likely to make mistakes is in stating the question you want to answer in probability terms. Though this step is hard, *it involves no mathematics*. This step requires only *hard, clear thinking;*

you cannot beg off by saying "I have no brain for math!" To flub this step is to admit that you have no brain for *clear thinking*, rather than no brain for mathematics.

We repeat, the hardest job in using probability statistics, and the most important, is to *translate* the scientific question into the form to which statistics can give a sensible answer. This translation is in the spirit of the discussion in Chapter 2 of the language of science and operational definitions; you must translate scientific questions into the appropriate form for *statistical operations*, so that you know which statistical operations to perform. This is the part of the job that requires hard, clear thinking—though nonmathematical thinking—and it is the part that someone else cannot easily do for you.

The best way to explain how to translate a scientific question into a statistical question is to illustrate the process.

ILLUSTRATION A

Are doctors' beliefs about the harmfulness of cigarette smoking (and doctors' own smoking behavior) affected by the *social* groups among whom they live (J. Simon, 1967–1968)? We decide to define the doctors' *reference groups* as the *states* in which they live, because data about doctors are available state by state (*Modern Medicine*). We can then translate this question into an operational and testable scientific hypothesis by asking this question: Do doctors in tobacco-economy states differ from doctors in other states in their smoking and beliefs about smoking?

But what numbers help us to answer this question, and how do we interpret them? We can now ask the *statistical* question: Do doctors in tobacco-economy states belong to the same universe (with respect to smoking) as do other doctors? That is, do doctors in tobacco-economy states have the same characteristics (at least of those we are interested in, smoking in this case) as do other doctors? Later we shall see that the way to proceed is to consider the statistical hypothesis that these doctors do indeed belong to that same universe; that hypothesis and the universe will be called "benchmark hypothesis" and "benchmark universe," respectively, though more conventional usage is "null hypothesis."

If the tobacco-economy doctors do indeed belong to the benchmark universe—that is, if the benchmark hypothesis is correct—then there is a 49/50 chance that doctors in some states *other* than the state in which tobacco is most important will have the highest rate of cigarette smoking. But in fact we observe that the state in which tobacco accounts for the largest proportion of the state's income—North Carolina—has a higher proportion of doctors who smoke than does any other state. (Furthermore, a lower proportion of doctors in North Carolina than in any other state say that they *believe* that smoking is a health hazard.)

Of course, it is possible that it is just *chance* that North Carolina doctors smoke most, but the chance is only 1 in 50 if the benchmark hypothesis is correct. Obviously, *some* state had to have the highest rate, and the chance for any other state was *also* 1 in 50. But, because our original *scientific* hypothesis was that North Carolina doctors' smoking rate would be highest and we then observed that it was highest, even though the chance was only 1 in 50, the observation is interesting and means something to us. It means that the chances are strong—49 in 50—that there is a connection between the importance of tobacco in the economy of a state and the rate of cigarette smoking among doctors living there.

To attack this problem from another direction, it would be rare for North Carolina to have the highest smoking rate for doctors if there were no special reason for it; in fact, it would occur only once in fifty times. But, if there *is* a special reason—and we hypothesize that the tobacco economy provides the reason—then it is *not* rare for North Carolina

to have the highest rate; therefore we choose to believe in the not-so-rare phenomenon that the tobacco economy causes doctors to smoke cigarettes.

ILLUSTRATION B

Does medicine CCC cure cancer? You begin with this scientific question and give the medicine to six patients who have cancer; you do not give it to six similar patients who also have cancer. Your sample is only twelve people because it is simply not feasible for you to obtain a larger one. Five of six "medicine" patients get well; two of six "no medicine" patients get well. Does the medicine cure cancer? That is, if future cancer patients take the medicine, will their rate of recovery be higher than if they did not take the medicine?

One way to translate the scientific question into a statistical question is to ask: Do the "medicine" patients belong to the same universe as do the "no medicine" patients? That is, we ask whether "medicine" patients still have the *same* chances of getting well from the cancer as do the "no medicine" patients, or whether the medicine has bettered the chances of those who took it and thus removed them from the original universe, with its original chances of getting well. The original universe, to which the "no medicine" patients must still belong, is the benchmark universe. Later we shall see that we proceed by making the benchmark hypothesis that they still belong to the benchmark universe (that is, still have the same chance of getting well as the "no medicine" patients).

We want to know whether the medicine does any good, which is the same thing as asking whether patients who take medicine are still in the same universe as "no medicine" patients or whether they belong to a different universe, one which now has different chances of getting well. To recapitulate our translations, we go from (a) Does the medicine cure cancer? to (b) Do "medicine" patients have the same chance of getting well as "no medicine" patients? and finally to (c) Do "medicine" patients belong to the same universe (population) as "no medicine" patients? Remember that "population" in this sense does *not* refer to the population at large but to a group of cancer sufferers (perhaps an infinitely large group) who have a given chance of getting well, on the average. Groups with different average chances of getting well are called "different populations" (universes). Later we shall see how to *answer* this statistical question.

We must keep in mind that our ultimate concern in cases like this one is *prediction of future results* of the medicine; that is, to predict whether use of the medicine will lead to a higher recovery rate than would be observed without the medicine.

ILLUSTRATION C

Is method A a better method of teaching reading than method B? That is, will method A produce a higher average reading score in the future than will method B? Twenty children who were taught to read with method A have an average reading score of 79, whereas twenty children who were taught with method B have an average score of 84. To translate this quite satisfactory *scientific* question into a statistical question we ask: Do children taught with method A come from the same universe (population) as children taught with method B? Again, "universe" (population) does *not* mean the town or social group the children come from, and indeed the experiment will make sense only if the children *do* come from the same population, in that sense. What we want to know is whether the children belong to the same population (universe), defined according to their *reading ability*, after they have studied with method A or method B.

Translating from a scientific question into a statistical question is mostly a matter of asking the probability that one or more samples come from some given benchmark universe. Notice

that we must (at least for general scientific testing purposes) ask about a *given* universe whose composition we assume to be *known*, rather than about a *range* of universes or a universe whose properties are unknown. In fact, there is really only one question that probability statistics can answer: Given some particular benchmark universe of some stated composition, what is the probability that an observed sample comes from it? A variation of this question is: Given two (or more) samples, what is the probability that they come from the *same* universe? In this latter case, the relevant universe is implicitly the universe whose composition is of the two samples combined.

The necessity for stating the characteristics of the universe in question becomes obvious when you think about it for a moment. Probability-statistical testing adds up to comparison of a sample with a particular benchmark universe and asking whether there is probably a difference between the sample and the universe. To carry out this comparison, we ask *how likely* it is that the benchmark universe would produce a sample like the observed sample. But, in order to find out whether a universe could produce a given sample, we must ask whether some *particular* universe—with stated characteristics—could produce the sample. There is no doubt that *some* universe could produce the sample by a random process; in fact, some universe did. The only sensible question, then, is whether a *particular* universe, with stated (or known) characteristics, is *likely* to produce such a sample. In the case of the medicine, the universe with which we compare the sample who took the medicine is the benchmark universe to which that sample would belong if the medicine had had no effect. This comparison leads to the benchmark (null) hypothesis that the sample comes from a population in which the medicine (or other experimental treatment) seems to have *no effect*. It is to avoid confusion inherent in the term "null hypothesis" that we replace it with "benchmark hypothesis."

The concept of the benchmark (null) hypothesis is hard to grasp.[4] The best way to learn its meaning is to see how it is used in practice. For example, we say we are willing to believe that the medicine has an effect if it seems very unlikely from the number who get well that the patients given the medicine still belong to the same benchmark universe as the patients given no medicine at all—that is, if the benchmark hypothesis is unlikely.

ILLUSTRATION D

If one plot is treated with fertilizer and another similar plot is not treated, the benchmark (null) hypothesis is that the corn raised on the treated plot is no different from the corn raised on the untreated plot; that is, that the corn from the treated plot comes from the same universe as the corn from the untreated plot. If our statistical test makes it seem very unlikely that a universe that produced the type of corn from the untreated plot would *also* produce corn such as that from the treated plot, then we are willing to believe that the fertilizer has an effect. For a psychological example, substitute the words "groups of children" for "plot," "special training" for "fertilizer" and "I.Q. score" for "corn."

There is nothing sacred about the benchmark (null) hypothesis of "no difference." You could just as well test the benchmark hypothesis that the corn comes from a universe that averages 110 bushels per acre, if you have reason to be especially interested in knowing whether the fertilizer produces more than 110 bushels per acre. But in many cases it is reasonable to test the likelihood that a sample comes from the population that does not receive the special treatment.

So far we have discussed the scientific question and the statistical question. Remember that there is always a generalization question too: Do the statistical results from this particular sample of, say, rats apply to a universe of humans? This question can be answered only with wisdom, common sense, and general knowledge.

6. Summary

This chapter begins with a discussion of the concepts of statistics, probability, independence, sample, and universe. Then it illustrates how scientific questions are translated into statistical questions. The translation is accomplished by specifying the relevant benchmark universe, and then asking the likelihood that the observed sample could have come from that universe. If you can soundly translate your scientific question into a statistical question, you have accomplished the hardest part of the task of statistical inference.

---

4. The classic discussion of the null hypothesis is by Fisher in his *The Design of Experiments* (1971: 18–19), but even that discussion is not at all satisfactory. Another useful treatment is by L. Neyman (1950: Chap. 5), who substitutes the term "test hypothesis" for "null hypothesis," however. The fact is that this concept is among the slipperiest in all scientific research and the hardest to learn. Don't despair if the notion eludes you at first. It will come clear as you work with it.

ADDITIONAL READING

Several articles in Tanur (1978) show how to turn scientific questions into statistical questions: Dunnett (1978) on how to determine whether a drug helps cure cancer; Zeisel and Kalven (1978) on the role of coincidence in legal proceedings; and Hooke on when it makes sense to bunt during a baseball game.

Probability and Hypothesis Testing by the Monte Carlo Method

31

1. Introductory Problems
2. The General Procedure
3. Hypothesis Testing
4. Summary

We have said that probability and statistical theory tells us the chance that something will (or will not) happen, expressed in the *odds* that it will (or will not) happen. Now let us see how we can *estimate* the odds of several concrete situations, using a new approach to basic problems in probability and statistics, the Monte Carlo method. (A formalization of similar methods has recently come to prominence in mathematical statistics under the label "bootstrap method" [Efron, 1982].)

1. Introductory Problems

A. EXAMPLE 1: AN INTRODUCTORY PROBLEM—POKER HANDS

Let us begin with a pure problem in odds: What is the chance (what are the odds) that the first five cards chosen from a complete deck of fifty-two bridge (poker) cards will contain two cards of the same denomination?

We shall estimate these odds the way that gamblers have estimated gambling odds for thousands of years. First, check that the deck is not a pinochle deck and is not missing any cards. (Overlooking such small but crucial mat-

ters often leads to errors in science.) Shuffle thoroughly until you are satisfied that the cards are randomly distributed. (It is surprisingly hard to shuffle well.) Then deal five cards and mark down whether the hand does or does not contain a pair of the same denomination. At this point, we must decide whether three of a kind, four of a kind, or two pairs meet our criterion for a pair; we decide *not* to count them.

Then replace the five cards in the deck, shuffle, and deal again. Again mark whether the hand contains one pair of the same denomination. Do this many times. (Table 31.1 shows 100 hands, which our assistant has just dealt.) Then count the number of hands with pairs, and figure the proportion (as a percentage) of all hands. In Table 31.1, 44 per cent of the hands contained pairs, and that is our estimate of the probability that one pair will turn up in a poker hand.

This experimental estimation (called "Monte Carlo estimation" for obvious reasons) does not require a deck of cards. For example, one might create a fifty-two sided die, one side for each card in the deck, and spin it five times to get a "hand." But note one important part of the procedure: No single "card" is allowed to

TABLE 31.1

Trial	1	2	3	4	5	6	7	8	9	10	11	12	13
Results	Y	Y	N	N	Y	Y	N	N	Y	N	N	Y	N
Trial	14	15	16	17	18	19	20	21	22	23	24	25	26
Results	N	Y	Y	Y	Y	Y	N	N	Y	N	Y	N	Y
Trial	27	28	29	30	31	32	33	34	35	36	37	38	39
Results	N	Y	N	Y	Y	N	Y	N	N	N	N	Y	N
Trial	40	41	42	43	44	45	46	47	48	49	50		
Results	N	N	N	N	Y	Y	Y	N	N	Y	N		

Subtotal: 23 Yes, 27 No = 46%

Trial	51	52	53	54	55	56	57	58	59	60	61	62	63
Results	N	Y	N	N	Y	N	Y	Y	N	N	N	Y	Y
Trial	64	65	66	67	68	69	70	71	72	73	74	75	76
Results	Y	N	N	Y	N	N	N	N	Y	N	Y	N	N
Trial	77	78	79	80	81	82	83	84	85	86	87	88	89
Results	N	N	N	N	Y	N	N	N	Y	Y	N	Y	N
Trial	90	91	92	93	94	95	96	97	98	99	100		
Results	Y	Y	N	N	Y	Y	Y	Y	N	Y	N		

Subtotal: 21 Yes, 29 No = 42%

Total: 44 Yes, 56 No = 44%

come up twice in the same set of five spins, just as no card can possibly appear twice in the same hand. If the same "card" did turn up twice or more in a die experiment, one could pretend that the spin had never taken place; this procedure is necessary to make the die experiment analogous to the actual card-dealing situation under investigation. Otherwise, the results will be slightly in error. This type of sampling is known as "sampling without replacement," because each card is *not replaced* in the deck each time it is dealt (until the end of the hand, that is).

Still another Monte Carlo method uses a *random-number table*, a sample of which is shown in Table 31.2. Arbitrarily designate the spades as numbers 01–13, the diamonds as 14–26, the hearts as 27–39, and the clubs as 40–52. Then proceed across a row (or down a column), writing down each successive two-digit number, except for numbers outside 01–52, and omitting duplication within sets of five numbers. Then translate them back into cards, and see how many "hands" of five "cards" contain one pair each. Table 31.3 shows six such hands, of which 2, 3, and 6 contain pairs.

How accurate are these Monte Carlo methods? The accuracy depends on the *number of hands* we deal—the more hands, the greater the accuracy. Mathematical calculations tell us that, if we were to deal millions of hands, 42 per cent would contain a pair each; that is, the chance of getting a pair in the long run is 42 per cent. The estimate of 44 per cent based on 100 hands in Table 31.1 is close, though whether it is close enough depends on one's needs, of course. If you need great accuracy, you should deal more hands.

How many trials (hands) should be made for the estimate? There is no easy answer. The best approach is to run several (perhaps ten) equal-sized sets of trials and then to examine whether the proportion of pairs found in the entire group of trials is very different from the proportion found in the various subgroup sets. If the proportions of pairs in the various

TABLE 31.2   Table of Random Digits

14900	77763	66045	91851	02199	34221	58116	06648	55779	50353	16401
14901	93968	57080	56566	05093	12677	02035	34393	28765	83709	60080
14902	96185	55327	46929	21087	08191	54583	17963	18599	57717	26689
14903	50956	13999	05475	02687	20207	28492	18203	53613	64035	69836
14904	42925	13489	61425	07510	92172	78063	78247	34647	37710	71779
14905	74102	76512	99800	27498	08257	71444	29192	73165	85985	58584
14906	25963	77276	01566	26830	83288	89183	03636	91176	04673	48271
14907	00336	28332	95442	45548	92764	69320	67663	74935	45673	89406
14908	97190	07021	54689	76464	07125	60376	96263	81957	98097	89311
14909	42508	33579	74511	37271	66533	14980	87997	46543	20445	29364
14910	15095	69719	62380	00947	13581	49929	23187	04410	11076	50274
14911	46426	40638	80584	14926	70877	76023	31838	32280	61814	43410
14912	18432	53552	44904	13591	53696	28658	09538	77232	23728	49210
14913	98828	28017	51152	39704	04560	20423	63072	94843	02544	70033
14914	81052	43812	38934	31109	94872	40069	70062	53044	24375	70147
14915	74325	73599	05533	99548	74035	63714	07222	08337	76768	32818
14916	90928	47761	02291	80702	83239	25189	89692	19820	22468	05036
14917	07510	62086	73335	06373	14326	08408	25356	55568	57104	01080
14918	91192	26484	00867	88759	10759	33681	65027	20204	86513	09961
14919	67338	60202	26494	65254	72875	19913	77183	67772	63750	00160
14920	85269	97756	56322	57967	67739	07247	43739	71253	20167	27559
14921	53369	93055	91402	49671	04836	76592	94506	36169	53691	29980
14922	41545	08255	77112	08226	59377	64281	78805	43935	89642	28246
14923	25149	61362	56824	03083	87188	24545	92615	02467	24037	30907
14924	07811	48013	21451	00027	24292	19821	61891	50220	58751	50149
14925	59136	72788	65822	92765	11578	41707	67454	53971	22142	42152
14926	39413	48108	16818	63717	28962	08592	14709	06238	05846	00185
14927	71779	00051	96502	23391	64072	62357	28655	24549	11676	47937
14928	41939	06052	07881	75888	74477	40449	59968	83495	62878	49038
14929	16852	18740	41590	28762	40054	10564	35447	68877	44619	61061
14930	04631	58241	41013	05634	63332	39191	97358	71011	11686	52933
14931	95217	80882	38875	03353	78129	48089	28134	99469	34177	72409
14932	80365	85981	85997	77118	04077	83723	50303	98313	01146	18326
14933	58855	05833	18794	52072	59851	01483	88374	36319	36368	26524
14934	22006	45586	23893	41542	62646	33970	54241	92550	88540	53154

Source: *A Million Random Digits*, p. 299, 1955; reprinted by permission of the RAND Corporation.

subgroups differ greatly from one another or from the overall proportion, then keep *quadrupling[1]* the number of trials until the overall

average is not changed much by the additional trials. In this case, Table 31.1 shows that the average of the total of 100 hands is not much different from the average of the first fifty hands, and so we could reasonably quit dealing after 100 hands.

The method of solution just discussed for this problem clearly is not difficult to do or to understand. In contrast, the conventional analytic method of solving this problem requires knowledge of the theory of permutations and

1. The reason for quadrupling is that *four* times as big a sample gives *twice* as much accuracy (as measured by the standard deviation, the most frequent measurement of accuracy). That is, the error decreases with the square root of the sample size. And a step that doubles accuracy is a comfortable arbitrary step in many cases. But if you see that you need *much* more accuracy, then *immediately* increase the sample size even more than four times.

TABLE 31.3

	Ace	Deuce	3	4	5	6	7	8	9	10	Jack	Queen	King
Spades	01	02	03	04	05	06	07	08	09	10	11	12	13
Diamonds	14	15	16	17	18	19	20	21	22	23	24	25	26
Hearts	27	28	29	30	31	32	33	34	35	36	37	38	39
Clubs	40	41	42	43	44	45	46	47	48	49	50	51	52
			1			10	09	25	33	52			
			2			01	35	34	36	48			
			3			17	39	29	27	49			
			4			45	20	48	05	47			
			5			42	24	52	40	37			
			6			20	04	02	29	16			

combinations, and it is not easy for the average student to understand, even though it is very elementary probability theory. It is even more true in the examples to follow that the Monte Carlo solution is simple and straightforward, whereas the conventional analytic solution is either difficult or impossible for the ordinary student, undergraduate or graduate.

B. EXAMPLE 2: ANOTHER INTRODUCTORY POKER PROBLEM

Which is more likely, poker hands with two pairs or with three of a kind? This is a *comparison* problem, rather than a problem in absolute estimation, as was Example 1.

In a series of 100 hands (using random numbers), four hands contained two pairs, and two hands contained three of a kind. Is it safe to say, on the basis of these 100 hands, that hands with two pairs are more frequent than hands with three of a kind? We do not think so. To check, we deal another 300 hands. In this 300, we see fifteen hands with two pairs (3.75 per cent) and eight hands with three of a kind (2 per cent), for a total of 19 to 10. Although the difference is not enormous, it is reasonably clear-cut. Another 400 hands might be advisable, but we shall not bother.

Earlier we obtained forty-four hands with *one* pair each out of 100 hands, which makes it quite plain that *one* pair is more frequent than

either two pairs or three of a kind. Obviously, we need *more* hands to compare the odds in favor of two pairs with the odds in favor of three of a kind than to compare those for one pair with those for either two pairs or three of a kind. Why? Because the difference in odds between one pair and either two pairs or three of a kind is much greater than the difference in odds between two pairs and three of a kind. This observation leads to a general rule: The closer the odds between two events, the *more trials* are needed to determine which has the higher odds.

Again it is interesting to compare the odds with the mathematical computations, which are 1 in 21 (4.75 per cent) for a hand containing two pairs and 1 in 47 (2.1 per cent) for a hand containing three of a kind—not too far from the estimate of 3.75 per cent and 2.0 per cent, based on 100 random hands.

We have dealt with these first two examples in an intuitive, unsystematic fashion. From here on, however, we will work in an explicitly systematic step-by-step manner.

C. EXAMPLE 3: FOUR DAUGHTERS AMONG FIVE CHILDREN (TWO-OUTCOME SAMPLING WITH EQUALLY LIKELY OUTCOMES WITH REPLACEMENT)

What is the probability that four of the first five children in a five-child family will be daughters?

The first step is to state the approximate probability that a single birth will produce a daughter as 50-50 (1 in 2). This estimate is not strictly correct because there are 106 male children born to every 100 female children, but the approximation is not too far off for most purposes, and the 50-50 split simplifies the job considerably. (Such "false" approximations are part of the everyday work of the scientist. The question is not whether a statement is "only" an approximation but whether it is a *good* approximation for your purposes.)

The chance of a fair coin's coming up heads is 50-50, as are the odds in favor of the birth of a single daughter. Therefore flip a coin in groups of five flips, and count how often all five of the flips produce *heads*. (You must decide in *advance* whether four heads mean four girls or four boys.) It is as simple as that.

In Monte Carlo estimation it is of the highest importance to work in a careful step-by-step fashion—to write down the steps in the estimation, and then to do the experiments just as described in the steps. (For classroom purposes, it is often sufficient for the student to write down the steps in the experiments, together with a very few experimental trials, rather than doing a full set of trials. The instructor can easily judge whether the student's method is correct.)

Here is a set of steps that will lead to a correct answer about the likelihood of getting four daughters among five children:

Step 1. Using coins, let "heads" equal "boy" and "tails" equal "girl."

Step 2. Throw five coins, and examine whether they fall with exactly four tails up. If so, write *yes* on a record sheet; otherwise write *no*.

Step 3. Repeat Step 2 perhaps a hundred times. Count the proportion of *yeses*. That proportion is an estimate of the likelihood of obtaining exactly four daughters in five children.

The first few experimental trials might appear in the record sheet as follows:

Number of Heads	Yes or No
1	No
1	No
4	Yes
3	No
2	No
3	No

The probability of getting four daughters in five births could also be found with a deck of cards, a random-number table, or a die. For example, half the cards in a deck are black, so the probability of dealing with a black card ("daughter") from a full deck is 1 in 2. Therefore, deal a card, record "daughter" or "son," *replace* the card, deal again, and so forth for sets of five cards. Then count the proportion of groups of five cards in which you got four daughters.

Notice that the procedure outlined in the steps would have been different if we had asked about the likelihood of *four or more* daughters rather than exactly four daughters among five children. For *four or more* daughters we would have scored *yes* for either *four or five* heads, rather than just for four heads.

In this case, in contrast to what occurred in Example 1, it is important that the card be replaced *each time*, so that each card is dealt from a full deck. This method is known as *sampling with replacement*. One samples with replacement whenever the successive events are *independent;* in this case, we assume that the chance of having a daughter remains the same (1 in 2), no matter how many sons or daughters the family has previously had.[2] But, if the first card dealt is black and is *not* replaced, the chance of the second card's being black is no longer 26 in 52 (1 in 2) but is only 25 in 51 (less

2. This assumption is slightly contrary to scientific fact. A better example would be the probability that four mothers delivering in a row in a hospital will all have daughters. But that example has other difficulties.

than 1 in 2). If the first *three* cards are black and are not replaced, then the chance of the fourth card's being black sinks to 23 in 49.

To take the illustration further, consider what would happen if we used a deck of only six cards, half (three) black and half (three) red, instead of a deck of fifty-two cards. If the cards were replaced each time, the six-card deck would produce the same results as a fifty-two-card deck; in fact, a two-card deck would do as well. But, if the sampling were done *without* replacement, it would be *impossible* to obtain four "daughters" with the six-card deck because there would be only three "daughters" in the deck. To repeat, then, whenever you want to estimate the probability of some series of events of which each is independent of the other, you must sample *with replacement*.

2. The General Procedure

Until now, the steps to follow in solving particular problems have been chosen to fit the facts of that problem. And so they must. But we can also describe the series of steps in a more general fashion so as to throw light on what we are doing when we construct a series of Monte Carlo problem-solving operations leading up to estimation of a probability. The general steps are lettered rather than numbered here, because more than one step in a particular Monte Carlo experiment *may be* necessary to complete a general step described here.

Step A. Construct a universe of random numbers or cards or dice or some other random generation mechanism that has similar composition and structural properties as does the universe whose behavior we wish to simulate and describe. The universe refers to the system that is relevant for a single simple event.

(a) A coin with two sides, or two sets of random numbers 1–5 and 6–0, simulate the system that produces a single male or female birth, when we are estimating the probability of four girls in the first five children. Notice that in this universe the probability of a girl remains the same from trial event to trial event—that is, the trials are independent—which is a universe from which we sample with replacement.

(b) A deck of twenty-five red and twenty-five black cards simulates a group of twenty-five boys and twenty-five girls from which we draw a sample of five students.

Hard thinking is required in order to decide just what the appropriate real universe is. Once this is done, however, it is relatively easy to choose the appropriate simulation model.

Step B. Specify the procedure that produces a sample that simulates the real-life sample we are interested in. That is, you must indicate the *rules* of procedure by which the sample is drawn from the simulated universe. These rules must correspond to the behavior of the real universe you are interested in. To put it another way, the simulation procedure must produce simple experimental events with the same probabilities that the simple events have in the real world.

In the case of four daughters in five children, the procedure is to draw a card *and then replace it*, if you are using cards. If you are using a random-numbers table, the random numbers automatically simulate replacement.

Recording the outcome of the sampling must be indicated as part of this step—record *yes* if girl, *no* if boy.

Step C. If several simple events must be combined into a composite event, and if the composite event was not described in the procedure in Step B, describe it now.

For the four girls in five children, the procedure for each simple event of a simple birth was described in Step B. Now we must specify repeating the simple event five times.

Recording *yes* or *no*, success or failure, is part of this step. This record indicates which set of events of interest to us—the outcome of the composite event, which is the Monte Carlo trial—occurs.

Step D. Calculate from the outcomes of the

Monte Carlo trials the proportion of *yes* or *no*, success or failure, that estimates the likelihood we wish to determine.

There is indeed more than one way to skin a cat. And there is always more than one way to correctly estimate a given probability. Therefore, when reading through the list of steps set forth here to estimate a given probability, please keep in mind that a particular list is not sacred or unique; other sets of steps will also do the trick.

A. EXAMPLE 4: THE BIRTHDAY PROBLEM (THE PROBABILITY OF DUPLICATION IN A MULTIOUTCOME SAMPLE FROM AN INFINITE UNIVERSE)

As an indication of how powerful *and* simple are Monte Carlo methods, consider this famous examination question used in courses on probability: What is the probability that two or more people among a roomful of, say, twenty-five people were born on the same day of the year (for example, November 26)? To answer, we may simply examine the first twenty-five numbers from the random-number table that fall between 001 and 365 (days in the year) and record whether there is a duplication among the twenty-five. Repeat the process enough times to get a reasonably stable probability estimate. Then pose the question to a mathematical friend of yours, watch him sweat for a while, and compare your answer to his. (We think you will find the correct answer very surprising. People who know how this problem works have been known to take advantage of this knowledge by making and winning big bets on it.)

More specifically, here are steps to handle this problem for the case of twenty-five people in the room:

Step 1. Let three-digit random numbers 001–365 stand for the 365 days in the year. (Ignore leap year for simplicity.)

Step 2. Examine the first twenty-five random numbers 001–365 to see if there is duplication (triplicates or higher-order repeats are counted as duplicates). If there is one or more duplicate, record *yes;* otherwise record *no.*

Step 3. Repeat perhaps a hundred times, and calculate the proportion of a duplicate birthday among twenty-five people.

Here is the first experiment from the random-number table on page 375, starting at the top left:

Experiment Numbers	Duplication
1) 021, 158, 116, 066, *353*, 164, 019 080, 312, 020, *353* . . .	Yes

3. Hypothesis Testing

The previous problems have been problems in probability theory—that is, problems in estimating the likelihood of a composite event resulting from a system in which we *know* the probabilities of the simple events. That is, we have been dealing with systems whose "parameters" we know.

Now we turn to inferential-statistical problems. These are problems in which *we seek to learn and estimate* the probabilities of a system—that is, the probabilities of its simple events and parameters.

This chapter begins a discussion of the group of problems in inferential statistics known as "hypothesis testing" problems. Subsequent chapters continue with hypothesis testing, and chapters that follow take up estimation of the *strength* of a relationship between two or more variables.

A. EXAMPLE 5: DOES IRRADIATION AFFECT THE SEX RATIO IN FRUIT FLIES? (WHERE THE BENCHMARK UNIVERSE MEAN IS KNOWN, IS THE MEAN OF THE POPULATION AFFECTED BY THE TREATMENT?)

You think you have developed a technique for irradiating the genes of fruit flies so that the sex ratio of the offspring will *not* be half males and half females. In the first twenty cases you treat, there are fourteen males and six females. Does this result confirm that the irradiation does work?

First convert the scientific question—whether the treatment affects the sex distribution—into a probability-statistical question: Is the observed sample likely to have come from a universe in which the sex ratio is one male to one female? The benchmark (null) hypothesis, then, is that the treatment makes no difference and that the sample comes from the 1-to-1 universe. (The concept of the benchmark hypothesis was discussed on page 370.) Therefore, we investigate how likely is a 1-to-1 universe to produce a distribution of fourteen males to six females.

A coin has a 1-to-1 (1 out of 2) chance of coming up tails. Therefore, we might flip a coin in groups of twenty flips and count the number of heads in each twenty flips. Or we can use a random-digit table. These steps will produce a sound estimate:

Step 1. Let heads = males, tails = females
Step 2. Flip twenty coins and count the number of males. If fourteen or more males occur, record *yes;* if thirteen or less, record *no*.
Step 3. Repeat Step 2 perhaps 100 times.
Step 4. Calculate the proportion of *yes* in the 100 trials. This proportion estimates the likelihood that a fruit-fly population with a mean of 50 per cent males will by chance produce as many as fourteen males in a sample of twenty flies.

Table 31.4 shows the results obtained in twenty-five trials of twenty flips each.

In two of the twenty-five trials (8 per cent) there were fourteen or more heads, which we shall call "males," and in one of the twenty-five trials (4 per cent) there were fourteen or more tails ("females"). We can therefore estimate that, even if the treatment does *not* affect the sex and even if the births over a long period are really 1 to 1, we would get fourteen or more of one sex or the other in three out of twenty-five times (12 per cent). Therefore,

TABLE 31.4

Trial of 20 Coin Flips	Number of Heads	Trial of 20 Coin Flips	Number of Heads	Trial of 20 Coin Flips	Number of Heads
1	11 = No	10	10 = No	18	12 = No
2	12 "	11	10 "	19	13 "
3	8 "	12	10 "	20	10 "
4	12 "	13	9 "	21	11 "
5	12 "	14	9 "	22	14 Yes
6	7 "	15	12 "	23	9 "
7	9 "	16	7 "	24	7 "
8	8 "	17	14 Yes	25	10 "
9	6 "				

finding fourteen males out of twenty births is not overwhelming evidence that the treatment has any effect, though it is suggestive.

How accurate is the estimate? Seventy-five more trials were made, and of the total 100 trials ten contained fourteen or more "males" (10 per cent), and seven trials contained fourteen or more "females" (7 per cent), a total of 17 per cent. So the first twenty-five trials gave a fairly reliable indication. As a matter of fact, a mathematical computation (not explaiend here) shows that the probability of getting fourteen or more females out of twenty births is .057 and, of course, the same for fourteen or more males from a 1-to-1 universe, a total probability of .114 of getting fourteen or more males *or* females.

Notice that the strength of the evidence for the effectivenss of the radiation treatment depends upon the original question, whether the treatment had *any* effect on sex. But if there were reason to believe at the start that the treatment could increase only the number of *males*, then we would focus our attention on the fact that in only two of our first twenty-five trials were there fourteen or more males. There would be only a ²⁄₂₅ probability of getting the observed results by chance if the treatment really has no effect, rather than the weaker odds against obtaining fourteen or more of *either* males or females.

Therefore, whether you decide to figure the odds for just fourteen or more males (what is called a "one-tail test") or for fourteen or more males *plus* fourteen or more females (a "two-tail test"), depends upon your advance knowledge of the treatment. If you have no reason to believe that the treatment will have an effect *only* in the direction of creating more males, and if you figure the odds for the one-tail test anyway, then you will be fooling yourself. Theory comes to bear here. If you have a strong hypothesis, deduced from a strong theory, that there will be more males, then you should figure one-tail odds, but if you have no

such theory you should figure the weaker two-tail odds.[3]

"Significance level" is a common term in probability statistics. It corresponds roughly to the probability that the observed sample does not come from a particular universe by chance. The results of Example 5 can be phrased as follows: The hypothesis that the radiation treatment affects the sex of fruit-fly offspring is accepted as true at the 17 per cent "level of significance." (A more common way of expressing this idea would be to say that the hypothesis is *not rejected* at the 17 per cent level of significance. But "not rejected" and "accepted" really do mean much the same thing, despite some arguments to the contrary.) This kind of statistical work is called *statistical testing*.

The question of *which* significance level should be said to be significant is difficult. How great must a coincidence be before you refuse to believe that it is only a coincidence? It has been conventional in social science to say that, if the probability that something happens by chance is less than 5 per cent, it is significant. But sometimes the stiffer standard of 1 per cent is used. Actually, *any* fixed cut-off significance level is an arbitrary construction. (And even the entire notion of saying that a hypothesis is true or is not true is sometimes not very useful.)

Before leaving this example, let us review our intellectual strategy in handling the problem. First we observe a result (14 males in 20 flies) that differs from the mean of the population (50 per cent males). Because we have treated this sample with irradiation and observed a result that differs from the untreated population's mean, we speculate that the irradiation caused the sample to differ from the untreated population. We wish to check whether this speculation is correct.

3. If you are very knowledgeable, you may do some in-between figuring (with what is known as "Bayesian analysis"), but leave this alone unless you know exactly what you are doing.

When asking whether this speculation is correct, we are implicitly asking whether future irradiation would also produce a proportion of males higher than 50 per cent. That is, we are implicitly asking whether irradiated flies would produce more samples with male proportions as high as $^{14}/_{20}$ than would occur by chance in the absence of irradiation.

If samples as far away as $^{14}/_{20}$ from the population mean would occur frequently by chance, then we are not impressed with the experimental evidence as proof that irradiation affects the sex ratio. Hence we set up a model that will tell us the frequency with which such samples as 14 males out of 20 births would be observed by chance. Carrying out the Monte Carlo procedure tells us that perhaps a tenth of the time such samples would be observed by chance. That is not frequent, but it is not infrequent either. Hence we would probably conclude that the evidence is provocative enough to justify further experimentation, but not so strong that we should immediately believe in the truth of this speculation.

B. EXAMPLE 6: DO ANY OF FOUR TREATMENTS AFFECT THE SEX RATIO IN FRUIT FLIES? (WHEN THE BENCHMARK UNIVERSE MEAN IS KNOWN, IS THE MEAN OF THE TWO-OUTCOME POPULATION AFFECTED BY ANY OF THE TREATMENTS?)

Suppose that, instead of trying just one type of radiation treatment on the flies, as in Example 5, you try *four* different treatments, which we shall label A, B, C, and D. In treatment A you get fourteen males and six females, but in treatments B, C, and D you get ten, eleven, and ten males, respectively. It is immediately obvious that there is no reason to think that treatment B, C, or D affects the sex ratio. But what about treatment A?

A frequent and dangerous mistake made by young scientists is to scrounge around in the data for the most extreme observation and then to treat it as if it were the only observation made. (This matter is discussed in more depth on page 242.) In the context of this example, it would be fallacious to think that the probability of the fourteen males–six females split observed for treatment A is the probability that we figured for a *single* experiment in Example 5. Instead, we must consider that our benchmark universe is composed of *four sets* of twenty trials, each trial having a 50-50 probability of coming out male. We can consider that old trials 1–4 in Example 5 constitute a single new trial, and each subsequent set of four old trials constitutes another new trial. We then ask how likely is a new trial of four sets of twenty flips to produce *one* set with fourteen or more of one or the other sex.

Let us make the procedure explicit, but using random numbers instead of coins this time:

Step 1. Let 1–5 = males, 6–0 = females
Step 2. Choose four groups of twenty numbers. If for *any* group there are fourteen or more males, record *yes;* if thirteen or less, record *no.*
Step 3. Repeat Step 2 perhaps 100 times.
Step 4. Calculate the proportion of *yes* in the 100 trials. This proportion estimates the likelihood that a fruit-fly population with a mean of 50 per cent males will produce as many as fourteen males in at least one of four samples of twenty flies.

We begin the trials with data from the previous examples.

In two of the six trials, a sample shows fourteen or more males. And another trial shows fourteen or more *females*. Without even concerning ourselves about whether we should be looking at males or females, or just males, or needing to do more trials, we can see that it would be very common indeed to have one of four treatments show fourteen or more of one sex just by chance. This discovery clearly indicates that a result that would be fairly unusual

Trial Number	Group A	Group B	Group C	Group D	Yes/No
1	11	12	8	12	No
2	12	7	9	8	No
3	6	10	10	10	No
4	9	9	12	7	No
5	14	12	13	10	Yes
6	11	14	9	7	Yes

(3 in 25) for a single sample is commonplace in one of four observed samples.

C. EXAMPLE 7: A PUBLIC-OPINION POLL (IS THE MEAN OF A POPULATION GREATER THAN A GIVEN VALUE?)

A municipal official wanted to determine whether the *majority* of a town's residents were for or against the awarding of a cable-television franchise, and he asked you take a poll. You judged that the telephone book was a fair representation of the universe in which the politician was interested, and you decided to interview by telephone. Of a sample of fifty people who expressed opinions, thirty were for the plan and twenty were against it. How conclusively do the results show that the people in town want cable television?

The benchmark (null) hypothesis is that 50 per cent of the town does not want the plan. (This statement really means that 50 per cent or *more* do not want the plan.)

This problem is very much like the one-group fruit fly irradiation problem in Example 5. The only difference is that now we are comparing the observed sample against an arbitrary value (50 per cent in this case, because that is the cut-off point in a situation where the majority decides), whereas in the fruit fly example we compared the observed sample against the normal population mean (also 50 per cent, because that is the normal proportion of males). But it really does not matter why we are comparing the observed sample to the figure of 50 per cent; the procedure is the same in both cases. (Please notice that there is noth-ing special about the 50 per cent figure; the same procedure would be followed for 20 per cent or 85 per cent.)

In brief, we designate 1–5 as *no* in the random number table, 6–0 as *yes*. We count the number of *yes* and *no* in the first fifty numbers and repeat for perhaps a hundred trials. Then we count the proportion of the trials in which a 50-50 universe would produce thirty or more *yes* answers.

In operational steps, the procedure is as follows:

Step 1. 1–5 = no, 6–0 = yes
Step 2. In fifty random numbers, if thirty or more are *no*, record it as *against*.
Step 3. Repeat Step 2 perhaps 100 times.
Step 4. Calculate the proportion of experimental trials *against*.

This estimates the likelihood that as many as thirty *nos* would be observed by chance in a sample of fifty people, *if* half (or more) are really for the plan.

In Table 31.5 we see the results of twenty trials; in four of twenty trials (20 per cent) 30 or more *nos* were observed by chance.

This is the probability that as many as thirty of fifty people would say yes by chance if the population were "really" split evenly. (If the population were split so that *more* than 50 per cent were against the plan, the probability would be even *less* that the observed result would occur by chance. In this sense, the benchmark hypothesis is conservative.)

This example suggests that the municipal official would be wise not to place very much

TABLE 31.5

Trial	Number of "No"s	Number of "Yes"es
1	23	27
2	25	25
3	26	24
4	22	28
5	22	28
6	20	30
7	25	25
8	21	29
9	28	22
10	19	31
11	28	22
12	19	31
13	18	32
14	23	27
15	34	16
16	27	23
17	22	28
18	26	24
19	28	22
20	27	23

confidence in the poll results, but rather ought to either act with caution or take a bigger sample.

D. EXAMPLE 8: COMPARISON OF POSSIBLE CANCER CURE TO PLACEBO EFFECT (DO TWO TWO-OUTCOME POPULATIONS DIFFER IN THEIR MEANS?)

Example 5 used an observed sample of male and female fruit flies to test the benchmark (null) hypothesis that the flies came from a universe with a 1-to-1 sex ratio. Now we want to compare *two samples with each other*, rather than comparing one sample with a hypothesized universe. That is, in this example we are not comparing one sample to a benchmark universe, but rather asking whether *both* samples come from the same universe. The universe from which both come, *if* both come from the same universe, may be thought of as the benchmark universe in this case.

The scientific question is whether pill P cures cancer. A researcher gave the pill to six patients selected randomly from a group of twelve cancer patients, of whom five got well. She gave an inactive placebo to the other six patients, and two of them got well. Does the evidence justify a conclusion that the pill has a curative effect?

(An identical statistical example could be constructed with an experiment on methods of teaching reading to children. But in such a case the researcher would respond to inconclusive results by running the experiment on more subjects, though in cases like the cancer-pill example the researcher often cannot obtain more subjects.)

The answer is to *combine* the two samples and then test both samples against the resulting combined universe. In this case, the universe is twelve subjects, seven $(5+2)$ of whom got well. Given such a universe, then, how likely would it be to produce two samples as far apart as five of six and two of six patients who get well? In other words, how often will two samples of six subjects each, drawn from a universe in which $7/12$ of the patients get well, be as far apart as $5-2=3$ patients in favor of the sample designated "pill"? This is obviously a one-tail test, for there is no reason to believe that the pill group might do less well than the placebo group.

Construct a twelve-sided die, seven of whose sides are marked "get well." Or use pairs of numbers from the random-number table, with numbers 01–07 corresponding to "get well," numbers 08–12 corresponding to "not get well," and all other numbers omitted. (If you wish to save time, you can work out a system that uses more and skips fewer of the numbers.) Designate the first six subjects "pill" and the next six subjects "placebo."

The more specific procedure might be as follows:

Step 1. 01–07 = get well, 08–12 = not get well

Step 2. Select two groups, "Pill" and "Placebo," of six random numbers from 01 to 12.

Step 3. Record how many "get well" in each group.

Step 4. Subtract the result in experimental placebo group from that in experimental pill group (the difference may be negative).

Step 5. Repeat Steps 1–4 perhaps 100 times.

Step 6. Compute the proportion of trials in which the pill is better by three or more cases. In the trials shown in Table 31.6 in three cases (12 per cent) the difference between the randomly drawn groups is three or greater. Apparently it is somewhat unusual for this universe to generate "pill" samples in which the number of recoveries exceeds the number in the "placebo" samples by three or more. Therefore the answer to the scientific question, based on these

samples, is that there is some reason to think that the medicine does have a favorable effect. But the investigator might sensibly await more data before reaching a firm conclusion about the pill's efficacy, given the 7 to 1 (12 per cent) odds.

This method is not the standard way of handling the problem; it is not even analogous to the standard analytic difference-of-proportions method. Though the method shown is quite direct and satisfactory, there are *many other* Monte Carlo methods that we might develop to solve the same problem. You should by all means invent your own statistics, rather than simply trying to copy the methods described here; the latter only illustrate the process of inventing statistics rather than offering solutions for all classes of problems.

TABLE 31.6

Trial	Pill	Placebo	Difference
1	4	4	0
2	3	5	−2
3	4	3	1
4*	5	2	3
5	4	3	1
6	2	5	−3
7	4	4	0
8	4	5	−1
9	4	4	0
10*	5	2	3
11	4	5	−1
12	5	3	2
13	3	5	−2
14	3	2	1
15	3	4	−1
16	5	4	1
17*	6	3	3
18	4	5	−1
19	3	4	−1
20	2	3	−1
21	4	4	0
22	4	4	0
23	3	5	−2
24	3	3	0
25	3	3	0

*The total of the asterisked trials is 3 differences as great as 3 in favor of pill.

E. EXAMPLE 9: DO FOUR PSYCHOLOGICAL TREATMENTS DIFFER IN EFFECTIVENESS? (DO SEVERAL TWO-OUTCOME SAMPLES DIFFER AMONG THEMSELVES IN THEIR MEANS?)

Consider now, not two but four different psychological treatments designed to rehabilitate juvenile delinquents. Instead of a score, there is only a *yes* or a *no* answer as to whether the juvenile has been rehabilitated or has gotten into trouble again. Label the treatments *P*, *R*, *S*, and *T*, each of which is administered to a separate group of twenty juvenile delinquents. The number of rehabilitations per group is P, seventeen; R, ten; S, ten; T, seven. Is it improbable that all four groups come from the same universe?

This problem is like the placebo-vs.-cancer-cure problem, but now there are more than two samples. It is also like the four-sample irradiated flies example, except that in this case we are *not* asking whether any or some of the samples differ from a *given universe* (50-50 sex ratio in that case). Rather, we are now asking whether there are differences among the samples themselves. Please keep in mind that we are still dealing with two-outcome (yes-or-no, well-or-sick) problems. Later we shall take up problems that are similar except that the outcomes are "quantitative."

If all four groups come from the same universe, that universe has an estimated rehabilitation rate of

$$\frac{17 + 10 + 10 + 7}{20 + 20 + 20 + 20} = \frac{11}{20} = \frac{55}{100}$$

because the observed data *taken as a whole* constitutes our best guess as to the nature of the universe from which they come—if they all come from the same universe. (Please think over this matter a bit because it is important though subtle. It may help you to notice the absence of any *other* information about the universe from which they all have come, if they have come from the same universe.)

Therefore, select twenty two-digit numbers for each group from the random-number table, marking *yes* for each number 1–55 and *no* for each number 56–100. Conduct a number of such trials. Then count the proportion of times that the difference between the highest and lowest groups is larger than the widest observed difference—that between P and T (17 − 7 = 10). Table 31.7 shows that none of the first six trials shows anywhere near as large a difference, suggesting that it would be rare for four treatments that are "really" similar to show so great a difference. There is thus reason to believe that P and T differ in their effects.

TABLE 31.7

Trial	P	R	S	T	Largest Minus Smallest
1	11	9	8	12	4
2	10	10	12	12	2
3	9	12	8	12	4
4	9	11	12	10	3
5	10	10	11	12	2
6	11	11	9	11	2

The conventional way to approach this problem would be with what is known as a "chi-square test."

F. EXAMPLE 10: IS ONE PIG RATION MORE EFFECTIVE THAN THE OTHER? (TESTING FOR A DIFFERENCE IN MEANS WITH A TWO-BY-TWO CLASSIFICATION)

Each of two new types of ration is fed to twelve pigs. A farmer wants to know whether ration A or ration B is better.[4] The weight gains for pigs fed on ration A are 31.0, 34.0, 29.0, 26.0, 32.0, 35.0, 38.0, 34.0, 30.1, 29.1, 32.0, and 31.0. The weight gains for pigs fed on ration B are 26.0, 24.0, 28.0, 29.0, 30.0, 29.0, 32.0, 26.0, 31.0, 29.0, 32.1, and 28.0.

The *statistical* question is whether the pigs fed on the different rations come from the same universe with respect to weight gains.

One approach is to adopt a strategy similar to that previously used in Example 9—though we now require a bit of arbitrariness. We can divide the pigs into two groups, those twelve with the higher weight gain, and those twelve with the lower weight gain. Then we check whether an unusually large number of high-weight-gain pigs were fed on one or the other of the rations.

We can make this test by ordering the twenty-four weights from high to low this way: 38.0 (ration A), 35.0 (A), 34.0 (A), 34.0 (A), 32.1 (B), 32.0 (A), 32.0 (A), 32.0 (B), 31.0 (A), 31.0 (B), 31.0 (A), 30.1 (A), 30.0 (B), 29.0 (A), 29.0 (A), 29.0 (B), 29.0 (B), 29.0 (B), 28.0 (B), 28.0 (B), 26.0 (A), 26.0 (B), 26.0 (B), and 24.0 (B).

Among the twelve high-gain pigs, nine were fed on ration A. Is this further from an even split than we are likely to get by chance?

Take twelve red and twelve black cards, shuffle them, and deal out twelve cards. Count

---

4. The data for this example are drawn from Dixon and Massey (1968: 117), who offer an orthodox method of handling the problem with a *t* test.

TABLE 31.8

Trial	Black	Red		Trial	Black	Red		Trial	Black	Red
1	7	5		19	5	7		37	6	6
2	7	5		20	5	7		38	5	7
3	6	6		21	4	8		39	7	5
4	6	6		*22	9	3		40	5	7
5	6	6		23	7	5		41	6	6
6	4	8		24	5	7		42	4	8
7	6	6		25	5	7		43	7	5
8	6	6		26	7	5		44	5	7
9	5	7		27	6	6		45	8	4
10	8	4		*28	9	3		46	5	7
11	6	6		29	7	5		47	5	7
12	7	5		30	7	5		48	6	6
13	8	4		31	8	4		49	6	6
14	5	7		*32	3	9		50	6	6
15	6	6		33	5	7				
16	7	5		34	6	6				
17	8	4		35	5	7				
18	8	4		36	5	7				

the proportion of times in which one color comes up nine or more times in the first twelve cards, to reflect ration A's appearance nine times among the highest twelve weight gains. More specifically:

Step 1. Constitute a deck of twelve red and twelve black cards.

Step 2. Deal out twelve cards, count the number of reds, and record *yes* if there are nine or more of *either* red or black.

Step 3. Repeat Step 2 perhaps fifty times.

Step 4. Compute the proportion of *yes*. This estimates the probability sought.

Table 31.8 shows the results of fifty hands. In three (marked by asterisks) of the fifty (6 per cent) there were nine or more either red or black cards in the first twelve cards. Again the results suggest that it would be *slightly unusual* for the results to favor one ration or the other so strongly just by chance if the universe were really the same.

4. Summary

This chapter demonstrates how problems in probability and hypothesis testing may be solved using the experimental Monte Carlo method. A systematic procedure is given and then illustrated in the handling of a variety of problems.

EXERCISE

1. Find an example of a misleading statistic in a newspaper or magazine.

Hypothesis Testing with Measured Data

The previous chapter discussed testing a hypothesis with data that are already in dichotomized form or data in situations where you have measurements but it is convenient to dichotomize the data. Now we move on to hypothesis testing with measured data.

A. EXAMPLE 11: THE PIG RATIONS AGAIN, USING MEASURED DATA (TESTING FOR THE DIFFERENCE BETWEEN MEANS OF TWO EQUAL-SIZED SAMPLES OF MEASURED-DATA OBSERVATIONS)

Another way to approach the pig-ration problem does not require converting the quantitative data into qualitative data and therefore loses no information. The term "to lose information" can be understood intuitively. Consider two sets of three sacks of corn each. The first set includes sacks weighing, respectively, one pound, two pounds, and three pounds. The second set includes sacks of one pound, two pounds, and a hundred pounds. If we *rank* the sacks by weight, the one-pound and two-pound sacks have ranks one and two in both cases, and their relative places in their sets are the same. But if we know not only that the one-pound sack is the smallest of its set and the three-pound or hundred-pound sack is the largest, but *also* that the largest sack is three pounds (or a hundred pounds), we have more information about the set than if we know only the ranks. The rank data are known as "ordi-

nal" or "ranked" data, whereas the data in pounds are known as "cardinal" or "measured" data. Converting from cardinal (measured) to ordinal (ranked) data loses information but may increase convenience.

We begin by observing that if the two rations are the same, then each of the observed weight gains came from the same universe. This is a basic tactic in our statistical strategy. We say that if the two rations came from the same universe, our best guess about the composition of the universe is that it is composed of weight gains like those of the twenty-four pigs we have observed. Since ours is a sample from an infinite (or at least very large) universe of possible weight gains, we assume that there are *many* weight gains in the universe just like the ones we have observed, in the same proportion as we have observed them. For example, we assume that 2/24 of the universe is composed of 34-pound weight gains, as seen in Figure 32.1.

Of course, we recognize that weight gains other than the exact ones we observed are possible, and in fact certainly would occur. And we could assume that the "distribution" of the weight gains would follow a regular "smooth" shape such as in Figure 32.2. But deciding just how to draw Figure 32.2 from the data in Figure 32.1 requires that we make some assumptions about unknown conditions. And if we were to draw Figure 32.2 in a form that would be sufficiently regular for conventional mathe-

FIGURE 32.1

Size of weight gain in pounds, observed

matical analysis, we might have to make some *strong* assumptions, going far beyond what we have observed.

If it were necessary to make such assumptions and draw a smooth curve such as Figure 32.2 from the raw data in Figure 32.1, it might well be done satisfactorily—if done with wisdom and good judgment. But there is no necessity to draw such a smooth curve, in this case or in most cases. We can proceed by assuming only that the benchmark universe—conventionally called the "null" or "hypothetical" universe, and which is the universe we shall compare our samples to—is composed only of elements similar to the observations we have in hand. We thereby lose no efficiency and avoid the probability of making misleading assumptions.

FIGURE 32.2

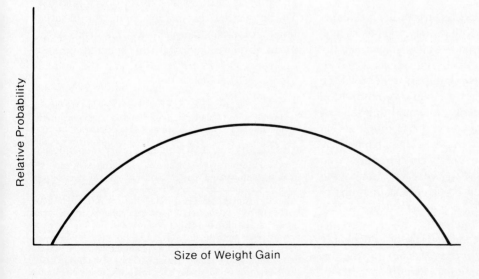

Size of Weight Gain

To execute our tactic, we write down each of the twenty-four weight gains on a separate, blank index card. We then have one card each for 31, 34, 29, 26, and so on. (Drop the decimal points that were arbitrarily added in Example 10 to break ties.) Shuffle the twenty-four cards thoroughly, and deal two hands of twelve cards each. Call the first "ration A" and the second "ration B." Reckon the average weight gain for the two hands, and record it as in Table 32.1. Reshuffle, and repeat several times.

In operational steps:

Step 1. Write down each observed weight gain on a card, such as 31, 34, 29, and so on.

Step 2. Shuffle and deal out groups A and B of twelve cards each. Calculate the mean weight gain of each group.

Step 3. Subtract the mean of group A from the mean of group B and record. If the figure is more positive than 3.08 or more negative than 3.08, record "more" or "less," respectively.

Step 4. Repeat Step 3 fifty times, and calculate the proportion of "more." This estimates the probability sought.

In none of the first ten trials did the difference in the means of the random hands exceed the observed difference (3.08 pounds, in the top line of the table) between rations A and B. (The difference between group *totals* tells the same story and is faster, requiring no division calculations.) Ordinarily we would quit dealing at such a point, confident that a difference in means that great is not likely to happen by chance. (Using the quick multiplication rule described on page 404, we can estimate the likelihood of such an occurrence happening by chance as $\frac{1}{2} \times \frac{1}{2} \times \frac{1}{2} \ldots = (\frac{1}{2})^{10} = \frac{1}{1024} \approx .001 = .1\%$, a small chance indeed.)

Table 32.1 shows fifty trials of which only one (the thirty-ninth) is as "far out" as the observed samples. These data give us an estimate of the probability that the two rations do not come from the same universe—approximately $\frac{49}{50}$, or 98 per cent. (Compare this estimate with the probability of roughly 99 per cent estimated with the conventional *t* test—that is, a signficance level of 1 per cent.) On the average, the test described in this section yields a significance level as high as such mathematical-probability tests as the *t* test; that is, it is just as efficient, though the test described in Example 10 is likely to be less efficient because it converts measured data to ranked, or classified, data.[1]

This example illustrates how the *dispersion within samples* affects the difficulty of finding out whether the samples differ from each other. For example, the average weight gain for ration A was 32 pounds, versus 29 pounds for ration B. If *all* the ration A-fed pigs had gained weight within a range of, say, 29.9 to 31.1 pounds, and if all the ration B-fed pigs had gained weight within a range of 28.9 to 29.1 pounds—that is, if the highest weight gain in ration B had been lower than the lowest weight gain in ration A—then there would be no question that ration A is better, and even fewer observations would have made this point clear. Variation (dispersion) is thus of great importance in statistics and in the social sciences. The larger the dispersion among the observations *within* the samples—as measured by the mean absolute deviation (the average absolute difference between the mean and the individ-

1. Note to statisticians: The test described in this section is nonparametric and therefore makes no assumptions about the shapes of the distributions, which is well because we would be on soft ground if we assumed normality in the pig-ration case, given the sample sizes. This test does not, however, throw away information as do the rank and median tests illustrated earlier. And indeed, this test proves to be more powerful than the other nonparametric tests. After developing this test, J. Simon discovered that its general logic follows the tradition of the "randomization" tests based on an idea by Fisher and worked out for the two-sample case by Pitman (1937). But the only mentions of *sampling* from the universe of possibilities are in Dwass (1957) and in Chung and Fraser (1958). J. Simon is grateful to J. Pratt for bringing the later literature to his attention.

TABLE 32.1

(1) Actually Observed Trial	Mean of First Twelve Observations (First Hand) (2) $381 \div 12 = 31.75$	Mean of Second Twelve Observations (Second Hand) (3) $344 \div 12 = 28.67$	Difference (4) = (2 − 3) 3.08	Greater or Less Than Observed Absolute Difference
1	$368 \div 12 = 30.67$	$357 \div 12 = 29.75$	.87	Less
2	$364 \div 12 = 30.33$	$361 \div 12 = 30.08$	.25	"
3	$352 \div 12 = 29.33$	$373 \div 12 = 31.08$	− 1.75	"
4	$378 \div 12 = 31.50$	$347 \div 12 = 28.92$	2.58	"
5	$365 \div 12 = 30.42$	$360 \div 12 = 30.00$	.42	"
6	$352 \div 12 = 29.33$	$373 \div 12 = 31.08$	− 1.75	"
7	$355 \div 12 = 29.58$	$370 \div 12 = 30.83$	− 1.25	"
8	$366 \div 12 = 30.50$	$359 \div 12 = 29.92$	.58	"
9	$360 \div 12 = 30.00$	$365 \div 12 = 30.42$	− .42	"
10	$355 \div 12 = 29.58$	$370 \div 12 = 30.83$	− 1.25	"
11	$359 \div 12 = 29.92$	$366 \div 12 = 30.50$	− .58	"
12	$369 \div 12 = 30.75$	$356 \div 12 = 29.67$	1.08	"
13	$360 \div 12 = 30.00$	$365 \div 12 = 30.42$	− .42	"
14	$377 \div 12 = 31.42$	$348 \div 12 = 29.00$	2.42	"
15	$365 \div 12 = 30.42$	$360 \div 12 = 30.00$	.42	"
16	$364 \div 12 = 30.33$	$361 \div 12 = 30.08$	.25	"
17	$363 \div 12 = 30.25$	$362 \div 12 = 30.17$	.08	"
18	$365 \div 12 = 30.42$	$360 \div 12 = 30.00$	.42	"
19	$369 \div 12 = 30.75$	$356 \div 12 = 29.67$	1.08	"
20	$369 \div 12 = 30.75$	$356 \div 12 = 29.67$	1.08	"
21	$369 \div 12 = 30.75$	$356 \div 12 = 29.67$	1.08	"
22	$364 \div 12 = 30.33$	$361 \div 12 = 30.08$	.25	"
23	$363 \div 12 = 30.25$	$362 \div 12 = 30.17$	.08	"
24	$363 \div 12 = 30.25$	$362 \div 12 = 30.17$	.08	"
25	$364 \div 12 = 30.33$	$361 \div 12 = 30.08$	.25	"
26	$359 \div 12 = 29.92$	$366 \div 12 = 30.50$	− .58	"
27	$362 \div 12 = 30.17$	$363 \div 12 = 30.25$	− .08	"
28	$362 \div 12 = 30.17$	$363 \div 12 = 30.25$	− .08	"
29	$373 \div 12 = 31.08$	$352 \div 12 = 29.33$	1.75	"
30	$367 \div 12 = 30.58$	$358 \div 12 = 29.83$	.75	"
31	$376 \div 12 = 31.33$	$349 \div 12 = 29.08$	2.25	"
32	$365 \div 12 = 30.42$	$360 \div 12 = 30.00$	.42	"
33	$357 \div 12 = 29.75$	$368 \div 12 = 30.67$	− 1.42	"
34	$349 \div 12 = 29.08$	$376 \div 12 = 31.33$	2.25	"
35	$356 \div 12 = 29.67$	$369 \div 12 = 30.75$	− 1.08	"
36	$359 \div 12 = 29.92$	$366 \div 12 = 30.50$	− .58	"
37	$372 \div 12 = 31.00$	$353 \div 12 = 29.42$	1.58	"
38	$368 \div 12 = 30.67$	$357 \div 12 = 29.75$	.92	"
39	$344 \div 12 = 28.67$	$381 \div 12 = 31.75$	− 3.08	More
40	$365 \div 12 = 30.42$	$360 \div 12 = 30.00$	.42	Less
41	$375 \div 12 = 31.25$	$350 \div 12 = 29.17$	2.08	"
42	$353 \div 12 = 29.42$	$372 \div 12 = 31.00$	− 1.58	"

TABLE 32.1 *Continued*

(1) Actually Observed Trial	Mean of First Twelve Observations (First Hand) (2) $381 \div 12 = 31.75$	Mean of Second Twelve Observations (Second Hand) (3) $344 \div 12 = 28.67$	Difference (4) = (2 − 3) 3.08	Greater or Less Than Observed Absolute Difference
43	$357 \div 12 = 29.75$	$368 \div 12 = 30.67$	− .92	"
44	$363 \div 12 = 30.25$	$362 \div 12 = 30.17$	.08	"
45	$353 \div 12 = 29.42$	$372 \div 12 = 31.00$	− 1.58	"
46	$354 \div 12 = 29.50$	$371 \div 12 = 30.92$	− 1.42	"
47	$353 \div 12 = 29.42$	$372 \div 12 = 31.00$	− 1.58	"
48	$368 \div 12 = 30.50$	$359 \div 12 = 29.92$	.58	"
49	$364 \div 12 = 30.33$	$361 \div 12 = 30.08$	.25	"
50	$370 \div 12 = 30.83$	$355 \div 12 = 29.58$	1.25	"

ual observations, treating both plus and minus differences as positive); the variance (the average *squared* difference between the mean and the observations); the standard deviation (the square root of the variance); the range (the difference between the smallest and largest observations); or some other device—the larger the *sample size* necessary to make a conclusive comparison between two groups or to make reliable estimates of summarization statistics.

Are you performing your tests by hand rather than by computer? In a few years everyone will be using computers right at his desk for such tasks. But in the meantime you might prefer to work with the median instead of the mean, for the median requires less computation. Simply compare the difference in medians of the Monte Carlo twelve-pig samples to the difference in medians of the actual samples, just as was done with the means. The only operational difference is to substitute the word "median" for the word "mean" in the steps previously listed on page 390. You may need a somewhat larger number of Monte Carlo trials when working with medians, however, for they tend to be less precise than means.

B. EXAMPLE 12: IS THERE A DIFFERENCE IN LIQUOR PRICES BETWEEN STATE-RUN AND PRIVATELY RUN SYSTEMS? (TESTING FOR DIFFERENCES BETWEEN MEANS OF UNEQUAL-SIZED SAMPLES OF MEASURED DATA)

The pig-ration example dealt with equal numbers of pigs in each litter. The general technique demonstrated in Example 11 is quite flexible, however, and can be used with unequal-sized samples. Consider the 1961 data for the price of a fifth of Seagram 7 Crown whisky in the various states. (Some states are omitted for technical reasons.) The question is whether the price is systematically different in the sixteen "monopoly" states in which the state government owns the retail liquor stores, compared to the twenty-seven states in which retail liquor stores are privately owned, or whether the observed differences might have occurred by chance. The prices for the sixteen monopoly states are $4.65, $4.55, $4.11, $4.15,

$4.20, $4.55, $3.80, $4.00, $4.19, $4.75, $4.74, $4.50, $4.10, $4.00, $5.05, and $4.20.

The prices for the private-enterprise states are $4.82, $5.29, $4.89, $4.95, $4.55, $4.90, $5.25, $5.30, $4.29, $4.85, $4.54, $4.75, $4.85, $4.85, $4.50, $4.75, $4.79, $4.85, $4.79, $4.95, $4.95, $4.75, $5.20, $5.10, $4.80, and $4.29.[2] Now write each of the *forty-two* prices on a separate card, to constitute the benchmark universe. The logic is the same as in Example 11: If the two samples do come from the same universe, then our best guess about the contents of that universe are the observations we have from it; the fact that the samples are of unequal size in this case makes no difference, if in fact they are from the same universe. From this universe we repeatedly deal out sixteen cards. The probability that monopoly states' prices are "really" lower than those of the private-enterprise states is estimated by the proportion of times that the sum (or average) of the sixteen prices dealt is less than (or equal to) the sum (or average) or the actual sixteen prices.

2. The data are from *The Liquor Handbook* (1962: 68). Eight states are omitted for various reasons.

The steps:

Step 1. Write each of the 42 prices on a separate card.
Step 2. Deal out groups of 16 and 26 cards. Calculate the mean price of each group.
Step 3. Calculate the difference between the groups in Step 2, and compare the experimental trial difference to the observed mean difference of $4.84 − $4.35 = $.49; if it is as great or greater, write *yes*, otherwise *no*.
Step 4. Repeat Steps 2 and 3 100 times.
Step 5. Calculate the proportion of *yes*, which estimates the probability we seek.[3]

This is another example of a Monte Carlo test used in a situation in which a *t* test is conventionally done.

3. Various tests indicate that the difference between the groups of states is highly significant. See J. Simon (1966b).

Correlation and Other Statistical Issues

33

1. Correlation and Association
2. Advantages and Disadvantages of the Monte Carlo Method
3. The Multiplication Rule
4. Evaluating the Significance of "Dredged-Up" Relationships
5. Summary

1. Correlation and Association

The questions in the previous examples have been stated in the following form: Does the independent variable (irradiation; type of pig ration) have an effect upon the dependent variable (sex of fruit flies; weight gain of pigs)? Another way to state this question, however, is: Is there a *causal relationship* between the independent variable(s) and the dependent variable?

A causal relationship cannot be defined perfectly neatly, as discussed in Chapter 35. Even an experiment does not determine perfectly whether a relationship deserves to be called "causal" because, among other reasons, the independent variable may not be clear-cut; for example, even if cigarette smoking experimentally produces cancer in rats, it might be the paper and not the tobacco that causes the cancer.

It is clear, however, that in any situation where we are interested in the possibility of causation, we must *at least* know whether there is a relationship (correlation) between

the variables of interest; the existence of a relationship is necessary for that relationship to be judged causal even if it is not sufficient to receive the causal label. And in other situations where we are not even interested in causality, but rather simply want to predict events or understand the structure of a system, we may be interested in the existence of relationships quite apart from questions about causation. Therefore, our next set of problems deals with the likelihood of there being a relationship between two measured variables—variables that can take on many values (say, the values on a test of athletic scores) rather than just two values (say, whether there has been irradiation).

Another way to think about such problems is to ask whether two variables are independent of each other—that is, whether you know anything about the value of one variable if you know the value of the other in a particular case—or whether they are not independent but rather are related.

A. EXAMPLE 13: IS ATHLETIC ABILITY DIRECTLY RELATED TO INTELLIGENCE? (IS THERE CORRELATION BETWEEN TWO VARIABLES OR ARE THEY INDEPENDENT?)

A scientist often wants to know whether two characteristics go together, that is, whether they are correlated (related or associated). For example, is athletic ability correlated with high I.Q.? That is, do youths with high athletic ability tend also to have high I.Q.s?

Physical-education scores of a group of ten high-school boys are shown, ordered from high to low, in Table 33.1, along with the I.Q. score for each boy. The ranks for each student's athletic and I.Q. scores are then shown in columns 3 and 4.

We want to know whether a high score on athletic ability tends to be found along with a high I.Q. score more often than would be expected by chance. Therefore, our strategy is to see how often high scores on both variables are found by chance. We do this dissociating the two variables and making two separate and independent universes, one composed of the athletic scores and another of the I.Q. scores. Then by drawing pairs of observations from the two universes at random, we can consider the experimental patterns to occur by chance, and can compare them to what actually occurs in the world.

The first testing scheme we shall use is similar to our first approach to the pig rations—splitting the results into just highs and lows. We take ten cards, one of each denomination from ace to ten, shuffle, and deal five cards to correspond to the first five athletic ranks. The face values then correspond to the I.Q. ranks. Under the benchmark hypothesis the athletic ranks will not be associated with the I.Q. ranks. Add the face values in the first five cards in each trial; the first hand includes 2, 4, 5, 6, and 9, so the sum is 26. Record, shuffle, and repeat perhaps ten times, as in Table 33.2.

Then compare the random results to the sum of the observed ranks of the five top athletes, which equals 17.

The following steps describe a slightly different procedure from that just described, because this one may be easier to understand:

Step 1. Convert the athletic and I.Q. scores to ranks. Then constitute a universe of spades, ace to ten, to correspond to the athletic ranks, and a universe of hearts, ace to ten, to correspond to the I.Q. ranks.

Step 2. Deal the well-shuffled cards into pairs, each pair with an athletic rank and an I.Q. rank.

Step 3. Locate the cards with the top five athletic ranks, and add the I.Q. rank

TABLE 33.1 Hypothetical Athletic and I.Q. Scores for High-School Boys

Athletic Score (1)	I.Q. Score (2)	Athletic Rank (3)	I.Q. Rank (4)
97	114	1	3
94	120	2	1
93	107	3	7
90	113	4	4
87	118	5	2
86	101	6	8
86	109	7	6
85	110	8	5
81	100	9	9
76	99	10	10

TABLE 33.2

Observed score: 17

Trial	Sum of I.Q. Ranks	Yes or No	Trial	Sum of I.Q. Ranks	Yes or No	Trial	Sum of I.Q. Ranks	Yes or No	Trial	Sum of I.Q. Ranks	Yes or No
1	26	No	11	35	No	21	30	No	31	30	No
2	23	No	12	36	No	22	31	No	32	21	No
3	22	No	13	31	No	23	35	No	33	25	No
4	37	No	14	29	No	24	25	No	34	19	No
*5	16	Yes	15	32	No	25	33	No	35	29	No
6	22	No	16	25	No	26	30	No	36	23	No
7	22	No	17	25	No	27	24	No	37	23	No
8	28	No	18	29	No	28	29	No	38	34	No
9	38	No	19	25	No	29	30	No	39	23	No
10	22	No	20	22	No	30	31	No	40	26	No

scores on their paired cards. Compare this sum to the observed sum of 17. If 17 or less, indicate *yes*, otherwise *no*. (Why do we use "17 or less" rather than "less than 17"? Because we are asking the likelihood of a score *this low or lower*.)

Step 4. Repeat Steps 2 and 3 forty times.

Step 5. Calculate the proportion of *yes*. This estimates the probability sought.

In Table 33.2 we see that the observed sum is lower than that in all but one (trial 5) of the ten random trials, which suggests that there is a good chance (9 to 1) that the five best athletes will not have I.Q. scores that high by chance. But it might be well to deal some more to get a more reliable average. We add thirty hands, and thirty-nine of the total forty hands exceed the observed rank value, so the likelihood that the observed correlation of athletic and I.Q. scores would occur by chance is about 2.5 per cent. In other words, the odds are 39 to 1 against there being no association between athletic ability and I.Q. score, and it therefore seems reasonable to believe that high athletic ability tends to accompany a high I.Q.

Some explanation is required for the procedure of adding ranks for the first *five* athletes and comparing them with the second five, rather than comparing the top three, say, with the bottom seven. We could indeed have compared the top three, two, four, or one with the rest. The first reason for splitting the group in half is that an even split provides fuller information and therefore greater efficiency. (We cannot prove this to you, but perhaps it makes intuitive sense.) A second reason is that getting into the habit of looking at an even split reduces the chances that you will pick and choose in such a manner as to fool yourself. For example, if the I.Q. ranks of the top five athletes were 3, 2, 1, 10, and 9, we would be kidding ourselves if, after looking the data over, we drew the line between athletes 3 and 4.

A simpler but less efficient approach to this same problem is to classify the top-half athletes by whether they were also in the top half of the I.Q. scores. (Of the first five athletes actually observed, *four* were in the top five I.Q. scores.) Then shuffle five black and five red cards and see how often four or more (that is, four or five) blacks come up with the first five cards. The proportion of times that four or more blacks occurs in the experiment is the likelihood that the observed scores come from the same universe—that is, the likelihood that there is no association between the two characteristics. Table 33.3 shows a proportion of

TABLE 33.3

Observed score: 4

Trial	Score	Yes or No	Trial	Score	Yes or No	Trial	Score	Yes or No	Trial	Score	Yes or No
1	4	Yes	6	2	No	11	3	No	16	3	No
2	2	No	7	4	Yes	12	1	No	17	2	No
3	2	No	8	3	No	13	3	No	18	2	No
4	2	No	9	3	No	14	3	No	19	2	No
5	3	No	10	4	Yes	15	4	Yes	20	4	Yes

five *yes* out of twenty trials, yielding a much weaker result than did the previous method.

We have proceeded on the theory that, if there is *any* relationship between athletes and I.Q., then the better athletes have higher rather than lower I.Q. scores. The justification for this assumption is that past research suggests that it is probably true. But, if we had *not* had the benefit of that past research, we would then have had to proceed somewhat differently; we would have had to consider the possibility that the top five athletes could have I.Q. scores either higher *or* lower than those of the other students. The results of the "two-tail" test would have yielded weaker odds than those we observed.

B. EXAMPLE 14: ATHLETIC ABILITY AND INTELLIGENCE, USING MEASURED DATA

Example 13 investigated the relationship between I.Q. and athletic scores by ranking the two sets of scores. But ranking of scores loses some efficiency because it uses only an "ordinal," rather than a "cardinal," scale; the numerical shadings and relative relationships are lost when we convert to ranks. Therefore, it is worth considering a test of correlation that uses the original cardinal numerical scores.

First a little background: Figures 33.1 and 33.2 show two hypothetical cases of very high association among the I.Q. and athletic scores used in previous examples.

Figure 33.1 indicates that the higher the I.Q. score, the higher the athletic score. Knowing a boy's athletic score, you can thus predict quite well his I.Q. score by means of the hand-drawn line—or vice versa. The same is true of Figure 33.2, but in the opposite way. (Notice that, even though athletic score is on the x axis (horizontal) and I.Q. score is on the y axis (vertical), the athletic score does not cause the I.Q. score. It is an unfortunate deficiency of such diagrams that *some* variable must arbitrarily be placed on the x axis, whether or not you intend to suggest causation.)

In Figure 33.3, which plots the scores as given in Table 33.1, the prediction of athletic score given I.Q. score, or vice versa, is less clear-cut than in Figure 33.2. On the basis of Figure 33.3 alone, one can say only that there *might* be some association between the two variables.

Now we can use a handy property of numbers. Consider the cases in Table 33.4, in which there is a perfect (linear) association between x (column 1) and y_1 (column 2), and between x and y_2 (column 4); the numbers shown in columns 3 and 5 are those that would be consistent with perfect associations. Notice the sum of the multiples of the x and y values. It is higher (xy_1) and lower (xy_2) than for any other possible way of arranging the y's. Any other arrangement of the y's $(y_3$, for example, chosen at random), when multiplied by the x's (for example, xy_3), produces a sum that falls

FIGURE 33.1   Hypothetical Data for a Group of Boys

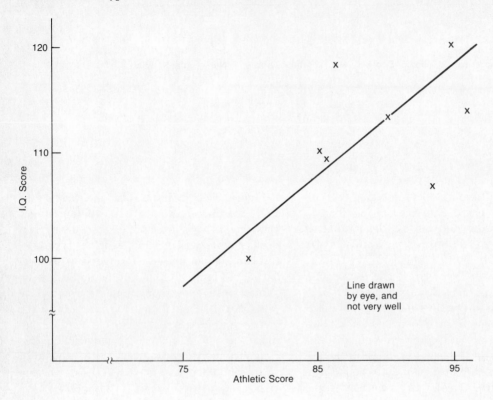

somewhere between the sums of xy_1 and xy_2, as is the case when y_3 is also less correlated with the x's. Column 7 in Table 33.4 shows how the sum of the products of another less-regular set of I.Q. scores multiplied by athletic scores (column 7) is *between* the sums that would occur if the I.Q. scores were ranked from best to worst (column 3) and worst to best (column 5). The extent of correlation (association) can thus be measured by whether the sum of the multiples of the observed x and y values is relatively high or low compared to random sums.

Now we attack the I.Q.–athletic-score problem in a different fashion. First multiply the x and y values of the observations, and sum them (95,759) as in Table 33.5. Then write the ten I.Q. scores on cards, and assign the cards

in random order to the ten athletes, as shown in Column 1 in Table 33.6. Multiply by the x's, and sum. If the I.Q. scores and athletic scores are *positively* associated–that is, if high I.Q.s and high athletic scores go together—then the sum of the multiplications for the observed sample will be higher than for most of the random trials. (If high I.Q.s go with low athletic scores, the sum of the multiplications for the observed sample will be *lower* than for most of the random trials.)

Step 1. Write the ten I.Q. scores on one set of cards, and the ten athletic scores on another set of cards.

Step 2. Pair the I.Q.- and athletic-score cards at random. Multiply the scores

FIGURE 33.2   Hypothetical Data for a Group of Boys

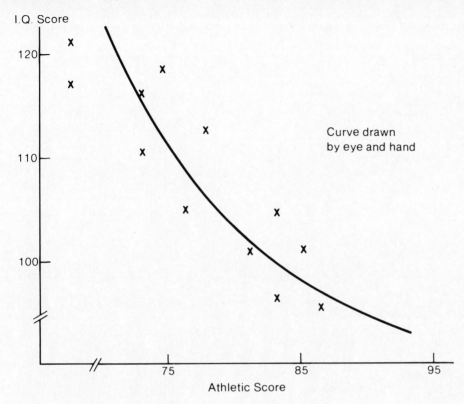

in each pair, and add the results of the ten multiplications.

Step 3. Compare the experimental sum in Step 2 to the observed sum, 95,759. If the experimental sum is as large or larger, record *yes*, otherwise *no*.

Step 4. Repeat Steps 2 and 3 twenty times.

Step 5. Compute the proportion of *yes*, which estimates the likelihood that an association as strong as that observed would occur by chance.

The sums of the multiplications for twenty trials are shown in Table 33.7. No random-trial sum was as high as the observed sum, which suggests that the probability of an association this strong happening by chance is very low,

approaching zero (an empirically observed probability is never actually zero).

C. EXAMPLE 15: IS THERE A RELATIONSHIP BETWEEN DRINKING BEER AND BEING IN FAVOR OF SELLING BEER? (TESTING FOR A RELATIONSHIP BETWEEN COUNTED-DATA VARIABLES)

The scores for athletic ability and I.Q. were measured data. Therefore, we could use them in their original "cardinal" form or split them into "high" and "low" groups. Often, however, the individual observations are recorded only as *yes* or *no*, which makes it more difficult to ascertain the existence of a relationship. Consider these answers to two public-opinion sur-

FIGURE 33.3   Hypothetical Data for a Class

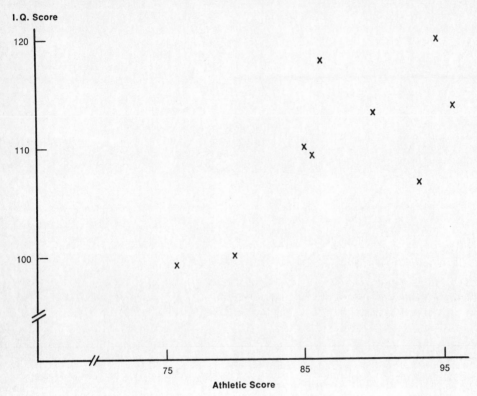

vey questions: "Do you drink beer?" and "Are you in favor of local option on the sale of beer?"[1]

1. These data are from an example in Dixon and Massey (1968: 242), in which the problem is tackled with a conventional test (the chi-square).

TABLE 33.4

1	2	3	4	5	6	7
x	Y_1	xy_1	y_2	xy_2	y_3	xy_3
2	2	4	10	20	4	8
4	4	16	8	32	8	32
6	6	36	6	36	6	36
8	8	64	4	32	2	16
10	10	100	2	20	10	100
		220		140		192

Here is the question: Is a person's opinion on local option related to whether he or she drinks beer? There are seventy-eight respondents, fifty-seven of whom approve local option and twenty-one of whom do not. Therefore, write *approve* on fifty-seven index cards and *disapprove* on twenty-one index cards. Now take *another* set of seventy-eight index cards, preferably of a different color, and write *yes* on fifty-two of them and *no* on twenty-six of them, corresponding to the numbers of people who do and do not drink beer in the sample. Now lay them down in random *pairs*, one from each pile.

If there is a high association between the variables, the observations will bunch up in the two diagonal cells on either diagonal. Therefore, subtract one sum of two diagonal

TABLE 33.5

1 Athletic Score	2 I.Q. Score	3 Column 1 × Column 2	4 I.Q. Score	5 Column 1 × Column 4	6 Actual I.Q.	7 Column 1 × Column 6
97	120	11640	99	9603	114	11058
94	118	11092	100	9400	120	11280
93	114	10602	101	9393	107	9951
90	113	10170	107	9630	113	10170
87	110	9570	109	9483	118	10266
86	109	9374	110	8460	101	8686
86	107	9202	113	9718	109	9374
85	101	8585	114	9690	110	9350
81	100	8100	118	9558	100	8100
76	99	7524	120	9120	99	7524
		95859		95055		95759

cells from the other sum for the observed case: $(37+6)-(20+15)=8$. Compare this difference to those found in random trials. The proportion of times that the trial differences do not exceed the observed difference is the probability that the observed association is not caused by chance. (Notice that, in this case, we are working on the assumption that beer drinking is *positively* associated with approval of local option and not the inverse. We are interested

TABLE 33.6

Athletic Score	1	2	3	4	5	6	7	8	9	10
97	114	109	110	118	107	114	107	120	100	114
94	101	113	113	101	118	100	110	109	120	107
93	107	118	100	99	120	101	114	99	110	113
90	113	101	118	114	101	113	100	118	99	99
87	120	100	101	100	110	107	113	114	101	118
86	100	110	120	107	113	110	118	101	118	101
86	110	107	99	109	100	120	120	113	114	120
85	99	99	104	120	99	109	101	107	109	109
81	118	120	114	110	114	99	99	100	107	100
76	109	114	109	113	109	118	109	110	113	110

Athletic Score	11	12	13	14	15	16	17	18	19	20
97	109	113	101	109	107	100	99	113	99	110
94	101	110	114	118	101	107	114	101	109	113
93	120	120	100	120	114	113	100	100	120	109
90	110	118	109	110	99	109	107	109	110	99
87	100	100	120	99	118	114	110	110	107	101
86	118	99	107	100	109	118	113	118	100	118
86	99	101	99	101	100	99	101	107	114	120
85	107	114	110	114	120	110	120	120	118	100
81	114	107	113	113	110	101	109	114	101	114
76	113	109	118	107	113	120	118	99	113	107

TABLE 33.7

Trial	Sum of Multiplications	Trial	Sum of Multiplications
1	95430	11	95406
2	95426	12	95622
3	95446	13	95250
4	95381	14	95599
5	95542	15	95323
6	95362	16	95308
7	95508	17	95220
8	95590	18	95443
9	95379	19	95421
10	95532	20	95528

only in differences that are equal to or exceed +8 when the northeast-southwest diagonal is subtracted from the northwest-southeast diagonal.)

Step 1. Write *approve* on fifty-seven red index cards and *disapprove* on twenty-one red index cards; write *drink* on fifty-two and *don't drink* on twenty-six white cards.

Step 2. Pair the cards randomly, and count the numbers of the four possible pairs: *approve-drink, disapprove-don't drink, disapprove-drink,* and *approve-don't drink*. Record the number of these combinations, as in Table 33.9, where columns 1–4 correspond to the four cells in Table 33.8.

Step 3. Add column 1 plus column 4. From this figure, subtract the sum of column 2 plus column 3. If the difference is equal to or greater than 8, record *yes*, otherwise *no*.

Step 4. Repeat Steps 2 and 3 perhaps a hundred times.

Step 5. Calculate the proportion of *yes*, which estimates the likelihood that

an association this great or greater would be observed by chance.

A series of ten trials in this case (see Table 33.9) indicates that the observed difference is very often exceeded, which suggests no relationship between beer drinking and opinion.

Though the test just described may generally be appropriate for data of this sort, a second thought casts doubt about whether it is appropriate in this case. Even if the test showed that an association existed, would we believe the test result to be meaningful? We think not. In Table 33.10 we see that nonbeer drinkers have a *higher* rate of approval of allowing beer drinking, which does not accord with experience or reason. Hence, without additional explanation we would not believe that a meaningful relationship exists among these variables even if the test showed one to exist. (Still another reason to doubt that a relationship exists is that the absolute differences are too small— there is only a 6 per cent difference in disapproval between *drink* and *don't drink* groups— to mean anything to anyone. On both grounds, then, it makes sense simply to act as if there were no difference between the two groups and to run *no test*).

The lesson to be learned from this is that one should inspect the data carefully before applying a statistical test, and only test for "significance" if the apparent relationships accord with theory and general understanding.

TABLE 33.8

Are You in Favor of Local Option on the Sale of Beer?	Do You Drink Beer?		
	Yes	**No**	**Total**
Approve	37	20	57
Disapprove	15	6	21
Total	52	26	78

TABLE 33.9

Trial	Approve Yes (1)	Approve No (2)	Disapprove Yes (3)	Disapprove No (4)	(Column 1 + Column 4) − (Column 2 + Column 3)* (5)
1	33	24	18	3	36 − 42 = −6
2	38	19	14	7	45 − 33 = 12
3	39	18	13	8	47 − 31 = 16
4	38	19	14	7	45 − 33 = 12
5	35	22	17	4	39 − 39 = 0
6	35	22	16	5	40 − 38 = 2
7	38	19	14	7	45 − 33 = 12
8	40	19	12	9	49 − 31 = 18
9	40	17	12	9	49 − 29 = 20
10	37	20	15	6	43 − 35 = 8

*In absolute figures.

2. Advantages and Disadvantages of the Monte Carlo Method

With card and dice experiments one can make many statistical tests without the mathematical theory of probability. But figuring the answer analytically is often *quicker*, especially for problems with many observations. For example, imagine that you want to know how often you will get two aces if you deal out hands of only two cards. A random experiment would take a while, but one can figure the answer in a hurry by multiplying $1/13 \times 1/13 = 1/269$, which tells us that, on the average, we shall get two aces in a hand of two cards once in 269 hands.

Mathematical methods can also be useful in more complex problems, though there are many problems that are *so* complex that mathematicians resort to random experiments for estimating the probabilities, using computers rather than cards or dice to run the experiments in a hurry.

Mathematical methods make handling cardinal quantitative data easy. But, as we demonstrated in the pig-ration example, sometimes card and dice experiments can also be run with quantitative data, without assuming as much as is necessary for the use of mathematical methods.

Though analytical methods may get an answer quicker than the Monte Carlo method, a person who does not expect to use probability statistics very often might find that, in the long run, it is more efficient to spend extra time on slow Monte Carlo trials than on studying the mathematical methods. On the other hand, anyone who plans to work in scientific research should eventually study probability statistics,

TABLE 33.10

	Percentage Approve	Percentage Disapprove	Total
Beer drinkers	71%	29%	100%
Nonbeer drinkers	77%	23%	100%

especially because that study deepens one's *intuition* about scientific and mathematical relationships.

A major advantage of the Monte Carlo method is that everything that you do is very explicit and you must think through each step. Such discipline reduces the probability of erroneous calculations from blindly plugging in the wrong method and formula.

It is an apparent disadvantage of the Monte Carlo method executed by hand that large sample sizes are clumsy to work with, as are very small probabilities; for example, it is difficult to work with data on the viewership of educational television stations because the probability of a given person watching may be only 1 in 1,000. But testing problems arise only when the samples are small; with large masses of data the conclusions are obvious without probability statistics. Furthermore, computers can easily be programmed to handle Monte Carlo methods.

One can avoid the tedious work of Monte Carlo experiments by getting the help of a statistician who will use mathematical methods. But—and it is a huge "but"—to be sure that the answer the statistician gives you is the answer you want, you must describe the Monte Carlo trial you would otherwise run to test your results. Then and only then can you be sure that the mathematical test the statistician performs is the right one. If you simply say, "I want to test whether these two samples are different," you are much more likely to get a misleading answer than if you describe a Monte Carlo experiment and then ask the statistician merely to perform the same task with mathematical analysis.

If you can say exactly what kind of Monte Carlo trial will give the test you want, you have performed 90 per cent of the work—and the hardest 90 per cent. It takes very hard, very clear thinking. Again, the job is *not* mathematical; if you tell yourself that you cannot do these and similar probability-statistical tests because you do not understand mathematics,

you are fooling yourself. If you cannot do correct tests of the type described in this chapter, it is because you are not willing to think hard and clearly. And you cannot shift the burden to a statistician, because then he or she will have to do the hard, clear thinking for you, without knowing what your study needs as well as you do. Furthermore, mathematical statisticians develop formulas to imitate the Monte Carlo trials you want to run, but they have no special training in deciding which Monte Carlo trials to perform. To repeat, that is the hard, clear thinking that you must do for yourself.

3. The Multiplication Rule

You should be familiar with two basic calculations in mathematical statistics, and you should know when they are applicable. The first calculation is the *rule of addition*. It states that, when two events are mutually exclusive, the probability of one event *or* the other event (*or* both) is the *sum* of the probabilities of each event happening alone. For example, the probability of drawing a spade is ¼, and the probability of a heart if ¼, and both cannot occur in the draw of one card. The probability of drawing *either* a spade *or* a heart is ¼ + ¼ = ½. Remember that the rule of addition should be used whenever you use the words "either . . . or (or both)" in the question.

The *multiplication rule* is the most important handy calculation in everyday statistical work. It is used whenever the question is, What is the probability that A *and* B will happen? For example, the probability of having a daughter the first time *and* a daughter the second time is ½ × ½ = ¼ (on the assumption that the sex of each newborn child is independent of that of the preceding ones). The probability of having four daughters in a row is ½ × ½ × ½ × ½ = 1/16, as we approximated earlier with card shuffling. If you want a more precise estimate using the data that 106 males are born for each 100 females, the appropriate calculation would be $(^{100}\!/_{206}) \times (^{100}\!/_{206}) \times (^{100}\!/_{206}) \times$

($^{100}/_{206}$). The multiplication rule is very handy for quick estimates of whether data result from chance. For example, if you compare the advertising effectiveness of large versus small firms in five separate years and if the small firms do better in each of the five years, the probability that this performance results from chance is $(\frac{1}{2})^5 = \frac{1}{2} \times \frac{1}{2} \times \frac{1}{2} \times \frac{1}{2} \times \frac{1}{2} = \frac{1}{32}$ (if you hypothesized that small firms do better). (If the data show that the smaller firms do better in seven years out of eight, however, you will need a more complicated calculation than the multiplication rule, and you had best use a Monte Carlo method.)

Another example: If the chance of my wife getting a job at a given university is .2, and my chance of getting a job at the same university is .15, then the chance of *both* of us getting jobs at that university is $.2 \times .15 = .03$.

4. Evaluating the Significance of "Dredged-Up" Relationships

In all the previous examples of hypothesis-testing statistics, we have assumed that the researcher had a specific hypothesis before examining the raw data and making the test. But there are other types of analysis, like secondary analysis, in which the researcher searches through the raw data in hopes of "dredging up" some relationships. Dredged-up relationships must *not* be tested with the probability apparatus described earlier in this chapter.

There are two ways to go astray in searching through raw data. The first is to seize upon the extreme observation of a *large* randomly generated sample distribution and to consider it unusual when in reality it is to be expected sometime. An example is the birth of ten daughters in a row. When you wonder whether it reveals something biological about a particular family, keep in mind that a pattern of ten girls in a row is no more and no less rare than a pattern of boy-girl-boy-girl-boy-girl-boy-girl-boy-girl. The second way to go astray results from the *smallness* of the sample rather than from its largeness: finding specious patterns that exist simply because *some* patterns must apparently occur. An example is bettors' finding patterns in a series of horse races. We shall take up these two fallacies in order.

A. "UNUSUAL" OCCURRENCES IN LARGE SAMPLES

If you are the dealer in a game of bridge and you deal yourself the ace, two, and three of spades; the four, five, and six of diamonds; the seven, eight, and nine of hearts; and the ten, jack, queen, and king of clubs, you probably will not think much of it. Now, will you think that there is a *pattern* (that is, a nonrandom deal) if you get thirteen spades? You will not think so if you yourself are dealing, because you will know that you did not cheat. But if *someone else* deals thirteen spades to himself, you may be suspicious and think the deal is a nonrandom (that is, cheating) deal. The point is that whether you think there is a pattern depends on more than the observed data; it also depends on what else you know—in this case, that you dealt and did not rig the cards.

To push the example further, remember that the first bridge hand we described did not surprise you much. But, if one of the players had *predicted* that you would get exactly that hand, you would be very surprised indeed. You would think that the hand was nonrandom and that the other person had either fixed the cards or was possessed of extrasensory perception. Again, your surprise depends on what you knew in advance—in this case, that your friend had predicted the exact hand.

Here is another example of the same sort:

> . . . On 16 May 1965, reading the San Francisco *Sunday Chronicle* I noticed an article on page 22 entitled "Ancient Men on the Nile." In scanning this story, I saw the phrase ". . . the expert appraisal of Philadelphia anthropologist Dr. Carleton S. Coon." To anyone who had been an undergraduate student at the University of Chicago

in the early 1930s, this unusual name would call up nostalgic memories of another Carleton Coon and his partner, Joe Sanders, whose popular Coon-Sanders dance band was then playing at the Blackhawk. So I found myself thinking about Joe Sanders, very probably for the first time in 30 years.

Less than five minutes later, having turned the pages of the paper to page 33, I saw an obituary notice headed "Joe Sanders." It read, ". . . died Friday. . . . [W]ith the late Carleton Coon . . . organized the Coon-Sanders band." These two closely spaced recollections of a person forgotten for 30 years, with the second event involving a death notice, is in the classical pattern; but it is obvious that no causal relationship could have existed between the two events.

The probability of a coincidental recollection of a known person in a 5-minute period just before learning of that person's death can easily be calculated, to within a factor of 10. Let us take a 30-year period, and assume that an average person would recognize the names of 3000 different people who might die in that period of time. . . . We assume that our subject will learn of the death of each of these persons at some time in the 30 years. If we restrict our attention to the time when our subject learns of the death of a particular person, we can then ask how probable it is, that in the 5 minutes just preceding that exact time of learning of the death, an unrelated recollection that is unique to the 30-year period will occur. This probability, to within a factor of 2, is the ratio of a 5-minute interval to a 30-year interval, or 3×10^{-7} [$3/10$ million]. (It is clear that if one thinks of the particular person once a year rather than once every 30 years, the probability will rise by a factor of 30, to about 10^{-5} [$1/100,000$].) The probability that one will have such an experience when learning of the death of any one of the 3000 recognizable persons is clearly 10^{-3} [$1/1000$] in a 30-year period, or approximately 3×10^{-5} per year. If we take the sample of 10^8 [100 million] adults in the United States, 3×10^3 [3000] experiences of the sort related above should occur per year, or about 10 per day. . . . With such a large sample to draw from, it is not surprising that some exceedingly astonishing coincidences are reported in the parapsychological literature as proof of extrasensory perception in one form or another. (Alvarez, 1965: 1541)

Still another example of the attribution of meaning to far-out observations occurs on the stock market from time to time. *Someone* must be lucky in a series of consecutive stock-market transactions, just by chance. When it happens, the fellow who hits it right by chance a large number of times assumes that the good results result from his *knowledge* and his method of stock analysis. Thereupon, he writes a book called *How I Made My Fortune in Stocks* and makes *another* small fortune in book royalties.[2]

The data in Table 33.11 illustrate this problem as it often appears in social-science research. The investigator collected data on three psychological characteristics of seven groups of people who exhibited different purchasing behavior, hoping to find characteristics that would distinguish the various groups. None of the three characteristics is *consistently* different for all seven groups of people.[3] But the investigator noticed a split of 71 per cent to 29 per cent in favor of the buyers of brand B on characteristic 2. *If* one treats this comparison as if it were the *only* comparison under examination, it appears to be very significant statistically and unlikely to occur by chance. The investigator offered the split as a valid finding from the data.

But there are twenty-one possible comparisons in the table (seven purchasing groups by three characteristics), which means that the likelihood of *one* comparison appearing to be significant is *much* higher than if only one comparison were examined (refer to Example 6 in Chapter 31). The investigator argued that, for *a priori* theoretical reasons, this was the only one of the twenty-one comparisons that he ex-

---

2. Thurow shows how important "luck" is in the creation of large fortunes (1975: Chap. 6), while Travers and Milgram (1969) discuss how likely it is for us to run into friends when we do not expect to.

3. Statistical tests conducted by the investigator indicate that none of the three characteristics in the seven groups is significant at the .05 level.

TABLE 33.11

Brand of Men's Suit Purchased	Psychological Characteristic I %		Psychological Characteristic II %		Psychological Characteristic III %	
	High	Low	High	Low	High	Low
A (26 buyers)	38(10)	62(16)	35(9)	65(17)	50(13)	50(13)
B (21 buyers)	38(8)	62(13)	71(15)	29(6)	57(13)	43(9)
C (7 buyers)	43(3)	57(4)	43(3)	57(4)	43(3)	57(4)
D (14 buyers)	43(6)	57(8)	43(6)	57(8)	28(4)	72(10)
E (19 buyers)	37(7)	63(12)	47(7)	53(10)	47(9)	53(10)
F (27 buyers)	48(13)	52(14)	52(14)	48(13)	41(11)	59(16)
Don't know (15 buyers)	27(4)	73(11)	20(3)	80(12)	47(7)	53(8)

pected to be significant, and a confirmation of his expectation would strengthen his case for the finding's significance. But the reader is entitled to be skeptical of such *post facto* discussion, and skepticism is reinforced by the small number of subjects in the comparison—only twenty-one.

To determine whether any meaning should be attached to the apparently unusual event is not easy. At the very least, one should remain alert to such events and explore them, rather than ignoring them; it would be foolish to shrug off a bridge dealer who twice deals himself a perfect hand. "An erroneous rejection of extreme observations profoundly affected the course of history when, shortly after seven o'clock on the morning of December 7, 1941, the officer in charge of a Hawaiian radar station ignored data solely because they seemed so incredible" (Wallis and Roberts, 1966: 170).

The examination of such "unusual" observations is known as "analysis of deviant cases" (Kendall and Lazarsfeld, 1950: 167), and it is an important source of scientific knowledge. For two examples, if a country has an unusually low rate of lung cancer or if an individual lives through a plague in which everyone else dies, an investigation of the causes of such an unusual occurrence may be instructive, *or* it may reveal only that the apparent exception is the result of random chance. One should con-

sider the unusual event as a clue that *may* lead to an explanation. And certainly keep your eyes open for a repetition of the event, just as you watch a card dealer whom you suspect.

But pay attention only to those events that have some importance; there is no sense in doing more than exclaiming about a card hand that has a peculiar combination of numbers but no special significance in the game.

A second way of dealing with an unusual event is to calculate just how unusual it really is. That is what Alvarez did with his memory of Joe Sanders, and he found that the event was not very unusual, considering all possible opportunities for it to happen in the United States. But, if the same thing had happened to Alvarez three times on successive days, the probability of the sequence's happening to anyone anywhere would be astronomically small, and he would not be likely to reason it away as he did. One could also calculate the probability of observing a split as wide as 15 to 6 for a single comparison among the twenty-one comparisons in Table 33.11. That calculation is rendered muddy, however, by the argument about the theoretical basis for that observation, as well as by the presentation of still other tables and data in the same study.

A third—and most important—way to evaluate unusual dredged-up events is to see if the same thing happens elsewhere. In Illustration

A in Chapter 30, North Carolina was seen to have both the biggest stake in tobacco growing *and* the highest rate of doctors' smoking. Assume that one had merely *noticed* this fact, rather than having sought these data to test a hypothesis. This observation *could* be a coincidence. But we can look to see if the same relationship holds elsewhere—as indeed it does for the other major tobacco-economy states—confirming our belief that the observed association for North Carolina is not just a fluke (J. Simon, 1967–1968). And in the study of psychological characteristics and purchasing behavior, the investigator should repeat the test on another sample from the group in question, to see if the same sort of finding appears again, before he places much confidence in the finding.

and then to see if it repeats itself in *different data*—data that you have not seen when you found the original pattern. If the pattern does repeat, you can use probability statistics to determine how likely the data would have been to repeat the pattern *had you predicted it in advance on the basis of finding your first pattern*.

Such a procedure points up the importance of theory once again. If you have a general theory about some subject matter, you can deduce specific hypotheses from it and then ask whether the data show the expected pattern. Without the theory your hypothesis will not be very strong, and therefore it will be more difficult to ask and answer a clear-cut question about whether the pattern of the data means anything.

B. PATTERNS IN SMALL SAMPLES

A second error in data dredging is reading a pattern into too small a sample. This is the error horse-racing fans frequently fall into. They look over the back records of races and find what they think is a pattern—say, that jockey A has been winning *every other race*. They then bet him to win after he loses his next race, and they are surprised when the "pattern" does not continue. Their error lies in not understanding how easy it is to think there is a pattern when there really is none, just as patterns apparently appear with randomly thrown dice or cards or random numbers.

Statistics offer little help in deciding whether a newly discovered pattern really means anything. If there were some way to calculate how many possible patterns might appear, then one might estimate the likelihood that *some* pattern of a particular strength would appear. But the possibilities of the human imagination in generating possible patterns are almost limitless, so even this statistical hope goes aglimmering.

The only safe test is to find the pattern *first*

C. NUMERICAL ARTIFACTS

Still another way to go astray in examining data is to discover artifacts—apparently interesting findings *that could not be otherwise*. An example is the children's teaser: "Did you know that exactly the same number of men got married last year as did women?" Sometimes this sort of artifact is not so obvious. Consider the observation that "Even though in the United States there are many fewer women than men with Ph.D. degrees, the data show that there were almost as many women with Ph.D. degrees who married men with Ph.D. degrees as men with such degrees who married women with such degrees." (Think about it!)

The famous "regression fallacy" is an artifact that occasionally slips into the work of even the wisest scientists. The regression fallacy takes its name from Galton's observation that the height of the population was "regressing to the mean." That is, Galton thought that the heights of people were becoming more uniform because the sons of the tallest fathers and of the shortest fathers were closer to the average than their fathers had been. What Galton

Industry	Advertising Expenditures-Sales Ratio	
	1948	**1962**
Primary metals	0.21%	0.39%
Fabricated structural metal products	0.54	0.59
Cutlery, hand tools and general hardware	1.91	3.28
Heating apparatus & plumbers' supplies	1.14	1.06
Miscellaneous fabricated metal products	0.54	0.92
Stone, clay & glass products	0.63	0.78
Construction, mining & material handling machinery and equipment	0.71	0.85
Metalworking machinery & equipment	1.03	0.91
Electrical generating, transmission, distribution & industrial apparatus	1.27	1.51
General industry machinery & equipment	1.02	1.09
Special industry machinery	0.77	0.94
Office, computing & accounting machines	1.25	0.72
Professional, scientific & controlling instruments, photographic & optical goods	1.93	2.15
Industrial organic & inorganic chemicals	0.72	1.24
Pulp, paper & paperboard	0.33	0.87
Converted paper & paperboard boxes	0.87	1.07
Motor freight transportation and warehousing	0.30	0.32

Source: "Advertising-to-sales ratios stabilizing: ABP economist," *Industrial Marketing*, June, 1966, copyright 1966 by Advertising Publications Inc., Chicago, Ill. Special credit to Dr. C. Y. Yang.

overlooked was that in each generation sons of *other* fathers are by chance much taller or shorter than are their fathers, so that each generation has equal numbers of very tall and very short people. One can avoid the regression fallacy by considering *all* the members of the universe (or sample) and not simply looking at selected members, for example, the sons of the tallest or shortest fathers.

Economics is often afflicted with the regression fallacy. Consider this conclusion based on the data that follow it:

. . . [S]ome pretty big variations in advertising-sales ratios between different industries seem to be narrowing. For example, a spread of 0.49% in 1948 between metalworking machinery and equipment, and fabricated structural metal products, had been reduced to 0.32% by 1962. (The metal-working ad-sales ratio declined from 1.03% to 0.91% during the period, while fabricated structural gained from 0.54% to 0.59%.)

Similarly, the advertising-sales ratios of other industries, such as pulp, paper and paperboard, have moved closer to the levels of other groups . . . the ratios [are] "quickly approaching the level of stability."

But, viewed in their entirety, the data do *not* show that the advertising ratios are moving together. One measure is the ratio of the range to the median:

$$\frac{1.93-0.21}{0.77} = 2.2 \text{ for the year 1948, and}$$

$$\frac{3.28-0.32}{0.94} = 3.2 \text{ for the year 1962.}$$

(Another measure of dispersion, the ratio of the standard deviation to the mean, is also higher in 1962 than in 1948.) To conclude that the ratios are "approaching stability" is therefore not reasonable.

We suspect that the regression fallacy is at

the root of many doubtful observations about changes in society over time. Consider, for example, the common observation that people are becoming more conformist with successive generations. (Put aside for now the difficulty of defining and measuring conformity.) Perhaps the writers who make this statement have themselves been nonconformists in their lives. It is likely that their own children are more conformist than they are, as the laws of chance would predict. Therefore, the writers observe a "trend toward conformity." But they are ignoring the nonconformist children that come out of conformist homes, children whom the writers do not see but yet who probably make up a generation that contains as many nonconformists as other generations do.

5. Summary

This and the previous chapter discuss statistical problems of determining whether there is a correlation between variables, and how to determine the strength of relationships, using the Monte Carlo method. Advantages and disadvantages of the Monte Carlo method are compared.

How one may evaluate the significance of relationships that are "dredged up" from a body of data is also discussed.

EXERCISES

1. What would be the probability of having three daughters in a row, if the probability of a girl child were 0.4?
2. You employ ten interviewers to ask people whether they prefer candy bar A to candy bar B. Each interviewer interviews twenty people and the preferences for candy bar A were 10, 14, 4, 16, 7, 3, 2, 15, 14, 5. Are the differences among interviewers those that might be expected by chance, or is there reason to believe that the interviewers differed in what they did?
3. Pick a problem randomly from a set of randomly chosen exercises in any basic statistics book, and solve the problem with Monte Carlo methods.
4. Three merchandising plans were tried out on a random sample of stores. Plan A raised sales by 2, 1, 0, 2, and 1 units in the five stores, respectively. Plan B raised sales by 1, 0, 0, 1, and 0 units in five stores. Plan C raised sales by 2, 0, 0, 0, and 1 units in five stores. What is the probability that plan A is "really" better than plans B and C?
5. What is the probability that four of your first five children will be daughters, assuming that you will have five children? What is the probability that you will have either four boys or five girls among your first five children?
6. What are the odds that three or more cards of any one suit (for instance, spades) will appear in a five-card poker hand from a well-shuffled deck? Give a numerical answer, as well as showing the steps by which you got the answer.
7. John tells you that with his old method of shooting foul shots in basketball his average (over a long period of time) was .6. Then he tried a new method of shooting and scored successes with nine of his first ten shots. Should he conclude that the new method is really better than the old method?
8. "If six fair coins are tossed, what is the probability that exactly three of them turn up heads?" (Adler, 1963: 92)
9. A football team played nine games during last season. It won the first, lost the next three, and then won the last five. A sportswriter concluded that the team had im-

proved during the season. Is that a good conclusion? Or is there a good chance that the team had the same six in nine chances of winning each game throughout the season? (This is a very tricky problem to set up.)

10. "If seven accidents occur at random on a highway during one week, what is the probability that one occurs each day of the week?" (Adler, 1963: 92)

11. Two different diets were tested on a randomly selected group of overweight people. The weight losses in pounds were:
    Diet A   0 5 10 9 6 4 1 3 8 7 3 4
    Diet B   4 6   4 1 1 3 2 8 5 9 1 2
    Judge whether diet A is better for losing weight than diet B is. Outline a procedure, discuss the logic of your procedure, and estimate.

12. Each of ten people secretly chooses a number between 1 and 100. What is the probability that at least two of them will choose the same number? State a procedure and an estimate.

13. What are the odds that two cards of the same denomination will appear in a five-card poker hand from a well-shuffled deck?

14. "On the average, how many times must a die be thrown before it comes up 6?" (Mosteller, 1965: 1)

15. There are ten boys in a grammar-school class, three black and seven white. In a foot race, the order of finishing is, from first to last (B = black, W = white), BWBWBWWWWW. Should one say that black boys are faster afoot than white boys are?

16. If we sent the manuscript of this book to five publishers chosen more or less randomly and if all five rejected it for publication, what would be a sensible probability that a sixth publisher (chosen in the same way) would accept it? (Hint: A sensible solution requires that you assume some additional information. This is what Mosteller calls a "problem without structure.")

17. You show me a jar that only you know has 4,322 stones in it, and you ask me to guess the number of stones. Estimate the probability that I shall guess correctly. (This is another problem without structure.)

ADDITIONAL READING

You may read more about "data-dredging" procedures in survey analysis in the article by Selvin and Stuart (1970).

Leamer (1978: Chaps. 1, 9, 10) analyzes what statisticians say about dredging up relationships (never do it), what people with no social science training do (almost always dredge up relationships), and what practical social scientists should do (dredge up relationships, but be careful).

An article on statistical methods related to those described above is Diaconis and Efron (1983).

How Big a Sample? $\boxed{34}$

1. Issues in Determining Sample Size
2. Some Practical Examples
3. Step-Wise Sample-Size Determination
4. Summary

1. Issues in Determining Sample Size

Sometime in the course of almost every study—preferably early in the planning stage—the researcher must decide how large a sample to take. Deciding the size of sample to take is likely to puzzle and distress you at the beginning of your research career. You have to decide somehow, but there are no simple, obvious guides for the decision.

For example, one of the first studies one of us worked on was a study of library economics (Fussler and Simon, 1961), which required taking a sample of the books from the library's collections. Sampling was expensive, and we wanted to take a "correct" sized sample. But how large should the sample be? The longer we searched the literature, and the more people we asked, the more frustrated we got because there just did not seem to be a clear-cut answer. Eventually we found out that, even though there are some fairly rational ways of fixing the sample size, most sample sizes in most studies are fixed simply (and irrationally) by the amount of money that is available or by the sample size that similar pieces of research have used in the past.

The rational way to choose a sample size is by weighing the benefits you can expect in information against the cost of increasing the sample size. In principle you should continue to increase the sample size until the benefit and cost of an additional sampled unit are equal.[1]

The benefit of additional information is not easy to estimate even in very applied research, and it is extraordinarily difficult to estimate in basic research, as discussed in Chapter 8. Therefore, it has been the practice of researchers to set up target goals of the *degree of accuracy* they wish to achieve, or to consider various degrees of accuracy that might be achieved with various sample sizes, and then to balance off a degree of accuracy with the cost of achieving that accuracy. The bulk of this

1. Schlaifer (1961) attacks the sample-size problem in the wider context of decision making, costs, and benefits. The statistically knowledgeable reader can find an excellent discussion of sample size in Hansen et al. (1953); Mace (1964) gives many examples of the appropriate calculation in an engineering framework.

chapter is devoted to learning how the sample size is related to accuracy in simple situations.

In complex situations, however, and even in simple situations for beginners, you are likely to feel frustrated by the difficulties of relating accuracy to sample size, in which case you cry out to a supervisor, "Don't give me complicated methods, just give me a rough number based on your greatest experience." Our inclination is to reply to you, "Sometimes life is hard and there is no shortcut." On the other hand, perhaps you can get more information than misinformation out of knowing sample sizes that have been used in other studies. Table 34.1 shows the middle (modal), 25th percentile, and 75th percentile scores for—please keep this in mind—*National Opinion Surveys* in the top panel. The bottom panel shows how subgroup analyses affect sample size.

Pretest sample sizes are smaller, of course, perhaps 25–100 observations. Samples in research for Master's and Ph.D. theses are likely to be closer to a pretest than to national samples.

Once again, the sample size ought to depend on the proportions of the sample that have the characteristics you are interested in, the extent to which you want to learn about subgroups as well as the universe as a whole, and of course the purpose of your study, the value of the information, and the cost. Also, keep in mind that the *added* information that you obtain from an additional sample observation tends to be smaller as the sample size gets larger. You must quadruple the sample to halve the error.

Now let us consider some specific cases. The first examples taken up here are from the descriptive type of study, and the latter deal with sample sizes in relationship research.

2. Some Practical Examples

A. EXAMPLE 16

What proportion of the homes in Countryville are tuned into television station WCNT's ten o'clock news program? That is the question your telephone survey aims to answer, and you

TABLE 34.1   Most Common Sample Sizes Used for National and Regional Studies, by Subject Matter

Subject Matter	National			Regional		
	Mode	Q$_3$	Q$_1$	Mode	Q$_3$	Q$_1$
Financial	1000+	—	—	100	400	50
Medical	1000+	1000+	500	1000+	1000+	250
Other behavior	1000+	—	—	700	1000	300
Attitudes	1000+	1000+	500	700	1000	400
Laboratory experiments	—	—	—	100	200	50

Typical Sample Sizes for Studies of Human and Institutional Populations

Number of Subgroup Analyses	People or Households		Institutions	
	National	Regional or Special	National	Regional or Special
None or few	1000–1500	200–500	200–500	50–200
Average	1500–2500	500–1000	500–1000	200–500
Many	2500+	1000+	1000+	500+

Source: From *Applied Sampling*, by Seymour Sudman, pp. 86–87. Copyright 1976 by Academic Press, reprinted by permission.

want to know how many randomly selected homes you must telephone to obtain a sufficiently large sample.

Begin by guessing the likeliest answer, say 30 per cent in this case. Do not worry if you are off by 5 per cent or even 10 per cent, and you will probably not be further off than that. Select a first-approximation sample size of perhaps 400; this number is selected from our general experience, but it is just a starting point. Then proceed through the first 400 numbers in the random-number table, marking down a *yes* for numbers 1–3 and *no* for numbers 4–10 (because 3/10 was your estimate of the proportion listening). Then add the number of *yes* and *no*. Carry out perhaps ten sets of trials. Table 34.2 shows the results of such trials.

Based on these ten trials, you can estimate that if you take a sample of 400 and if the "real" viewing level is 30 per cent, your average percentage error will be 1.375 per cent on either side of 30 per cent. That is, with a sample of 400, half the time your error will be greater than 1.375 per cent if 3/10 of the universe is listening.

Now you must decide whether the estimated error is small enough for your needs. If you want greater accuracy than a sample of 400 will give you, increase the sample size, using this important rule of thumb: To cut the error in half, you must *quadruple* the sample size. In other words, if you want a sample that will give you an error of only 0.55 per cent on the average, you must increase the sample size to 1,600 interviews. Similarly, if you cut the sample size to 100, the average error will be only 2.75 per cent (double 1.375 per cent) on either side of 30 per cent. If you are distrustful of this rule of thumb, run ten or so trials on sample sizes of 100 or 1,600, and see what error you can expect to obtain on the average.

If the "real" viewership is 20 per cent or 40 per cent, instead of 30 per cent, the accuracy you will obtain from a sample size of 400 will not be very different from an "actual" viewership of 30 per cent, so do not worry about that too much, as long as you are in the right general vicinity.

Accuracy is *slightly* greater in smaller universes but *only* slightly. For example, a sample of 400 would give *perfect* accuracy if Countryville had only 400 residents. And a sample of 400 will give *slightly* greater accuracy for a town of 800 residents than for a city of 80,000 residents. But, beyond the point at which the sample is a *large fraction* of the total universe, there is no difference in accuracy with increases in the size of universe. This point is very important. For any given level of accu-

TABLE 34.2

Trial	Number "Yes"	Number "No"	% Difference From Expected Mean of 30% (120 "Yes")
1	115	285	1.25
2	119	281	0.25
3	116	284	1.00
4	114	286	1.50
5	107	293	3.25
6	116	284	1.00
7	132	268	3.00
8	123	277	.75
9	121	279	.25
10	114	286	1.50
Mean			1.375

racy, *identical* sample sizes give the same level of accuracy for Podunk (population 8,000) or New York City (population 8 million). The *ratio* of the sample size to the population of Podunk or New York City means nothing at all, even though it intuitively seems to be important.

The size of the sample must depend upon which population or subpopulations you wish to describe. For example, Kinsey's sample size would have seemed large, by customary practice, for generalizations about the United States population as a whole. But, as Kinsey explains: "The chief concern of the present study is an understanding of the sexual behavior of *each segment of the population*, and it is only secondarily concerned with generalization for the population as a whole" (Kinsey et al., 1948: 82, italics added). Therefore Kinsey's sample had to include subsamples large enough to obtain the desired accuracy in *each* of these subuniverses. The U.S. Census offers a similar illustration. When the U.S. Bureau of the Census aims to estimate only a total or an average for the United States as a whole—as, for example, in the Current Population Survey estimate of unemployment—a sample of perhaps 50,000 is big enough. But the decennial census aims to make estimates for all the various communities in the country, estimates that require adequate subsamples in each of these subuniverses; such is the justification for the decennial census' sample size of so many millions.

Television ratings illustrate both types of purpose. Nielsen ratings, for example, are sold primarily to national network advertisers. These advertisers on national television networks usually sell their goods all across the country and are therefore interested primarily in the total United States viewership for a program, rather than in the viewership in various demographic subgroups. The appropriate calculations for Nielsen sample size will therefore refer to the total United States sample. But other organizations sell rating services to *local*

television and radio stations for use in soliciting advertising over the local stations rather than over the network as a whole. Each local sample must then be large enough to provide reasonable accuracy, and, considered as a whole, the samples for the local stations therefore add up to a much larger sample than the Nielsen and other nationwide samples.

B. EXAMPLE 17

This is the first example of sample-size estimation for *probability* (testing) statistics, rather than the summarization statistics dealt with in Example 16. Recall the problem of the sex of fruit-fly offspring discussed in Chapter 31 (Example 5). The question now is, How big a sample is needed to determine whether the radiation treatment results in a sex ratio other than a 50-50 male-female split?

The first step is, as usual, difficult but necessary. As the researcher, you must *guess* what the sex ratio will be if the treatment *does* have an effect. Let's say that you use all your general knowledge of genetics and of this treatment and that you guess the sex ratio at 75 per cent males and 25 per cent females *if* the treatment alters the ratio from 50-50.

Look at the random-number table, and let 1–25 stand for females and 26–00 for males (0 stands for 10, 00 for 100 and so forth, when all 10, all 100 and so forth, numbers are being used). Take twenty successive pairs of numbers for each trial, and run perhaps fifty trials, as in Table 34.3.

In Example 5 we found that, if a sample of twenty flies contained fourteen or more males, we could estimate the odds at 23 to 2 (92 per cent) that the ratio is not "really" 50-50. Now Table 34.3 tells us that, if the ratio is really 75 to 25, then a sample of twenty will show fourteen or more males 42 of 50 times (84 per cent of the time). If we take a sample of twenty flies and if the ratio is *really* 75-25, we will make the correct decision by deciding that the split is not 50-50 84 per cent of the time.

TABLE 34.3

Trial	Females	Males	Trial	Females	Males	Trial	Females	Males
1	4	16	18	7	13	34	4	16
2	6	14	19	3	17	35	6	14
3	6	14	20	7	13	36	3	17
4	5	15	21	4	16	37	8	12
5	5	15	22	4	16	38	4	16
6	3	17	23	5	15	39	3	17
7	7	13	24	8	12	40	6	14
8	6	14	25	4	16	41	5	15
9	3	17	26	1	19	42	2	18
10	2	18	27	5	15	43	8	12
11	6	14	28	3	17	44	4	16
12	1	19	29	8	12	45	6	14
13	6	14	30	8	12	46	5	15
14	3	17	31	5	15	47	3	17
15	1	19	32	3	17	48	5	15
16	5	15	33	4	16	49	3	17
17	5	15				50	5	15

Perhaps you are not satified with reaching the right conclusion only 84 per cent of the time. In that case, still assuming that the ratio will really be 75-25 if it is not 50-50, you need to take a sample larger than twenty flies. How much larger? That depends on how much surer you want to be. Follow the same procedure for a sample size of perhaps eighty flies. First work out for a sample of eighty, as was done in Chapter 31 for a sample of twenty, the number of males (or more) out of eighty that you would need to find for the odds to be, say, 9 to 1 that the universe is not 50-50; your estimate turns out to be forty-eight males, say. Then run fifty trials of eighty flies each on the basis of 75-25 probability, and see how often you would not get as many as forty-eight males in the sample. Table 34.4 shows the results we got. No trial was anywhere near as low as forty-eight, which suggests that a sample of eighty is bigger than necessary if the split is really 75-25.

It is obvious that, if the split you guess at is 60 to 40 rather than 75 to 25, you will need a bigger sample to obtain the "correct" result with the same probability. For example, run some eighty fly random-number trials with 1–40 representing males and 51–100 representing females. Table 34.5 shows that only twenty-four of fifty (48 per cent) of the trials reach the necessary cut-off at which one would judge that a sample of eighty really does not come from a universe that is split 50-50; therefore, a sample of eighty is not big enough if the split is 60-40.

To review the main principles of this example: First, the closer together the two possible universes from which you think the sample might have come (50-50 and 60-40 are closer together than are 50-50 and 75-25), the bigger the sample needed to distinguish between them. Second, the surer you want to be that you reach the right decision based on the sample evidence, the bigger the sample you need.

C. EXAMPLE 18

Referring back to Example 7, on the cable-television poll, in Chapter 31, how large a sample *should* you have taken? Pretend that the data have not yet been collected. You need *some* estimate of how the results will turn out before you can select a sample size. But you have not the foggiest idea of how the results will turn out. Therefore, go out and take a very small

TABLE 34.4

Trial	Females	Males	Trial	Females	Males	Trial	Females	Males
1	21	59	18	13	67	34	21	59
2	22	58	19	19	61	35	17	63
3	13	67	20	17	63	36	22	58
4	15	65	21	17	63	37	19	61
5	22	58	22	18	62	38	21	59
6	21	59	23	26	54	39	21	59
7	13	67	24	20	60	40	21	59
8	24	56	25	16	64	41	21	59
9	16	64	26	22	58	42	18	62
10	21	59	27	16	64	43	19	61
11	20	60	28	21	59	44	17	63
12	19	61	29	22	58	45	13	67
13	21	59	30	21	59	46	16	64
14	17	63	31	22	58	47	21	59
15	22	58	32	19	61	48	16	64
16	22	58	33	10	70	49	17	63
17	17	63				50	21	59

sample, maybe ten people, to give you some idea of whether people will split quite evenly or quite unevenly. Seven of your ten initial interviews say they are for CATV. How big a sample do you need to provide an answer of which you can be fairly sure?

Using the techniques of the previous chapter, we estimate roughly that from a sample of fifty people at least thirty-two would have to vote the same way for you to believe that the odds are at least 19 to 1 that the sample does not misrepresent the universe, that is, that the sample does not show a majority different from that of the whole universe if you polled everyone. That estimate comes from the Monte Carlo experiment whose results are in Table

TABLE 34.5

Trial	Females	Males	Trial	Females	Males	Trial	Females	Males
1	35	45	18	32	48	34	35	45
2	36	44	19	28	52	35	36	44
3	35	45	20	32	48	36	29	51
4	35	45	21	33	47	37	36	44
5	36	44	22	37	43	38	36	44
6	36	44	23	36	44	39	31	49
7	36	44	24	31	49	40	29	51
8	34	46	25	27	53	41	30	50
9	34	46	26	30	50	42	35	45
10	29	51	27	31	49	43	32	48
11	29	51	28	33	47	44	30	50
12	32	48	29	37	43	45	37	43
13	29	51	30	30	50	46	31	49
14	31	49	31	31	49	47	36	44
15	28	52	32	32	48	48	34	46
16	33	47	33	34	46	49	29	51
17	36	44				50	37	43

31.5, page 384. That table shows that, if half the people (or more) are against cable television, only one in twenty times will thirty-two (or more) people of a sample of fifty say that they are for cable television; that is, only one of twenty trials with a 50-50 universe will produce as many as thirty-two *yeses* if a majority of the population is against it. Therefore, designate numbers 1–30 as *no* and 31–00 as *yes* in the random-number table (that is, 70 per cent, as in your estimate based on your presample of ten), work through a trial sample size of fifty, and count the number of *yeses*. Run through perhaps ten or fifteen trials, and reckon how often the observed number of *yeses* exceeds thirty-two, the number you must get for a result you can rely on. In Table 34.6 we see that a sample of fifty respondents, from a universe split 70-30, will show that many *yeses* a preponderant proportion of the time—in fact, in fifteen of fifteen experiments; therefore, the sample size of fifty is large enough if the split is "really" 70-30.

D. EXAMPLE 19

How large a sample is needed to determine whether there is any difference between the two pig rations in Examples 10 and 11 in Chapters 31 and 32? The first step is to guess the results of the tests. You estimate that the average for ration A will be a weight gain of thirty-two pounds. You further guess that twelve pigs on ration A might gain thirty-six,

thirty-five, thirty-four, thirty-three, thirty-three, thirty-two, thirty-two, thirty-one, thirty-one, thirty, twenty-nine, and twenty-eight pounds. This set of guesses has an equal number of pigs above and below the average and more pigs close to the average than further away. That is, there are more pigs at thirty-three and thirty-one pounds than at thirty-six and twenty-eight pounds. This would seem to be a reasonable distribution of pigs around an average of thirty-two pounds. In similar fashion, you guess an average weight gain of twenty-eight pounds for ration B and a distribution of thirty-two, thirty-one, thirty, twenty-nine, twenty-nine, twenty-eight, twenty-eight, twenty-seven, twenty-seven, twenty-six, twenty-five, and twenty-four pounds.

Let us review the basic strategy. We want to find a sample size large enough so that a large proportion of the time it will reveal a difference between groups big enough to be accepted as not attributable to chance. First, then, we need to find out how big the difference must be to be accepted as evidence that the difference is not attributable to chance. We do so from trials with samples that size from the benchmark universe. We state that a difference larger than the benchmark universe will usually show is not attributable to chance.

In this case, let us try samples of twelve pigs on each ration. First we draw two samples from a combined benchmark universe made up of the results that we have guessed will come from ration A and ration B. (The procedure is the same as was followed in Example 11 on page 388.) We find that in nineteen out of twenty trials the difference between the two drawn groups of twelve was three pounds or less. Now we investigate how often samples of twelve pigs each, drawn from the *separate* universes, will show a mean difference as large as three pounds. We do so by making up a twenty-five- or fifty-card deck for *each* of the twelve hypothesized A's and each of the twelve B's, with the ration name and the weight gain written on it; that is, a deck of, say, 300 cards

TABLE 34.6

Trial	No	Yes	Trial	No	Yes
1	13	37	9	15	35
2	14	36	10	9	41
3	18	32	11	15	35
4	10	40	12	15	35
5	13	37	13	13	37
6	11	39	14	14	36
7	13	37	15	17	33
8	7	43			

for each ration. Then from each deck we draw two sets of twelve cards at random, record the group averages, and find the difference. The differences in the fifteen trials turn out invariably to be four pounds or larger. Therefore, two samples of twelve pigs each are clearly large enough, and, in fact, even smaller samples might be sufficient if the universes are really like those we guessed at. If, on the other hand, the differences in the guessed universes had been smaller, then twelve-pig groups would have seemed too small, and we would then have had to try out bigger sample sizes, say forty-eight pigs in each group and perhaps 200 pigs in each group if forty-eight were not enough. And so on until the sample size is large enough to promise the accuracy we want. (In that case, the decks would also have to be much larger, of course.)

If we had guessed different universes for the two rations, then the sample sizes required would have been larger or smaller. If we had guessed the averages for the two samples to be closer together, then we would have needed bigger samples. Also, if we had guessed the weight gains *within* each universe to be less spread out, the samples could have been smaller and vice versa.

We hope that the examples in this chapter have not seemed unpleasantly complex or tedious. One cannot estimate necessary sample size without going through procedures like those we have illustrated, though mathematical methods can speed up the tedious shuffling-and-dealing phase. There is just no easy answer to the question of how large a sample to take.

3. Step-Wise Sample-Size Determination

Often it is wisest to determine the sample size as you go along, rather than fixing it firmly in advance. In sequential sampling, which was discussed briefly in Chapter 9, you *continue* sampling until the split is sufficiently even to make you believe you have a reliable answer.

Related techniques work in a series of *jumps* from sample size to sample size. Step-wise sampling makes it less likely that you will take a sample that is much larger than necessary. For example, in the cable-television case, if you took a sample of perhaps fifty you could see whether the split was as wide as 32-18, which you figure you need for 9 to 1 odds that your answer is right. If the split were not that wide, you would sample another fifty, another 100, or however large a sample you needed until you reached a split wide enough to satisfy you that your answer was reliable and that you really knew which way the entire universe would vote.

Step-wise sampling is not always practical, however, and the cable-television telephone-survey example is unusually favorable for its use. One major pitfall is that the *early* responses to a mail survey, for example, do *not* provide a random sample of the whole, and therefore it is a mistake simply to look at the early returns when the split is not wide enough to justify a verdict. If you have listened to early radio or television reports of election returns, you know how misleading the reports from the first precincts can be if we regard them as a fair sample of the whole.[2]

Stratified sampling is another device that helps reduce the sample size required, by balancing the amounts of information you obtain in the various strata. Chapter 9 discussed the general idea of stratified sampling. (Cluster sampling does not reduce the sample size.

2. See Lorie and Roberts (1951: 155–57) for more discussion of the limitations of sequential sampling. And Hansen and his associates warn against the danger of increasing the sample size in this fashion:

> The investigator examines the returns from an initial sample to determine whether they appear acceptable to the investigator; if they do, he uses the results as they are; if they do not, he discards the sample results [or keeps the old sample] and draws a new sample, perhaps by a different method, in the hope that he will obtain a result more nearly like the one he expected. Such an approach can be utilized to obtain almost any results desired, or can "prove" any point even when unbiased and consistent methods of selecting the sample and making the individual estimates are used if the initial results are subject to relatively large sampling errors. (Hansen et al. 1953: 78)

Rather, it aims to reduce the cost of obtaining a sample that will produce a given level of accuracy.)

4. Summary

Sample sizes are too often determined on the basis of convention or of the available budget. A more rational method of choosing the size of the sample is by balancing the diminution of error expected with a larger sample, and its value, against the cost of increasing the sample size. The relationship of various sample sizes to various degrees of accuracy can be estimated with Monte Carlo methods, which are illustrated here.

ADDITIONAL READING

Tull and Hawkins (1976, Chap. 6) summarize various approaches to determining sample size, but you must know a little about elementary conventional statistics to understand that chapter.

W. Williams (1978) provides practical advice on sampling and sample size, with examples; Cochran et al. (1970) provide a more thorough and technical treatment.

The Concept of Causality in Social Science, with Notes on Prediction, Law, Explanation, and Function

What *is* a cause-and-effect relationship? The main purpose of this chapter[1] is to establish a workable definition of "causality";[2] the chapter also explores the related ideas of prediction, law, explanation, and function.

1. Causality

The task boils down to a search for an *operational* definition of "causality." This is perhaps the most important point of all and the hardest to understand and accept. Of course, the operational definition must fit social scientists'

hypothetical conception of causality. Furthermore, it ought to accord with common scientific usage; that is, the definition should fit situations in which scientists commonly do say that something causes something else or that something is an effect of something else. This definition need *not* also fit the everyday speech of laypersons, which is what has led many philosophers into trouble, we believe.

A definition of "causality" seems unnecessary in everyday life. No one is in much doubt about whether to say that a baseball causes a window to break or that yeast causes the cake to rise. And even when we say we do not know whether two events are causally related—for example, whether walking under a ladder causes bad luck or night air causes disease—our doubt seems to be about our knowledge of the world and not about the meaning of the word "cause."

1. The first part of this chapter on causality owes a debt to Wold. It was two unpublished manuscripts of his (1966a, 1966b) that provoked Simon to develop this view in apparent opposition to his. And subsequent correspondence has made clear to us both that our views are complementary and refer to different aspects of the subject. Discussions with J. W. Carey have also been helpful in clarifying these ideas.

2. "Causality," "causation," and "causal relationship" are used as synonyms in this chapter.

It is useful to speculate on why the term "cause" and the causal concept are *not* puzzling or vague in everyday life. Much of the explanation is probably that we use causal terms all day long in our common speech—not only the term "cause" itself, but also synonyms like "influence," "produce," and "create" and related words like "smash," "build," and "fix." This common conversational practice teaches us quite accurately *what these terms mean to other people*. Our sure-footed use of the term in everyday speech—as contrasted with our confusion in scientific speech—may also stem from the one-to-one quality of most everyday relationships called "causal." We are not so concerned with whether baseballs cause windows to break but rather with whether *that* baseball caused *that* window to break. In our everyday speech we are not so concerned with general statements about groups of events—for example, whether a rise in price causes fewer people to buy or heat causes riots[3]—as we are in social science.

For the most part, defining causality is not a troubling problem when the scientist can run an experiment. As we shall see, the actual experiment is itself *close* to a complete operational definition of causality—though it is *not* a complete definition. It is when the scientist cannot experiment but must deal instead with the data as the world presents them to him or her that an operational definition of "causality" is most acutely needed—and most difficult to create. That is the job of this chapter. To create a satisfactory operational definition of "causality" for nonexperimental situations, we must, first, trace some philosophic history; second, go further into the nature of definitions to see why we seek an *operational* definition; and, third, and most important, explore the use of the causality concept in the social sciences, in order to find out what a *valid* operational definition of causality should be.

To explicate the term "causality" and the concept for which it stands in social-scientific usage, we must start with the most basic notion in science—the observed *association* or *correlation* or *relationship*, all of which are used as synonyms. To say that there is an association is simply to say that, when A has occurred in the past, B has also occurred more often than would have been expected from chance. Or to put it another way, an association is shown if B has occurred more often when A was present than when A was not present.[4]

This definition of an association does not necessarily exclude historical statements, even though they refer to single occurrences of A and B. There is nothing logically wrong with saying that war with Japan in 1941 occurred more often than it would have if Japan had not bombed Pearl Harbor.

The rest of this chapter is simply (!) a subclassification of various types of observed associations (relationships) into those that can also be called "predictions," "causal relationships," "laws," "functional relationships," and so forth. These categories are not intended to be mutually exclusive.

2. Causation and Prediction

Causation and prediction have often been confused, so we must first talk a bit about prediction. Many—but not all—observed associations can be interpreted as bases for *predictions*. A prediction is the expressed belief that an asso-

---

3. But notice that we are not saying that everyday relationships are completely determinate or nonprobabilistic. A tumbler does not shatter *every* time it is dropped, but we do not have difficulty saying that a given fall *did* cause it to break.

4. The definition is framed in terms of dichotomous presence-absence variables only for convenience, and it can easily be generalized to quantitative variables. It uses the past tense to emphasize that it refers only to events that have already been observed and excludes predictive elements.

ciation will also hold in the future; a person predicts if he or she believes that the general background conditions will not change drastically from the observation period to the prediction period. For example, if one observes that sales of drug D have been associated with the number of cases of angina pectoris in previous years, one may predict that, if angina pectoris cases rise this year, sales of drug D will also rise—unless one has reason to doubt *ceteris paribus*. But, if one learns that some important condition no longer holds–for example, that a new drug for angina pectoris has been introduced—one will no longer interpret the past observed association as basis for a prediction. One is willing to make a prediction if one believes that the future is an unbiased sample from the same universe as that of the past period on which the prediction is based. (See Chapter 25 for more discussion of the assumption of *ceteris paribus* in predicting.)

Notice that the basis for the interpretation of an association as prediction *cannot be found in the data themselves*.[5] Rather it is in one's general knowledge of the situation. This is the reason for the word "belief" in our definition of prediction.

It is at this point that David Hume makes his mighty entrance. Hume argued that all that one can know is that there has been an association—a "constant conjunction"—in the past. He asserted that there is no *logical* basis for prediction of the future on the basis of the past; one can never prove an induction in any formal logical fashion. And our definition of a prediction is in agreement with that point of view. But then Hume also stated that to call an association a "causal relationship" is to assert

nothing more than constant conjunction.[6] He argued that no one could ever demonstrate a "necessary connexion" between a cause and an effect. In other words, he denied that anyone could show a material or "ontological"[7] relationship between a cause and an effect, and therefore he argued that it is not sensible to say that something is a "real" cause of something else.

One reason why it is impossible to make an air-tight case for an ontological causal relationship is that the possibility of a third factor always exists, and that possibility cannot be dismissed logically. Equally important, there are always conceptual intermediates. If one person says that the bicycle pedals make the bicycle go, another can argue that it is the linkage of the chain and sprockets that makes the bicycle go. Someone else can argue on the level of friction, another on a molecular level, and so on. One simply cannot demonstrate a "real" cause-and-effect relationship in a material sense. That is why an actual experiment is not a *complete* operational definition of a cause-and-effect relationship.

This view of the causal relationship is called a "subjective" view because it asserts that the connection between the two events is a product of the mind of the observer. It asserts that *it is the observer who pairs the two events and calls the relationship a "causal" relationship*. The Humean view does *not* assert there is *not* a material relationship between A and B. Rather, it asserts that we can never determine and isolate some *unique* material relationship between them that we should call "causal." Also, the label "subjective" may be confusing; the word does not imply that the pairing of two events is strictly private and unknown to other

---

5. Nor is there basis for the prediction in an operation, as is the case with generalizations on the basis of randomly drawn samples. The generalization to the colors of balls in an urn based on a random sample from the urn is based on the operation of drawing the sample randomly. But we can never draw the future randomly from the past.

6. "We may define a cause to be an object, followed by another, and where all the objects similar to the first are followed by objects similar to the second."

7. By "ontological" we mean physical, material, existential, being *qua* being.

people. The Humean view is compatible with a wide consensus that the association between a particular pair of events should be called a "causal relationship." "Subjective" simply implies that the pairing is a result of people's *perceptions* and that many people can share a common perception—or at least say they do.

The central point of the Humean view is that, when someone says "A causes B," that person expresses some *reflection in his or her mind* of the material objective world and not the material world directly. It is as if the person is talking of a moving picture of a footrace or a landscape, rather than of the footrace or landscape itself. The moving picture can be very public, and almost all of us might agree on what the picture is "of," just as a prediction that the sun will come up tomorrow is quite public and agreed upon. But the moving picture is humanly produced, just as the association or prediction is humanly produced, in the sense that it requires an observer to notice the association or to interpret the association in a prediction.

We are *not* saying that there is not a real world in which things grow, push one another, and decay; in which air inflates balloons, baseballs crack windows, people hurt one another, babies make mothers laugh, and so on. What we are saying is that, when scientists *observe* an association and abstract from the real world to make a scientific statement, that statement is not the *same* thing as what they are observing; it is a product of their minds or a picture of the world filtered through their perceptions, if you like. This is true not only of causal statements; it is true also of every association. Furthermore, every *word* in the language is such a picture of the world and represents such an abstraction from the world.

To repeat, then, a discussion of cause-and-effect relationships, or of associations generally, is a discussion of how people use language in response to various kinds of situations that confront them. This discussion is about language and not about the material world. It is the confusion between those two levels of discussion that is responsible for the confusion about the term "causality."

We must ask, What does "causality" *mean?* When we ask what a word means, we are asking *what people refer to* when they use the word. The definition can never be perfect, of course, because there are always borderline cases, even for such relatively clear-cut words as "chair." Is a stool a chair? Not all people will classify the same instances in the same way. The test of a definition is whether there is some *consensus* among people in their use of the word and whether an operational definition can be formulated that will capture the basis of that consensus.

The unamended Humean view is that there is no difference between statements of cause and effect and all other statements of association, or, as the view is propounded today by Friedman in economics, that there is no difference between predictions[8] and cause-and-effect statements. But this unvarnished Humean view is not very satisfactory, for social scientists talk and act as if some associations are of a different sort from other associations and as if some predictions are of a different sort from other predictions. A statement that the flight of birds overhead precedes rain seems to be a different sort than the statement that activating the starter of the automobile precedes the starting of the engine; indeed, we react very differently toward these two statements.

To take an example from economics, we sense a difference between the observed association between prices on the Dutch stock exchange and the number of houses built in the United States, on one hand, and the observed association between mortgage interest rates in the United States and the number of houses

---

8. Friedman talks about predictions and associations almost interchangeably, as if predictions were automatically implied by associations (pp. 7–13). In fact, the link between associations and predictions is not logically dissimilar to the link between associations and cause-and-effect statements.

built in the United States, on the other. Similarly, in sociology there seems to be a difference between a statement that the birth rate is high in districts in Europe where there are many storks and the statement that the birth rate is high where child mortality is high.

3. The Problem of Definition

The *nature* of the differences between these statements is something of which we have so far said nothing. We have only asserted that we seem to act and talk *as if there are* such differences.

A detour about definitions is necessary now. Several sorts of definition of a term are possible, and some are relevant here. First, one can define a term by giving synonyms for it. For example, Blalock says that "causality is conceived [in his discussion] as involving the notion of production, that is, causes produce effects . . ." (1972: 173). "Production" is a synonym for "causation." Giving synonyms like this one can be useful in clarifying for a foreigner what the word "cause" means in English or in explaining the term to a child. But synonymization obviously does not suffice to solve basic scientific problems of causal labeling.

Second, one may define by *naming some properties* of the concept one is trying to get at. This sort of definition aims to say what causality *is*. It is an "ontological" definition in terms of material properties of the world. Such definitions can help one person to convey to another a general feeling of what he or she is talking about. They are also often used successfully with children or foreigners—or even in making clearer to another scientist what one has in mind. An example is saying that "an automobile is a device with four wheels, an internal combustion engine, and so on" or "conformity is the act of patterning one's behavior to make it like the behavior of the group." This type of definition of causality has been tried by philosophers for thousands of years, with a no-

table lack of success. And, as noted in Chapter 2, Bridgman argued that it was because physicists had defined their words in terms of properties that there had grown up the wall to understanding that Einstein shattered—by achieving definitions in terms of *operations* to substitute for definitions in terms of *properties*.

What Hume did was to demonstrate the flaws in an ontological definition of causality. But he did not offer a substitute definition in terms of operations. Rather, he suggested that the term "causality" was useless and ought to be dispensed with. This has been the prevailing view among the most influential of twentieth-century philosophers, including B. Russell.

Third, definition by *denotation* can be helpful under some circumstances. Most of the definitions of terms in this book have been defined denotatively, that is, with examples. But again, we need more than denotation to clarify the scientific notion of causality.

Fourth, when scientists disagree about the application of a term and wish to increase the likelihood that they will apply the same terms to the same empirical phenomena, they *must* turn to operational definitions. The entire purpose of this chapter is to develop useful operational definitions of "causality" and related terms. We shall see that, if experimentation is possible, an operational definition of causality is reasonably easy with the following procedure.

1. Vary the stimulus and observe the variations in the response.
2. Try many other stimuli to see if the same response occurs.
3. If both steps yield appropriate results, call the relationships between stimulus and response "causal."

Furthermore, we must also try to define "causality" operationally in nonexperimental situations. Success of this endeavor is measured in two ways: Does the operational definition result in many scientists reaching the same judgment on whether to apply the term "causal" in a given situation? And does the definition accord with common usage and intuitive "property definitions" held by social scientists? That is, does the proposed operational definition fit closely the hypothetical concept of causality held by most scientists?

We think that causal relationships are a subclass of associations, that is, that all causal relationships are associations but that not all associations are causal relationships. This is a slight (but important) amendment of the point made by Wold (1966b) that causal relationships are a subclass of *predictions*.

A cause-and-effect statement is a type of scientific *explanation*, but not all explanations are causal statements, as we interpret common usage.

It is at this point that the real work begins. After we have said that causal relationships are a subclass of associations and that each causal statement is a humanly produced concept, just as are all words and ideas, then what? *How does one distinguish between those associations that are and those that are not within the subclass of causal statements?* This is the job of creating an operational definition of causality.

There have been various attempts to find a method for deciding whether a particular association should be called "causal," that is, a method for partitioning the class of associations into causal and noncausal associations. But none of the authors has described his proposed method as an "operational definition of causality." We shall briefly mention some of the attempts.

First, many writers have said that all those associations that can be *verified experimentally* deserve to be called "causal"—and no others. This is quite congenial to the scientific intuition, and it has been a very useful rule in much of science. But it is not a perfect rule—that is, it does not work in every case—for at least two

reasons: (1) In any experiment a hidden third factor, rather than changes in the presumed independent "test variable," might account for the changes in the dependent variable; and (2) in many situations experimentation is not possible.

Because a hidden third factor may always turn out to be the "real" cause, a single experiment does not provide a *complete* operational definition of causality. Rather, one must also run related experiments varying various parameters of the situation, and only when one has exhausted the important possibilities should he or she say that the experimental stimulus causes the experimental response. In the Hawthorne experiment, for example, a single experiment varying light intensities and observing work output was not sufficient; the researchers also had to vary such parameters as their own presence in the work situation to establish a causal relationship.

To restate, then, the operational definition of "causality" when experimentation is possible is this: If the response follows the experimental stimulus and if this experimental relationship persists when other elements of the situation are varied, the experimentally observed relationship may be called "causal."

From here on the discussion will be concerned with the case in which no experiment is possible, as in some of psychology, most of sociology, and almost all of economics and anthropology. It is here that the stickiest questions about causal statements occur.

A second proposed method is that of Wold, who attempted to bring nonexperimental situations within the reach of the experimental-verification principle by asking whether a nonexperimental situation is a "fictitious," or "hypothetical," experiment, meaning that the natural situation has most of the elements of an actual experiment (Wold, 1966b). But this conceptualization has two shortcomings. To begin with, the essence of the experiment as an operational definition of causality is that it is the actual observed results of a real experiment that serve to determine whether the relationship is called "causal." The other shortcoming is that one might say that the very act of choosing to label the relationship as causal is an operation that defines "causality." But such an operational definition has little validity because it does not go far toward resolving disagreements among people on what should be called "causal." That is, it carries us little further than the present ill-defined situation.[9]

A third approach is that of logician-philosophers who have tried various combinations of conditional statements of the "if-then" variety, what they call "counterfactual conditionals," and discussions of necessary and sufficient conditions. They have attempted to find some *logical* formulation that successfully distinguishes between causal and noncausal associations. But Shapere's assessment that this quest has so far failed completely is surely fair and accurate (1965: 24). We think the failure results from the philosophers' failure to recognize that an *operational* definition is needed.

Fourth, H. Simon (1959, 1979), Blalock (1972), and others, abstracting from original work by Lazarsfeld, have investigated how the correlations between and among three or more variables can help one sort out which of these variables can be said to "cause" which. This is an amplification and formalization of the analysis presented in Chapter 25 to investigate whether a hidden third factor is "responsible"

for the correlation between two other variables.[10]

The study of "causal ordering," as it is called, is useful and important, but it does not do the whole job, as H. Simon points out (1957: 41). For example, if the investigator starts out with three variables, none of which should really be said to be the "cause" of another, the analysis can tell us nothing about whether the relationship between two given variables should be called a "causal" relationship. These schemes for labeling relationships as "causal" or "noncausal" depend on the use of *outside knowledge* to help sort out the relationships, for example, the knowledge that one event precedes all the others in time and therefore cannot be the result of all the others. This position boils down to the assertion that a relationship is causal unless proved not causal by tests for spuriousness. Such an analytic scheme does *not* provide an operational definition that indicates whether a *given* relationship should be called causal; at best, it tells us that, within a set of variables and relationships, one relationship is "more causal" than another.[11]

For now it is necessary to note that no definition has been created that fits customary scientific usage, even though this is the stated aim of all of them (H. Simon, 1957: 60; Wold, 1966b: 267). On reflection, it is not surprising that no perfect or near-perfect definition of "cause-and-effect relationship" has yet been

9. Orcutt's extension of the pragmatic point of view to the definition of causality is related (1952a, 1952b). Orcutt argues that a relationship should be called "causal" only *if the relationship can be manipulated for policy purposes*. By this test, the relationship between the money supply and inflation might be called "causal" because the money supply can be manipulated to influence inflation. This point of view has much in common with the experimental-validation test for causality, but it does not demand experimental validation *before* calling the relationship "causal." Also, it does not permit us to refer to a relationship as "causal" if the investigator is interested in the phenomenon just for "pure science" and not for immediate policy manipulation.

10. Hyman (1955) and Hirschi and Selvin (1967) have gone far beyond the formal Lazarsfeld analytic scheme in somewhat the same direction that we are going here. Part II of the Hirschi-Selvin volume is the most painstaking and perceptive discussion of causality extant, though we do not agree with its point of view entirely. Its strength is its firm root in empirical material, though its limited focus on juvenile delinquency will turn away many who could profit from it.

11. Wold has also explored a related and important area. *Assuming* that a given variable *is* causal, Wold investigates which econometric transformations do and do not permit subsequent causal inference (1966a).

created. It is difficult to create perfect auto- matic rules for discriminating even such gen- erally understood concepts as "chair" and "tree" and "money"; even the best operational definition does not lead everyone to classify all examples of such concepts in exactly the same way; there are always exceptions at the border- line. It is natural, then, that such a term as "cause and effect," which is so much more complex and abstract than are the other terms, will be much harder to define satisfactorily and will have many more borderline cases on which people disagree when classifying situa- tions as causal and noncausal.

In order to develop a definition of "causal- ity" that is *valid* as well as *operational*, we must examine actual scientific usage. There- fore, let us consider a set of situations relating to sales in department stores, to see how the causal concept is used.

A. EXAMPLE 1. INCOME AND TOY DEMAND IN DEPARTMENT STORES

Assume that per capita income in a community rises from period 0 to period 1. *Ceteris pari- bus*, a rise in the *sales of toys* probably will also occur between periods 0 and 1. This is merely the statement of an association.

Should one say that increased income causes an increase in toy demand? Our observation is that, except for those who completely reject the use of the causal concept, no economist will boggle at saying that increased income causes increased toy demand.

Upon casual examination, this relationship seems to have three elements that seem to fit intuitive notions of causality:

1. High predictive reliability.
2. A set of theoretical links—the economic theory of consumer preference, in this case—give us the feeling that we "under- stand" the relationship.
3. Few or no qualifications to the statement seem to be required.

For now these are only clues; later we shall examine them with care.

This example was chosen because of its ex- treme simplicity and the general acceptance of the causality of this kind of relationship.

B. EXAMPLE 2. SEASONAL TOY DEMAND IN DEPARTMENT STORES

We hypothesize that a Chicago department store will sell more toys in December than in January, subject only to such further condi- tions as that the store stays in business, no nat- ural calamity like war or earthquake occurs, and so forth. We do *not* specify that advertis- ing or price be held constant because variation in them does not change the pattern enough to render the statement untrue. The (hypotheti- cal) observed association is between sales and the calendar months. To put the hypothesis in other words, if the store is in business and un- less there is a calamity, there is an overwhelm- ingly high probability that the demand for toys will be higher in December than in January, and the probability of any such condition as a calamity or the store's not being in business is very small.

How might this situation be characterized in terms of the causality concept in normal eco- nomic usage? In the policy-making situation, the manager of the store acts upon this knowl- edge when she orders more toys for December than for January because she expects higher demand in December. One could say that the manager uses the association as a predictive device; such Humean language is the simplest and least restrictive interpretation of the situa- tion. Furthermore, the manager would act in the same way if she believed that there was a real and material connection between Decem- ber and demand or if she believed that De- cember was only a predictive index like birds that predict rain. The distinction does not mat- ter to the manager because she cannot manip- ulate the independent variable. But we would not be surprised if she used causal language and said that December causes toy demand to be higher than does January.

An economic analysis that provides information about relative demand in December and January is certainly of value to policy makers, and therefore the pragmatist should approve the label "causal." It is not, however, a situation in which the independent variable (the calendar change from month to month) is subject to human control. Therefore, Orcutt's pragmatic definition of "causality" does not seem to fit this example. Nor does this situation fit the requirement that a relationship labeled "causal" should be a reasonable analogy to an experiment. It is difficult even to conceptualize an experiment that might test whether the relationship would hold if the "causal" variable were manipulated. How does a researcher manipulate December or seasonality?

Economists might also study the pattern of seasonal demand merely because it is interesting and they want to understand it, rather than because they want to help department stores make sound decisions. Or they might wish to estimate seasonal demand for use in seasonal adjustments. If an economist is addicted to causal language, he may say that the seasonal pattern "causes" demand to be higher in December, even though he knows that Christmas and various religious and social beliefs and attitudes mediate between seasonality and toy demand; by using the word "cause" he surely does not mean to imply "complete and ultimate cause," and therefore his knowledge of intermediate links does not weaken the claim of the seasonal patterns to be called "causal."

This example offers good ground for a discussion of time, antecedence, and the causal concept. We have written as if the *time period* called "December" (or the change from December to January) might be called the "cause" of the changed demand, but time itself is only a matrix in which the real cause is embedded, and therefore it is questionable that time can ever be called a "cause," an issue discussed in Section 7 of this chapter.

C. EXAMPLE 3. THE HOURLY PATTERN OF TOTAL DEPARTMENT-STORE DEMAND

In this example, we shall discuss the hypothesis that in a department store the total demand for all goods (and for every good) *after* the store doors have been unlocked is greater than the demand before the doors are unlocked. This example and those that follow may seem trivial or bizarre, because more realistic examples are harder to handle briefly. It is worth noting, however, that these examples are nowhere near as trivial as the usual examples in logical discussions, for instance, "John wears his raincoat because it rains."

The hypothesized association between door unlocking and increased sales presupposes various normal conditions, for instance, that the door opens within thirty minutes of 8:30 A.M., that no strike is in progress, and that the day is not Sunday. In other words, unlocking the door will be followed by a sudden increase in demand *if a good many other conditions are specified*. Side conditions were also specified in Example 2 (for example, the store's being in business), but the present example differs in that the side conditions might very well not be met a good part of the time (for instance, it is often Sunday) and could be changed arbitrarily (for example, the management might decide not to stay open Wednesday). Another difference is that the "cause" variable (unlocking the door) could be put into operation quixotically, for instance, by a drunken manager. We do not know what the probability is that a given door-unlocking event will take place when the various inputs hold. A compulsive janitor may unlock and relock the doors every hour on the hour, with no sales resulting.

This situation differs from those in Examples 1 and 2 in that neither a decision maker nor a scientist is likely to consider the relationship between door unlocking and increased demand a causal relationship. The reasons are instructive. The difference between Example 3 and Examples 1 and 2 that would seem to explain the difference in the appropriateness of the causal concept is that many of the side conditions necessary for the association in Example 3 to be highly predictable are themselves not very predictable and are subject to change. To put it another way, *given* the various conditions, the association is highly predictable. But, *without knowledge* of whether the various side conditions hold, the association of Example 3 is much less predictable than are those in Examples 1 and 2, and it is more difficult to determine whether the side conditions hold in Example 3 compared to Examples 1 and 2.

Note that the difference between Examples 2 and 3 is *not* that Example 3 is a case of multicausation; if anything, the opposite is true. In Example 3, but *not* in Example 1, it is possible to hold everything constant, vary only the "independent" variables, and observe the association.

D. EXAMPLE 4. THE EFFECT ON DEMAND OF A WARNING BUZZER

In a particular department store, a buzzer is sounded in all employees' spaces as warning that the doors will open in five minutes. The hypothesis that we shall discuss in this section is that sales in the hour starting ten minutes after the bell sounds will be greater than sales in the hour before the bell sounds. Again this statement requires that we specify further conditions, including the same ones specified in Examples 2 and 3, as well as some others: that the buzzer is never buzzed except to warn employees of the beginning of the business day, except to test it; that the situation described is not a test; and so forth.

In this example there are two major possibilities. The first is that the buzzer would be activated only in conjunction with an unlocking of the door. If so, the probabilities are *exactly the same* as those for unlocking alone, as in the previous example. There is also, however, a second set of possibilities in which the buzzer and the lock would *not* be activated together. If it should prevail, there is no reason to be-

lieve that demand will be higher or lower after the buzzing; that is, the association will then not hold.

Example 4 is a classic hidden-third-factor situation (that is, an example of spurious correlation or specification error). It is not possible to specify (as one could in Example 3) even a very limited set of conditions under which experimental control can be applied with a high degree of probability—*unless* a condition (unlocking) is specified that can *also* be interpreted as the "active" variable in the experiment. Then the latter variable will have an identical observed association with buzzing, provided that one more condition (unlocking) is specified for the buzzing association than for the unlocking association. (Speaking loosely, this distinction gives us a criterion for choosing *between* two variables which one we should call the "more real" cause. The more real cause does not include the other as a side condition, but the other does include the more real one.)

In general, the buzzing example has the same characteristics as does the unlocking example but to a greater degree, because there is no reason to think that we can guess accurately what the conjunction or disjunction of lock and buzzer will be. This important change could take place quixotically and arbitrarily, a characteristic that surely disqualifies the association as a causal relationship. Yet the association can be manipulated experimentally and under rigidly specified conditions. The outcome can be predicted with such high accuracy as to be almost a fully determinate relationship rather than a "mere" statistical relationship.

It is illuminating to make a few more assumptions and then to consider how a person without the usual experience and knowledge might react. Assume that the door locks are electric and are activated by a central switch. Assume also that the switch is wired so that it is pushed to buzz the warning buzzer and that, after a five-minute delay, the doors are automatically unlocked. Because she is from another planet or merely from some "backward" country, the person who pushes the switch thinks that it activates the buzzer, and she does not know about the door-unlocking action. In her perception, the state of demand for toys under each set of conditions will be exactly the same as ours for door unlocking, except that she will believe that the buzzing of the buzzer is the immediate predecessor of increased toy demand. (Stranger *post hoc, ergo propter hoc* superstitions have been held, both by Skinner's pigeons and by humans.) Note that in this case the relationship can be manipulated and apparently tested experimentally. To reveal this specification error there is no recourse except to subject-matter knowledge; for example, doctors used leeches for a long time because no one did any satisfactory empirical investigation to determine their effectiveness.

4. Generalization About the Meaning of "Cause and Effect"

Now it is time to see what reasonable generalizations can be drawn from the examples. Whether a situation is closely analogous to a controlled experiment clearly does not provide a complete definition of causality. Example 3 could be studied experimentally by varying the time of unlocking the door, whereas it would be difficult to carry out a validating experiment for the seasonal effects of Example 2. Yet it is Example 2 that economists probably will consider causal, rather than Example 3.

Furthermore, even in the controlled experiment there is often no help for specification error except subject-matter knowledge. In the example of the men who got drunk successively on bourbon and soda, scotch and soda, and brandy and soda and concluded that soda causes drunkenness, nothing except substantive knowledge or scientific intuition would have led them to the recognition that it is the alcohol rather than the soda that made them drunk, *as long as they always took soda with their drinks*. And no statistical procedure can suggest to them that they ought to experiment with the presence and absence of soda. If this is true for an experiment, it must also be true

for an uncontrolled study, a point illustrated by Examples 3 and 4.

Surety of prediction is not a satisfactory definition of causality. In Example 3, one may predict that increased demand will follow door unlocking with a probability closely approaching 1.0, but the situation is not one that would be considered causal. One important reason why accuracy of prediction is not a complete test of causality is that the scientist can and does arrange side situations in various ways that change the observed and theoretical probabilities. More specifically, by fixing enough side conditions an investigator can force probabilities very high, but the fixing of many side conditions reduces the claim of the relationship to be called "causal."

We hazard the following as a working definition:

(1) A causal relationship is expressed in a statement that has these important characteristics: It is an association that is strong enough so that the observer believes it to have a predictive (explanatory) power great enough to be scientifically useful or interesting. For example, one is not likely to say that wearing glasses causes (or is a cause of) auto accidents if the observed correlation is .07, even if the sample is large enough to make the correlation statistically significant. In other words, unimportant relationships are not likely to be labeled causal.

Observers may differ in judging whether an association is strong enough to be important and therefore "causal." And the particular academic field in which the observer works may affect this judgment. This indicates that whether a relationship is dubbed "causal" involves a good deal of human judgment and is subject to dispute.

(2) The side conditions must be sufficiently *few* and sufficiently observable so that the relationship will apply under a wide enough range of conditions to be considered useful or interesting. In other words, *the relationship must not require too many "ifs", "ands", and "buts" in order to hold*. For example, one

might say that an increase in income caused an increase in the birth rate if this relationship were observed everywhere. But if the relationship were found to hold only in developed countries, among the educated classes, and among the higher-income groups, then it would be less likely to be called "causal"— even if the correlation were extremely high once the specified conditions had been met. A similar example can be made of the relationship between income and happiness.

(3) For a relationship to be called "causal," there should be a good reason to believe that, even if the control variable were not the "real" cause (and it never is), other relevant "hidden" and "real" cause variables must also change *consistently* with changes in the control variables. That is, a variable being manipulated may reasonably be called "causal" if the real variable for which it is believed to be a proxy must always be tied intimately to it. (Between two variables, v may be said to be the "more real" cause and w a "spurious" cause, if v and w require the same side conditions, except that v does not require w as a side condition.) This third criterion (nonspuriousness) is of particular importance to policy makers. The difference between it and the previous criterion for side conditions is that a plenitude of very restrictive side conditions may take the relationship out of the class of causal relationships, *even though the effects of the side conditions are known*. This criterion of nonspuriousness concerns variables that are as yet *unknown and unevaluated* but that have a *possible* ability to *upset* the observed association.

Examples of spurious relationships and hidden-third-factor causation are commonplace. For a single example, toy sales rise in December. There is no danger in saying that December causes an increase in toy sales, even though it is "really" Christmas that causes the increase, because Christmas and December practically always accompany each other.

Belief that the relationship is not spurious is increased if *many* likely variables have been investigated and none removes the relationship.

This is a further demonstration that the test of whether an association should be called "causal" cannot be a logical one; there is no way that one can express in symbolic logic the fact that many other variables have been tried without changing the relationship in question.

(4) The more tightly a relationship is bound into (that is, deduced from, compatible with, and logically connected to) a general framework of theory, the stronger is its claim to be called "causal." To take an example from economics, observed positive relationships between the interest rate and business investment and between profits and investment are more likely to be called "causal" than is the relationship between liquid assets and investment. This is so because the first two statements can be deduced from classical price theory, whereas the third statement cannot. Connection to a theoretical framework provides support for belief that the side conditions necessary for the statement to hold true are not restrictive and that the likelihood of spurious correlation is not great; because a statement is logically connected to the rest of the system, the statement tends to stand or fall as the rest of the system stands or falls. And, because the rest of the system of economic theory has, over a long period of time and in a wide variety of tests, been shown to have predictive power, a statement connected with it is cloaked in this mantle.[12]

The social sciences other than economics do not have such well-developed bodies of deductive theory, and therefore this criterion of causality does not weigh as heavily in sociology, for instance, as in economics. Rather, the other social sciences seem to substitute a weaker and more general criterion, that is, whether the statement of the relationship is accompanied by other statements that seem to "explain" the "mechanism" by which the relationship operates. Consider, for example, the relationship between the phases of the moon

---

12. Wilson (1952: 160) makes a similar point about "generalizations" in physics and chemistry.

and the suicide rate. The reason that sociologists do not call it causal is that there are no auxiliary propositions that explain the relationship and describe an operative mechanism. On the other hand, the relationship between broken homes and juvenile delinquency is often referred to as "causal" in large part because a large body of psychoanalytic theory serves to explain why a child raised without one or another parent or in the presence of parental strife should not adjust readily.

Few social-scientific statements except those in economics can claim to be unambiguous deductions from generally accepted principles because the disciplines do not meet Letwin's test:

> . . . [I]f the explanation and prediction follow necessarily from a few principles that explain many other phenomena as well, it is nevertheless [even if inaccurate] a scientific theory. On the other hand, the mere isolated statement of one of those principles, or even an exhaustive list of all of them, is not a scientific theory. . . .[13] (Letwin, 1975: vi; see also Homans, 1964: 11–12)

This operational definition of "causality" is long, involved, and imprecise, demonstrating our central argument that there is not, and cannot be, *any* simple test or definition of the term. Rather, there must be several criteria, and they cannot be very objective but must be as subjective as each person's own background and experience. It is on such a subjective basis—though presumably guided and influenced by some reasonably clear idea of what the causality concept means to other people—that each person must render his or her own judgment on whether to *call* a given scientific statement "causal."

To describe the definition of "causality" in another way, we can say that causal relations are a subclass of associations that meet several qualifying tests or conditions. The job of the definition is to establish appropriate tests, which are the conditions a relationship must meet to be considered causal.

The term "causal" has, and probably should have, different meanings to the decision maker and to the scientist. The decision maker will call a relationship "causal" if he expects to be able to manipulate it successfully. Cigarette smoking may be considered causal by the decision maker who wishes to reduce deaths from lung cancer and other diseases statistically related to smoking, which was the meaning of the Surgeon General's committee's use of the word "cause." But to the scientist *qua* investigative scientist the word "cause" is likely to mean that the situation does not require further and deeper exploration; in the case of cigarettes, perhaps only one ingredient in the cigarettes does the damage, and the scientist searching for this ingredient may chose to withhold the word "cause" from the cigarettes themselves.

The difference in meaning and use of the causal concept between decision-making and "pure" investigative situations is just one illustration of the general proposition that the attribution of causality depends on one's purpose.[14]

---

13. This is certainly not a claim that the nonexperimental social sciences are scientifically inferior to economics. We believe that, for example, sociology's relative lack of success in developing a deductive structure is a necessary result of the complexity of the subject matter sociologists deal with and especially of the irreducible multiplicity of motives that influence the human behavior they want to study. Braithwaite makes a similar point about psychology, though in our limited knowledge of the fields, it is not as true of recent psychology as of sociology:

> The aesthetic defect of psychological theory as a scientific deductive system is that it has a vast number of separate highest-level hypotheses; up to the present [1949] it has succeeded hardly at all in unifying itself by the use of colligating concepts, as physical theory did in the seventeenth century. (1953: 307)

Northrop tells us why economics meets this aesthetic and scientific requirement:

> Any deductive theory in any subject whatever must possess relations as well as elements among its primitive concepts. The fundamental entities of economic theory are economic goods, or wants, or valuations. Its fundamental relation is that of "preference." (1965: 239)

14. This proposition is the subject of a major debate among legal scholars. The question is whether a question of negligence can or should be broken up into a neutral question about the material facts of causation and a legal question about whether the causal act is negligent. It seems to us that the much better arguments belong to those who argue that it is impossible to ask a neutral and "nonevaluative" question about causality.

Not only may the particular *occasion* of the term's use differ between policy makers and "pure" investigators, but also the frequency of its use may differ, for there seems to be a difference in the *necessity* of the causal concept for people in these different roles. The causal concept is perhaps most necessary for a policy maker, especially when he or she is considering changing one variable in hopes of achieving change in another variable. The classification of causal versus noncausal is an attempt to discriminate between situations that he or she believes allow such control and those that do not. On the other hand, the causal concept is not at all necessary for the forecaster, for he or she has no interest in trying to manipulate the independent variables. The causal concept may or may not be necessary to the "pure" investigator; most contemporary physicists apparently believe that it is neither necessary nor useful in the physical sciences. Many nonpolicy scholars in the social sciences, however, seem to find the concept useful in classifying situations for future research.

The difference among disciplines in the variables to call "causal" also illustrates how causal labeling depends on purpose. In those cases in which the variables are complementary—like the achievement motive and capital investment in discussions of economic development—it is perhaps unnecessary for either the economist or the psychologist to deny the causal label to one variable in order to apply it to another variable. But when the variables are hierarchical—for example, badly designed auto, slippery highway, going too fast, braking too sharply on curve (see 91)—then the variables may be causally incompatible, and particular investigators and disciplines must then choose which level to study and call "causal" on the basis of the level they consider most fruitful.

We began by saying that, to find out what "causality" means, we must investigate how social scientists use the term. That we have done. We believe that there is considerable consensus among scientists on which relationships are causal and which are not, and we believe that we have isolated the most important characteristics of the causal relationships. Given that the characteristics listed earlier successfully distinguish causal from noncausal relationships, one can use these characteristics as guides to labeling associations. It is important to use language in accord with accepted scientific usage, and causal language is no exception. These characteristics, then, are prescriptions, as well as descriptions.

Before leaving the subject of causality, let us try out the definition on disputes about the causal status of some variables associated with juvenile delinquency.[15] Many investigators have found the following variables correlated with juvenile delinquency: broken homes, poverty, poor housing, lack of recreation facilities, poor physical health, race, and working mothers. All these variables were long considered causes of delinquency, but recently the causal status of each has been called into question.

First, each of these variables, alone and in combination with other variables, have predicted delinquency with some success. None is perfectly correlated with delinquency, of course, but to demand such a perfect prediction would be a false criterion of causality, as Hirschi and Selvin point out. Therefore, each of these associations meets the first criterion given.

Second, each of these variables except race has been shown to be associated with delinquency in a wide variety of conditions. The range of these conditions is certainly wide enough so that the associations are of interest to both "pure" sociologists and policy-oriented sociologists and social workers. But in those conditions in which no other variable in the list is favorable for delinquency—especially poverty and broken homes—race is *not* associated with delinquency, and therefore race fails to

15. This section draws heavily upon material presented in Hirschi and Selvin's "False Criteria of Causality in Delinquency Research."

meet the second test of causality: that the relationship holds under a wide variety of conditions.[16] The other variables do meet this test, however.

The third test is that of spuriousness and the certainty of connection between the given variable and the "more real" variable. Consider the matter of working mothers, for example. It is reasonable to suppose that *lack of the mother's interest and attention* is the "real" variable (more real than the working-mother variable) associated with delinquency. Mothers who are highly motivated to spend maximum time with their children will be less likely to go to work than will other mothers, even when financial need is great. Another possible connection is that the very fact that she works may reduce the attention a mother can pay to her children. So both these chains are relevant:

reduced
interest and → going to work →delinquency
attention

               reduced
going to work → interest and →delinquency
               attention

It was long believed that we need not worry about the relationship between the mother's working and her interest and attention. The former was seen as a thoroughly reliable proxy for the latter. If the amount of attention the mother devotes is high, she will not be working. As the real variable is not likely to be dissociated from the variable in question (working mothers), we do not disqualify the working-mothers variable from being called "causal." (Its impact is now more doubtful, when a majority of mothers work, than was the case when Hirschi and Selvin wrote, however.) All the other variables except race seem to pass this test, though considerable discussion would be required to demonstrate these relationships.

The fourth characteristic of a causal statement in economics is that the statement be tied in with the rest of formal deductive theory. In sociology, however, this test can seldom, if ever, be met. Instead, some sociologists demand that the two variables in the association must be related with intervening variables, that is, that the relationship be able to be explained with ad hoc theory. For example, one might suppose that lack of recreational facilities is associated with delinquency because recreation can occupy adolescents' leisure time and thereby keep them out of trouble. All the variables under consideration can be explained in this fashion. The trouble is that it is too easy to concoct such ad hoc explanations for almost any relationship, and one must therefore be uneasy about the causal status of all the variables in question.[17]

A fifth point is relevant for decision makers more than for pure scientists. Race, unlike the other variables, cannot be manipulated by a social planner who wants to reduce delinquency. Therefore, the policy maker is not likely to consider the association between race and delinquency a cause-and-effect relationship.

5. Causality and Functional Relationships

Now let us move on to another troublesome concept, that of *function* or *functional relationship*, which is a particular type of association important in anthropology, sociology, social psychology, and clinical psychology. It has nothing to do with the functional form, $y=f(x)$, with which it shares only the label. Rather, this concept refers to such statements as "A function of the bus driver is to drive the bus."

Some writers (for example, Homans, 1964; Hagen, 1962: 512–513) believe that *no* set of data should be said to demonstrate a functional relationship, for the data *by themselves* can never show more than an association. This ar-

---

16. Hirschi and Selvin do not agree with this test of causality and, consequently, with any judgment on the causal status of race.

17. Again, Hirschi and Selvin would not agree that the causal status of these variables is thereby weakened.

gument is perfectly analogous to the argument that no data should be called "causal." It is quite correct that function cannot be expressed in formal symbolic logic, but associations that sociologists, anthropologists, and psychologists call "functional" do have some characteristics in common, just as causal statements do; and a statement of these characteristics constitutes a meaningful definition of "functional relationship." These characteristics are all contextual, that is, they depend on general knowledge of the situation under investigation, the sort of knowledge that cannot be expressed or proved in formal quantitative terms.

Here is a set of criteria for a functional relationship.[18]

First, a functional relationship is an association between the survival or nonsurvival (or effectiveness) of a group or individual and any other variable. For example, there is an association between the survival, continued existence, and effectiveness of Boy Scout troops and the presence of an adult leader. The association is statistical, of course, and there may be exceptions.

Second, the association must meet all the criteria spelled out for causal relationships; the relationship is always that survival (or effi-

ciency) is the effect variable and the other variable is the cause.[19] It may often seem awkward to say that the independent variable causes survival; it is more natural to say that the absence of the independent variable causes the death (or diminished efficiency) of the group organization or the individual. For example, the absence of an adult leader causes the Boy Scout troop to fall apart.

Third, one important condition might be that some compensating mechanism is not working. For example, the absence of a bus driver will not stop the bus if a passenger jumps into the driver's seat or if an automatic piloting mechanism goes into operation. To demonstrate that a relationship is functional in such a case, it must be demonstrated that the association *will* hold if the compensating mechanism is prevented from operating and that under some actual conditions the compensating mechanism would fail to operate. For example, sometimes no passenger will jump into the bus driver's seat, and then the bus will not move.

Fourth, the statement of the association must be accompanied by a full account of the working of the mechanism through which the independent variable exerts its influence in maintaining the existence of the group organization. This requirement is closely allied to the causality requirement that the statement be connected with the body of theory, though in sociology or anthropology the requirement for a deductive theoretical framework is not as strong as in economics.[20]

The anthropological-sociological concept of function is patterned after the same concept in biology, as Merton emphasizes. In social science, however, it is much more difficult to define the terms "survival" and "efficiency" without troublesome value terms. For example,

---

18. These criteria were not developed from a direct empirical inspection of sociological and anthropological statements labeled "functional" but rather from the following paragraph in Merton's "Manifest and Latent Functions." The rest of Merton's remarkable essay contains a good linguistic analysis of the functional concept.

> If the logic of this approach is stated in its more general terms, the following interrelated sequence of steps becomes evident. First of all, certain functional requirements of the organisms are established, requirements which must be satisfied if the organism is to survive, or to operate with a given degree of effectiveness. Second, there is a concrete and detailed description of the arrangements (structures and processes) through which these requirements are typically met in "normal" cases. Third, if some of the typical mechanisms for meeting these requirements are destroyed, or are found to be functioning inadequately, the observer is sensitized to the need for detecting compensating mechanisms (if any) which fulfill the necessary function. Fourth, and implicit in all that precedes, there is a detailed account of the structure *for which* the functional requirements hold, as well as a detailed account of the arrangements *through which* the function is fulfilled. (Merton, 1968: 103)

19. Brown (1963: 110) makes the same point.

20. But functional statements do appear in economics. Stigler tells us that the function of a market is to bring together buyers and sellers. And one of the most famous passages by Knight is entitled "Social Economic Organization and Its Five Primary Functions" (1951: 3–14).

one might say that the function of the fiddler is to make a successful party. But some people might call the party a success even without fiddling, though it might be a different sort of party. Nor can one say that it is a compensating mechanism that keeps the party from failing, for the compensating mechanism would have to be defined so loosely that the definition means nothing at all.[21]

Functional statements may have either of two purposes. One purpose may be to inform a policy maker which elements of a situation are necessary for it to continue to exist (or "function") or which elements should be removed if he wishes to break up the group (or individual). The second purpose is to increase scientific understanding of the conditions of social survival, efficiency, and equilibrium.

6. Association, Cause, Prediction, and Law

To summarize, the relationships among the most important types of statements found in the social sciences, as we interpret common scientific usage, are shown in Figure 35.1.

First, *associations* are a very general type of scientific statement. Important subclasses of associations are cause-and-effect statements, predictions, empirical generalizations (laws), and functional relationships.

Second, some *explanations* are not associations; they are the logical (tautological) and nonempirical explanations, for example, the explanation[22] of why $(a+b)^2 = a^2 + 2ab + b^2$. Motivational explanations are another nonassociation type of explanation. For instance, to the question "Why did you go out?" one answer might be "I wanted to go to the drug store." Explanations are statements that make one understand, which associations do not always do;

that is why some associations do not furnish explanations, for example, the association between moon cycles and murders.

Third, not all *facts* are associations, either, for example, such descriptive one-variable statements as that there are more than 200 million people in the United States. Conversely, not all associations are facts; hypothetical associations are important statements, but they are not factual.

Fourth, *cause-and-effect relationships* are a subclass of associations. They include only those associations that meet the criteria specified earlier in this chapter.

Fifth, relationships that yield *predictions* are another subclass of associations, those that are taken as forecasts for time periods later than the time of prediction. Not all predictions are causal; empirical generalizations that do not explain a phenomenon can often be used for successful predictions of the phenomenon. And not all causal relationships yield predictions, because the situation to which the relationship applies may change.

Sixth, *functional relationships* are a subclass of causal relationships. They include only those causal relationships that refer to survival or efficiency of equilibrium systems and that meet the criteria just spelled out.

Seventh, *laws* are empirically observed, factual associations. They need not be causal relationships. Conversely, hypothetical associations are not laws because they have not been established in fact.

7. Time, Antecedence, and Causality

This chapter has been primarily concerned with *whether* there is a causal relation, rather than with the *direction* of causality, and arguments of time order arise mainly in the latter issue. But time order can also be relevant to issues of *whether* a relationship is causal. For example, if it is otherwise assumed that causality in the relationship discussed is possible only in one direction, time order might then

21. Homans goes further in damming the concept of survival in functional sociological theory (1964: 812–813).

22. Example from Kaplan (1964: 336). We follow him in this distinction between explanation and association.

FIGURE 35.1   The Interrelations Among Types of Scientific Statements (For instance, cause-and-effect statements are a subclass of association statements in common scientific usage, as interpreted by the authors of this book.)

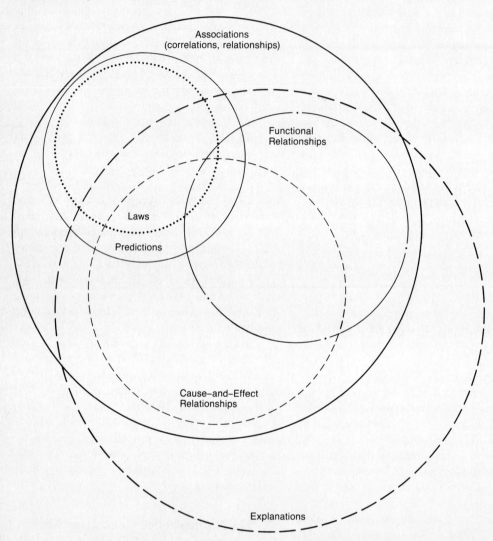

be adduced as an argument that even an otherwise possible causal relationship is impossible.

Many writers state that, even if there are no other logically conclusive tests of causality, time precedence may be considered a satisfactory test on logical grounds. Wold, for example, says, "There is usually a lapse of time be-

tween cause and effect, and in any event the effect cannot precede the cause in the flow of time" (1967b). The task of this section is to show that time order is not a logical golden key to causality but rather that it is a freqently useful hypothesis that must itself be supported with other subject-matter knowledge.

The first problem with time order as the test

of causal direction is that it is often difficult to make a practical determination of which event comes first. Even Hyman, who is a strong supporter of the time-order test of causality, notes that "guesses [about time order] on the basis of inspection of the nature of the variables are dangerous. The complexities of behavior are such that bizarre time orders are possible" (Hyman, 1955: 194). And Hyman notes several types of variables that give special difficulties (pp. 195 ff.). It is especially difficult to make sound judgments of time order in anthropology and archaeology.

A second problem is that, when the two variables are repetitive, and one does not *already* know which causes which, one does not know which events in the repetitive series are relevant for dating. For example, we know that there is a relationship between the price of corn in the fall and the amount of corn planted in the spring. But which causes which, and which comes first? The 1966 corn planting precedes the 1966 corn price, but the 1966 corn price precedes the 1967 corn planting. Time order alone will not establish the direction of causality in such cases.

Third, there may be several possible proxies for the "real" cause or effect, and these proxies may have very different dates. For example, refer to the toy-demand situation, except that now the hypothesis is that *wholesale* demand for toys in *November* will be higher than it was in *October*. It is reasonable to explain this relationship causally by saying that it is really *Christmas* that causes the upsurge in toy demand in November. That would be a satisfactory explanation except that Christmas follows November (or at least the Christmas that we refer to follows November). If one wishes to regard Christmas as the cause, and we see no logical reason not to do so, then cause *follows* effect rather than preceding it. This seems to indicate that time dating cannot be an automatic test of the direction of causal influence.

As always when there are apparent empirical deviations from a law, there are two possible ways to respond: We can junk the law, or we can explain the deviations in such a way as to leave the law intact though more restricted. The abandonment of the phlogiston theory in the face of new evidence is an example of the one possibility; the retention of the law of gravity in the face of evidence that balloons rise and leaves fall more slowly than Newton's law predicts is an example of the other possibility. In the Christmas-toy-demand example, it is possible to maintain the law of time order and causality by using some *other* proxy (Christmas is itself a proxy for the desire to give gifts), especially by arguing that "expectations" or "anticipations" of Christmas precede the demand. This might not be a very difficult explanation to swallow if, as H. Simon suggests, the concept of the future is applied only to human beings. But not so. A bird may be said to build its nest because it is expecting young. Even plant life and mechanical things can be usefully anthropomorphized by having expectations attributed to them. What we have, then, is an avoidance of reverse time data by a device that cannot be tested empirically (except possibly for humans). Because this device can be used to explain anything, it explains nothing. Therefore, it might be better, because of such examples, to drop the law of time order and causality, rather than to try to amend it.

Fourth, in a very formal way we can always say that, if an event occurred at time t, then the absence of the event (which has the same *logical* nature as the event itself) prevailed before time t. For example, we could say that a woman goes to the maternity ward because she has *not yet* had the baby. In a similar way we can *always* find a negative event to precede another occurrence; we can pick and choose events and their negatives to set up any time order we want—thereby vitiating time order as an automatic test of causality.

Fifth, nor does a discussion of time itself give any reason to believe in a useful logical relationship between time order and causality. Appropriate time dating of a variable or the choice of a combination of a variable and a time system seems to depend *upon the information that is available to us*. As Ashby points out, complete knowledge of the present state of a system renders unnecessary any reference to past states to explain the system's behavior. It is "only if a determinate system is only partly observable, and thereby becomes (for that observer) not predictable, the observer [would then want] to restore predictability by taking the system's past history into account . . ." (Ashby, 1968: 114).

Of course one cannot consider all determinants of an effect as being *simultaneous* with the effect, or the system would never be able to change. But one can think of the proximate cause in the time-order sequence as *approaching* simultaneity with the effect, just as the segment of rope that is proximately causal of the tension at point *p* is the infinitesimal segment that is infinitely close to point *p;* that is, if there is no tension in the infinitely close segment, there cannot be tension at point *p*, even if there is tension in more distant segments.

If we accept that time order is not an *automatic* logical test of causality, where does it leave us? Just because there is no *logical* connection, it does *not* follow that time lags are of no help in establishing causality. First, we must recognize that to use a time lag to infer the direction of causality in a particular relationship is, as Orcutt puts it, to make "use of one of the most general inferences that has been made from all the experimentation that has been done; namely, that actions taken in the present do not *appear* to modify the past" (1952b: 310; italics added). But this is a statistical empirical hypothesis with known exceptions, as we have discussed. Therefore, to make *sensible* use of this inference, one must offer additional reason why the hypothesis (or "law") should be believed to apply in the particular case. Consider the relationship between market price in year *t* and crop planting in year *t* + 1. We are willing to accept a normal time order as a test of causality, that is, that price

causes planting, rather than vice versa. But we accept time order as a test only because we have no reasons arising from our knowledge of the *subject matter* not to accept it *in this case*. Ultimately, then, time order as a clue to causality has no logical superiority over other subject-matter clues but must itself be considered as subject-matter information, with the possible imperfections that all subject-matter information must have in a complex world.

8. Summary

Causality is a key concept in science, and a most confusing one. Following in the line of Hume, the key to removing the confusion is to understand that causality is not an intrinsic property. The basis for an interpretation of causality cannot be found in the data themselves, even in an experiment, but rather depends on our general understanding of the situation together with our research purposes. That is, the label "causality" is a judgment.

What we need, then, is a good operational definition of "causality." We hazard the following as a working definition:

First, it is an association that is strong enough so that the observer believes it to have a predictive (explanatory) power great enough to be scientifically useful or interesting.

Second, the side conditions must be sufficiently *few* and sufficiently observable so that the relationship will apply under a wide enough range of conditions to be considered useful or interesting. In other words, *the relationship must not require too many "ifs," "ands," and "buts" in order to hold*.

Third, for a relationship to be called "causal," there should be a good reason to believe that, even if the control variable were not the "real" cause (and it never is), other relevant "hidden" and "real" cause variables must also change *consistently* with changes in the control variables. That is, a variable being manipulated may reasonably be called "causal" if the real variable for which it is believed to be a proxy must always be tied intimately to it. (Between two variables, v may be said to be the "more real" cause and w a "spurious" cause, if v and w require the same side conditions, except that v does not require w as a side condition.) This third criterion (nonspuriousness) is of particular importance to policy makers. The difference between it and the previous criterion for side conditions is that a plenitude of very restrictive side conditions may take the relationship out of the class of causal relationships, *even though the effects of the side conditions are known*. This criterion of nonspuriousness concerns variables that are as yet *unknown and unevaluated* but that have a *possible* ability to *upset* the observed association.

Fourth, the more tightly a relationship is bound into (that is, deduced from, compatible with, and logically connected to) a general framework of theory, the stronger is its claim to be called "causal."

In brief, one can never decide with perfect surety whether in any given situation one variable "causes" a particular change in another variable. At best, given your particular purposes in investigating a phenomenon, you may be safe in judging that very likely there is causal influence. It is correct to say (as it is so often said) that correlation does not prove causation—if we add the word "completely" to make it "correlation does not *completely* prove causation." On the other hand, causation can *never* be "proven" *completely* by correlation or *any other* tool or set of tools, including experimentation. The best we can do is make informed judgments about whether to call a relationship causal.

EXERCISES

1. Discuss the following statement:
   Somebody once went to a good deal of trouble to find out if cigarette smokers make lower college grades than nonsmokers. It turned out that they did. This pleased a good many people and they have been making much of it ever since. The road to good grades, it would appear, lies in giving up smoking; and, to carry the conclusion one reasonable step further, smoking makes dull minds. (Huff, 1954: 87)
2. Give two examples in your field of close relationships between two variables that turn out not to be causal because a "hidden third factor" explains them both.
3. Give two examples of relationships in your field that you believe ought to be called "causal," and show how they fit the operational definition of "causal" given in this chapter; that is, justify applying the label "causal" to the relationships.
4. Give an example of a functional relationship in your field. Justify its being called "functional."
5. Give an example of a relationship that cannot be tested for causality by examining to see which variable occurred first.

ADDITIONAL READING

Hirschi and Selvin (1966) convey an excellent understanding of the nature of causation, supported by a great many examples from delinquency research. Their analysis of the nature of the causal concept has much in common with that presented here but also diverges from it significantly.

Part Five

Epilogue

The Nature, Powers, and Limits of Social Science

1. What Makes an Investigation Scientific?
2. What Can Empirical Research Do?
3. The Necessity of Knowing the Purpose of the Research
4. The Special Powers and Limitations of Social-Science Research
5. The Ethics of Research
6. The Present and Future of Social-Science Research

This chapter is a grab bag of topics. It is something of an indulgence for us because—except for the pages about the necessity of knowing the purpose of the research—it does not have the practical aim of helping you to do better empirical research. With this warning, you can decide whether to read or skip, though we do hope that these topics that we think important will seem important to you too.

1. What Makes an Investigation Scientific?

First of all, scientific research is a form of learning, a way of increasing one's knowledge about the world. And it is a type of *rational* learning; it depends upon the human *reasoning* powers. Though we value rational learning and it seems to be useful in many cases, we should not deprecate other modes of human knowledge. Such nonrational (but not irrational) mental states as artistic feeling, emotion, and spiritual feeling are not competitors of rational learning. We do not urge you to seek rational

answers to all important questions. What we do urge is that, *if* you want a rational answer, scientific methods can help you to get it; this book has tried to help you apply empirical scientific methods.

Second, not all rational attempts to "get the facts" by observing nature are scientific. All of us learn a great deal about the world around us by hit-or-miss methods, rather than by formal scientific investigation. You find out what a restaurant is serving by asking the waitress or looking at the menu. You find out whether it is raining by sticking your hand out the window. As a baby, you learn that the stove may be hot by getting your hand burned and that your parents will usually come when you cry. These common-sense[1] methods of obtaining factual knowledge are generally quite satisfactory for our purposes.

Common sense has limitations, however,

---

1. We won't bother to define "common sense," but, as some wag has said, it is not always sensible and never common.

sometimes such severe limitations that it produces misinformation or no facts at all. Common-sense observation is often the basis of misleading superstition. And common sense breaks down when the question you want to answer is very complex or is otherwise difficult to investigate.

Scientific research takes up where common sense is forced to leave off. Scientific research is an *extension* of everyday methods of getting information, rather than a replacement for them. Furthermore, common-sense general knowledge is frequently an important point of departure for the good researcher, and an important test of the results. Scientific research must always simplify, which is both its major advantage and an important disadvantage in comparison with common sense. If common sense contradicts your scientific findings, check your scientific findings again. Sometimes you will find that, indeed, your common sense is dead wrong.[2] But sometimes you will find that common sense and your sound intuition prevent scientific mistakes. For example, if a complicated statistical technique tells you that half the smokers will quit if the price of a pack of cigarettes goes up two cents, your good common sense will refuse to accept these results and will save you from a major error.

How can you judge whether a piece of empirical research is scientific? The judgment is never open and shut. It is better to ask whether a piece of research is more or less scientific, rather than whether it is or is not scientific. Here are some of the marks of scientific empirical research:

In scientific research you describe the empirical work in such a way that other people could repeat exactly what you did. If you have not described what you did sufficiently clearly and specifically and if subsequent researchers cannot expect to get the same results, then we cannot call the research "scientific."

As an example, consider a newspaper's public-opinion research. Often a reporter will try to find out what "the man in the street" thinks by going out into the street and asking people. There are many ways the reporter could select people to ask, and the opinion received will often depend on the way the reporter selects people. Unless you know exactly how the people were selected, it is not likely that you can go into the street and arrive at the same conclusions.

The more that the observer *interprets* what he or she sees, the less repeatable is the study. Sociology has largely worked its way beyond relying on impressions and judgments of the observer, but anthropology has not yet gotten so far. For example, different observers of the Zuñi Indians reached entirely different assessments of the kind of people the Zuñi are, because of different impressions gained in living with the Zuñi. And an impartial observer cannot either examine the raw data to reach his or her own conclusions or go to the Zuñi and repeat exactly what the prior observers did.

But repeatability alone is not sufficient to make research scientific. If a man tries to find out whether men or women are safer drivers, he can ask his wife for the answer, and he can tell you exactly how he got his answer, namely, by asking his wife. You can surely repeat exactly what he did, by also asking his wife, but *neither* of you will be doing scientific research.

A second mark of a scientific investigation is that it fits in with work that is being done by other scientists. In other words, we are more likely to say that a study is scientific *if it means something to other scientists* than if it has no connection with what anyone else is doing or with the thinking of any field. This may seem unfair or parochial to you at first, but take our word for it (just this one time). And, of course, we should not be dogmatic about denying the

2. A fascinating illustration of how fallible our common sense can be and of how what seem to be obvious findings of the social sciences are often not so obvious at all is given by Lazarsfeld (1949). He fools the reader by listing several very obvious findings from the famous study of *The American Soldier* (Stouffer et al., 1949) and then points out that the *opposites* were really found to be true. The findings were not so obvious after all, and common sense was not enough to arrive at the correct answers. See also Marwell (1966).

label "scientific" to purely applied studies whose results have only practical value and no implication for science. An example would be a market-research study of which color package sells more detergent. In other words, if work uses scientific methods, that is sufficient for us to call it "scientific," even if its goals are not the goals of the scientific enterprise and the scientific community.

A third mark of a scientific study is that it conforms with established research procedures and avoids the obstacles to knowledge.[3]

2. What Can Empirical Research Do?

Let us now summarize what the knowledge derived from empirical research can and cannot do. Thoughts that appeared in many places throughout the book now can be drawn together. Empirical research can increase our knowledge of nature and its workings and can be a source of power for individuals and institutions. For example, knowledge of the workings of the weather helps you to decide whether to go on a picnic. The Rothschilds increased their power in financial negotiation because they developed a clever system of collecting information in Europe and transmitting it across the Channel to England by lights at night. An army increases its military power

when it increases the skills of its intelligence sections. And obviously, advances in medical research increase the physician's power to control the physical human condition. The power in all these examples stems from increased ability to plan future actions.

Much social-science research aims to help make better decisions. Research is used for planning in advertising and national propaganda. Judges, bureaucrats, and legislators often ask for research on which to base judgments, regulations, and legislation.

Empirical research also serves as part of the general scientific enterprise. Empirical facts are inextricably entangled with conceptualization in science, as we mentioned earlier. Hypotheses most often follow from *some* observations about nature, whether from formal or informal research.[4] Furthermore, *after* the theoretical scientist has stretched his or her imagination to make interesting guesses about what's what, empirical research serves to determine whether the guesses are sound.[5] It is widely accepted among scientists and philosophers that, unless a scientific idea is *capable* of being tested, it has no meaning.[6] Of course, an idea is immensely more valuable after it *has* been tested and found to be in accord with the empirical facts.

Still another use of research fits the classically romantic notion of science: to satisfy curiosity. But do not worry if at first you are not consumed with curiosity about the outcome of your research. Your interest will often mount as your work continues, and the moment when

---

3. This whole definition of "scientific" research is very crude. Philosophers of science give much more subtle definitions; see, for example, M. Cohen and Nagel (1962: 391 ff.). But this definition will serve for most of the unsubtle problems that we shall meet. Just as only the thorny legal problems go to the Supreme Court, we need call upon the philosophy of science only when we are forced to deal with the subtleties. H. Reichenbach points out that "indifference to philosophy has turned out to be a wholesome attitude for the scientist, though perhaps only as a matter of good luck. Success is often with those who act rather than reflect about what they should do" (1951: 93). Kaplan also makes the same point vigorously (1964: 22–24). But this may be truer at some stages in the history of a science than at others. Also, because *indifference* to philosophy has sometimes turned out well, *ignorance* of scientific philosophy is foolish and dangerous. In our opinion, Kaplan's book is by far the best introduction to philosophy of science for the student of social science.

4. An important practical aside: When you cannot come up with satisfactory hypotheses and you feel stumped, go back to your original observation or your raw data, and soak yourself in them. Pore over the pages of your statistical data until you notice some relationships. Or go out and talk casually to people about what you are interested in, if your problem is one of human behavior. And ideas *will* come!

5. We do not mean to suggest that the theoretician and the empiricist should be separate people. Ivan King claims that every great astronomer has been both a theorist and an empiricist.

6. Kaplan criticizes this concept very sharply and with point (1964: 39–42).

at last you examine your results can have high drama and excitement.[7]

In this discussion of what scientific research can do, it is appropriate to say something about the limitations of research. Laypersons sometimes overestimate the power of scientific study and underestimate the difficulty of finding things out, as do students when they begin their first research project. Consider this comment by a medical expert on testing drugs: "Very few people, be they laymen or practicing physicians, have any . . . comprehension of the extraordinary complexity and the great difficulty of establishing even the smallest scientific fact . . ." (Bean, 1961: 267).

A case in point is investigation by one of us of whether liquor prices are higher or lower in the sixteen states in which the stores are state-owned than in the other states, where liquor is sold in privately owned stores. Apparently this is the simplest possible task, especially as the prices of many individual brands are easily available for most states. Nevertheless, this simple task took weeks and weeks and some fancy statistical analysis. For example, the prices for only eight brands were available in published form, the price of no single brand was available in *all* the states, and for some states there were no published data at all. This meant that some further data had to be obtained from liquor firms and state liquor-control boards, and, even so, some states' price levels had to be estimated on the basis of the price of one brand and others' on the basis of prices of other brands. (And of course the work had to come to grips with the fact that the price level estimated on the basis of one brand or eight brands is not, by a long shot, a perfect estimate of the average price level for *all* liquor sold in a state.)

It is useful to understand the limitations of a particular branch of science at a particular

time. Much error, trouble, and argument result from scientists' trying to overgeneralize a theory, that is, trying to squeeze too many phenomena within the compass of the theory. It is not well for a science to be too modest and for scientific thinking to be nothing but a collection of anecdotes. On the other hand, it is not well to be too ambitious and to try to explain too much with a theory. It is our experience that, when two social scientists vehemently disagree on whether a hypothesis is correct, the argument can often be settled by showing that the hypothesis holds for some part of the universe—which is the part the hypothesis maker had in mind—and does not hold for the part of the universe that the objector was thinking of. Often the argument hinges on differing *purposes* that the arguers have in mind for the hypothesis—for instance, policy decisions versus pure understanding.

An example from communications research: The famous two-step flow-of-influence hypothesis suggests this process of modifying people's behavior or attitudes through the mass media: A few opinion leaders are affected directly by the media; then most other people who are affected at all are influenced by the opinion leaders, rather than directly by the media. Evidence to confirm the hypothesis was found in the drug-prescribing habits of physicians in a small city. But many communications theorists talk as though *all* the mass media's effects take place in two steps. This is demonstrably not true for, say, the sales of marriage books by mail order from advertisements in magazines; in fact, the very "one-step" privacy of the sale stimulates purchasing ("in plain brown wrapper"). The simple fact is that some behavior is acquired from the media in two steps, other behavior in one step. Furthermore, acknowledgment of this fact can help eliminate the arguments over whether the two-step flow hypothesis is or is not valid.

To drop down one level of abstraction so that a theory fits the facts much better is what Merton, for example, has in mind when he talks

---

7. Curiosity is necessary to a researcher in the long run, however. As Einstein said, "If you don't itch, you can't scratch."

about "sociology of the middle range," in contrast to "grand theory." It can often be a creative and useful accomplishment in all disciplines to show how a theory can be vastly improved and an argument settled with a qualification or two—though this accomplishment is seldom applauded by anyone.

> Time and again the industrial development of Europe has been described in terms of a general pattern constructed upon the empirical material gleaned from English history. Such an approach is not without merit. Precisely because there are common features in all industrializations, it possessed and still possesses some explanatory and even predictive value. To concentrate upon these general aspects of industrialization may be quite useful for some purposes. But it is equally true, as always when the level of generality is pitched very high, that as one moves deeper and deeper into the subject one is bound to come across things in one area or another that do not fit the general model. When that happens, the historian, after he has refused to ignore the uncomfortable irregularities, is faced with two alternatives. He may regard those things as exceptions and treat them as such. Or else he can attempt to systematize the deviations from the original pattern by bringing them into a new, although necessarily more complicated, pattern. (Gerschenkron, 1965: 41)

Good science is not only limited; it is also messy. Scientific reports are logical and neat, as they ought to be, but the work process that leads up to them is much less logical and neat. In many cases the researcher cannot clearly state the problem when beginning the work. The research seldom follows the neat stages discussed by philosophers of science (for instance, Northrop, 1965: 28–29). Often the results of the first experiments or surveys are muddy and inconclusive. And often the researcher must make technical decisions with insufficient information. In short, scientific research is not a sacred ritual with strict rules of procedure laid down in an official dogma. Rather, it is a body of useful methods to go beyond common sense when common sense is not good enough.

3. The Necessity of Knowing the Purpose of the Research

Scientists often like to characterize their work as a disinterested search for objective truth. But we shall argue that this goal is not enough; one must also have the knowledge for some *purpose*, and the purpose must go beyond curiosity.[8] Our argument is not on grounds of social value but on practical ones; we believe that a specified purpose is necessary in order to do useful and meaningful research.

We shall develop this point of view through the example of the relationship of income to family size. As noted earlier, the various relevant studies have shown both positive and negative relationships between fertility and income. The approach of most recent writers has been to try to clear away as many other variables as possible in order to get at the "pure" relationship of income to fertility. They have sought objective estimates of the "structural parameter" relating income and fertility. But, even if the investigator does succeed in this abstracting process, he or she will not necessarily have a useful answer. That is, even if "ideally" the "direct effect" of an increase in income is to raise fertility, there almost surely are important classes of nonideal situations (for instance, the presently underdeveloped countries) in which an increase in per capita income has an overall effect (direct and indirect) in the direction of *reducing* fertility.

Unraveling the puzzle and choosing a sensible conclusion require that you first decide what your purpose is. For example, perhaps you want to estimate the effect on the birth

8. Kaplan (1964: 42–47 and elsewhere) argues this point of view very well, but he labels it "pragmatism," which—as he notes—is a misleading name because of the common too-narrow interpretation of the pragmatist's requirement that the knowledge be related to some purpose and intended action.

rate of giving family-allowance payments to all parents in the United States. Or perhaps you want to forecast the effect on the birth rate of the likely rise in per capita income in the underdeveloped countries of Africa. Or perhaps you want to know whether the ratio of children born to upper-income families to those born to lower-income familes will change as knowledge of contraception is more widely diffused in Latin America. Or perhaps you want to know how the birth rate will be affected if education increases along with per capita income in Africa.

In any of these exemplary situations, you want to know the relationship between income and family size, but the answer differs from situation to situation. It is not sufficient for you, as a researcher, to seek disinterestedly the structural parameters of the general system of income and family size. Rather, you must decide in advance which system of income and family size you are interested in among the many possible that you could explore. And you can make that decision sensibly only if you first clarify your purpose, which most often means asking what kind of a decision depends upon the knowledge you develop, for instance, whether family-allowance payments are contemplated. The system the investigator chooses to explore should be most analogous to the situation about which the decision will be made.

This is a problem not only in survey research. The experimenter, too, makes decisions that affect the estimates obtained, the most important of which are the choices of the *range* over which the stimulus will be varied and of the *conditions* under which the experiment will be run. At one degree of food deprivation, the rat may run faster when made even hungrier. At another degree of deprivation, further deprivation may slow him down. Furthermore, it may matter whether the experiment is run in a heated or a cool room.

The fact is that nature has no parameters to be estimated. Some researcher must mark off boundaries around some chunk of nature and must specify particular characteristics to be considered before any parameter can be estimated. To search for structural parameters is tantamount to denying that the parameters will be different, depending upon the choice of system and its boundaries. And, given that we must make a rather arbitrary choice about which system to study, it makes sense to refer to one's larger purpose for criteria on which system to work with.

Some scientists argue that one should explore the most universal system possible. But this cannot be a sufficient criterion. What would be encompassed in the most universal estimate of the relationship of income to family size—all people who ever lived or who ever will live? Even if one could obtain such an estimate, it would be irrelevant, not only for most practical decisions that one might make, but also for almost any theoretical purpose. "In my view a useful model will usually be appropriate only in particular circumstances and, even then, only for the analysis of particular problems. Clearly, where greater generality can be achieved without loss of content, we must approve of it—but this can rarely be possible" (Baumol, 1959: 3).[9]

The argument of this section is still another example of a very general idea that has appeared in various guises throughout the book: The scientist's world is very much what he or she makes of it, and results depend heavily upon what he or she chooses to look at and how he or she chooses to look at it. One important example was the definition of causality, in which we suggested that a judgment of causality depends on the scientist's purpose and point of view.

9. This statement should not be construed as an argument against idle curiosity as a wellspring of science. The very best of work may well originate in a scientist's desire "to know how it works." But, in the course of development of the idea, a more disciplined scientific purpose usually emerges, and that emergent purpose serves to guide decisions on research strategy.

Sociologists and psychologists have been more sophisticated and less confused by this aspect of science than have economists; indeed, this confusion has caused serious problems in economics. An example is the hassle over whether "utility" can be measured, which has been a roadblock in the development of welfare economics. This confusion is interwoven with economists' impatience with discussions of scientific philosophy and method (as distinguished from statistical method). And economists' preoccupation with the analogy of their discipline to what they think is objective physical science helps to account for this unsound point of view. It is therefore instructive to note that, even in physics since Einstein and Gibbs, there has taken place ". . . a shift in the point of view of physics in which the world as it actually exists is replaced in some sense or other by the world as it happens to be observed, and the old naïve realism of physics gives way" . . . (Wiener, 1954: 20).

4. The Special Powers and Limitations of Social-Science Research

At this point in the history of social science it is unnecessary to discuss whether the social sciences are real sciences. What is more interesting now is whether the social sciences are *more* scientific than are the natural sciences; as far as methodology[10] goes, we think there is good reason to think that the social sciences are far ahead of the natural sciences. The reason is that social scientists have to fight harder to achieve procedures and results that are satisfactorily scientific. Samuelson puts it this way:

A physicist or chemist need not be much of a methodologist: his disciplines have a logic of

10. Notice that this is the first time we use the word "methodology" in this book and also one of the last. One of the less attractive features of the social sciences is occasional pretentiousness, a symptom of which is the addition of three extra and mostly incorrect syllables to the perfectly good word "method."

their own which often will unobtrusively point the way. It is otherwise with the "softer" social sciences. So little spontaneous guidance is provided by the subject matter, that in some of these disciplines substantive research is displaced by repetitious and inconclusive discussion of methodology. (Samuelson, 1959: 189)

A simple example: A physicist rarely has to worry about his experiment being contaminated by his own bad mood on the day of the experiment, by the occurrence of a newspaper strike or a war that day, or by his having inadvertently given his subjects too much information—and on and on. But those and many, many other such factors must be carefully controlled to ensure that a social scientist does not foul up his research.

It is worth recapitulating a few of the properties of the subject matter that offer special problems for social science. First, the results are statistical, rather than of an all-or-nothing kind. Of course, *no* research is perfectly determinate; if a chemist mixes hydrogen and oxygen, he might *rarely* fail to get water for various experimental reasons, but it is fair to say that getting H_2O from H and O is practically invariable. But the results of a social-science study seldom are so clear-cut. A new method of teaching reading may work better than the old method did with 60 per cent of children. Or middle-sized business firms may produce more inventions per dollar size than do small or large firms but by only a small margin. These small percentage differences make it much harder to make fair comparisons.

Second, social-science problems usually involve more than one important variable, and often it is very difficult to disentangle the variables to study their effects separately. The difficulty is especially great—and sometimes insoluble—when these multiple variables go hand in hand and also cannot be subjected to experiment. For example, when people receive more education, they usually achieve higher incomes also. Therefore, it is difficult to determine whether highly educated people travel more than other people do because of their education or because of their income or because of both together.

Third, researchers themselves frequently affect the subject matter, thereby changing the whole situation.

A further difference between the natural and social sciences is that a complete *system* can seldom be constructed fruitfully in the social sciences other than economics. An electronics engineer can discuss and set up equations for the entire system in which electrons flow in a radio circuit. And a refrigeration engineer can follow the refrigeration in an air conditioner back and forth from cycle to cycle. But communications among people, for example, cannot be described so easily in this manner.[11] This is because human systems are constantly *open* to new and disturbing influences. That is, social-science systems *leak* so much that it is seldom possible to predict a long-time course of events from the starting point. Once the refrigeration cycle begins, nothing much affects it except some loss of energy; that is, the system is *closed*, except for loss of energy. But, when human beings interact with one another, a great many new influences come into play with each interchange. It is therefore difficult to describe more than one or two steps at a time, and the idea of system is rendered less useful.

Sometimes it seems as if social scientists labor very hard to bring forth only small mouse-like pieces of knowledge. To the extent that this is so, there may be two causes that, like scissor blades, slice from both directions. On one hand, many of the biggest problems of human civilization have barely been scratched: Why do wars occur? What influences will reduce human anxiety? What factors will be efficient in getting underdeveloped countries on the road of development? What is consciousness? Why do people retreat into their own

skins as they grow older and have less intimate contact with other people? Of course, the social sciences have made vast gains in some fields like smoothing out business cycles and reducing unemployment. But many huge problems in social science are still almost untouched.

The other scissors blade is that we learn so much about our social world in very simple fashion. Most social questions can be answered very easily. Why have most coal mines in Illinois closed? Because their veins have been worked out. Why don't blacks go to a particular restaurant? Because they know they will be insulted or not served or thrown out. Why are there fewer buses after midnight? Why is the factory shut down on Sunday? These and many other *important* questions can be answered quite well either by consulting our own experience or by asking others. Notice that these questions are *not* trivial, but many of them have single clear answers; in each case, a single factor accounts for what happens, to an overwhelmingly large degree. In the natural sciences it is a major task to unravel even those problems that have single sharp answers: why colds end after five days, or how the genetic code carries information. These questions are much harder to answer than is one about why the factories are closed on Sunday.

Because the easy-to-solve problems do not demand scientific methods, those that are left for social science are all tough problems. It is this that makes social science seem weak and powerless.

Beside the questions that are tough but soluble *in principle,* there is a class of questions that *may* lie beyond the reach of social-scientific techniques. These are questions of the causation of major historical events. Schlesinger argues that:

> . . . there seem to me two main troubles with this effort—with an effort, for example, to solve quantitatively the problem of the causes of the Civil War. One is that most of the variables in an historical equation are not susceptible to com-

11. For a valiant conceptual effort to do so, see Carey (1963).

mensurable quantification; the other is that the observer is too mixed up with the phenomena observed to eliminate the subjective element. (Schlesinger; 1962: 770)

Furthermore, such historical events are non-repetitive, in the sense that it is usually not sensible to put the American Civil War in a category with other civil wars and to treat them all as a homogeneous group. Without a sample of some reasonable size, social-science investigation is helpless.

The limits of social science in explaining historical events are related to the limits on social science's ability to predict large changes, as discussed in Chapter 29.

Nor are these historical questions trivial. As a historian, Schlesinger tries to restore the balance:

The *mystique* of empirical social research, in short, leads its acolytes to accept as significant only the questions to which the quantitative magic can provide answers. As an humanist, I am bound to reply that almost all important questions are important precisely because they are *not* susceptible to quantitative method. What he denies is that it can handle everything which the humanist must take into account; what he condemns is the assumption that things which quantitative methods can't handle don't matter. I would suggest that these are the things that matter most. (Schlesinger, 1962: 770)

5. The Ethics of Research

For many kinds of problems empirical social-scientific methods can be very powerful. But just because they can be powerful does not mean that they and their findings are automatically good. The sciences may have justifiably scourged some of the superstitious aspects of religion, like miracles and amulets. But, as already noted, the importance of religion and other nonrational aspects of life is not obviated by science, though some people may choose to make a type of substitute religion out of science itself. Also, social-science research can at

times have ill effects on aspects of social and personal life that we value.

The possible ill effects of social-science research are of many kinds.[12] Research might affect the results of elections by publicizing correct or incorrect poll estimates before the election. Research can affect the lives and mental welfare of subjects in some psychological experiments and surveys (Kelman, 1966; Bachrach, 1972: 93–108), and governmental fund-granting agencies have already recognized this problem to the extent of requiring certain safeguards and approval for some types of research. Here are some relevant excerpts from a report by an august group convened to study the subject:

. . . The right to privacy is the right of the individual to decide for himself how much he will share with others his thoughts, his feelings, and the facts of his personal life. . . .

From our examination of the relation of behavioral science research to the right to privacy, we have been led to the following conclusions.

1. While most current practices in the field pose no significant threat to the privacy of research subjects, a sufficient number of exceptions have been noted to warrant a sharp increase in attention to procedures that will assure protection of this right. The increasing scale of behavioral research is itself an additional reason for focusing attention in this area.

2. Participation of subjects must be voluntary and based on informed consent to the extent that this is consistent with the objectives of the research. It is fully consistent with the protection of privacy that, in the absence of full information, consent be based on trust in the qualified investigator and the integrity of his institution.

3. The scientists has an obligation to insure that no permanent physical or psychological harm will ensue from the research procedures, and that temporary discomfort or loss of privacy will be remedied in an appropriate way during the course of the research or at its completion. To

12. For extended discussion of this topic see E. Shils (1959).

merit trust, the scientist must design his research with a view of protecting, to the fullest extent possible, the privacy of the subjects. If intrusion on privacy proves essential to the research, he should not proceed with his proposed experiment until he and his colleagues have considered all of the relevent facts and he has determined, with support from them, that the benefits outweigh the costs.

4. The scientist has the same responsibility to protect the privacy of the individual in published reports and in research records that he has in the conduct of the research itself. . . . (Panel on Privacy and Behavioral Research Report, 1967: 535–538)

There is much more that can be said about the ethics of research (e.g. Reynolds, 1979; Cook, 1969). But better than—or best of all, in addition to—consideration of the ethical principles involved is a discussion of your proposed work with colleagues and laypersons. If all agree that what you plan to do is ethical, then you can feel reasonably secure, even though standards and ethical consciousness do change from decade to decade.

The results of empirical research might lead to manipulation and exploitation by government and private firms.[13] It is a scientific disadvantage of free societies that governments respect the wish of individuals and private institutions to keep their records private. The Soviet Union has much more complete economic data of many sorts than does the United States. And data that the United States government does collect—Internal Revenue tax data, for example—are available broken down only for *groups* of firms. This confidentiality is very frustrating to the social scientist at times. On the other hand, totalitarian societies keep much data secret for what they consider to be reasons of state security. This is equally frustrating.

---

13. See Chapter 00 for an eighteenth-century warning against the dangers of a census.

6. The Present and Future of Social-Science Research

The very extent of public-opinion research gives one pause. Lerner estimates that "more than half of the American annual expenditure on all types of social research—in business, government, universities—is now spent on attitude research. So crucial, for our mode of self-observation, is information about the will of the governed" (Lerner, 1959: 26). This large volume of research may affect us directly by conveying our wishes so that what is offered to us "is the result of the demand on the part of the public," as learned through preference surveys, says the president of General Motors (Kefauver, 1965: 100). On the other hand, surveys can help firms force upon us what we have no special preference for but what we can be induced to accept. The president of American Motors put it thus:

> A small company could not have made the wraparound windshield a successful thing because when you get right down to the guts of it, it has no basic advantages over the straight windshield, and yet through advertising and promotion you can make an item of that type become absolutely the hallmark of a modern car, if you have got a large enough percentage of the total market to do it. (Kefauver, 1965: 101)

It is interesting to speculate why it was not until the last hundred years or so that scientific methods were applied to social and behavioral questions. Unlike the development of the natural sciences, the development of social science was not held back by the lack of measuring instruments or the absence of sophisticated theories; the obvious ingredients existed for surveys and experiments to have been conducted 2,000 years ago. Why, then, was social-science research not done then?

Actually, censuses and descriptive social science have been carried on almost as far back as history was first recorded (Carr-Saunders, 1925: A2). It is *relationship* research, and especially research into cause and effect, that has not been done until recently. We hazard as part of the explanation that, until recently in the Western world, most people have not thought about the possibility of changing the structure of their social world for the better, except for the possibility of overthrowing a government or waging a war. The kinds of changes that people contemplated were not the kinds of changes that science can easily evaluate. Most especially, these kinds of changes did not lend themselves to study by experimentation. In sum, then, the rise of social science probably awaited the idea of progress.

The future of social science is not clear to us. Certainly there will be increasingly more so-cial-science research of the kind that is done today. But what else? Will social science also break entirely new ground and try to solve different sorts of problems entirely? We wish we knew.

As to whether social science will help create better lives for the world's people, our crystal ball is murky. One question is whether the new problems we cause for ourselves—especially, more fiendish ways of killing one another without improved political safeguards—increase faster than our ability to handle the problems. Another question is whether an easier world is a better world. All one can do is hope—and we hope that it will be a more *human* world.

AFTERTHOUGHT

"Anyway, it goes like this: there's this desert prison, see, with an old prisoner, resigned to his life, and a young one just arrived. The young one talks constantly of escape, and, after a few months, he makes a break. He's gone a week, and then he's brought back by the guards. He's half dead, crazy with hunger and thirst. He describes how awful it was to the old prisoner. The endless stretches of sand, no oasis, no signs of life anywhere. The old prisoner listens for a while, then says, 'Yep, I know. I tried to escape myself, twenty years ago.' The young prisoner says, 'You did? Why didn't you tell me, all these months I was planning my escape? Why didn't you let me know it was impossible?' And the older prisoner shrugs, and says, 'So who publishes negative results?' " M. Crichton, 1968.

EXERCISES

1. What is your guess about the future of social science?
2. Give three research examples from your field in which *deception* is unethical and three examples in which it is ethically acceptable. Give other examples of ill effects of social-scientific research.
3. Give an example in which common sense corrected a wrong finding of social-science research.
4. Should a newspaperwoman collect public opinion in such a manner that her procedure will be replicable?
5. What problems in your field *cannot* be solved by social-science research?
6. What do you think of the proposal to collect much available information about United States citizens in a central repository as a "data bank" for research?

ADDITIONAL READING

Lerner (1959) presents a collection of interesting articles about the nature of social science.

For more on the place and purpose of research, see Selltiz et al. (1976: 1–11).

Barber (1952) analyzes the relationship of science to society in an illuminating fashion.

Kaplan's (1964) Part V on "values in research" clarifies many important ideas.

On the ethics of research, Cook (in Selltiz et al., 1976) is excellent. For a wider-ranging discussion, see the spring 1969 issue of *Daedulus.* A provocative discussion of ethics and research, urging very strict standards, is that of Kelman (1966). See also Reynolds (1979).

An interesting discussion of what was to have been a large U.S. government-funded research project to study revolution and various countries, Project Camelot, is discussed by Horowitz (1965). This project caused it to abort.

References

Aaron, Henry J. *Politics and the Professors.* Washington, D.C.: Brookings Institution, 1978.

Abrams, Jack. "Evaluation of Alternate Rating Devices for Consumer Research." *Journal of Marketing Research,* 3 (May 1966), 189–193.

Abrams, Robert. *Foundations of Political Analysis.* New York: Columbia University Press, 1980.

Abramson, Paul R. *Political Attitudes in America.* San Francisco: W. H. Freeman, 1983.

Agnew, Neil McK., and Sandra W. Pyke. *The Science Game,* Englewood Cliffs, N.J.: Prentice-Hall, 1969.

Alba, Richard D., and Gwen Moore. "Ethnicity in the American Elite." *American Sociological Review,* 47 (June 1982), 373–382.

Allen, R. G. D. *Mathematical Economics,* 2nd ed. New York: St. Martin's, 1959.

Allport, Gordon, *The Nature of Prejudice.* Cambridge, Mass.: Addison-Wesley, 1954.

Alvarez, Luis W. "A Pseudo Experience in Parapsychology." *Science,* 148 (June 18, 1965), 1541.

Alwin, Duane. "Making Errors in Surveys: an Overview." *Sociological Methods and Research,* 6 (November 1977), 131–150.

———, and Robert M. Hauser. "The Decomposition of Effects in Path Analysis." *American Sociological Review,* 40 (February 1975), 37–47.

American Psychiatric Association. *Diagnostic and Statistical Manual of Mental Disorders,* 2nd. ed. Washington, D.C.: American Psychiatric Association, 1980.

Andrews, Frank M., and Stephen B. Withey. *Social Indicators of Well-Being: Americans' Perceptions of Life Quality.* New York: Plenum Press, 1976.

Armer, Michael, and Allen Grimshaw (eds.). *Comparative Social Research.* New York: Wiley, 1973.

Armstrong, Jon S. *Long Range Forecasting.* New York: Wiley, 1978.

Arndt, Johan. "Haire's Shopping List Revisited." *Journal of Advertising Research,* 13 (October 1973), 57–62.

Aronson, Elliot, and J. Merrill Carlsmith. "Experimentation in Social Psychology," in Gardner Lindzey and Elliot Aronson (eds.), *Handbook of Social Psychology,* 2nd ed. Vol. II. Reading, Mass.: Addison-Wesley, 1968, pp. 1–79.

Ashby, W. Ross. *An Introduction to Cybernetics.* London: Chapman & Hall, 1968.

Ayer, A. J. "Chance." *Scientific American,* 213 (October 1965), pp. 44–54.

Babbie, Earl R. *Survey Research Methods.* Belmont, Calif.: Wadsworth, 1973.

Bachrach, Arthur J. *Psychological Research: An Introduction,* 3rd ed. New York: Random House, 1972.

Bailey, Kenneth D. "Cluster Analysis," in David Heise (ed.), *Sociological Methodology, 1974.* San Francisco: Jossey-Bass, 1974, 59–128.

Baker, J. Stannard. "A Framework for Assessment of Causes of Automobile Accidents," in Paul F. Lazarsfeld and Morris Rosenberg (eds.), *The Language of Social Research.* New York: Free Press, 1955, pp. 438–448.

Balch, George. "The Stick, the Carrot, and Other Strategies," in John Brigham and Don W. Brown (eds.), *Policy Implementation: Penalties or Incentives.* Beverly Hills, Calif.: Sage, 1980, pp. 43–68.

Bane, Mary Jo. *Here to Stay: American Families in the 20th Century.* New York: Basic Books, 1976.

Banks, Seymour. *Experimentation in Marketing.* New York: McGraw-Hill, 1965.

Barber, Bernard. *Science and the Social Order,* Glencoe, Ill.: Free Press, 1952.

Bart, Pauline, and L. Frankel. *The Student Sociologist Handbook.* Cambridge, Mass.: Schenkman, 1975.

Barzun, Jacques. *Teacher in America*. Garden City, N.Y.: Doubleday, 1954.

Baumol, William J. *Business Behavior, Value, and Growth*. New York: Macmillan, 1959.

Bean, William B. Testimony Before the Subcommittee on Antitrust and Monopoly of the Committee on the Judiciary, Part I (1961), p. 267.

Belden, G. C., *et al. The Protein Paradox*. Boston: Management Reports, 1964.

Belsley, David, Edwin Kuh, and Roy E. Welsch. *Regression Diagnostics*. New York: Wiley, 1980.

Berenson, Conrad, and Raymond Colton. *Research and Report Writing for Business and Economics*. New York: Random House, 1971.

Bernikow, Louise. "Alone: Yearning for Companionship in America." *New York Times Magazine*, August 15, 1982, 24ff.

Bernstein, Jeremy. "Profile (Marvin Minsky)." *The New Yorker*, 57 (December 14, 1982), 50–128.

———. *The Analytical Engine*. New York: Random House, 1964.

Beveridge, W. I. B. *The Art of Scientific Investigation*, 3rd ed. New York: Random House, 1960.

Biernacki, Patrick, and Dan Waldorf. "Snowball Sampling: Problems and Techniques of Chain Referral Sampling." *Sociological Methods and Research*, 10 (October 1981), 141–163.

Blalock, Hubert M., Jr. *Causal Inference in Non-Experimental Research*. New York: Norton, 1972.

———, (ed.). *Measurement in the Social Sciences*. Chicago: Aldine, 1974.

———. "Measurement and Conceptualization Problems: The Major Obstacle to Integrating Theory and Research." *American Sociological Review*, 44 (December 1979), 881–894.

———. *Conceptualization and Measurement in the Social Sciences*. Beverly Hills, Calif.: Sage, 1982.

Bloom, Howard S., and H. Douglas Price. "Voter Response to Short-Run Economic Conditions." *American Political Science Review*, 69 (December 1975), 1240–1254.

Bogdan, Robert, and Stephen J. Taylor. *Introduction to Qualitative Research Methods*. New York: Wiley, 1975.

Bohrnstedt, George W. "A Quick Method for Determining the Reliability and Validity of Multiple-Item Scales." *American Sociological Review*, 34 (1969), 542–548.

Bollen, Kenneth A., and Burke D. Grandjean. "The Dimension(s) of Democracy." *American Sociological Review*, 46 (October 1981), 651–659.

Bonacich, Philip, and John Light. "Laboratory Experimentation in Sociology." *Annual Review of Sociology*, 4 (1978) 145–170.

Boulding, Kenneth E. "Welfare Economics," in B. F. Haley (ed.), *A Survey of Contemporary Economics*, Vol. II. Homewood, Ill.: Irwin, 1952.

Boyd, Harper, and Stanley F. Stasch. *Marketing Research: Text and Cases* 4th ed. Homewood, Ill.: Irwin, 1977.

Bradburn, Norman M. "Summary of *In Pursuit of Happiness*." Chicago: (mimeographed), 1963.

———, and David E. Berlew. "Need for Achievement and English Industrial Growth." *Economic Development and Cultural Change* (October 1961), pp. 8–20.

Bradburn, Norman M., and David Caplovitz. *Reports on Happiness*. Chicago: Aldine, 1965.

Bradburn, Norman, Seymour Sudman, and associates. *Improving Interview Method and Questionnaire Design*. San Francisco: Jossey-Bass, 1979.

Braidwood, Robert J. "The Biography of a Research Project." *Chicago Today*, II (Autumn 1965), 14–27.

Braithwaite, Richard B. *Scientific Explanation*. New York: Harper, 1953.

Breiger, Ronald L. "Career Attributes and Network Structure." *American Sociological Review*, 41 (February 1976), 117–135.

Bridge, R. Gary, Leo Reeder, David Kanouse, Donald Kinder, Vivian Tong Nagy, and Charles M. Judd. "Interviewing Changes Attitudes—Sometimes." *Public Opinion Quarterly*, 41 (1977), 56–64.

Bridgman, P. W. "The Prospect for Intelligence." *Yale Review*, XXXIV (Spring 1945), 444–461.

Brodbeck, May (ed.). *Readings in the Philosophy of the Social Sciences*. New York: Macmillan, 1968.

Brooks, Andree. "It's a Return to Tradition for Many Young Marrieds." *Nashville Tennessean* (December 17, 1981), p. 64.

Bross, Irwin. *Design for Decision*. New York: Free Press, 1965.

Brown, Robert. *Explanation in Social Science*. Chicago: Aldine, 1963.

Brownlee, K. A. "Smoking and Health," *Journal of the American Statistical Association*, 60 (September 1965), 722–739.

Brunner, Ronald D., and Klaus Liepelt. "Data Analysis, Process Analysis, and System Change." *Midwest Journal of Political Science*, XVI (November 1972), 538–569.

Burstein, Paul. "A New Method for Measuring Legislative Content and Change." *Sociological Methods and Research*, 6 (February 1978), 337–364. (a)

———. "Social Cleavages and Party Choice in Israel." *American Political Science Review*, 72 (March 1978), 96–109. (b)

———. "Equal Employment Opportunity Legislation and the Incomes of Women and Nonwhites." *American Sociological Review*, 44 (June 1979), 367–391.

———, and Margo MacLeod. "Prohibiting Employment Discrimination." *American Journal of Sociology*, 86 (November 1980), 512–533.

Campbell, Donald T. "Factors Relevant to the Validity of Experiments in Social Settings," in Carl Backman and P. Secord (eds.), *Problems in Social Psychology*. New York: McGraw-Hill, 1966

———. "Reforms as Experiments." *American Psychologist*, 24 (April 1969), 409–429.

———, and Julian C. Stanley. "Experimental and Quasi-Experimental Designs for Research in Teaching," in N. L. Gage (ed.), *Handbood of Research in Teaching*. Chicago: Rand McNally, 1963.

Cannell, Charles F., Peter V. Miller, and Lois Oksenberg. "Research on Interviewing Techniques," in Samuel Leinhardt (ed.), *Sociological Methodology 1981*. San Francisco: Jossey-Bass, 1981, 389–437.

Cannon, Walter B. *The Way of an Investigator*. Boston: Houghton Mifflin, 1965. Reprint of 1945 edition.

Cantril, Hadley. *Gauging Public Opinion*. Port Washington, N.Y.: Kennikat Press, 1971.

Carey, Alex. "The Hawthorne Studies: A Radical Criticism." *American Sociological Review*, 32 (June 1967), 403–447.

Carey, James W. "Communication Systems and Social Systems." Unpublished doctoral dissertation, University of Illinois, 1963.

Carmines, Edward G., and Richard A. Zeller. *Reliability and Validity Assessment*. Beverly Hills, Calif.: Sage, 1980.

Carr-Saunders, A. M. *Population*. London: Oxford, 1925.

Cartter, Allan M. *An Assessment of Quality in Graduate Education*. Washington, D.C.: American Council on Education, 1966.

Chatterjee, Samprit, and Bertram Price. *Regression Analysis by Example*. New York: Wiley, 1977.

Cherlin, Andrew J. *Marriage, Divorce, Remarriage*. Cambridge: Harvard University Press, 1981.

Chung, J. H., and D. A. S. Fraser. "Randomization Tests for a Two-Sample Problem." *Journal of the American Statistical Association*, 53 (September 1958), 729–735.

Coale, Ansley, J., and F. F. Stephan. "The Case of the Indians and the Teen-Age Widows." *Journal of the American Statistical Association*, 57 (June 1962), 338–347.

Cochran, William C., Frederick Mosteller, and John W. Tukey. "Statistical Problems of the Kinsey Report." *Journal of the American Statistical Association*, 48 (December 1953), 673–716. Excerpted in Jcrome Himelhoch and Sylvia Fleis Fava. *Sexual Behavior in American Society*. New York: Norton, 1955.

———. "Principles of Sampling." *Journal of the American Statistical Association*, 49 (March 1954), 13-35. Reprinted in Dennis P. Forcese and Stephen Richer (eds.). *Stages of Social Research: Contemporary Perspectives*. Englewood Cliffs, N.J.: Prentice-Hall, 1970, pp. 168–186.

Cohen, Jerome B. "The Misuse of Statistics." *Journal of the American Statistical Association*, 33 (December 1938), 657–674.

Cohen, Morris R., and Ernest Nagel. *An Introduction to Logic and Scientific Method*. New York: Harcourt, 1962.

Cohen, Stanley E. "U.S. Tests Use of Direct Mail in Data Gathering for 1970 Census." *Advertising Age* (February 22, 1965), p. 82.

Colby, K. M. *An Introduction to Psychoanalytic Research*. New York: Basic Books, 1960.

Cole, Jonathan R. *Fair Science: Women in the Scientific Community*. New York: Free Press, 1979.

Cole, Stephen. *The Sociological Method*, 3rd ed. Boston: Houghton Mifflin, 1980.

Coleman, James S., Elihu Katz, and Herbert Menzel. *Medical Innovation*. Indianapolis: Bobbs-Merrill, 1966.

Conant, James Bryant. *Two Modes of Thought*. New York: Pocket Books, 1965.

Congressional Information Service. *American Statis-*

tics Index. Washington, D.C.: Congressional Information Service.

Congressional Information Service. *Congressional Information Service Annual*. Washington, D.C.: Congressional Information Service.

Connell, Christopher. "SAT Scores Show 300-Point Variation Across U.S." *Nashville Tennessean*, November 2, 1981, 12.

Converse, Jean M., and Howard Schuman. *Conversations at Random: Survey Reserach as Interviewers See It*. New York: Wiley, 1974.

Converse, Philip, Jean Dotson, Wendy Hoag, William McGee III. *American Social Attitudes Data Sourcebook, 1947–1978*. Cambridge: Harvard University Press, 1980.

Cook, Stuart W. "Ethical Issues in the Conduct of Research in Social Relations," in Claire Selltiz, Lawrence S. Wrightsman, and Stuart W. Cook. *Research Methods in Social Relations*, 3rd ed. New York: Holt, 1976, Chapter 7.

Cooley, William, and Paul Lohnes. *Multivariate Data Analysis*. New York: Wiley, 1971.

Coombs, Clyde H. "Theory and Methods of Social Measurement," in Leon Festinger and Daniel Katz (eds.). *Research Methods in the Behavioral Sciences*. New York: Holt, 1953, Chapter 11.

Cooper, Sanford L. "Random Sampling by Telephone—An Improved Method." *Journal of Marketing Research*, 1 (November 1964), 45–48.

Cootner, Paul (ed.). *The Random Character of Stock Market Prices*. Cambridge, Mass.: M.I.T. Press, 1964.

Crichton, Michael. *A Case of Need*. New York: Signet, 1968.

Cummings, E. E. *Poems 1923–1954*. New York: Harcourt, 1954.

Dahl, Robert. *Who Governs?* New Haven: Yale University Press, 1961.

Dantzig, Tobias. *Number: The Language of Science*, 4th ed. New York: Free Press, 1967.

Dawson, Richard E. "Simulation in the Social Sciences," in Harold Guetzkow (ed.). *Simulation in Social Science*. Englewood Cliffs, N.J.: Prentice-Hall, 1962.

Deming, W. Edwards. "On Errors in Surveys." *American Sociological Review*, 9 (August 1944), 359–369.

————. *Sample Design in Business Research*. New York: Wiley, 1960.

DeNeufville, Judith. *Social Indicators and Public Policy*. New York: Elsevier, 1975.

Dentler, Robert, and Marvin B. Scott. *Schools on Trial: An Inside Account of the Boston Desegregation Case*. Cambridge: Abt Books, 1981.

Denzin, Norman K. *The Research Act*. Chicago: Aldine, 1970. (a)

————. *Sociological Methods: A Source Book*. Chicago: Aldine, 1970. (b)

Diaconis, Persi, and Bradley Efron. "Computer-Intensive Methods of Statistics." *Scientific American*, 248 (May 1983), 116–130.

Diesing, Paul. *Patterns of Discovery in the Social Sciences*. Chicago: Aldine, 1971.

Dillman, Don A. *Mail and Telephone Surveys: The Total Design Method*. New York: Wiley, 1978.

Distilled Spirits Institute. *Public Revenues from Alcoholic Beverages, 1961*. Washington, D.C.: Distilled Spirits Institute, 1962.

Dixon, W. J. (ed.). *BMDP Statistical Software 1981*. Berkeley: University of California Press, 1981.

————, and Frank J. Massey, Jr. *Introduction to Statistical Analysis*, 3rd ed. New York: McGraw-Hill, 1968.

Downs, Anthony. *An Economic Theory of Democracy*. New York: Harper & Row, 1957.

Dulles, Allen. *The Craft of Intelligence*. New York: New American Library, 1965.

Duncan, O. D. "Partials, Partitions, and Paths," in Edgar Borgatta and George Bohrnstedt (eds.). *Sociological Methodology 1970*. San Francisco: Jossey-Bass, 1970.

————. *Introduction to Structural Equation Models*. New York: Academic Press, 1975.

Duncan, O. D., Archibald Haller, and Alejandro Portes. "Peer Influences on Aspirations." *American Journal of Sociology*, 74 (September 1968), 119–137.

Duncan, O. D., David L. Featherman, and Beverly Duncan. *Socioeconomic Background and Achievement*. New York: Seminar, 1972.

Duncan, Otis Dudley, Ray P. Cuzzort, and Beverly Duncan. *Statistical Geography*. New York: Free Press, 1961.

Dunnett, Charles W. "Drug Screening: The Never-Ending Search for New and Better Drugs," in Judith Tanur (ed.). *Statistics: A Guide to the Unknown*, 2nd ed. San Francisco: Holden-Day, 1978, pp. 26–37.

Dunnette, Marvin D. "Fads, Fashions, and Folderol in Psychology." *American Psychologist,* 21 (April 1, 1966), 343–352.

Durand, John D. *Labor Force in Economic Development.* Princeton, N.J.: Princeton University Press, 1975.

Dwass, Meyer. "Modified Randomization Tests for Nonparametric Hypothesis." *Annals of Mathematical Statistics,* 28 (March 1957), 181–187.

Easterlin, Richard. "Effects of Population Growth in the Economic Development of Developing Countries." *Annals of the American Academy of Political and Social Science,* 369 (January 1967), 98–108.

Ebbinghaus, Hermann. *Memory: A Contribution to Experimental Psychology.* Translated by H. A. Ruger and C. E. Bussenius. New York: Columbia University Teachers College, 1913.

Edwards, Allen L. *Techniques of Attitude Scale Construction.* New York: Appleton, 1957.

Efron, Bradley. *The Jackknife, the Bootstrap, and Other Resampling Plans.* Philadelphia: SIAM, 1982.

Ehrenberg, A.S.C. *Data Reduction.* New York: Wiley, 1975.

Emerson, Robert M. "Observational Field Work." *Annual Review of Sociology,* 7 (1981), 351–378.

Enthoven, Alain C. "Economic Analysis in the Department of Defense." *American Economic Review,* LIII (May 1963), 413–423.

Entwisle, Doris R., and Susan G. Doering. *The First Birth: A Family Turning Point.* Baltimore: Johns Hopkins University Press, 1981.

Evan, William M. (ed.). *Organizational Experiments.* New York: Harper, 1971.

Evans, Franklin B. "An Analysis of Automobile Purchasers: The Discriminatory Efficacy of Objective and Psychological Variables." Unpublished doctoral dissertation, University of Chicago, 1959.

———. "Correlates of Automobile Shopping Behavior." *Journal of Marketing,* 26 (October 1962), 74–77.

Ezekiel, Mordecai. *Methods of Correlation and Regression Analysis.* New York: Wiley, 1930.

Fair, Roy C. "An Analysis of the Accuracy of Four Macroeconomic Models." *Journal of Political Economy,* 87 (1979), 701–718.

Featherman, David L., and Robert M. Hauser. *Opportunity and Change.* New York: Academic Press, 1978.

Fein, Rashi. *The Economics of Mental Illness.* New York: Basic Books, 1958.

Fenno, Richard. *Home Style: House Members in their Districts.* Boston: Little, Brown, 1978.

Ferber, Robert, and Hugh G. Wales. *A Basic Bibliography on Marketing Research.* Chicago: American Marketing Association, 1963.

Ferber, Robert, and P. J. Verdoorn. *Research Methods in Economics and Business.* New York: Macmillan, 1962.

Ferguson, Allen R., and E. Philip LeVeen (eds.). *The Benefits of Health and Safety Regulation.* Cambridge: Ballinger, 1981.

Festinger, Leon. "Laboratory Experiments," in Festinger and Danile Katz (eds.). *Research Methods in the Behavioral Sciences.* New York: Holt, 1953, pp. 140–146. Reprinted in Billy J. Franklin and Harold W. Osborne (eds.). *Research Methods: Issues and Insights.* Belmont, Calif.: Wadsworth, 1971, pp. 325–330.

Fiedler, Judith. *Field Research: A Manual for Logistics and Management of Scientific Studies in Natural Settings.* San Francisco: Jossey-Bass, 1978.

Firebaugh, Glenn. "The Case of the *Missing-Values* Card and Other Mysteries." *American Sociological Review,* 45 (February 1980), 137–145. (a)

———. "Cross-National versus Historical Regression Models." *Comparative Social Research.* 3 (1980), 333–344. (b)

Fisher, R. A. *The Design of Experiments,* 8th ed. New York: Hafner, 1971.

Franck, Frederick. *The Zen of Seeing.* New York: Vintage, 1973.

Franke, Richard, and James D. Kaul. "The Hawthorne Experiments: First Statistical Interpretation." *American Sociological Review,* 43 (October 1978), 623–642.

Freeman, John, and Edgar Butler. "Some Sources of Interviewer Variance in Surveys." *Public Opinion Quarterly,* 40 (1976), 79–91.

Freilich, Morris (ed.). *Marginal Natives: Anthropologists and Work.* New York: Harper, 1970.

Friedman, Lawrence M., Robert A. Kagan, Bliss Cartwright, Stanton Wheeler. "State Supreme Courts: A Century of Style and Citation." *Stanford Law Review,* 33 (May 1981), 773–818.

Friedman, Milton. "The Methodology of Positive Economics," in Friedman. *Essays in Positive Economics*. Chicago: University of Chicago Press, 1953, Chapter 1.

Fromm, Erich. *The Sane Society*. New York: Holt, 1955.

Fuchs, Douglas A. "Election Day Newscasts and Their Effects on Western Voter Turnout." *Journalism Quarterly*, XLI (Winter 1965), 22–28.

Fussler, Herman H., and Julian L. Simon. *Patterns in the Use of Books in Large Research Libraries*. Chicago: University of Chicago Library, 1961.

Galanter, E. H., quoted in S. S. Stevens. "Measurement, Psychophysics, and Utility," in C. W. Churchman and Philburn Ratoosh (eds.). *Measurement: Definitions and Theories*. New York: Wiley, 1959, Chapter 2.

Gallup, George. *A Guide to Public Opinion Polls*. Princeton, N.J.: Princeton University Press, 1948.

––––––. *The Sophisticated Poll Watcher's Guide*. Princeton, N.J.: Princeton Opinion Press, 1976.

Gamson, William A. *The Strategy of Social Protest*. Homewood, Ill.: Dorsey Press, 1975.

––––––, Bruce Fireman, and Steven Rytina. *Encounters with Unjust Authority*. Homewood, Ill.: Dorsey Press, 1982.

Gelles, Richard J., and Murray A. Straus. "Violence in the American Family," *Journal of Social Issues*, 35 (Spring 1979), 15–39.

Georgescu-Roegen, Nicholas. "The Economics of Production." *American Economic Review*, LX (May 1970), 1 ff.

Gerschenkron, Alexander. *Economic Backwardness in Historical Perspective: A Book of Essays*. New York: Praeger, 1965.

Gilbert, Dennis, and Joseph A. Kahl. *The American Class Structure*. Homewood, Ill.: Dorsey, 1982.

Ginsberg, Yona. *Jews in a Changing Neighborhood*. New York: Free Press, 1975.

Glasser, Gerald J., and Dale D. Metzger. "Random-Digit Dialing as a Method of Telephone Sampling." *Journal of Marketing Research*, 9 (February 1972), 59–64.

Glazer, Myron. *The Research Adventure: Promise and Problems of Fieldwork*. New York: Random House, 1972.

Glenn, Norval. "Trend Studies with Available Data: Opportunities and Pitfalls," in Philip Hastings and Jessie Southwick (eds.). *Survey Data for Trend Analysis*. Williamstown, Mass.: Roper Public Opinion Center, 1974, pp. 16–150.

––––––. *Cohort Analysis*. Beverly Hills, Calif.: Sage, 1977.

Goldberg, Lewis R. "The Effectiveness of Clinicians' Judgments: The Diagnosis of Organic Brain Damage from the Bender Gestalt Test." *Journal of Consulting Psychology*, 23 (February 1959), 25–33.

Goodman, Leo. "Generalizing the Problem of Prediction," in Paul Lazarsfeld and Morris Rosenberg (eds.). *The Language of Social Research*. New York: Free Press, 1955, pp. 277–281.

Gorden, Raymond L. *Interviewing: Strategy, Techniques, and Tactics*. Homewood, Ill.: Dorsey, 1969.

Gould, Stephen Jay. *The Mismeasure of Man*. New York: Norton, 1981.

Governor's Commission on the Los Angeles Riots (known as the McLane Commission). *Violence in the City*. Los Angeles: State of California, 1965.

Granovetter, Mark. "Network Sampling: Some First Steps." *American Journal of Sociology*, 81 (May 1976), 1287–1303.

Green, Paul E., and Donald S. Tull. *Research for Marketing Decisions*, 3rd ed. Englewood Cliffs, N.J.: Prentice-Hall, 1975.

Griswold, Wendy. "American Character and the American Novel." *American Journal of Sociology*, 86 (January 1981), 740–765.

Groves, Robert, and Robert Kahn. *Surveys by Telephone: A National Comparison with Personal Interviews*. New York: Academic Press, 1979.

Guetzkow, Harold (ed.). *Simulation in Social Science*. Englewood Cliffs, N.J.: Prentice-Hall, 1962.

Hagen, Everett E. *On the Theory of Social Change: How Economic Growth Begins*. Homewood, Ill.: Dorsey, 1962.

Haire, Mason. "Projective Techniques in Marketing Research." *Journal of Marketing*, 14 (April 1950), 649–656.

Halacy, D. S., Jr. *Computers: The Machines We Think With*, rev. ed. New York: Harper, 1969.

Hall, R. J., and C. J. Hitch. "Price Theory and Business Behavior." *Oxford Economic Papers*, II (1939), 12–45.

Hamblin, Robert L. "Social Attitudes: Magnitude Measurement and Theory," in H. M. Blalock, Jr. (ed.). *Measurement in the Social Sciences*. Chicago: Aldine, 1974, pp. 61–120.

Hammond, Philip E. (ed.). *Sociologists at Work*. New York: Basic Books, 1964.

Hannan, Michael T., Nancy Brandon Tuma, and Lyle P. Groeneveld. "Income and Independence Effects on Marital Dissolution." *American Journal of Sociology*, 84 (November 1978), 611–633.

Hansen, Morris H., W. N. Hurwitz, and W. G. Madow. *Sample Survey Methods and Theory*, Vol. I. New York: Wiley, 1953.

Hartwig, Frederick, with Brian E. Dearing. *Exploratory Data Analysis*. Beverly Hills, Calif.: Sage, 1979.

Hastings, Philip, and Jessie Southwick (eds.). *Survey Data for Trend Analysis*. Williamstown, Mass.: Roper Public Opinion Center, 1974.

Heilbroner, Robert. *The Quest for Wealth*. New York: Simon and Schuster, 1956.

———. *The Economic Problem*. Englewood Cliffs, N.J.: Prentice-Hall, 1968.

Heise, David R. *Understanding Events: Affect and the Construction of Social Action*. New York: Cambridge University Press, 1979.

Hirschi, Travis, and Hanan C. Selvin. "False Criteria of Causality in Delinquency Research." *Social Problems*, 13 (Winter 1966), 254–268.

Hite, Shere. *The Hite Report*. New York: Macmillan, 1976.

Hoinville, Gerald, and Roger Jowell. *Survey Research Practice*. London: Heinemann Educational Books, 1978.

Holdren, Bob R. *The Structure of a Retail Market and the Market Behavior of Retail Units*. Englewood Cliffs, N.J.: Prentice-Hall, 1960.

Homans, George C. "Bringing Men Back In." *American Sociological Review*, 29 (December 1964), 809–818.

Hooke, Robert. "Statistics, Sports, and Some Other Things," in Judith Tanur (ed.). *Statistics: A Guide to the Unknown*, 2nd ed. San Francisco: Holden-Day, 1978, pp. 297–305.

Horowitz, Irving Louis. "Life and Death of Camelot." *Trans-action*, 3 (November-December 1965), 3–7, 44–47. Reprinted in Billy J. Franklin and Harold W. Osborne (eds.). *Research Methods: Issues and Insights*. Belmont, Calif.: Wadsworth, 1971, pp. 75–92. Also reprinted in Dennis P. Forcese and Stephen Richer (eds.). *Stages of Social Research: Contemporary Perspectives*. Englewood Cliffs, N.J.: Prentice-Hall, 1970, pp. 228–243.

Hovland, Carl. "Reconciling Conflicting Results Derived from Experimental and Survey Studies of Attitude Change." *American Psychologist*, 14 (January 1959), 8–17. Reprinted in Norman K. Denzin. *Sociological Methods: Source Book*. Chicago: Aldine, 1970, pp. 476–494.

Hovland, Carl, Arthur Lumsdaine, and Fred Sheffield. *Experiments in Mass Communication*. Princeton, N.J.: Princeton University Press, 1949.

Howell, Joseph T. *Hard Living on Clay Street*. Garden City, N.Y.: Doubleday, 1973.

Huber, Joan, and Glenna Spitze. "Wives' Employment, Household Behaviors, and Sex-Role Attitudes." *Social Forces*, 60 (September 1981), 150–169.

Huff, Darrell. *How to Lie with Statistics*. New York: Norton, 1954.

Hume, David. *An Enquiry Concerning Human Understanding*. London: 1758.

Humphreys, Paul, and Joseph Berger. "Theoretical Consequences of the Status Characteristics Formulation." *American Journal of Sociology*, 86 (March 1981), 953–983.

Hunt, Morton. "A Fraud that Shook the World of Science." *New York Times Magazine*, November 1, 1981, 42ff.

Hyman, Herbert H. *Interviewing in Social Research*. Chicago: University of Chicago Press, 1954.

———. *Survey Design and Analysis*. Glencoe, Ill.: Free Press, 1955.

———. "Problems in the Collection of Opinion-Research Data." *American Journal of Sociology*, 55 (January 1950), pp. 362–370. Reprinted in Milton L. Barron (ed.). *Contemporary Sociology: An Introductory Textbook of Readings*. New York: Dodd, Mead, 1964, pp. 513–523.

———. *Secondary Analysis of Sample Surveys: Principles, Procedures, and Potentialities*. New York: Wiley, 1972.

Ishii, Ryoichi. *Population Pressure and Economic Life in Japan*. London: P. S. King, 1937.

Jaffe, A. J., and Charles D. Stewart. *Manpower Resources and Utilization*. New York: Wiley, 1951, pp. 62–73. Reprinted in Paul F. Lazarsfeld and Morris Rosenberg. *The Language of Social Research*. New York: Free Press, 1955, pp. 28–34.

Janowitz, Morris. "Content Analysis and the Study of Sociopolitical Change." *Journal of Communication*, 26 (1976), 10–26.

Jenkins, J. Craig, and Charles Perrow. "Insurgency of the Powerless: Farm Worker Movements (1946–1972)." *American Sociological Review*, 42 (April 1977), 249–267.

Jennings, M. Kent, and Richard G. Niemi. *Generations and Politics: A Panel Study of Young Adults and Their Parents*. Princeton, N.J.: Princeton University Press, 1981.

Johnston, J. *Econometric Methods*, 2nd ed. New York: McGraw-Hill, 1972.

Jones, Arnold Hugh Martin. *Ancient Economic History: An Inaugural Lecture Delivered at University College, London*. London: Lewis, 1948.

Kagan, Robert, Bliss Cartwright, Lawrence Friedman, and Stanton Wheeler. "The Evolution of State Supreme Courts." *Michigan Law Review*, 76 (1978), 961–1005.

Kahn, Robert L., and Charles F. Cannell. *The Dynamics of Interviewing*. New York: Wiley, 1967.

Kaplan, Abraham. *The Conduct of Inquiry*. San Francisco: Chandler, 1964.

Kappel, Geofrey, and W. H. Saufley, Jr. *Introduction to Design and Analysis: a Student's Handbook*. San Francisco: W. H. Freeman, 1980.

Katona, George. *The Powerful Consumer*. New York: McGraw-Hill, 1960.

Kefauver, Estes. *In a Few Hands: Monopoly Power in America*. Baltimore: Penguin, 1965.

Kelman, Herbert C. "Deception in Social Research." *Trans-action*, 3 (July–August 1966), 20–24.

Kendall, Maurice, and William R. Buckland. *A Dictionary of Statistical Terms*. London: Oliver & Boyd, 1957.

Kendall, Patricia L., and Paul F. Lazarsfeld. "Problems of Survey Analysis," in Robert K. Merton and Paul F. Lazarsfeld (eds.). *Continuities in Social Research*. New York: Free Press, 1950, pp. 133–196.

Keyfitz, Nathan. "Explaining the Salaries of Managers." *Contemporary Sociology*, 10 (January 1981), 85–87.

Kim, Jae-On, and Charles W. Mueller. *Factor Analysis: What It is and How to Do It*. Beverly Hills, Calif.: Sage, 1978.

———. *Factor Analysis: Statistical Methods and Practical Issues*. Beverly Hills, Calif.: Sage, 1978.

Kinder, Donald R., and D. Roderick Kiewiet. "Economic Discontent and Political Behavior." *American Journal of Political Science*, 23 (December 1979), 495–527.

Kinsey, Alfred C., Wardell B. Pomeroy, and Clyde E. Martin. *Sexual Behavior in the Human Male*. Philadelphia: Saunders, 1948.

———, and Paul H. Gebhard. *Sexual Behavior in the Human Female*. Philadelphia: Saunders, 1953; New York: Pocket Books, 1965.

Kish, Leslie. *Survey Sampling*. New York: Wiley, 1965.

Knight, Frank H. *The Economic Organization*. New York: Harper, 1951.

Knoke, David, and Peter J. Burke. *Log-Linear Models*. Beverly Hills, Calif.: Sage, 1980.

Kroeber, A. L. *Anthropology*. New York: Harcourt, 1948.

Kruskal, Joseph B., and Myron Wish. *Multidimensional Scaling*. Beverly Hills, Calif.: Sage, 1978.

Kruskal, William. "Statistics in Society: Problems Unsolved and Unformulated." *Journal of the American Statistical Association*, 76 (1981), 505–515.

———, and Frederick Mosteller. "Ideas of Representative Sampling," in D. Fiske (ed.). *New Directions for Methodology of Social and Behavioral Science*. San Francisco: Jossey-Bass, 1981, pp. 3–24.

Kuhn, Thomas S. *The Structure of Scientific Revolutions*, 2nd ed. Chicago: University of Chicago Press, 1970.

Kumar, Joginder. *Population and Land in World Agriculture*. Berkeley, Calif.: University of California Press, 1973.

Kuznets, Simon. *National Income: A Summary of Findings*. New York: National Bureau of Economic Research, 1946.

Land, Kenneth. "Principles of Path Analysis," in Edgar Borgatta (ed.). *Sociological Methodology 1969*. San Francisco: Jossey-Bass, 1968, pp. 3–37.

Laumann, Edward O. *Bonds of Pluralism*. New York: Wiley, 1973.

Lazarsfeld, Paul F. "The Art of Asking Why." *National Marketing Review* (now *Journal of Marketing*), I (Summer 1935), 26–38.

Lazarsfeld, Paul F., Bernard Berelson, and Hazel Gaudet. *The People's Choice: How the Voter Makes Up His Mind in a Presidential Campaign*. New York: Columbia University Press, 1948.

———. "The American Solider—An Expository Review." *Public Opinion Quarterly*, XIII (Fall 1949), 377–404.

———. "Evidence and Inference in Social Research." *Daedalus*, 87 (1958), 99–129. Reprinted in May Brodbeck (ed.). *Readings in the Philosophy of the Social Sciences*. New York: Free Press, 1968, pp. 608–634.

Leamer, Edward E. *Specification Searches*. New York: Wiley, 1978.

Lerner, Daniel. "Social Science: Whence and Whither?" in D. Lerner (ed.). *The Human Meaning of the Social Sciences*. New York: Meridan, 1959, pp. 13–42.

Letwin, William. *The Origins of Scientific Economics*. Westport, Conn.: Greenwood Press, 1975.

Levine, Joel H. "The Sphere of Influence." *American Sociological Review*, 37 (February 1972), 14–27.

Liebow, Elliot. *Tally's Corner*. Boston: Little, Brown, 1967.

Lipset, Seymour Martin. "Predicting the Future of Post-Industrial Society," in Seymour Martin Lipset (ed.). *The Third Century*. Chicago: University of Chicago Press, 1979, pp. 3–35.

Lipset, Seymour Martin, Martin Trow, and James S. Coleman. *Union Democracy*. Garden City, N.Y.: Doubleday, 1956.

Locke, John. *Essay on Human Understanding*. Chicago: Regnery, 1956.

Lodge, Milton. *Magnitude Scaling*. Beverly Hills, Calif.: Sage, 1981.

Lorie, James H., and Harry V. Roberts. *Basic Methods of Marketing Research*. New York: McGraw-Hill, 1951.

McCallister, L., and Claude S. Fischer. "A Procedure for Surveying Personal Networks," *Sociological Methods and Research*, 8 (1978), 131–148.

Mace, Arthur E. *Sample Size Determination*. New York: Reinhold, 1964.

Machlup, Fritz. "The Characteristics and Classifications of Oligopoly." *Kyklos* V (1951–1952), 145–165. Reprinted in Machlup, *The Economics of Sellers' Competition*. Baltimore: Johns Hopkins Press, 1952.

———. "The Problem of Verification in Economics." *Southern Economic Journal*, XXII (July 1955), 1–21.

Maclay, Howard, and Charles E. Osgood. "Hesitation Phenomena in Spontaneous English Speech." *Word*, XV (April 1959), 19–44.

Madge, John. *The Origins of Scientific Sociology*. New York: Free Press, 1962.

Madow, W. G., H. H. Hyman, and R. J. Jessen. *Evaluation of Statistical Methods Used in Obtaining Broadcast Ratings*. Washington, D.C.: American Statistical Association, 1961.

Malinowski, Bronislaw. *Argonauts of the Western Pacific*. New York: Dutton, 1961.

Malmquist, S. *A Statistical Analysis of the Demand for Liquor in Sweden*. Uppsala, Sweden: University of Uppsala, 1948.

Malthus, Thomas. *Principle of Population*, 5th ed. Homewood, Ill.: Irwin Paperback Classics in Economics, 1817–1963.

Mangione, Thomas, Ralph Hingson, and Jane Barrett. "Collecting Sensitive Data: a Comparison of Three Survey Strategies." *Sociological Methods and Research*, 10 (February 1982), 337–346.

Markus, Gregory B. *Analyzing Panel Data*. Beverly Hills, Calif.: Sage, 1979.

Marshall, Alfred. *Principles of Economics*, 9th (variorum) ed. New York: Macmillan, 1961.

Marwell, Gerald. "Introducing Introductory Sociology: The Social Awareness Test." *The American Sociologist*, 1 (November 1966), 253–254.

Maslow, Abraham H., and James M. Sakoda. "Volunteer Error in the Kinsey Study," in Jerome Himelhoch and Sylvia Fleis Fava. *Sexual Behavior in American Society*. New York: Norton, 1955.

Mason, Stephen. *A History of the Sciences*, rev. ed. New York: Collier, 1962.

Masserman, Jules H. "Neurosis and Alcohol: An Experimental Study." *American Journal of Psychiatry*, 101 (November 1944), 389–399.

Matheson, Douglas. *Experimental Psychology: Research, Design, and Analysis*, 3rd ed. New York: Holt, Rinehart & Winston, 1978.

Mead, Margaret. *People and Places*. New York: Bantam, 1963.

Meier, Richard L. *Science and Economic Development*, 2nd ed. Cambridge, Mass.: M.I.T. Press, 1966.

Melitz, Jack. "Friedman and Machlup on the Significance of Testing Economic Assumptions." *Journal of Political Economy*, 73 (February 1965), 37–60.

Merton, Robert K. *Social Theory and Social Structure*. New York: Free Press, 1968.

Merton, Robert K., James S. Coleman, and Peter H. Rossi (eds.). *Qualitative and Quantitative Social Research: Papers in Honor of Paul F. Lazarsfeld*. New York: Free Press, 1979.

Michener, H. A., I. J. Ginsberg, and K. Yuen. "Effects of Core Properties in Four-Person Games with Side Payments." *Behavioral Science,* 24 (1979), 263–280.

Milgram, Stanley. *Obedience to Authority.* New York: Harper & Row, 1974.

Miller, Delbert C. *Handbook of Research Design and Social Measurement,* 3rd ed. New York: David McKay, 1977.

Miller, Robert G. "The Probability of Rain," in Judith Tanur (ed.). *Statistics: A Guide to the Unknown,* 2nd ed. San Francisco: Holden-Day, 1978.

Miller, S. M., et al. *America's Uncounted People.* Washington, D.C.: National Academy of Sciences, 1972.

Mills, C. Wright. *The Sociological Imagination.* New York: Oxford University Press, 1959.

Mises, Richard von. *Positivism: A Study of Human Understanding.* Cambridge, Mass.: Harvard University Press, 1951.

Mitchell, Wesley. *What Happens During Business Cycles: A Progress Report.* New York: National Bureau of Economic Research, 1951.

Modern Medicine, March 2, 1964, and *Modern Medicine* press release of February 24, 1964.

Moore, Geoffrey H. "Accuracy of Government Statistics," *Harvard Business Review,* 25 (Spring 1947), 306–317.

Moore, Kristin A., and Sandra L. Hofferth. "Women and their Children," in Ralph E. Smith (ed.). *The Subtle Revolution.* Washington, D.C.: Urban Institute, 1979, pp. 129–158.

Morgan, J. N. "Factors Relating to Consumer Saving When It Is Defined as a Net-Worth Concept," in Lawrence R. Klein et al.. *Contributions of Survey Methods to Economics.* New York: Columbia University Press, 1954, pp. 89–156.

Morgan, James N., and Greg J. Duncan. *Five Thousand American Families, Volume 7, Analyses of the First Ten Years of the Panel Study of Income Dynamics.* Ann Arbor: Institute for Social Research, University of Michigan, 1979.

Morgenstern, Oskar. *On the Accuracy of Economic Observations,* 2nd ed. Princeton, N.J.: Princeton University Press, 1963.

Morrison, Donald. "Discriminant Analysis," in Robert Ferber (ed.). *Handbook of Marketing Research.* New York: McGraw-Hill, 1974.

Moser, C. A., and G. Kalton. *Survey Methods in Social Investigation,* 2nd ed. New York: Basic Books, 1972.

Moses, Lincoln E., and Frederick Mosteller. "Safety of Anesthetics," in Judith Tanur (ed.). *Statistics: A Guide to the Unknown,* 2nd ed. San Francisco: Holden-Day, 1978, 16–25.

Mosteller, Frederick. *The Pre-Election Polls: Report to the Committee on Analysis of Pre-Election Polls.* New York: Social Science Research Council, 1949.

———, Robert E. K. Rourke, and George B. Thomas, Jr. *Probability with Statistical Applications,* 2nd ed. Reading, Mass.: Addison-Wesley, 1970.

Mosteller, Frederick, and John W. Tukey. *Data Analysis and Regression.* Reading, Mass.: Addison-Wesley, 1977.

National Science Foundation. *Guide to Programs, Fiscal Year 1981.* Washington, D.C.: U.S. Government Printing Office, 1981.

Neibuhr, Reinhold. *Moral Man and Immoral Society.* New York: Scribners, 1936.

Neuman, Russell. "Differentiation and Integration: Two Dimensions of Political Thinking." *American Journal of Sociology,* 86 (May 1981), 1236–1268.

Neyman, Jerzy. *First Course in Probability and Statistics.* New York: Holt, 1950.

Nie, Norman H., C. Hadlai Hull, Karin Steinbrenner, and Dale H. Bent. *Statistical Package for the Social Sciences,* 2nd ed. New York: McGraw-Hill, 1975.

Nock, Steven L., and Peter H. Rossi. "Ascription versus Achievement in the Attribution of Family Social Status." *American Journal of Sociology,* 84 (November 1978), 565–590.

Northrop, F. S. C. *The Logic of the Sciences and the Humanities.* Cleveland: World, 1965.

Oppenheim, A. N. *Questionnaire Design and Attitude Measurement.* New York: Basic Books, 1966.

Orcutt, Guy H. "Toward Partial Re-direction of Econometrics." *Review of Economics and Statistics,* XXXIV, No. 3 (August 1952), 211–213. (a).

———. "Actions, Consequences, and Causal Relations." *Review of Economics and Statistics,* XXXIV, No. 4 (November 1952), 305–313. (b)

———, et al. "A Stochastic Microanalytic Model of a Socioeconomic System," in Orcutt et al.. *Microanalysis of Socioeconomic Systems: A Simulation Study.* New York: Harper, 1961, Chapter 2. Reprinted in R. E. Frank, A. A. Kuehn, and W. F. Massy (eds.). *Quantitative Techniques in Mar-*

keting Analysis. Homewood, Ill.: Irwin, 1962, pp. 481–501.

Panel on Privacy and Behavioral Research. "Report." *Science*, 155 (February 3, 1967), 535–538.

Parten, Mildred Bernice. *Surveys, Polls, and Samples: Practical Procedures*. New York: Harper, 1950.

Paul, B. D. "Interview Techniques and Field Relationships," in Alfred L. Kroeber (ed.). *Anthropology Today: An Encyclopedia Inventory*. Chicago: University of Chicago Press, 1953.

Pavlov, Ivan Petrovich. *Essential Works of Pavlov*, ed. Michael Kaplan. New York: Bantam Books, 1966.

Payne, Stanley L. *The Art of Asking Questions*. Princeton, N.J.: Princeton University Press, 1951.

Peck, Jon K. *PEC User's Manual*. New Haven: Yale University, 1981.

Pitman, E. J. G. "Significance Tests Which May Be Applied to Samples from Any Population." *Journal of the Royal Statistical Society*, Supplement 4 (1937), 119–130. (a)

———. "Significance Tests Which May Be Applied to Samples from Any Population: III. The Analysis of Variance Test." *Biometrika*, 29 (June 1937), 322–335. (b)

Pohlman, Edward. *Incentives and Compensations in Birth Planning*. Chapel Hill, N.C.: Carolina Population Center, 1971.

Politz, Alfred. *Reach and Frequency*. New York: Politz Research Inc., Communication Report 4, 1964.

Polya, G. *How to Solve It*, 2nd ed. Garden City, N.Y.: Doubleday, 1957.

Prest, A. R. "Some Experiments in Demand Analysis." *Review of Economics and Statistics*, XXXI (February 1949), 33–49.

Price, Derek J. DeSolla. *Science Since Babylon*. New Haven: Yale University Press, 1961.

Przeworski, Adam, and Henry Teune. *The Logic of Comparative Social Inquiry*. New York: Wiley, 1970.

Raiffa, Howard. *Decision Analysis*. Reading, Mass.: Addison-Wesley, 1968.

RAND Corporation, *A Million Random Digits*. New York: Free Press, 1955.

Rao, Potluri, and Roger L. Miller. *Applied Econometrics*. Belmont, Calif.: Wadsworth Publishing, 1971.

Reichenbach, Hans. *The Rise of Scientific Philosophy*. Berkeley: University of California Press, 1951.

Reiss, David. *The Family's Construction of Reality*. Cambridge: Harvard University Press, 1981.

Rensberger, Boyce. "Fraud in Research Is a Rising Problem in Science." *New York Times*, January 23, 1977, pp. 1, 44.

Reskin, Barbara F. "'Fair Science': A Fair Test?" *Contemporary Sociology*, 9 (November 1980), 793–795.

Reynolds, Paul Davidson. *Ethical Dilemmas and Social Science Research*. San Francisco: Jossey-Bass, 1979.

Richardson, Stephen A., et al. *Interviewing: Its Forms and Functions*. New York: Basic Books, 1965.

Riecken, Henry, and R. F. Boruch. "Social Experiments." *Annual Review of Sociology*, 4 (1978), 511–532.

Riesman, David. "Ethical and Practical Dilemmas of Fieldwork in Academic Settings," in Robert K. Merton, James S. Coleman, and Peter H. Rossi (eds.). *Qualitative and Quantitative Social Research*. New York: Free Press, 1979, pp. 210–231.

Riley, Matilda White, and Edward E. Nelson (eds.). *Sociological Observation*. New York: Basic Books, 1974.

Robinson, John P. *How Americans Use Time*. New York: Praeger, 1977.

Roethlisberger, F. J., and W. J. Dickson. *Management and the Worker*. Cambridge: Harvard University Press, 1949.

Romney, A. Kimball, Roger N. Shepard, and Sara Beth Nerlove (eds.). *Multidimensional Scaling: Volume II, Applications*. New York: Seminar, 1972.

Rosenberg, Morris. *The Logic of Survey Analysis*. New York: Basic Books, 1968.

Rosenfeld, Leonora D. *Portrait of a Philosopher: Morris R. Cohen in Life and Letters*. New York: Harcourt, 1962.

Rosenham, D. L. "On Being Sane in Insane Places." *Science*, 179 (January 1973), 250–258.

Rosenthal, Robert. *Experimenter Effects in Behavioral Research*. New York: Century, 1966.

Rossi, Peter H. "The Presidential Address: The Challenge and Opportunities of Applied Social

Research." *American Sociological Review*, 45 (December 1980), 889–904.

———, and Andy Anderson. "The Factorial Survey Approach," in Peter Rossi and Steven Nock (eds.). *Measuring Social Judgments*. Beverly Hills, Calif.: Sage, 1982, pp. 15–68.

Roth, Julius. "Hired-Hand Research." *American Sociologist*, 1 (August 1966), 190–196.

Rowntree, B. S. *Poverty: A Study of Town Life*, 2nd ed. London: Macmillan, 1902.

Saiger, George L. "Errors of Medical Studies." *Journal of the American Medical Association*, 173 (June 11, 1960), 678–681.

Samuelson, Paul A. "What Economists Know," in Daniel Lerner (ed.). *The Human Meaning of the Social Sciences*. New York: Meridan, 1959, pp. 183–213.

Sandage, C. H. "Do Research Panels Wear Out?" *Journal of Marketing*, 20 (April 1956), 397–401.

Schiffman, Susan S., M. Lance Reynolds, and Forrest W. Young. *Introduction to Multidimensional Scaling*. New York: Academic Press, 1981.

Schlaifer, Robert. *Probability and Statistics for Business Decisions: An Introduction to Managerial Economics Under Uncertainty*. New York: McGraw-Hill, 1959.

———. *Introduction to Statistics for Business Decisions*. New York: McGraw-Hill, 1961.

Schlei, Barbara L., and Paul Grossman. *Employment Discrimination Law*. Washington, D.C.: Bureau of National Affairs, 1976.

Schlesinger, Arthur, Jr. "The Humanist Looks at Empirical Social Science." *American Sociological Review*, 27 (December 1962), 768–771.

———. "A Middle Way Out of Vietnam." *New York Times Magazine*, September 18, 1966, pp. 47–49+.

Schultz, Theodore W. *Economic Crisis in World Agriculture*. Ann Arbor: University of Michigan Press, 1965.

Schuman, Howard, and Stanley Presser. *Questions and Answers in Attitude Surveys*. New York: Academic Press, 1981.

Selltiz, Claire, Lawrence S. Wrightsman, and Stuart W. Cook. *Research Methods in Social Relations*, 3rd ed. New York: Holt, 1976.

Seltzer, Carl C. "Morphologic Constitution and Smoking." *Archives of Environmental Health*, 17 (July 1968), 143–147.

Selvin, Hanan C., *The Effects of Leadership*. New York: Free Press, 1960.

———. "Durkheim's Suicide: Further Thoughts on a Methodological Classic," in Robert A. Nisbet (ed.). *Emile Durkheim*. Englewood Cliffs, N.J.: Prentice-Hall, 1965.

———, and Alan Stuart. "Data-Dredging Procedures in Survey Analysis." *Journal of the American Statistical Association*, 61 (June 1966), 20–23. Reprinted in Dennis P. Forcese and Stephen Richer (eds.). *Stages of Social Research: Contemporary Perspectives*. Englewood Cliffs, N.J.: Prentice-Hall, 1970, pp. 326–332.

Shapere, Dudley. *Philosophical Problems of Natural Science*. New York: Macmillan, 1965.

Sheatsley, Paul. "An Analysis of Interviewer Characteristics and Their Relationship to Performance," in Seymour Sudman. *Reducing the Cost of Surveys*. Chicago: National Opinion Research Center, 1967, pp. 105–106.

Shepard, Roger N., A. Kimball Romney, and Sara Beth Nerlove (eds.). *Multidimensional Scaling: Volume I. Theory*. New York: Seminar, 1972.

Shils, Edward A. "Social Inquiry and the Autonomy of the Individual," in Daniel Lerner (ed.). *The Human Meaning of the Social Sciences*. New York: Meridan, 1959, Chapter 5, pp. 114–157.

———, (ed.). *Criteria for Scientific Development: Public Policy and National Goals*. Cambridge, Mass.: M.I.T. Press, 1968 (especially "Criteria for Scientific Choice" by Alvin M. Weinberg).

Simon, Herbert A. *Models of Men*. New York: Wiley, 1957.

———. "The Meaning of Causal Ordering," in Robert K. Merton, James S. Coleman, and Peter Rossi (eds.). *Qualitative and Quantitative Social Research*. New York: Free Press, 1979.

Simon, Julian L. "The Cause of the Newspaper Rate Differential: A Subjective-Demand-Curve Analysis." *Journal of Political Economy*, LXXIII (October 1965), 536–539.

———. "The Demand for Liquor in the U.S., and a Simple Method of Determination." *Econometrica*, 34 (January 1966), 193–205. (a)

———. "The Economic Effect of State Monopoly of Packaged Liquor Retailing." *Journal of Political Economy*, LXXIV (April 1966), 188–194. (b)

———. "A Reply on 'Smoking and Health,'" *American Statistician* (October 1966), 35–36. (c)

———. "Doctors, Smoking, and Reference Groups." *Public Opinion Quarterly*, 31 (Winter 1967–1968), 646–647.

———. "Toward Formal Evaluation of Scientific Research Projects: A Case Study in Population Control." *Policy Sciences*, 3 (July 1972), 177–181.

———. *The Effects of Income on Fertility*. Chapel Hill, N.C.: Carolina Population Center, 1974.

———. *The Ultimate Resource*. Princeton, N.J.: Princeton University Press, 1981.

Simon, Julian, Carlos Puig, and John Ashcoff. "Duopoly Simulations and Theory." *Review of Economic Studies*, 40 (1973), 353–366.

Simon, Julian, and Rita Simon. "The Effect of Money Incentives on Family Size: A Hypothetical-Question Study." *Public Opinion Quarterly*, 38 (1975), 585–595.

Simon, Julian L., David T. Atkinson, and Carolyn Shevokas. "Probability and Statistics: Experimental Results of a Radically Different Teaching Method." *The American Mathematical Monthly*, 83 (November 1976), 733–739.

Simon, Rita. "Murder, Juries, and the Press." *Trans-action*, 3 (May–June 1966), 40–42.

———. *The Jury and the Plea of Insanity*. Boston: Little, Brown, 1967.

Sjoberg, Gideon, and Roger Nett. *A Methodology for Social Research*. New York: Harper, 1968.

Smith, H. W. *Strategies of Social Research*. Englewood Cliffs, N.J.: Prentice-Hall, 1975.

Smith, T. Lynn. *Fundamentals of Population Study*. Philadelphia: Lippincott, 1960.

Smith, Vernon L. "An Experimental Study of Competitive Market Behavior." *Journal of Political Economy*, LXX (April 1962), 111–137.

Sneath, Peter H. A., and Robert R. Sokal. *Principles of Numerical Taxonomy,* 2nd ed. San Francisco: Freeman, 1973; first ed. 1963.

Snow, C. P. "On Albert Einstein." *Commentary*, 43 (March 1967), 45–55.

Snyder, David, and William R. Kelly. "Conflict Intensity, Media Sensitivity, and the Validity of Newspaper Data." *American Sociological Review*, 42 (February 1977), 105–123.

Snyder, David, and Edward L. Kick. "Structural Position in the World System and Economic Growth, 1955–1970." *American Journal of Sociology*, 84 (March 1979), 1096–1126.

Sobol, M. G. "Panel Mortality and Panel Bias." *Journal of the American Statistical Association*, 54 (March 1959), 52–68.

Sonquist, John A., and William C. Dunkelberg. *Survey and Opinion Research: Procedures for Processing and Analysis*. Englewood Cliffs, N.J.: Prentice-Hall, 1977.

Spencer, Herbert. *The Study of Sociology*. New York and London: Appleton, 1912.

Starch, Daniel. *Measuring Product Sales Made by Advertising*. Mamaroneck, N.Y.: Daniel Starch, 1961.

Steiner, Gary A. "The People Look at Commercials: A Study of Audience Behavior." *Journal of Business*, 39 (April 1966), 272–304.

Stephan, Frederick J., and Philip J. McCarthy. *Sampling Opinion*, 2nd ed. New York: Wiley, 1963.

Stevens, S. S. "Measurement, Psychophysics, and Utility," in C. W. Churchman and Philburn Ratoosh (eds.). *Measurement: Definitions and Theories*. New York: Wiley, 1959, pp. 18–63.

Stewman, Shelby, and D. Lincoln. "Recombinant DNA Breakthroughs in Agriculture, Industry, and Medicine—A Delphi Study." *Futures*, 13 (1981), 128–140.

Stigler, George. "The Kinky Oligopoly Demand and Rigid Prices," in George Stigler and Kenneth E. Boulding (eds.). *Readings in Price Theory*. Homewood, Ill.: Irwin, 1952, pp. 410–435.

———. *Essays in the History of Economics*. Chicago: University of Chicago Press, 1965.

Stinchcombe, Arthur. *Constructing Social Theories*. New York: Harcourt, 1968.

Stone, Richard. *The Role of Measurement in Economics*. Cambridge, Mass.: Harvard University Press, 1952.

Stouffer, Samuel B. "Afterthoughts of a Contributor," in Robert K. Merton and Paul F. Lazarsfeld (eds.). *Continuities in Social Research*. New York: Free Press, 1950, pp. 197–211.

Stouffer, Samuel, et al. *The American Soldier,* Vols. I–IV. Princeton, N.J.: Princeton University Press, 1949.

Streuning, E., and Marcia Guttentag (eds.). *Handbook of Evaluation Research*. Beverly Hills, Calif.: Sage, 1975.

Strunk, William, and E. B. White. *The Elements of Style*, 8th ed. New York: Macmillan, 1972.

Sudman, Seymour. "New Uses of Telephone Methods in Survey Research." *Journal of Marketing Research,* 3 (May 1966), 163–167.

———. *Reducing the Cost of Surveys.* Chicago: Aldine, 1967.

———. "The Uses of Telephone Directories for Survey Sampling." *Journal of Marketing Research,* 10 (May 1973), 204–207.

———. *Applied Sampling.* New York: Academic Press, 1976.

———, Norman Bradburn, Ed Blair, and Carol Stocking. "Modest Expectations: the Effects of Interviewers' Prior Expectations on Responses." *Sociological Methods and Research,* 6 (November 1977), 171–182.

Suits, Daniel B. "The Demand for New Automobiles in the United States." *Review of Economics and Statistics,* XL (August 1958), 273–280.

———. *Statistics: An Introduction to Quantitative Economic Research.* Chicago: Rand McNally, 1963.

Sullivan, John L., and Stanley Feldman. *Multiple Indicators.* Beverly Hills, Calif.: Sage, 1979.

Summers, Gene F. *Attitude Measurement.* Chicago: Rand McNally, 1970.

Tanur, Judith (ed.). *Statistics: A Guide to the Unknown,* 2nd ed. San Francisco: Holden-Day, 1978.

———, et al. (eds.). *Statistics: A Guide to Unknown.* San Francisco: Holden-Day, 1972.

Tanur, Judith. "Advances in Methods for Large-Scale Surveys and Experiments," in National Science Foundation (ed.). *The Five-Year Outlook on Science and Technology 1981.* Washington, D.C.: U.S. Government Printing Office, 1981, pp. 589–620.

Telser, Lester G. "Advertising and Cigarettes." *Journal of Political Economy,* LXX (October 1962), 471–499.

Terman, Lewis M. *Genetic Studies of Genius,* 2nd ed. Stanford, Calif.: Stanford University Press, 1976.

Thernstrom, Stephan. *The Other Bostonians.* Cambridge, Mass.: Harvard University Press, 1973.

Thurow, Lester. *Generating Inequality.* New York: Basic Books, 1975.

Tilly, Charles. *From Mobilization to Revolution.* Reading, Mass.: Addison-Wesley, 1978.

———. *As Sociology Meets History.* New York: Academic Press, 1981.

Tintner, Gerhard. *Econometrics.* New York: Wiley, 1965.

Torgerson, W. S. *Theory and Methods of Scaling.* New York: Wiley, 1958.

Toynbee, Arnold. *The Industrial Revolution.* Boston: Beacon, 1956.

Travers, Jeffrey, and Stanley Milgram. "An Experimental Study of the Small World Problem." *Sociometry,* 32 (1969), 425–443.

Treiman, Donald. *Occupational Prestige in Comparative Perspective.* New York: Academic Press, 1977.

Tufte, Edward R. *Data Analysis for Politics and Policy.* Englewood Cliffs, N.J.: Prentice-Hall, 1974.

Tukey, John W. *Exploratory Data Analysis.* Reading, Mass.: Addison-Wesley, 1977.

Tull, Donald S., and Dell I. Hawkins. *Marketing Research: Meaning, Measurement and Method.* New York: Macmillan, 1976.

Ulam, Stanislaw M. *Adventures of a Mathematician.* New York: Scribners, 1976.

Underwood, Benton J. *Psychological Research.* New York: Appleton, 1957.

———, and John J. Shaughnessy. *Experimentation in Psychology.* New York: Wiley, 1975.

U.S. Bureau of the Census. *Statistical Abstract of the United States 1980,* 101st ed. Washington, D.C.: U.S. Government Printing Office, 1980.

U.S. Federal Trade Commission. *U.S.F.T.C. vs. Procter & Gamble,* docket 6901, 1963, pp. 45–46.

U.S. Public Health Service. *Smoking and Health: Report of the Advisory Committee to the Surgeon General of the Public Health Service.* Washington, D.C.: U.S. Department of Health, Education and Welfare, 1964.

Usher, Abbott Payson. "The History of Population and Settlement in Eurasia," in J. J. Spengler and O. D. Duncan (eds.). *Demographic Analysis.* New York: Free Press, 1956, pp. 3–25. Originally published in *Geographical Review,* 20 (January 1930), 110–132.

Vanneman, Reeve. "The Occupational Composition of American Classes." *American Journal of Sociology,* 82 (January 1977), 783–807.

Waite, Linda. "Projecting Female Labor Force Participation from Sex-Role Attitudes." *Social Science Research,* 7 (December 1978), 299–318.

Wallis, W. Allen. "Statistics of the Kinsey Report."

Journal of the American Statistical Association, 44 (December 1949), 463–484.

———, and Harry V. Roberts. *The Nature of Statistics*, rev. ed. New York: Free Press, 1966.

Warburton, Clark. *The Economic Effects of Prohibition*. New York: Columbia University Press, 1932.

Warwick, Donald P. *The Teaching of Ethics in the Social Sciences*. Hastings-on-Hudson, N.Y.: Hastings Center, 1980.

Wasserman, Paul, and Jacqueline O'Brien (eds.). *Statistics Sources, 6th ed., A Subject Guide to Data on Industrial, Business, Social, Educational, Financial, and Other Topics for the United States and Internationally*. Detroit: Gale Research, 1980.

Watson, James D. *The Double Helix*. New York: New American Library, 1968.

Webb, Eugene J., et al. *Unobtrusive Measure: Nonreactive Research in the Social Sciences*. Chicago: Rand McNally, 1966.

Weber, Max. *The Theory of Social and Economic Organization*. Glencoe, Ill.: Free Press, 1947.

West, Morris. *The Ambassador*. New York: Dell, 1965.

White, Harrison. *Chains of Opportunity*. Cambridge: Harvard University Press, 1970.

White, Harrison, Scott Boorman, and Ronald Breiger. "Social Structure from Multiple Networks." *American Journal of Sociology*, 81 (January 1976), 730–780.

Whitney, Frederick L. *The Elements of Research*, 3rd ed. New York: Prentice-Hall, 1950.

Whyte, William Foote. *Street Corner Society: The Social Structure of an Italian Slum*, 2nd ed. Chicago: University of Chicago Press, 1961.

Wiener, Norbert. *The Human Use of Human Beings*, rev. ed. Garden City, N.Y.: Doubleday, 1954.

Wilensky, Harold. *The Welfare State and Equality*. Berkeley, Calif.: University of California Press, 1975.

Williams, Thomas R. *Field Methods in the Study of Culture*. New York: Holt, 1967.

Williams, William H. *A Sampler on Sampling*. New York: Wiley, 1978.

Wilson, E. Bright. *An Introduction to Scientific Research*. New York: McGraw-Hill, 1952.

Wold, Herman O. A. "The Approach of Model Building," in Wold (ed.). *Model Building in the Human Sciences*. Monaco: Centre International d'Etude des Problèmes Humains, 1966. (a)

———. "On the Definition and Meaning of Causal Concepts," in Wold (ed.). *Model Building in the Human Sciences*. Monaco: Centre International d'Etude des Problèmes Humains, 1966. (b)

———. "Time as the Realm of Forecasting." Paper presented at Symposium on the Interdisciplinary Perspectives of Time, New York Academy of Sciences, January 20, 1966. (c)

Wolfe, Linda. *The Cosmo Report*. New York: Arbor House, 1981.

Wolins, Leroy. "Responsibility for Wrong Data." *American Psychologist*, 17 (September 1962), 657–658.

Wonnacott, Ronald J., and Thomas H. Wonnacott. *Econometrics*, 2nd ed. New York: Wiley, 1979.

Wood, Gordon. *Fundamentals of Psychological Research*. Boston: Little, Brown, 1974.

Wright, Charles R., and Herbert H. Hyman. "The Evaluators," in Philip E. Hammond (ed.). *Sociologists at Work*. New York: Doubleday Anchor, 1964–1967, pp. 140–163.

Wright, Erik O. *Class Structure and Income Determination*. New York: Academic Press, 1979.

Young, James Webb. *A Technique for Producing Ideas*, 4th ed. Chicago: Crain Communications, 1977.

Young, Pauline V. *Scientific Social Surveys and Research: An Introduction to the Background, Content, Methods, and Analysis of Social Studies*, 4th ed. Englewood Cliffs, N.J.: Prentice-Hall, 1966.

Zeisel, Hans. "Review of *Sexual Behavior in the Human Female*." *University of Chicago Law Review*, XXI (1953), 517–525.

———. *Say It with Figures*, 5th ed. New York: Harper, 1968.

———, and Harry Kalven, Jr. "Parking Tickets and Missing Women: Statistics and the Law," in Judith Tanur (ed.). *Statistics: A Guide to the Unknown*, 2nd ed. San Francisco: Holden-Day, 1978, pp. 139–149.

Zeller, Richard A., and Edward G. Carmines. *Measurement in the Social Sciences*. New York: Cambridge University Press, 1980.

Zuckerman, Harriet. *Scientific Elite: Nobel Laureates in the United States*. New York: Free Press, 1977.

Index

About the Authors

Paul Burstein received his B.A. from the University of Chicago and his Ph.D. from Harvard University. After having served as Associate Director of the sociology program at the National Science Foundation, he is currently associate professor of sociology and Senior Research Associate at the Institute for Public Policy Studies at Vanderbilt University. In addition to publishing many articles in sociology and political science, he is the author of *Discrimination, Jobs, and Politics*, a book about the struggle for equal opportunity in the United States since the New Deal. He has also served on the editorial boards of *The American Sociological Review* and *The American Journal of Sociology*.

Julian L. Simon teaches at the University of Maryland. His special interest is the economics of population. In addition to the earlier editions of this book, he is the author of *How to Start and Operate a Mail-Order Business*, *Patterns of Use of Books in Large Research Libraries* (with Herman H. Fussler), *Issues in the Economics of Advertising*, *The Management of Advertising*, *The Effects of Income on Fertility*, *Applied Managerial Economics*, *The Economics of Population Growth*, and *The Ultimate Resource*.